BUSINESS ACCOUNTING AND FINANCE

ONE WEEK LOAN

questions to test your understanding

...dies

...ional exercises

...ards to test yo... ...rms

■ Links to relevant sites on the World Wide Web
■ Author biographies

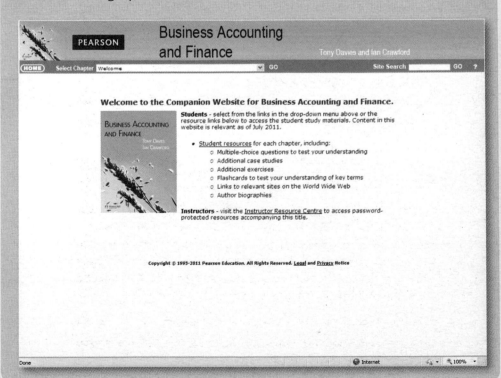

PEARSON

Business Accounting and Finance

Tony Davies and Ian Crawford

HOME Select Chapter Welcome GO Site Search GO ?

Welcome to the Companion Website for Business Accounting and Finance.

Students - select from the links in the drop-down menu above or the resource links below to access the student study materials. Content in this website is relevant as of July 2011.

- **Student resources** for each chapter, including:
  - Multiple-choice questions to test your understanding
  - Additional case studies
  - Additional exercises
  - Flashcards to test your understanding of key terms
  - Links to relevant sites on the World Wide Web
  - Author biographies

Instructors - visit the Instructor Resource Centre to access password-protected resources accompanying this title.

Done   Internet   100%

BUSINESS ACCOUNTING AND FINANCE

TONY DAVIES

and

IAN CRAWFORD

**Financial Times
Prentice Hall**
is an imprint of

Harlow, England • London • New York • Boston • San Francisco • Toronto • Sydney • Singapore • Hong Kong
Tokyo • Seoul • Taipei • New Delhi • Cape Town • Madrid • Mexico City • Amsterdam • Munich • Paris • Milan

Pearson Education Limited
Edinburgh Gate
Harlow
Essex CM20 2JE
England

and Associated Companies throughout the world

Visit us on the World Wide Web at:
www.pearsoned.co.uk

First published by Pearson Education Limited in 2011

ISBN: 978-0-273-72312-7

British Library Cataloguing-in-Publication Data
A catalogue record for this book is available from the British Library

Library of Congress Cataloging-in-Publication Data
Davies, Tony.
  Business accounting and finance/Tony Davies and Ian Crawford.
    p. cm.
  ISBN 978-0-273-72312-7 (pbk.)
  1. Accounting.   2. Business enterprises—Finance.   I. Crawford, Ian (Ian Peter)   II. Title.

  HF5636.D38 2011
  657—dc22   2011004813

10 9 8 7 6 5 4 3 2 1
14 13 12 11
Typeset in 9.5/13 pt ITC Charter by 73
Printed and bound by Rotolito Lombarda, Italy

Brief contents

Contents

Supporting resources

Visit www.pearsoned.co.uk/daviestony to find valuable online resources

Companion Website for students
- Multiple-choice questions to test your understanding
- Additional case studies
- Additional exercises
- Flashcards to test your understanding of key terms
- Links to relevant sites on the World Wide Web
- Author biographies

For instructors
- Teaching notes for each chapter
- Debriefs to all case studies in the book
- Additional case studies and debriefs
- Solutions to all chapter-end exercises
- Additional exercises and solutions
- PowerPoint presentations for each chapter, including all illustrations from the book

Also: The Companion Website provides the following features:
- Search tool to help locate specific items of content
- E-mail results and profile tools to send results of quizzes to instructors
- Online help and support to assist with website usage and troubleshooting

For more information please contact your local Pearson Education sales representative or visit www.pearsoned.co.uk/daviestony

Features

Case studies

Press extracts

Figures

Preface

Accounting and finance are of critical importance in the support of all business activities. The formal study of accounting and finance is exciting because it introduces a toolkit that allows a better understanding of the performance of businesses, and the decisions and problems they face. These issues are discussed daily by managers and in the media. This textbook provides you with the toolkit and shows you how to apply it in practice, utilising a comprehensive range of learning features, illustrative examples and assessment material to support and reinforce your study.

This textbook is aimed primarily at students who are not majoring in accounting or finance, but who are undertaking an introductory-level module as part of their degree or diploma course in business management, economics or any other subject. Our main objective was to produce a tightly written, clear and engaging text which distils the core principles of accounting and finance for those students who do not have the luxury of devoting all their time to its study.

Content and structure

The content and structure of the text have been carefully researched to follow closely the typical requirements of introductory undergraduate and MBA modules. This text assumes no prior knowledge of the subject: we start at square one and take you step-by-step through the concepts and application of techniques, with clear explanations and numerous worked examples.

The text comprises 16 chapters, and is structured into two parts. Each of the two parts of the book, and their component chapters, are outlined in the introductory section to each part of the text, and cover the main areas of accounting and finance:

- **financial accounting** which is broadly concerned with the recording and analysis of historical financial data, the presentation of information on financial performance, and compliance with legislation, and accounting rules and standards
- **financial management** which includes management accounting: mainly involved in dealing with current problems and in looking ahead, and includes the roles of costing and pricing of products and services, and support of the planning, control and decision-making functions, and business finance: which includes capital investment decision-making, alternative ways of financing the business, and the management of the assets that the organisation has at its disposal.

A further key objective in writing this text was to provide a flexible study resource. There is a linkage between each of the chapters, which follow a structure that has been designed to facilitate effective learning of the subject in a progressive way. However, each chapter may also be used on a stand-alone basis; equally, chapters may be excluded from study if they relate to subjects that are not essential for a specific course. Therefore, the text is intended to be suitable for modules of either one or two semesters' duration.

Just as the principles and practice of genetics or information technology are steadily progressing, so accounting and finance continue to develop, sometimes in exciting ways. Some of the chapters introduce topics typically not covered in some more traditional and technical introductory accounting texts, for example corporate governance, sustainability and corporate social responsibility reporting. A number of contemporary issues and areas of increasing importance are also included such as the balanced scorecard and activity based costing.

Given that this text has been written primarily for non-specialist students, each chapter aims to help students understand the broader context and relevance of accounting and finance in the business environment, and how accounting statements and financial information can be used to improve the quality of management decision-making. We have therefore provided numerous examples and commentary on company activity within each chapter, including at least one press extract. Companies featured include Liverpool FC, General Motors, Ryanair, Sony, Royal Bank of Scotland, British Airways, Kraft, Revlon, Berkshire Hathaway, EasyDate, Bosch, and Marks & Spencer. In addition, two of the chapters feature extracts and analysis of the actual Report and Accounts 2010 of Johnson Matthey Plc.

Using this book

To support your study and reinforce the topics covered, we have included a comprehensive range of learning features and assessment material in each chapter, including:

- learning objectives
- introduction
- highlighted key terms
- fully worked examples
- integrated progress checks
- key points summary
- questions
- discussion points
- exercises.

Within each chapter we have also included numerous diagrams and charts that illustrate and reinforce important concepts and ideas. The double-page Guided Tour of the Book that follows on pages (xxiii–xxv) summarises the purpose of these learning features and the chapter-end assessment material. To gain maximum benefit from this text and to help you succeed in your study and exams, you are encouraged to familiarise yourself with these elements now, before you start the first chapter.

It is easy, but mistaken, to read on cruise control, highlighting the odd sentence and gliding through the worked examples, progress checks and chapter-end questions and exercises. Active learning needs to be interactive: if you haven't followed a topic or an example, go back and work through it again; try to think of other examples to which particular topics may be applied. The only way to check you have a comprehensive understanding of things is to attempt all the integrated progress checks and worked examples, and the chapter-end assessment material, and then to compare with the text and answers provided. Fully worked solutions are given for each worked example, and solutions to about 45% of the chapter-end exercises (those with their numbers in colour) are provided in Appendix 3. Additional self-assessment material is available on the book's accompanying website (see page i).

Case studies

The book includes six case studies that may be tackled either individually or as a team. The case studies are a little more weighty than the chapter-end exercises; in addition, they integrate many of the topics included in the chapters in each part of the text to which they relate, although not exclusively. Each case study therefore gives you an opportunity to apply the knowledge and techniques gained from each part of the book, and to develop these together with the analytical skills and judgement required to deal with real-life business problems. Additional cases are provided on the accompanying website.

We hope this textbook will enhance your interest, understanding and skills. Above all, relax, learn and enjoy!

Guided tour of the book

Learning objectives

Listed at the start of each chapter, these bullet points identify the core learning outcomes you should have acquired after completing each chapter.

Learning objectives

Completion of this chapter will enable you to:

- explain the convention of double-entry bookkeeping
- describe what is meant by 'debit' and 'credit'
- enter business transactions into accounts
- account for closing inventories and other accounting adjustments
- explain the balancing of accounts
- extract a trial balance from a company's accounts
- prepare an income statement, balance sheet and statement of cash flows from a trial balance
- appreciate the concepts of accrual accounting and cash accounting
- explain and account for payments in advance (prepayments) and charges not yet received (accruals)
- appreciate the importance of accounting periods.

Introduction

This section gives you a brief overview of the coverage and purpose of each chapter, and how it links to the previous chapter.

Introduction

This chapter begins by explaining what is sometimes referred to as the dual aspect rule. This rule recognises that for all transactions there is a two-sided effect within the entity. A manager in a non-accounting role may not be expected to carry out the recording of transactions in this way, but an appreciation of how accounting data has been recorded will be extremely helpful in the interpretation of financial information. We will go on to describe the processes that deal with the two sides of each transaction, the 'debits' and 'credits' of double-entry bookkeeping.

Don't worry if at first these topics seem a little difficult and confusing. They will become clearer as we follow through some transactions step-by-step into the accounts of a business and show how these accounts are kept in balance.

The chapter continues with an introduction to the way in which each of the accounts is held in what are termed the books of account and ledgers of the business. The balances on all the accounts in an entity are summarised in what is called a trial balance. The trial balance may be adjusted to allow for payments in advance, charges not yet received, and other adjusting entries. From this information we will show how to prepare a simple income statement, balance sheet and statement of cash flows.

This chapter refers to some of the accounting concepts introduced in Chapter 1. In that context we will look at the time period chosen by a business, to which the financial reporting relates – the accounting period.

Key terms

These are colour-highlighted the first time they are introduced, alerting you to the core concepts and techniques in each chapter. A full explanation is contained in the glossary of key terms section at the end of the book.

Cash book

The cash book is a book of account that in theory should match exactly with the regular statements issued by the entity's bank. In practice, the cash book is prepared partly from company internally generated **cash payments** information and available information relating to **cash receipts**. Some transactions may appear in the bank account without prior notification, for example bank charges, and so the cash book may also be partly prepared with reference to information from the bank statement.

There is a need to periodically check cash book balances against the balances shown on the bank statements supplied by the bank. The two numbers are rarely the same and so the differences between them need to be reconciled to ensure that cash book balances are correct. The regular preparation of a **bank reconciliation** on at least a monthly basis is therefore a necessary function of the finance department.

There are five main reasons for differences between cash book balances and the balances shown on bank statements:

- cash book arithmetic errors and incorrect postings of receipts and payments
- cash book omissions of items shown on the bank statements such as bank charges, standing orders, direct debits, and dishonoured (returned) cheques

Worked examples

The numerous worked examples in each chapter provide an application of the learning points and techniques included within each topic. By following and working through the step-by-step solutions, you have an opportunity to check your knowledge at frequent intervals.

Worked example 3.2

Mr Bean decides to set up a wholesale business, Ayco, on 1 January 2010. He has his own cash resources for the purpose of setting up the business and has estimated that an initial £50,000 would be required for this purpose. During the first four-week period in business, January 2010, Ayco will enter into the following transactions:

		£
Week 1	Receipt of cheque from Mr Bean	50,000
Week 1	Purchase for cash the freehold of a shop	30,000
Week 1	Purchase for cash the shop fittings	5,000
Week 2	Cash paid for printing and stationery used	200
Week 3	Purchases of inventory, from Beeco Ltd, of Aymen toys, payable two months later (12,000 toys at £1 each)	12,000
Week 3	Sales of Aymen toys to Ceeco Ltd for cash (1,000 toys at £2 each)	2,000
Week 4	Sales of Aymen toys to Deeco Ltd, receivable one month later (8,000 toys at £2 each)	16,000

		Week 1 £	Total £
Profit and loss account	Sales revenue	0	0
	Cost of sales	0	0

Progress checks

Each topic within each chapter includes one or more of these short questions that enable you to check and apply your understanding of the preceding key topics before you progress to the next one in the chapter.

Progress check 4.6

What are the various methods that may be used to depreciate an asset? Describe two of the most commonly used methods.

The amount of depreciation calculated for an accounting period is charged as a cost reflected in the income statement, the depreciation charge. A corresponding amount is also reflected in an account in the balance sheet, the cumulative depreciation provision account, the effect of which is to reduce the original, historical cost of the non-current assets at the end of each accounting period.

The difference between depreciation cost and other costs such as wages and salaries is that it is not a cash expense, that is it does not represent a cash outflow. The only cash outflow relating to depreciation took place when the asset was originally purchased. The depreciation is really only the 'memory' of that earlier cash outflow.

Progress check 4.7

Why are assets depreciated and what factors influence the decision as to how they may be depreciated?

Press extracts

Included in every chapter, these topical extracts feature real company examples from the press, including commentary that highlights the practical application of accounting and finance in the business environment.

The press extract below illustrates the factors involved in (and the implications of) making investment decisions. When Bosch opened its alternator factory in Cardiff in 1989 the decision was aided by the belief that the UK was undergoing a renaissance as an automobile manufacturer. In addition, more than £20m of grants were received by Bosch from the Welsh Development Agency in a bid to

The impact of high UK costs on investments by large foreign companies

About 900 jobs are to be lost in South Wales as Bosch prepares to shut a car parts factory next year.

The privately owned German engineering group blamed its decision to pull out of Wales on the economic slump, which has hit the car industry hard. The Unite union described the news as a 'terrible blow'.

Management confirmed the closure to workers at the plant in Miskin near Cardiff on Thursday, after a three-month consultation, during which they had to decide whether to shed 300 jobs and carry on with a smaller operation, or close the plant completely in 2011.

The division in charge of the plant will now recommend to the Bosch board that production should be phased out. The consultation is being extended until February as unions and staff try to thrash out redundancy terms.

The factory, which makes alternators for German carmakers including BMW and Daimler's Mercedes-Benz, is scheduled to shut in the summer of next year. Production will be transferred to Hungary, where labour costs are 65% of those in Cardiff.

The move is a serious blow to south Wales. The other major employer in the region is Corus, the steelmaker, which itself is cutting more than 1,000 [...] Talbot, along the M4 from Miskin.

several divisions of Bosch, he added: 'Everyone is bitterly disappointed that there's not a hope of something being retained.'

Bosch, which is set to make its first operating loss for six decades, said demand for alternators had dropped dramatically, with sales down 45% last year.

The global recession has hit carmakers around the world, with General Motors and Chrysler going bankrupt last year and needing US government aid to survive. The luxury marques BMW and Daimler both saw sales slip by 13%, according to figures released yesterday, as government scrappage schemes led to a move towards smaller and more fuel-efficient vehicles.

'I deeply regret that we could not find a solution for the Cardiff plant', said Stefan Asenkerschbaumer, president of the Bosch starter motors division, who rejected the alternative plan to keep the plant open with the loss of 300 jobs.

'I have spent time in a previous role as plant manager in Cardiff and I know first-hand the dedication and commitment of the employees here. Therefore, this is for me personally one of the toughest decisions in my career.'

The worst economic downturn for many decades had 'left its mark' on the Bosch group, he said.

The Welsh assembly government offered [...] full support.

Summary of key points

Following the final section in each chapter there is a comprehensive summary of the key points in terms of the learning outcomes listed at the start of each chapter. These allow you to check that you understand all the main points covered before moving on to the next chapter.

Summary of key points

- Standard costing can be used to calculate costs of units or processes that may be used in budgeted costs.
- Not all budgeted amounts are standard amounts, as the latter will be precise by nature, unlike budgeted amounts.
- Standard costing provides the basis for performance evaluation and control from comparison of actual performance against budget through the setting of predetermined cost estimates.
- A flexed budget reflects the costs or revenues expected as a result of changes in activity levels from those planned in the master budget.
- A flexed budget provides a more realistic basis for comparison of actual performance against planned performance.
- Flexed budgets enable comparison of actual costs and revenues on a like-for-like basis through the calculation of differences, or variances.
- Variances are the differences between planned, budgeted or standard costs (or revenues) and actual costs incurred and may be summarised in an operating statement to reconcile budget with actual performance.
- Variances between actual and standard performance may be investigated to explain the reasons for the differences through preparation of a complete analysis of all variances, or alternatively through the use of exception reporting that highlights only significant variances.
- Inaccuracies in original budgets may be identified through planning variances, and actual performance may then be compared with a subsequently revised budget to show operational variances.

Questions

These are short narrative-type questions that encourage you to review and check your understanding of all the key topics. There are typically 7 to 10 of these questions at the end of each chapter.

Assessment material

Questions

Q13.1 How is standard costing used in the preparation of budgets?

Q13.2 (i) What are the benefits of using standard costing?
(ii) What type of standard may best ensure that those benefits are achieved?
(iii) How are standards used to achieve those benefits?

Q13.3 Describe and illustrate the technique of flexible budgeting.

Q13.4 (i) What is management by exception?
(ii) How is variance analysis used to support this technique?

Q13.5 (i) Outline the main variances that may be reported using the bases of absorption costing and marginal costing.
(ii) What do these variances tell us about direct labour, direct materials and overhead costs?

Q13.6 Describe the main reasons why usage and efficiency variances may occur and illustrate these with some examples.

Q13.7 What are mix and yield variances?

Q13.8 (i) Explain some of the problems associated with traditional variance reporting.
(ii) What are planning and operational variances?

Discussion points

This section typically includes 2 to 4 thought-provoking ideas and questions that encourage you to critically apply your understanding and/or further develop some of the topics introduced in each chapter, either individually or in team discussion.

Discussion points

D13.1 'We set the budget once a year and then compare the actual profit after the end of the financial year. If actual profit is below budget, then everyone needs to make more effort to ensure this doesn't happen the following year.' Discuss.

D13.2 'The standard-setting process is sometimes seen as management's way of establishing targets that demand better and better manufacturing performance.' To what extent do you think that is true, and if it is true how effectively do you think the standard-setting process achieves that objective?

D13.3 To what extent do you think that the techniques of flexed budgets and variance analysis complicate the otherwise simple process of comparing the various areas of actual performance against budget?

D13.4 'Traditional variance analysis tends to focus on cutting costs and increasing output in a way that is detrimental to product and service quality and the longer-term viability of the business.' Discuss.

Exercises

These comprehensive examination-style questions are graded by their level of difficulty, and also indicate the time typically required to complete them. They are designed to assess your knowledge and application of the principles and techniques covered in each chapter. There are typically 6 to 8 exercises at the end of each chapter. Full solutions to the colour-highlighted exercise numbers are provided in Appendix 3 to allow you to self-assess your progress.

Exercises

Solutions are provided in Appendix 3 to all exercise numbers highlighted in colour.

Level I

F13.1   *Time allowed – 60 minutes*

Nilbog Ltd makes garden gnomes. It uses standard costs and has budgeted to produce and sell 130,000 Fishermen (their top-of-the-range gnome) in 2010. Nilbog's budget for the year is phased over 13 four-week periods, and production and sales revenues are spread evenly in the budget.

Budgeted standard costs and selling prices for the Fisherman are:

		£
Direct materials	3 cubic metres at £3.60 per cubic metre	10.80
Direct labour	2 hours at £6.60 per hour	13.20
Variable overheads	2 hours at £2.40 per hour	4.80
Fixed overheads	2 hours at £4.80 per hour	9.60
Standard cost of one Fisherman		38.40
Standard profit		9.60
Standard selling price		48.00

The actual results for period five, a four-week period, were:

Revenue	9,000 Fishermen at £48 each
Production	9,600 Fishermen
Purchase of direct materials	30,000 cubic metres at a cost of £115,200
Direct materials usage	28,000 cubic metres
Direct labour cost	£142,560 for 22,000 hours
Variable overhead	£44,000
Fixed overhead	£100,000

There was no work-in-progress at the start or at the end of period five. Finished goods and materials inventories are valued at standard cost.

Glossary of key terms

At the end of the book a glossary of key terms in alphabetical order provides full definitions of all main terms that have been introduced. The numbers of the pages on which key term definitions appear are colour-highlighted in the index.

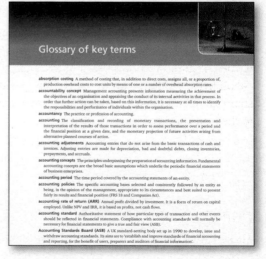

Glossary of key terms

absorption costing A method of costing that, in addition to direct costs, assigns all, or a proportion of, production overhead costs to cost units by means of one or a number of overhead absorption rates.

accountability concept Management accounting presents information measuring the achievement of the objectives of an organisation and appraising the conduct of its internal activities in that process. In order that further action can be taken, based on this information, it is necessary at all times to identify the responsibilities and performance of individuals within the organisation.

accountancy The practice or profession of accounting.

accounting The classification and recording of monetary transactions, the presentation and interpretation of the results of those transactions in order to assess performance over a period and the financial position at a given date, and the monetary projection of future activities arising from alternative planned courses of action.

accounting adjustments Accounting entries that do not arise from the basic transactions of cash and invoices. Adjusting entries are made for depreciation, bad and doubtful debts, closing inventories, prepayments, and accruals.

accounting concepts The principles underpinning the preparation of accounting information. Fundamental accounting concepts are the broad basic assumptions which underlie the periodic financial statements of business enterprises.

accounting period The time period covered by the accounting statements of an entity.

accounting policies The specific accounting bases selected and consistently followed by an entity as being, in the opinion of the management, appropriate to its circumstances and best suited to present fairly its results and financial position (FRS 18 and Companies Act).

accounting rate of return (ARR) Annual profit divided by investment. It is a form of return on capital employed. Unlike NPV and IRR, it is based on profits, not cash flows.

accounting standard Authoritative statement of how particular types of transaction and other events should be reflected in financial statements. Compliance with accounting standards will normally be necessary for financial statements to give a true and fair view (ASB).

Accounting Standards Board (ASB) A UK standard-setting body set up in 1990 to develop, issue and withdraw accounting standards. Its aims are to 'establish and improve standards of financial accounting and reporting, for the benefit of users, preparers and auditors of financial information'.

This book is dedicated to my dad
Phil Davies

Acknowledgements

Thank you to the lecturers who were involved in either the initial market research and/or in providing useful review comments and technical checks of the draft chapters during the development phase of this project.

Thank you to CIMA (the Chartered Institute of Management Accountants) for their permission to include material from their Management Accounting Official Terminology 2005 edition.

Thank you to Johnson Matthey Plc for their permission to use extracts of their Report and Accounts 2010 as an excellent example of the information provided to shareholders by a major UK plc. Thanks also to *The Times, The Independent, The Guardian,* and the *Daily Telegraph, Financial Times, Sunday Herald, Business Week, Daily Mail, Huddersfield Daily Examiner, Birmingham Post,* and *Sunday Express* for their permissions to use extracts from their publications.

Thank you to Katie Rowland for her support and encouragement in the writing of this book and the development of the website, and to Colin Reed, Philippa Fiszzon and Gemma Papageorgiou for their design and production wizardry.

Publisher's acknowledgements

We are grateful to the following for permission to reproduce copyright material:

Figures

Figure 10.10 from *Kaizen*, McGraw-Hill (Masaaki Imai 1986) © The McGraw-Hill Companies, Inc.; Figure 10.11 from The Weir Group PLC Annual Report 2008, page 27, http://www.weir.co.uk/investors/financial_information/annual_reports/2008.aspx., Source: The Weir Group PLC.; Figure 10.14 adapted from "Using the balanced scorecard as a strategic management system", *Harvard Business Review*, Jan/Feb, 75–85 (Kaplan, R.S. and Norton, D.P. 1996), © 1996 by the Harvard Business School Publishing Corporation; all rights reserved.; Figure 13.4 from *CIMA Official Terminology*, 2005 ed., CIMA Publishing, Elsevier p.34, Copyright CIMA; Figure 13.5 from *CIMA Official Terminology*, 2005 ed., CIMA Publishing, Elsevier p.35, Copyright CIMA.

Text

Article on page 10 from Liverpool slide further into red, *Daily Telegraph*, 08/05/2010 (Rory Smith), © Telegraph Media Group Limited 2010; Article on page 41 from Greek crisis deepens with S&P downgrade; worry about true scale of undisclosed military spending adds to concern, *Daily Telegraph*, 17/12/2009 (Ambrose Evans-Pritchard), © Telegraph Media Group Limited 2009; Article on page 98 from Persimmon returns to profit after revaluation, *Daily Telegraph*, 03/03/2010 (Dominic Midgley), © Telegraph Media Group Limited 2010; Article on page 99 from The value of 5,000 years of history? £51m, *Daily Telegraph*, 25/05/2010 (Myra Butterworth), © Telegraph Media Group Limited 2010; Article on page 141 from Northgate stuns market with profit warning; Business in brief, *The Independent*, 26/02/2009, © The Independent 2009; Article on page 151 from Hill & Smith; QUESTOR, *Daily Telegraph*, 10/03/2010 (Garry White), © Telegraph Media Group Limited 2010;

Extract 5. from Tesco annual report and accounts 2009; Article on page 216 from The small cases that will have a big influence on the way we work; Gary Slapper reflects on the deaths that have led to changes in corporate manslaughter law, *The Times*, 11/07/2009 (Gary Slapper), © Gary Slapper/ The Times/nisyndication; Article on page 231 from Farewell then . . . floppy disks, *Daily Mail*, 28/04/2010 (Chris Beanland); Article on page 241 from Late payments mean bigger write-offs for small businesses, *Daily Telegraph*, 15/04/2010 (Roland Gribben), © Telegraph Media Group Limited 2010; Article on page 266 from Johnson Matthey cautious on recovery, *Daily Telegraph*, 25/11/2009 (Garry White), © Telegraph Media Group Limited 2009; Article on page 357 from Firm shows iron will to net major award, *Huddersfield Daily Examiner*, 03/07/2010 (Henryk Zientek); Article on page 386 from BA reports worst ever loss of £531m: This year's break-even hopes hit by strike threat, *The Guardian*, 22/05/2010 (Dan Milmo), Copyright Guardian News & Media Ltd 2010.; Article on page 419 from Why lean accounting stands fat chance in UK, *Birmingham Post*, 21/10/2008; Article on page 441 from Kraft is 'truly sorry' for U-turn over closure of Somerdale plant, *The Independent*, 17/03/2010 (James Thompson), © The Independent 2010; Article on page 446 from Revlon chief goes as new product line fails to shine, *The Times*, 19/09/2006 (Tom Bawden), © Tom Bawden/ The Times/nisyndication; Article on page 479 from Fighter jet costs rise to £260bn, *Sunday Express*, 06/06/2010 (Tracey Boles); Article on page 518 from How short-term thinking causes whirlpool effect, *The Sunday Herald*, 30/07/2006 (Ken Symon); Article on page 554 from Online dating site seeks to woo investors, *Daily Telegraph*, 18/05/2010 (Philip Smith), © Telegraph Media Group Limited 2010; Article on page 607 from 'Terrible blow' to Wales as car parts factory is shut with loss of 900 jobs: Bosch plant near Cardiff to close in Summer of 2011, *The Guardian*, 16/01/2010 (Julia Kollewe), Copyright Guardian News & Media Ltd 2010.; Article on page 635 from Christmas chopping: Stores hacking prices to make Britain defy the credit crunch, *Sunday Express*, 23/11/2008 (David Jarvis and Emily Fox); Various extracts from the Johnson Matthey Annual Report and Accounts 2010, reproduced in Chapters 6 and 8, including: pages 40–42 (Corporate governance), 46–57 (Nomination Committee Report, Audit Committee Report, Remuneration Report, Responsibility of directors), 0 (Financial highlights), 2–3 (Chairman's statement), 4–5 (Chief Executive's statement), 7–27 (Business review), 63–7 (Accounting policies), 58–62 (Financial statements), 68–70 (Notes on the accounts [Note 1]), 28–37 (Sustainability), 108 (Independent auditors' report) and 109 (five year record). Also in Chapter 8: Consolidated income statement for the year ended 31 March 2010, http://www.matthey.com/AR10/pdf/Johnson_Matthey_AR10.pdf – Thank you to Johnson Matthey Plc for their kind permission to use these extracts from their Report and Accounts 2010 as an excellent example of the information provided to shareholders by a major UK plc.

The Financial Times

Article on page 17 from Push for accounting convergence threatened by EU reform drive, *Financial Times*, 05/04/2010 (Rachel Sanderson).

Photographs

Getty Images: Aaron Graubart 671, Adam Gault 439, Creativ Studio Heinemann 515, David Gould 225, David Leahy 183, EschCollection 549, J.A. Kraulis 677, Jamie Grill 39, MARK SYKES/Science Photo Library 383, Martin Barraud 355, Medioimages/Photodisc 69, Paper Boat Creative 477, Peter Sherrard 111, Rosemary Calvert 585, Yamada Taro 149; **Pearson Education Ltd:** Photodisc. Cybermedia 342, Trevor Clifford 349, Photodisc. Getty Images 620, Photodisc. Photolink 547, 668.

In some instances we have been unable to trace the owners of copyright material, and we would appreciate any information that would enable us to do so.

Part I

FINANCIAL ACCOUNTING

Outline of Part I

Part I is about financial accounting. **Chapter 1** begins with an introduction to the fundamentals of accounting and finance and the next four chapters deal with the three key financial statements: income statement; balance sheet; statement of cash flows (previously called the cash flow statement), and in particular those relating to limited companies. In most respects these also apply to other profit-making and not-for-profit organisations in both the private and public sectors.

Chapter 2 shows how commercial transactions are accounted for. It is about the system used to record accounting transactions and accounting data and provides the fundamental basis for the further analysis and reporting of financial information. It provides an introduction to double-entry bookkeeping. Bookkeeping is a process that records accounting data in such a way that allows subsequent preparation of financial reports in appropriate formats which inform shareholders and others about the financial position and the financial performance of the business.

Chapter 3 looks in detail at the balance sheet.

Chapter 4 looks in detail at the income statement. It looks at how to recognise that a profit (or loss) has been made and how it is linked with the balance sheet and statement of cash flows.

Chapter 5 deals with the statement of cash flows, which shows from where an organisation has received cash during an accounting period and how cash was used.

In **Chapter 6** we broaden the scope of our study of accounting and finance to provide an introduction to corporate governance. This is a topic that has become increasingly important as the behaviour of directors and managers towards their shareholders and to society in general receives greater and greater attention and comes under closer and closer scrutiny by investors, the media, governments and the general public. The burden also lies with management to run businesses in strict compliance with statutory, regulatory and accounting requirements, so it is crucial that directors are aware of the rules and codes of practice in place to regulate the behaviour of directors of limited companies.

Chapter 7 is headed *Financial statements analysis*. The three financial statements provide information about business performance. Much more may be gleaned about the performance of the business through further analysis of the financial statements, using financial ratios and other techniques, for example trend analysis, industrial analysis and inter-company analysis.

Chapter 8 looks at the analysis and interpretation of the annual report and accounts of a business. It uses the report and accounts for the year ended 31 March 2010 of Johnson Matthey Plc to illustrate the type of financial and non-financial information provided by a major UK public company.

1

The importance of accounting and finance

Contents

Learning objectives

Completion of this chapter will enable you to:

- outline the uses and purpose of accounting and the practice of accountancy
- explain the development of the conceptual frameworks of accounting
- outline the contents of the UK Statement of Principles (SOP)
- explain the main UK accounting concepts and accounting and financial reporting standards
- appreciate the meaning of true and fair view
- consider the increasing importance of international accounting standards
- explain what is meant by financial accounting, management accounting and financial management
- illustrate the different types of business entity: sole traders, partnerships, private limited companies, public limited companies
- explain the nature and purpose of financial statements
- identify the wide range of users of financial information
- consider the issues of accountability and financial reporting.

Introduction

This chapter explains why accounting and finance are such key elements of business life. Both for aspiring accountants, and those of you who may not continue to study accounting and finance beyond the introductory level, the fundamental principles of accounting and the ways in which accounting is regulated to protect owners of businesses, and the public in general, are important topics. A broad appreciation will be useful not only in dealing with the subsequent text, but also in the context of the day-to-day management of a business.

This chapter will look at why accounting is needed and how it is used and by whom. Accounting and finance are wide subjects, which often mean many things to many people. They are broadly concerned with the organisation and management of financial resources. Accounting and accountancy are two terms which are sometimes used to mean the same thing, although they more correctly relate separately to the subject and the profession.

Accounting and accountancy are generally concerned with measuring and communicating the financial information provided from accounting systems, and the reporting of financial results to shareholders, lenders, creditors, employees and Government. The owners or shareholders of the wide range of business entities that use accounting may be assumed to have the primary objective of maximisation of shareholder wealth. Directors of the business manage the resources of the business to meet shareholders' objectives.

Accounting operates through basic principles and rules. This chapter will examine the development of conceptual frameworks of accounting, which in the UK are seen in the Statement of Principles (SOP). We will discuss the rules of accounting, which are embodied in what are termed accounting concepts and accounting standards.

Over the past few years there has been an increasing focus on trying to bring together the rules, or standards, of accounting that apply in each separate country, into one set of accounting standards. For example, with effect from January 2005 all the stock exchange listed companies within the European Union were required to comply with one such set of accounting standards relating to the way in which they report financial information. We will discuss how this may affect the topics we shall be covering in this book.

We will consider the processes used in accounting and look at an overview of the financial statements used in financial reporting, and the way in which financial reporting is used to keep shareholders informed. The timely and accurate disclosure of accounting information is a fundamental requirement in the preparation of appropriate statements of the financial performance and the financial position of a business. Directors and managers are responsible for running businesses and their accountability to shareholders is maintained through their regular reporting on the activities of the business.

A large number of accounting concepts and terms are used throughout this book, the definitions of which may be found in the glossary of key terms at the end of the book.

What is accounting, and what are its uses and purposes?

The original, basic purposes of **accounting** were to classify and record monetary transactions (see Chapter 2) and present the financial results of the activities of an entity, in other words the scorecard that shows how the business is doing. The accounting profession has evolved and accounting techniques have been developed for use in a much broader business context. To look at the current nature of accounting and the broad purposes of accounting systems we need to consider the three questions these days generally answered by accounting information:

- how are we doing, and are we doing well or badly?   **a scorecard (like scoring a game of cricket, for example)**
- which problems should be looked at?   **attention-directing**
- which is the best alternative for doing a job?   **problem-solving**

Although accountants and the accounting profession have retained their fundamental roles they have grown into various branches of the profession, which have developed their own specialisms and responsibilities.

Accounting is a part of the information system within an organisation (see Chapter 2, which explains double-entry **bookkeeping**, and how data are identified, recorded and presented as information in the ways required by the users of financial information). Accounting also exists as a service function, which ensures that the financial information that is presented meets the needs of the users of financial information. To achieve this, accountants must not only ensure that information is accurate, reliable and timely but also that it is relevant for the purpose for which it is being provided, consistent for comparability, and easily understood (see Fig. 1.1).

In order to be useful to the users of financial information, the accounting data from which it is prepared, together with its analysis and presentation, must be:

- accurate – free from error of content or principle
- reliable – representing the information that users believe it represents
- timely – available in time to support decision-making
- relevant – applicable to the purpose required, for example a decision regarding a future event or to support an explanation of what has already happened

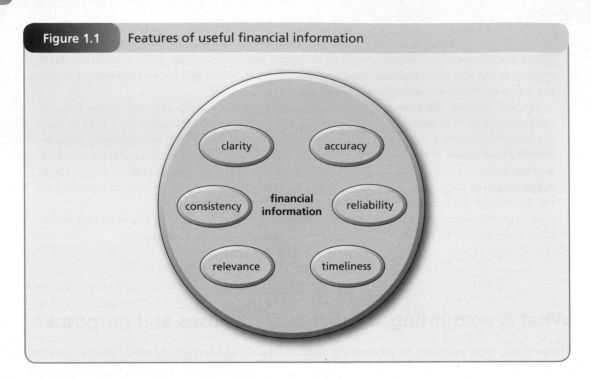

Figure 1.1   Features of useful financial information

■ consistent – the same methods and standards of measurement of data and presentation of information to allow like-for-like comparison
■ clear – capable of being understood by those for whom the information has been prepared.

In the next few sections we will see just how important these features are, and the ways they are included in the development of various **conceptual frameworks of accounting**, and the accounting policies selected by companies.

The conceptual frameworks of accounting

How can the credibility and usefulness of accounting and financial information be ensured? Accounting operates within a framework. This framework is constantly changing and evolving as new problems are encountered, as new practices and techniques are developed, and the objectives of users of financial information are modified and revised.

The search for a definitive conceptual framework, a theoretical accounting model, which may deal with any new accounting problem that may arise, has resulted in many conceptual frameworks having been developed in a number of countries worldwide. The basic assumption for these conceptual frameworks is that **financial statements** must be useful. The general structure of conceptual frameworks deals with the following six questions:

1. What is the purpose of financial statement reporting?
2. Who are the main users of accounting and financial information?
3. What type of financial statements will meet the needs of these users?
4. What type of information should be included in financial statements to satisfy these needs?
5. How should items included in financial statements be defined?
6. How should items included in financial statements be recorded and measured?

In 1989 the **International Accounting Standards Board (IASB)** issued a conceptual framework ◀▥
that largely reflected the conceptual framework of the Financial Accounting Standards Board of the
USA issued in 1985. This was based on the ideas and proposals made by the accounting profession
since the 1970s in both the USA and UK. In 1999 the **Accounting Standards Board (ASB)** in the UK ◀▥
published its own conceptual framework called the **Statement of Principles (SOP) for Financial** ◀▥
Reporting.

> **Progress check 1.1**
>
> What is meant by a conceptual framework of accounting?

The Statement of Principles (SOP)

The 1975 Corporate Report was the first UK attempt at a conceptual framework. This, together
with the 1973 Trueblood Report published in the USA, provided the basis for the conceptual framework issued by the IASB in 1989, referred to in the previous section. It was followed by the publication of the SOP by the ASB in 1999. The SOP is a basic structure for determining objectives,
in which there is a thread from the theory to the practical application of accounting standards to
transactions that are reported in published accounts. The SOP is not an accounting standard and
its use is not mandatory, but it is a statement of guidelines; it is, by virtue of the subject, constantly
in need of revision.

The SOP identifies the main users of financial information as:

- investors
- lenders
- employees
- suppliers
- customers
- Government
- the general public.

The SOP focuses on the interests of investors and assumes that each of the other users of financial
information is interested in or concerned about the same issues as investors.

The SOP consists of eight chapters that deal with the following topics:

1. The objectives of financial statements, which are fundamentally to provide information that is
   useful for the users of that information.
2. Identification of the entities that are required to provide financial statement reporting by virtue of
   the demand for the information included in those statements.
3. The qualitative characteristics required to make financial information useful to users:
   - **materiality** (inclusion of information that is not material may distort the usefulness of other ◀▥
     information)
   - relevance
   - reliability
   - comparability (enabling the identification and evaluation of differences and similarities)
   - comprehensibility.
4. The main elements included in the financial statements – the 'building blocks' of accounting such
   as assets and liabilities.

5. When transactions should be recognised in financial statements.
6. How assets and liabilities should be measured.
7. How financial statements should be presented for clear and effective communication.
8. The accounting by an entity in its financial statements for interests in other entities.

The UK SOP can be seen to be a very general outline of principles relating to the reporting of financial information. The SOP includes some of the basic concepts that provide the foundations for the preparation of financial statements. These accounting concepts will be considered in more detail in the next section.

Progress check 1.2

What are the aims of the UK Statement of Principles and how does it try to achieve these aims?

Accounting concepts

The accounting framework revolves around the practice of accounting and the accountancy profession, which is bounded by rules, or concepts (see Fig. 1.2, in which the five most important concepts

Figure 1.2 Accounting concepts

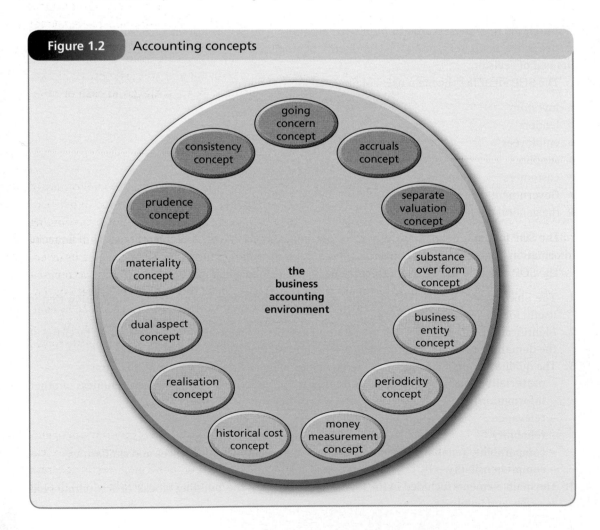

are shown in a darker colour) of what data should be included within an accounting system and how that data should be recorded.

Accounting concepts are the principles underpinning the preparation of accounting information relating to the ethical rules, boundary rules, and recording and measurement rules of accounting. Ethical rules, or principles, are to do with limiting the amount of judgement (or indeed creativity) that may be used in the reporting of financial information. Boundary rules are to do with which types of data, and the amounts of each, that should be held by organisations, and which elements of financial information should be reported. Recording and measurement rules of accounting relate to how the different types of data should be recorded and measured by the organisation.

Fundamental accounting concepts are the broad, basic assumptions, which underlie the periodic financial accounts of business enterprises. The five most important concepts, which are discussed in FRS 18, Accounting Policies, are as follows.

The prudence concept

Prudence means being careful or cautious. The **prudence concept** is an ethical concept that is based on the principle that revenue and profits are not anticipated, but are included in the income statement only when realised in the form of either cash or other assets, the ultimate cash realisation of which can be assessed with reasonable certainty. Provision must be made for all known liabilities and expenses, whether the amount of these is known with certainty or is a best estimate in the light of information available, and for losses arising from specific commitments, rather than just guesses. Therefore, companies should record all losses as soon as they are known, but should record profits only when they have actually been achieved in cash or other assets.

The consistency concept

The **consistency concept** is an ethical rule that is based on the principle that there is uniformity of accounting treatment of like items within each accounting period and from one period to the next. However, as we will see in Chapter 3, judgement may be exercised as to the application of accounting rules to the preparation of financial statements. For example, a company may choose from a variety of methods to calculate the **depreciation** of its machinery and equipment, or how to value its inventories. Until recently, once a particular approach had been adopted by a company for one accounting period then this approach should normally have been adopted in all future accounting periods, unless there were compelling reasons to change. The ASB now prefers the approaches adopted by companies to be revised by them, and the ASB encourages their change, if those changes result in showing a truer and fairer picture. If companies do change their approaches then they have to indicate this in their annual reports and accounts.

The going concern concept

The **going concern concept** is a boundary rule that assumes that the entity will continue in operational existence for the foreseeable future. This is important because it allows the original, historical costs of assets to continue to be used in the balance sheet on the basis of their being able to generate future income. If the entity was expected to cease functioning then such assets would be worth only

Financial mismanagement makes fans see Red

Liverpool chairman Martin Broughton has been forced to offer assurances to the Premier League that the club will fulfil their fixtures next season after their accounts, published yesterday, revealed record losses of £54.9million and soaring debts of £351million.

Broughton, appointed as non-executive chairman last month, had to provide proof that Liverpool could meet strict financial guidelines laid down by the Premier League and Uefa and that they would be able to continue trading as a going concern throughout the 2010–11 campaign.

It is believed the Royal Bank of Scotland, the club's banker, has provided reassurances that Liverpool will have sufficient funds to survive until the sale of owners Tom Hicks's and George Gillett's stakes can be finalised.

Though Broughton, in an interview with the club's television channel, yesterday insisted that process would take 'a matter of months', the publication of Liverpool's financial position will hardly help.

Accounts for the club's holding company for the year ending in July 2009 show spiralling interest payments of £40million, wages breaking the £100million-a-season barrier, a record loss of £54.9million and an increase in the club's debt of £51.5million.

Liverpool now stand £351million (net) in the red. Some £233million of that is owed to the government-owned RBS and the US investment bank Wachovia, while £144.4million is owed to Hicks and Gillett's parent company, Kop Cayman.

Much of Liverpool's losses - increased by £14million to July 2009 - can be attributed to the interest payments on that debt, which have cost the club a little over £40million alone, or almost £110,000 a day.

But the greatest concern is that Liverpool's financial picture can be so bleak in a year when the club's turnover was £185million, an increase of £20million on the previous year, thanks to the television rights and money accrued for last season's second-place finish in the Premier League and run to the Champions League quarter-finals.

Liverpool will finish no higher than sixth in the Premier League this season and were eliminated from the Champions League at the group stage. Though the club remain confident much of that loss will be compensated for by an £80million, four-year sponsorship deal with Standard Chartered, it is believed that some of that money is performance-related.

Twice this year Liverpool were forced to extend their credit facility on a short-term basis with RBS, while auditors KPMG expressed a 'material uncertainty' about the club's ability to continue for the second year running.

Source: **Liverpool slide further into red,** by Rory Smith
© *Daily Telegraph,* 8 May 2010

On 15 October 2010 the US Company New England Sports Ventures completed a £300 million takeover of the club from the former owners, Gillett and Hicks, which effectively cleared the club of all the debt that had been accrued by the former owners.

what they would be expected to realise if they were sold off separately (their break-up values) and therefore usually considerably less.

Even the most high-profile enterprises are not immune to the threat of failure to continue to trade. In February 2007 American tycoons George Gillett and Tom Hicks acquired Liverpool football club including its £44.8m debts. Both men already owned ice hockey and baseball clubs in the USA and guaranteed to invest £200m in the club. However, much of the capital for the takeover was financed by debt, bringing with it massive interest payments. This together with the club's decline in fortunes in the 2009/2010 season gave rise to grave concerns by the summer of 2010 over the ability of the club to continue to operate over the next season (see the press extract above).

The accruals concept

The **accruals concept** (or the matching concept) is a recording and measurement rule that is based on the principle that revenues and costs are recognised as they are earned or incurred, are matched with one another, and are dealt with in the income statement of the period to which they relate, irrespective of the period of receipt or payment. It would be misleading to report profit as the difference between cash received and cash paid during a period because some trading and commercial activities of the period would be excluded, since many transactions are based on credit.

Most of us are users of electricity. We may use it over a period of three months for heating, lighting, and running our many home appliances, before receiving an invoice from the electricity supplier for the electricity we have used. The fact that we have not received an invoice until much later doesn't mean we have not incurred a cost for each month. The costs have been accrued over each of those months, and we will pay for them at a later date.

The separate valuation concept

The **separate valuation concept** is a recording and measurement rule that relates to the determination of the aggregate amount of any item. In order to determine the aggregate amount of an asset or a liability, each individual asset or liability that makes up the aggregate must be determined separately. This is important because material items may reflect different economic circumstances. There must be a review of each material item to comply with the appropriate accounting standards:

- IAS 16 (Property, Plant and Equipment)
- IAS 36 (Impairment of Assets)
- IAS 37 (Provisions, Contingent Liabilities and Contingent Assets).

(See the later section, which discusses UK and international accounting and financial reporting standards called **Financial Reporting Standards (FRSs)**, **International Financial Reporting Standards (IFRSs)**, and **International Accounting Standards (IASs)**.)

Note the example of the Millennium Dome 2000 project, which was developed in Greenwich, London, throughout 1999 and 2000 and cost around £800m. At the end of the year 2000 a valuation of the individual elements of the attraction resulted in a total of around £100m.

The further eight fundamental accounting concepts are as follows.

The substance over form concept

Where a conflict exists, the **substance over form concept**, which is an ethical rule, requires the structuring of reports to give precedence to the representation of financial or economic reality over strict adherence to the requirements of the legal reporting structure. This concept is dealt with in IAS 17, Leases. When a company acquires an asset using a finance lease, for example a machine, it must disclose the asset in its balance sheet even though not holding legal title to the asset, whilst also disclosing separately in its balance sheet the amount that the company still owes on the machine. The reason for showing the asset in the balance sheet is because it is being used to generate income for the business, in the same way as a purchased machine. The substance of this accounting transaction (treating a leased asset as though it had been purchased) takes precedence over the form of the transaction (the lease itself).

The business entity concept

➠ The **business entity concept** is a boundary rule that ensures that financial accounting information relates only to the activities of the business entity and not to the other activities of its owners. An owner of a business may be interested in sailing and may buy a boat and pay a subscription as a member of the local yacht club. These activities are completely outside the activities of the business and such transactions must be kept completely separate from the accounts of the business.

The periodicity concept

➠ The **periodicity concept** (or time interval concept) is a boundary rule. It is the requirement to produce financial statements at set time intervals. This requirement is embodied, in the case of UK companies, in the Companies Act 2006 (all future references to the Companies Act will relate to the Companies Act 2006 unless otherwise stated). Both annual and interim financial statements are re-
➠ quired to be produced by **public limited companies (plcs)** each year.

Internal reporting of financial information to management may take place within a company on a monthly, weekly, daily, or even an hourly basis. But owners of a company, who may have no involvement in the running of the business or its internal reporting, require the external reporting of their company's accounts on a six-monthly and yearly basis. The owners of the company may then rely on the regularity with which the reporting of financial information takes place, which enables them to monitor company performance, and compare figures year on year.

The money measurement concept

➠ The **money measurement concept** is a recording and measurement rule that enables information relating to transactions to be fairly compared by providing a commonly accepted unit of converting quantifiable amounts into recognisable measures. Most quantifiable data are capable of being converted, using a common denominator of money, into monetary terms. However, accounting deals only with those items capable of being translated into monetary terms, which imposes a limit on the scope of accounting to report such items. You may note, for example, that in a university's balance sheet there is no value included for its human resources, that is its lecturers, managers, and secretarial and support staff.

The historical cost concept

➠ The **historical cost concept** is a recording and measurement rule that relates to the practice of valuing assets at their original acquisition cost. For example, you may have bought a mountain bike two years ago for which you were invoiced and paid £150, and may now be wondering what it is currently worth. One of your friends may consider it to be worth £175 because they feel that the price of new mountain bikes has increased over the past two years. Another friend may consider it to be worth only £100 because you have used it for two years and its condition has deteriorated. Neither of your friends may be incorrect, but their views are subjective and they are different. The only measure of what your bike is worth on which your friends may agree is the price shown on your original invoice, its historical cost.

Although the historical cost basis of valuation may not be as realistic as using, for instance, a current valuation, it does provide a consistent basis for comparison and almost eliminates the need for any subjectivity.

The realisation concept

The **realisation concept** is a recording and measurement rule and is the principle that increases in value should only be recognised on realisation of assets by arm's-length sale to an independent purchaser. This means, for example, that sales revenue from the sale of a product or service is recognised in accounting statements only when it is realised. This does not mean when the cash has been paid over by the customer; it means when the sale takes place, that is when the product or service has been delivered, and ownership is transferred to the customer. Very often, salespersons incorrectly regard a 'sale' as the placing of an order by a customer because they are usually very optimistic and sometimes forget that orders can get cancelled. Accountants, being prudent individuals, ensure that sales are correctly recorded through the issuing of an invoice when services or goods have been delivered (and installed).

The dual aspect concept

The **dual aspect concept** is the recording and measurement rule that provides the basis for double-entry bookkeeping. It reflects the practical reality that every transaction always includes both the giving and receiving of value. For example, a company may pay out cash in return for a delivery into its warehouse of a consignment of products that it subsequently aims to sell. The company's reduction in its cash balance is reflected in the increase in its inventory of products.

The materiality concept

Information is material if its omission or misstatement could influence the economic decisions of users taken on the basis of the financial statements. Materiality depends on the size of the item or error judged, its significance, in the particular circumstances of its omission or misstatement. Thus, materiality provides a threshold or cut-off point rather than being a primary qualitative characteristic that information must have if it is to be useful. The **materiality concept** is the overriding recording and measurement rule, which allows a certain amount of judgement in the application of all the other accounting concepts. The level of materiality, or significance, will depend on the size of the organisation and the type of revenue or cost, or asset or liability being considered. For example, the cost of business stationery is usually charged as an expense regardless of whether or not all the items have been used; it would be pointless to try and attribute a value to such relatively low-cost unused items.

True and fair view

The term **true and fair view** was introduced in the Companies Act 1947, requiring that companies' reporting of their accounts should show a true and fair view. It was not defined in that Act and has not been defined since. Some writers have suggested that conceptually it is a dynamic concept but over the years it could be argued that it has failed, and various business scandals and collapses have occurred without users being alerted. The concept of true and fair was adopted by the European Community Council in its fourth directive, implemented by the UK in the Companies Act 1981, and subsequently in the implementation of the seventh directive in the Companies Act 1989 (sections 226 and 227). Conceptually the directives require additional information where individual provisions are insufficient.

In practice true and fair view relates to the extent to which the various principles, concepts and standards of accounting have been applied. It may therefore be somewhat subjective and subject to change as new accounting rules are developed, old standards replaced and new standards introduced. It may be interesting to research the issue of derivatives and decide whether the true and fair view concept was invoked by those companies that used or marketed these financial instruments, and specifically consider the various collapses or public statements regarding losses incurred over the past few years. Before derivatives, the issue which escaped disclosure in financial reporting under true and fair view was leasing.

UK accounting and financial reporting standards

A number of guidelines, or standards (some of which we have already discussed), have been developed by the accountancy profession to ensure truth, fairness and consistency in the preparation and presentation of financial information.

A number of bodies have been established to draft accounting policy, set accounting standards, and to monitor compliance with standards and the provisions of the Companies Act. The Financial Reporting Council (FRC), whose chairman is appointed by the Secretary of State for Business, Innovation and Skills and the Bank of England, develops accounting standards policy and gives guidance on issues of public concern. The ASB, which is composed of members of the accountancy profession, and on which the Government has an observer status, has responsibility for development, issue and withdrawal of accounting standards.

The accounting standards are called Financial Reporting Standards (FRSs). Up to 1990 the **accounting standards** were known as **Statements of Standard Accounting Practice (SSAPs)**, and were issued by the Accounting Standards Committee (ASC), the forerunner of the ASB. Although some SSAPs have now been withdrawn there are, in addition to the new FRSs, a large number of SSAPs that are still in force.

The ASB is supported by the Urgent Issues Task Force (UITF). Its main role is to assist the ASB in areas where an accounting standard or Companies Act provision exists, but where unsatisfactory or conflicting interpretations have developed or seem likely to develop. The UITF also deals with issues that need to be resolved more quickly than through the issuing of an accounting standard. A recent example of this was the guidance on the accounting aspects of a recent EU directive which makes producers of electrical equipment responsible for financing waste management costs of their products, such as the costs of collection, treatment and environmentally sound disposal. The Financial Reporting Review Panel (FRRP) reviews comments and complaints from users of financial information. It enquires into the annual accounts of companies where it appears that the requirements of the Companies Act, including the requirement that annual accounts shall show a true and fair view, might have been breached. The Stock Exchange rules covering financial disclosure of publicly quoted companies require such companies to comply with accounting standards and reasons for non-compliance must be disclosed.

Pressure groups, organisations and individuals may also have influence on the provisions of the Companies Act and FRSs (and SSAPs). These may include some Government departments (for example HM Revenue & Customs and the Office of Fair Trading) in addition to the Department for Business, Innovation and Skills (BIS) and employer organisations such as the Confederation of British

Industry (CBI), and professional bodies like the Law Society, Institute of Directors, and Chartered Management Institute.

There are therefore many diverse influences on the form and content of company accounts. In addition to legislation, standards are continually being refined, updated and replaced and further enhanced by various codes of best practice. As a response to this the UK Generally Accepted Accounting Practices (UK GAAP), first published in 1989, includes all practices that are considered to be permissible or legitimate, either through support by statute, accounting standard or official pronouncement, or through consistency with the needs of users and of meeting the fundamental requirement to present a true and fair view, or even simply through authoritative support in the accounting literature. UK GAAP is therefore a dynamic concept, which changes in response to changing circumstances.

Within the scope of current legislation, best practice and accounting standards, each company needs to develop its own specific **accounting policies**. Accounting policies are the specific accounting bases selected and consistently followed by an entity as being, in the opinion of the management, appropriate to its circumstances and best suited to present fairly its results and financial position. Examples are the various alternative methods of valuing inventories of materials, or charging the cost of a machine over its useful life, that is, its depreciation.

The accounting standard that deals with how a company chooses, applies and reports on its accounting policies is called FRS 18, Accounting Policies, and was issued in 2000 to replace SSAP 2, Disclosure of Accounting Policies. FRS 18 clarified when profits should be recognised (the realisation concept), and the requirement of 'neutrality' in financial statements in neither overstating gains nor understating losses (the prudence concept). This standard also emphasised the increased importance of the going concern concept and the accruals concept. The aims of FRS 18 are:

- to ensure that companies choose accounting policies that are most suitable for their individual circumstances, and incorporate the key characteristics stated in Chapter 3 of the SOP
- to ensure that accounting policies are reviewed and replaced as necessary on a regular basis
- to ensure that companies report accounting policies, and any changes to them, in their annual reports and accounts so that users of that information are kept informed.

Whereas FRS 18 deals with the disclosure by companies of their accounting policies, FRS 3, Reporting Financial Transactions, deals with the reporting by companies of their financial performance. Financial performance relates primarily to the income statement, whereas financial position relates primarily to the balance sheet. FRS 3 aims to ensure that users of financial information get a good insight into the company's performance during the period to which the accounts relate. This is in order that decisions made about the company may be made on an informed basis. FRS 3 requires the following items to be included in company accounts to provide the required level of reporting on financial performance (which will all be discussed in greater detail in Chapter 4 which is about the income statement, and Chapter 8, which looks at published reports and accounts):

- analysis of sales, cost of sales, operating expenses and profit before interest
- exceptional items
- extraordinary items
- statement of recognised gains and losses (a separate financial statement along with the balance sheet, income statement and statement of cash flows).

> **Progress check 1.3**
>
> What is meant by accounting concepts and accounting standards, and why are they needed? Give some examples.

International accounting standards

The International Accounting Standards Committee (IASC), set up in 1973, which is supported by each of the major professional accounting bodies, fosters the harmonisation of accounting standards internationally. To this end each UK FRS (Financial Reporting Standard) includes a section explaining its relationship to any relevant international accounting standard.

There are wide variations in the accounting practices that have been developed in different countries. These reflect the purposes for which financial information is required by the different users of that information, in each of those countries. There is a different focus on the type of information and the relative importance of each of the users of financial information in each country. This is because each country may differ in terms of:

- who finances the businesses – individual equity shareholders, institutional equity shareholders, debenture holders, banks, etc.
- tax systems either aligned with or separate from accounting rules
- the level of government control and regulation
- the degree of transparency of information.

The increase in international trade and globalisation has led to a need for convergence, or harmonisation, of accounting rules and practices. The IASC was created in order to develop international accounting standards, but these have been slow in appearing because of the difficulties in bringing together differences in accounting procedures. Until 2000 these standards were called International Accounting Standards (IASs). The successor to the IASC, the IASB (International Accounting Standards Board), was set up in April 2001 to make financial statements more comparable on a worldwide basis. The IASB publishes its standards in a series of pronouncements called International Financial Reporting Standards (IFRSs). It has also adopted the body of standards issued by the IASC, which continue to be designated IASs.

The chairman of the IASB, Sir David Tweedie, has said that 'the aim of the globalisation of accounting standards is to simplify accounting practices and to make it easier for investors to compare the financial statements of companies worldwide'. He also said that 'this will break down barriers to investment and trade and ultimately reduce the cost of capital and stimulate growth' (*Business Week*, 7 June 2004). On 1 January 2005 there was convergence in the mandatory application of the IFRSs by listed companies within each of the European Union member states. The impact of this should be negligible with regard to the topics covered in this book, since UK accounting standards have already moved close to international standards. The reason for this is that the UK SOP was drawn up using the 1989 IASB conceptual framework for guidance. A list of current IFRSs and IASs is shown in Appendix 2 at the end of this book.

At the time of writing this book, major disagreements between the EU and accountants worldwide over the influence of the EU on the process of developing International Accounting Standards are causing concern that the dream of the globalisation of accounting standards may not be possible (see the article below from the 5 April 2010 edition of the *Financial Times*).

Who controls the IASB?

FT

The European Union's new internal market commissioner has proposed reforms to the body that sets international accounting rules, infuriating accountants and potentially scotching fragile hopes of global convergence.

In an apparent power grab by Brussels, Michel Barnier has suggested future funding of the International Accounting Standards Board might depend on whether it bows to political pressure from the European Commission to make changes to its governance.

Mr Barnier's suggestion, made at a meeting of top accountants and regulators in London, stunned the accounting community by raising questions about IASB independence during crucial talks to establish an international set of accounting rules.

The Group of 20 most industrialised nations last September pledged support for a single set of accounting standards to improve capital flows and reduce cross-border arbitrage in response to the financial crisis. However, achieving consensus is proving increasingly difficult.

Crucially, many European policymakers believe prudential regulators should be more involved in IASB governance so that accounting can be used as a tool for financial stability.

But accountants and business leaders – particularly in the US and Japan – argue that accounts should not be the subject of regulatory intervention but should focus on providing an accurate snapshot of a company's value.

During an increasingly tense meeting on future funding for the IASB, Mr Barnier said that "the two issues of financing and governance can be linked".

"We want to see more issuers – more banks and more companies – and more prudential regulators represented on the governing board [of the IASB]", he said.

Mr Barnier went on to say that it was "premature" to expect the EU to increase its annual £4.3m ($6.5m) budget contribution for the IASB. Moreover, Brussels intended to reconsider its funding annually.

Senior accountants said Mr Barnier's salvo could bring Brussels into conflict with the US and Asia and derail the convergence process.

More than 110 countries, including most of Europe and Asia, use the International Financial Reporting Standards drawn up by the IASB. US companies continue to report under Generally Accepted Accounting Principles while regulators consider whether to endorse IFRS.

Source: **Push for accounting convergence threatened by EU reform drive,** by Rachel Sanderson © *Financial Times,* 5 April 2010

Progress check 1.4

What is the significance of the International Financial Reporting Standards (IFRSs) that have been issued by the IASB?

Worked example 1.1

Young Fred Osborne decided that he would like to start to train to become an accountant. Some time after he had graduated (and after an extended backpacking trip across a few continents) he registered with the Chartered Institute of Management Accountants (CIMA). At the same time Fred started employment as part of the graduate intake in the finance department of a large engineering group. The auditors came in soon after Fred started his job and he was intrigued and a little confused at their conversations with some of the senior accountants. They talked about accounting concepts and this standard and that standard, SSAPs, FRSs, and IFRSs, all of which meant very little to Fred. Fred asked his boss, the Chief Accountant Angela Jones, if she could give him a brief outline of the framework of accounting one evening after work over a drink.

Angela's outline might have been something like this:

- Accounting is supported by a number of rules, or concepts, that have evolved over many hundreds of years, and by accounting standards to enable consistency in reporting through the preparation of financial statements.
- Accounting concepts relate to the framework within which accounting operates, ethical considerations and the rules relating to measurement of data.
- A number of concepts relate to the boundaries of the framework: business entity; going concern; periodicity.
- A number of concepts relate to accounting principles or ethics: consistency; prudence; substance over form.
- A number of concepts relate to how data should be measured and recorded: accruals; separate valuation; money measurement; historical cost; realisation; materiality; dual aspect.
- Accounting standards are formulated by a body comprised of members of the accounting institutes (Accounting Standards Board – ASB) and are guidelines which businesses are recommended to follow in the preparation of their financial statements.
- The original standards were the Statements of Standard Accounting Practice (SSAPs) which have been and continue to be superseded by the Financial Reporting Standards (FRSs).
- The aim of the SSAPs/FRSs is to cover all the issues and problems that are likely to be encountered in the preparation of financial statements and they are the authority to ensure that 'financial statements of a **reporting entity** give a true and fair view of its state of affairs at the balance sheet date and of its profit or loss for the financial period ending on that date' (as quoted from the ASB foreword to *Accounting Standards*).

- SSAPs were promulgated by the Accounting Standards Committee (ASC) and FRSs are promulgated by the ASB.
- In recent years the International Accounting Standards Board (IASB) which is an independent standard setting board based in the UK has sought to develop a set of high quality globally accepted financial reporting standards based upon clearly articulated accounting principles.
- From 2005 all listed companies in the EU have been required to prepare their financial statements in accordance with the standards of the IASB, which are called International Financial Reporting Standards (IFRSs).

There is considerable convergence between the international and UK standards and indeed the ASB develops and amends its standards in the light of IFRSs.

Financial accounting, management accounting and financial management

The provision of a great deal of information, as we shall see as we progress through this book, is mandatory; it is needed to comply with, for example, the requirements of Acts of Parliament, and HM Revenue & Customs. However, there is a cost of providing information that has all the features that have been described, which therefore renders it potentially useful information. The benefits from producing information, in addition to mandatory information, should therefore be considered and compared with the cost of producing that information to decide on which information is 'really' required.

Accountants may be employed by accounting firms, which provide a range of accounting-related services to individuals, companies, public services and other organisations. Alternatively, account-ants may be employed within companies, public services and other organisations. Accounting firms may specialise in **audit**, corporate taxation, personal taxation, VAT, or consultancy (see the right-hand column of Fig. 1.3). Accountants within companies, public service organisations etc., may be employed in the main functions of **financial accounting**, **management accounting**, and **treasury management** (see the left-hand column of Fig. 1.3), and also in general management. Accounting skills may also be required in the areas of **financial management** and corporate finance. Within companies this may include responsibility for investments, and the management of cash and foreign currency risk. External to companies this may include advice relating to mergers and acquisitions, and Stock Exchange **flotations**.

Financial accounting

Financial accounting is primarily concerned with the first question answered by accounting informa-tion, the scorecard function. Taking a car-driving analogy, financial accounting makes greater use of the rear-view mirror than the windscreen; financial accounting is primarily concerned with historical information.

Financial accounting is the function responsible in general for the reporting of financial in-formation to the owners of a business, and specifically for preparation of the periodic external reporting of financial information, statutorily required, for shareholders. It also provides simi-lar information as required for Government and other interested third parties, such as potential

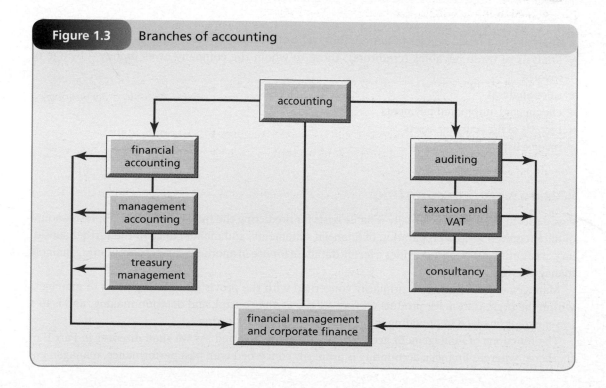

Figure 1.3   Branches of accounting

investors, employees, lenders, suppliers, customers and financial analysts. Financial accounting is concerned with the three key financial statements: the **balance sheet**; **income statement**; **statement of cash flows**. It assists in ensuring that financial statements are included in published reports and accounts in a way that provides ease of analysis and interpretation of company performance.

The role of financial accounting is therefore concerned with maintaining the scorecard for the entity. Financial accounting is concerned with the classification and recording of the monetary transactions of an entity in accordance with established concepts, principles, accounting standards and legal requirements and their presentation, by means of income statements, balance sheets and statements of cash flows, during and at the end of an **accounting period**.

Within most companies, the financial accounting role usually involves much more than the preparation of the three main financial statements. A great deal of analysis is required to support such statements and to prepare information both for internal management and in preparation for the annual audit by the company's external **auditors**. This includes sales analyses, bank reconciliations, and analyses of various types of expenditure.

A typical finance department has the following additional functions within the financial accounting role: control of **accounts payable** to suppliers (the **purchase ledger**); control of **accounts receivable** from customers (the **sales ledger**), and credit control; control of cash (and possible wider treasury functions) including cash payments, cash receipts, managers' expenses, petty cash, and banking relationships. The financial accounting role also usually includes responsibility for payroll, whether processed internally or by an external agency. However, a number of companies elect to transfer the responsibility for payroll to the personnel, or human resources department, bringing with it the possibility of loss of **internal control**.

The breadth of functions involved in financial accounting can require the processing of high volumes of data relating to purchase invoices, supplier payments, sales invoices, receipts from customers, other cash transactions, petty cash, employee expense claims and payroll data. Control and monitoring of these functions therefore additionally requires a large number of reports generated by the accounting systems, for example:

■ analysis of trade receivables (debtors): those who owe money to the company – by age of debt
■ analysis of trade payables (creditors): those to whom the company owes money – by age of invoice
■ sales analyses
■ cheque and automated payments
■ records of non-current assets
■ invoice lists.

Management accounting

Past performance is never a totally reliable basis for predicting the future. However, the vast amount of data required for the preparation of financial statements, and maintenance of the further subsidiary accounting functions, provides a fertile database for use in another branch of accounting, namely management accounting.

Management accounting is primarily concerned with the provision of information to managers within the organisation for product costing, planning and control, and decision-making, and is to a lesser extent involved in providing information for external reporting.

The functions of management accounting are wide and varied. As we shall discover in Part II of this book, whereas financial accounting is primarily concerned with past performance, management accounting makes use of historical data, but focuses almost entirely on the present and the future. Management accounting is involved with the scorecard role of accounting, but in addition is particularly concerned with the other two areas of accounting, namely problem-solving and attention-directing. These include cost analysis, decision-making, sales pricing, forecasting and budgeting, all of which will be discussed later in this book.

Financial management

Financial management has its roots in accounting, although it may also be regarded as a branch of applied economics. It is broadly defined as the management of all the processes associated with the efficient acquisition and deployment of both short- and long-term financial resources. Financial management assists an organisation's operations management to reach its financial objectives. This may include, for example, responsibility for corporate finance and treasury management, which is concerned with cash management, and the management of interest rate and foreign currency exchange rate risk.

The management of an organisation generally involves the three overlapping and inter-linking roles of strategic management, risk management and operations management. Financial management supports these roles to enable management to achieve the financial objectives of the shareholders. Financial management assists in the reporting of financial results to the users of financial information, for example shareholders, lenders and employees.

The responsibility of the finance department for financial management includes the setting up and running of reporting and control systems, raising and managing funds, the management of relationships with financial institutions, and the use of information and analysis to advise management regarding planning, policy and capital investment. The overriding requirement of financial management is to ensure that the financial objectives of the company are in line with the interests of the shareholders; the underlying fundamental objective of a company is to maximise shareholder wealth.

Financial management, therefore, includes both accounting and treasury management. Treasury management includes the management and control of corporate funds, in line with company policy. This includes the management of banking relationships, borrowings and investment. Treasury management may also include the use of the various financial instruments, which may be used to hedge the risk to the business of changes in interest rates and foreign currency exchange rates, and advising on how company strategy may be developed to benefit from changes in the economic environment and the market in which the business operates. This book will identify the relevant areas within these subjects, which will be covered as deeply as considered necessary to provide a good introduction to financial management.

As management accounting has continued to develop its emphasis on decision-making and strategic management, and broaden the range of activities that it supports, it has now come to be regarded as an integral part of financial management.

Worked example 1.2

A friend of yours is thinking about pursuing a career in accounting and would like some views on the major differences between financial accounting, management accounting and financial management.

The following notes provide a summary that identifies the key differences.

Financial accounting: The financial accounting function deals with the recording of past and current transactions, usually with the aid of computerised accounting systems. Of the various reports prepared, the majority are for external users, and include the income statement, balance sheet, and the statement of cash flows. In a plc, such reports must be prepared at least every 6 months, and must comply with current legal and reporting requirements.

Management accounting: The management accounting function works alongside the financial accounting function, using a number of the day-to-day financial accounting reports from the accounting system. Management accounting is concerned largely with looking at current issues and problems and the future in terms of decision-making and forecasting, for example the consideration of 'what if' scenarios during the course of preparation of forecasts and budgets. Management accounting outputs are mainly for internal users, with much confidential reporting, for example to the directors of the company.

Financial management: Financial management may include responsibilities for corporate finance and the treasury function. This includes the management and control of corporate funds, within parameters specified by the board of directors. The role often includes the management of company borrowings, investment of surplus funds, the management of both interest rate and exchange rate risk, and giving advice on economic and market changes and the exploitation of opportunities. The financial management function is not necessarily staffed by accountants. Plcs report on the treasury activities of the company in their periodic reporting and financial review.

Some of the important functions in which management accounting and financial management may be involved include:

■ forecasting revenues and costs
■ planning activities
■ managing costs
■ identifying alternative sources and costs of funding
■ managing cash
■ negotiations with bankers
■ evaluation of investments
■ measurement and control of performance
■ union negotiations
■ negotiating with government
■ costing compliance with social, environmental and sustainability requirements.

Progress check 1.5

What are the main differences between financial accounting, management accounting and financial management?

Accounting and accountancy

Accounting is sometimes referred to as a process of identifying, measuring and communicating economic information to permit informed judgements and decisions by users of the information, and also to provide information, which is potentially useful for making economic and social decisions. The term 'accounting' may be defined as:

- the classification and recording of monetary transactions
- the presentation and interpretation of the results of those transactions in order to assess performance over a period and the financial position at a given date
- the monetary projection of future activities arising from alternative planned courses of action.

Accounting processes are concerned with how data are measured and recorded and how the accounting function ensures the effective operation of accounting and financial systems. Accounting processes follow a system of recording and classification of data, followed by summarisation of financial information for subsequent interpretation and presentation. An accounting system is a series of tasks and records of an entity by which the transactions are processed as a means of maintaining financial records. Such systems identify, assemble, analyse, calculate, classify, record, summarise and report transactions.

Most companies prepare an accounting manual that provides the details and responsibilities for each of the accounting systems. The accounting manual is a collection of accounting instructions governing the responsibilities of persons, and the procedures, forms and records relating to preparation and use of accounting data.

There may be separate accounting manuals for the constituent parts of the accounting system, for example:

- financial accounting manual – general ledger and coding
- management accounting manual – budget and cost accounting
- financial management/treasury manual – bank reconciliations and foreign currency exposure management.

Accountancy is defined as the practice of accounting. A **qualified accountant** is a member of the accountancy profession, and in the UK is a member of one of the six professional accountancy bodies (see Fig. 1.4). An accountant becomes qualified within each of these institutes through passing a large number of extremely technically demanding examinations and completion of a mandatory period of three years' practical training. The examination syllabus of each of the professional bodies tends to be very similar; each body provides additional emphasis on specific areas of accounting.

Chartered Management Accountants (qualified members of CIMA) receive their practical training in industrial and commercial environments, and in the public sector, for example the NHS. They are involved in practical accounting work and development of broader experience of strategic and operational management of the business. Certified Accountants (qualified members of ACCA) and Chartered Accountants (qualified members of ICAEW, ICAS, or ICAI) usually receive training while working in a practising accountant's office, which offers services to businesses and the general public, but may also receive training while employed in industrial and commercial organisations. Training focuses initially on auditing, and may then develop to include taxation and general business advice. Many accountants who receive training while specialising in central and local government usually, but not exclusively, are qualified members of CIPFA.

There are also a number of other accounting bodies like the Association of Accounting Technicians (AAT), Association of International Accountants, and Association of Authorised Public Accountants. The AAT, for example, provides bookkeeping and accounting training through examination and

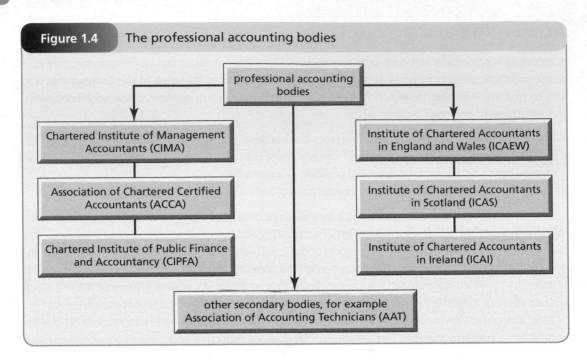

Figure 1.4 The professional accounting bodies

experience to a high level of competence, but short of that required to become a qualified accountant. Treasury management is served by the Association of Corporate Treasurers (ACT). This qualification has tended to be a second qualification for accountants specialising in corporate funding, cash and working capital management, interest rate and foreign currency exchange rate risk management. In the same way, the Institute of Taxation serves accountants who are tax specialists.

Progress check 1.6

What services does accounting offer and why do businesses need these services?

Worked example 1.3

Of which professional bodies are accountants likely to be members if they are employed as auditors, or if they are employed in the industrial and commercial sectors, or if they are employed in local government?

The following list of each of the types of professional accounting bodies links them with the sort of accounting they may become involved in.

Chartered Institute of Management Accountants (CIMA): management accounting and financial accounting roles with a focus on management accounting in the industrial and commercial sectors, and strategic and operational management

Institutes of Chartered Accountants (ICAEW, ICAS, ICAI): employment within a firm of accountants, carrying out auditing, investigations, taxation and general business advice – possible opportunities to move into an accounting role in industry

Chartered Institute of Public Finance and Accountancy (CIPFA): accounting role within central government or local government

Association of Chartered Certified Accountants (ACCA): employment either within a firm of accountants, carrying out auditing etc., or management accounting and financial accounting roles within commerce/industry

Association of Corporate Treasurers (ACT): commercial accounting roles with almost total emphasis on treasury issues: corporate finance; funding; cash management; working capital management; financial risk management

Types of business entity

Business entities are involved either in manufacturing (for example, food and automotive components) or in providing services (for example retailing, hospitals or television broadcasting). Such entities include profit-making and not-for-profit organisations, and charities. The main types of entity, and the environments in which they operate are represented in Figure 1.5. The four main types of profit-making organisations are explained in the sections that follow.

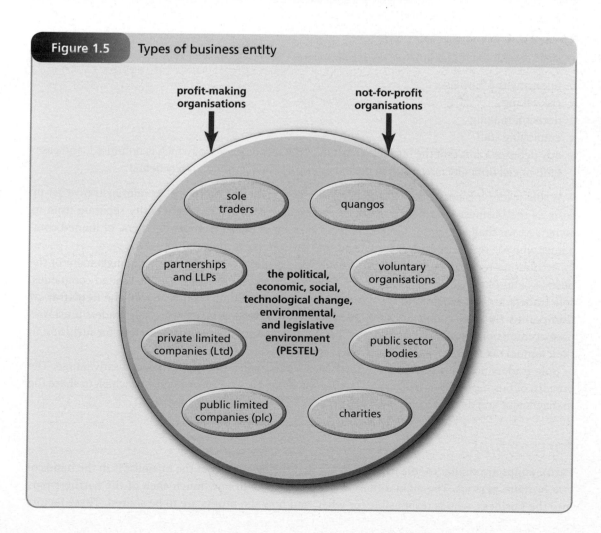

Figure 1.5   Types of business entity

The variety of business entities can be seen to range from quangos (quasi-autonomous non-government organisations) to partnerships to limited companies. Most of the topics covered in this book apply to any type of business organisation that has the primary aim of maximising the wealth of its owners: limited liability companies, both private (Ltd) companies and public (plc) limited companies, sole traders, and partnerships.

Progress check 1.7

What are the different types of business entity? Can you think of some examples of each?

Sole traders

A sole trader entity is applicable for most types of small business. It is owned and financed by one individual, who receives all the profit made by the business, even though more than one person may work in the business.

The individual sole trader has complete flexibility regarding:

■ the type of (legal) activities in which the business may be engaged
■ when to start up or cease the business
■ the way in which business is conducted.

The individual sole trader also has responsibility for:

■ financing the business
■ risk-taking
■ decision-making
■ employing staff
■ any debts or loans that the business may have (the responsibility of which is unlimited, and cases of financial difficulty may result in personal property being used to repay debts).

A sole trader business is simple and cheap to set up. There are no legal or administrative set-up costs as the business does not have to be registered since it is not a legal entity separate from its owner. As we shall see, this is unlike the legal position of owners, or shareholders, of limited companies who are recognised as separate legal entities from the businesses they own.

Accounting records are needed to be kept by sole traders for the day-to-day management of the business and to provide an account of profit made during each tax year. Unlike limited companies, sole traders are not required to file a formal report and accounts each year with the **Registrar of Companies** (in some countries called the chamber of commerce). However, sole traders must prepare accounts on an annual basis to provide the appropriate financial information for inclusion in their annual tax return for submission to HM Revenue & Customs.

Sole traders normally remain quite small businesses, which may be seen as a disadvantage. The breadth of business skills is likely to be lacking since there are no co-owners with which to share the management and development of the business.

Partnerships

Partnerships are similar to sole traders except that the ownership of the business is in the hands of two or more persons. The main differences are in respect of how much each of the partners puts into the business, who is responsible for what, and how the profits are to be shared. These factors are normally set out in formal partnership agreements, and if the partnership agreement is not specific then the provisions of the Partnership Act 1890 apply. There is usually a written partnership agreement (but this is not absolutely necessary) and so there are initial legal costs of setting up the business.

A partnership is called a firm and is usually a small business, although there are some very large partnerships, for example firms of accountants like PriceWaterhouseCoopers. Partnerships are formed by two or more persons and, apart from certain professions like accountants, architects and solicitors, the number of persons in a partnership is limited to 20.

A partnership:

- can carry out any legal activities agreed by all the partners
- is not a legal entity separate from its partners.

The partners in a firm:

- can all be involved in running the business
- all share the profits made by the firm
- are all jointly and severally liable for the debts of the firm
- all have unlimited liability for the debts of the firm (and cases of financial difficulty may result in personal property being used to repay debts)
- are each liable for the actions of the other partners.

Accounting records are needed to be kept by partnerships for the day-to-day management of the business and to provide an account of profit made during each tax year. Unlike limited companies, partnership firms are not required to file a formal report and accounts each year with the Registrar of Companies, but partners must submit annual returns for tax purposes to HM Revenue & Customs.

A new type of legal entity was established in 2001, the limited liability partnership (LLP). This is a variation on the traditional partnership, and has a separate legal identity from the partners, which therefore protects them from personal bankruptcy.

One of the main benefits of a partnership is that derived from its broader base of business skills than that of a sole trader. A partnership is also able to share risk-taking, decision-making and the general management of the firm.

Limited companies

A **limited company** is a legal entity separate from the owners of the business, which may enter into contracts, own property, and take or receive legal action. The owners limit their obligations to the amount of finance they have put into the company by way of the share of the company they have paid for. Normally, the maximum that may be claimed from shareholders is no more than they have paid for their shares, regardless of what happens to the company. Equally, there is no certainty that shareholders may recover their original investment if they wish to dispose of their shares or if the business is wound up, for whatever reason.

A company with unlimited liability does not give the owners, or members, of the company the protection of limited liability. If the business were to fail, the members would be liable, without limitation, for all the debts of the business.

The legal requirements relating to the registration and operation of limited companies is contained within the Companies Act 2006. Limited companies are required to be registered with the Registrar of Companies as either a private limited company (designated Ltd) or a public limited company (designated plc).

Private limited companies (Ltd)

Private limited companies are designated as Ltd. There are legal formalities involved in setting up a Ltd company which result in costs for the company. These formalities include the drafting of the company's Memorandum and Articles of Association (M and A) that describe what the company is and what it is allowed to do, registering the company and its director(s) with the Registrar of Companies, and registering the name of the company.

The shareholders provide the financing of the business in the form of share capital, of which there is no minimum requirement, and are therefore the owners of the business. The shareholders must appoint at least one director of the company, who may also be the company secretary, who carries out the day-to-day management of the business. A Ltd company may only carry out the activities included in its M and A.

Limited companies must regularly produce annual accounts for their shareholders and file a copy with the Registrar of Companies, and therefore the general public may have access to this information. A Ltd company's accounts must be audited by a suitably qualified accountant, unless it is exempt from this requirement, currently (with effect from 6 April 2008) by having annual sales of less than £6.5m and a balance sheet total of less than £3.26m. The exemption is not compulsory and having no audit may be a disadvantage: banks, financial institutions, customers and suppliers may rely on information from Companies House to assess creditworthiness and they are usually reassured by an independent audit. Limited companies must also provide copies of their annual accounts for Her Majesty's Revenue & Customs (HMRC) and also generally provide a separate computation of their profit on which corporation tax is payable. The accounting profit of a Ltd company is adjusted for:

- various expenses that may not be allowable in computing taxable profit
- tax allowances that may be deducted in computing taxable profit.

Limited companies tend to be family businesses and smaller businesses with the ownership split among a few shareholders, although there have been many examples of very large private limited companies. The shares of Ltd companies may be bought and sold but they may not be offered for sale to the general public. Since ownership is usually with family and friends there is rarely a ready market for the shares and so their sale usually requires a valuation of the business.

The Companies Act 2006 removed the requirement of a private limited company to hold an annual general meeting (AGM). However, if companies' Articles of Association require an AGM, then they must continue to be held unless the Articles are amended. Under the provisions of the Companies Act 2006, directors or 10% of the shareholders of a company may at any time request a general meeting to be held.

Public limited companies (plc)

Public limited companies are designated as plc. A plc usually starts its life as a Ltd company and then becomes a plc by applying for a listing of its shares on the Stock Exchange or the Alternative Investment Market, and making a public offer for sale of shares in the company. Plcs must have a minimum issued share capital of (currently) £50,000. The offer for sale, dealt with by a financial institution and the company's legal representatives, is very costly. The formalities also include the redrafting of the company's M and A, reflecting its status as a plc, registering the company and its director(s) with the Registrar of Companies, and registering the name of the plc.

The shareholders must appoint at least two directors of the company, who carry out the day-to-day management of the business, and a suitably qualified company secretary to ensure the plc's compliance with company law. A plc may only carry out the activities included in its M and A.

Plcs must regularly produce annual accounts, which they copy to their shareholders. They must also file a copy with the Registrar of Companies, and therefore the general public may have access to this information. The larger plcs usually provide printed glossy annual reports and accounts which they distribute to their shareholders and other interested parties. A plc's accounts must be audited by a suitably qualified accountant. Plcs must also provide copies of their annual accounts for HM Revenue & Customs and also generally provide a separate computation of their profit on which corporation tax is payable. The accounting profit of a plc is adjusted for:

- various expenses that may not be allowable in computing taxable profit
- tax allowances that may be deducted in computing taxable profit.

The shareholders provide the financing of the plc in the form of share capital and are therefore the owners of the business. The ownership of a plc can therefore be seen to be spread amongst many shareholders (individuals and institutions like insurance companies and pension funds), and the shares may be freely traded and bought and sold by the general public.

Worked example 1.4

Ike Andoowit is in the process of planning the setting up of a new residential training centre. Ike has discussed with a number of his friends the question of registering the business as a limited company, or being a sole trader. Most of Ike's friends have highlighted the advantages of limiting his liability to the original share capital that he would need to put into the company to finance the business. Ike feels a bit uneasy about the whole question and decides to obtain the advice of a professional accountant to find out:

(i)   the main disadvantages of setting up a limited company as opposed to a sole trader
(ii)   if Ike's friends are correct about the advantage of limiting one's liability
(iii) what other advantages there are to registering the business as a limited company.

The accountant may answer Ike's questions as follows:

Setting up as a sole trader is a lot simpler and easier than setting up a limited company. A limited company is bound by the provisions of the Companies Act 2006, and for example, may be required to have an independent annual audit. A limited company is required to be much more open about its affairs.

The financial structure of a limited company is more complicated than that of a sole trader. There are also additional costs involved in the setting up, and in the administrative functions of a limited company.

Running a business as a limited company requires registration of the business with the Registrar of Companies.

As Ike's friends have pointed out, the financial obligations of a shareholder in a limited company are generally restricted to the amount he or she has paid for his or her shares. In addition, the number of shareholders is potentially unlimited, which widens the scope for raising additional capital.

It should also be noted that:

- a limited company is restricted in its choice of business name
- if any director or 10% of the shareholders request it, a limited company is required to hold a general meeting at any time
- any additional finance provided for a company by a bank is likely to require a personal guarantee from one or more shareholders.

There are some differences between those businesses that have been established as sole traders and those established as partnerships, and likewise there are differences between private limited companies and public limited companies. What are these differences, and what are the similarities?

An introduction to financial statement reporting

Limited companies produce financial statements for each accounting period to provide adequate information about how the company has been doing. There are three main financial statements – balance sheet, income statement (or **profit and loss account**), and statement of cash flows. Companies are also obliged to provide similar financial statements at each year end to provide information for their shareholders, HMRC, and the Registrar of Companies. This information is frequently used by City analysts, investing institutions and the public in general.

After each year end companies prepare their **annual report and accounts** for their shareholders. Copies of the annual report and accounts are filed with the Registrar of Companies and copies are available to other interested parties such as financial institutions, major suppliers and other investors. In addition to the income statement and statement of cash flows for the year and the balance sheet as at the year end date, the annual report and accounts includes notes to the accounts, and much more financial and non-financial information such as company policies, financial indicators, corporate governance compliance, directors' remuneration, employee numbers, business analysis, and segmental analysis. The annual report also includes an operating and financial review of the business, a report of the auditors of the company, and the chairman's statement.

The auditors' report states compliance or otherwise with accounting standards and that the accounts are free from material misstatement, and that they give a true and fair view prepared on the assumption that the company is a going concern. The chairman's statement offers an opportunity for the chairman of the company to report in unquantified and unaudited terms on the performance of the company during the past financial period and on likely future developments. However, the auditors would object if there was anything in the chairman's statement that was inconsistent with the audited accounts.

What are the three main financial statements reported by a business? How are business transactions ultimately reflected in financial statements?

Fred Osborne soon settled into his graduate trainee role in the finance department of the large engineering group, and pursued his CIMA studies with enthusiasm. Although Fred was more interested in business planning and getting involved with new development projects, his job and his studies required him to become totally familiar with, and to be able to prepare, the financial statements of a company. Fred was explaining the subject of financial statements and what they involve to a friend of his, Jack, another graduate trainee in human resources. Where? – you've guessed it – over an after-work drink.

Fred explained the subject of financial statements to Jack, bearing in mind that he is very much a non-financial person.

Limited companies are required to produce three main financial statements for each accounting period with information about company performance for:

- shareholders
- HMRC
- banks
- City analysts
- investing institutions
- the public in general.

The three key financial statements are the:

(a) balance sheet
(b) income statement (or profit and loss account)
(c) statement of cash flows.

(a) Balance sheet: a financial snapshot at a moment in time, or the financial position of the company comparable with pressing the 'pause' button on a DVD. The DVD in 'play' mode shows what is happening as time goes on second by second, but when you press 'pause' the DVD stops on a picture; the picture does not tell you what has happened over the period of time up to the pause (or what is going to happen after the pause). The balance sheet is the consequence of everything that has happened up to the balance sheet date. It does not explain how the company got to that position.

(b) Income statement: this is the DVD in 'play' mode. It is used to calculate whether or not the company has made a gain or deficit on its operations during the period, its financial performance, through producing and selling its goods or services. Net earnings or net profit is calculated from revenues derived throughout the period between two 'pauses', minus costs incurred in deriving those revenues.

(c) Statement of cash flows: this is the DVD again in 'play' mode, but net earnings is not the same as cash flow, since revenues and costs are not necessarily accounted for when cash transfers occur. Sales are accounted for when goods or services are delivered and accepted by the customer but cash may not be received until some time later. The income statement does not reflect non-trading events like an issue of shares or a loan that will increase cash but are not revenues or costs. The statement of cash flows summarises cash inflows and cash outflows and calculates the net change in the cash position for the company throughout the period between two 'pauses'.

Users of accounting and financial information

Financial information is important to a wide range of groups both internal and external to the organisation. Such information is required, for example, by individuals outside the organisation to make decisions about whether or not to invest in one company or another, or by potential suppliers who wish to assess the reliability and financial strength of the organisation. It is also required by managers within the organisation as an aid to decision-making. The main users of financial information are shown in Figure 1.6.

Figure 1.6	Users of financial and accounting information

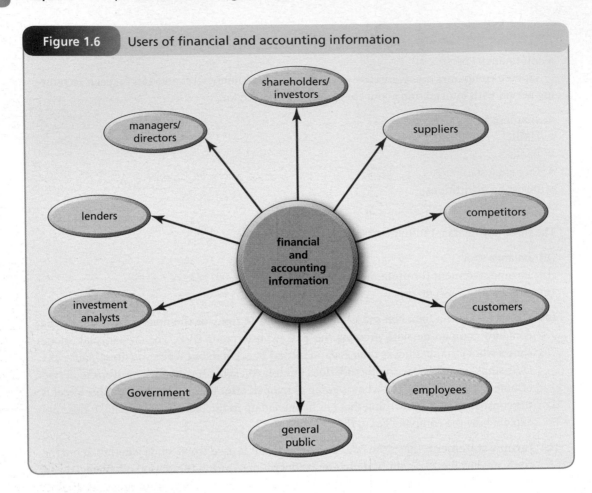

How many users of financial information can you think of and in what ways do you think they may use this information?

Worked example 1.6

Kevin Green, a trainee accountant, has recently joined the finance department of a newly formed public limited company. Kevin has been asked to work with the company's auditors who have been commissioned to prepare some alternative formats for the company's annual report.

As part of his preparation for this, Kevin's manager has asked him to prepare a draft report about who is likely to use the information contained in the annual report, and how they might use such information.

Kevin's preparatory notes for his report included the following:

- **Competitors** as part of their industry competitive analysis studies to look at market share, and financial strength
- **Customers** to determine the ability to provide a regular, reliable supply of goods and services, and to assess customer dependence

- **Employees** to assess the potential for providing continued employment and assess levels of remuneration
- **General public** to assess general employment opportunities, social, political and environmental issues, and to consider potential for investment
- **Government value added tax (VAT)** and corporate taxation, Government statistics, grants and financial assistance, monopolies and mergers
- **Investment analysts** investment potential for individuals and institutions with regard to past and future performance, strength of management, risk versus reward
- **Lenders** the capacity and the ability of the company to service debt and repay capital
- **Managers/directors** to a certain extent an aid to decision-making, but such relevant information should already have been available internally
- **Shareholders/investors** a tool of accountability to maintain a check on how effectively the directors/managers are running the business, and to assess the financial strength and future developments
- **Suppliers** to assess the long-term viability and whether the company is able to meet its obligations and pay suppliers on an ongoing basis.

Accountability and financial reporting

When we talk about companies we are generally referring to limited companies, as distinct from sole traders and partnerships (or firms – although this term is frequently wrongly used to refer to companies). As we have discussed, limited liability companies have an identity separate from their owners, the shareholders, and the liability of shareholders is limited to the amount of money they have invested in the company, that is their shares in the company. Ownership of a business is separated from its stewardship, or management, by the shareholders' assignment to a board of directors the responsibility for running the company. The directors of the company are accountable to the shareholders, and both parties must play their part in making that accountability effective.

The directors of a limited company may comprise one or more professionally qualified accountants (usually including a finance director). The directors of the company necessarily delegate to middle managers and junior managers the responsibility for the day-to-day management of the business. It is certainly likely that this body of managers, who report to the board of directors, will include a further one or more qualified accountants responsible for managing the finance function.

Accountability is maintained by reporting on the financial performance and the financial position of the business to shareholders on both a yearly and an interim basis. The reporting made in the form of the financial statements includes the balance sheet, income statement, and statement of cash flows, which will be considered in detail in Part I of this book.

You may question why all the accounting regulation that we have discussed in the earlier sections of this chapter is necessary at all. Well, there are a number of arguments in favour of such regulation:

- It is very important that the credibility of financial statement reporting is maintained so that actual and potential investors are protected as far as possible against inappropriate accounting practices.
- Generally, being able to distinguish between the good and not so good companies also provides some stability in the financial markets.
- The auditors of companies must have some rules on which to base their true and fair view of financial position and financial performance, which they give to the shareholders and other users of the financial statements.

External auditors are appointed by, and report independently to, the shareholders. They are professionally qualified accountants who are required to provide objective verification to shareholders and other users that the financial statements have been prepared properly and in accordance with legislative and regulatory requirements; that they present the information truthfully and fairly; and that they conform to the best accounting practice in their treatment of the various measurements and valuations.

The audit is defined by the Auditing Practices Board (APB) as 'an independent examination of, and expression of an opinion on, the financial statements of the enterprise'. There is a requirement for all companies registered in the UK to have an annual audit, except for those companies that (currently) have annual sales revenue of less than £6.5m and a balance sheet total of less than £3.26m.

The financial reporting of the company includes preparation of the financial statements, notes and reports, which are audited and given an opinion on by the external auditors. A regulatory framework exists to see fair play, the responsibility for which is held jointly by the Government and the private sector, including the accountancy profession and the Stock Exchange.

The Government exercises influence through bodies such as the Department for Business, Innovation and Skills (BIS) and through Parliament by the enactment of legislation, for example the Companies Act. Such legal regulation began with the Joint Stock Companies Act 1844.

Subsequent statutes exerted greater influence on company reporting: the Companies Acts 1948, 1967, 1981 and 1985, amended in 1989. The provisions included in these Acts were consolidated into the Companies Act 2006. The Companies Act 2006 contains the overall current legal framework.

It may be argued that the increasing amount of accounting regulation itself stifles responses to changes in economic and business environments, and discourages the development of improved financial reporting. We have already seen that the development of various conceptual frameworks indicates that there is wide disagreement about what constitutes accounting best practice. The resistance to acceptance of international accounting standards may be for political reasons, the rules perhaps reflecting the requirements of specific interest groups or countries.

It is also true that despite increasing accounting regulation there have been an increasing number of well-publicised financial scandals in the USA in particular, where the accounting systems are very much 'rule-based', as well as in the UK, Italy and Japan. However, these scandals have usually been the result of fraudulent activity. This leads to another question as to why the auditors of such companies did not detect or prevent such fraud. The answer is that, despite the widespread perception of the general public to the contrary, auditors are not appointed to detect or prevent fraud. Rather, they are appointed by the shareholders to give their opinion as to whether the financial statements show a true and fair view and comply with statutory, regulatory, and accounting and financial reporting standards requirements.

Progress check 1.11

In what ways may the reliability of financial reporting be ensured?

Worked example 1.7

You are thinking of changing jobs (within marketing) and moving from a local, well-established retailer that has been in business for over 20 years. You have been asked to attend an interview at a new plc that started up around two years ago. The plc is a retailer via the Internet. Your family has suggested that you investigate the company thoroughly before your interview, paying particular attention to its financial resources. There is a chance the plc may not be a going concern if its business plan does not succeed.

You will certainly want to include the following questions at your interview.

(a) Are any published accounts available for review?

(b) What is the share capital of the company (for example, is it £50,000 or £1,000,000)?

(c) Is the company profitable?

(d) Does the company have loan commitments?

(e) Is the company working within its bank overdraft facilities?

(f) Are any press analyses of the company available?

(g) What is the current customer base?

The answers may suggest whether the company can continue trading for the foreseeable future.

Summary of key points

- The three main purposes of accounting are: to provide records of transactions and a scorecard of results; to direct attention to problems; to evaluate the best ways of solving problems.

- Accountancy is the practice of accounting.

- Conceptual frameworks of accounting have been developed in many countries and the UK conceptual framework is embodied in the Statement of Principles (SOP).

- The framework of accounting is bounded by concepts (or rules) and standards, covering what data should be included within an accounting system and how that data should be recorded.

- International Financial Reporting Standards (IFRSs) have been developed, which have been adopted by listed companies within the European Union with effect from 1 January 2005.

- The main branches of accounting within commercial and industrial organisations are financial accounting, management accounting, treasury management, financial management and corporate finance.

- The main services, in addition to accounting, that are provided by accountants to commercial and industrial organisations are auditing, corporate taxation, personal taxation, VAT advice and consultancy.

- The large variety of types of business entity includes profit and not-for-profit organisations, both privately and Government owned, involved in providing products and services.

- The four main types of profit-making businesses in the UK are sole traders, partnerships, limited companies (Ltd) and public limited companies (plc).

- Accounting processes follow a system of recording and classifying data, followed by a summarisation of financial information for subsequent interpretation and presentation.

- The three main financial statements that appear within a business's annual report and accounts, together with the chairman's statement, directors' report and auditors' report, are the balance sheet, income statement and statement of cash flows.

- There is a wide range of users of financial information external and internal to an organisation. External users include: potential investors; suppliers; financial analysts. Internal users include: managers; shareholders; employees.

- Accountability is maintained by the reporting to shareholders on a yearly and half-yearly basis of sales and other activities and profits or losses arising from those activities, and the audit function.

Assessment material

Questions

Q1.1 **(i)** How many different types of business entity can you think of?
(ii) In what respect do they differ fundamentally?

Q1.2 **(i)** Why are accountants required to produce financial information?
(ii) Who do they produce it for and what do they do with it?

Q1.3 Describe the broad regulatory, professional, and operational framework of accounting.

Q1.4 What are conceptual frameworks of accounting?

Q1.5 **(i)** What are accounting concepts?
(ii) What purpose do they serve?

Q1.6 What is the UK Statement of Principles (SOP)?

Q1.7 **(i)** What is accountancy?
(ii) What is an accountant?
(iii) What do accountants do?

Q1.8 What do accountants mean by SSAPs and FRSs, and what are they for?

Q1.9 What are IASs and IFRSs and why are they important?

Q1.10 **(i)** What is financial management?
(ii) How does financial management relate to accounting and perhaps other disciplines?

Q1.11 How do financial statements ensure accountability for the reporting of timely and accurate information to shareholders is maintained?

Discussion points

D1.1 The managing director of a large public limited company stated: 'I've built up my business over the past 15 years from a one man band to a large plc. As we grew we seemed to spend more and more money on accountants, financial managers, and auditors. During the next few months we are restructuring to go back to being a private limited company. This will be much simpler and we can save a fortune on accounting and auditing costs.' Discuss.

(Hint: You may wish to research Richard Branson and, for example, Virgin Air, on the Internet to provide some background for this discussion.)

D1.2 The managing director of a growing private limited company stated: 'All these accounting concepts and standards seem like a lot of red tape to me, and we've got financial accountants and management accountants as well as auditors. Surely all I need to know at the end of the day is how much have we made.' Discuss.

D1.3 Is accounting objective? Discuss with reference to at least six different accounting concepts.

Exercises

Exercises E1.1 to E1.10 require an essay-type approach. You should refer to the relevant sections in Chapter 1 to check your solutions.

Level I

E1.1   *Time allowed – 15 minutes*

> **Discuss the implications of preparation of the income statement if there were no accounting concepts.**

E1.2   *Time allowed – 30 minutes*

At a recent meeting of the local branch of the Women's Institute they had a discussion about what sort of organisation they were. The discussion broadened into a general debate about all types of organisation, and someone brought up the term 'business entity'. Although there were many opinions, there was little sound knowledge about what business entities are. Jane Cross said that her husband was an accountant and she was sure he wouldn't mind spending an hour one evening to enlighten them on the subject. Chris Cross fished out his textbooks to refresh his knowledge of the subject and came up with a schedule of all the different business entities he could think of together with the detail of their defining features and key points of difference and similarity.

> **Prepare the sort of schedule that Chris might have drafted for his talk and identify the category that the Women's Institute might fall into.**

E1.3   *Time allowed – 30 minutes*

Mary Andrews was an accountant but is now semi-retired. She has been asked by her local comprehensive school careers officer to give a talk entitled: 'What is an accountant and what is accounting, and what are its use and its purpose?'.

> **Prepare a list of bullet points that covers everything necessary for Mary to give a comprehensive and easy-to-understand presentation to a group of sixth-formers at the school.**

Level II

E1.4   *Time allowed – 30 minutes*

Accounting standards in general are reasonably clear and unambiguous.

> **Are there any major areas where accountants may disagree in balance sheet accounting?**

E1.5   *Time allowed – 30 minutes*

Financial statements are produced each year by businesses, using prescribed formats.

> **Should major plcs be allowed to reflect their individuality in their own financial statements?**

E1.6   *Time allowed – 45 minutes*

Professionals in the UK, for example, doctors, solicitors, accountants etc., normally work within partnerships. Many tradesmen, such as plumbers, car mechanics, carpenters, and so on, operate as sole traders. Software engineers seem to work for corporations and limited companies.

> **Consider the size of operation, range of products, financing, the marketplace and the geographical area served, to discuss why companies like Microsoft and Yahoo! should operate as plcs.**

E1.7   *Time allowed – 60 minutes*

Bill Walsh has just been appointed Finance Director of a medium-sized engineering company, Nutsan Ltd, which has a high level of exports and is very sensitive to economic changes throughout the UK and the rest of the world. One of the tasks on Bill's action list is a review of the accounting and finance function.

> **What are the senior financial roles that Bill would expect to be in place and what are the important functions for which they should be responsible?**

E1.8   *Time allowed – 60 minutes*

Wembley Stadium II (the Football Association's replacement for the original iconic Wembley Stadium) was planned to open in 2003 but due to numerous problems financing the construction, problems in the general day-to-day operations, and changes of contractor, it finally opened in March 2007. There were many crises reported in the press during the course of the project and the development finally cost over £1 billion.

> **You are required to research into the Wembley Stadium II project using the BBC, *Financial Times*, and the other serious newspapers, and the Internet, and summarise the financial aspects of the project that you gather. You should focus on the attitudes expressed by the general public, Government ministers, and the Football Association management, and consider examples of bias, non-timeliness, and lack of transparency.**

E1.9   *Time allowed – 60 minutes*

Conceptual frameworks of accounting have been developed over many years and in many countries.

> **Explain how these culminated in the publication of the UK Statement of Principles (SOP) in 1999, and discuss the implications of each of the eight chapters.**

E1.10   *Time allowed – 60 minutes*

The International Accounting Standards Board (IASB) decreed the adoption of the International Financial Reporting Standards (IFRSs) by all listed companies within the European Union mandatory with effect from 1 January 2005.

> **Discuss the practical and political issues surrounding this decision.**

2

Classifying and recording financial transactions

Contents

Learning objectives

Completion of this chapter will enable you to:

■ explain the convention of double-entry bookkeeping

■ describe what is meant by 'debit' and 'credit'

■ enter business transactions into accounts

■ account for closing inventories and other accounting adjustments

■ explain the balancing of accounts

■ extract a trial balance from a company's accounts

■ prepare an income statement, balance sheet and statement of cash flows from a trial balance

■ appreciate the concepts of accrual accounting and cash accounting

■ explain and account for payments in advance (prepayments) and charges not yet received (accruals)

■ appreciate the importance of accounting periods.

Introduction

This chapter begins by explaining what is sometimes referred to as the dual aspect rule. This rule recognises that for all transactions there is a two-sided effect within the entity. A manager in a non-accounting role may not be expected to carry out the recording of transactions in this way, but an appreciation of how accounting data has been recorded will be extremely helpful in the interpretation of financial information. We will go on to describe the processes that deal with the two sides of each transaction, the 'debits' and 'credits' of double-entry bookkeeping.

Don't worry if at first these topics seem a little difficult and confusing. They will become clearer as we follow through some transactions step-by-step into the accounts of a business and show how these accounts are kept in balance.

The chapter continues with an introduction to the way in which each of the accounts is held in what are termed the books of account and ledgers of the business. The balances on all the accounts in an entity are summarised in what is called a trial balance. The trial balance may be adjusted to allow for payments in advance, charges not yet received, and other adjusting entries. From this information we will show how to prepare a simple income statement, balance sheet and statement of cash flows.

This chapter refers to some of the accounting concepts introduced in Chapter 1. In that context we will look at the time period chosen by a business, to which the financial reporting relates – the accounting period.

Theory and practice of double-entry bookkeeping

Double-entry bookkeeping has a long history, having been created by the father of modern accounting, the Franciscan monk Luca Pacioli in Italy in the late fifteenth century. His publication, *Summa de Arithmetica, Geometria, Proportioni et Proportionalita* (Everything about Arithmetic, Geometry and Proportion), published in 1494, was the first printed work dealing with algebra and also contained the first text on bookkeeping, entitled *Particularis de Computis et Scripturis*. Bookkeeping then spread throughout the world by a series of plagiarisms and imitations of Pacioli's work. If Pacioli were around today he would be very disappointed to see the extent to which double-entry has apparently not been practised in Greece in more recent times. During 2009 and 2010 the Greek economy was in severe economic difficulty. It may be significant that a large part of the Greek public sector does not use double-entry bookkeeping at all (see the press extract below).

It is important to remember that the idea of double-entry is a convention. There are two main objectives of bookkeeping: to have a permanent record of transactions; to show the effect of each transaction and the combined effect of all the transactions on the financial position of the entity.

The fundamental idea of double-entry bookkeeping is that all business transactions of a business entity, for example, cash and invoices, should be recorded twice in the entity's business records. It is based on the principle that every financial transaction involves the simultaneous receiving and giving of value, and is therefore recorded twice. Transactions of course involve both services and goods. We

Look what happens when you neglect double entry!

Standard & Poor's has become the second rating agency to downgrade Greek sovereign debt to near junk levels of BBB1, issuing a withering verdict on spartan plans unveiled this week by premier George Papandreou.

'The downgrade reflects our opinion that the measures to reduce the high fiscal deficit are unlikely, on their own, to lead to a sustainable reduction in the public debt burden. If political considerations and social pressures hamper progress, we could lower the ratings further', it said.

The move came as Spyros Papanikolaou, head of Greece's Public Debt Management Agency, held back-to-back meetings with bankers in London in a bid to stop the crisis spiralling out of control.

Yields on 10-year Greek bonds surged to 5.75pc, a spread of 254 basis points over German Bunds. Borrowing costs are nearing levels that risk setting off an interest compound spiral. The public debt is already 113pc of GDP. S&P said it is likely to reach 138pc by 2012. 'The increasing debt-service burden narrows the scope for debt stabilisation', it said.

Fitch Ratings precipitated the Greek crisis earlier this month with a surprisingly harsh downgrade to BBB1, accompanied by a 'negative outlook'.

It emerged yesterday that Greece had raised euro2bn (£1.77bn) at a premium of 30 basis points in a private placement shortly after the Fitch move, avoiding the public glare of an auction.

To make matters worse, there were fresh concerns yesterday about the true scale of Greek military spending, which is kept off the books of the debt agency.

'Greek military accounts seem to be regarded as a state secret', said Chris Pryce, Fitch's director of sovereign ratings.

'In every other EU country we can find out how much they spend on defence, but we don't know for Greece. All we know is that their military spending is very large, around 5pc of GDP', he said.

Analysts who have probed deeply into Greek accounts have been astonished to discover that parts of the public sector lack double-entry bookkeeping, 700 years after it was invented by the Venetians.

Given Greece has misled the bond markets and Brussels in the past over its deficits, analysts suspect that Athens may try to hide problems behind a military veil. Mr Papandreou admits that Greece has lost "every shred of credibility".

Greece has already cut defence this year. It announced in September that it would not take delivery of four submarines built by Thyssen-Krupp, alleging technical faults. This has led to accusations Athens is effectively defaulting on a euro520m contract. Last week it cancelled tenders for a flight of maritime aircraft worth up to euro250m.

Source: **Greek crisis deepens with S&P downgrade; worry about true scale of undisclosed military spending adds to concern**, by Ambrose Evans-Pritchard © *Daily Telegraph*, 17 December 2009

shall find out later in this chapter that there are other accounting entries which do not result directly from invoice or cash transactions but which also result in double-entry records being created. These ⟶ **accounting adjustment** entries relate, for example, to accounting for depreciation, **bad debts**, and ⟶ **doubtful debts**.

The convention of double-entry assumes that in all business transactions equal and opposite values are exchanged. For example, if a company purchases materials for £1,000 for cash it adds to its inventory of materials to the value of £1,000, but reduces its cash balance also to the value of £1,000. The convention uses two terms for convenience to describe the two aspects of each transaction. These terms are debit and credit.

There is sometimes confusion in the use of the terms debit and credit used in bookkeeping when they are compared with the same terms used on bank statements. Bank statements traditionally refer to a receipt of cash as a credit, whereas a receipt of cash in bookkeeping terms is referred to as a debit. The reason for this is that customer accounts are presented from the bank's point of view; as far as the bank is concerned, account holders are creditors, to whom the bank will eventually have to repay any money deposited by them.

Debits and credits

The explanation of debits and credits in terms of value received and value given respectively is not perhaps one that provides the clearest understanding. Neither is the explanation that debits are in the left-hand column and credits are in the right-hand column, or debits are on the side of the room closest to the window!

Debits and credits do represent certain types of account, as we will see later, in both the balance ⟶ sheet: **assets** and **liabilities**, and the income statement: **costs** and sales. However, for the purpose of clarity of explanation we shall propose a couple of basic assumptions with which to work from as we go through some elementary accounting entries.

If we initially consider all business transactions as either goods or services then it is reasonable to assume (unless we are in a barter society) that all these transactions will ultimately end up with cash (or cash equivalents, such as cheques, bank transfers, etc.) changing hands. We can also assume that all these transactions will involve a document being raised, as a record of the transaction and an indi- ⟶ cation of the amount of cash that will change hands, namely an invoice. A **purchase invoice** records ⟶ a purchase from a third party and so it represents an account to be payable at some time. A **sales invoice** records a sale to a third party and so it represents an account to be receivable at some time.

Business entities themselves have a separate identity from the owners of the business. When we consider double-entry bookkeeping we will now assume that all the entries we are discussing relate to those of the business entity, in whatever form the entity takes: sole trader; partnership; limited company; public limited company (see Chapter 1).

For the business entity, we shall define the following business transactions:

Transaction		Accounting entries	
CASH RECEIPT	=	DEBIT CASH	and credit something else
CASH PAYMENT	=	CREDIT CASH	and debit something else
PURCHASE INVOICE	=	CREDIT ACCOUNTS PAYABLE	and debit something else
SALES INVOICE	=	DEBIT ACCOUNTS RECEIVABLE	and credit something else

These are definitions within the convention of double-entry bookkeeping, which may be usefully re-membered as a basis for establishing whether all further subsequent transactions are either debits or credits. It is suggested that the above four statements are kept filed in permanent memory, as a useful aid towards the understanding of further accounting entries.

Outline what is meant by double-entry bookkeeping.

An elementary method of representing and clarifying double-entry is known as the T account. We shall use this method to demonstrate double-entry in action using a simple example. (Note that in the UK there are many computerised accounting packages that automate the double-entry for a business, for example Sage. The purpose of this extensive worked example is to illustrate how such transactions take place.)

Worked example 2.1

Mr Bean decides to set up a wholesale business, Ayco, on 1 January 2010. He has his own cash resources available for the purpose of setting it up and has estimated that an initial £50,000 would be required for this purpose. During the first month in business, January 2010, *Ayco* (as distinct from Mr Bean) will enter into the following transactions:

	£
Receipt of cheque from Mr Bean	50,000
Purchase the freehold of a shop for cash	30,000
Purchase the shop fittings for cash	5,000
Cash expenses on printing and stationery	200
Purchases of inventory, from Beeco, of Aymen toys, payable two months later	
(12,000 toys at £1 each)	12,000
Sales of Aymen toys to Ceeco for cash (1,000 toys at £2 each)	2,000
Sales of Aymen toys to Deeco, receivable one month later	
(8,000 toys at £2 each)	16,000

We shall consider each of these transactions in detail and subsequently represent them in T account format for clarity, with debits on the left and credits on the right of the middle line of the T. We will repeatedly refer to the earlier four key double-entry definitions in order to establish the entries required for each transaction.

Receipt of cheque from Mr Bean £50,000 – transaction 1

Ayco will have needed to open a bank account to pay in the money received from Mr Bean. This represents a receipt of cash of £50,000 to Ayco, and so:

Debit cash account   **£50,000 and credit what?**

This money represents the capital that Mr Bean, as the sole investor in the business, has invested in Ayco and so the account is called the capital account. So:

Debit cash account   **£50,000**
Credit capital account   **£50,000**

Worked example 2.2

Purchase for cash the freehold of a shop £30,000 – transaction 2

This represents a cash payment for the purchase of a shop, something which is called a non-current asset: an asset acquired for retention by the entity for the purpose of providing a service to the business, and not held for resale in the normal course of trading.

Credit cash account	£30,000 and debit what?

A payment of cash of £30,000 is a credit to the cash account, and so:

Credit cash account	£30,000
Debit non-current assets – shop account	£30,000

Worked example 2.3

Purchase for cash the shop fittings £5,000 – transaction 3

This represents a cash payment for the shop fittings, which are also non-current assets, but a different category of non-current asset from the freehold shop.

A payment of cash of £5,000 is a credit to the cash account, and so:

Credit cash account	£5,000
Debit non-current assets – fittings account	£5,000

Worked example 2.4

Cash expenses on printing and stationery £200 – transaction 4
This represents a payment of cash of £200 by Ayco in the month, and so:

Credit cash account	£200 and debit what?

This money was paid out on day-to-day expenses that have been made to support the business, and is a charge for printing and stationery expenses. So:

Credit cash account	£200
Debit printing and stationery expenses account	£200

Worked example 2.5

Purchases of inventory, from Beeco, of Aymen toys, payable two months later £12,000 – transaction 5

This represents a purchase on credit from Beeco. An invoice is assumed to have been received from Beeco along with the receipt of inventory. The invoice from Beeco is a purchase invoice for £12,000 to Ayco, and so:

Credit accounts payable	£12,000 and debit what?

This represents a purchase of inventory which are goods held for resale, and so:

Credit accounts payable	£12,000	
Debit inventories account	£12,000	a purchase of inventory may alternatively be initially debited to the purchases account and then subsequently transferred to the inventories account.

Worked example 2.6

Sales of Aymen toys to Ceeco for cash £2,000 – transaction 6
This represents a sale for cash to Ceeco. An invoice will be issued by Ayco to Ceeco along with the delivery of inventory. The invoice to Ceeco is a sales invoice for £2,000 from Ayco, and so:

Debit accounts receivable	£2,000	and credit what?

This represents sales of inventory which are called sales, or sales revenue, and so:

Debit accounts receivable	£2,000
Credit sales revenue account	£2,000

But as a cash sale this sales invoice is being paid immediately with a cash receipt of £2,000, and so:

Debit cash account	£2,000	and credit what?

This £2,000 is immediately paying accounts receivable, and so

Debit cash account	£2,000
Credit accounts receivable	£2,000

which means that on this transaction the net balance of accounts receivable is zero.

This transaction may be short cut by directly crediting the sales revenue account and debiting cash. However, it is normally recorded in the way described in order to create and record a value added tax (VAT) sales invoice.

Worked example 2.7

Sales of Aymen toys to Deeco, receivable one month later £16,000 – transaction 7
This represents sales on credit to Deeco. An invoice will be issued by Ayco to Deeco along with the delivery of inventory.

The invoice to Deeco is a sales invoice for £16,000 from Ayco, and so as above:

Debit accounts receivable	£16,000
Credit sales revenue account	£16,000

This is different from the transaction in Worked example 2.6 because the account receivable will not be paid until the following month.

Closing inventories adjustment

In the Ayco example, one further accounting entry needs to be considered, which relates to the inventory of toys sold during the period. It is called a **closing inventories** adjustment, which is illustrated in Worked example 2.8.

Worked example 2.8

We represented the purchase of 12,000 toys into the inventory of Ayco as a debit of £12,000 to the inventories account. Ayco sold 1,000 toys for cash and 8,000 toys on credit. The physical inventory of 12,000 toys at 31 January 2010 has therefore been reduced to only 3,000 (12,000 − 1,000 − 8,000). We may value these units that are left in inventory at cost, for the purpose of this example, at 3,000 × £1, or £3,000. Ayco sold a total of 9,000 units during January at a selling price of £2 per unit. These 9,000 units cost £1 each and so these sales have cost Ayco £9,000: cost of sales £9,000. A double-entry accounting transaction is necessary to represent this for two reasons: to show the cost of the 9,000 toys that matches the sale of 9,000 toys; to ensure that the inventories account represents only the physical toys that are actually held in inventory.

The entries for the original purchase of inventory were:

Credit accounts payable	£12,000
Debit inventories account	£12,000

We know that the inventories account should now be £9,000 less than the original £12,000, representing the £9,000 cost of sales. Therefore we need to credit the inventories account to reduce it and debit something else. The something else is the cost of sales account.

Transaction 8

Credit inventories account	£9,000
Debit cost of sales account	£9,000

Accounting adjustments

The diagram in Figure 2.1 includes all the main types of accounting transactions that may be recorded in an accounting system. The shaded items represent the prime entries (the first record of transactions) and cash entries. The non-shaded items are the five main accounting adjustment entries.

The closing inventories adjustment, illustrated in Worked example 2.8, is one of the five main accounting adjustment entries that are shown in Figure 2.2, which may or may not be incorporated into the **trial balance**.

Accounting adjustments are made to the trial balance and prior to preparation of the income statement and balance sheet. The other four adjusting entries are **accruals** and **prepayments** (covered later in this chapter), depreciation, and bad and doubtful debts and the **doubtful debt provision** (which are covered together with further detail on closing inventories in Chapter 4).

Each of the T accounts for Ayco in Figure 2.3 shows the detailed movement through the month and each account represents the balance on each account at the 31 January 2010, the end of the first month of trading.

Figure 2.1   Accounting transactions

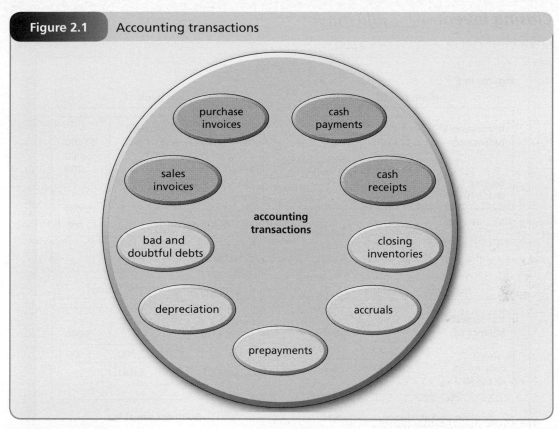

Figure 2.2   The five accounting adjustments and their impact on the profit and loss account and the balance sheet

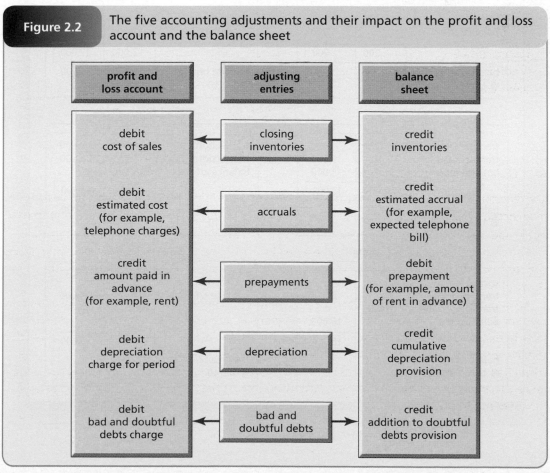

Figure 2.3   T account representation of the January 2010 transactions of Ayco

Figures in £

share capital

transaction 1		50,000
balance c/f	50,000	
	50,000	50,000
balance b/f @ 1/2/10		50,000

cash book

transaction 1	50,000	
transaction 2		30,000
transaction 3		5,000
transaction 4		200
transaction 6	2,000	
balance c/f		
		16,800
	52,000	52,000
balance b/f @ 1/2/10	16,800	

non-current assets – shop

transaction 2	30,000	
balance c/f		30,000
	30,000	30,000
balance b/f @ 1/2/10	30,000	

non-current assets – fittings

transaction 3	5,000	
balance c/f		5,000
	5,000	5,000
balance b/f @ 1/2/10	5,000	

printing and stationery – expenses

transaction 4	200	
balance c/f		200
	200	200
balance b/f @ 1/2/10	200	

accounts payable

transaction 5		12,000
balance c/f	12,000	
	12,000	12,000
balance b/f @ 1/2/10		12,000

inventories

transaction 5	12,000	
transaction 8		9,000
balance c/f		3,000
	12,000	12,000
balance b/f @ 1/2/10	3,000	

sales revenue

transaction 6		2,000
transaction 7		16,000
balance c/f	18,000	
	18,000	18,000
balance b/f @ 1/2/10		18,000

accounts receivable

transaction 6	2,000	
transaction 6		2,000
transaction 7	16,000	
balance c/f		16,000
	18,000	18,000
balance b/f @ 1/2/10	16,000	

cost of sales

transaction 8	9,000	
balance c/f		9,000
	9,000	9,000
balance b/f @ 1/2/10	9,000	

Explain broadly what is meant by accounting adjustment entries.

Books of account and the ledgers in action

We saw in the previous section how the principle of double-entry bookkeeping operates to record the detail of transactions. We represented these records in T accounts to provide some clarity in seeing how each entry has been made and the interrelation of the entries. In practice, accounting records are kept along the same lines but in books of account and ledgers rather than T accounts on a piece of paper. The old-fashioned manually prepared ledgers maintained by companies have long since been superseded by **computerised accounting systems**. Nevertheless, the same principles apply and the same books of account and ledgers are maintained albeit in an electronic format.

The chart shown in Figure 2.4 shows the relationship between the main ledger, the general ledger (or nominal ledger) and the other books of account, and subsidiary ledgers:

- **cash book** (receipts and payments)
- **purchase invoice daybook** and accounts payable (or purchase ledger)
- **sales invoice daybook** and accounts receivable (or sales ledger).

It also shows the main sources of data input for these ledgers and the basic reporting information produced out of these ledgers and books of account.

Figure 2.4 The general ledger and its relationship with the cash book, accounts payable and accounts receivable

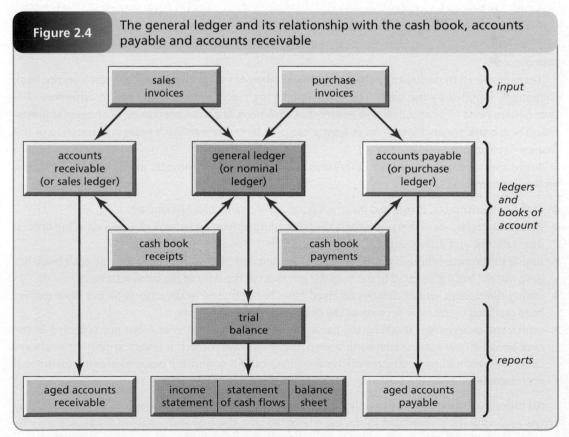

Source: Based on *CIMA Official Terminology*, 2005 ed., CIMA Publishing, Elsevier p.58.

General ledger

In smaller businesses, wages and salaries data are usually recorded in the cash book and subsequently posted to the general ledger. In larger companies, wages and salaries usually have their own ledgers and control accounts in the general ledger.

The main ledger of any company, in which the results of all transactions made by the entity are recorded, is called the **general ledger** or nominal ledger. This ledger is set up to include all accounts whether they are assets, liabilities, sales (or revenues), or costs (or expenses). The detail of every transaction finds its way into this ledger, or is posted to it (to use the technical term), in much the same way as we saw in the T accounts. The general ledger may be said to be the collection of every T account within the entity.

Within the general ledger one account or more will be established to represent cash transactions (including cheques, drafts, bank transfers, etc.). These entries are posted to the general ledger from the analysis of entries made into the cash book. The cash book is a book of original entry maintained to show the detail of all receipts and payments made by the entity; it records the dates, values and unique references of all receipts and payments, and what they are for. These include, for example, payment of salaries, receipts from customers, purchase of non-current assets, etc.

Cash book

The cash book is a book of account that in theory should match exactly with the regular statements issued by the entity's bank. In practice, the cash book is prepared partly from company internally generated **cash payments** information and available information relating to **cash receipts**. Some transactions may appear in the bank account without prior notification, for example bank charges, and so the cash book may also be partly prepared with reference to information from the bank statement.

There is a need to periodically check cash book balances against the balances shown on the bank statements supplied by the bank. The two numbers are rarely the same and so the differences between them need to be reconciled to ensure that cash book balances are correct. The regular preparation of a **bank reconciliation** on at least a monthly basis is therefore a necessary function of the finance department.

There are five main reasons for differences between cash book balances and the balances shown on bank statements:

- cash book arithmetic errors and incorrect postings of receipts and payments
- cash book omissions of items shown on the bank statements such as bank charges, standing orders, direct debits, and dishonoured (returned) cheques
- timing differences where cheques have been written and issued and entered in the cash book but have not yet been presented to the bank for payment at the date of the bank statement
- timing differences where cheques received have been entered in the cash book but have not yet been credited to the bank account at the date of the bank statement
- errors and overcharges made by the banks included in their statements but not reflected in the cash book (do not assume that bank statements are always correct: it is very important to always check interest and bank charges calculations in detail on a monthly basis, to identify errors and overcharges made by the banks).

All differences between the cash book and bank statement balance must be identified and any errors and omissions corrected in the cash book so that the updated cash book balance may be reconciled with the bank statement balance as follows:

	balance per cash book
plus:	**cheques paid but not yet presented**
minus:	**receipts not yet credited**
=	**balance per bank statement**

Each payment and each receipt is posted from the cash book to the cash account in the general ledger as a credit or debit to cash. The opposite entry, either debit or credit, is posted at the same time to its relevant account in the general ledger, for example accounts payable, printing and stationery expenses, accounts receivable, etc. In the days when accounting ledgers were maintained manually such postings were made weekly or monthly. With computerised, integrated accounting systems postings may be made simultaneously to the cash book and the general ledger from the same source but avoiding any duplication of effort.

It is most important that the balance on the cash book, the net of all receipts and payments, at all times equals the balance of the cash book represented in the cash account within the general ledger, and that all the opposite entries have also been posted to their relevant accounts. In this way, the equality of total debits and total credits is maintained. The use of computerised accounting systems should guarantee this.

Worked example 2.9

The debit balance on the cash book of Renfrew Ltd at 31 May 2010 is £4,800, but the bank statement at the same date shows a balance of £6,768. A comparison of the company's cash book with the bank statements has identified the following differences at 31 May 2010:

Cheques received amounting to £1,986 have been entered in the cash book prior to 31 May 2010 and paid into the bank but have not been credited to Renfrew's account until 5 June.

Cheques paid amounting to £4,364 have been entered in the cash book but not presented for payment and shown on the bank statement until after 31 May 2010.

Bank charges of £180 have been included in the bank statement but have not been entered in the cash book.

Dividends received of £220 appear on the bank statement but have not been entered into the cash book.

A cheque received from a credit customer for £450 was entered in the cash book and paid into the bank, but on 30 May this was returned unpaid because the customer had fled to South America.

First, we need to make the appropriate corrections to the cash book.

		£
	balance per cash book	4,800
plus:	dividends received	220
minus:	bank charges	180
	returned cheque	450
		4,390

We can now prepare a bank reconciliation as at 31 May 2010.

		£
	balance per cash book	4,390
plus:	cheques paid but not yet presented	4,364
minus:	receipts not yet credited	1,986
	balance per bank statement	6,768

Accounts payable

Payables are recorded in a ledger, the accounts payable account, which represents all supplier account balances owed by the entity. Within the general ledger one account or more (control accounts) will be established to represent trade payables transactions, the purchases by the entity for which invoices have been rendered by suppliers, or vendors. All supplier invoices are recorded in accounts payable and analysed into the various items of expense by allocating them to a specific general ledger control account. These entries are debited to the appropriate general ledger accounts from the analysis of supplier invoices that are posted to accounts payable. The totals of these entries are credited to the control account representing accounts payable in the general ledger.

The accounts payable ledger is maintained to show the detail of all invoices received from and cash paid to suppliers. In addition to its functions of posting the totals of invoices to the accounts payable control account in the general ledger, and the analysis of what the invoices represent to the appropriate accounts in the general ledger, accounts payable may be analysed to show all invoices, credit notes, cash payments, etc. and grouped by supplier.

Payments made to suppliers are recorded in the cash book, and are credited to the cash account and debited to the accounts payable control account in the general ledger. They are also recorded in detail by amount, date and supplier within the trade payables supplier accounts. In this way it can be seen that the total balances at any one time of all supplier accounts within accounts payable equal the balance on the accounts payable control account in the general ledger.

Accounts receivable

Receivables are recorded in another ledger – the accounts receivable account, which represents all customer account balances owed to the entity. Within the general ledger one account or more will be established (control accounts) to represent accounts receivable transactions – the sales by the entity for which invoices have been issued to customers. All customer invoices are recorded in accounts receivable and analysed into the various items of sale or revenue by allocating them to a specific general ledger control account. These entries are credited to the appropriate general ledger accounts from the analysis of customer invoices posted to accounts receivable. The totals of these entries are debited to the control account(s) representing accounts receivable in the general ledger.

The accounts receivable ledger is maintained to show the detail of all invoices issued to and cash received from customers. The totals of customer invoices are posted to the accounts receivable control account in the general ledger. The analyses of what the invoices represent are posted to the appropriate accounts in the general ledger. The sales ledger may also enable each invoice to be analysed and grouped by customer.

Receipts from customers are recorded in the cash book, and are debited to the cash account and credited to the accounts receivable control account in the general ledger. They are also recorded in detail by amount, date and customer within the accounts receivable customer accounts. In this way the total balances at any one time of all customer accounts within accounts receivable equal the balance on the accounts receivable control account in the general ledger.

The cash accounts, accounts payable and accounts receivable control accounts in the general ledger are referred to as control accounts because they provide control over the same transactions which are also represented in some further detail, and which must agree in total, in what are termed the books of account and subsidiary ledgers: the cash book, accounts payable (purchase ledger), and accounts receivable (sales ledger).

Progress check 2.3

What are the usual books of account and ledgers you would expect to be used in a company's accounting system?

The trial balance

A **trial balance** is a list of account balances in a double-entry system. If the records have been correctly maintained, the sum of the debit balance accounts will be equal and opposite to the sum of the credit balance accounts, although certain errors such as omission of a transaction or erroneous entries will not be apparent in the trial balance.

Worked example 2.10

If we turn again to the Ayco example, we can see that each of the T accounts we have prepared represents the general (or nominal) ledger balances of the entity. These balances may be listed to form a trial balance for Ayco as at 31 January 2010.

The trial balance for Ayco as at 31 January 2010:

	Debit £	Credit £
Capital		50,000
Cash	16,800	
Non-current assets – shop	30,000	
Non-current assets – fittings	5,000	
Printing and stationery expenses	200	
Accounts payable		12,000
Inventories	3,000	
Sales revenue		18,000
Accounts receivable	16,000	
Cost of sales	9,000	
	80,000	80,000

From this simple trial balance it is possible to derive three reports that tell us something about the business: the income statement; the balance sheet; the statement of cash flows.

How do we know which items in the trial balance are balance sheet items and which are income statement items? Well, if an item is not a cost (expense) or a sales revenue item, then it must be an asset or a liability. The expenses and revenues must appear in the income statement and the assets and liabilities must appear in the balance sheet. Even a computerised accounting system must be told the specific classification of a transaction.

Worked example 2.11

Let's examine each of the items in the Ayco trial balance as at 31 January 2010.

	Debit £	Credit £
Capital account		50,000
This represents the original money that the investor Mr Bean put into Ayco – not revenue or expense.		
Cash account	16,800	
This represents the total cash that Ayco has at its disposal at 31 January, an asset – not revenue or expense.		
Non-current assets – shop account	30,000	
This represents assets purchased out of cash to help run the business – not revenue or expense.		
Non-current assets – fittings account	5,000	
This represents assets purchased out of cash to help run the business – not revenue or expense.		
Printing and stationery expenses account	200	
This represents costs incurred on disposable items used in running the business through January – expense.		
Accounts payable		12,000
This represents debts which Ayco must pay in the next two months, a liability – not revenue or expense.		
Inventories account	3,000	
This represents items held in inventory to sell to customers over future periods, an asset – not revenue or expense.		
Sales revenue account		18,000
This represents the value of toys delivered to customers in January – revenue.		
Accounts receivable	16,000	
This represents debts for which Ayco will receive payment next month, an asset – not revenue or expense.		
Cost of sales account	9,000	
This represents the cost of toys delivered to customers in January – expense.		
	80,000	80,000

Income statement

The income statement shows the profit or loss generated by an entity during an accounting period by deducting all costs from total sales. Within the trial balance we may extract the balances on the costs (expenses) and sales revenue accounts in order to construct the income statement. The total sum of these accounts will then result in a balance which is a profit or a loss, and which may be inserted back into a restated trial balance in summary form in place of all the individual profit and loss items which make up that balance.

Worked example 2.12

The expense and revenue items, or the income statement items, may be extracted from Ayco's trial balance and summarised as follows:

	Debit £	Credit £
Sales		18,000
Cost of sales	9,000	
Printing and stationery expenses	200	
Balance representing a profit for January	8,800	
	18,000	18,000

Although the £8,800 is shown in the debit column to balance the account, it is in fact a credit balance that is carried forward, that is a balance resulting from £18,000 total credits less total debits of £9,200.

Ayco income statement for January 2010

	£	£
Sales	18,000	
less		
Cost of sales	9,000	
Gross profit (gross margin)		9,000
Printing and stationery expenses		200
Net profit for January 2010		8,800

Balance sheet

The balance sheet of an entity discloses the assets (debit balances), and liabilities and shareholders' capital (credit balances), and profits (gains) or losses as at a given date. A gain or profit is a credit balance, and a loss is a debit balance. The revised trial balance, which includes the net balance of profit or loss, then forms the basis for the balance sheet. The balance sheet may then be constructed by rearranging the balances into an established format.

Worked example 2.13

Ayco's profit for January 2010 is a credit balance of £8,800, and if we substitute this back into Ayco's trial balance to replace the individual revenue and expense items we have:

	Debit £	Credit £
Capital		50,000
Cash	16,800	
Non-current assets – shop	30,000	
Non-current assets – fittings	5,000	
Accounts payable		12,000
Inventory	3,000	
Accounts receivable	16,000	
Profit for January		8,800
	70,800	70,800

To construct a balance sheet this needs to be rearranged into a more usual sort of format:

Ayco balance sheet as at 31 January 2010

Assets	£	£	Liabilities	£	£
Non-current assets		35,000	Owner's investment		
			Capital	50,000	
			Profit and loss account	8,800	
					58,800
Current assets			Short-term liabilities		
Accounts receivable	16,000		Accounts payable		12,000
Inventories	3,000				
Cash	16,800				
		35,800			
		70,800			70,800

Progress check 2.6

Outline what a balance sheet tells us about a company.

Statement of cash flows

The final report, the **statement of cash flows**, is simply a report on the detail of the movement
within the cash account in the trial balance. This starts with the opening balance, shows the receipts
and payments during the accounting period, and results in the closing balance.

Worked example 2.14

The final report, the statement of cash flows, may be constructed by looking at the elements that
are included in Ayco's cash T account, that is the elements which make up the total movements
in the cash account in the general ledger:

	Debit £	Credit £
Cash balance at 1 January 2010	–	
Receipt from Mr Bean – capital for business	50,000	
Payment for freehold shop		30,000
Payment for shop fittings		5,000
Payment for printing and stationery expenses		200
Receipt from customers	2,000	
Cash balance at 31 January 2010		16,800
	52,000	52,000

The £16,800 debit balance brought forward represents a positive cash position of £16,800.

The aim of the last few sections has been to explain the basics of double-entry bookkeeping and
the sources of accounting data, and to provide an introduction to the accounting ledgers and books
of account. This begins to show how the information from double-entry bookkeeping records may be
effectively used. The inclusion of the rudimentary financial statements shown above illustrates the
importance of the:

- accuracy
- timeliness
- completeness

of the financial data included in the double-entry system.

Progress check 2.7

Outline what a statement of cash flows tells us about a company.

Accrual accounting and cash accounting

We have already covered a number of important accounting ideas and concepts, one of which is that profit does not necessarily equal cash. This was apparent from the Ayco worked examples. The net cash movement in the month of January was an inflow, a positive of £16,800. However, the income statement showed a gain, a profit of £8,800. The reason that they were not identical was first (as shown in the statement of cash flows) due to cash items other than those associated with trading, for example receipt of the original capital, and expenditure on non-current assets. Second, the trading or operational transactions were not all converted into cash within the month of January; they were held as trade payables, inventory and trade receivables.

The approach that we took in the Ayco examples demonstrated compliance with the accruals concept, or matching concept, the principle that revenues and costs are:

- recognised as they are earned or incurred
- matched with one another
- dealt with in the income statement of the period to which they relate, irrespective of the period of cash receipt or cash payment.

Progress check 2.8

In what way does a company's income statement differ from the movements on its cash account during an accounting period?

Accruals

It may be that an expense has been incurred within an accounting period, for which an invoice may or may not have been received. For example, electricity used, telephone charges incurred, or stationery supplies received and used. We have talked about the concept of matching costs with sales revenues. Costs not necessarily related to sales cannot be matched in that way. Such charges must be matched to the accounting period to which they relate, and therefore an estimate of the cost (an accrual) must be made and included as an accounting adjusting entry in the accounts for that period.

Figure 2.5 shows an invoice dated 15 April 2010 received by a company from its communications provider for charges of £2,000 for the period January to March 2010. At the end of April 2010 the company had not yet received its bill for the next quarter even though it had use of telephone lines and had incurred call charges. We may assume that the company's accounting year runs from January to December. Therefore, before finalising its income statement for January to April the company needed to estimate its telephone costs for April, which are shown as £700.

The estimate of £700 has been charged, or debited, to telephone costs in the profit and loss account, and a temporary payable, an accrual, credited in the balance sheet for £700. The total telephone costs charged to the profit and loss account for January to April 2010 are therefore £2,700. The accrual carried forward at the end of April would normally be reversed and the position assessed again at the end of May, and the same procedure followed at the end of June. By the end of July the invoice would normally be expected to have been received covering the period April to June and so no accrual will be necessary. However, an accrual will be required for the month of July.

Figure 2.5	T account illustration of accounting for accruals

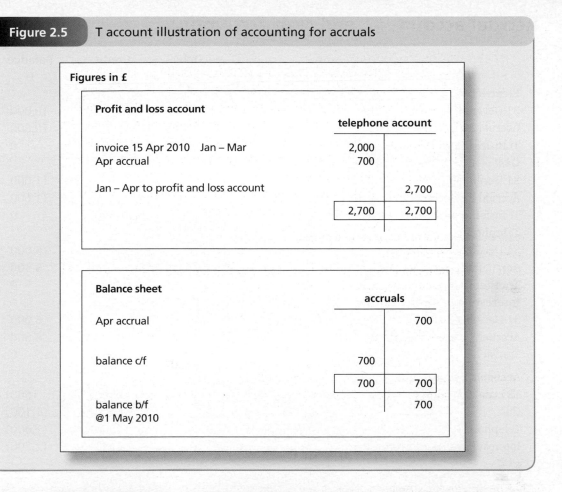

Figures in £

Profit and loss account

telephone account

invoice 15 Apr 2010 Jan – Mar	2,000	
Apr accrual	700	
Jan – Apr to profit and loss account		2,700
	2,700	2,700

Balance sheet

accruals

Apr accrual		700
balance c/f	700	
	700	700
balance b/f		700
@1 May 2010		

Worked example 2.15

From the following information we are required to prepare three-column accounts (in an Excel **spreadsheet** or in a Word table) to reflect the current balances on each account, which are then required to be adjusted for the accruals at 31 December 2010 to show the total transfer to the profit and loss account. We are also required to show a summary of the accruals as at 31 December 2010.

	£
Balances at 31 December 2010	
Electricity	10,000
Gas	11,000
Telephone	5,000
Interest on overdraft	6,000
Accruals required at 31 December 2010	
Electricity	500
Gas	600
Telephone	500
Interest on overdraft	600

Accruals adjustments at 31 December 2010:

	Debit £	Credit £	Balance £
Electricity			
31 December 2010			10,000
Accrual 31 December 2010	500		10,500
Transfer to profit and loss account		(10,500)	0
Gas			
31 December 2010			11,000
Accrual 31 December 2010	600		11,600
Transfer to profit and loss account		(11,600)	0
Telephone			
31 December 2010			5,000
Accrual 31 December 2010	500		5,500
Transfer to profit and loss account		(5,500)	0
Interest payable on overdraft			
31 December 2010			6,000
Accrual 31 December 2010	600		6,600
Transfer to profit and loss account		(6,600)	0
Accruals 31 December 2010			
Electricity		(500)	(500)
Gas		(600)	(1,100)
Telephone		(500)	(1,600)
Interest payable on overdraft		(600)	(2,200)

The same sort of exercise is carried out within a company for all the categories of expense for which accruals are likely to be required. Worked example 2.16 explains how accruals may have been dealt with in Ayco.

Worked example 2.16

The accruals concept could have been further illustrated in the Ayco scenario by the introduction of a number of additional factors. Assume, for example, that Ayco had used more than £200 of stationery in the month, say £1,000. We know that Ayco had been invoiced for and paid for £200 worth of stationery.

If £500 worth of the additional stationery had been used, and an invoice had been received but not processed through the ledgers, what would be the impact on Ayco? If £300 worth of the additional stationery had been used, and an invoice had not yet been received but was in the mail what would be the impact on Ayco?

The answer is that both would have to be debited to printing and stationery expenses for a total of £800, and credited not to accounts payable but to accruals.

Accruals are treated in a similar way to accounts payable but the invoices for these charges have not yet been processed by the entity. They are charges which are brought into the period because, although goods (or services) have been provided, they have not yet been included in the suppliers' accounts.

Expense recognition is an important concept. Expenses should be recognised immediately they are known about. Ayco knew they had used stationery for which there was a cost even though an invoice may not have been processed. On the other hand, revenues or profits should not be recognised until they are earned.

The net impact of the above on Ayco would have been a reduction in profit, a debit of £800 and an increase in liabilities, a credit of £800 to accruals. The accruals entries would need to be exactly reversed at the beginning of the following month to avoid a doubling up since the actual transactions will also be processed.

Prepayments

It may be that an expense has been incurred within an accounting period that related to future period(s). For example, property taxes, rents or vehicle licence fees paid in advance. As with accruals, these costs are not necessarily related to sales and cannot be matched with sales. Such charges must also be matched to the period to which they relate and therefore the proportion of the charges that relates to future periods (a prepayment) must be calculated and included as an adjustment in the accounts for that period. Figure 2.6 shows a charge of £6,000 that has been incurred by a company from its landlord on 1 January 2010 for rent for the period January to June 2010. At the end of

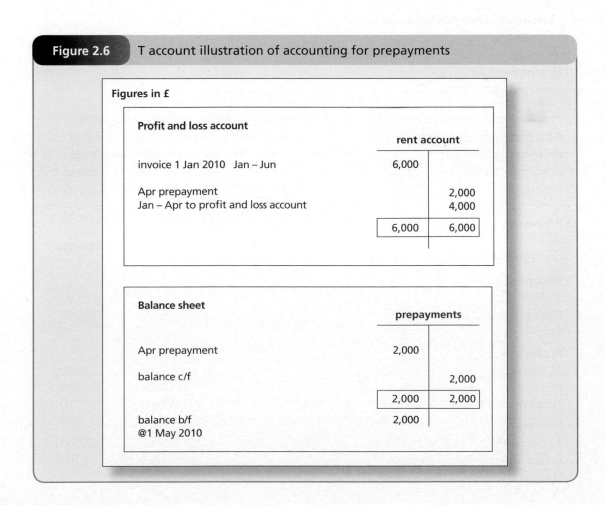

Figure 2.6   T account illustration of accounting for prepayments

Figures in £

Profit and loss account

rent account

invoice 1 Jan 2010 Jan – Jun	6,000	
Apr prepayment		2,000
Jan – Apr to profit and loss account		4,000
	6,000	6,000

Balance sheet

prepayments

Apr prepayment	2,000	
balance c/f		2,000
	2,000	2,000
balance b/f	2,000	
@1 May 2010		

April 2010 the company had paid rent not only for January to April, but rent in advance for May and June. Therefore, before finalising its profit and loss account for January to April the company needed to calculate the rent in advance for May and June, which is shown as £2,000.

The rent in advance of £2,000 has been credited to the rent account and a temporary receivable, a prepayment, created in the balance sheet for £2,000. The total rent costs charged to the profit and loss account for January to April 2010 are therefore £4,000. The prepayment carried forward at the end of April would normally be reversed and the position assessed again at the end of May, and the same procedure followed at the end of June. By the end of July a charge would normally be expected to have been received covering the period July to December and so a prepayment will be necessary at the end of July for the period August to December.

Worked example 2.17

From the following information we are required to prepare three-column accounts (in an Excel spreadsheet or in a Word table) to reflect the current balances on each account, which are then required to be adjusted for the prepayments, deferred income and accrued income at 31 December 2010, to show the total transfer to the profit and loss account. We are also required to show a summary of the prepayments and accrued income, and accruals and deferred income as at 31 December 2010.

£

Balances at 31 December 2010

	£
Rent paid	12,000
Property taxes paid	13,000
Interest received	7,000 (credit)
Rent received	8,000 (credit)

Prepayments, accrued income, and deferred income required at 31 December 2010

Rent paid	700 (normally paid in advance)
Property taxes paid	800 (normally paid in advance)
Interest receivable	700 (normally received in arrears)
Rent received	800 (normally received in advance)

Prepayments and accruals adjustments at 31 December 2010

	Debit £	Credit £	Balance £
Rent payable			
31 December			12,000
Prepayment 31 December 2010		(700)	11,300
Transfer to profit and loss account		(11,300)	0
Property taxes			
31 December			13,000
Prepayment 31 December 2010		(800)	12,200
Transfer to profit and loss account		(12,200)	0
Interest receivable			
31 December			(7,000)
Accrued income 31 December 2010		(700)	(7,700)
Transfer to profit and loss account	7,700		0

Rent receivable		
31 December		(8,000)
Deferred income 31 December 2010	800	(7,200)
Transfer to profit and loss account	7,200	0
Prepayments and accrued income		
31 December 2010		0
Rent paid	700	700
Property taxes paid	800	1,500
Interest receivable	700	2,200
Accruals and deferred income		
31 December 2010		0
Rent received	(800)	(800)

The same sort of exercise is carried out within a company for all the categories of expense for which prepayments are likely to be required. Worked example 2.18 explains how prepayments may have been dealt with in Ayco.

Worked example 2.18

Assume, for example, that Ayco had received an invoice for £2,000 for advertising in January to be paid in March, but the advertising was not taking place until February. An invoice may have been received and processed through the ledgers, but what would be the impact on Ayco?

The answer is that accounts payable would have been credited with £2,000 and advertising expenses debited with £2,000 in the month of January. However, because the advertising had not taken place, the charge of £2,000 would be considered as being in advance, or to use its technical term a prepayment. The accounts payable entry remains as a credit of £2,000, but an additional entry is required to credit advertising expenses with £2,000 and debit prepayments with £2,000.

A prepayment is expenditure on goods (or services) for future benefit, which is to be charged to future operations. Such amounts are similar to trade receivables and are included in current assets in the balance sheet.

The net impact of the above on Ayco would have been no charge to profit. The prepayment entry would need to be exactly reversed at the beginning of the following month.

Progress check 2.9

What are accruals and prepayments and why are such adjusting entries needed?

Accounting periods

In the Ayco worked examples we were introduced to the idea of an accounting period. An accounting period is that covered by the accounting statements of an entity. Different periods may be chosen within the financial year, for example 13 periods of four weeks, 12 periods using a four, four, five week quarter basis, or 12 calendar periods. The Ayco worked examples assumed 12 periods on a calendar basis. Once an accounting period basis has been chosen, consistency must be maintained. This is an example of both the periodicity concept and the consistency concept (see Chapter 1).

Progress check 2.10

What is an accounting period?

Summary of key points

- Double-entry bookkeeping is a convention, the two main objectives of which are to have a permanent record of transactions, and to show the effect of each transaction and the combined effect of all the transactions upon the financial position of the entity.
- Double-entry bookkeeping data are recorded as transactions described as 'debits' and 'credits'.
- The meaning of a debit and a credit may most usefully be remembered using the following rule, applying to entries reflected in the accounts of a company:

Cash receipt	= debit cash account and credit another account
Cash payment	= credit cash account and debit another account
Purchase invoice	= credit accounts payable and debit another account
Sales invoice	= debit accounts receivable and credit another account.

- The main ledger held within the accounting system of a company is called the general ledger, or nominal ledger, in which the results of all transactions made by the company are recorded either in summary or in detail.
- The original books of account, and subsidiary ledgers: cash book (receipts and payments); purchase invoice daybook and accounts payable (or purchase ledger); sales invoice daybook and accounts receivable (or sales ledger), hold the details of transactions that are reflected in the general ledger.
- Wages and salaries data are recorded in the cash books and posted to the general ledger.
- Adjusting accounting entries, such as those relating to closing inventories valuations, are made to the accounts prior to preparation of the income statement and balance sheet.
- There are five main accounting adjustments that are made prior to preparation of the income statement and balance sheet:
  - closing inventories
  - accruals: charges not yet received
  - prepayments: payments in advance (and income accrued)
  - depreciation
  - bad and doubtful debts.
- The balances on the individual accounts recorded within the general ledger may be summarised in a trial balance, the total of the debit balances being equal to the total of the credit balances.

- The income statement of an entity shows the profit or loss generated by the entity during an accounting period by deducting all expenses from all revenues.

- The balance sheet of an entity discloses the assets (debit balances) and liabilities and shareholders' capital (credit balances), and gains (credits) or losses (debits) as at a given date.

- The statement of cash flows is a report on the detail of the movement within the cash account in the trial balance, starting with the opening balance and adding the receipts and deducting the payments during the accounting period, resulting in the closing balance.

- The accounting period chosen by a business is the period covered by its financial statements.

Assessment material

Questions

Q2.1 What are the four basic business transactions and what are their corresponding debit and credit accounting entries under the convention of double-entry bookkeeping?

Q2.2 (i) Name each of the books of account and ledgers in an accounting system.
(ii) What are they used for?

Q2.3 Describe the use and purpose of the five main accounting adjusting entries.

Q2.4 (i) At a specific point in time, what does a company's trial balance show?
(ii) What may the trial balance not show?

Q2.5 How may the financial performance of a company be ascertained from its trial balance?

Q2.6 How may the financial position of a company be ascertained from its trial balance?

Q2.7 How may the cash position of a company be ascertained from its trial balance?

Q2.8 Why is the profit made during an accounting period not necessarily equal to the cash flow during that period?

Q2.9 In what ways do businesses adjust their accounts for accruals and prepayments?

Q2.10 What is the relevance of the accounting period?

Discussion points

D2.1 'Managers who are non-accounting specialists don't need to learn about bookkeeping, debits and credits, etc.' Discuss.

D2.2 Computerised accounts and information systems have speeded up the recording of accounting data and the presentation of information. What are the other advantages over manual accounting systems and what are the disadvantages?

Exercises

Solutions are provided in Appendix 3 to all exercise numbers highlighted in colour.

Level I

E2.1 *Time allowed – 30 minutes*

Extracts from the ledgers of Hall Ltd have provided the following information for 2009 and 2010.

	£
Sales revenue 2009	11,000
Sales revenue 2010	12,000
Purchases 2009	7,100
Purchases 2010	8,300
Expenses 2009	2,500
Expenses 2010	2,800
Inventories 1 January 2009	600
Inventories 31 December 2009	700
Inventories 31 December 2010	800
Obsolete inventories included in 31 December 2010 inventories	200

> **You are required to prepare a basic income statement for the years ended 31 December 2009 and 2010.**

E2.2 *Time allowed – 30 minutes*

> (a) **Explain why there are always problems at the year end in the assessment of the costs associated with electricity, gas and telephone.**
> (b) **Using the information below, prepare the appropriate year-end accounting entries.**

Electricity charges account balance at 15 December 2010: £10,000
Gas charges account balance at 20 December 2010: £5,000
Estimated consumption
Electricity 16 December to 31 December 2010: £300
Gas 21 December to 31 December 2010: £150

E2.3 *Time allowed – 30 minutes*

Arthur Moment set up a table-making business, Forlegco, on 1 July 2010. He had £10,000 available to invest, which is the amount he estimated was required for setting up costs. In the first month of trading Forlegco entered into the following transactions:

	£
£10,000 from Arthur Moment	10,000
Purchase of hand tools for cash	2,000
Purchase of lathe, power saw and drill on one month's credit	6,000
Purchase of printing and stationery – invoice received for half the order	100

The total order is £200, and it was all delivered in July and used
Purchase of advertising flyers for cash 2,000 at 50p each, of which 1,000 will be used in July, and 500 in August and September

Purchases of timber, glue and varnish, from Woodco, payable within the month £1,500 – half of this inventory will be on hand at 31 July 2010

Sales of tables to Gardenfurnco for settlement one month later (10 tables at £700 each)

You are required to present these transactions in T account format, and then prepare a trial balance for Forlegco for 31 July 2010.

E2.4   *Time allowed – 30 minutes*

From the trial balance for Forlegco for 31 July 2010 (Exercise E2.3)

(i)   **Prepare a simple income statement for the month of July 2010.**

(ii) **Has Forlegco made a profit in July?**

(iii) **If Forlegco has not made a profit, why not?**

E2.5   *Time allowed – 30 minutes*

From the trial balance for Forlegco for 31 July 2010 (Exercise E2.3) prepare a simple balance sheet at that date.

E2.6   *Time allowed – 30 minutes*

From the trial balance for Forlegco for 31 July 2010 (Exercise E2.3) prepare a simple statement of cash flows for the month of July 2010.

E2.7   *Time allowed – 30 minutes*

You are required to prepare the appropriate correcting entries in a company's accounts at 31 December 2010 for the following:

(i)   **A cheque paid for rent amounting to £2,400 has been entered into the car hire account in error.**

(ii) **A cheque for £980 was received from a customer in full settlement of a balance of £1,000, but no accounting entry for the discount has been made.**

(iii) **A cheque paid for insurance on the company cars amounting to £1,200 has been entered in the cost of motor cars account in error.**

(iv) **An invoice from a builder for £3,500 has been entered in the buildings cost account, but in fact it related to redecoration of the reception area of the office and should be treated as a building repair.**

Level II

E2.8   *Time allowed – 60 minutes*

David (Dai) Etcoak decided to set up a drinks wholesale business, Etcoakco, on 1 December 2009. He had £100,000 available to invest, which is the amount he felt was required to set up the business. In the first month of trading Etcoakco entered into the following transactions:

	£
£100,000 from Dai Etcoak	100,000
Purchase for cash the freehold of a shop	50,000
Purchase for cash the shop fittings	7,000

	£
Purchase of a labelling machine payable one month later	20,000
Cash expenses on printing and stationery	400
Purchases of inventory, from Gasco, of bottles of pop, payable three months later	
(25,000 bottles at £1.25 each)	31,250
Sales of bottles of Etcoak to Boozah for settlement one month later	
(10,000 bottles at £2.30 each)	23,000
Sales of bottles of Etcoak to Disco30, receivable in the month	
(12,000 bottles at £2.30 each)	27,600

You are required to:

(i)   look at these transactions in detail and then present them in T account format, and

(ii) state any assumptions you have made particularly relating to how you have valued inventories transactions.

Also:

(iii) Do you think £100,000 was enough money or too much to invest in the business?

(iv) What alternative courses of action are open to Dai?

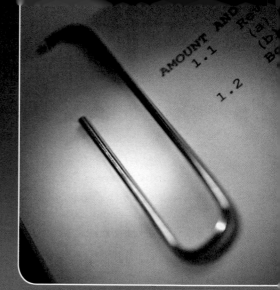

3

Balance sheet

Contents

Learning objectives

Completion of this chapter will enable you to:

■ explain the differences in accounting treatment of capital expenditure and revenue expenditure

■ identify the financial information shown in the financial statements of a company: balance sheet; income statement; statement of cash flows

■ construct simple financial statements

■ outline the structure of the balance sheet of a limited company

■ classify the broad balance sheet categories of shareholders' equity, liabilities, and assets

■ outline the alternative balance sheet formats

■ prepare a balance sheet

■ evaluate some of the alternative methods of asset valuation

■ appreciate the limitations of the conventional balance sheet.

Introduction

We talked about business entities in general in Chapter 1. The financial accounting and reporting of limited companies are similar to those of sole traders and partnerships, except that they are more detailed and require a greater disclosure of information. This is to comply with current legislation and the requirements for reporting of financial information to the owners of the business (the shareholders).

Each type of business is required to prepare periodic financial statements in one form or another for internal control purposes, the shareholders and, for example, HM Revenue & Customs. The current chapter and Chapters 4 and 5 provide a comprehensive coverage of financial statements, which are the basis for the subsequent chapters about business performance analysis and published reports and accounts.

We will be looking in a little more detail at the profit and loss account and income statement in Chapter 4 and the balance sheet later in this chapter. The terms income statement and profit and loss account have often been used interchangeably. To conform with International Accounting Standards (IASs) and International Financial Reporting Standards (IFRSs) requirements, the financial statement that companies in the UK and many other countries had hitherto called the profit and loss account is now called the income statement. The financial statements in this book comply with that requirement. However, the term profit and loss account is still used throughout this book but essentially to describe that part of the general ledger that includes all the revenue and cost accounts, as distinct from all the asset, liability and equity accounts which are included within the balance sheet part of the general ledger.

Each of the financial statements includes expenditure of one form or another. This chapter begins by broadly looking at types of expenditure and explaining what is meant by revenue expenditure and capital expenditure. Most items may be clearly identified in terms of revenue or capital expenditure, but there are also a number of uncertain areas in these classifications with regard to the rules used in accounting and in the way that expenditure may be analysed for taxation purposes.

Before dealing specifically with the balance sheets of limited companies we will discuss the subject of financial statements that was introduced in Chapter 1. We will see how these are constructed and interrelated, by working through a comprehensive example that illustrates how transactions are reflected in the income statement, balance sheet and statement of cash flows of a business.

This chapter deals with how balance sheets are structured and how the accounts within the balance sheet are categorised. Each of the items within each of the balance sheet categories will be described in detail and form the basis that enables the preparation of a balance sheet of a limited company in the appropriate format.

The chapter closes by illustrating the subjective nature of the balance sheet and considers the areas in which this is apparent through looking at examples of the alternative methods for valuation of assets that are available to companies.

Capital expenditure and revenue expenditure

Expenditure made by an entity falls generally within two types:

- **revenue expenditure**
- **capital expenditure**.

Revenue expenditure relates to expenditure incurred in the manufacture of products, the provision of services or in the general conduct of the company, which is normally charged to the profit and loss account in the accounting period in which it is incurred or when the products and services are sold. This expenditure includes repairs and depreciation of non-current assets as distinct from the provision of these assets. Revenue expenditure relates to expenditure on those items where the full benefit is received within the normal accounting period. The accruals (matching) concept says that sales must be recognised in the period in which they are earned, and the costs incurred in achieving those sales must also be recognised in the same period. Therefore the costs of revenue expenditure appear under the appropriate headings within the profit and loss account of the period in which the benefits are consumed and the costs are therefore incurred.

In some circumstances expenditure, which would normally be treated as revenue expenditure, is not written off in one period. This is called deferred revenue expenditure and relates to, for example, extensive expenditure on an advertising campaign over a period of months.

Capital expenditure (not to be confused with share capital or capital account, which are something completely different) relates to the cost of acquiring, producing or enhancing non-current assets. Capital expenditure is extremely important because it is usually much higher in value and follows the appropriate authorisation of expenditure on items of plant or equipment, or on a specific project. Such expenditure is usually expected to generate future earnings for the entity, protect existing revenue or profit levels, or provide compliance with, for example, health and safety or fire regulation requirements. Capital expenditure does not necessarily relate directly to sales derived in the period that the expenditure was made. It relates to expenditure on those items where the benefit from them is received over a number of future accounting periods. Therefore, capital expenditure items are held and carried forward to subsequent accounting periods until such time as their costs must be matched with sales or other benefits derived from their use. Accordingly, such items should appear in the balance sheet under the heading non-current assets. The values of these items are reduced during each subsequent accounting period as the appropriate portions of their cost are charged to the profit and loss account to match the sales or other benefits deriving from their use. Receipts from the disposal of non-current assets also appear under the non-current assets heading in the balance sheet. They are not treated as sales in the profit and loss account.

Control over capital expenditure is maintained through procedures for authorisation and subsequent monitoring of capital expenditure. Capital expenditure proposals are formal requests for authority to incur capital expenditure. Organisations usually require capital expenditure proposals to be supported by detailed qualitative and quantitative justifications for the expenditure, in accordance with the company's capital investment criteria. Levels of authority for expenditure must be clearly defined. The reporting structure of actual expenditure must also be aligned with the appropriate authority levels.

In addition to the actual plant or equipment cost some revenue-type expenditure such as delivery, installation and financing costs may also, where appropriate, be treated as capital expenditure. Such expenditure is described as being capitalised. In many circumstances revenue items must be capitalised as they are considered part of the acquisition cost, and in other circumstances revenue items may optionally be capitalised as part of the acquisition cost. In many circumstances it is not always possible to provide a clear ruling.

The general rule is that if the expenditure is as a result of: (a) a first-time acquisition, delivery and commissioning of a non-current asset; or relates to (b) improving the asset from when it was first acquired, then it is capital expenditure. If the expenditure is neither of these two types then it is normally revenue expenditure. The following examples of expenditure illustrate some of the circumstances that may prompt the question 'is it revenue or capital expenditure?'

Repairs are usually treated as revenue expenditure, but if, for example, some second-hand plant is purchased and some immediate repair costs are incurred necessary to make it efficient for the company's purpose, then such repairs become capital expenditure and are therefore added to the plant cost as part of the acquisition cost. Salaries and wages are revenue items. However, salaries and wages paid to employees to erect and fit some new machinery that has been acquired must be considered as an addition to the cost of the machinery.

Legal expenses are usually treated as revenue expenditure. But the legal expenses of conveyancing when purchasing a factory must be treated as part of the cost of the factory. Finance changes incurred during, say, the building of a factory or installation of plant and machinery may be capitalised so long as such a policy is applied consistently.

Apportionment of expenditure

Some items of expenditure require an apportionment of costs. This means that part of the cost is charged as capital expenditure and the balance is written off immediately as revenue expenditure. This is frequently the case within the uncertain area of improvements, alterations and extensions to plant and buildings. Capitalisation of the whole may not be prudent, since the value of the plant or building may not be enhanced to anything near the amount of money that may have been spent. The prudent policy may be not to permanently capitalise any expenditure that is not represented by assets, although legally this may be acceptable.

You may question why the distinction between capital and revenue expenditure is so important. We have already touched on the prudence concept and the consistency concept. The matching concept requires a company to match income, or sales revenue, and costs as closely as possible to the time period to which they relate. If the expected life of a non-current asset acquired to generate income is, say, five years then the costs of that asset should be spread over five years to match the realisation of the income it generates. It is therefore important to ensure that all the costs associated with the acquisition, installation and commissioning of the asset are included as part of its capitalised cost.

The amount of corporation tax that a company must pay on the profits it has generated is not computed simply as a percentage of profit. Depending on the tax rules currently in force, many revenue items may be disallowable expenses so far as taxable profit is concerned. In a similar way the treatment of capital expenditure in terms of allowances against taxation also has an impact on the amount of tax payable by the company.

Worked example 3.1

The following table illustrates how various items of expenditure are normally classified as either capital expenditure or revenue expenditure.

Revenue expenditure	Capital expenditure
Wages and salaries	Computer software
Interest payable	Goodwill
Travel expenses	Enhancement of a moulding machine
Repairs to the factory building	Patents
Professional fees	Office desk

Financial statements of limited companies

In Chapter 1 we introduced the topic of the financial statements that businesses need to prepare for each accounting period to provide adequate information about the financial performance and the financial position of the business.

We will now look in more detail at the three key financial statements (see Fig. 3.1): balance sheet, income statement and statement of cash flows.

Balance sheet

The balance sheet summarises the financial position of the business; it is a financial snapshot at a moment in time. It may be compared to looking at a DVD. In 'play' mode the DVD is showing what is happening as time goes on second by second. If you press 'pause' the DVD stops on a picture. The

Figure 3.1   The three key financial statements

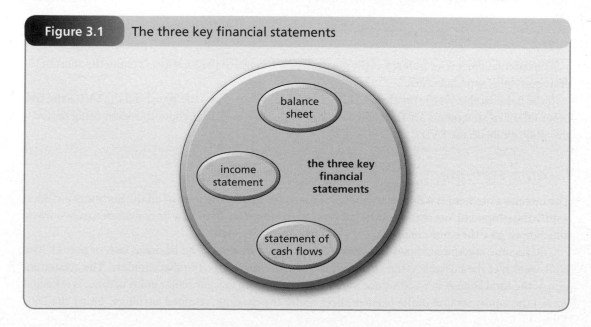

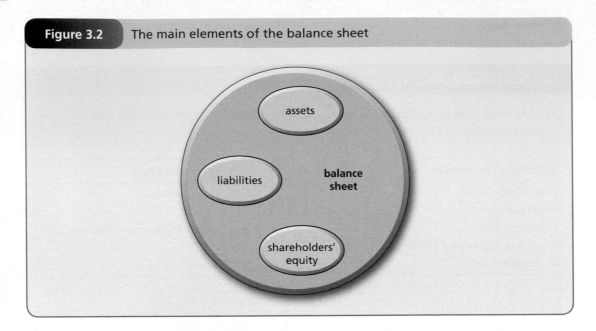

Figure 3.2 The main elements of the balance sheet

picture does not tell you what has happened over the period of time up to the pause (or what is going to happen after the pause). The balance sheet is the financial position of the company at the 'pause' position. It is the consequence of everything that has happened up to that time. It does not explain how the company got to that position, it just shows the results of financial impacts of events and decisions up to the balance sheet date. The year end may be 31 December, but other dates may be chosen. A company's year end date is (normally) the same date each year.

The balance sheet comprises a number of categories, within the three main elements (see Fig. 3.2), which are labelled **assets, liabilities** or shareholders' equity (usually referred to as just **equity**). The assets are debit balances and the liabilities and shareholders' equity are credit balances. (Note: the concepts of debit and credit, and double-entry bookkeeping were fully covered in Chapter 2.) The balance sheet is always in balance so that

$$\text{total assets (TA)} = \text{equity (E)} + \text{total liabilities (TL)}$$

The balance sheet is a summary of the general ledger in which the total assets equal the shareholders' equity plus total liabilities.

If the balance sheet is the financial snapshot at a moment in time – the 'pause' on the DVD – the two other financial statements are the equivalent of what is going on throughout the accounting period – the 'play' mode on the DVD.

Income statement

The income statement is a financial statement that summarises the total of all the accounts included within the profit and loss section of the general ledger. Profit (or loss) may be considered in two ways, which both give the same result.

The income statement shows the change in the book wealth of the business over a period. The book wealth of the business is the amount it is worth to the owners, the shareholders. The accumulation of the total change in wealth since the business began, up to a particular point in time, is reflected within the equity section of the balance sheet under the heading 'retained earnings'. Using the DVD

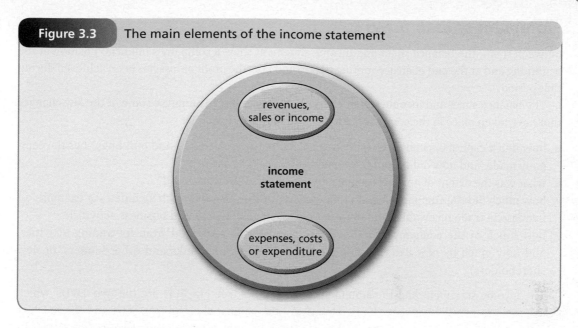

Figure 3.3 The main elements of the income statement

analysis, the income statement measures the change in the balance sheet from one 'pause' to another. An increase in equity is a profit and a decrease in equity is a loss.

The income statement may also be considered in its measurement of the trading performance of the business (see Fig. 3.3). The income statement calculates whether or not the company has made a profit or loss on its operations during the period, through producing and selling its goods or services. The result, the earnings, net income or **profit** (or loss), is derived from deducting expenses incurred from revenues derived throughout the period between two 'pauses'. The income statement is dealt with in detail in Chapter 4.

The profit and loss account comprises the total of the expenses (debits) accounts and revenues (credits) accounts within the general ledger. The total of these may be a net debit or a net credit. A net debit represents a loss and a net credit represents a profit. The profit or loss is reflected in the balance sheet of the business under the heading retained earnings, which is part of shareholders' equity. All the other accounts within the general ledger, other than expenses and revenues, may be summarised into various other non-profit and loss account categories and these represent all the other balances that complete the overall balance sheet of the business.

There are three main points to consider regarding the income statement and how it differs from the statement of cash flows. First, revenues (or sales, or sales revenues, or income) and expenses (or costs or expenditure) are not necessarily accounted for when cash transfers occur. Sales are normally accounted for when goods or services are delivered and accepted by the customer. Cash will rarely be received immediately from the customer, except in businesses like high-street retailers and supermarkets; it is normally received weeks or months later.

Second, the income statement does not take into account all the events that impact on the financial position of the company. For example, an issue of new **shares** in the company, or a loan to the company, will increase cash but they are neither revenue nor expenses.

Third, non-cash flow items, for example depreciation and provisions for doubtful debts, reduce the profit, or increase the loss, of the company but do not represent outflows of cash. These topics will be covered in detail in the next chapter.

Therefore it can be seen that net profit is not the same as cash flow. A company may get into financial difficulties if it suffers a severe **cash** shortage even though it may have positive net earnings (profit).

Statement of cash flows

Between them, the balance sheet and income statement show a company's financial position at the beginning and at the end of an accounting period and how the profit or loss has been achieved during that period.

The balance sheet and income statement do not show or directly analyse some of the key changes that have taken place in the company's financial position, for example:

- how much capital expenditure (for example, equipment, machinery and buildings) has the company made, and how did it fund the expenditure?
- what was the extent of new borrowing and how much **debt** was repaid?
- how much did the company need to fund new **working capital** (which includes, for example, an increase in trade receivables and **inventories** as a result of increased business activity)?
- how much of the company's funding was met by funds generated from its trading activities, and how much by new external funding (for example, from banks and other lenders, or new shareholders)?

The income statement and the statement of cash flows (see Fig. 3.4) are the two 'DVDs' which are running in parallel between the two 'pauses' – the balance sheets at the start and the finish of an accounting period. However, the statement of cash flows goes further in answering the questions like those shown above. The aim of the statement of cash flows is to summarise the cash inflows and outflows and calculate the net change in the cash position of the company throughout the period between two 'pauses'.

Progress check 3.1

Explain the fundamental differences between the types of information presented in each of the three key financial statements.

Figure 3.4   The main elements of the statement of cash flows

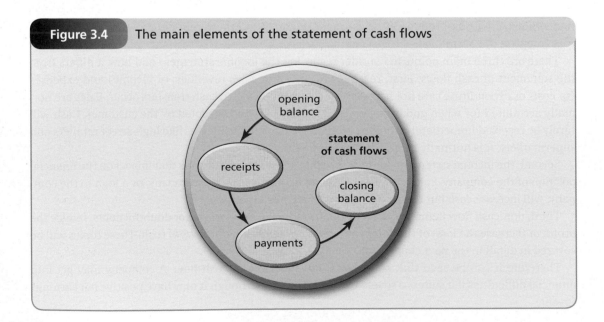

Construction and use of financial statements

An example will best illustrate how financial statements may be constructed. We will use the example of Mr Bean's business, Ayco (see also Worked example 2.1, Chapter 2), to track how some simple transactions are reflected in the income statement, statement of cash flows and balance sheet.

Worked examples 3.2 to 3.5 will look at the four one-week periods during Ayco's first month of trading and show the income statement reflecting the trading transactions of the business. The result, the change in wealth of the business, is shown as the resources held at the end of each period and reflected in the balance sheet. The example will show the statement of cash flows as movements in cash and changes to the cash balance, which is reflected in the balance sheet that gives a summary of the financial position of the company at the end of each period.

Worked example 3.2

Mr Bean decides to set up a wholesale business, Ayco, on 1 January 2010. He has his own cash resources for the purpose of setting up the business and has estimated that an initial £50,000 would be required for this purpose. During the first four-week period in business, January 2010, Ayco will enter into the following transactions:

		£
Week 1	Receipt of cheque from Mr Bean	50,000
Week 1	Purchase for cash the freehold of a shop	30,000
Week 1	Purchase for cash the shop fittings	5,000
Week 2	Cash paid for printing and stationery used	200
Week 3	Purchases of inventory, from Beeco Ltd, of Aymen toys, payable two months later (12,000 toys at £1 each)	12,000
Week 3	Sales of Aymen toys to Ceeco Ltd for cash (1,000 toys at £2 each)	2,000
Week 4	Sales of Aymen toys to Deeco Ltd, receivable one month later (8,000 toys at £2 each)	16,000

		Week 1 £	Total £
Profit and loss account	Sales revenue	0	0
	Cost of sales	0	0
	Gross profit	0	0
	Expenses	0	0
	Profit/(loss)	0	0
	Cumulative profit/(loss)	0	0
Cash flow	Opening balance	0	0
	Cash received ex Mr Bean	50,000	50,000
	Cash received from customers	0	0
	Cash paid for shop freehold	(30,000)	(30,000)
	Cash paid for shop fittings	(5,000)	(5,000)
	Cash paid for stationery	0	0
	Closing balance	15,000	15,000

Balance sheet		Week 1 £	Total £
	Cash closing balance	15,000	15,000
	Freehold shop	30,000	30,000
	Shop fittings	5,000	5,000
	Inventories	0	0
	Accounts receivable	0	0
	Accounts payable	0	0
	Total wealth	50,000	50,000
	Represented by:		
	Mr Bean's original capital	50,000	50,000
	Profit/(loss) to date	0	0
	Total capital	50,000	50,000

The statement above shows that no trading took place during the first week of January. Mr Bean paid £50,000 of his personal funds into the bank account of Ayco, representing his capital invested in Ayco. The company immediately used £35,000 of this to purchase the freehold of a shop together with shop fittings.

We can summarise the financial position at the end of the first week as follows:

- There was neither a profit nor a loss.
- Cash has been increased by Mr Bean's capital invested, less payments for the shop and fittings, to give a closing cash (bank) balance of £15,000.
- The wealth of the business at the end of the first week was Mr Bean's original capital of £50,000. Wealth had not been increased or decreased as there was no profit or loss.
- The wealth was represented by the shop, its fittings and the closing bank balance.
- Totals for the month to date are of course the same as for week 1.

Let's look at Ayco for the subsequent three weeks accounting periods, one week at a time, beginning with week 2.

Worked example 3.3

Accounting period week 2.

Profit and loss account		Week 1 £	Week 2 £	Total £
	Sales revenue	0	0	0
	Cost of sales	0	0	0
	Gross profit	0	0	0
	Expenses	0	(200)	(200)
	Profit/(loss)	0	(200)	(200)
	Cumulative profit/(loss)	0	(200)	(200)

		Week 1 £	Week 2 £	Total £
Cash flow	Opening balance	0	15,000	0
	Cash received ex Mr Bean	50,000	0	50,000
	Cash received from customers	0	0	0
	Cash paid for shop freehold	(30,000)	0	(30,000)
	Cash paid for shop fittings	(5,000)	0	(5,000)
	Cash paid for stationery	0	(200)	(200)
	Closing balance	15,000	14,800	14,800
Balance sheet	Cash closing balance	15,000	14,800	14,800
	Freehold shop	30,000	30,000	30,000
	Shop fittings	5,000	5,000	5,000
	Inventories	0	0	0
	Accounts receivable	0	0	0
	Accounts payable	0	0	0
	Total wealth	50,000	49,800	49,800
	Represented by:			
	Mr Bean's original capital	50,000	50,000	50,000
	Profit/(loss) to date	0	(200)	(200)
	Total capital	50,000	49,800	49,800

We can summarise the financial position at the end of the second week as follows:

- There was still no trading but printing and stationery had been used, and there was a charge for their expense to the profit and loss account, therefore there was a loss for the week. The cumulative two weeks is obtained by adding across each line in the profit and loss account, which is also the sum of the totals, to give a cumulative two-week loss of £200.
- Cash was reduced in week 2 by the cash paid for printing and stationery expenses to give a closing balance of £14,800. It can be seen that the two-week cumulative cash position is calculated by starting with the week 1 opening balance and then adding across all the payment and receipt elements. The sum of the total column will give the same closing balance as that shown for week 2.
- The book wealth of the business at the end of the second week was Mr Bean's original capital reduced by the cumulative loss of £200 to give £49,800. The wealth was represented by the shop, its fittings and the closing bank balance.

Note that the cumulative balance sheet at the end of week 2 is exactly the same as that shown in the week 2 column and not the totals of each of the elements added across in weeks 1 and 2. This is always true for however many weeks or any other period we may be looking at, which is what we would expect since the balance sheet does show the financial position at a point in time, in this example the position at the end of week 2.

Progress check 3.2

How can a business have made a loss during an accounting period if it hasn't been involved in any trading during the period?

Worked example 3.4

Let's now look at accounting period week 3.

		Week 1 £	Week 2 £	Week 3 £	Total £
Profit and loss account	Sales revenue	0	0	2,000	2,000
	Cost of sales	0	0	(1,000)	(1,000)
	Gross profit	0	0	1,000	1,000
	Expenses	0	(200)	0	(200)
	Profit/(loss)	0	(200)	1,000	800
	Cumulative profit/(loss)	0	(200)	800	800
Cash flow	Opening balance	0	15,000	14,800	0
	Cash received ex Mr Bean	50,000	0	0	50,000
	Cash received from customers	0	0	2,000	2,000
	Cash paid for shop freehold	(30,000)	0	0	(30,000)
	Cash paid for shop fittings	(5,000)	0	0	(5,000)
	Cash paid for stationery	0	(200)	0	(200)
	Closing balance	15,000	14,800	16,800	16,800
Balance sheet	Cash closing balance	15,000	14,800	16,800	16,800
	Freehold shop	30,000	30,000	30,000	30,000
	Shop fittings	5,000	5,000	5,000	5,000
	Inventories	0	0	11,000	11,000
	Accounts receivable	0	0	0	0
	Accounts payable	0	0	(12,000)	(12,000)
	Total wealth	50,000	49,800	50,800	50,800
	Represented by:				
	Mr Bean's original capital	50,000	50,000	50,000	50,000
	Profit/(loss) to date	0	(200)	800	800
	Total capital	50,000	49,800	50,800	50,800

We can summarise the financial position at the end of the third week as follows:

■ There was some trading, which gave a profit for the week of £1,000. The cumulative three weeks is obtained by adding across each line in the profit and loss account, which is also the sum of the totals, to give a cumulative three-week profit of £800.

- Cash was increased in week 3 by the cash received from customers, and with no cash payments the closing balance was £16,800. It can be seen that the three-week cumulative cash position is calculated by starting with the week 1 opening balance and then adding across all the payment and receipt elements. The sum of the total column will give the same closing balance as that shown for week 3.
- The book wealth of the business at the end of the third week was Mr Bean's original capital increased by the cumulative profit of £800 to give £50,800. The wealth was represented by the shop, its fittings, the closing bank balance, plus inventories less trade payables (two new categories introduced in this example). The first category is inventories. Inventories had been purchased in the month, but had been reduced by the amount used in trading. The second new category is the result of the purchase of inventory for £12,000, which had not yet been paid out in cash but nevertheless was a claim against the company. This claim is an amount due to be paid to suppliers – accounts payable by the business – and therefore a reduction in the wealth of the company.

The amount of inventories used in trading to provide the sales of £2,000 is called **cost of sales**, which in this example is £1,000. Note again that the cumulative balance sheet at the end of week 3 is exactly the same as that shown in the week 3 column and not the totals added across each of the elements in weeks 1, 2 and 3.

Worked example 3.5

Let's now look at the final accounting period, week 4.

		Week 1 £	Week 2 £	Week 3 £	Week 4 £	Total £
Profit and loss account	Sales revenue	0	0	2,000	16,000	18,000
	Cost of sales	0	0	(1,000)	(8,000)	(9,000)
	Gross profit	0	0	1,000	8,000	9,000
	Expenses	0	(200)	0	0	(200)
	Profit/(loss)	0	(200)	1,000	8,000	8,800
	Cumulative profit/ (loss)	0	(200)	800	8,800	8,800
Cash flow	Opening balance	0	15,000	14,800	16,800	0
	Cash received ex Mr Bean	50,000	0	0	0	50,000
	Cash received from customers	0	0	2,000	0	2,000
	Cash paid for shop freehold	(30,000)	0	0	0	(30,000)
	Cash paid for shop fittings	(5,000)	0	0	0	(5,000)
	Cash paid for stationery	0	(200)	0	0	(200)
	Closing balance	15,000	14,800	16,800	16,800	16,800

		Week 1 £	Week 2 £	Week 3 £	Week 4 £	Total £
Balance sheet	Cash closing balance	15,000	14,800	16,800	16,800	16,800
	Freehold shop	30,000	30,000	30,000	30,000	30,000
	Shop fittings	5,000	5,000	5,000	5,000	5,000
	Inventories	0	0	11,000	3,000	3,000
	Accounts receivable	0	0	0	16,000	16,000
	Accounts payable	0	0	(12,000)	(12,000)	(12,000)
	Total wealth	50,000	49,800	50,800	58,800	58,800
	Represented by:					
	Mr Bean's original capital	50,000	50,000	50,000	50,000	50,000
	Profit/(loss) to date	0	(200)	800	8,800	8,800
	Total capital	50,000	49,800	50,800	58,800	58,800

We can summarise the final financial position at the end of the fourth week as follows:

■ There was further trading, which gave a profit for the week of £8,000. The cumulative four weeks is obtained by adding across each line in the profit and loss account, which is also the sum of the totals, to give a cumulative four-week profit of £8,800.

■ No cash was received or paid during week 4, and so the closing balance remained at £16,800. It can be seen that the four-week cumulative cash position is calculated by starting with the week 1 opening balance and then adding across all the payment and receipt elements. The sum of the total column will give the same closing balance as that shown for week 4.

■ The book wealth of the business at the end of the fourth week was Mr Bean's original capital increased by the cumulative profit of £8,800 to give £58,800. The wealth was represented by the shop, its fittings, closing bank balance, inventories, less accounts payable, and now another additional element: accounts receivable. Sales of £16,000 had been made in the month, none of which had been paid in cash. The amount remaining due from customers – accounts receivable by the company – at the end of the week was £16,000 which represented an element of the wealth of Ayco. The inventories used for those sales had reduced the inventories from the end of the previous week £11,000 to £3,000 at the end of week 4.

Note again that the cumulative balance sheet at the end of week 4 is exactly the same as that shown in the week 4 column and not the totals of each of the elements added across in weeks 1, 2, 3 and 4.

Progress check 3.3

Why is there usually a difference between profit and cash in an accounting period?

Worked Examples 3.2 to 3.5 introduced a number of terms relating to financial statements. Whilst they gave an introduction to the principles and put things in context they were by no means exhaustive. In this chapter and the next two, we will consider each of the financial statements in more detail, beginning with the balance sheet.

Balance sheet formats

IAS 1, Presentation of Financial Statements, allows considerable flexibility in the way that a balance sheet may be presented. The Companies Act 2006 indicates that the balance sheet and income statement for all reporting entities must comply with the current relevant accounting or financial reporting standards. The Companies Act 2006 does not specify the format of the financial statements. There is a general requirement for the reporting of comparative previous year numbers. These are normally shown in a column to the right of the current year's numbers.

Assets and liabilities must both be classified as current and non-current. IAS 1 provides a choice in presentation of the balance sheet between separating current and non-current assets and liabilities, or presenting assets and liabilities in order of their liquidity (or in reverse order of liquidity) without a current and non-current distinction. Liquidity presentation of assets and liabilities is required only when it provides a more relevant and reliable presentation.

Sometimes an asset or liability may be classified as current even if it is not due to be settled within twelve months of the balance sheet date, if it is expected to be settled within the company's normal operating cycle.

While IAS 1 does not stipulate the precise format of balance sheets, it does require a minimum of information that should be presented on the face of the balance sheet, which includes:

- property, plant and equipment
- investment property
- investments (financial assets, for example shares and loans)
- inventories
- **trade receivables** (accounts receivable net of any doubtful debt provision)
- other receivables
- cash and cash equivalents
- **trade payables** (net accounts payable)
- other payables
- provisions
- tax liabilities
- equity (issued share capital and retained earnings).

Additional items or sub-classification of items may need to be included because of their size or nature, or in order to comply with some other financial reporting standard or to present fairly the company's financial position or when such presentation is relevant to an understanding of the company's financial performance. This may include classifications of:

- assets, such as property, plant, equipment and inventories
- liabilities, such as provisions
- equity, such as share numbers and par values, retained earnings, and **reserves**.

In order to keep the balance sheet presentation clear, such additional information may be included in the notes on the accounts.

What does the balance sheet tell us?

In theory the balance sheet of a private limited company or a public limited company should be able to tell us all about the company's financial structure and liquidity – the extent to which its assets and liabilities are held in cash or in a near cash form (for example, bank accounts and deposits). It should also tell us about the assets held by the company, the proportion of **current assets** and the extent to which they may be used to meet current obligations. In later chapters we will look at many of the important ratios used to evaluate the strength of a company's balance sheet. We will also see what the balance sheet tells us about the financial structure of companies and the sources of such financing.

An element of caution should be noted in analysing balance sheet information. The balance sheet is a historical document. It may have looked entirely different six months or a year ago, or even one week ago. There is not always consistency between the information included in one company's balance sheet and that of another company. Two companies even within the same industry are usually very difficult to compare. Added to that, different analysts very often use the same ratios in different ways.

We will look at some of the variety of methods used to value the various items contained in the balance sheet. However, in addition to the wide choice of valuation methods, the information in a typical published balance sheet does not tell us anything about the quality of the assets, their real value in money terms or their value to the business.

Off balance sheet financing and **window dressing** are two terms that often crop up in discussions about the accuracy of balance sheet information. The former relates to the funding of operations in such a way that the relevant assets and liabilities are not disclosed in the balance sheet of the company concerned. The latter is a **creative accounting** practice in which changes in short-term funding have the effect of disguising or improving the reported liquidity (cash and near cash) position of the reporting organisation.

Structure of the balance sheet

Assets are acquired by a business to generate future benefits, for example from trading or whatever activities the business has been set up to provide. To acquire assets the business must first raise the necessary funds primarily from shareholders. In doing so the claims or obligations are created in the form of shareholders' equity.

Shareholders' equity and also **non-current liabilities** and **current liabilities** represent claims, or obligations, on the company to provide cash or other benefits to third parties. Equity, or shareholders' capital, represents a claim by the owners, or shareholders of the business, against the business.

Liabilities represent claims by persons, other than the owners of the business, against the business. These claims arise from transactions relating to the provision of goods or services, or lending money to the business.

An example of a balance sheet format adopted by a limited company, Flatco plc, is shown in Figure 3.5. It is shown in what is termed a horizontal format in order to illustrate the grouping of the assets categories, the total of which equals the total of the liabilities and equity categories. In practice, UK companies adopt the vertical format (see Fig. 3.7), rather than the horizontal format balance sheet, which we shall discuss in a later section of this chapter.

Figure 3.5   A horizontal balance sheet format showing the balancing of assets with liabilities and equity

Flatco plc
Balance sheet as at 31 December 2010

	Assets	£000		Liabilities	£000	
	Non-current assets			**Equity**		
operational	Tangible	1,884		Share capital	1,200	financial
operational	Intangible	416		Share premium account	200	financial
operational	Investments	248		Retained earnings	1,594	financial
	Total non-current assets	2,548		**Total equity**	2,994	
				Non-current liabilities		
				Borrowings and finance leases	173	financial
				Trade and other payables	154	operational
				Deferred tax liabilities	–	operational
				Provisions	222	operational
				Total non-current liabilities	549	
	Current assets			**Current liabilities**		
operational	Inventories	311		Borrowings and finance leases	50	financial
operational	Trade and other receivables	1,162		Trade and other payables	553	operational
				Current tax liabilities	50	operational
financial	Cash and cash equivalents	327		Provisions	152	operational
	Total current assets	1,800		**Total current liabilities**	805	
	Total assets	4,348		**Total liabilities and equity**	4,348	

The detail of each of the categories within the balance sheet will be explained in the sections that follow. As we have shown in Figure 3.5, each balance sheet category, both assets and liabilities, may be described as either financial or operational. **Equity**, borrowings and finance leases, and cash and cash equivalents are financial resources, whereas **non-current assets**, inventories, trade and other receivables, non-current liabilities and current liabilities are operational, relating to the manufacturing, commercial and administrative activities of the company.

We will now look at each of the balance sheet categories in detail, beginning with shareholders' equity and liabilities.

Equity

Shareholders' equity is usually simply called equity. It represents the total investment of the shareholders in the company, the total book wealth of the business. Equity broadly comprises share capital, the share premium account and retained earnings. The cost of shareholders' equity is generally related to the **dividends** paid to shareholders, the level of which is usually dependent on how well the company has performed during the year.

Share capital

The nominal value of a share is the value of each share, decided at the outset by the promoters of the company. The nominal value is the same for each of the shares and may be, for example, 25p, 50p or £1 (the usual maximum). The initial **share capital** is the number of shares in the company multiplied by the nominal value of the shares (for example, two million shares at 50p per share is £1,000,000, or at £1 per share is £2,000,000). Each share is a title of ownership of the assets of the company. This is an important issue in respect of control and growth of the company.

Worked example 3.6

Arthur King is setting up a small limited company, Round Table Ltd, for which he needs initial capital of £10,000. Arthur creates 100 shares each having a nominal value of £100. Arthur decides to start off as king of his empire and keep 90% of the shares for himself and so buys 90 shares at £100 each and pays £9,000 out of his personal bank account into the bank account of the new company, Round Table Ltd. Arthur owns 90% of the company. The remaining 10 shares are purchased by 10 of Arthur's friends each for £100. Each friend owns 1% of the company, has 1% of the voting rights at shareholders' meetings and will receive 1% of dividends paid by the company.

Round Table Ltd does well and after some time considers that it needs additional capital of a further £10,000 to fund its growth. The company may issue 100 new shares at £100 each.

We may discuss the implications for Arthur if he is unable to afford any additional shares himself and the new shares are sold to new investors. The total number of shares will become 200, of which he will own 90, that is 45%.

Because Arthur will have less than 50% of the shares we may say that he therefore loses control of the company. There are two main considerations regarding the issue of shares and control.

The first point is that the founder of a growing business must face a difficult dilemma: growing but losing control, or keeping control but losing growth opportunities. An alternative may be to go to the bank and fund growth with a loan. However, along with this goes a vulnerability to failure at the first cash crisis the company may face.

The second point is that the issue of new shares at the same price as the existing original shares may be considered unfair. When Round Table Ltd was created it was worth only the money that the original shareholders invested in it. The company's credibility has now been built up through successful operations and an understanding of the market. Surely this must have a value so that the new share issue should be made at a higher price? The difference in price between the original nominal value and the price new investors will have to pay is the share premium.

Share premium account

The **share premium account** may be best illustrated with a worked example.

Worked example 3.7

Using the company in Worked Example 3.6, let's assume that for potential investors the value of one share is now £400. This means that 25 shares of £400 would be needed to raise additional capital of £10,000.

We will look at how these new shares should appear in the company's balance sheet.

(i)   These new shares cannot appear in the balance sheet with a nominal value of £400 because it would then mean that legally the shareholders would have voting and dividend rights four times those of the £100 nominal shares.

(ii)   The capital in the balance sheet will need to be increased by 25 times £100, the nominal value of the shares, that is £2,500.

(iii) A new category, the share premium account, is required on the balance sheet.

(iv)   The share premium account will have a value of 25 (£400 − £100), that is £7,500.

Retained earnings

Retained earnings is the final element within the equity of the company. The profit or net income generated from the operations of the company belongs to the shareholders of the company. It is the directors who recommend how much of those earnings are distributed to shareholders as dividends, the balance being held as retained earnings and reinvested in the business. The retained earnings of the company are increased by the annual net profit less any dividends payable; they are part of the wealth of the company and therefore appear within the equity of the company. Similarly, any losses will reduce the retained earnings of the company.

Liabilities

Current liabilities

Current liabilities are items that are expected to become payable within one year from the balance sheet date. These comprise borrowings and finance leases, trade and other payables, current tax liabilities and **provisions**.

Borrowings and finance leases

Borrowings and finance leases are the elements of bank overdrafts, loans and leases that are payable within one year of the balance sheet date.

Trade and other payables

Whereas there is a cost associated with equity and borrowings in the form of dividends and interest payable, trade payables are sometimes considered 'free' of such cost. This, however, is rarely true. Trade payables, the accounts payable to suppliers net of any adjustments such as credit notes due, are not a free source of finance. This is because when credit is extended this is usually accompanied by an increase in the price of the product or service being provided.

Worked example 3.8

A supplier may offer to a company payment terms of three months from delivery date.

We will look at the effect of the company proposing to the supplier payment terms of two months from delivery date, for which the supplier may for example offer 1% or 2% early settlement discount.

A discount of 1% for settlement one month early is equivalent to over 12% per annum. Consequently, it becomes apparent that the supplier's selling price must have included some allowance for financial charges; accounts payable to suppliers are therefore not a free debt.

Other payables include for example employee and social costs payable and also accruals, which are allowances made for costs and expenses incurred and payable within one year of the balance sheet date but for which no invoices have yet been processed through the accounts. This is in line with the matching (or accruals) concept we discussed in Chapter 1. Expense recognition is an important concept. Expenses should be recognised immediately they are known about. Accruals are treated in a similar way to payables but the invoices for these charges have not yet been processed by the entity. They are charges or expenses that are brought into the period because, although goods (or services) have been provided, they have not yet been included in the supplier's accounts. Some examples are telephone and electricity charges which are incurred but for which invoices may not normally be received until the end of each quarter. On the other hand, revenues or profits should not be recognised until they are earned.

Worked example 3.9

We know that in the Ayco example the business had used and had been invoiced for and paid for £200 worth of stationery. If we assume, for example, that more than £200 worth of stationery had been used in the month of January, say £1,000, we can consider:

(i)   What would be the impact on Ayco if £500 worth of the additional stationery had been used, and an invoice had been received but not processed through the ledgers?
(ii) What would be the impact on Ayco if £300 worth of the additional stationery had been used, and an invoice had not yet been received but was still in the mail?

Both amounts would have to be charged to printing and stationery expenses for a total of £800. The balancing entries that would have to be made would be to credit a total of £800 to accruals. Ayco knew they had used stationery for which there was a cost even though an invoice may not have been processed.

The net impact of the above on Ayco would have been a reduction in profit, a debit of £800 and an increase in liabilities, a credit of £800 to accruals.

Current tax liabilities

Corporation tax assessed on the current year profit is shown as a liability for tax to be paid within one year following the balance sheet date and may be shown as income tax payable. This is based on a tax computation that may not necessarily be agreed by HMRC and so the exact amount of tax paid may be more or less than that stated in the balance sheet.

Provisions

A provision that is classified as a current liability is an amount charged against profit to provide for an expected liability or loss even though the amount of the liability or loss is uncertain, but which is expected to materialise within the next year. This is in line with the prudence concept we discussed in Chapter 1.

Non-current liabilities

Non-current liabilities are items that are expected to become payable after one year from the balance sheet date. These comprise borrowings and finance leases, trade and other payables, deferred tax liabilities and provisions.

Borrowings and finance leases

Items included within the non-current liabilities category of borrowing and finance leases are the elements of loans and finance leases that are not payable within one year following the balance sheet date but are payable some time after that year. To help the company finance its operations it may take on further financial debt, or loans, for a limited period of time. The company has to pay interest on financial debt, over the period of the loan, regardless of how well or not the company performs, that is, regardless of whether it has made a profit or a loss.

Financial debt, provided by various financial institutions such as banks, may take the form of loans, **debentures** and leases. Interest rates vary according to the risk of the investment. The level of interest payable, and thus the choice of which type of debt the company may wish to take on, will be determined by how risky the potential lender regards this particular company.

A banker or investor may wish to invest in Government securities, which are risk-free, and receive the low rate of return offered by such investments. For a company, which is not risk-free, the investor will expect a higher rate of interest as an incentive or compensation for the risk being taken. The higher the risk of a security, the higher the expected rate of return (see Fig. 3.6).

| Figure 3.6 | An illustration of the relationship between risk and return |

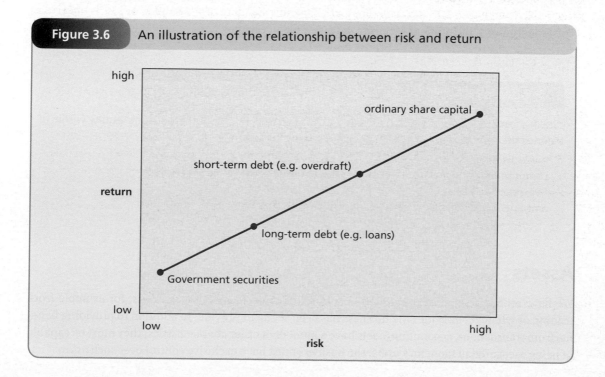

The difference between the interest rate paid on Government securities and the interest rate that a company pays on loans is called the risk premium. Shareholders' equity is even riskier than shorter-term corporate debt (for example, a loan made to the company). Therefore, the company should not only make a profit but the level of profit should be such that the shareholders get a return in line with their level of **risk**. This should be the return on Government securities plus a risk premium which is even higher than the risk premium payable on the corporate debt.

Trade and other payables

Trade and other payables after one year mainly comprise accounts payable to suppliers of goods and services provided to the company that may typically be, for example, relating to capital projects taking place over an extended period for which stage payments may have been agreed.

Deferred tax liabilities

Deferred tax is the difference between the tax ultimately payable on the profits recognised in an accounting period and the actual amount of tax payable for the same accounting period. The former figure will be based on the tax implications of accounting profit and the carrying amounts of assets and liabilities. The latter figure will be based on a calculation of profits as recognised by the tax authorities.

The deferred tax liability is the amount of income taxes payable in future periods in respect of taxable temporary differences. Similarly, a deferred tax asset is the amount of income taxes recoverable in future periods in respect of deductible temporary differences, carried forward unused tax losses, and unused tax credits (IAS 12, Income Taxes).

Provisions

A provision that is classified as a non-current liability is an amount charged against profit to provide for an expected liability or loss even though the amount and date of the liability or loss is uncertain. This is in line with the prudence concept we discussed in Chapter 1.

Progress check 3.4

Which of the following do you think may be classified as liabilities or shareholders' equity within a balance sheet, and under which headings should they appear?

- bank overdraft
- computer
- five-year bank loan
- amounts owed by customers
- accruals
- amounts owed to suppliers
- ordinary shares
- share premium

Assets

We have seen that assets are acquired by a business to generate future benefits, for example from trading or whatever activities the business has been set up to provide. In addition to providing benefits from transactions, accounting assets have a number of other characteristics: they must be capable of being measured in monetary units; the business must have exclusive control over such assets.

The assets sections of the balance sheet are more homogeneous than the equity and liabilities sections of the balance sheet. The liabilities sections of the balance sheet generally describe where the financing comes from, whereas the assets sections generally represent how the money has been used.

Non-current assets

Non-current assets include land and buildings, equipment, machinery, furniture, fittings, computers, software and motor vehicles, which the company has purchased to enable it to meet its strategic objectives. They have a very important common feature, namely that they are not renewed within the operating cycle (see current assets below), which may be measured in months, weeks, days, or even hours. Non-current assets have a longer life of usually much more than one year.

A building may have a life of 20 years, whereas a personal computer may have a life of three years, both being longer than the cycle in which raw materials and packaging are renewed, for example. Regardless of this, non-current assets are 'consumed' on a day-to-day basis. The measure of this consumption is called depreciation.

Non-current assets comprise tangible non-current assets, **intangible non-current assets** and long-term investments (or financial assets).

Tangible non-current assets

Tangible non-current assets are long-term assets that one can touch, for example land, buildings, equipment, machinery, computers, fixtures and fittings. Their costs are apportioned, or depreciated, over the estimated economic life of each asset.

Intangible non-current assets

Intangible non-current assets are the long-term assets that one cannot touch, for example computer software, patents, trademarks and **goodwill**. A business must decide if the useful lives of its intangible assets (other than goodwill) are indefinite or finite, in accordance with IAS 38, Intangible Assets. An indefinite life means that there is no foreseeable limit to the period over which the asset is expected to generate net cash inflows for the business. A finite life means there is a limited period of benefit to the business.

If a business decides that the useful economic life of the asset is finite then the costs, net of their residual values, are amortised (or apportioned) over the estimated economic life of each asset. The **amortisation** method used should reflect the time pattern over which the benefits are received from the use of the asset. If the asset is considered to have an indefinite life then it should not be amortised. Goodwill is always assumed to have an indefinite life, and both finite and indefinite life assets should be subject to annual **impairment** reviews (see page 102).

Investments

Investments are long-term financial assets that include loans to **subsidiary companies**, investments in associate companies and non-associated companies.

Current assets

In addition to the investment in its whole long-term, and relatively fixed, environment (buildings, equipment, machinery, computers and furniture), the company has to invest additional funds in its **operating cycle**. The operating cycle involves the management of the company's current assets and current liabilities, which may be measured in months, weeks, days, or even hours. The operating cycle is the period of time between the point at which cash starts to be spent on production and the collection of cash from customers who have been supplied with finished product. We will look in detail at the operating cycle in Chapter 16 when we look at the management of working capital.

Current assets comprise inventories, trade and other receivables, and cash and cash equivalents.

Inventories

Inventories generally include raw materials, work in progress and finished goods. They may also include sundry other consumable items purchased for use over a period of time such as stationery, replacement parts, spare parts and cleaning materials, if these are of any significant value, so that the inclusion of their total cost on acquisition would provide a distortion in the income statement.

Trade and other receivables

Trade and other receivables include accounts receivable, net of any doubtful debt provision, due from customers and others including subsidiaries, and also prepayments and accrued income.

A prepayment is expenditure on goods (or services) for future benefit, which is to be charged to future operations. Such amounts are similar to accounts receivable which is why they are included in the current assets section of the balance sheet.

Prepayments include prepaid expenses for services not yet used, for example rent, insurance, subscriptions, or electricity charges in advance, and also accrued income. Accrued income relates to sales of goods or services that have occurred and have been accounted for within the trading period but have not yet been invoiced to the customer. This is in accord with the matching (or accruals) concept discussed in Chapter 1.

Cash and cash equivalents

Cash and cash equivalents includes bank balances and deposits in addition to actual cash held in the form of notes and coins.

Other financial assets

Current assets may also include short-term financial assets such as foreign exchange contracts and options, currency swaps and other derivatives.

Worked example 3.10

In the Ayco example we may assume, for example, that Ayco had received an invoice in January for £2,000 for advertising to be paid in March, but the advertising was not taking place until February.

An invoice may have been received and processed through the ledgers, which has an additional impact on Ayco.

Accounts payable would be increased by (or credited with) £2,000 and advertising expenses charged with (or debited with) £2,000 in the month of January. However, because the advertising had not yet taken place the charge of £2,000 would be considered as being in advance, or to use its technical term, a prepayment. The accounts payable entry remains as a credit of £2,000, but an additional entry is required to credit advertising expenses with £2,000 and debit prepayments with £2,000.

The net impact of the above on Ayco would have been no change to profit.

Progress check 3.5

(i) Which of the following items do you think may be classified as assets within a balance sheet?
(ii) Which ones are non-current assets and which ones are current assets?
(iii) In which categories should the assets appear?

- long-term loan
- computer printer
- goodwill
- share premium
- water charges paid in advance
- an invoice not yet received for photocopy expenses already incurred
- materials held to be used in production
- products for sale to customers

The summary balance sheet that we saw in Figure 3.5 is known as the horizontal format. Although now rarely used in practice within businesses, it was a conventional format in which assets are shown in one column, and liabilities and shareholders' equity in the other column. Such a presentation clearly illustrated how total assets equalled the total of liabilities plus shareholders' equity.

The horizontal balance sheet format can be represented by the equation

$$\text{total assets (TA)} = \text{equity (E)} + \text{total liabilities (TL)}$$
$$TA = E + TL$$

or

$$\text{non-current assets (NCA)} + \text{current assets (CA)}$$
$$= \text{equity (E)} + \text{non-current liabilities (NCL)} + \text{current liabilities (CL)}$$
$$NCA + CA = E + NCL + CL$$

Using the above equation, companies generally present their balance sheets in a vertical format. IAS 1 does not prescribe the exact order or format in which a company presents individual items in the balance sheet and so companies may therefore present their balance sheets in a variety of different ways. A company arranges each item and presents its balance sheet in a way that it feels is most appropriate to its comprehensibility. A commonly used vertical format rearranges the above equation to become:

$$NCA + CA - CL - NCL = E$$

Each element in the equation is represented vertically with total assets minus total liabilities equal to net assets, and represented by the shareholders' equity of the company.

Using the data from Figure 3.5 the balance sheet for Flatco plc is shown in a vertical format in Figure 3.7. The total book wealth of the company is represented by the **net assets** of the business. Net assets is derived by deducting total liabilities from total assets, and therefore equals the shareholders' equity of the business. A balance sheet is probably easier to read down the page

Figure 3.7   A vertical format balance sheet

Flatco plc

Balance sheet as at 31 December 2010

Assets	£000
Non-current assets	
Tangible	1,884
Intangible	416
Investments	248
Total non-current assets	2,548
Current assets	
Inventories	311
Trade and other receivables	1,162
Cash and cash equivalents	327
Total current assets	1,800
Total assets	4,348
Liabilities	
Current liabilities	
Borrowings and finance leases	50
Trade and other payables	553
Current tax liabilities	50
Dividends payable	70
Provisions	82
Total current liabilities	805
Non-current liabilities	
Borrowings and finance leases	173
Trade and other payables	154
Deferred tax liabilities	—
Provisions	222
Total non-current liabilities	549
Total liabilities	1,354
Net assets	2,994
Equity	
Share capital	1,200
Share premium account	200
Retained earnings	1,594
Total equity	2,994

rather than across, and the vertical format does clearly highlight each of the main sections of the balance sheet.

In Chapter 2, the concept of the trial balance, and its links with the income statement and balance sheet are examined in detail. Worked example 3.11 uses the trial balance of Perfecto Ltd to identify the various categories of assets, liabilities and shareholders' equity (the debits and the credits).

Worked example 3.11

The balances extracted from the trial balance of Perfecto Ltd at 30 September 2010 are presented in an alphabetical list:

	£000
Accruals	100
Bank and cash balances	157
Intangible non-current assets	203
Inventories of finished goods	95
Inventories of materials	37
Long-term loans	85
Prepaid expenses and accrued income	295
Profit and loss account to 30 September 2010 (profit)	130
Provisions	103
Retained earnings at 30 September 2009	525
Share capital	600
Share premium account	105
Tangible non-current assets	902
Trade payables due after one year	77
Trade payables due within one year	277
Trade receivables	284
Work in progress	29

It should be remembered that a loss is a debit. If the total of the debit balances is equal to the total of the credit balances it may be assumed that the information is complete.

- First, we need to identify which are assets (debit balances) and which are liabilities and shareholders' equity (credit balances).
- Second, we can check that the trial balance is actually in balance, and if there is any missing information.
- Third, we can prepare a balance sheet for Perfecto Ltd as at 30 September 2010 using a vertical format.

	Assets (debits) £000	Liabilities and equity (credits) £000
Accruals		100
Bank and cash balances	157	
Trade payables due within one year		277
Trade payables due after one year		77
Trade receivables	284	
Intangible non-current assets	203	
Long-term loans		85
Prepaid expenses and accrued income	295	
Profit and loss account year to September 2010 (profit)		130
Provisions		103
Retained earnings at 30 September 2009		525
Ordinary share capital		600
Share premium		105

	Assets (debits) £000	Liabilities and equity (credits) £000
Inventories of finished goods	95	
Inventories of materials	37	
Tangible non-current assets	902	
Work in progress	29	
Total	2,002	2,002

The total of the assets is £2,002,000, which is equal to the total of the liabilities plus shareholders' equity. The trial balance is therefore in balance and there doesn't appear to be any information missing. However, errors of omission, for example, or transposed figures, may not be spotted from the information given. There could be equal and opposite debit and credit balances that have been excluded from the list in error.

Given that the data is correct, an accurate balance sheet for Perfecto Ltd as at 30 September 2010 may be prepared.

Perfecto Ltd
Balance sheet as at 30 September 2010

	£000
Non-current assets	
Tangible	902
Intangible	203
Total non-current assets	1,105
Current assets	
Inventories	161
Trade receivables	284
Prepayments	295
Cash and cash equivalents	157
Total current assets	897
Total assets	2,002
Current liabilities	
Trade payables	277
Accruals	100
Total current liabilities	377
Non-current liabilities	
Borrowings and finance leases	85
Trade and other payables	77
Provisions	103
Total non-current liabilities	265
Total liabilities	642
Net assets	1,360
Equity	
Share capital	600
Share premium account	105
Retained earnings	655
Total equity	1,360

What does the horizontal format balance sheet tell us? Why is the vertical format balance sheet now used by most large companies?

Many of the larger businesses in the UK consist of a number of companies rather than just one company. The control of such companies, or groups of companies, rests with a parent company, which is called the holding company. The other companies within the group are called subsidiaries. The holding company holds the required number of shares in each of the subsidiaries to give it the required control.

Businesses operate in a group structure for a variety of reasons. It may be because they cover different countries, different products, or different market sectors; it may be to provide independence, or separate accountability, or may very often be a result of successive takeovers or mergers of businesses.

IAS 27, Consolidated and Separate Financial Statements, requires group accounts to be prepared for the holding company in addition to the accounts that are required to be prepared for each of the individual companies within the group. These **consolidated accounts** exclude all transactions between companies within the group, for example inter-company sales revenue and purchases, to avoid double counting of transactions. In most other respects, the group consolidated accounts reflect an amalgamation of each of the components of the balance sheets of all the companies within the group.

Valuation of assets

The question of valuation of assets at a specific balance sheet date arises in respect of choosing the most accurate methods relating to non-current assets, inventories and receivables (and similarly payables), which support the fundamental requirement to give a true and fair view. Companies must be very careful to ensure that their assets are valued in a way that realistically reflects their ability to generate future cash flows. This applies to both current assets such as inventories, and non-current assets such as land and buildings. The balance sheets of companies rarely reflect either the current market values of non-current assets, or their future earnings potential, since they are based on historical costs.

During 2008 the house building market suffered greatly as property prices fell and the demand for new housing diminished. We saw several house builders failing or being the subject of takeover bids. One of the UK's largest house builders, Persimmon (see the press extract below), recorded a loss of £780m in 2008. However, in 2009 they reported a profit of £77.8m.

In 2008 Persimmon had written down the value of the land they held by £664.1m, which largely explained the huge loss for that year. In 2009, following a review of the value of the company's land, the directors decided to reverse £74.8m of these write-offs, which was added back to profit. Directors of companies must take care in such valuation increases that reflect the impact of property price inflation, which may not be sustained, and which ignore the future earning potential of the assets. The effect on Persimmon was that the shareholders, and the market, were delighted at the tremendous reversal in fortunes in the year, particularly as rival house builder Taylor Wimpey reported a £640m pre-tax loss in 2009.

Differences between the methods chosen to value various assets (and liabilities) at the end of accounting periods may have a significant impact on the results reported in the income statement for those periods. Examples of this may be seen in:

- non-current assets and depreciation
- inventories valuations and cost of sales
- valuations of trade payables and trade receivables denominated in foreign currencies
- provisions for doubtful debts.

The real value of a company's assets

Britain's biggest house builder gave the troubled sector a lift yesterday by returning to profitability following a torrid period in which it was forced to wipe £600m off the value of its assets.

York-based Persimmon posted a profit of £77.8m – boosted by a windfall of £74.8m from a revaluation of its land bank – on sales of £1.42bn. This compares with a loss last year of £780m. The company also reported a sharp reduction in its debt – cut by more than half from £601m to £268m.

John White, the chairman, described the results as 'a major turnaround' and the market responded well to the news with Persimmon's share price rising 29 to 429p at one point, despite the lack of a dividend.

While Persimmon's profit would have been a modest £7m without the write-back – a steep fall on last year's pre-exceptionals profit of £127m – one analyst suggested that the company's revaluation veered on the side of caution.

Mike Farley, the group chief executive, agreed there was scope for further write-backs but was inclined to wait and see before making any further changes. 'We come into this year with a strong forward order book of £900m, up 29pc on the same period last year', he said. 'We are going to open 90 new sites in the first half of 2010 and, to put that into context, we opened 90 in the whole of 2009.

'That said, there's an election campaign coming up and whichever party gets in there could be cuts in Government spending and increases in taxation and they could have knock-on effects for the economy as a whole.'

Mr Farley does look forward to a further reduction in Persimmon's debts over the next 12 months, however. 'We'd like to see debt below £100m if things remain as they are', he said. 'If things improve, we may have to invest more cash. We're comfortable with our debt. Our gearing is at 16pc and we have £1bn of facilities and so have plenty of headroom.'

Both the chairman and chief executive yesterday failed to issue outright denials to speculation that they would use this 'headroom' to mount a takeover of smaller rival Bovis – expected to be at £600m – taking refuge in the line that their focus is on debt reduction.

But Mr Farley added fuel to the rumours by saying: 'You can never say never, can you?' He also held out hope for a dividend next year. 'That's not something we are going to decide at this point', he said. 'We recognise [the loyalty of] our shareholders and we are one of the few companies in our sector who haven't asked for extra cash. That's something we'll review as the year goes on.'

Source: **Persimmon returns to profit after revaluation,** by Dominic Midgley © *Daily Telegraph*, 3 March 2010

The valuation of assets and liabilities will all be covered in detail in Chapter 4 when we look at the income statement. The rules applicable to the valuation of balance sheet items are laid down in the international accounting standards and UK financial reporting standards (IASs and FRSs). These rules allow companies to prepare their financial statements under the historical cost convention (the gross value of the asset being the purchase price or production cost), or alternative conventions of historical cost modified to include certain assets at a revalued amount or current cost.

Under alternative conventions, the gross value of the asset is either the market value at the most recent valuation date or its current cost: tangible non-current assets should be valued at market value or at current cost; investments (non-current assets) are valued at market value or at any value considered appropriate by the directors; short-term investments are valued at current cost; inventories are valued at current cost. If a reduction in value of any non-current assets is expected to be permanent then provision for this must be made. The same applies to investments even if the reduction is not expected to be permanent.

Non-current assets with finite lives are subject to depreciation charges. Current assets must be written down to the amount for which they could be disposed of (their **net realisable value**), ⬅||| if that value is lower than cost or an alternative valuation. It should be noted that provisions for reductions in value no longer considered necessary must be written back to the profit and loss account.

There is an element of choice between alternative valuation methods that may be adopted by businesses. Because of this, difficulties may arise in trying to provide consistent comparisons of the performance of companies even within the same industrial sectors. If changes in accounting policies have been introduced, further inconsistencies arise in trying to provide a realistic comparison of just one company's performance between one accounting period and another.

The difficulty of accurately valuing assets was clearly made by a recent story in the *Daily Telegraph* shown below.

Accounting concepts and the IASs and UK FRSs provide rules and guidance for the valuation of balance sheet items. We will look at some of the most important valuation rules in respect of non-current assets and current assets.

Non-current assets

IAS 16, Property, Plant and Equipment, and IAS 38, Intangible Assets, and IAS 40, Investment Property, define non-current assets as those assets intended for use on a continuing basis in

The real value of an asset – priceless!

Its value as a 5,000-year-old monument to British heritage is priceless. But should Stonehenge be sold on the open market it would fetch £51million, according to estate agents. Ever willing to put a pound sign beside any available assets, property marketeers have valued a host of national landmarks, should the Government or the Crown be tempted to sell them.

According to a survey of 500 estate agents, 10 Downing Street is worth £5.2million and Windsor Castle £390.9million.

The exercise by the property website FindaProperty.com also valued Brighton's Royal Pavilion at £51.9million and Blackpool Tower at £60million.

Nigel Lewis, a property analyst at FindaProperty.com, said: 'Based on these valuations, the Government and Crown probably own enough land and property to pay down the national debt pretty significantly.

'Of course, we know these landmarks will never be put up for sale, but with property prices shooting up 10 per cent in value over the past year we thought it would be fun to see what the market consensus was about their values.

'It's quite a challenge for estate agents more used to valuing suburban semis to put an accurate valuation on a royal castle or ancient monument, but there was a surprising amount of agreement between the different agents we spoke to.' The valuations were based on location, transport links, available land and the potential for renovation and reuse.

Other landmarks valued included Birmingham's Bull Ring, which estate agents said would cost £750million; Coventry Cathedral, worth £50million, and Leeds Town Hall, which would be listed for an estimated £30million on the open market.

Source: **The value of 5,000 years of history? £51m,** by Myra Butterworth © *Daily Telegraph*, 25 May 2010

the company's activities. As we have already discussed, non-current assets comprise tangible assets, intangible assets and investments (financial assets). Within tangible non-current assets there are various categories of asset: land and buildings (freehold, long leasehold and short leasehold); plant and machinery; fixtures, fittings, tools and equipment; assets in the course of construction.

Capital expenditure relates to acquisition of non-current assets and includes all the costs of putting an asset into service with the company so that the company will benefit from the services of the asset for more than one trading period.

Interest charges incurred in the financing of the production of an asset may be added to and included in the total cost of the asset. Such charges are said to have been capitalised, and if they are included in the total non-current asset cost this must be disclosed in a note to the financial statements.

Which other acquisition costs should be added to the asset price to give the total acquisition cost? The total amount recorded in the accounts of a company, the capitalised cost, for each category of non-current asset, should include various acquisition costs in addition to the purchase price of the asset, as follows:

■ land
   – agent's commissions
   – legal fees
   – survey fees
   – draining, clearing, landscaping, demolition costs
■ buildings
   – repair, alteration and improvement costs
■ other assets
   – freight costs
   – customs duty
   – installation charges
■ building construction
   – subcontract work
   – materials costs
   – labour costs
   – direct construction overheads
   – excavation costs
   – construction offices
   – professional fees
■ own-built plant and machinery
   – materials costs
   – labour costs
   – production overheads.

Overheads that may be capitalised relate to costs of wages, salaries and expenses not directly incurred in the construction of buildings or machinery, but which nevertheless are necessary costs incurred to enable construction to take place. Examples may be a proportion or the full costs of management and supervision of projects, and a share of electricity or similar charges incurred on such projects.

Worked example 3.12

We have been asked to decide which of the following items should be disclosed in the balance sheet and which should be disclosed in the income statement.

	£
1. Extension to the factory	500,000
2. New plant	100,000
3. Architect's fee for supervising the building of the extension	10,000
4. Haulier's invoice for delivering the plant	5,000
5. Invoice from decorators for painting the reception area	2,000
6. Insurance premium for twelve months on new cars	15,000
7. Invoice from garage for ten new cars	200,000

The disclosure should be as follows:

	£
1. Balance sheet – non-current assets	500,000
2. Balance sheet – non-current assets	100,000
3. Balance sheet – non-current assets	10,000
4. Balance sheet – non-current assets	5,000
5. Income statement – repairs	2,000
6. Income statement – insurance	15,000
7. Balance sheet – non-current assets	200,000

A valuation problem arises with regard to non-current assets because such assets have been 'consumed' over time and will currently be worth less than at the time of acquisition. The total cost of using a non-current asset over its life is generally defined as the original investment less a portion of its cost recovered (its residual value) at the end of the asset's useful life. Depreciation is allocated to charge a fair proportion of the total cost (or valuation) of the asset to each accounting period expected to benefit from its use. The net non-current asset figure reported in each period's balance sheet will reflect the reduction to the historical cost, or revalued amount, of the asset using the depreciation calculated for each period.

Intangible assets include: deferred development costs; concessions; patents; licences; trademarks; goodwill; brand names. Investments (financial assets) primarily include shares and loans in non-consolidated group companies.

Progress check 3.7

Does it really matter if the year-end balance sheet of a company shows non-current assets at cost, less depreciation and amortisation, but ignores any change in their value? This should be discussed from the points of view of an investor and a lender as two major users of financial statements.

Brand names

Some organisations have included brand names for products like chocolate bars and beers in their balance sheets as intangible assets, therefore inflating the totals of their balance sheets. Examples of companies that have capitalised brand names have been:

- Ranks Hovis McDougall (1991) capitalised non-purchased brand names
- Guinness (1993) capitalised purchased brand names.

Capitalisation of purchased brand names is permitted under IAS 38. Although brands purchased by a company may be capitalised, non-purchased brands are specifically prohibited from being capitalised. The IASB has viewed the inclusion of non-purchased brands as undesirable because of the difficulty in ascertaining historical costs and the inappropriateness of trying to capitalise the earnings or cash flows which have been generated by the brand names. If the value of possible intangible asset cannot be measured reliably it cannot be capitalised in the balance sheet. Purchased brands have proved to be as desirable as traditional tangible non-current assets, and so should be disclosed in the balance sheet.

Goodwill

IAS 22 provided for two methods of accounting for business combinations: the pooling of interests method or merger method; the purchase method or acquisition method. IFRS 3, Business Combinations, has replaced IAS 22. Under IFRS 3 the merger method is no longer used and it is only the acquisition method that should be applied.

IFRS 3 defines goodwill as the difference between the consideration (purchase price) paid for the business and the fair value of the assets acquired. It can only appear on the balance sheet if a business has been acquired for a value in either cash or shares, so a company may not capitalise internally generated goodwill. IFRS 3 explains that if the value of the assets acquired are greater than the consideration then the gain is recognised immediately as a 'bargain purchase' in the profit and loss account. If, as is more usual, the consideration paid has a greater value than the assets acquired then the difference (the goodwill) is capitalised in the balance sheet as an intangible non-current asset. Unlike other intangible non-current assets goodwill is not amortised over its useful economic life but is tested for impairment annually, or more frequently if events or changes in circumstances indicate that the asset might be impaired, in accordance with IAS 36 Impairment of Assets.

Impairment requires the goodwill to be evaluated to see if its value in the balance sheet is greater than the net income that could be derived from the goodwill either from its continued use in the business or from sale. It must then be reduced to the lower figure and the difference charged as an expense to the profit and loss account.

Research and development costs

Research and development are activities directed to the development of knowledge. Development costs do not include research costs.

A development cost is defined in IAS 38, Intangible Assets, as the cost of the application of research findings or other knowledge to a plan or design for the production of new or substantially improved materials, devices, products, processes, systems or services before the start of commercial production or use. Development expenditure on new products or services is normally undertaken with an expectation of future commercial benefits, from either increased profits or reduced costs. Development costs are therefore matched against future revenues. IAS 38 indicates that once an intangible asset arising from development activity can be recognised it is capitalised as an intangible asset in the balance sheet. The cost of the intangible asset is then charged in proportion to the revenues derived from this development activity period by period over the life of the project.

Examples of development activities that might create intangible assets include:

- design, construction and testing of pre-production prototypes
- design of equipment that uses new technology
- a pilot project involving design, construction and operation of a new plant.

Research costs are defined in IAS 38 as the costs of original and planned investigation undertaken with the prospect of gaining new scientific or technical knowledge and understanding.

Examples of activities classified as research include:

- activities aimed at obtaining new knowledge
- the search for applications of research findings or other knowledge
- the search for alternatives for materials, devices, products, processes, systems or services.

In general, no one particular period rather than another is expected to benefit from research activities and so their costs should be charged to the profit and loss account as they are incurred.

Inventories

Problems arise in the area of valuation of inventories for three main reasons. First, homogeneous items within various inventory categories are purchased continuously and consumed continuously in the manufacturing processes. The purchase prices of these homogeneous items may vary considerably. How do we know the specific prices of each item as we take them from inventory and use them?

The general rule is that inventories must be valued at the lower of purchase cost (or production cost) and their net realisable value. IAS 2, Inventories, allows alternative methods to be used to match the cost of inventory items with their usage: FIFO (first in first out, where the oldest items of inventory or their costs are assumed to be the first to be used); weighted average cost.

LIFO (last in first out, where the most recently acquired items of inventory or their costs are assumed to be the first to be used) is not permitted in IAS 2, and is not acceptable for taxation purposes in the UK.

Second, materials may be purchased from a variety of geographical locations. Additional costs such as duty, freight and insurance may be incurred. How should these be accounted for? The costs of inventories should comprise the expenditure that has been incurred in the normal course of business in bringing the product or service to its present location and condition.

Third, as materials, packaging and other consumable items are used during the production processes to manufacture work in progress, partly finished product and fully finished product, how should costs be correctly apportioned to give a true cost? Which costs should be included and which should be excluded?

Inventories are disclosed as a main heading in the balance sheet and comprise raw materials and consumables, work in progress, and finished goods. IAS 2 requires that companies must disclose accounting policies adopted in respect of inventories and work in progress.

Trade receivables

Trade receivables are normally paid to the company according to contractual terms of trading agreed at the outset with each customer. However, economic and trading circumstances may have changed.

Can the company be sure that it will receive payment in full against all outstanding receivables? If not, what is a more realistic valuation of such receivables?

Trade receivables may need to be reduced by an assessment of individual accounts receivable that will definitely not be paid (bad debts), or individual accounts receivable that are unlikely ever to be paid (doubtful debts). Bad and doubtful debts and their impact on profit and trade receivables will be examined in detail in Chapter 4, which looks at the income statement.

When goods or services are supplied to a customer they are invoiced at the agreed price and on the trading terms that have been contracted. The trading terms may be, for example 30 days. In this case the sales value will have been taken into the current period profit and loss account but the debt, or the account receivable, will remain unpaid in the accounts receivable ledger until it is settled after 30 days.

Foreign currency transactions

A general factor that may impact on the valuation of all asset types (and liability types) is foreign currency exchange rate risk. For example, a customer in the USA may insist on being invoiced by the company in US$, say 10,000 US$. At the time of delivery of the goods or services the value of the US$ sale in £ at the exchange rate on the day may be say £6,250 (£ = 1.60 US$). The sales invoice may be issued a few days later and the exchange rate may have changed, for example £6,173 (£ = 1.62 US$). The customer may have agreed to settlement two months later, by which time the exchange rate may have moved again, say £5,714 (£ = 1.75 US$). What value should have been attributed to the account receivable at the balance sheet date?

The value attributed to a sales invoice is its £ value on the day if invoiced in £ sterling. If a sales invoice is rendered in foreign currency IAS 21 requires it to be valued at the exchange rate at the date of the transaction, or at an average rate for the period if exchange rates do not fluctuate significantly. If the transaction is to be settled at a contracted exchange rate then the exchange rate specified in the contract should be used. Such a trading transaction is then said to be covered by a matching forward contract.

Progress check 3.8

UK International Ltd invoiced a customer in the USA for goods to the value of 100,000 US$ on 31 December 2009. The US$ cheque sent to UK International by the customer was received on 31 January 2010 and was converted into £ sterling by the bank at 1.55 US$ to £1. Discuss the two transactions, the invoice and its settlement, and their impact on UK International Ltd's income statement and its balance sheet as at 31 December 2009.

A foreign exchange forward contract is a contract, for example between a company and a bank, to exchange two currencies at an agreed exchange rate. Note also the foreign exchange forward option contract which extends this idea to allow the bank or the company to call for settlement of the contract, at two days' notice, between any two dates that have been agreed between the bank and the company at the time of agreeing the contract.

At the end of each accounting period, all receivables denominated in foreign currency should be translated, or revalued, using the rates of exchange ruling at the period-end date, or where appropriate, the rates of exchange fixed under the terms of the relevant transactions. Where there are related or matching forward contracts in respect of trading transactions, the rates of exchange specified in those contracts may be used. A similar treatment should be applied to all monetary assets and liabilities denominated in a foreign currency, that is cash and bank balances, loans, and amounts payable and receivable.

An exchange gain or loss will result during an accounting period if a business transaction is settled at an exchange rate which differs from that used when the transaction was initially recorded, or where appropriate that used at the last balance sheet date. An exchange gain or loss will also arise on unsettled transactions if the rate of exchange used at the balance sheet date differs from that used previously. Such gains and losses are recognised during each accounting period and included in the profit or loss from ordinary activities.

Summary of key points

- Items of expenditure may be generally classified as either capital expenditure or revenue expenditure, although some items may need to be apportioned between the two classifications.

- Limited companies are required to prepare periodically three main financial statements: balance sheet; income statement; statement of cash flows.

- Financial statements are required for the shareholders and the Registrar of Companies, and are also used by, for example, analysts, potential investors, customers, suppliers.

- Categories within the balance sheet are classified into shareholders' equity, liabilities and assets.

- With regard to the structure of the balance sheet, assets and liabilities must both be classified as current and non-current but IAS 1 provides a choice in presentation of the balance sheet between separating current and non-current assets and liabilities, or presenting assets and liabilities in order of their liquidity (or in reverse order of liquidity) without a current and non-current distinction.

- Valuation of the various items within the balance sheet is covered by the accounting concepts, International Accounting Standards (IASs) and UK Financial Reporting Standards (FRSs), but nevertheless gives rise to problems and differences in approach.

- Within the rules, alternative methods may be used to value the different categories of assets (and liabilities) within the balance sheet.

- There are limitations to the conventional balance sheet arising not only from the fact that it is a historical document, but from inconsistencies in its preparation between companies and industries, the employment of various asset valuation methods, off-balance sheet financing and window dressing.

Assessment material

Questions

Q3.1 (i) What are the three main financial statements?
     (ii) What is their purpose?
     (iii) What does the statement of changes in equity show?

Q3.2 Consider two ways of looking at the profit of a business: an increase in the book wealth of the company; and the net result of the company's trading operations (revenue less expenses). What do these terms mean, and is the result different using the two approaches?

Q3.3   Explain the format and structure of the balance sheet of a typical limited company.

Q3.4   Explain what assets, liabilities and shareholders' equity are, and give some examples of the items included in each of these categories.

Q3.5   Illustrate the difference between current liabilities and non-current liabilities by giving some examples of each.

Q3.6   (i)   What accounting convention is generally used in the valuation of non-current assets?
      (ii)   What additional costs may sometimes be included within non-current assets costs and to which assets may these be applied?

Q3.7   Why are current assets and non-current assets shown under different balance sheet classifications?

Q3.8   Describe what is meant by intangible assets and give some examples of how they may be valued.

Q3.9   What factors influence the accurate valuation of a company's trade receivables?

Q3.10   Why should a potential investor exercise caution when analysing the balance sheets of potential companies in which to invest?

Discussion points

D3.1   'Surely the purchase of non-current assets is expenditure just like spending on stationery or photocopy expenses so why should it appear as an entry in the balance sheet?' Discuss.

D3.2   'It has often been said that the value of every item in a balance sheet is a matter of opinion and the cash and bank balances are the only numbers that can truly be relied upon.' Discuss.

Exercises

Solutions are provided in Appendix 3 to all exercise numbers highlighted in colour.

Level I

E3.1   *Time allowed – 30 minutes*

Mr IM Green – Manager Ian admired the sign on the door to his new office, following his appointment as manager of the human resources department. The previous manager left fairly suddenly to join another company but had left Ian with some papers about the costs of his department, which showed a total of £460,000 together with a list of items of expenditure. This seemed rather a high figure to Ian for a department of five people. Ian's boss muttered something to him about capital expenditure and revenue expenditure, but this was an area about which Ian had never been very clear. The list left with Ian by his predecessor was as follows:

	£
Legal fees	42,000
Five personal computers	15,000
Specialist HR software	100,000

	£
Three laser printers	10,000
Salaries	158,000
Employee benefit costs	16,000
Pension costs	14,000
Building repairs	25,000
Equipment repairs	8,000
Health and safety costs	20,000
Staff recruitment fees	10,000
Training costs	20,000
Subsistence and entertaining	10,000
Office furniture	12,000
	460,000

Assume that you are the finance manager whom Ian has asked for advice and provide him with a list that separates the items into capital expenditure and revenue expenditure.

E3.2   *Time allowed – 30 minutes*

The balances in the accounts of Vertico Ltd at 31 July 2010 are as follows:

	£000
Accrued expenses	95
Bank overdraft	20
Accounts receivable	275
Plant and equipment	309
Inventories of finished products	152
Computer system	104
Petty cash	5
Equity share capital	675
Accounts payable	293
Final payment on computer system due 1 September 2011	52
Loan for a factory building	239
Buildings	560
Raw materials	195

(i)   An important number has been omitted. What is that?
(ii) Using the data provided and the missing data prepare a balance sheet for Vertico Ltd as at 31 July 2010.

E3.3   *Time allowed – 45 minutes*

You are required to prepare a balance sheet for Trainer plc as at 31 December 2010 using the trial balance at 31 December 2010 and the additional information shown on the next page.

	Debit £000	Credit £000
Bank balance	73	
Ordinary share capital		320
Land and buildings at cost	320	
Plant and machinery at cost	200	
Cumulative depreciation provision (charge for year 2010 was £20,000)		80
Inventories	100	
Revenue		1,000
Cost of sales	600	
Operating expenses	120	
Depreciation	20	
Bad debts written off	2	
Accounts receivable	100	
Accruals		5
Accounts payable		130
	1,535	1,535

Additional information: the company will be paying £20,000 for corporation tax on the 2010 profit during 2011.

E3.4   *Time allowed – 45 minutes*

The following information relates to Major plc at 31 December 2010 and the comparative numbers at 31 December 2009.

	2009 £000	2010 £000
Accruals	800	1,000
Bank overdraft		16,200
Cash at bank	600	
Plant and machinery at cost	17,600	23,900
Debenture loan (interest at 15% per annum)	600	750
Plant and machinery depreciation	9,500	10,750
Proposed dividends	3,000	6,000
Ordinary share capital	5,000	5,000
Preference share capital	1,000	1,000
Prepayments	300	400
Retained earnings	3,000	10,100
Inventories	5,000	15,000
Tax payable	3,200	5,200
Accounts payable	6,000	10,000
Accounts receivable	8,600	26,700

Prepare a balance sheet in the format adopted by most of the leading UK plcs showing the previous year comparative figures.

E3.5   *Time allowed – 60 minutes*

From the trial balance of Gremlins plc at 31 March 2010 identify the assets and expenses (debit balances) and income, liabilities and equity (credit balances). Confirm that the trial balance is in balance, then prepare a balance sheet for Gremlins Ltd as at 31 March 2010.

	£000
Depreciation on office equipment and furnishings (administrative expenses)	156
Bank overdraft	609
Accountancy and audit fees	30
Electricity paid in advance	45
Computer system (net book value)	441
Advertising and promotion	135
Share premium account	240
Interest received	15
Plant and equipment (net book value)	927
Amount for final payment on factory machine due March 2012	252
Accounts receivable	1,110
Goodwill	204
Twelve-year lease on factory	330
Rents received	63
Prepaid expenses	885
Interest paid	120
Office electricity	66
Retained earnings at 1 April 2009	513
Inventories of materials at 31 March 2010	585
Telephone	87
Distribution costs	162
Other office utilities	72
Cost of goods sold	1,659
Administrative salaries	216
Sales department salaries	267
Furniture and fixtures (net book value)	729
Revenue	3,267
Office rent	165
Finished products at 31 March 2010	84
Debenture loan	750
Accounts payable	1,257
Bank and cash	51
Share capital	1,560

Level II

E3.6   *Time allowed – 60 minutes*

Prepare a balance sheet as at 31 December 2010 for Gorban Ltd based on the following trial balance, and the further information shown below.

	£	£
Equity share capital		200,000
Retained earnings		108,968
Building at cost	130,000	
Machinery at cost	105,000	
Provision for depreciation as at 31 December 2010		30,165
Provision for doubtful debts at 31 December 2010		1,725
Accounts payable		35,112
Accounts receivable	42,500	
Bank balance	67,050	
Loan		20,000
Inventories as at 31 December 2010	51,420	
	395,970	395,970

You are given the following additional information, which is not reflected in the above trial balance.

(a) The authorised and issued share capital is divided into 200,000 shares at £1 each.
(b) Wages unpaid at 31 December 2010 amounted to £1,173.
(c) Inventories at 31 December 2010 were found to have been undervalued by £48,000.
(d) The provision for doubtful debts is to be increased by £1,870.
(e) Additional machinery was purchased on 31 December 2010 for cash at a cost of £29,368.
(f) The company issued 50,000 £1 ordinary shares at par on 31 December 2010.
(g) A customer owing £10,342 went into liquidation on 9 January 2011 – a bad debt which had not previously been provided for.
(h) The loan was repaid on 31 December 2010.

E3.7   *Time allowed – 60 minutes*

> **You are required to prepare a balance sheet as at 31 December 2010 from the following summary of Pip Ltd's financial position at 31 December 2010.**

Brands worth £10,000 (directors' opinion)
Reputation in the local area £10,000 (directors' opinion)
Inventories at cost £50,000 and resale value £85,000, with obsolete inventories £5,000 within the £50,000
Bank overdraft facility £20,000 agreed by the bank manager
Cash in the office £1,000
Cash in the bank number one current account £10,000
Overdraft on the bank number two current account £10,000, per the bank statement
Land and buildings at cost £100,000
Plant and equipment at cost £150,000
Plant and equipment cumulative depreciation £50,000
Plant and equipment market value £110,000
Accounts payable £81,000
Invoices outstanding by all customers £50,000, including an invoice of £5,000 owed by a customer in liquidation (Pip Ltd has been advised by the receiver that 1p in the £1 will be paid to creditors)
Past profits reinvested in the business £110,000
Ordinary shares issued £100,000 (authorised ordinary shares £200,000)

4

Income statement

Contents

Learning objectives

Completion of this chapter will enable you to:

- describe what is meant by profit (or loss)
- outline the structure of the income statement of a limited company
- classify the categories of income and expenditure that make up the income statement
- appreciate the alternative income statement formats
- prepare an income statement
- explain the links between the income statement and the balance sheet, particularly with regard to the valuation of non-current assets and depreciation, inventory and cost of sales, and accounts receivable and the doubtful debt provision
- explain the links between the income statement and cash flow
- appreciate the subjective aspects of profit measurement.

Introduction

In Chapter 3 we looked at how to prepare simple financial statements from transactions carried out by a business during an accounting period. We then looked in a little more detail at the first of these financial statements, namely the balance sheet. This chapter will be concerned with the second of the financial statements, the income statement (or profit and loss account). Although income statements are prepared by all forms of business entity, this chapter, in a similar way to Chapter 3, deals primarily with the income statements of limited companies, both private and public.

This chapter deals with how income statements are structured and how the accounts within the income statement are categorised. Each of the items within each of the income statement categories will be described in detail and form the basis to enable the preparation of an income statement of a limited company in the appropriate format.

We will look at the relationship between the income statement and the balance sheet and provide an introduction to the relationship between profit (or loss) and cash flow. Like the balance sheet, the income statement is subjective largely because of the impact on costs of the variety of approaches that may be taken to the valuation of assets and liabilities.

What does the income statement tell us?

The income statement of a private limited company or a public limited company should be able to tell us all about the results of the company's activities over specified accounting periods. The income statement shows us what revenues have been generated and what costs incurred in generating those revenues, and therefore the increase or decrease in wealth of the business during the period.

The same note of caution we mentioned in Chapter 3 that should be exercised in the analysis of balance sheet information, applies to income statement information. The income statement is a historical statement and so it does not tell us anything about the ability of the business to sustain or improve upon its performance over subsequent periods.

There is not always consistency between the information included in one company's income statement and that of another company. As with the balance sheet, the income statements of two companies even within the same industry may be very difficult to compare. This will be illustrated by the wide variety of methods of depreciation calculations and inventory valuation methods examined in this chapter. In addition, the bases of financial ratios (to be examined in detail in Chapter 7) used by analysts in looking at a company's income statement may often be different.

It is often said of income statements, as well as of balance sheets, that the value of every item included in them is a matter of opinion. This is due not only to the alternative inventory valuation and depreciation methods, but also because of the subjective assessment of whether the settlement of a customer account is doubtful or not, and the sometimes imprecise evaluation of accruals and provisions.

What is profit?

We saw from the worked examples in Chapter 2 that profit (or loss) may be considered from two perspectives. We may consider these perspectives to illustrate the links between the income statement and the balance sheet.

The first perspective, which is not suggested as a method for calculating profit in practice, compares the balance sheet of an entity at the start of an accounting period with the balance sheet at the end of the accounting period. We may see from these that the values of each of the components of the balance sheet may have changed. For example, levels of inventory, accounts receivable, accounts payable, cash, non-current assets and accruals may have changed during an accounting period. We have seen that the net value of the assets and liabilities in the balance sheet represents the capital, or equity, or the wealth of the business at a point in time. The change in wealth over an accounting period between the beginning and end of the accounting period is the profit or loss for the period reflected in the retained earnings category in the balance sheet.

Profit (or loss) considered in this way can be represented in the equation:

$$\text{total assets (TA)} - \text{total liabilities (TL)} = \text{equity (E)} + \text{retained profit (RP)}$$

Worked example 4.1

Using the balance sheet as at 1 March 2010 below and the further transactions (a) and (b), we are able to:

(i) show how the balance sheet will appear at the end of March after these transactions and events have taken place

(ii) identify the profit which the shareholders should consider is potentially distributable as a dividend.

Balance sheet as at 1 March 2010	£
Non-current assets	100,000
Current assets	100,000
less	
Current liabilities	(100,000)
Net assets	100,000
Equity	100,000

During March

(a) the non-current assets were re-valued from £100,000 to £120,000

(b) all the inventories of £20,000 were sold for £40,000 cash (that is, not on credit).

(i)

Balance sheet as at 31 March 2010

	£
Non-current assets [100,000 + 20,000]	120,000
Current assets [100,000 − 20,000 + 40,000]	120,000
less	
Current liabilities [no change]	(100,000)
	140,000
Equity [100,000 + 20,000 + 20,000]	140,000

(ii)

The revised balance sheet reflects two profits:

- The revaluation surplus of £20,000 is a paper profit; as no cash has been involved it is not prudent to pay a dividend from this profit (and legally it is not permitted).
- The other £20,000 profit is from trading and is a cash profit; it is quite prudent to pay a dividend from this profit.

The balance sheets show each of the categories of assets, liabilities and equity, but it can be seen there must be an analysis of the movements between the balance sheets to appreciate their fundamental nature.

The second perspective, as we discussed in Chapter 3, considers profit by summarising all the trading and non-trading transactions that have occurred during an accounting period (see Fig. 4.1). This is the method used in practice to calculate the profit or loss for an accounting period. This gives the same result as that derived by simply looking at the change in wealth between the beginning and end of the accounting period. It is the same because all the transactions relating to items contained in the profit and loss account are also all reflected in some way within one or more balance sheet categories. For example, sales revenues are reflected in trade receivables, expenses are reflected in trade payables, cost of goods that have been sold are reflected as a reduction of inventories.

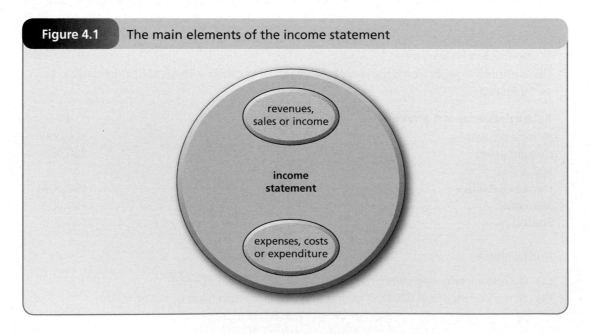

Figure 4.1   The main elements of the income statement

Profit (or loss) considered in this way can be represented in the equation:

$$\textbf{profit (P)} \; = \; \textbf{total revenue (TR)} \; - \; \textbf{total costs (TC)}$$

and it should be noted that

$$\textbf{retained profit (RP)} \; = \; \textbf{profit (P)} \; - \; \textbf{dividends}$$

Worked example 4.2

A trading company, Squirrel Ltd, has an accounting period that covers the 12 months to 31 December 2010. During that period the company entered into the following transactions:

Sales revenue of £1,300,000 included a sales invoice for January 2011 amounting to £100,000. Expenses of £1,000,000 included a payment of £60,000 for rent relating to the six months to 31 March 2011.

The expenses excluded some heating costs relating to the last two weeks of December 2010, for which the estimated cost was around £5,000. The quarterly invoice covering that period was not expected until late March 2011.

The above information may be used to look at why the annual net profit should be revenues less expenses, and why there should be accounting concepts applied to the treatment of those expenses.

The income statement for a year tries to match revenues and expenses for that year (complying with the matching concept – see Chapter 1). Profit means the difference between revenues and expenses. Gross profit or gross margin is derived from sales revenue less the costs of those sales, and profit is derived from deducting expenses from gross profit. Profit is not the difference between cash receipts and cash payments. Cash inflows and outflows suffer from timing differences.

The reported sales revenue for the year must relate only to the 12 months to 31 December. Sales revenue for Squirrel Ltd for the year 2010 is £1,200,000 (£1,300,000 less £100,000). Using the matching concept, the expenses must also be for 12 months. So the estimated heating costs of £5,000 for the last two weeks of December 2010 must be added, and the rent relating to January to March 2011 of £30,000 (£60,000/2) must be deducted from the total expenses of £1,000,000. Without these adjustments, the expenses would not represent 12 months' expenses.

Profit for the 12 months to 31 December 2010 for Squirrel Ltd is therefore:

Revenue	£1,200,000	[£1,300,000 less £100,000]
less		
Expenses	£975,000	[£1,000,000 plus £5,000 less £60,000 plus £30,000]
Which equals	£225,000	

There must be an application of accounting concepts and standard practices in arriving at profit, otherwise users of financial information would not have reasonable confidence in the amounts being shown in the financial statements reported by companies, large or small.

In this chapter we will look at the income statement from the second perspective. We will look at how an income statement is constructed and prepared by deducting total costs from total revenues, as the second of the three key financial statements that are required to be prepared by a limited company.

Progress check 4.1

Explain the perspectives from which we may consider the profit (or loss) of a business.

Income statement formats

The format of the income statement is explained in IAS 1 Presentation of Financial Statements. IAS 1 outlines the minimum information that should be disclosed on the face of the income statement, which gives a little flexibility to the ways in which individual companies report, rather than setting out a rigid format that must be adopted by every company.

IAS 1 does include the minimum information that should be disclosed on the face of the income statement, which includes:

- revenue
- finance costs
- profits or losses arising from discontinued operations
- income tax expense
- profit or loss for the year.

IAS 1 recommends two alternative ways of presenting costs and expenses on the face of the income statement:

- according to business functions, for example distribution costs and administrative expenses
- according to their nature, for example employee expenses, depreciation etc.

The income statement in the example adopted by Flatco plc (see Fig. 4.4) has been based on the format that presents expenses and costs according to business functions, and this format will be adopted generally throughout this book. Directors of companies will adopt this format if they believe that presenting how much of the revenue of the company was 'used' by particular functions of the business may provide more relevant and accurate information and a better impression of the efficiency of the business.

It is not always a straightforward matter to allocate costs within a company to specific functions. The costs of shared resources are often allocated between functions on a fairly arbitrary basis. The alternative presentation of the income statement which presents costs and expenses according to their nature, for example employee expenses, depreciation etc., may be adopted by companies. Certainly for management reporting within the company this analysis is far more useful in support of forecasting and planning.

Unlike FRS 3, Reporting Financial Performance, and UK GAAP, IAS 1 does not use the term 'exceptional items'. Exceptional items relate to material (significant), non-recurring items of income and expense of abnormal size and incidence arising from infrequent circumstances but which are derived from the ordinary activities of the business. FRS 3 required exceptional items to be included under the statutory format headings to which they relate and disclosed separately on the face of the income statement if necessary to give a true and fair view.

Although it does not refer to them as exceptional items, IAS 1 makes it clear that such material items of income and expense must be separately disclosed if they are relevant to an understanding of the financial performance of the business. These need not be shown on the face of the income statement so long as they appear within the notes on the financial statements. The material, non-recurring income and expense items that require separate disclosure include:

- write-downs of inventories to net realisable value, and reversals of such write-downs
- write-downs of property, plant and equipment to net realisable value, and reversals of such write-downs

- restructuring of the activities of the company
- reversals of provisions
- disposals of property, plant and equipment
- disposals of investments
- discontinued operations
- litigation settlements.

Another separate term, 'extraordinary items' as distinct from exceptional items, is defined as material income or costs which are derived or incurred from unusual events or transactions outside the ordinary activities of the company which like exceptional items are infrequent and therefore not expected to occur frequently or regularly. The costs resulting from the complete destruction of a factory may be sufficiently material and infrequent and possess such a high degree of abnormality as to warrant its disclosure as an extraordinary item.

Up until 2004, IAS 1 required extraordinary items to be disclosed in a separate line on the income statement. A company's ordinary activities have now been defined so broadly that the disclosure of extraordinary items is now prohibited by IAS 1. US GAAP still requires extraordinary items to be disclosed in the income statement if they are unusual and infrequent.

Earnings per share (eps) are dealt with in IAS 33, Earnings per Share, which requires basic earnings per share and diluted earnings per share to be presented on the face of the income statement with equal prominence. Both should be presented relating to:

- the profit or loss from continuing operations attributable to ordinary equity shareholders of the parent company

and

- for total profit or loss attributable to such shareholders.

Earnings per share from discontinued operations should be shown either on the face of the income statement or in the notes on the accounts.

Basic earnings per share are calculated by dividing earnings, or profit of the year, by the weighted average number of ordinary shares in issue over the year. Diluted earnings per share are calculated by adjusting for a reduction in the earnings per share for the year caused by an increase or potential increase in the number of shares in issue, for example through the conversion of convertible securities into ordinary shares.

Earnings per share should also be presented for each class of ordinary shares that has a different right to participate in the profit of the company.

Group financial statements must to be prepared for the holding company in addition to the financial statements which are required to be prepared for each of the individual companies within the group. Consolidated financial statements exclude all transactions between companies within the group, for example inter-company sales and purchases. In most other respects the group consolidated financial statements reflect an amalgamation of each of the components of the income statements, balance sheets and statements of cash flows of all the companies within the group.

Progress check 4.2

There are broadly two income statement formats that are outlined in IAS 1. How do these formats differ? Which format appears to be favoured by the majority of large companies?

Structure of the income statement

As we have seen previously, the income statement measures whether or not the company has made a profit or loss on its operations during the period, through producing or buying and selling its goods or services. It measures whether total revenues are higher than the total costs (profit), or whether total costs are higher than total revenues (loss).

The total revenue of a business is generated from the provision of goods or services and may include, for example:

- sales of goods or services
- interest received (on loans)
- rents (from property)
- subscriptions (for example to TV channels)
- fees (for example professional subscriptions)
- royalties (payable on books and CDs)
- dividends received (from investments).

The total costs of a business include the expenditure incurred as a result of the generation of revenue. The total costs of a business include, for example:

- costs of goods purchased for resale
- costs of manufacturing goods for sale
- transport and distribution costs
- advertising
- promotion
- insurance
- costs of the 'consumption' of non-current assets over their useful lives (depreciation)
- wages and salaries
- interest paid
- stationery costs
- photocopy costs
- communications costs
- electricity
- water and effluent costs
- travel expenses
- entertaining expenses
- postage.

Each of the above examples of costs (which is by no means an exhaustive list) incurred in the generation of revenue by a business appears itself as a separate heading, or is grouped within one or other of the other main headings within the income statement. Figure 4.2 shows each of the levels of profit that are derived after allowing for the various categories of revenues and expenses.

We will look at how a basic income statement is constructed to arrive at the profit for the year after taxation (or net profit) for the company. Profit is also sometimes called earnings, or net income, from which may be deducted dividends payable to ordinary shareholders. The net result is then the retained earnings (or retained profit) for the financial year.

Each of the levels of profit shown in Figure 4.2 can be examined to show the categories of revenue and costs included in the income statement. These are illustrated in Figure 4.3, which is completely consistent with the headings shown in Figure 4.2.

Figure 4.2	Levels of profit within the income statement

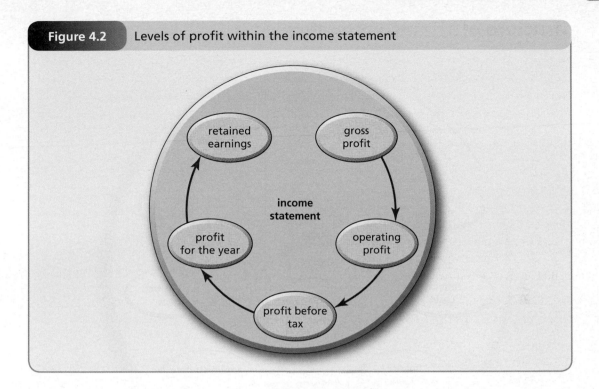

We will look at each of the headings included within the income statement as shown in Figures 4.2 and 4.3 in a little more detail.

Revenue

The main source of income for a company is its **revenue**, primarily comprising sales of its products and services to third-party customers. Revenues and costs are not necessarily accounted for when cash receipts and payments are made. Sales revenues are normally accounted for when goods or services are delivered and invoiced, and accepted by the customer, even if payment is not received until some time later, even in a subsequent trading period.

Cost of sales (COS)

It should be noted that a cost or expense is the financial result of the 'consumption' that occurred during the accounting period that relates directly or indirectly to the production or sales of the goods or services, and is accounted for as it is incurred rather than on a cash payment basis. Costs may be cash-related, invoiced costs such as raw materials, or non-cash items like depreciation charges.

The sum of direct costs of goods sold plus any manufacturing expenses relating to the sales revenue is termed cost of sales, or production cost of sales, or cost of goods sold. These costs include:

■ costs of raw material inventories used
■ costs of inward-bound freight paid by the company
■ packaging costs
■ direct production salaries and wages
■ production expenses, including depreciation of trading-related non-current assets.

Figure 4.3   Elements of the income statement

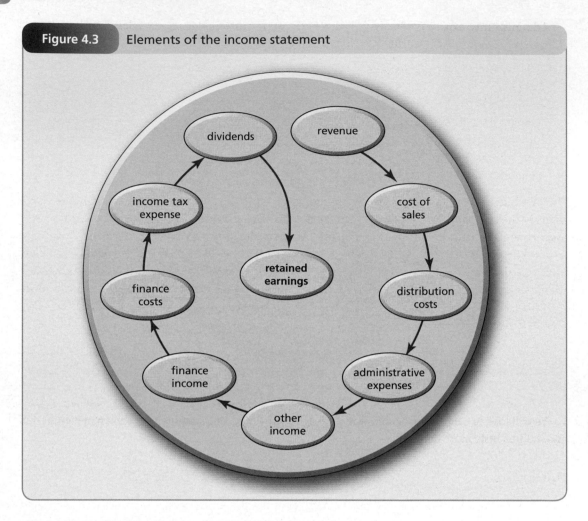

Gross profit (or gross margin)

The difference between revenue and cost of sales (COS) is **gross profit** or gross margin. It needs to be positive and large enough to at least cover all other expenses.

Distribution costs and administrative expenses

Although not directly related to the production process, but contributing to the activity of the company, are further costs that are termed 'other operating expenses'. These include distribution costs and selling costs, administrative expenses, and research and development costs (unless they relate to specific projects and the costs may be deferred to future periods).

Distribution costs include the costs of selling and delivering goods and services. Such costs may include:

- advertising
- market research
- promotion
- costs of the sales department
- outbound freight costs
- delivery vehicles fleet costs
- costs of the warehouse and goods outward department.

Administrative expenses effectively include all costs not included in cost of sales, distribution costs and financial costs. They may include, for example:

- costs of service departments such as
  - finance
  - human resources
  - research and development
  - engineering
- telephone costs
- computer costs.

Distribution costs and administrative expenses include all expenses related to the 'normal' operations of the company, except those directly related to manufacturing like the costs of the purchasing department, logistics department and quality department. They also exclude the share of overhead costs, for example heating and lighting, business property taxes, water and effluent costs, relating to manufacturing activities. Administrative expenses exclude financial expenses and revenues, because these are really a function of the financial structure of the company (the extent of its funding by owners' share capital and by lenders' debt, or loans), and exclude any other non-operational expenses and revenues.

Other income

Other income includes all other revenues that have not been included in other parts of the income statement. It does not include sales of goods or services, reported within sales revenue, or any sort of interest receivable.

Operating profit (OP)

operating profit (OP)
= revenue − COS − distribution costs − administrative expenses + other income

The operating profit is the net of all operating revenues and costs, regardless of the financial structure of the company and whatever exceptional events occurred during the period that resulted in exceptional costs. The disclosure of operating profit is not listed as a requirement in IAS 1 but it is one of the specific recommendations within the UK standard FRS 3, Reporting Financial Performance.

Operating profit is a measure of the profitability of the operations of a company regardless of the amount of interest payable and receivable on overdrafts and loans, and regardless of the amount of corporation tax it may have to pay. It is therefore an extremely important profit or loss subtotal because it allows inter-company comparisons of companies operating in the same markets but having different financial policies.

Finance income

Finance income includes interest receivable, and dividends receivable from subsidiary companies and from **non-related companies**.

Finance costs

Finance costs include interest paid and interest payable, and other financial costs like bank charges and costs of transferring funds. The overall level of finance costs will be dependent on the type of company and level of interest rates and debt and equity mix within the funding of the company.

Profit before tax (PBT)

profit before tax (PBT) = OP + finance income − finance costs

Income tax expense

Corporation tax is payable on profits of limited companies. The companies, as entities, are responsible for the tax, rather than individuals as with sole traders and partnerships. Tax is shown in the income statements, balance sheets and statements of cash flows of limited companies.

The corporation tax shown on the face of the income statement will have been based on a computation carried out prior to the exact amount payable having been agreed with HMRC. There may therefore be some differences from year to year between the tax payable numbers reported and tax actually paid.

Figure 4.4 shows an example of the income statement format adopted by a public limited company, Flatco plc.

Profit for the year

profit for the year = PBT − income tax expense

Figure 4.4   Income statement format in compliance with IAS 1

Flatco plc
Income statement for the year ended 31 December 2010

	£000
Revenue	3,500
Cost of sales	(2,500)
Gross profit	1,000
Distribution costs	(300)
Administrative expenses	(250)
Other income	100
Operating profit	550
Finance income	111
Finance costs	(71)
Profit before tax	590
Income tax expense	(50)
Profit for the year from continuing operations	540
Profit for the year from discontinued operations	–
Profit for the year	540

Profit for the year is the net profit, or net income, or earnings, on ordinary activities after tax. The final charge that a company has to suffer, provided it has made sufficient profits, is therefore corporate taxation.

The profit for the year has resulted from the following processes. The assets, owned by the shareholders, have generated the operating profit. Operating profit has been used to pay interest to bankers and other lenders, and corporation tax to HMRC. What is left, the profit for the year, 'belongs' to the equity ordinary shareholders.

The directors of the company then recommend and propose to the shareholders how the profit for the year may be appropriated. It may be paid out to shareholders in dividends, or it may be held in equity as retained earnings for reinvestment in the operations of the company, or it may be appropriated in any combination of both dividends and retained earnings. The shareholders vote on whether to accept or reject the directors' proposal. The profit for the year is therefore used to provide the shareholders' returns in terms of the dividends they receive from their total investment in the equity of the company; so, not only does the profit of the year have to be positive, but it has to be high enough to reward the risk the shareholders took in investing in the company. In some circumstances a dividend may be paid out of retained earnings, even though the company may have made a loss during the period. This is obviously only acceptable in the short term and cannot be continued for successive accounting periods.

Progress check 4.3

What exactly do we mean by cost of sales? What types of expense does cost of sales include and what types of expense does it exclude?

Dividends on ordinary shares

Dividends for the year paid on equity shares are disclosed in the financial statement, Statement of Changes in Equity as a deduction from retained earnings. IAS 1, Presentation of Financial Statements, implies that dividends are usually deducted from the profit for the financial year in arriving at the profit retained for the year. Dividends include any interim payment that may have been made and any final dividend proposed by the directors to be paid to shareholders later in the year.

Dividends on preference shares

Some companies issue preference shares as well as equity shares. These pay a dividend at a set percentage on face value and payments are made to preference shareholders before the payment of equity dividends. IAS 32, Financial Instruments, requires that dividends paid on preference shares with a set maturity date be treated as a finance cost and charged directly to the income statement, whereas dividends paid on preference shares which do not have a maturity date are treated just like dividends paid on ordinary shares and deducted from retained earnings in the Statement of Changes in Equity.

Retained earnings

The **retained earnings** (or retained profit) for the year is what is left from profit for the year after deducting dividends for the year. The remainder is added to cumulative retained earnings and forms part of the total equity (or shareholders' funds) of the company. It is a requirement included in IAS 1, Presentation of Financial Statements, that the company's annual report and accounts includes a statement that discloses the reconciliation of the movement on shareholders' funds that has taken place between the beginning and the end of the financial year, called the Statement of Changes in Equity (see Fig. 4.5). This financial statement is a combination of the two previously required statements in the UK called the statement of recognised gains and losses, and the reconciliation of movements in shareholders' funds.

Progress check 4.4

The profit or loss that a business has earned or incurred during an accounting period may be ascertained by deducting the total costs from the total revenues for the period. Identify in which category of the income statement the following items may appear.

- interest received
- share premiums
- interest paid
- depreciation of factory machinery for the year
- CD royalties received
- outward freight costs
- sales of redundant inventories
- travel and subsistence

- accountancy fees
- electricity standing charge
- rents received
- telephone charges
- advertising and promotion
- raw materials purchases
- inventory of work in progress
- sales of finished product

Figure 4.5   Statement of changes in equity

Flatco plc
Statement of changes in equity
for the year ended 31 December 2010

	Share capital £000	Share premium £000	Revaluation reserve £000	Translation reserve £000	Retained earnings £000	Total £000
Balance at 1 January 2010	1,000	200	–	–	1,124	2,324
Changes in equity for 2010						
Gain on revaluation of property	–	–	–	–	–	–
Exchange differences on translation of foreign operations	–	–	–	–	–	–
Net income recognised directly to equity	–	–	–	–	–	–
Profit for the period	–	–	–	–	540	540
Total recognised income and expense for the period	–	–	–	–	540	540
Dividends	–	–	–	–	(70)	(70)
Issue of share capital	200	–	–	–	–	200
Balance at 31 December 2010	1,200	200	–	–	1,594	2,994

Worked example 4.3

The relevant profit and loss account balances, representing the costs and revenues for the year to date as extracted from the trial balance of Perfecto Ltd at 30 September 2010, are presented below in an alphabetical list:

	£000
Advertising and promotion	54
Corporation tax	70
Costs of administrative departments	146
Costs of production departments	277
Costs of purchasing and logistics departments	77
Depreciation of factory machinery	284
Depreciation of office equipment	35
Direct labour cost of sales	203
Freight out costs	230
Interest paid	20
Interest received	10
Materials cost of sales	611
Rent and utilities (2/3 factory, 1/3 office)	48
Sales revenue	2,279
Warehousing and goods outward costs	84

We will prepare an income statement for Perfecto Ltd for the year to 30 September 2010, using the format that presents expenses and costs according to business functions which complies as far as possible with the requirements of IAS 1.

Perfecto Ltd
Income statement for the year ended 30 September 2010

	£000
Revenue	2,279
Cost of sales [277 + 77 + 284 + 203 + 611 + 32 (2/3 of 48)]	(1,484)
Gross profit	795
Distribution costs [54 + 230 + 84]	(368)
Administrative expenses [146 + 35 + 16 (1/3 of 48)]	(197)
Operating profit	230
Finance income	10
Finance costs	(20)
Profit before tax	220
Income tax expense	(70)
Profit for the year	150

Profit and loss and the balance sheet

The balance sheet and the income statement, whilst they are both historical statements, are not alternatives or competing options. They show different financial information, as we have discussed. The balance sheet shows the financial position at the start and at the end of an accounting period, and the income statement shows what has happened during the period, the financial performance.

The income statement and the balance sheet are linked in two ways:

■ the cumulative balance on the profit and loss account of the company is reflected within the equity, or the shareholders' funds, category of the balance sheet representing the increase in the book wealth of the business
■ some of the items contained in the profit and loss account are also all reflected in some way within one or more balance sheet categories.

In Chapter 3 we saw how the balance on the profit and loss account was reflected in retained earnings, within the equity of the company. We will now look at some of the types of adjusting entries used to prepare the income statement, which are also reflected in the balance sheet. Two of these types of adjusting entries, accruals and prepayments, were described in Chapter 2.

In this chapter we will look at some further categories of adjusting entries:

■ depreciation, the depreciation provision and non-current assets
■ the cost of sales and the valuation of inventories
■ bad and doubtful debts and accounts receivable.

Worked example 4.4

Ronly Bonly Jones Ltd, or RBJ, buys and sells giftware. It made a profit of £10,000 during the month of January 2010.

We will use the balance sheet as at 1 January 2010 as the starting point and then look at how each of the elements in the income statement for January is reflected in the balance sheet to derive the balance sheet as at 31 January 2010.

The income statement for January 2010 and the balance sheet as at 1 January 2010 are as follows:

Income statement for January 2010	£000	£000
Revenue		650
Cost of goods sold		
Opening inventories	45	
Purchases	424	
	469	
less: Closing inventories	79	(390)
Gross profit		260
Depreciation		(5)
Expenses		(245)
Profit for January [650 − 390 − 5 − 245]		10

Additional information

RBJ acquired non-current assets in January for £20,000 cash, and raised additional share capital of £10,000.

Suppliers (trade payables) were paid £422,000 in the month and £632,000 was received from customers (trade receivables). The bank account at the end of January 2010 was overdrawn by £39,000.

Balance sheet as at 1 January 2010

	£000
Non-current assets at cost	130
Depreciation provision	(20)
Inventories	45
Trade receivables	64
Cash and bank	6
	225
Trade payables	(87)
Share capital	(50)
Retained earnings	(88)
	(225)

Let's derive the 31 January 2010 balance sheet from the information that has been provided.

Figures in £000	Non-curr. assets	Depn.	Inventories	Trade rec'bles	Cash	Trade payables	Equity share capital	Retained earnings
1 January 2010	130	(20)	45	64	6	(87)	(50)	(88)
Sales revenue				650				(650)
Cash from customers				(632)	632			0
Purchases			424			(424)		0
Cash to suppliers					(422)	422		0
Inventory sold			(390)					390
Depreciation		(5)						5
Expenses					(245)			245
Non-current asset additions	20				(20)			0
Issue of shares					10		(10)	0
31 January 2010	150	(25)	79	82	(39)	(89)	(60)	(98)

Ronly Bonly Jones Ltd
Balance sheet at 1 January 2010 and at 31 January 2010 is as follows:

	1 January 2010 £000	31 January 2010 £000
Non-current assets at cost	130	150
Depreciation provision	(20)	(25)
Inventories	45	79
Trade receivables	64	82
Cash and bank	6	–
	225	286
Trade payables	(87)	(89)
Bank overdraft	–	(39)
Share capital	(50)	(60)
Retained earnings	(88)	(98)
	(225)	(286)

Worked example 4.4 shows the changes in the balance sheet that have taken place over the month of January. The 31 January 2010 balance sheet has been derived from considering each element in the income statement for January and the additional information we were given and their impact on the balance sheet, and movements between accounts within the balance sheet:

- sales to customers on credit are the starting point for the income statement, which also increase trade receivables
- cash received from customers increases cash and reduces trade receivables
- purchases of goods on credit for resale increase inventories and increase trade payables
- cash paid to suppliers reduces cash and reduces trade payables
- inventory sold reduces inventories and is a cost in the income statement
- depreciation of non-current assets increases the depreciation provision and is a cost in the income statement
- payments of expenses reduce cash and are a cost in the income statement
- payments for additions to non-current assets increase non-current assets and reduce cash
- issues of ordinary shares increase equity share capital and increase cash.

In Worked example 4.4, depreciation is a relatively small number. Normally, income statement movements may have significant impacts on the balance sheet in the areas of both inventories and depreciation. Real-life cases that illustrate this are:

- during the years 2009 and 2010 several major retailers had to announce that their profits would be lower due to their inventories having to be heavily discounted (for example, JJB Sports plc)
- depreciation of an automotive assembly line may need to be changed due to a revision in its estimated useful economic life following a reassessment of the life cycle of a vehicle.

Progress check 4.5

Describe the ways in which a company's income statement and its balance sheet are linked.

We have already discussed the links between the various categories in the income statement and those within the balance sheet. Consequently, the ways in which specific balance sheet items are valued have a significant impact on the profit reported for an entity for a particular period. The requirement for the valuation, or revaluation of, for example, assets like machinery, raw materials and finished product may be a result of their consumption or being used up; it may be because of their deterioration or obsolescence, or significant changes in their market value. For whatever reason, such changes in the valuation of assets must be reflected in the income statement in the period in which they occur. We will focus here on the valuation of the three key areas of:

- non-current assets, reflected in the income statement within *depreciation*
- inventories, reflected in the income statement within *cost of sales*
- trade receivables, reflected in the income statement within *bad and doubtful debts*.

Depreciation

Generally, the total cost of using a non-current asset over its life may be defined as the original investment less an estimate of the portion of its cost that may be recovered (its residual value) at the end of the asset's useful life. IAS 16 calls this the depreciable amount and defines depreciation as the systematic allocation of the depreciable amount of an asset over its useful life. In accordance with the accruals (matching) concept a fair proportion of the total cost (or valuation) of a non-current asset, its depreciation, should be charged to the profit and loss account during each period that sales revenue or other benefits are received from the use of that asset. At the same time as the depreciation charge is made to the profit and loss account, the value of the non-current asset is reduced by the same amount from a corresponding entry to credit the cumulative **depreciation provision** account. The cumulative balance at any point in time on the depreciation provision account for a non-current asset is deducted from its historical cost to provide its net value shown in the balance sheet at that time.

Worked example 4.5

Many companies operate and succeed in one market for many years. One of many business 'facts of life' is that recurring profits can come to an abrupt end, when a successful business model develops a basic flaw. Changes in technology can cause a change in trading or force a complete review of the equipment, systems or methods of trading that have been highly profitable in the past. In January 2008 William Hill plc (the sports betting company) brought in an outside technology company to install a system to allow customers to place bets on events that are in progress. William Hill had spent two years developing software in-house but it would have taken several more years to develop, while already available software could be installed within the year. The effect was that the company had to write off £26m already spent on the development against profits for the year. Had the company not cancelled its in-house development the £26m would have been recognised as an intangible non-current asset. The company blamed the pressure of the rapid growth in Internet betting which had caused their share of the market to decline over the previous 18 months.

There a number of reasons why this type of equipment review might affect the annual profits:

(i)   The income statement for a year aims to match revenues and expenses for that year, complying with the matching concept (see Chapter 1). Additionally, when it is clear that an asset is no longer capable of generating economic benefits it should be written out of the accounts immediately following the prudence principle (see Chapter 1).

(ii)   One of a company's expenses relates to the use of non-current assets, which aims to spread the economic use of the asset over its useful life, and is called depreciation.

(iii)   The choice of method of depreciating an asset will result in differing amounts of depreciation for the year and so the annual income statement can be quite different because of this subjective decision (which involves opinions that may vary from manager to manager, and company to company).

(iv)   The International Accounting Standards Board (IASB) introduced IAS 36, Impairment of Assets, which requires companies to formally review their non-current assets for any changes in circumstances (impairment is not recurring, whereas depreciation is recurring).

(v)   In the William Hill circumstances outlined above, the company would have had to acknowledge that the development it had already paid for would not bring the future benefits it had anticipated because of the sudden and unexpected change in customer preferences. The company would have to reduce its asset values to reflect the fact that its software development no longer had value because market circumstances had changed significantly and the costs had therefore to be written off against the current profits.

The useful life of an asset is the period of its service relevant to the business entity. With regard to the useful life of the asset, there are a number of problems in dealing with depreciation of non-current assets:

- determining the useful life of the asset
- determining the correct way to spread the total cost of the asset over the useful life
- physical limitations regarding the useful life
  – intensity of use of the asset
  – the actions of the elements
  – adequacy of maintenance
  – the simple passage of time (e.g. legal rights or patents)
- economic limitations in respect of useful life
  – technological developments
  – business growth.

Three of the many depreciation methods include:

- straight line
- reducing balance
- sum of the digits.

We will consider each of these in detail in Worked example 4.6. However, the straight line and the reducing balance methods are the ones that are most frequently used by companies.

Straight-line depreciation is calculated by deducting the residual value from the acquisition cost to obtain the net cost of the asset (the depreciable amount) and then dividing the result by the life of the asset.

The reducing balance method is used to derive the rate required (d) to reduce the cost of the asset, period by period, to the residual value by the end of its life. This may be expressed as:

$$d = 1 - \sqrt[\text{life}]{\text{residual value/original cost}}$$

The sum of the digits method considers the life of the asset, say for example five years, and allocates the net cost of the asset (acquisition cost less residual value) over that period as follows:

For a five-year life the sum of digits is $5 + 4 + 3 + 2 + 1 = 15$

So each year's depreciation is calculated:

1st year $5/15 \times$ (acquisition cost − residual value)
2nd year $4/15 \times$ (acquisition cost − residual value)
3rd year $3/15 \times$ (acquisition cost − residual value)
4th year $2/15 \times$ (acquisition cost − residual value)
5th year $1/15 \times$ (acquisition cost − residual value)

Worked example 4.6

Castle Ltd purchased an item of equipment for £16,000 and estimated its residual value, at the end of its useful economic life of five years, at £1,000. At the start of year one the net book value (NBV) is the acquisition cost of the asset £16,000.

Annual depreciation charges and net book values may be derived by using each of the three methods:

- straight line
- reducing balance
- sum of the digits.

Straight line depreciation divides the acquisition cost less the residual value by the number of years of economic life, in this case 5.

Reducing balance depreciation calculates:

$$d = 1 - \sqrt[5]{1,000/16,000} = 42.57\%$$

The sum of the digits is $(5 + 4 + 3 + 2 + 1) = 15$.

Figures in £000

	Straight line			Reducing balance			Sum of the digits		
Year	Start NBV	Depn	End NBV	Start NBV	Depn	End NBV	Start NBV	Depn	End NBV
1	16,000	3,000	13,000	16,000	6,810	9,190	16,000	5,000	11,000
2	13,000	3,000	10,000	9,190	3,912	5,278	11,000	4,000	7,000
3	10,000	3,000	7,000	5,278	2,247	3,031	7,000	3,000	4,000
4	7,000	3,000	4,000	3,031	1,290	1,741	4,000	2,000	2,000
5	4,000	3,000	1,000	1,741	741	1,000	2,000	1,000	1,000

The resultant cost of £1,000 in the balance sheet under the non-current assets category at the end of year five is the same using each of the methods. This cost is likely to be offset exactly by the proceeds of £1,000 expected to be received on disposal of the asset.

In addition to the methods already discussed, it should be noted that there are many alternative methods that may be used to account for depreciation. We will not look at the detailed calculations of any further methods, but you may consider Worked example 4.7, which serves only to illustrate the wide variations in yearly depreciation (and therefore net book values) that may be derived from a selection of alternative methods, compared with the straight line method.

Worked example 4.7

Consider a company van, which cost £20,000 to purchase new. Its residual value is estimated will be zero at the end of its useful life of five years. The rate of inflation is 10% and the cost of capital (see Chapter 14) is 15%.

The depreciation for the first year and the net book value (NBV) at the end of year one may be evaluated using six alternative methods, including straight-line depreciation.

	Depreciation calculation	Depreciation in year 1	NBV at end of year 1
1. Straight-line depreciation over five years, i.e. 20% per annum using a historical cost of £20,000	£20,000 × 20%	£4,000	£16,000
2. Constant purchasing power, which means allowing for an inflationary price increase (in this case 10%), and using straight-line depreciation at 20% per annum	£20,000 × 1.10 × 20%	£4,400	£17,600
3. Replacement value for an identical one-year-old van based on used van market value of say £17,000	£20,000 − £17,000	£3,000	£17,000
4. Replacement cost of a new van less one year's depreciation based on an estimated replacement cost of say £21,600	£21,600 × 20%	£4,320	£17,280
5. Net realisable value; the net proceeds from a trade auction of say £16,000	£20,000 − £16,000	£4,000	£16,000
6. Economic value; the estimated future cash flows from using the van: £6,000 per year for years 1, 2, 3, and 4, and the calculation of their present values using a cost of capital of 15% per annum (see the discounted cash flow technique in Chapter 15) $£6,000/1.15 + £6,000/1.15^2 + £6,000/1.15^3 + £6,000/1.15^4$ = £17,130	£20,000 − £17,130	£2,870	£17,130

We have already seen from Worked example 4.6 that there may be large variations in the amounts of depreciation charged to the profit and loss account, in each year, dependent on which method is adopted by a company. Worked example 4.7 further illustrates the wide variation in first-year depreciation, from £2,840 to £4,400 on an asset costing £20,000, using six alternative methods of calculation. The particular depreciation method used by a company, therefore, may result in widely differing levels of profit reported each year. This sometimes makes it difficult to compare the profit of a company from one year to the next on a like-for-like basis. Likewise, it may sometimes be difficult to accurately compare the yearly performance of two or more businesses, which may be similar in every respect other than the difference in the methods they have used to depreciate their non-current assets.

Whichever method of depreciation is used, it must be consistent from one accounting period to another. The depreciation method adopted must be disclosed within the company's accounting policies that accompany the financial statements in its annual report and accounts and include the depreciation rates applied to each of the categories of non-current asset.

Progress check 4.6

What are the various methods that may be used to depreciate an asset? Describe two of the most commonly used methods.

The amount of depreciation calculated for an accounting period is charged as a cost reflected in the income statement, the depreciation charge. A corresponding amount is also reflected in an account in the balance sheet, the cumulative depreciation provision account, the effect of which is to reduce the original, historical cost of the non-current assets at the end of each accounting period.

The difference between depreciation cost and other costs such as wages and salaries is that it is not a cash expense, that is it does not represent a cash outflow. The only cash outflow relating to depreciation took place when the asset was originally purchased. The depreciation is really only the 'memory' of that earlier cash outflow.

Progress check 4.7

Why are assets depreciated and what factors influence the decision as to how they may be depreciated?

Cost of sales

As we saw in Chapter 3, inventories of **raw materials**, **work in progress**, **finished product**, spare parts, consumable stores, etc., pose problems in their valuation for three main reasons:

■ raw materials may be purchased from a variety of geographical locations, and additional costs such as duty, freight and insurance may be incurred – the costs of inventories should comprise the expenditure that has been incurred in the normal course of business in bringing the product or service to its present location and condition

- packaging and other consumable items, in addition to raw materials, are used during the production processes to manufacture work in progress, partly-finished product and fully-finished product, and such costs must be correctly apportioned to give a true cost – inventories are disclosed as a main heading in the balance sheet and comprise raw materials and consumables, work in progress, finished goods, and long-term contracts
- homogeneous items within various inventory categories are purchased continuously and consumed continuously in the manufacturing processes and the purchase prices of these homogeneous items may vary considerably – inventories must be valued at the lower of purchase cost (or production cost) and their net realisable value (IAS 2).

There are many alternative methods that may be used to determine the cost of inventories. Four methods that are most commonly used by businesses are:

- **first in first out (FIFO)**
- **last in first out (LIFO)**
- weighted average cost
- market value.

The choice of method adopted by individual companies depends largely on their particular requirements and will be influenced by a number of factors:

- ease of use
- volumes of inventories
- costs of inventories
- management information requirements.

The FIFO method of inventory valuation is by far the most popular and is permitted by IAS 2, Inventories. FIFO (first in first out, where the oldest items of inventory, and their costs, are assumed to be the first to be used) assumes that costs are matched with the physical flow of inventory (although this may not actually be true).

LIFO (last in first out, where the most recently acquired items of inventory, and their costs, are assumed to be the first to be used) matches current costs with current revenues. LIFO is not permitted by IAS 2, and is not acceptable for UK taxation purposes.

The weighted average cost method is permitted by IAS 2. This method smoothes income and inventory values and assumes that individual units cannot be tracked through the system. The use of market values begs the questions as to which market value is most appropriate and whether replacement or realisable values be used.

Progress check 4.8

What factors must be considered regarding the valuation of inventories?

The following worked example looks at the four main methods of inventory valuation to enable us to provide a comparison in numerical terms and represent this graphically.

Worked example 4.8

A retailing company at 1 January 2010 has 400 units in inventory of a product that cost £3 each, and therefore a total cost of £1,200. The company's purchases over January and February were:

	Units	Price £	Value £	
January	600	4.00	2,400	
	800	5.00	4,000	Total £6,400
February	200	6.00	1,200	
	1,000	4.00	4,000	Total £5,200

and its sales over the same periods were:

	Units	Price £	Value £
January	1,400	12.00	16,800
February	1,400	12.00	16,800

The market value of a unit of each product was:

	Price £
January	6.00
February	3.00

FIFO — first in first out, matching costs with physical inventory flows

	Units	£		Units	£
January opening inventories	400	1,200	Sales	1,400	16,800
Purchases	1,400	6,400			
	1,800	7,600			
January closing inventories	400	2,000			
Cost of goods sold	1,400	5,600			
Gross profit		11,200			
		16,800			16,800
February opening inventories	400	2,000	Sales	1,400	16,800
Purchases	1,200	5,200			
	1,600	7,200			
February closing inventory	200	800			
Cost of goods sold	1,400	6,400			
Gross profit		10,400			
		16,800			16,800

Note that purchases are always valued at their actual cost regardless of which inventory valuation method is used.

There were 400 units in inventory at the beginning of January that cost £3 each and then 600 units were purchased at £4 each and then 800 purchased at £5 each. On a FIFO basis it is assumed that the 1,400 units sold in January first used the 400 opening inventory and then the 600 units first purchased and then 400 of the 800 units next purchased. The cost of these units was (400 × £3) + (600 × £4) + (400 × £5) = £5,600. The 400 units of inventory remaining at the end of January (which becomes the opening inventory at the beginning of February) are the 400 units left from the purchase of 800 units at £5 each and so are valued at £2,000. Using the same basis, the cost of the 1,400 units sold in February was (400 × £5) + (200 × £6) + (800 × £4) = £6,400. The 200 units of inventory remaining at the end of February are the 200 units left from the purchase of 1,000 units at £4 each and so are valued at £800.

The result is a gross profit of £11,200 for January and £10,400 for February.

LIFO − last in first out, matching current costs with current revenues

	Units	£		Units	£
January opening inventories	400	1,200	Sales	1,400	16,800
Purchases	1,400	6,400			
	1,800	7,600			
January closing inventories	400	1,200			
Cost of goods sold	1,400	6,400			
Gross profit		10,400			
		16,800			16,800
February opening inventories	400	1,200	Sales	1,400	16,800
Purchases	1,200	5,200			
	1,600	6,400			
February closing inventories	200	600			
Cost of goods sold	1,400	5,800			
Gross profit		11,000			
		16,800			16,800

There were 400 units in inventory at the beginning of January that cost £3 each and then 600 units were purchased at £4 each and then 800 purchased at £5 each. On a LIFO basis it is assumed that the 1,400 units sold in January used the 800 last purchased at £5 each and then the 600 units purchased at £4 each. The cost of these units was (800 × £5) + (600 × £4) = £6,400. The 400 units of inventory remaining at the end of January (which becomes the opening inventory at the beginning of February) are the 400 units left from opening inventory at £3 each and so are valued at £1,200. Using the same basis, the cost of the 1,400 units sold in February was (1,000 × £4) + (200 × £6) + (200 × £3) = £5,800. The 200 units of inventory remaining at the end of February are the 200 units left from the opening inventory of 400 units at £3 each and so are valued at £600.

The result is a gross profit of £10,400 for January and £11,000 for February.

Weighted average cost − smoothing of revenues and inventories values, assuming that individual units purchased cannot be followed through to actual sales so total purchases are combined to calculate an average cost per unit

	Units	£		Units	£
January opening inventories	400	1,200	Sales	1,400	16,800
Purchases	1,400	6,400			
	1,800	7,600			
January closing inventories	400	1,689			
Cost of goods sold	1,400	5,911			
Gross profit		10,889			
		16,800			16,800

Weighted average cost per unit for January $= \dfrac{(1,200 + 6,400)}{(400 + 1,400)} = \dfrac{7,600}{1,800} = £4.222$

January closing inventories $= 400 \times \dfrac{7,600}{1,800} = £1,689$

	Units	£		Units	£
February opening inventories	400	1,689	Sales	1,400	16,800
Purchases	1,200	5,200			
	1,600	6,889			
February closing inventories	200	861			
Cost of goods sold	1,400	6,028			
Gross profit		10,772			
		16,800			16,800

Weighted average cost per unit for February $= \dfrac{(1,689 + 5,200)}{(400 + 1,200)} = \dfrac{6,889}{1,600} = £4.305$

February closing inventories $= 200 \times \dfrac{6,889}{1,600} = £861$

The result is a gross profit of £10,889 for January and £10,772 for February.

The lower of FIFO or market value

	Units	£		Units	£
January opening inventories	400	1,200	Sales	1,400	16,800
Purchases	1,400	6,400			
	1,800	7,600			
January closing inventories	400	2,000			
Cost of goods sold	1,400	5,600			
Gross profit		11,200			
		16,800			16,800
February opening inventories	400	2,000	Sales	1,400	16,800
Purchases	1,200	5,200			
	1,600	7,200			
February closing inventories	200	600			
Cost of goods sold	1,400	6,600			
Gross profit		10,200			
		16,800			16,800

The value of January closing inventories using FIFO is £2,000. Using market value, January closing inventory is 400 units at £6 per unit — £2,400. Using the lower value, inventory at the end of January is £2,000. February closing inventory using FIFO is £800. Using market value, February closing inventory is 200 units at £3 per unit — £600. Using the lower value, inventory at the end of February is £600.

The result is a gross profit of £11,200 for January and £10,200 for February.

Summary of inventory valuation methods

	FIFO £	LIFO £	Weighted average cost £	Lower of FIFO or market value £
Profit				
January	11,200	10,400	10,889	11,200
February	10,400	11,000	10,772	10,200
Inventories **valuation**				
January	2,000	1,200	1,689	2,000
February	800	600	861	600

Graphical representations of the summary of inventory valuation methods used in Worked example 4.8 are shown in Figure 4.6 and Figure 4.7.

Figure 4.6 Profit comparison from the use of various inventory valuation methods

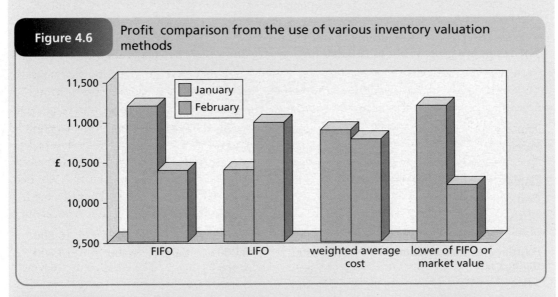

Figure 4.7 Inventory value comparison from the use of various inventory valuation methods

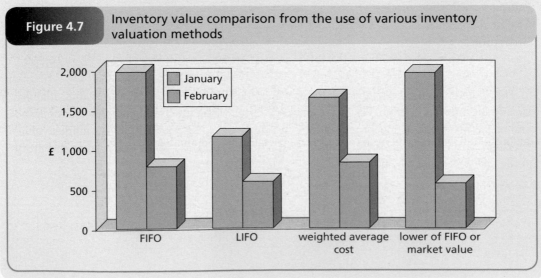

It can be seen from the summary of results in Worked example 4.8 that wide variations in profit may be reported from period to period. However, over the long run the total result will eventually be the same, when all inventories become used up. It is important to stress that a method may not be chosen to give, for example, a required result for one period. There must be consistency in the use of inventory valuation method from one period to the next.

Bad and doubtful debts

The term 'provision' often means very much the same thing as accrued expenses. The difference is that a provision is normally an amount charged against profit to provide for an expected liability or loss even though the amount or date of the liability or loss is uncertain. However, the word 'provision' is sometimes used in a different context, most commonly the depreciation provision relating to a non-current asset. It is also used in dealing with accounts receivable at the end of an accounting period.

When goods or services are sold to a customer on credit, an invoice is issued to record the transaction and to obtain settlement. The sale is reflected in the profit and loss account within the sales revenue of the business for the relevant period. The 'other side' of the accounting transaction is debited to accounts receivable, appearing as an amount due from the customer in line with the agreed payment terms. Most customers pay in accordance with their agreed terms, whether it is for example within 10 days, one month, or two months of invoice date. Unfortunately, there may sometimes be slow payers; there may be customers, for a variety of reasons, from whom payment will never be received. In the event of an invoice not being settled at all, as soon as this is known with reasonable certainty, the debt is deemed to be a bad debt and must be written off as a cost. The effect of this in the profit and loss account is not a reduction to sales revenue. It is a cost charged to the bad debt account. The accounting double entry is to the customer account to cancel the appropriate account receivable.

At the end of each accounting period accounts receivable still unpaid, falling outside their normal credit terms, must be reviewed as to the likelihood of their not paying in full or at all. If non-payment is certain then the debt must be written off. If there is uncertainty as to whether or not a debt will be settled then a provision for doubtful debts may be made on a specific basis, based on knowledge of particular customers, or on a general basis, say as a percentage of total accounts receivable, based on past trading experience.

An amount in respect of estimated doubtful debts that is charged to an account in the profit and loss account, the bad and doubtful debt account, is also reflected as a credit to an account in the balance sheet, the doubtful debt provision. The effect of the provision for doubtful debts is to reduce the value of accounts receivable in the balance sheet but without permanently eliminating any customer balances. Accounts receivable that are deemed to be bad debts are actually written off (charged as a cost in the profit and loss account) and the debts are permanently eliminated from accounts receivable.

Worked example 4.9

Accounts receivable on the books of Sportswear Wholesalers Ltd at 31 January 2010 were £429,378: current month £230,684, month two £93,812, three to six months £64,567, over six months £40,315. On 18 January 2010 one of Sportswear's customers, Road Runner Ltd, had gone into liquidation owing Sportswear £15,342, which had been invoiced over six months previously. Sportswear's policy was to provide for doubtful debts on the basis of three to six months' debts 5%, and over six months' debts 10%.

Let's consider what entries would appear in Sportwear's cumulative profit and loss account to January 2010 and its balance sheet at 31 January 2010 in respect of bad and doubtful debts. We may assume that no other debts have been written off during the year to date.

Road Runner Ltd had gone into liquidation owing Sportswear £15,342, of which it is assumed there was no chance of any recovery; therefore it had to be written off as a bad debt in the profit and loss account in January 2010.

The effect of the bad debt write-off was to reduce accounts receivable by £15,342, and the debts over six months old would reduce down to £24,973 [£40,315 − £15,342].

The doubtful debt provision at 31 January in line with Sportswear's policy was therefore:

5% × £64,567 = £3,228
10% × £24,973 = £2,497
Total   = £5,725 (assuming no opening doubtful debt provision at 1 January 2010)

Profit and loss account for the year to 31 January 2010:
Bad and doubtful debts

Road Runner Ltd write off 31 January 2010	£15,342
Doubtful debt provision at 31 January 2010	£5,725
Balance at 31 January 2010	£21,067

Balance sheet as at 31 January 2010:
Accounts receivable:

Balance 1 January 2010	£429,378
Road Runner Ltd write off 31 January 2010	£15,342
Balance at 31 January 2010	£414,036

Doubtful debt provision:

Doubtful debt provision at 31 January 2010	£5,725
Balance at 31 January 2010	£5,725

Trade receivables presented in Sportswear's published balance sheet as at 31 January 2010 would be £408,311 [£414,036 − £5,725].

Such bad and doubtful debt entries would not be individually apparent from inspection of Sportswear Wholesalers Ltd's financial statements. Bad and doubtful debt charges are normally included under the income statement heading *Distribution Costs,* and the corresponding balance sheet entries are reflected within the total *Trade Receivables* heading.

Profit and loss and cash flow

During the last decade of the twentieth century there was a great deal of activity in the birth and growth of so-called dot.com companies. Their aim was to exploit the use of the Internet to provide opportunities to sell products and services in wider markets and on an increasingly global basis.

The apparent success of the majority of these businesses was initially based on growth of potential in both market share and profitability reflected in the numbers of subscribers attracted to their websites. Actual and potential profitability do not necessarily inevitably result in a healthy cash position. Such companies invariably required large amounts of cash for them to continue operating for extended periods prior to achieving profitability and to generate their own cash flows. Many dot.com businesses from that era failed to survive and flourish, but there were also many successes, for example Google.com, Amazon.com, Sportingbet.com, and Lastminute.com.

In Chapter 3 we discussed how profit and cash flow do not mean the same thing. In fact, the profit earned and the net cash generated during an accounting period are usually very different, and often significantly different. How often do we see cases reported of businesses in serious financial difficulties because of severe cash shortages, even though they may appear to be trading profitably?

Profit is a matter of opinion. Cash flow is a matter of fact.

However, it is invariably the reported profits, or more usually estimated profits, that are closely monitored by investors and financial analysts. It is these numbers on which analysts base their business forecasts, and which influence investor confidence in a business, and therefore its share price.

While research by accountants Ernst & Young showed that profit warnings reached a six-year high in 2007, two years later the same researchers reported that profit warnings in 2009 had fallen to a six-year low. In spite of the reductions in the number of profit warnings issued, there were still some high profile companies such as Aer Lingus, Sony Ericsson and National Express, who issued warnings. The issue of a profit warning can have serious effects on the share values of the companies concerned, as illustrated in the press extract below.

Profit is important, but cash flow is very important. There is a relationship between cash and profit, and it is possible to identify and quantify the factors within this relationship. The profit or loss made by a business during an accounting period differs from the net cash inflows and outflows during the period because of:

- cash expected to be paid or received relating to transactions during a period may in fact not be paid or received until the following or subsequent periods
- cash may have been paid or received in advance of goods or services being received or provided and invoices being received or issued

Profits warning – the writing on the wall

The van hire company Northgate stunned the market yesterday with a profit warning. The shares lost almost half their value after the company said full-year profits would be significantly lower than expected, adding that it is in talks with its banks as its debt covenants come under increasing strain.

Northgate said trading conditions in its key markets in the UK and Spain continued to deteriorate on slumping demand for vehicle rental. The Darlington-based company added that the worsening economy means it may need to write down the value of its assets and that the pound's weakness is also putting its debt covenants under pressure. The company has conducted a review of its businesses in Britain and Spain and said it expects to conclude that they had declined in value. Northgate, which issued profit warnings in September and December, said it anticipates writing down about £86m goodwill on acquisitions and £60m from the value of its assets. Its shares fell 30p to 39p.

Source: **Northgate stuns market with profit warning; Business in brief** © *The Independent*, 26 February 2009

- cash may have been paid or received relating to non-manufacturing, non-trading or non-profit items – for example cash received for shares in the business and cash paid out on capital expenditure
- profit will have been calculated to include the impact of non-cash items such as depreciation.

When we look at the statement of cash flows in the next chapter we shall see that one of the schedules that is required to be prepared in support of the statement of cash flows is in fact a reconciliation of profit to operating cash flow. Prior to that, we can consider the following example, which is not in strict compliance with the cash flow reconciliation schedule requirement, but will serve to illustrate how profit and cash flow are linked and how the links may be identified.

Worked example 4.10

In Worked example 4.4 we saw that Ronly Bonly Jones Ltd made a profit of £10,000 during the month of January 2010. A summary of its balance sheet at 1 January 2010, and the 31 January 2010 balance sheet that we derived, are as follows:

	1 January 2010 £000	31 January 2010 £000
Non-current assets at cost	130	150
Depreciation provision	(20)	(25)
Inventories	45	79
Trade receivables	64	82
Cash and bank	6	–
	225	286
Trade payables	(87)	(89)
Bank overdraft	–	(39)
Share capital	(50)	(60)
Retained earnings	(88)	(98)
	(225)	(286)

We can provide a reconciliation of Ronly Bonly Jones profit for the month of January with the cash flow for the same period.

	January 2010 £000
Profit for the month	10
Add back non-cash item:	
Depreciation for month	5
	15
Cash gained from:	
Increase in trade payables	2
Additional share capital	10
	27
Cash reduced by:	
Purchase of non-current assets	(20)
Increase in inventories	(34)
Increase in trade receivables	(18)
	(72)
Cash outflow for month	(45)
Cash and bank 1 January 2010	6
Cash outflow for month	(45)
Bank overdraft 31 January 2010	(39)

Worked example 4.10 shows that despite making a profit of £10,000 during the accounting period the company in fact had a shortfall of cash of £45,000 for the same period. After adjusting profit for the non-cash item of depreciation and adding the increase in share capital it effectively had an increase in funds during the month of £25,000. It then had to finance the purchase of non-current assets of £20,000 and finance an increase in its working capital requirement of £50,000 (inventories £34,000 plus trade receivables £18,000 less trade payables £2,000). This resulted in its cash deficit for the month of £45,000. The company therefore went from having a positive cash balance of £6,000 at the start of the month to a bank overdraft of £39,000 at the end of the month.

Both the company and its bankers would obviously need to monitor RBJ's performance very closely over future months! A company will normally continuously review its cash, bank overdraft, trade payables and trade receivables position. The bank manager will regularly review a company's balances and require advance notice of potential breaches of its overdraft limits.

Progress check 4.11

In what way does the profit earned by a business during an accounting period differ from the cash generated during the same period? In what ways are profit and cash affected by the settlement (or not) of their accounts by the customers of the business?

Summary of key points

■ An income statement is a summary report of the movements for the accounting period on each of the accounts in the profit and loss account section of the general ledger of a business.

■ The profit (or loss) of an entity may be considered from two perspectives: by considering the change in book wealth between the start and end of an accounting period; by deducting total costs from total revenues (sales) generated during the accounting period.

■ In accordance with IAS 1, costs and expenses on the face of the income statement may be presented according to business functions, and classified into revenue, cost of sales, other operating costs (distributions costs and administrative expenses), other income, finance costs, finance income and income tax expense.

■ In accordance with IAS 1, costs and expenses on the face of the income statement may alternatively be presented according to their nature, and classified into revenue, employee expenses, depreciation etc.

■ The profit for the year reported in the income statement 'belongs' to the equity shareholders and may be used either to pay dividends to shareholders or to retain as retained earnings. The company may use profit for either dividends or retained earnings or both.

■ The profit and loss account (and therefore the income statement) is closely linked with the balance sheet in two ways: they both reflect the change in the book wealth of the business; most transactions are reflected once in the income statement and once in the balance sheet.

■ Valuation of the various items within the balance sheet in accordance with accounting concepts and accounting and financial reporting standards has a significant impact on the level of profit (or loss) earned by a business during an accounting period.

- The profit (or loss) earned during an accounting period is not the same as the cash flow generated during the period, but the links between the two measures may be quantified and reconciled.
- There are limitations to the income statement, which like the balance sheet is a historical document, primarily due to the impact on costs of the employment of alternative methods of valuation of assets and liabilities.

Assessment material

Questions

Q4.1 How would you define the profit (or loss) earned by a business during an accounting period?

Q4.2 Outline an income statement showing each of the main category headings using the business functions format.

Q4.3 (i) Which accounting or financial reporting standard contains provisions relating to the format of the income statement?
(ii) What are the requirements that are relevant to the formats of the income statement of a limited company?

Q4.4 The income statement and the balance sheet report on different aspects of a company's financial status. What are these different aspects and how are they related?

Q4.5 (i) Why are the methods used for the valuation of the various types of assets so important?
(ii) Describe the three main categories of asset that are most relevant to asset valuation.

Q4.6 What is depreciation and what are the problems encountered in dealing with the depreciation of non-current assets?

Q4.7 Describe three of the most commonly used methods of accounting for depreciation.

Q4.8 Describe four of the most commonly used methods of valuing inventory.

Q4.9 How does the valuation of trade receivables impact on the income statement of a business?

Q4.10 Profit does not equal cash, but how can the one be reconciled with the other for a specific accounting period?

Discussion points

D4.1 'My profit for the year is the total of my pile of sales invoices less the cash I have paid out during the year.' Discuss.

D4.2 'The reason why companies make a provision for depreciation of their non-current assets is to save up enough money to buy new ones when the old assets reach the end of their lives.' Discuss.

D4.3 Why is judgement so important in considering the most appropriate method to use for valuing inventories? What are the factors that should be borne in mind and what are the *pros* and *cons* of the alternative methods?

Exercises

Solutions are provided in Appendix 3 to all exercise numbers highlighted in colour.

Level I

E4.1   *Time allowed – 30 minutes*

Mr Kumar's chemist shop derives income from both retail sales and from prescription charges made to the NHS and to customers. For the last two years to 31 December 2009 and 31 December 2010 his results were as follows:

	2009 £	2010 £
Sales and prescription charges to customers	196,500	210,400
Prescription charges to the NHS	48,200	66,200
Purchases of inventories	170,100	180,600
Opening inventories at the start of the year	21,720	30,490
Closing inventories at the end of the year	30,490	25,300
Wages	25,800	27,300
Mr Kumar's drawings*	20,500	19,700
Rent and property taxes	9,400	13,200
Insurance	1,380	1,620
Motor vehicle expenses	2,200	2,410
Other overheads	14,900	15,300

*Note that Mr Kumar's drawings are the amounts of money that he has periodically taken out of the business for his own use and should be shown as a deduction from the profits earned by the business rather than an expense in the income statement.

Rent for the year 2009 includes £2,400 paid in advance for the half year to 31 March 2010, and for 2010 includes £3,600 paid in advance for the half year to 31 March 2011. Other overheads for 2009 do not include the electricity invoice for £430 for the final quarter (included in 2010 other overheads). There is a similar electricity invoice for £510 for 2010. Depreciation may be ignored.

(i)   **Prepare an income statement for the two years to 31 December.**
(ii) **Why do you think that there is a difference in the gross profit to sales % between the two years.**
(iii) **Using Mr Kumar's business as an example, explain the accruals accounting concept and examine whether or not it has been complied with.**

E4.2   *Time allowed – 30 minutes*

Discuss the concepts that may apply and practical problems that may be encountered when accounting for:

(i)   the acquisition of desktop personal computers, and
(ii) popular brands of products supplied by retailers

with specific comments regarding their depreciation reported in the income statement and their net book values reported in the balance sheet.

E4.3 *Time allowed – 30 minutes*

A friend of yours owns a shop selling CDs and posters for the 12- to 14-year-old market. From the following information advise him on the potential problems that may be encountered in the valuation of such items for balance sheet purposes:

(a) greatest hits compilation CDs have sold consistently over the months and cost £5,000 with a retail value of £7,000

(b) sales of specific group CDs, which ceased recording in the previous year, have now dropped off to zero and cost £500 with a total retail value of £700

(c) specific band CDs, which are still constantly recording and selling in the shop every week cost £1,000 with a total retail value of £1,400

(d) specific artist posters are currently not selling at all (although CDs are), and cost £50 with a retail value of £100.

E4.4 *Time allowed – 30 minutes*

The Partex company began trading in 2008, and all sales are made to customers on credit. The company is in a sector that suffers from a high level of bad debts, and a provision for doubtful debts of 4% of outstanding accounts receivable is made at each year end.

Information relating to 2008, 2009 and 2010 is as follows:

	Year to 31 December		
	2008	**2009**	**2010**
Outstanding accounts receivable at 31 December*	£88,000	£110,000	£94,000
Bad debts to be written off during year	£4,000	£5,000	£4,000

*before bad debts have been written off

You are required to state the amount that will appear:

(i) in the balance sheet for trade receivables, and

(ii) in the income statement for bad debts.

E4.5 *Time allowed – 45 minutes*

Tartantrips Ltd, a company in Scotland, operates several ferries and has a policy of holding several in reserve, due to the weather patterns and conditions of various contracts with local authorities. A ferry costs £5 million and has an estimated useful life of 10 years, at which time its realisable value is expected to be £1 million.

Calculate and discuss three methods of depreciation that the company may use:

(i) sum of the digits

(ii) straight line

(iii) reducing balance.

E4.6   *Time allowed — 60 minutes*

From the following financial information that has been provided by Lazydays Ltd, for the year ended 31 March 2010 (and the corresponding numbers for the year to 31 March 2009), construct an income statement, using the format adopted by the majority of UK plcs, including comparative figures.

	2010	2009
	£	£
Administrative expenses	22,000	20,000
Depreciation	5,000	5,000
Closing inventories	17,000	15,000
Distribution costs	33,000	30,000
Dividends paid	32,000	30,000
Dividends received from non-related companies	5,000	5,000
Interest paid	10,000	10,000
Interest received	3,000	3,000
Opening inventories	15,000	10,000
Purchases	99,000	90,000
Redundancy costs	5,000	–
Sales revenue	230,000	200,000
Taxation	25,000	24,000

(a) Depreciation is to be included in administrative expenses
(b) Redundancy costs are to be regarded as an exceptional item to be included in administrative expenses

Level II

E4.7   *Time allowed — 60 minutes*

Llareggyb Ltd started business on 1 January 2010 and its year ended 31 December 2010. Llareggyb entered into the following transactions during the year.

Received funds for share capital of £25,000

Paid suppliers of materials £44,000

Purchased 11,000 units of a product at £8 per unit, which were sold to customers at £40 per unit

Paid heating and lighting costs for cash £16,000

Further heating and lighting costs of £2,400 were incurred within the year, but still unpaid at 31 December 2010

Mr D Thomas loaned the company £80,000 on 1 January 2010 at 8% interest per annum

Loan interest was paid to Mr Thomas for January to June 2010

8,000 product units were sold to customers during 2010

Customers paid £280,000 to Llareggyb for sales of its products

Rent on the premises £60,000 was paid for 18 months from 1 January 2010, and local business property taxes of £9,000 were also paid for the same period

Salaries and wages were paid for January to November 2010 amounting to £132,000 but the December payroll cost of £15,000 had not yet been paid as at 31 December 2010

A lorry was purchased for £45,000 on 1 January 2010 and was expected to last for five years after which it was estimated that it could be sold for £8,000

The company uses the straight line method of depreciation.

> Prepare an income statement for Llareggyb Ltd for the year ended 31 December 2010.

E4.8   *Time allowed – 60 minutes*

> From the trial balance of Retepmal Ltd at 31 March 2010 shown below prepare an income statement for the year to 31 March 2010 and a balance sheet as at 31 March 2010 using the formats used by most UK companies.

	£
Premises (net book value)	95,000
Accounts receivable	75,000
Purchases of inventories	150,000
Retained earnings at 31 March 2009	130,000
Inventories at 31 March 2009	15,000
Furniture and fixtures	30,000
Sales revenue	266,000
Distribution costs	40,000
Administrative expenses	50,000
Accounts payable	54,000
Motor vehicles (net book value)	40,000
Cash and bank	35,000
Equity share capital	80,000

Additional information:

(a) Inventories at 31 March 2010 were £25,000.

(b) Dividend proposed for 2010 was £7,000.

(c) An accrual for distribution costs of £3,000 was required at 31 March 2010.

(d) A prepayment of administrative expenses of £5,000 was required at 31 March 2010.

(e) Corporation tax estimated to be payable on 2009/2010 profit was £19,000.

(f) Annual depreciation charges on premises and motor vehicles for the year to 31 March 2010 are included in administrative expenses and distribution costs, and in the cumulative depreciation provisions used to calculate the net book values of £95,000 and £40,000 respectively, shown in the trial balance at 31 March 2010.

The furniture and fixtures balance of £30,000 relates to purchases of assets during the year to 31 March 2010. The depreciation charge in administrative expenses and the corresponding depreciation provision are not included in the trial balance at 31 March 2010. They are required to be calculated on a straight line basis for a full year to 31 March 2010, based on a useful economic life of eight years and an estimated residual value of £6,000.

5

Statement of cash flows

Contents

Learning objectives

Completion of this chapter will enable you to:

■ describe what is meant by cash flow

■ outline the structure of the statement of cash flows for a limited company, and its supporting schedules

■ classify the categories of cash inflows and cash outflows that make up the statement of cash flows

■ illustrate how both the direct and indirect cash flow approaches are used to derive net cash flows from operating activities

■ prepare a statement of cash flows

■ explain the links between the statement of cash flows and the balance sheet

■ explain the links between the statement of cash flows and the income statement

■ consider the merits of cash flow versus profit as a measure of financial performance.

Introduction

Chapters 3 and 4 have been concerned with the first two of the three key financial statements required to be prepared periodically by limited companies: the balance sheet and the income statement. This chapter will be concerned with the third of the key financial statements, the statement of cash flows. It should be noted that IAS 7, Statement of Cash Flows, has now revised the formally reported heading of the cash flow statement to the statement of cash flows. Throughout this book, and in this chapter in particular we may use both headings interchangeably to mean exactly the same thing.

The statement of cash flows, in one form or another, is prepared and used as an important management tool by all businesses. However, as in the previous two chapters, this chapter deals primarily with the statement of cash flows of limited companies, both private and public.

Chapter 5 looks at how statements of cash flows are structured and how each of the different types of cash inflows and cash outflows are categorised. This forms the basis to enable the preparation of a statement of cash flows of a limited company, and its supporting schedules, in the appropriate format.

We will look at the relationship between the statement of cash flows and the balance sheet and the income statement. In Chapters 3 and 4 we have seen the subjective aspects of both the balance sheet and the income statement. Cash flow is not subjective in any way but is a matter of fact.

What does the statement of cash flows tell us?

Cash is a crucial requirement for any business to develop and survive, whether it is involved in the public services, retailing or manufacturing (see the press extract below that illustrates the importance of cash management).

The current serious economic recession clearly demonstrates the need for companies to undertake realistic and timely cash planning through the preparation of regular, clearly understood cash reports. Such cash planning and reporting can help managers to survive through the most difficult periods and to provide a solid financial base from which to take advantage of new projects and opportunities once the worst of the financial crisis is over.

Cash planning is crucial for success

Midlands-based industrial group Hill & Smith has weathered the downturn pretty well – and its focus on cash management has put it in a strong position.

Last year's results, released yesterday, came in ahead of expectations. Revenues fell by 7pc to £389m but pre-tax profits rose to £39.7m from £35.1m in 2008 – hitting a record high in one of the toughest years the industry has seen for some time. This is a credit to the group's cost-cutting and cash-management drive.

The group even managed to slash its **net debt** to £87.6m from £146.2m over the 12-month period.

Hill & Smith operates in three divisions – infrastructure, galvanising and building and construction products. It is exposed to stimulus spend on both sides of the Atlantic.

The roads operation of its infrastructure business has been strong throughout the downturn. It currently has all of its road barriers – which stretch to 173,000 miles – in use on the UK roads network. With its contracts for roadworks on the M1 and M25, it has 45pc of business for this operation for the next three years.

Derek Muir, the group's chief executive, told Questor yesterday that its galvanising business was stable and the group has started to see a pick up in its construction operations.

It has also recently won contracts for new street lighting columns in Hampshire and Surrey and it is bidding for contracts in Oldham, Rochdale and Coventry.

Moreover, the company is seeking to expand. It is already one of the country's largest suppliers of galvanised steel, with Mr Muir looking for a move into renewables.

Solar panels need to be attached to buildings in steel frames and this is the main area of interest but the company also wants business in utilities.

Hill is expanding its operations in the US, India and China. Its first US galvanising plant in Delaware had a successful first year and it has introduced its temporary vehicle restraint system, Zoneguard, into Canada.

Source: **Hill & Smith; QUESTOR,** by Garry White
© *Daily Telegraph*, 10 March 2010

The definition of cash includes not only cash in hand but also deposits and overdrafts, including those denominated in foreign currencies, with any bank or other financial institutions. A bank overdraft, which is **repayable on demand**, is a borrowing facility where interest is paid only to the extent of the facility that is actually used. Deposits repayable on demand include any kind of account where additional funds may be deposited at any time or funds withdrawn at any time without prior notice. All charges and credits on these accounts such as bank interest, bank fees, deposits or withdrawals, other than movements wholly within them, represent cash inflows and outflows of the reporting entity.

Virtually all transactions are conducted ultimately by cash or near cash (for example bank accounts and credit cards). Sales of goods or services, or any other business assets, whether they are settled immediately or settled at some future date, are settled by cash or cash equivalents. Cash is an asset like any other asset, such as a non-current asset like machinery, or current assets like accounts receivable. Cash has the same properties as other assets, but also many more.

Cash is:

- a unit of measurement – we evaluate transactions and report financial information in £ sterling or whatever other foreign currency denominated
- a medium of exchange – rather than using the exchange or barter of other assets, cash is used as the accepted medium, having itself a recognisable value
- a store of value – cash may be used for current requirements or held for future use.

The inability of a business to pay its creditors and other claims on the business, is invariably the reason for that business to fail. Cash, therefore, is a key asset and different from all other assets, which is why the performance of cash as a measure of business performance is so important.

In Chapters 3 and 4 we have discussed how the balance sheet and the income statement do not show or directly deal with some of the key changes that have taken place in the company's financial position and financial performance. We will see in this chapter how the statement of cash flows addresses this shortfall of information seen from the other two key financial statements, by answering questions like:

- How much capital expenditure (for example on machines and buildings) has the company made, and how did it fund the expenditure?
- What was the extent of new borrowing and how much debt was repaid?
- How much did the company need to fund new **working capital requirements** (for example increases in trade receivables and inventory requirements as a result of increased business activity)?
- How much of the company's **financing** was met by funds generated from its trading activities, and how much met by new external funding (for example, from banks and other lenders, or new shareholders)?

We introduced the DVD analogy in Chapters 3 and 4 with regard to the balance sheet and the income statement. In the same way as profit (or loss), cash represents the dynamic DVD of changes in the cash position of the business throughout the period between the two 'pauses' – the balance sheets at the start and the finish of an accounting period. The statement of cash flows summarises the cash inflows and outflows and calculates the net change in the cash position throughout the period. In this way it provides answers to the questions shown above. Analysis and summary of the cash inflows and outflows of the period answers those questions by illustrating:

- changes in the level of cash between the start and end of the period
- how much cash has been generated, and from where
- for what purpose cash has been used.

The basic purpose of a statement of cash flows, as we saw in Chapter 3, is to report the cash receipts and cash payments that take place within an accounting period (see Fig. 5.1), and to show how the

---

Figure 5.1   The main elements of the statement of cash flows

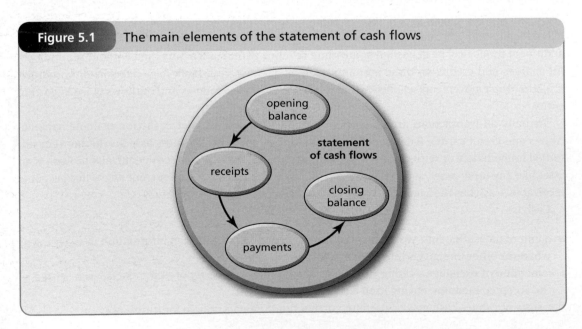

cash balance has changed from the start of the period to the balance at the end of the period. This can be seen to be objective and clearly avoids the problems of allocation associated with the preparation of a conventional income statement.

However, a more useful presentation would describe:

■ how the company generated or lost cash
■ how the company financed its growth and investments
■ the extent to which the company was funded by debt and equity.

The statement of cash flows should ensure that companies:

■ report their cash generation and cash absorption for a period by highlighting the significant components of cash flow in a way that facilitates comparison of the cash flow performances of different businesses
■ provide information that assists in the assessment of their liquidity, solvency and financial adaptability.

Progress check 5.1

What questions should a statement of cash flows set out to answer?

Statement of cash flows format

The objective of IAS 7, Statement of Cash Flows, is the presentation of information about the historical changes in cash and cash equivalents of an entity by means of a statement of cash flows, which classifies cash flows during the period according to:

■ operating activities
■ investing activities
■ financing activities.

Cash flows from operating activities are the main revenue-producing activities of the company that are not investing or financing activities, so operating cash flows include cash received from customers and cash paid to suppliers and employees. There are two methods of calculating cash flows from operating activities: the direct method; the indirect method. In IAS 7 the direct method of presentation is encouraged, but the indirect method is acceptable (see the section below about the direct method and indirect method of calculating operating cash flow).

Cash flows from investing activities are the acquisition and disposal of long-term assets and other investments that are not considered to be cash equivalents.

Cash flows from financing activities result from changes to the equity capital and borrowing structure of the company.

Interest and dividends received and paid may be classified as operating, investing, or financing cash flows, provided that they are classified consistently from period to period. Cash flows arising from taxes on income are normally classified as operating, unless they can be specifically identified with financing or investing activities.

All companies that prepare financial statements which conform with IFRSs are required to present a statement of cash flows.

The statement of cash flows analyses changes in cash and cash equivalents during a period. Cash and cash equivalents comprise cash on hand and demand deposits, together with short-term, highly liquid investments that are readily convertible to a known amount of cash, and that are subject to an insignificant risk of changes in value. An investment normally meets the definition of a cash equivalent when it has a maturity of three months or less from the date of acquisition. Equity investments are normally excluded, unless they are in substance a cash equivalent, for example preference shares acquired within three months of their specified redemption date. Bank overdrafts, which are repayable on demand, usually form an integral part of a company's cash position are also included as a component of cash and cash equivalents.

The exchange rate used for translation of transactions denominated in a foreign currency should be the rate in effect at the date of the cash flows.

Aggregate cash flows relating to acquisitions and disposals of subsidiaries and other business units should be presented separately and classified as investing activities.

Investing and financing transactions which do not require the use of cash should be excluded from the statement of cash flows, but they should be separately disclosed elsewhere in the financial statements.

The components of cash and cash equivalents should be disclosed, and a reconciliation presented to amounts reported in the balance sheet.

The amount of cash and cash equivalents held by the entity that is not available for use by the group should be disclosed, together with a commentary by management.

Progress check 5.2

What are the aims and purposes of the statement of cash flows?

Direct and indirect cash flow

As we discussed earlier, the heading relating to cash flow from operating activities can be presented by using either the direct method or indirect method. We shall consider both methods in a little more detail, although the indirect method is by far the easier to use in practice and is the method used by most companies.

Cash flows from operating activities include the cash effects of transactions and other events relating to the operating or trading activities of the business. They are the movements in cash and cash equivalents of the operations that are included in the income statement to derive operating profit. Net cash flows from operating activities include the cash effects only and not all the revenues and costs that together represent the income statement.

Reference to the **direct method** and the **indirect method** relates to the choice of two options that are available for a business to derive the net cash flows from operating activities. Each method in one way or another involves individual identification of each of the cash items during the period that have been included in the income statement.

Direct method

The direct method provides an analysis of all the cash transactions for the appropriate period to identify all receipts and payments relating to the operating activities for the period. The analysis therefore shows the relevant constituent cash flows, operating cash receipts and cash payments including in particular cash receipts from customers, cash payments to suppliers, cash payments to and on behalf of employees, and other cash payments.

The direct method shows each major class of gross cash receipts and gross cash payments. The operating cash flows section of the statement of cash flows under the direct method would appear something like this:

Operating activities

Cash receipts from customers	xxx
Cash paid to suppliers	xxx
Cash paid to employees	xxx
Cash paid for other operating expenses	xxx
Cash generated from operations	xxx
Interest paid	xxx
Income taxes paid	xxx
Net cash generated from operating activities	xxx

Using data provided from Flatco plc's cash records for the year ended 31 December 2010 an example of the direct method is illustrated in Figure 5.2. IAS 7 requires a reconciliation between profit and cash flow from operating activities (using the indirect cash flow method – see below), even where the direct method is adopted. Because of the amount of time and other resources required to analyse the relevant cash information, the direct method has not been popular with many companies, although it does provide some very useful information.

Figure 5.2 shows cash generated from operations during the year ended 31 December 2010. Interest paid of £71,000 and tax paid of £44,000 must be deducted from cash generated from operations to determine cash flows from operating activities of £821,000.

Indirect method

The indirect method is by far the one more frequently adopted by UK companies. The basis of this approach is that operating revenues and costs are generally associated with cash receipts and cash payments and so profits earned from operating activities during an accounting period will approximate

Figure 5.2   Cash generated from operations – direct method

Flatco plc
Cash generated from operations for the year ended 31 December 2010
Direct cash flow method

	£000
Operating activities	
Cash receipts from customers	3,472
Cash paid to suppliers	(1,694)
Cash paid to employees	(631)
Cash paid for other operating expenses	(211)
Cash generated from operations	936
Interest paid	(71)
Income taxes paid	(44)
Net cash generated from operating activities	821

the net cash flows generated during the period. The cash generated from operations may be determined by adjusting the profit before tax reported in the income statement for non-cash items:

■ depreciation
■ amortisation

and also changes in working capital during the period:

■ inventories
■ trade receivables
■ trade payables.

As we saw in the direct method, interest paid and tax paid during the accounting period must be deducted from the cash generated from operations to determine cash flows from operating activities.

The operating cash flows section of the statement of cash flows under the indirect method would appear something like this:

Operating activities	
Profit before tax	xxx
Add back depreciation and amortisation	xxx
Adjust net finance income/costs	xxx
Increase/decrease in trade and other receivables	xxx
Increase/decrease in inventories	xxx
Increase/decrease in trade and other payables	xxx
Cash generated from operations	xxx
Interest paid	xxx
Income taxes paid	xxx
Net cash generated from operating activities	xxx

Using the income statement for 2010 and balance sheet for the year ended 31 December 2010 for Flatco plc (see Figs 3.7 and 4.4), an example of the indirect method is illustrated in Figure 5.3.

In the same way as in the direct method shown in Figure 5.2, the indirect method also shows cash generated from operations during the year ended 31 December 2010. Interest paid of £71,000 and tax paid of £44,000 must be deducted from cash generated from operations to determine cash flows from operating activities of £821,000.

Figure 5.3   Cash generated from operations – indirect method

Flatco plc
Cash generated from operations for the year ended 31 December 2010
Indirect cash flow method

	£000
Profit before tax	590
Depreciation and amortisation charges	345
Adjust finance (income)/costs [71 – 11 – 100]	(40)
Increase in inventories	(43)
Increase in trade and other receivables	(28)
Increase in trade and other payables, and provisions	112
Cash generated from operations	936
Interest paid	(71)
Income taxes paid	(44)
Net cash generated from operating activities	821

Worked example 5.1

Indirect Ltd earned profit before tax of £247,000 during 2009/2010, and its retained profit for the year was also £247,000. Indirect Ltd had acquired non-current assets totalling £290,000 during the year and had made no disposals of non-current assets. Indirect Ltd received no finance income and paid no interest or tax during the year ended 30 June 2010. Indirect Ltd's balance sheets as at 1 July 2009 and 30 June 2010 were as follows:

	1 July 2009 £000	30 June 2010 £000
Non-current assets	385	525
Inventories	157	277
Trade receivables	224	287
	766	1,089
Trade payables	(305)	(312)
Bank overdraft	(153)	(222)
Equity	(308)	(555)
	(766)	(1,089)

The indirect method may be used to calculate the net cash flow from operating activities:

Calculation of depreciation	£000
Non-current assets at the start of the year were	385
Additions during the year were	290
Disposals during the year were	zero
	675
Non-current assets at the end of the year were	525
Therefore, depreciation for the year was	150

Indirect Ltd
Cash generated from operations for the year ended 30 June 2010
Indirect cash flow method

	£000
Profit before tax	247
Depreciation charge	150
Adjust finance (income)/costs	–
Increase in inventories [277−157]	(120)
Increase in trade and other receivables [287−224]	(63)
Increase in trade and other payables [312−305]	7
Cash generated from operations	221
Interest paid	–
Income taxes paid	–
Net cash generated from operating activities	221

Worked example 5.1 shows how the cash generated from operations of £221,000 was calculated by starting with the profit before tax for the year of £247,000 and adjusting for changes in depreciation and working capital over the year. Because no interest or taxes were paid during the year net cash generated from operating activities is also £221,000. The only other cash activity during the year is the acquisition of non-current assets totalling £290,000. If we deduct that from the net cash generated from operating activities of £221,000 the result is the net decrease in cash and cash equivalents and bank overdrafts of £69,000. This agrees with the movement in the bank overdraft for the year, seen from the balance sheet, which has worsened from an overdraft of £153,000 at the beginning of the year to an overdraft of £222,000 at the end of the year.

Progress check 5.3

Describe the direct and the indirect cash flow methods that may be used to derive cash generated from operating activities, and their differences and their purpose.

Structure of the statement of cash flows

As we have seen, IAS 7 requires that a company's statement of cash flows should list its cash flows for the period and classify them under three standard headings. These headings and their detailed components are illustrated in Figure 5.4. We will look at each of these and how they are used to provide an analysis of the cash movements of the business over an accounting period.

Figure 5.4   Cash inflows and cash outflows reflected in the statement of cash flows

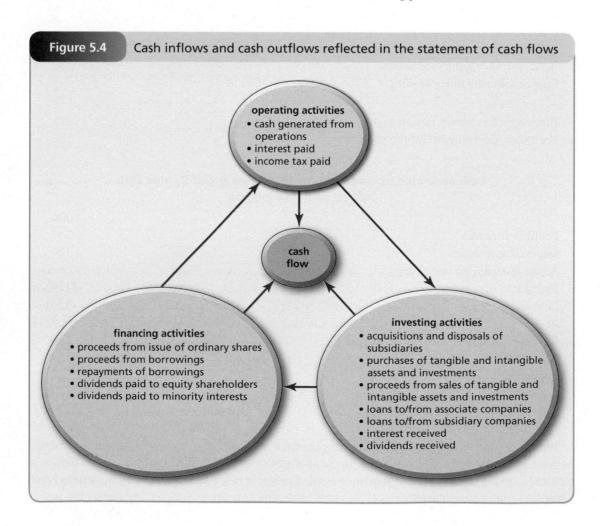

Cash generated from operations

Cash generated from operations includes the cash effects of transactions and other events relating to the operating or trading activities of the business. We have seen above how this may be calculated using the direct method or indirect method.

Interest paid

Interest paid relates to payments of cash to providers of finance, and includes interest paid on bank overdrafts and long-term and short-term loans.

Income tax paid

Income tax paid includes all items in respect of taxes on revenue and capital profits. These include all payments relating to corporation tax, and receipts from rebate claims, overpayments, etc. Payments and receipts in respect of value added tax (VAT) are not included within the taxation heading. VAT payments and receipts are netted against the cash flows to which they relate, for example operating activities and non-current assets investments.

Acquisitions and disposals of subsidiaries

Cash payments and receipts for acquisitions and disposals of subsidiaries relate to the acquisition and sale of investments in subsidiary undertakings, or investment and sales of investments in other undertakings. This does not include any income derived from these investments, which is included within dividends received.

Purchases and sales of tangible and intangible assets and investments

Purchases and sales of tangible and intangible assets and investments relate to the acquisition and disposal of long-term assets and other investments not included in cash equivalents.

Loans to and from associate companies

Associate companies are companies in which a company has a substantial stake in the form of share ownership but does not have a controlling interest. Associate companies do not form part of a group for the purposes of consolidated accounts. This section of the statement of cash flows includes cash advances and loans made to associate companies and cash receipts from the repayment of advances and loans made to associate companies.

Loans to and from subsidiary companies

A parent company controls a subsidiary company by owning a majority of the voting shares in the subsidiary or by agreement to have the right to appoint or remove a majority of the board of directors. The parent company (the controlling company) and its subsidiary companies form a group for the purposes of consolidated accounts. This section of the statement of cash flows includes cash advances and loans made to subsidiary companies and cash receipts from the repayment of advances and loans made to subsidiary companies.

Interest received

This includes interest received on long-term and short-term loans.

Dividends received

Dividends received include receipts of cash that result from owning an investment and exclude all other returns included elsewhere in the statement of cash flows under operating activities, investing or financing activities.

Proceeds from issue of ordinary shares

These are the cash proceeds from issuing ordinary shares and the cash payments to shareholders to acquire or redeem the company's shares.

Proceeds from and repayments of borrowings

This includes cash proceeds from issuing debentures, loans, notes, bonds, mortgages and other short-term or long-term borrowings and cash repayments of amounts borrowed.

Loans are amounts borrowed that have fixed payments, and notes are borrowings that allow the lender to receive regular payments over a set time period ending on a specified date when the full amount is repaid. Bonds are debt instruments issued for periods of more than one year and mortgages are loans raised usually to purchase property with specified payment periods and interest rates. Short term generally means anything less than one year, whilst long term generally means anything more than one year. A debenture is a type of bond, which is made in writing and under the company's seal.

Dividends paid to ordinary shareholders

This heading includes all dividends actually paid in cash during the accounting period to ordinary shareholders. It does not include proposed dividends or dividends declared, which will not be paid until a subsequent accounting period, and it does not include preference share dividends.

Dividends paid to minority interests

This heading includes all dividends paid to other than ordinary shareholders, which are preference shareholders and minority interests.

Worked example 5.2

The following is a list of some of the different types of cash inflows and cash outflows of a typical plc. We will identify within which of the statement of cash flows headings they would normally be reported.

- sale of a subsidiary
- dividends paid to ordinary shareholders
- VAT
- interest paid
- purchase of a copyright (intangible non-current asset)
- interest received
- issue of debenture loans
- short-term Government loans (for example Treasury Stock)

- corporation tax
- purchase of a building
- income from investments
- receipts from customers (accounts receivable)
- payments to suppliers (accounts payable)
- purchase of factory machinery
- issue of ordinary shares

Cash flow from operating activities

Receipts from customers (trade receivables)

Payments to suppliers (trade payables)

Interest paid

Corporation tax

VAT? No, because VAT is netted against the cash flow to which it relates

Cash flow from investing activities

Purchase of a copyright

Purchase of a building

Purchase of factory machinery

Sale of a subsidiary

Short-term Government loans

Interest received

Income from investments

Cash flow from financing activities

Issue of ordinary shares

Issue of debenture loans

Dividends paid to ordinary shareholders

Progress check 5.4

Explain what cash inflows and outflows are reflected within each of the three main headings in the statement of cash flows.

Figures 5.5 and 5.6 illustrate the format of the statement of cash flows, and analysis of cash and cash equivalents and bank overdrafts, and have been prepared from the balance sheet and income statement for Flatco plc included in Chapter 3 and Chapter 4 (see Figs 3.7 and 4.4). IAS 7 requires the comparative figures for the previous year to be disclosed in columns to the right of the current year's figures (although these are not shown in the Flatco illustration).

Figure 5.5	Statement of cash flows

Flatco plc
Statement of cash flows for the year ended 31 December 2010

	£000
Cash flows from operating activities	
Cash generated from operations	936
Interest paid	(71)
Income tax paid	(44)
Net cash generated from operating activities	821
Cash flows from investing activities	
Acquisition of subsidiary	–
Disposal of subsidiary	–
Purchases of tangible assets	(286)
Proceeds from sales of tangible assets	21
Purchases of intangible assets	(34)
Proceeds from sales of intangible assets	–
Purchases of investments	–
Proceeds from sales of investments	–
Loans to/from associate companies	–
Loans to/from subsidiary companies	–
Interest received	11
Dividends received	100
Net cash outflow from investing activities	(188)
Cash flows from financing activities	
Proceeds from issue of ordinary shares	200
Proceeds from borrowings	173
Repayments of borrowings	–
Dividends paid to equity shareholders	(67)
Dividends paid to minority interests	–
Net cash inflow from financing activities	306
Increase in cash and cash equivalents in the year	939
Cash and cash equivalents and bank overdrafts at beginning of year	(662)
Cash and cash equivalents and bank overdrafts at end of year	277

Figure 5.6	Analysis of cash and cash equivalents and bank overdrafts

Flatco plc
Analysis of cash and cash equivalents and bank overdrafts
as at 31 December 2010

	At 1 January 2010 £000	At 31 December 2010 £000
Cash and cash equivalents	17	327
Bank overdrafts	(679)	(50)
Cash and cash equivalents and bank overdrafts	(662)	277

Worked example 5.3

The reconciliation of profit to net cash flow from operating activities shown below is an extract from the published accounts of BAE Systems plc, which is a global defence, security and aerospace company that places very strong emphasis on research and development. In the financial year 2009 BAE Systems spent £1,153m on research and development as well as unveiling a range of new products to the market.

We can use the reconciliation to identify a number of key aspects of the company's operations during the financial year 2009.

	2009 £m	2008 £m
(Loss)/profit for the year	(45)	1,768
Taxation expense	327	603
Share of results from investments	(203)	(139)
Net financing costs	700	(653)
Depreciation and impairment	1,600	755
Gains on disposals of assets	(33)	(225)
Changes in provisions	(605)	(387)
Decrease in inventories	6	46
Decrease/(increase) in receivables	52	(5)
Increase in payables	433	246
	2,232	2,009
Interest paid	(252)	(254)
Taxation paid	(350)	(261)
Net cash inflow from operating activities	1,630	1,494

The nature of BAE Systems' business means that much of the costs it incurs can be capitalised as intangible assets. According to IAS 38, development costs are capitalised only after technical and commercial feasibility of the asset for sale or use have been established. Once these costs are capitalised the asset must be amortised over the period from which economic benefit is estimated to flow from the asset. In 2009 a number of new products came on stream and we can see the impact of this in the very high depreciation charges in 2009. In addition, some products were developed but failed to gain sufficient orders and were subsequently cancelled. £592m is attributed to such write-offs. These costs are partly responsible for the dramatic change from a £1,768m profit in 2008 to a £45m loss in 2009.

It is important for any business to maintain a healthy cash flow from operations and the great change from profit to loss may deflect from the underlying health of the company. We can see from the reconciliation above that in fact BAE turned in a very healthy £1,630m cash inflow from operating activities (partly the result of the improved sales revenues generated by the new products). The net cash inflow actually increased by £136m over 2008 despite profits falling by £1,813m.

BAE Systems is a conservatively run company and its attention to sustainable cash flows from operations can clearly be seen from the reconciliation. Indeed, the company was able to increase its dividend payment to shareholders by 10% in 2009.

The nature of BAE Systems' business means that it maintains a relatively stable level of inventory and although contract work can lead to fluctuations in the levels of working capital, it can be seen that BAE Systems maintains relatively tight control over these fluctuations.

Worked example 5.4

The extract shown below is from the leading UK supermarket retailer, Tesco plc, for the year to 28 February 2009. It is an analysis of its net debt that supports its statement of cash flows.

Figures in £m	Opening balance 1 Mar 2008	Cash flow	Closing balance 28 Feb 2009
Cash and cash equivalents	1,788	1,721	3,509
Overdrafts	–	(37)	(37)
	1,788	1,684	3,472
Short-term investments	851	2,502	3,353
Short-term loans	(2,527)	(1,427)	(3,954)
Long-term loans	(6,294)	(6,177)	(12,471)
Net debt	(6,182)	(3,418)	(9,600)

We will discuss each of the elements in this analysis and comment briefly on the cash flow movements over the year.

(a) Cash and cash equivalents have almost doubled during the year. This apparent policy of increasing balances of cash and cash equivalents may be questioned. The actual policy may be established by looking at the trends over several years and any comments made by the company in its published report and accounts, but in an industry which generates substantial amounts of cash on a daily basis there seems little reason to hold large cash balances.

(b) The short-term investments were increased substantially, possibly to take advantage of the interest rates being paid on the money markets.

(c) The company is obviously making use of short-term loans to finance the business. The users of financial information usually require information on the timing of repayments of loans (in this case the bulk of the £3,954 million short-term debt is owed to banks), which plcs are required by the Companies Act to disclose in their published reports and accounts.

(d) The most striking aspect of this analysis is the increase in long-term debt during the financial year. The company now has over £12 billion of long-term debt, which would normally be used to fund long-term projects. The company has a policy of increasing debt to exploit new opportunities and then to reduce that debt when the new opportunities begin to deliver profits.

(e) All major UK plcs provide an overview of their treasury activities in their published reports and accounts, which links current policies with the components of net debt (for example, banking facilities).

(f) The financial press sometimes comment on companies' net debt movements. These may vary from year to year and comments vary from one analyst to another. A typical comment might be 'the increase in Tesco's net debt to £9.6bn was partly to finance higher capital expenditure, including overseas investments. The level of net debt was also affected by adverse currency movements and property market weakness, which made capital-raising measures more difficult.'

The Companies Act 2006 requires group financial statements to be prepared for the holding company in addition to the financial statements that are required to be prepared for each of the individual companies within the group. These 'consolidated' financial statements exclude all transactions between companies within the group, for example, inter-company sales and purchases. Undertakings preparing consolidated financial statements should prepare a consolidated statement of cash flows and related notes; they are not then required to prepare an entity statement of cash flows, that is the holding company (parent company) in isolation.

Progress check 5.5

Explain why the statement of cash flows is so important.

Worked example 5.5

We may use the following data, extracted from the financial records of Zap Electronics plc, to prepare a statement of cash flows in compliance with the provisions of IAS 7. The data relate to the financial statements prepared for the year ended 31 July 2010.

	£000
Dividends paid on ordinary shares	49
Purchases of Government bills (short-term investments)	200
Issue of ordinary share capital	100
Reduction in inventories	25
Corporation tax paid	120
Interest paid	34
Operating profit	830
Bank and cash balance 31 July 2010	527
Purchase of machinery	459
Sales of Government bills	100
Interest received	18
Purchase of a copyright (intangible non-current asset)	78
Depreciation charge for the year	407
Purchase of a building	430
Sale of a patent (intangible non-current asset)	195
Increase in trade receivables	35
Decrease in trade payables	85
Bank and cash balance 1 August 2009	342

Zap Electronics plc
Cash generated from operations for the year ended 31 July 2010
Indirect cash flow method

	£000
Profit before tax [830 − 34 + 18]	814
Depreciation charge	407
Adjust finance (income)/costs	16
Decrease in inventories	25
Increase in trade and other receivables	(35)
Decrease in trade and other payables	(85)
Cash generated from operations	1,142
Interest paid	(34)
Income taxes paid	(120)
Net cash generated from operating activities	988

Statement of cash flows for the year ended 31 July 2010

	£000
Cash flows from operating activities	
Cash generated from operations	1,142
Interest paid	(34)
Income tax paid	(120)
Net cash generated from operating activities	988
Cash flows from investing activities	
Purchases of tangible assets [430 + 459]	(889)
Purchases of intangible assets	(78)
Proceeds from sales of intangible assets	195
Purchases of investments	(200)
Proceeds from sales of investments	100
Interest received	18
Net cash outflow from investing activities	(854)
Cash flows from financing activities	
Proceeds from issue of ordinary shares	100
Dividends paid to equity shareholders	(49)
Net cash inflow from financing activities	51
Increase in cash and cash equivalents in the year	185
Cash and cash equivalents and bank overdrafts at beginning of year	342
Cash and cash equivalents and bank overdrafts at end of year	527

**Analysis of cash and cash equivalents and bank overdrafts
as at 31 December 2010**

	At 1 August 2009 £000	At 31 July 2010 £000
Cash and cash equivalents	342	527
Bank overdrafts	–	–
Cash and cash equivalents and bank overdrafts	342	527

Worked example 5.6

**Perfecto Ltd
Income statement for the year ended 30 September 2010**

	£000
Revenue	2,279
Cost of sales	(1,484)
Gross profit	795
Distribution costs	(368)
Administrative expenses	(197)
Operating profit	230
Finance costs	(10)
Profit before tax	220
Income tax expense	(70)
Profit for the year	150

Perfecto Ltd
Balance sheet as at 30 September 2010

	2010 £000	2009 £000
Non-current assets		
Tangible	902	193
Intangible	203	1,071
Total non-current assets	1,105	1,264
Current assets		
Inventories	161	142
Trade receivables	284	193
Prepayments	295	278
Cash and cash equivalents	157	–
Total current assets	897	613
Total assets	2,002	1,877
Current liabilities		
Borrowings and finance leases	–	20
Trade payables (including income tax payable 2010: 70, 2009: 55)	277	306
Accruals	100	81
Total current liabilities	377	407
Non-current liabilities		
Borrowings and finance leases	85	126
Trade and other payables	77	184
Provisions	103	185
Total non-current liabilities	265	495
Total liabilities	642	902
Net assets	1,360	975
Equity		
Share capital	600	450
Share premium account	105	–
Retained earnings	655	525
Total equity	1,360	975

During the year Perfecto Ltd acquired new plant and machinery for £150,000, bought a patent for £10,000, and made no disposals of either tangible or intangible non-current assets.

Perfecto Ltd paid an interim dividend of £20,000 during the year and declared a final dividend of £20,000. Interest paid was £20,000 and interest received was £10,000. The company paid corporation tax of £55,000 during the year.

We have all the data required to prepare statement of cash flows and analysis of cash and cash equivalents and bank overdrafts for the year ended 30 September 2010 complying with IAS 7.

	£000
Non-current assets at the start of the year were	1,264
Additions during the year were [150 + 10]	160
Disposals during the year were	zero
	1,424
Non-current assets at the end of the year were	1,105
Therefore, depreciation for the year was	319

	30 Sep 2009 £000	30 Sep 2010 £000	Difference £000
Inventories	142	161	19 increase
Trade receivables, and prepayments	471 [193 + 278]	579 [284 + 295]	108 increase
Trade payables, accruals, and provisions	701 [306 − 55 + 81 + 184 + 185]	487 [277 − 70 + 100 + 77 + 103]	214 decrease

Perfecto Ltd
Cash generated from operations for the year ended 30 September 2010
Indirect cash flow method

	£000
Profit before tax	220
Depreciation charge	319
Adjust finance (income)/costs	10
Increase in inventories	(19)
Increase in trade and other receivables	(108)
Decrease in trade and other payables	(214)
Cash generated from operations	208
Interest paid	(20)
Income taxes paid	(55)
Net cash generated from operating activities	133

Statement of cash flows for the year ended 30 September 2010

	£000
Cash flows from operating activities	
Cash generated from operations	208
Interest paid	(20)
Income tax paid	(55)
Net cash generated from operating activities	133
Cash flows from investing activities	
Purchases of tangible assets	(150)
Purchases of intangible assets	(10)
Interest received	10
Net cash outflow from investing activities	(150)
Cash flows from financing activities	
Proceeds from issue of ordinary shares [600 + 105 − 450]	255
Repayments of borrowings [126 − 85]	(41)
Dividends paid to equity shareholders	(20)
Net cash inflow from financing activities	194
Increase in cash and cash equivalents in the year	177
Cash and cash equivalents and bank overdrafts at beginning of year	(20)
Cash and cash equivalents and bank overdrafts at end of year	157

**Analysis of cash and cash equivalents and bank overdrafts
as at 30 September 2010**

	At 30 September 2009 £000	At 30 September 2010 £000
Cash and cash equivalents	–	157
Bank overdrafts	(20)	–
Cash and cash equivalents and bank overdrafts	(20)	157

Cash flow links to the balance sheet and income statement

The diagram shown in Figure 5.7 is a simple representation of the links between cash flow and the income statement, and their relationship with the balance sheet. It shows how for example:

- a purchase of non-current assets for cash of £50 has
  - increased non-current assets in the balance sheet from the opening balance of £100 to the closing balance of £150
  - decreased the opening cash balance by £50
- a profit of £100, that has been realised in cash, has
  - increased by £100 the opening cash balance of £100 which, less the outflow of £50 for non-current assets, gives a closing balance of £150
  - increased the profit and loss account from the opening balance of £100 to the closing balance of £200.

The effect of the above transactions is:

- cash has increased by £50
- non-current assets have been increased by £50
- profit has increased by £100
- the balance sheet is still in balance with increased total assets and total liabilities.

Figure 5.7	Some simple links between cash flow and the income statement, and the balance sheet

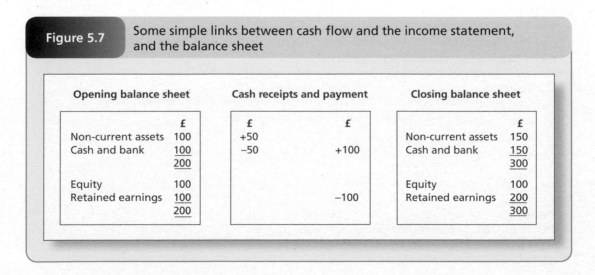

We may see from the more detailed information given as part of statement of cash flows reporting how cash flow may be appreciated in the context of the information given by the balance sheet and the income statement. IAS 7, Statement of Cash Flows, requires companies to provide two reconciliations included as part of the statement of cash flows reporting, between:

■ profit and the cash flow

and between:

■ cash and cash equivalents and bank overdrafts at the beginning and end of the accounting period,

which are provided in supporting schedules.

The reconciliation of cash flow and the income statement may be seen from profit adjusted for non-cash items and the changes in working capital to arrive at cash generated from operations.

The reconciliation of cash and cash equivalents and bank overdrafts at the beginning and end of the accounting period is a simple matter of adding the increase or decrease in cash during the accounting period to the opening balance of cash and cash equivalents and bank overdrafts to agree the closing balance of cash and cash equivalents and bank overdrafts.

Progress check 5.6

What are the schedules that are used to support the main statement of cash flows and what is their purpose?

Worked example 5.7

Detailed below are the direct method operating cash flow, indirect method operating cash flow and statement of cash flows for Ronly Bonly Jones Ltd for the month of January 2010, and its balance sheet as at 1 January 2010.

Rather than deriving a statement of cash flows from an income statement and a balance sheet this example aims to derive the following information from a statement of cash flows:

(i) revenue, costs of sales, depreciation, and expenses for the month
(ii) an income statement for the month
(iii) the changes in the balance sheet during the month from the 1 January balance sheet
(iv) a balance sheet as at 31 January 2010.

Ronly Bonly Jones Ltd
Cash generated from operations for the month ended 31 January 2010
Direct cash flow method

	£000
Operating activities	
Cash receipts from customers	632
Cash paid to suppliers	(422)
Cash paid to employees	(190)
Cash paid for other operating expenses	(55)
Cash generated from operations	(35)

Cash generated from operations for the month ended 31 January 2010
Indirect cash flow method

	£000
Operating activities	
Profit before tax	10
Depreciation charge	5
Increase in inventories	(34)
Increase in trade and other receivables	(18)
Increase in trade and other payables	2
Cash generated from operations	(35)

Statement of cash flows for the month ended 31 January 2010

	£000
Cash flows from operating activities	
Cash generated from operations	(35)
Net cash generated from operating activities	(35)
Cash flows from investing activities	
Purchases of tangible assets	(20)
Net cash outflow from investing activities	(20)
Cash flows from financing activities	
Proceeds from issue of ordinary shares	10
Net cash inflow from financing activities	10
Decrease in cash and cash equivalents in the year	(45)

Balance sheet as at 1 January 2010

	£000
Non-current assets at cost	130
Depreciation provision	(20)
Inventories	45
Trade and other receivables	64
Cash and cash equivalents	6
	225
Trade and other payables	(87)
Equity share capital	(50)
Retained earnings	(88)
	(225)

(i) We may reconcile elements of cash flow for the month with the profit for the month as follows:

	January 2010 £000
Increase in trade and other receivables during the month	18
Cash received from customers	632
Revenue for the month	650

Increase in inventories during the month	(34)	
Purchases from suppliers	424	[increase in trade and other payables 2 + cash paid to suppliers 422]

Cost of goods sold in the month	390
Depreciation charge in the month	5
Cash paid to employees	190
Cash paid for other operating expenses	55
Expenses for the month	245

(ii) Therefore:

Income statement for January 2010

	£000
Revenue	650
Cost of goods sold	(390)
Depreciation	(5)
Expenses	(245)
Profit for January	10

(iii) Let's derive the 31 January 2010 balance sheet from the information that has been provided:

Figures in £000

	Non-curr. assets	Depn.	Inventories	Trade & other rec'bles	Cash & cash equiv.	Trade & other payables	Equity share capital	Retained earnings
1 January 2010	130	(20)	45	64	6	(87)	(50)	(88)
Revenue				650				(650)
Cash from customers				(632)	632			0
Purchases			424			(424)		0
Cash to suppliers					(422)	422		0
Inventory sold			(390)					390
Depreciation		(5)						5
Expenses					(245)			245
Non-current asset additions	20				(20)			0
Issue of shares					10		(10)	0
31 January 2010	150	(25)	79	82	(39)	(89)	(60)	(98)

(iv) Therefore:

Balance sheets as at 1 January 2010 and at 31 January 2010

	1 January 2010 £000	31 January 2010 £000
Non-current assets at cost	130	150
Depreciation provision	(20)	(25)
Inventories	45	79
Trade and other receivables	64	82
Cash and cash equivalents	6	–
	225	286
Trade and other payables	(87)	(89)
Bank overdraft	–	(39)
Equity share capital	(50)	(60)
Retained earnings	(88)	(98)
	(225)	(286)

In Worked example 5.7, we have:

- used the statement of cash flows to derive the income statement for the month,

and we have then used the

- 1 January 2010 balance sheet
- income statement for the month of January 2010
- non-profit and loss items also shown in the January statement of cash flows

to derive the balance sheet for 31 January 2010.

In this way, we can see how the balance sheet, income statement and statement of cash flows of a business are inextricably linked.

Worked example 5.8

We can use the indirect cash flow analysis from Worked example 5.7 to provide an explanation to shareholders in Ronly Bonly Jones Ltd of the net cash outflow of £45,000.

During January 2010 there was a profit before depreciation of £15,000 (£10,000 + £5,000). This, together with the increase in share capital of £10,000, provided a total cash inflow for the month of £25,000. However, there was a net outflow of cash on increased working capital of £50,000 (£34,000 + £18,000 − £2,000) and capital expenditure of £20,000. This all resulted in a net cash outflow of £45,000 (£25,000 − £50,000 − £20,000).

The net cash outflow may be in line with what the company had planned or forecast for January 2010. Alternatively, the outflow may not have been expected. Changes in trading circumstances and management decisions may have been the reason for the difference between the actual and expected cash flow for January 2010.

The shareholders of Ronly Bonly Jones Ltd need to be reassured that the current cash position is temporary, and under control, and within the overdraft facility agreed with the company's bankers. The shareholders must also be reassured that the company is not in financial difficulty or that if problems are being experienced then the appropriate remedial actions are in place.

Progress check 5.7

How is the statement of cash flows of a business related to its other financial statements, the income statement and the balance sheet?

Summary of key points

■ Cash flow includes not only cash in hand but also bank deposits and bank overdrafts (which are repayable on demand) with any bank or other financial institutions.

■ The statement of cash flows lists the inflows and outflows of cash and cash equivalents for a period classified under the standard headings of: operating activities; investing activities; financing activities.

■ IAS 7 requires all reporting entities that prepare financial statements which conform with IFRSs to prepare a statement of cash flows.

■ There is only one standard format for the statement of cash flows prescribed by IAS 7, comprising a main statement of cash inflows and outflows (divided into those cash flows from operating activities, investing activities and financing activities), supported by a calculation of cash generated from operations, and an analysis of cash and cash equivalents and bank overdrafts.

■ Cash generated from operations may be derived using the direct method or the indirect method, with both methods giving the same result.

■ The statement of cash flows is directly related to both the income statement and the balance sheet and the links between them may be quantified and reconciled.

■ The preparation of the statement of cash flows is a highly objective exercise, in which all the headings and amounts are cash based and therefore easily measured.

■ The cash flow generated during an accounting period is a matter of fact and does not rely on judgement or the use of alternative conventions or valuation methods.

Assessment material

Questions

Q5.1   (i)   How would you define cash generated by a business during an accounting period?
(ii) Which International Accounting Standard (IAS) deals with cash flow?

Q5.2   Give an example of a statement of cash flows showing each of the main categories.

Q5.3   Give an example of the supporting analyses and notes that are prepared in support of the main statement of cash flows.

Q5.4   Describe the ways in which both the direct method and the indirect method may be used by a business to derive cash generated from operations during an accounting period.

Q5.5 (i) Which cash analysis is used to link the statement of cash flows to the income statement?
(ii) How does it do that?

Q5.6 (i) Which cash analysis is used to link the statement of cash flows to the balance sheet?
(ii) What are the links?

Q5.7 Why is cash so important, compared to the other assets used within a business?

Q5.8 (i) What questions does the statement of cash flows aim to answer?
(ii) How far does it go towards answering them?

Discussion points

D5.1 Why is the information disclosed in the income statement and the balance sheet not considered sufficient for users of financial information? What is so important about cash flow that it has an International Accounting Standard, IAS 7, devoted to it?

D5.2 'Forget your income statements and balance sheets, at the end of the day it's the business's healthy bank balance that is the measure of its increase in wealth.' Discuss.

Exercises

Solutions are provided in Appendix 3 to all exercise numbers highlighted in colour.

Level I

E5.1 *Time allowed – 60 minutes*

Candice-Marie James and Flossie Graham obtained a one-year lease on a small shop which cost them £15,000 for the year 2010, and in addition agreed to pay rent of £4,000 per year payable one year in advance. Candyfloss started trading on 1 January 2010 as a florist, and Candice and Flossie bought a second-hand, white delivery van for which they paid £14,500. The business was financed by Candice and Flossie each providing £9,000 from their savings, and receipt of an interest-free loan from Candice's uncle of £3,000. Candice and Flossie thought they were doing OK over their first six months but they weren't sure how to measure this. They decided to try and see how they were doing financially and looked at the transactions for the first six months:

Cash transactions:

	£
Cash sales of flowers	76,000
Rent paid	4,000
Wages paid	5,000
Payments for other operating expenses	7,000
Purchases of inventories of flowers for resale	59,500
Legal expenses paid for the lease acquisition	1,000

In addition, at 30 June 2010:

The business owed a further £4,000 for the purchase of flowers and £1,000 for other operating expenses.

Customers had purchased flowers on credit and the sum still owed amounted to £8,000.

One customer was apparently in financial difficulties and it was likely that the £1,500 owed would not be paid.

Inventories of flowers at 30 June 2010 valued at cost were £9,500.

They estimated that the van would last four years, at which time they expected to sell it for £2,500, and that depreciation would be spread evenly over that period.

> (i) Prepare a statement of cash flows for Candyfloss for the first six months of the year 2010 using the direct method.
> (ii) Prepare an income statement for Candyfloss for the first six months of the year 2010, on an accruals basis.
> (iii) Why is the profit different from the cash flow?
> (iv) Which statement gives the best indication of the first six months' performance of Candyfloss?

E5.2   *Time allowed – 60 minutes*

> Using the information from Exercise E5.1 prepare a statement of cash flows for Candyfloss for the first six months of the year 2010, using the indirect method.

E5.3   *Time allowed – 60 minutes*

Jaffrey Packaging plc have used the following information in the preparation of their financial statements for the year ended 31 March 2010.

	£000
Dividends paid	25
Issue of a debenture loan	200
Reduction in inventories	32
Corporation tax paid	73
Interest paid	28
Operating profit for the year	450
Cash and cash equivalents 31 March 2010	376
Purchase of factory equipment	302
Dividends payable at 31 March 2010	25
Interest received	5
Depreciation charge for the year	195
Purchase of a new large computer system	204
Sale of a patent (intangible non-current asset)	29
Increase in trade and other receivables	43
Reduction in trade and other payables	62
Cash and cash equivalents 1 April 2009	202

> You are required to prepare a cash generated from operations statement for Jaffrey Packaging Ltd using the indirect method, and a statement of cash flows for the year ended 31 March 2010 in compliance with the provisions of IAS 7, and also an analysis of cash and cash equivalents for the same period.

E5.4   *Time allowed – 60 minutes*

> From the income statement for the year ended 31 December 2010 and balance sheets as at 31 December 2009 and 31 December 2010, and the additional information shown below, prepare a statement of cash flows for Medco Ltd for the year to 31 December 2010.

Income statement	2010
	£
Operating profit	2,500
Interest paid	(100)
Profit before tax	2,400
Income tax paid	(500)
Profit for the year	1,900

Balance sheet as at 31 December	2010	2009
	£	£
Non-current assets	28,000	20,000
Current assets		
Inventories	6,000	5,000
Trade and other receivables	4,000	3,000
Investments	5,100	3,000
Cash and cash equivalents	2,150	5,000
Total current assets	17,250	16,000
Total assets	45,250	36,000
Current liabilities		
Borrowings and finance leases	(6,000)	(2,000)
Trade and other payables	(4,000)	(6,000)
Current tax liabilities	(500)	(400)
Dividend (proposed)	(600)	(450)
Total current liabilities	(11,100)	(8,850)
Non-current liabilities		
Borrowings and finance leases	(2,000)	(1,000)
Total liabilities	(13,100)	(9,850)
Net assets	32,150	26,150
Equity		
Ordinary share capital	14,000	10,000
Share premium account	6,000	5,000
Retained earnings	12,150	11,150
Total equity	32,150	26,150

During the year 2010 the company:

(a) acquired new non-current assets that cost £12,500
(b) issued new share capital for £5,000
(c) sold non-current assets for £2,000 that had originally cost £3,000 and had a net book value of £2,500
(d) depreciated its non-current assets by £2,000
(e) paid an interim dividend of £300,000 during the year and proposed a final dividend of £600,000.

Level II

E5.5   *Time allowed – 90 minutes*

Llareggyb Ltd started business on 1 January 2010 and its year ended 31 December 2010. Llareggyb entered into the following transactions during the year.

Received funds for share capital of £25,000

Paid suppliers of materials £44,000

Purchased 11,000 units of a product at £8 per unit, which were sold to customers at £40 per unit

Paid heating and lighting costs for cash £16,000

Further heating and lighting costs of £2,400 were incurred within the year, but still unpaid at 31 December 2010

Mr D Thomas loaned the company £80,000 on 1 January 2010 at 8% interest per annum

Loan interest was paid to Mr Thomas for January to June 2010

8,000 product units were sold to customers during 2010

Customers paid £280,000 to Llareggyb for sales of its products

Rent on the premises £60,000 was paid for 18 months from 1 January 2010, and local business property taxes of £9,000 were also paid for the same period

Salaries and wages were paid for January to November 2010 amounting to £132,000 but the December payroll cost of £15,000 had not yet been paid as at 31 December 2010

A lorry was purchased for £45,000 on 1 January 2010 and was expected to last for five years after which it was estimated that it could be sold for £8,000

The company uses the straight line method of depreciation.

> **You are required to:**
>
> (i)   prepare a balance sheet for Llareggyb Ltd as at 31 December 2010.
> (ii) prepare a statement of cash flows for Llareggyb Ltd for the year ended 31 December 2010.
>
> (Note: you may use the profit or loss figure calculated in Exercise E4.7 to complete this exercise.)

E5.6   *Time allowed – 90 minutes*

The balance sheets for Victoria plc as at 30 June 2009 and 30 June 2010 are shown below:

Victoria plc
Balance sheet as at 30 June

	£000	£000
	2009	**2010**
Non-current assets		
Cost	6,900	9,000
Depreciation provision	900	1,100
Total non-current assets	6,000	7,900
Current assets		
Inventories	2,600	4,000
Trade and other receivables	2,000	2,680
Cash and cash equivalents	200	–
Total current assets	4,800	6,680
Total assets	10,800	14,580

Current liabilities

Borrowings and finance leases	–	600
Trade and other payables	2,000	1,800
Current tax liabilities	300	320
Dividend payable	360	480
Total current liabilities	2,660	3,200
Non-current liabilities		
Borrowings and finance leases	1,000	1,000
Total liabilities	3,660	4,200
Net assets	7,140	10,380
Equity		
Ordinary share capital	4,000	5,500
Share premium account	–	1,240
Retained earnings	3,140	3,640
Total equity	7,140	10,380

The following information is also relevant:

1. During the years 2009 and 2010 Victoria plc disposed of no non-current assets.
2. Interim dividends were not paid during the years ended 30 June 2009 and 2010.
3. Non-current liabilities borrowing is a 10% £1m debenture and loan interest was paid on 10 February in each year.

You are required to:

(i) Calculate:

 (a) profit before tax for the year ended 30 June 2010
 (b) operating profit for the year ended 30 June 2010

(ii) Prepare for Victoria plc for the year to 30 June 2010 a statement of cash generated from operations using the indirect method, and a statement of cash flows for the year ended 30 June 2010 in compliance with IAS 7, and also an analysis of cash and cash equivalents for the same period.

E5.7 *Time allowed – 90 minutes*

Sparklers plc have completed the preparation of their income statement for the year ended 31 October 2010 and their balance sheet as at 31 October 2010. During the year Sparklers sold some non-current assets for £2m that had originally cost £11m. The cumulative depreciation on those assets at 31 October 2009 was £7.6m.

You have been asked to prepare a statement of cash flows for the year ended 31 October 2010 in compliance with IAS 7. The directors are concerned about the large bank overdraft at 31 October 2010, which they believe is due mainly to the increase in trade receivables as a result of apparently poor credit control. What is your assessment of the reasons for the increased short-term borrowings?

Sparklers plc
Income statement for the year ended 31 October 2010

	£m	£m
	2010	**2009**
Operating profit	41.28	18.80
Interest paid	(0.56)	–
Interest received	0.08	0.20
Profit before tax	40.80	19.00
Income tax expense	(10.40)	(6.40)
Profit for the year	30.40	12.60
Dividends:		
Preference paid	(0.20)	(0.20)
Ordinary: interim paid	(4.00)	(2.00)
final proposed	(12.00)	(6.00)
Retained profit for the year	14.20	4.40

Sparklers plc
Balance sheet as at 31 October 2010

	2010	2009
	£m	£m
Non-current assets		
Tangible at cost	47.80	35.20
Depreciation provision	(21.50)	(19.00)
Total non-current assets	26.30	16.20
Current assets		
Inventories	30.00	10.00
Trade and other receivables	54.20	17.80
Cash and cash equivalents	–	1.20
Total current assets	84.20	29.00
Total assets	110.50	45.20
Current liabilities		
Borrowings and finance leases	32.40	–
Trade and other payables	22.00	13.60
Dividends payable	12.00	6.00
Income tax payable	10.40	6.40
Total current liabilities	76.80	26.00
Non-current liabilities		
Debenture loan	1.50	1.20
Total liabilities	78.30	27.20
Net assets	32.20	18.00
Equity		
Ordinary share capital – £1 ordinary shares	10.00	10.00
Preference share capital – £1 preferences shares 10%	2.00	2.00
Retained earnings	20.20	6.00
Total equity	32.20	18.00

E5.8 *Time allowed – 90 minutes*

Dimarian plc's income statement for the year ended 31 December 2010, and its balance sheets as at 31 December 2010 and 2009, are shown below. Dimarian plc issued no new ordinary shares during the year.

During 2010 Dimarian plc spent £100,000 on non-current assets additions. There were no non-current assets disposals during 2010.

Dimarian plc
Income statement for the year ended 31 December 2010

Figures in £000

Revenue	850
Cost of sales	(500)
Gross profit	350
Distribution costs and administrative expenses	(120)
	230
Other operating income	20
Operating profit	250
Interest paid	(30)
	220
Interest received	10
Profit before tax	230
Income tax expense	(50)
Profit for the year	180
Retained profit 1 January 2010	230
	410
Proposed dividends	(80)
Retained earnings 31 December 2010	330

Dimarian plc
Balance sheet as at 31 December 2010

Figures in £000	2010	2009
Non-current assets		
Tangible	750	800
Intangible	40	50
Total non-current assets	790	850
Current assets		
Inventories	50	60
Trade and other receivables	190	200
Cash and cash equivalents	20	10
Total current assets	260	270
Total assets	1,050	1,120

Current liabilities

Borrowings and finance leases	20	10
Trade and other payables	70	80
Dividends payable	80	70
Income tax payable	50	30
Total current liabilities	220	190
Non-current liabilities		
Debenture loan	100	300
Total liabilities	320	490
Net assets	730	630
Equity		
Share capital	260	260
Share premium account	50	50
Revaluation reserve	90	90
Retained earnings	330	230
Total equity	730	630

You are required to prepare:

(i) An indirect statement of cash flows for the year to 31 December 2010.

(ii) A statement of cash flows for the year ended 31 December 2010, in the format required by IAS 7.

(iii) An analysis of cash and cash equivalents for the years ended 31 December 2009 and 31 December 2010.

6

Corporate governance

Contents

Learning objectives

Completion of this chapter will enable you to:

- describe the agency problem and how the framework for establishing good corporate governance and accountability has been established in the UK Corporate Governance Code, developed from the work of the Cadbury, Greenbury, Hampel and Turnbull Committees

- explain the statutory requirement for the audit of limited companies, the election by shareholders of suitably qualified, independent auditors, and the role of the auditors

- outline directors' specific responsibility to shareholders, and responsibilities to society in general, for the management and conduct of companies

- recognise the fiduciary duties that directors have to the company, and their duty of care to all stakeholders and to the community at large, particularly with regard to the Companies Act 2006, Health and Safety at Work Act 1974, Health and Safety (Offences) Act 2008, and Financial Services Act 1986

- explain the implications for companies and their directors that may arise from the UK Government's newly-enacted legislation on the issue of corporate manslaughter

- appreciate the importance of directors' duties regarding insolvency, the Insolvency Act 1986 and the Enterprise Act 2002

- consider the implications for directors of wrongful trading, and recognise the difference between this and the offence of fraudulent trading, and the possibility of criminal penalties

- outline the implication for directors of the Company Directors Disqualification Act 1986

- explain the actions that directors of companies should take to ensure compliance with their obligations and responsibilities, and to protect themselves against possible non-compliance.

Introduction

In Chapter 8 we will see that a large part of Johnson Matthey Plc's report and accounts 2010 is devoted to the subject of corporate governance, the systems by which companies are directed and controlled. This chapter turns to the statutory and non-statutory rules that surround the accounting for limited companies.

In earlier chapters we discussed the way in which the limited company exists in perpetuity as a legal entity, separate from the lives of those individuals who both own and manage it. The limited company has many rights, responsibilities and liabilities in the same way as individual people. As a separate legal entity the company is responsible for its own liabilities. These liabilities are not the obligations of the shareholders who have paid for their shares, this being the limit of their obligations to the company.

The directors of a limited company are appointed by, and are responsible to, the shareholders for the management of the company, maintained through their regular reporting on the activities of the business. The responsibilities of directors, however, are wider than to just the shareholders. They are also responsible for acting correctly towards their employees, suppliers and customers, and to the public at large. Indeed these responsibilities are considered so vital that the Companies Act 2006 introduces the legal requirement that 'a director of a company must exercise reasonable care, skill and diligence'.

The annual audit of the accounts is a statutory requirement for all limited companies, excluding smaller limited companies. As with directors, the auditors of a limited company are also appointed by, and are responsible to, the shareholders. Their primary responsibility is to make an objective report to shareholders and others as to whether, in their opinion, the financial statements show a true and fair view, and compliance with statutory, regulatory and accounting standard requirements. Therefore, the management and regulation of a company as a separate legal entity lies with the directors and the auditors. The directors are within, and part of, the company, and the auditors are external to, and not part of, the company.

This chapter will look at roles and responsibilities of directors and auditors. It will also consider the obligations of directors, who are the agents of the shareholders (who are the principals). We will consider this agent–principal relationship and where it breaks down – the agency problem – and particularly with regard to the UK Corporate Governance Code, and the many Acts that are now in place to regulate the behaviour of directors of limited companies. The chapter closes with a look at some of the steps that directors may take to protect themselves against possible non-compliance.

The agency problem

Shareholder wealth maximisation is the primary objective of a business, reflected in increases in share prices and dividends. But can we assume that the managers and **directors** of the business are making decisions and taking actions that are consistent with the objective of maximising shareholder wealth? Certainly managers and directors should make decisions consistent with the objective of shareholder wealth maximisation, because that is what they are appointed to do by the shareholders. In practice, this may not actually happen, because their goals may be different and they may be seeking to enhance their status, secure their positions, or maximise their own wealth rather than that of the shareholders.

The agency problem occurs when directors and managers are not acting in the best interests of shareholders. Directors and managers of a company run the business day to day and have access to internal management accounting information and financial reports, but shareholders only see the external annual and six-monthly reports. Annual and interim reporting may also, of course, be subject to manipulation by management.

The agency problem of directors not acting in the best interests of shareholders may be seen in, for example:

- a high retention of profits and cash by directors to provide a cushion for easier day-to-day management of operations, rather than for investment in new projects
- an unwillingness by directors to invest in risky projects in line with shareholders' required returns, because of fear of failure and possibly losing their jobs, particularly if they are close to retirement age and wish to protect their pension benefits
- receipt of high salaries, benefits and perks by directors and chief executives, regardless of how well, or not, the business has performed
- participation by directors and managers in profit or eps-related bonus and incentive schemes, which encourage short-term profit maximisation rather than creation of shareholder wealth.

Why should the agency problem exist? Well, it is management who are in the position, and who have the opportunity, to pursue the maximisation of their own wealth without detection by the owners of the business. Additionally, both financial analysts and managers and directors of companies have an obsession with profit as the measure of financial performance. This is despite the fact that profit is a totally subjective measure and that it is future cash flows and not short-term profit from which the real value of a business is determined.

A growth in profit does not necessarily translate into a sustained increase in shareholder wealth. For example, diversified multinational companies, conglomerates, have in the past acquired many businesses to effectively 'buy' additional profits. This has invariably not resulted in an increase in the share prices of such conglomerates.

The agency problem manifests itself through a conflict of interest. There may be different views about risks and returns, for example. The shareholders may be interested in the long term, whereas the rewards paid to managers, for example, may be based on short-term performance. To address the agency problem between agents and principals – managers and shareholders – a number of initiatives may be implemented to encourage the achievement of goal congruence:

- audit of results
- reporting of manager performance
- work shadowing of managers and directors
- the use of external analysts.

Worked example 6.1

Directors of companies are concerned with the important issues of agency-related problems and their impact. What is the basis of discussions they may have to consider what actions they may implement to try and minimise the impact of such problems?

Their discussions may include the following:

- The agency problem emerges when directors or managers make decisions that are inconsistent with the objective of shareholder wealth maximisation.
- There are a number of alternative approaches a company can adopt to minimise the possible impact of such a problem, which may differ from company to company. In general, such approaches would range between:
  - the encouragement of goal congruence between shareholders and managers through the monitoring of managerial behaviour and the assessment of management decision outcomes and
  - the enforcement of goal congruence between shareholders and managers through the incorporation of formalised obligations and conditions of employment into management contracts.

Any such approach would invariably be associated with some form of remuneration package to include an incentive scheme to reward managers, such as performance-related pay, or executive share options.

Progress check 6.1

What are the conflicts that may arise between the directors and the shareholders of a business?

In addition to the agency problem relating to the directors and shareholders of a company, there may be a conflict between shareholders, and the lenders to a company, who may try to exploit their relationship with lenders. The agency problem here is that shareholders may prefer the use of debt for investments by the company in new high-risk projects. Shareholders then subsequently benefit from the rewards gained from the success of such investments, but it is the debt holders (lenders) who bear the risk. Debt holders may protect their interests by having security over specific assets or the assets in general of the company. They may also include restrictive covenants in their loan agreements with the company, for example with regard to decision-making, and levels of debt taken on the company.

Outline how the agency problem may occur between the shareholders, directors and lenders of a business.

There has been an increasing influence of institutional investors in the UK, which to some degree has helped in dealing with the agency problem. Institutional shareholders like banks, pension funds and fund management companies have been getting tougher with companies who do not comply with the appropriate standards of behaviour, and in particular with the appropriate **corporate** **governance** requirements.

Corporate governance is concerned with the relationship between company management, its directors, and its owners, the shareholders. It is the structure and the mechanisms by which the owners of the business 'govern' the management or the directors of the business. Its importance has been highlighted as a result of the increasing concern about the conduct of companies, following the spate of financial scandals, but also by concerns about senior executive remuneration.

Corporate governance code of practice

Concerns about financial reporting and accountability, and the impact on the business community (see Fig. 6.1), grew during the 1980s following increasing numbers of company failures and financial scandals.

Figure 6.1   The business community

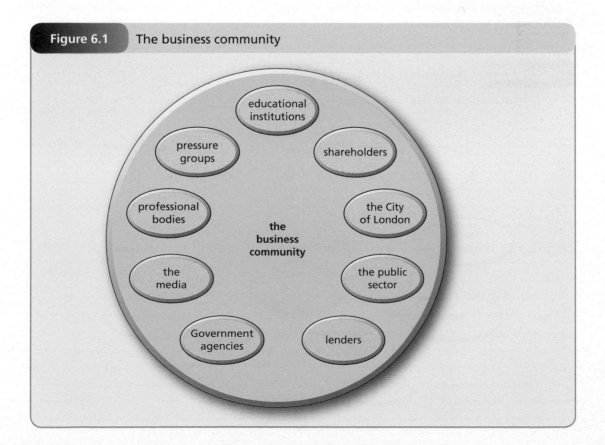

During the 1980s and 1990s there was huge concern within the business community following the financial scandals surrounding for example Polly Peck (1990), the Robert Maxwell companies (1991), BCCI (1991), and Barings Bank – Nick Leeson (1995).

The concerns increased as we saw in the 2000s even larger scandals involving companies such as Enron (2001), Marconi (2001), WorldCom (2002) and Parmalat (2004) and particularly the involvement of the consulting arms of major accounting firms like Arthur Andersen. These concerns resulted in a growing lack of confidence in financial reporting, and in shareholders and others being unable to rely on auditors to provide the necessary safeguards for their reliance on company annual reports.

The main factors underlying the lack of confidence in financial reporting were:

- loose accounting standards, which allowed considerable latitude (an example has been the treatment of extraordinary items and exceptional items in financial reporting)
- lack of a clear framework to ensure directors were able to continuously review business controls
- competitive pressure within companies and on auditors, making it difficult for auditors to maintain independence from demanding boards
- lack of apparent accountability regarding directors' remuneration and compensation for loss of office.

The Cadbury Committee, chaired by Sir Adrian Cadbury, was set up in May 1991 by the Financial Reporting Council, the London Stock Exchange, and the accounting profession, to address these concerns and make recommendations on good practice.

The Cadbury Committee defined corporate governance (see Fig. 6.2) as 'the system by which companies are directed and controlled. Boards of directors are responsible for the governance of their companies. The shareholders' role in governance is to appoint the directors and the auditors and to satisfy themselves that an appropriate governance structure is in place. The responsibilities of the board include setting the company's strategic aims, providing the leadership to put them into effect, supervising the management of the business and reporting to shareholders on their stewardship. The board's actions are subject to laws, regulations and the shareholders in general meeting.'

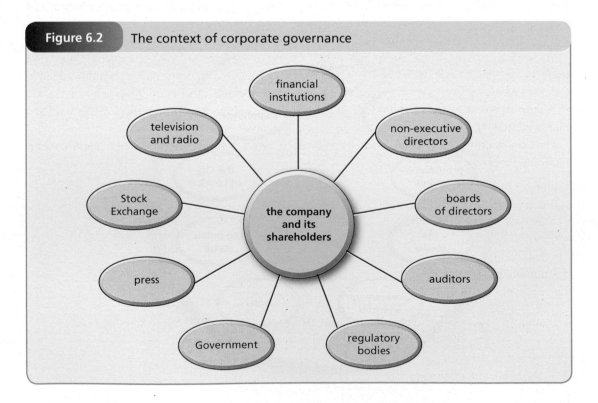

Figure 6.2 **The context of corporate governance**

The financial aspects within the framework described by Cadbury are the ways in which the company's board sets financial policy and oversees its implementation, the use of financial controls, and how the board reports on activities and progress of the company to shareholders.

The framework for establishing good corporate governance and accountability set up by the Cadbury Committee was formulated as the Committee's Code of Best Practice, published in December 1992. This provided a benchmark against which to assess compliance. The Cadbury Code was updated in 1998 by the **Hampel Committee**, to include their own Committee's work, and the Greenbury Committee report on directors' remuneration (published July 1995). In September 1999 the Turnbull Committee report on *Internal Control: Guidance for Directors on the Combined Code* was published by the ICAEW.

In May 2000 the original Cadbury Code and subsequent reports were all consolidated by the Committee on Corporate Governance and published in the **Combined Code of Practice**.

The underlying principles of the Code are:

- openness
- integrity
- accountability.

Openness

Openness from companies is constrained within the limits of their competitive position but is the basis for the confidence that needs to exist between business and all those who have a stake in its success. Openness in disclosure of information adds to the effectiveness of the market economy. It forces boards to take action and allows shareholders and others to be able to look more closely and thoroughly into companies.

Integrity

Integrity means straightforward dealing and completeness. Financial reporting should be honest and present a balanced view of the state of the company's affairs. The integrity of the company's reports will depend on the integrity of the people responsible for preparing and presenting them.

The annual reports and financial statements of the majority of UK plcs now include a section headed *Corporate Governance*. These sections of the annual reports are required to aim to comply with provisions set out in a Combined Code of Practice (principles of good governance and code of best practice), embracing the principles of the Cadbury, Greenbury and Hampel Committees, appended to the Listing Rules of the London Stock Exchange.

The corporate governance section of a company's annual report and accounts should contain details under the following headings:

- directors' biographies
- board responsibilities
- board composition and functions
- board committees
  - audit committee
  - nomination committee
  - remuneration committee
  - IT committee
  - capital expenditure committee
  - **non-executive directors'** committee
- directors' remuneration
- relations with shareholders

- internal financial control
- incentive compensation
- directors' pensions
- corporate strategy.

This may not be a complete list but it gives a broad indication of the areas of compliance under the Combined Code of Practice. This compliance can be seen as set out in the annual reports and accounts of UK plcs.

Accountability

Accountability of boards of directors to their shareholders requires the commitment from both to make the accountability effective. Boards of directors must play their part by ensuring the quality of information that is provided to shareholders. Shareholders must exercise their responsibilities as owners of the business. The major investing institutions (for example, pension funds and insurance companies) are in regular contact with the directors of UK plcs to discuss past, current and future performance.

Subsequent to 1998, further reviews of various aspects of corporate governance were set up:

- *Review of the role and effectiveness of non-executive directors*, by Derek Higgs and published January 2003
- *Audit Committees Combined Code guidance*, by a group led by Sir Robert Smith and published January 2003.

The above reviews were undertaken during a period in which investor confidence had been badly shaken both by lapses in corporate governance and by the high-profile failure of some corporate strategies, and were very much in response to these events. The reviews were reflected in a revision to the 2000 Combined Code of Practice, which was published by the Financial Reporting Council (FRC) in July 2003 – the Combined Code on Corporate Governance.

The Combined Code on Corporate Governance was revised by the FRC several times up to June 2008. Following an extensive consultation process, in June 2010 the FRC issued a new code of corporate governance entitled the **UK Corporate Governance Code**. This Code was to be effective for the financial years beginning after 29 June 2010.

The consultation was initiated by the world-wide financial crisis. The FRC, whilst it acknowledges the quality of the Combined Code, highlight an increasing problem within organisations in that 'it seems that there is almost a belief that complying with the Code in itself constitutes good governance'. The FRC, therefore, insists that to 'follow the spirit of the Code to good effect, boards must think deeply, thoroughly and on a continuing basis, about their overall tasks and the implications of these for the roles of their individual members'. The new Code then follows a 'comply or explain' approach to corporate governance that was introduced by the Cadbury Committee, and concentrates on developing sound mechanisms which the FRC believes to be central to effectively following the five key principles of corporate governance. These five key principles, which all listed companies must report to shareholders on how they have applied them, are: leadership; effectiveness; accountability; remuneration; relations with shareholders.

Companies listed on the London Stock Exchange are requested to comply with the Code, but other companies may also benefit from compliance. It is not compulsory for any company, but rather a target of best practice to aim for. The Combined Code on Corporate Governance also promoted the 'comply or explain' approach. This meant that companies listed on the London Stock Exchange were required to include in their annual report and accounts a statement to confirm that they had complied with the relevant provisions throughout the accounting period, or to provide an explanation if that were not the case.

Progress check 6.3

What is corporate governance and how is it implemented?

Let's take a look at the Johnson Matthey section on corporate governance, included in pages 40 to 42 and pages 46 to 57 of their report and accounts 2010, and reproduced on pages 192–206 of this book. This section includes the corporate governance report itself, and the audit committee report, remuneration committee report, remuneration of the directors, and the responsibility of the directors' report. The company states that 'The group was in compliance with the provisions of the Code throughout the year'.

A number of the headings required as part of corporate governance reporting are not included within Johnson Matthey Plc's main corporate governance report, but are shown elsewhere in the report and accounts. For example, the composition and functions of the board, and directors' biographies are shown on pages 38 to 39 of the report and accounts 2010, and are not reproduced in this book.

Worked example 6.2

What are the basic problems that may be encountered by shareholders with small shareholdings as they enter a new relationship with the company they effectively part-own?

Most of the major UK plcs are owned by both individual and institutional shareholders. Some shareholders have large shareholdings, and some have small shareholdings, the analysis of which can be found in their companies' annual reports and accounts.

Usually within a very short time of acquiring their shares, most new small shareholders realise they have neither influence nor power.

As plcs have increasingly engaged in wider ranges of activities and become global businesses, so their directors have become more and more distanced from their shareholders. Compare the large multinational banks, for example, with locally based building societies.

During the move towards growth and expansion by companies, particularly during the 1980s, considerable disquiet regarding accountability emerged in the business community. In response to this the UK Government appointed the Committee on the Financial Aspects of Corporate Governance (Cadbury Committee), which produced its report in December 1992.

At the same time, there was also a great deal of unease regarding remuneration, bonus schemes, option schemes and contracts. Various other committees on corporate governance, subsequent to Cadbury, such as the Greenbury, Hampel and Turnbull committees, have reviewed each of these areas.

Non-executive directors are represented on all Johnson Matthey's main committees, except the chief executive's committee. The company does not appear to have an information technology (IT) committee or a capital expenditure committee, and so IT and capital expenditure are presumably the responsibility of the chief executive's committee.

The importance of **corporate social responsibility (CSR)** is emphasised in the business review section of the report and accounts 2010 headed sustainability on pages 28 to 37 and reproduced in this book on pages 320 to 329 (see Chapter 8).

Together with the section covering corporate governance, the reports of Johnson Matthey Plc's nomination committee, audit committee, remuneration committee, and the sustainability report are included in this book for reference.

CORPORATE GOVERNANCE

Statement of Compliance with the Combined Code

This statement describes how the Main Principles of the Combined Code on Corporate Governance, issued by the Financial Reporting Council dated June 2008 (the Code), have been applied.

During the year ended 31st March 2010, the company has complied with all relevant provisions set out in Section 1 of the Code throughout the year except the following:

- A.3.2 – At least half the board, excluding the chairman, should comprise non-executive directors determined by the board to be independent.

  During the period from 22nd June 2009, following the appointment of Mr R J MacLeod as Group Finance Director designate, to 21st July 2009, the board comprised five independent non-executive directors and six executive directors and therefore less than half of the board comprised independent non-executive directors. On 21st July 2009, following the retirement of Dr P N Hawker and Mr D W Morgan from the board and the appointment of Mr W F Sandford as an executive director, the number of executive directors was reduced to five. Since the retirement of Mr J N Sheldrick as Group Finance Director on 7th September 2009, more than half of the board has comprised independent non-executive directors. The board considers the one month period of non-compliance with this provision to be immaterial and was necessary in order to ensure orderly board succession.

- D.1.1 – The senior independent director should attend sufficient meetings with a range of major shareholders to listen to their views in order to help develop a balanced understanding of the issues and concerns of major shareholders.

  During the year the board has taken the view that it is not necessarily practical, efficient or desired by shareholders for the Senior Independent Director to attend meetings with major shareholders in order to learn their issues and concerns unless such discussions are requested by shareholders. The methods by which major shareholders' views are communicated to the board as a whole are discussed under 'Relations with Shareholders' on page 41.

Directors and the Board

The board is responsible to the company's shareholders for the group's system of corporate governance, its strategic objectives and the stewardship of the company's resources and is ultimately responsible for social, environmental and ethical matters. The board held seven meetings in the year and in addition met separately to review the group's long term strategy. The board delegates specific responsibilities to board committees, as described below. The board reviews the key activities of the business and receives papers and presentations to enable it to do so effectively. The Company Secretary is responsible to the board, and is available to individual directors, in respect of board procedures.

The board comprises the Chairman, the Chief Executive, three other executive directors and five independent non-executive directors. Mr N A P Carson is the Chief Executive. Sir John Banham is the Chairman. Sir John's other commitments are disclosed on page 38. The roles of Chairman and Chief Executive are separate. The Chairman leads the board, ensuring that each director, particularly each non-executive director, is able to make an effective contribution. He monitors, with assistance from the Company Secretary, the information distributed to the board to ensure that it is sufficient, accurate, timely and clear. The Chief Executive maintains day-to-day management responsibility for the company's operations, implementing group strategies and policies agreed by the board.

The role of non-executive directors, who are appointed for specified terms subject to re-election and to Companies Acts provisions relating to the removal of a director, is to enhance independence and objectivity of the board's deliberations and decisions. Mr A M Thomson is the Senior Independent Director. Each non-executive director is considered by the board to be independent in character and

judgment and there are no relationships or circumstances which are likely to affect, or could appear to affect, the director's judgment.

The executive directors have specific responsibilities, which are detailed on pages 38 and 39, and have direct responsibility for all operations and activities.

In accordance with the company's Articles of Association, all directors submit themselves for re-election at least once every three years. The board composition allows for changes to be made with minimum disruption.

Regular business presentations from senior managers at board meetings assist the non-executive directors in familiarising themselves with the group's businesses. The board also usually holds at least one board meeting per year at one of the group's operational sites and takes the opportunity to tour the site and discuss issues with local senior and middle management. During the year ended 31st March 2010 the board visited the new methanol synthesis catalyst manufacturing plant in Clitheroe, UK and the Emission Control Technologies' manufacturing facilities in Royston, UK. Individual non-executive directors also undertake site visits. Such presentations, meetings and site visits help to give a balanced overview of the company. They enable the non-executive directors to build an understanding of the company's businesses, the markets in which the company operates and its main relationships and to build a link with the company's employees. This is important in helping the non-executive directors to continually develop and refresh their knowledge and skills to ensure that their contribution to the board remains informed and relevant. Account is taken of environmental, social and governance matters in the training of directors.

During the year the board undertook a formal evaluation of its performance and the performance of its committees and the individual directors. The Deputy Company Secretary conducted face to face interviews with each individual director based on a standard questionnaire. The interviews focused on the operation of the board and its committees and on individual directors' contributions. Separately, the Chairman held a series of one to one discussions with each director to provide them with an opportunity to expand on their responses, to raise any broader issues and to review their performance. A report was prepared on the findings of these interviews and it also contained a number of recommendations designed to ensure that the current high standards of governance and processes were maintained. The report has been considered by the board and the board approved its recommendations. The report concluded that the board and its committees continue to work effectively.

Led by the Senior Independent Director, the non-executive directors met without the Chairman present to appraise the Chairman's performance, taking into account the views of the executive directors.

Committees of the Board

The Chief Executive's Committee is responsible for the recommendation to the board of strategic and operating plans and on decisions reserved to the board where appropriate. It is also responsible for the executive management of the group's business. The Committee is chaired by the Chief Executive and meets monthly (except in August). During the year it comprised the executive directors and six senior executives of the company.

The Audit Committee is a committee of the board whose purpose is to assist the board in the effective discharge of its responsibilities for financial reporting and corporate control. The Audit Committee meets quarterly and is chaired by Mr A M Thomson. It comprises all the independent non-executive directors with the group Chairman, the Chief Executive, the Group Finance Director and the external and internal auditors attending by invitation. A report from the Audit Committee on its activities is given on page 47. Mr Thomson has recent and relevant financial experience as former Finance Director of Smiths Group plc and currently as President of the Institute of Chartered Accountants of Scotland.

CORPORATE GOVERNANCE

Committees of the Board (continued)

Attendance at the board and board committee meetings in 2009/10 was as follows:

Director	Full Board		MDRC		Nomination Committee		Audit Committee	
	Eligible to attend	Attended	Eligible to attend	Attended	Eligible to attend	Attended	Eligible to attend	Attended
Sir John Banham	7	7	4	4	2	2	–	4[1]
N A P Carson	7	7	–	4[1]	–	2[1]	–	4[1]
Sir Thomas Harris	7	7	4	4	2	2	4	4
P N Hawker	3	3	–	–	–	–	–	–
R J MacLeod	5	5	–	–	–	–	–	3[1]
D W Morgan	3	3	–	–	–	–	–	–
L C Pentz	7	7	–	–	–	–	–	–
M J Roney	7	7	4	4	2	2	4	4
W F Sandford	5	5	–	–	–	–	–	–
J N Sheldrick	3	3	–	–	–	–	–	2[1]
D C Thompson	7	6[2]	4	4	2	2	4	4
A M Thomson	7	7	4	4	2	2	4	4
R J W Walvis	7	7	4	4	2	1	4	4

Notes

[1] Includes meetings attended by invitation for all or part of meeting.

[2] Absence due to illness.

The Nomination Committee is a committee of the board responsible for advising the board and making recommendations on the appointment and, if necessary, dismissal of executive and non-executive directors. The Nomination Committee is chaired by Sir John Banham, the group Chairman, and also comprises all the independent non-executive directors. A report from the Nomination Committee on its activities is given on page 46.

The Management Development and Remuneration Committee (MDRC) is a committee of the board which determines on behalf of the board the fair remuneration of the executive directors and the Chairman and assists the board in ensuring that the current and future senior management of the group are recruited, developed and remunerated in an appropriate fashion. The MDRC is chaired by Mr R J W Walvis and comprises all the independent non-executive directors together with the group Chairman. The Chief Executive and the Director of Human Resources attend by invitation except when their own performance and remuneration are discussed. Further details are set out in the Remuneration Report on pages 48 to 56.

Directors' Remuneration

The Remuneration Report on pages 48 to 56 includes details of remuneration policies and of the remuneration of the directors.

Relations with Shareholders

The board considers effective communication with shareholders, whether institutional investors, private or employee shareholders, to be extremely important.

The company reports formally to shareholders when its full year and half year results are published. These results are posted on Johnson Matthey's website (www.matthey.com). At the same time, executive directors give presentations on the results to institutional investors, analysts and the media in London and other international centres. Live audiocasts of the results presentations in London are available on the company's website and copies of major presentations are also posted on the company's website.

The company's Annual General Meeting takes place in London and formal notification is sent to shareholders at least 20 working days in advance of the meeting. The directors are available for questions, formally during the Annual General Meeting and informally afterwards. Details of the 2010 Annual General Meeting are set out in the notice of the meeting accompanying this Annual Report.

Contact with major shareholders is principally maintained by the Chief Executive and the Group Finance Director, who ensure that their views are communicated to the board as a whole. The Chairman is also available to discuss governance and other matters directly with major shareholders. The board believes that appropriate steps have been taken during the year to ensure that the members of the board, and in particular the non-executive directors, develop an understanding of the views of major shareholders about the company. The board is provided with brokers' reports at every board meeting and feedback from shareholder meetings on a six-monthly basis. The canvassing of major shareholders' views for the board in a detailed investor survey is usually conducted every two years by external consultants. The board has taken the view that these methods, taken together, are a practical and efficient way both for the Chairman to keep in touch with major shareholder opinion on governance and strategy and for the Senior Independent Director to learn the views of major shareholders and to develop a balanced understanding of their issues and concerns. The Senior Independent Director and other non-executive directors are available to attend meetings with major shareholders if requested, however no such meetings were requested during the year.

Accountability, Audit and Control

In its reporting to shareholders, the board aims to present a balanced and understandable assessment of the group's financial position and prospects. The statement of the Responsibility of Directors for the preparation of the Annual Report and Accounts is set out on page 57.

The group's organisational structure is focused on its three divisions. These are all separately managed but report to the board through a board director. The executive management team receives monthly summaries of financial results from each division through a standardised reporting process. The group has in place a comprehensive annual budgeting process including forecasts for the next two years. Variances from budget are closely monitored.

The Group Control Manual, which is distributed to all group operations, clearly sets out the composition, responsibilities and authority limits of the various board and executive committees and also specifies what may be decided without central approval. It is supplemented by other specialist policy and procedures manuals issued by the group, divisions and individual businesses or departments. The high intrinsic value of many of the metals with which the group is associated necessitates stringent physical controls over precious metals held at the group's sites.

CORPORATE GOVERNANCE

Accountability, Audit and Control (continued)

The board has overall responsibility for the group's systems of internal control, including in respect of the financial reporting process, and for reviewing their effectiveness. The internal control systems are designed to meet the group's needs and manage the risks to which it is exposed, although these cannot be eliminated. Such systems can only provide reasonable but not absolute assurance against material misstatement or loss.

There is a continuous process for identifying, evaluating and managing the significant risks faced by the company. This process has been in place during the financial year and up to the date of approval of the Annual Report and Accounts. The board regularly reviews this process.

The assessment of group and strategic risks is reviewed by the board and updated on an annual basis. At the business level, the processes to identify and manage the key risks are an integral part of the control environment. Key risks and internal controls are the subject of regular reporting to the Chief Executive's Committee.

The Audit Committee monitors and reviews the effectiveness of the group's systems for internal financial control and risk management, considering regular reports from management and internal audit. The Audit Committee also considers reports from the external auditors on their evaluation of the systems of internal financial control and risk management. Amongst other matters, the Audit Committee reviews the group's credit control procedures and risks, controls over precious metals, IT controls and the group's corporate social responsibility reporting arrangements and whistleblowing procedures. The Audit Committee also reviews the performance of both the internal and external auditors.

The internal audit function is responsible for monitoring the group's systems of internal financial controls and the control of the integrity of the financial information reported to the board. The Audit Committee approves the plans for internal audit reviews and receives the reports produced by the internal audit function on a regular basis. Actions are agreed with management in response to any issues raised by the internal audit reports produced. Internal audit follows up the implementation of its recommendations, including any recommendations to improve internal controls, and reports the outcome to senior management and to the Audit Committee.

In addition, significant businesses provide assurance on the maintenance of financial and non-financial controls and compliance with group policies. These assessments are summarised by the internal audit function and a report is made annually to the Audit Committee. A report from the Audit Committee on its activities and on the work of internal audit is given on page 47.

The directors confirm that the system of internal controls for the year ended 31st March 2010 and the period up to 2nd June 2010 has been established in accordance with the revised Turnbull Guidance on Internal Control published by the Financial Reporting Council included with the Code. The directors have reviewed the effectiveness of the group's system of internal controls, including financial, operational and compliance controls and risk management systems. No significant failings or weaknesses were identified.

Corporate Social Responsibility

Measures to ensure responsible business conduct and the identification and assessment of risks associated with social, ethical and environmental matters are managed in conjunction with all other business risks and reviewed at regular meetings of the board, the Audit Committee and the Chief Executive's Committee.

A review of the group's policies and targets for corporate social responsibility (CSR) is set out in the Sustainability section of the Business Review on pages 29 to 37. A full version of the Sustainability Report is available on the company's website.

The identification and monitoring of environment, health and safety (EHS), social and governance risks are the responsibility of the CSR Compliance Committee, which is a sub-committee of the Chief Executive's Committee. It comprises the division directors, the Director of EHS, the Company Secretary and senior representatives of Group Legal, Internal Audit, Group EHS and other group functions. The Committee has specific responsibility for setting and overseeing compliance with the standards for group CSR performance through the development, dissemination, adoption and implementation of appropriate group policies and other operational measures. EHS performance is monitored using monthly statistics and detailed site audit reports. EHS performance is reviewed on a regular basis by the Chief Executive's Committee and an annual review is undertaken by the board.

Risks from employment and employee issues are identified and assessed by the Chief Executive's Committee and reported to the board.

Employment contracts, handbooks and policies specify acceptable business practices and the group's position on ethical issues. The Group Control Manual and security manuals provide further operational guidelines to reinforce these.

The Audit Committee reviews risks associated with corporate social responsibility on an annual basis and monitors performance through the annual control self-assessment process conducted by the internal audit function.

NOMINATION COMMITTEE REPORT

Role of the Nomination Committee

The Nomination Committee is a committee of the board whose purpose is to advise the board on the appointment and, if necessary, dismissal of executive and non-executive directors. The full terms of reference of the Nomination Committee are provided on the company's website at www.matthey.com.

Composition of the Nomination Committee

The Nomination Committee comprises all the independent non-executive directors together with the group Chairman. The quorum necessary for the transaction of business is two, each of whom must be an independent non-executive director. Biographical details of the independent directors and the group Chairman are set out on pages 38 and 39. Their remuneration is set out on page 51.

The group Chairman acts as the Chairman of the Nomination Committee, although the group Chairman may not chair the Nomination Committee when it is dealing with the matter of succession to the chairmanship of the company. A non-executive director may not chair the Nomination Committee when it is dealing with a matter relating to that non-executive director.

Only members of the Nomination Committee have the right to attend Nomination Committee meetings. However, the Chief Executive, the Director of Human Resources, external advisers and others may be invited to attend for all or part of any meeting as and when appropriate.

The Company Secretary is secretary to the Nomination Committee.

The Nomination Committee has the authority to seek any information that it requires from any officer or employee of the company or its subsidiaries. In connection with its duties, the Nomination Committee is authorised by the board to take such independent advice (including legal or other professional advice, at the company's expense) as it considers necessary, including requests for information from or commissioning investigations by external advisers.

Main Activities of the Nomination Committee

The Nomination Committee met twice during the financial year ended 31st March 2010; on 2nd February and 30th March 2010.

The Nomination Committee met on 2nd February 2010 to discuss board succession and consider proposed recommendations to the board for extensions to the terms of appointment of Mr M J Roney, Mrs D C Thompson and Mr R J W Walvis. After full review, the Nomination Committee recommended second three year terms for Mr Roney and Mrs Thompson and an extension of the term for Mr Walvis of one year (taking his term of appointment to nine years). After review, the board accepted these recommendations at its meeting on 30th March 2010.

Also at its meeting on 2nd February 2010, the Nomination Committee noted that the Chairman, Sir John Banham, would serve as Chairman until the Annual General Meeting in July 2011 in accordance with the terms of his appointment and that he would not be seeking a further term beyond that date. Consideration therefore needed to be given to the appointment of a successor and it was agreed that a draft specification for the role should be prepared. This was subsequently prepared and, at its meeting on 30th March 2010, the Nomination Committee considered the draft specification and also considered initial proposals from a number of executive search consultants to assist in the recruitment process. The draft specification was approved and it was agreed that the selection process, including the selection of executive search consultants, should be led by the Senior Independent Director and the Chief Executive, assisted by the Director of Human Resources. At both meetings, the Senior Independent Director chaired the discussions relating to the Chairman's successor.

Also at its meetings on 2nd February and 30th March 2010, the Nomination Committee discussed the prospective retirement in September 2011 of Mr A M Thomson, the Senior Independent Director and Chairman of the Audit Committee, and Mr R J W Walvis, Chairman of the Management Development and Remuneration Committee. It was agreed that the process for succession should be instigated later in the year.

On behalf of the Nomination Committee:

Sir John Banham
Chairman of the Nomination Committee

AUDIT COMMITTEE REPORT

Role of the Audit Committee

The Audit Committee is a committee of the board whose responsibilities include:

- Reviewing the half-yearly and full year accounts and results announcements of the company and any other formal announcements relating to the company's financial performance and recommending them to the board for approval.

- Reviewing the group's systems for internal financial control and risk management.

- Monitoring and reviewing the effectiveness of the company's internal audit function and considering regular reports from internal audit on internal financial controls and risk management.

- Considering the appointment of the external auditors, overseeing the process for their selection and making recommendations to the board in relation to their appointment to be put to shareholders for approval at a general meeting.

- Monitoring and reviewing the effectiveness and independence of the external auditors, agreeing the nature and scope of their audit, agreeing their remuneration, and considering their reports on the company's accounts, reports to shareholders and their evaluation of the systems of internal financial control and risk management.

The full terms of reference of the Audit Committee are provided on the company's website at www.matthey.com.

Composition of the Audit Committee

The Audit Committee comprises all the independent non-executive directors. Biographical details of the independent directors are set out on pages 38 and 39. Their remuneration is set out on page 51. The Chairman of the Audit Committee is Mr A M Thomson, who was formerly Finance Director of Smiths Group plc and is currently President of the Institute of Chartered Accountants of Scotland. The group Chairman, Chief Executive, Group Finance Director, Head of Internal Audit and external auditors (KPMG Audit Plc) attend Audit Committee meetings by invitation. The Committee also meets separately with the Head of Internal Audit and with the external auditors without management being present. The Company Secretary is secretary to the Audit Committee.

Main Activities of the Audit Committee

The Audit Committee met four times during the financial year ended 31st March 2010. At its meeting on 29th May 2009 the Committee reviewed the company's preliminary announcement of its results for the financial year ended 31st March 2009, and the draft report and accounts for that year. The Committee received reports from the external auditors on the conduct of their audit, their review of the accounts, including accounting policies and areas of judgment, and their comments on risk management and control matters.

The Audit Committee met on 20th July 2009 to receive reports on internal controls from both the internal and external auditors and approve amendments to the Group Control Manual. The external auditors also presented their proposed fees and scope for the forthcoming year's audit. The Committee also assessed the performance of both the internal and external auditors. The review of the external auditors was used to confirm the appropriateness of their reappointment and included assessment of their independence, qualification, expertise and resources, and effectiveness of the audit process. The Committee recommended to the board the reappointment of KPMG Audit Plc as auditors. In addition, the Committee received a presentation on the group's taxation management processes and strategy from the group's Director of Tax. The group's Sustainability Report 2008/09 was also reviewed, which is available on the company's website at www.matthey.com.

At its meeting on 23rd November 2009 the Audit Committee reviewed the company's half-yearly results, the half-yearly report and the external auditors' review and also papers on credit control and credit risk and on litigation affecting the group. The Committee received a presentation on the risks facing the Emission Control Technologies business from the Environmental Technologies Division Finance Director.

At its meeting on 2nd February 2010 the Audit Committee reviewed management's and internal audit's reports on the effectiveness of the company's systems for internal financial control and risk management. The Committee reviewed the group's credit control procedures and risks, controls over precious metals and IT controls. The group's corporate social responsibility reporting arrangements and whistleblowing procedures were also reviewed. Changes to the Group Control Manual were ratified. The Committee also received a presentation on the risks facing the Precious Metal Products Division from the Division Finance Director.

Since the year end the Committee has met to review the company's preliminary announcement of its results and draft report and accounts for the financial year ended 31st March 2010, and also the company's assessment of going concern.

Independence of External Auditors

Both the board and the external auditors have for many years had safeguards in place to avoid the possibility that the auditors' objectivity and independence could be compromised. Our policy in respect of services provided by the external auditors is as follows:

- Audit related services – the external auditors are invited to provide services which, in their position as auditors, they must or are best placed to undertake. This includes formalities relating to borrowings, shareholders' and other circulars, various other regulatory reports and work in respect of acquisitions and disposals.

- Tax consulting – in cases where they are best suited, we use the external auditors. All other significant tax consulting work is put out to tender.

- General consulting – in recognition of public concern over the effect of consulting services on auditors' independence, our policy is that the external auditors are not invited to tender for general consulting work where we believe it would compromise their audit independence and objectivity.

The split between audit and non-audit fees for the year ended 31st March 2010 and information on the nature of non-audit fees appear in note 5 on the accounts.

Internal Audit

During the year the Audit Committee reviewed the performance of the internal audit function, the findings of the audits completed during the year and the department's resource requirements and also approved the internal audit plan for the year ending 31st March 2011.

Internal audit independently reviews the risks and control processes operated by management. It carries out independent audits in accordance with an internal audit plan which is agreed with the Audit Committee before the start of the financial year.

The plan provides a high degree of financial and geographical coverage and devotes significant effort to the review of the risk management framework surrounding the major business risks.

Internal audit reports include recommendations to improve internal controls together with agreed management action plans to resolve the issues raised. Internal audit follows up the implementation of recommendations and reports progress to senior management and the Audit Committee.

The Audit Committee receives reports from the Head of Internal Audit on the department's work and findings.

The effectiveness of the internal audit function is reviewed and discussed on an annual basis with the Head of Internal Audit.

On behalf of the Committee:

Alan Thomson

Alan Thomson
Chairman of the Audit Committee

REMUNERATION REPORT

Remuneration Report to Shareholders

Management Development and Remuneration Committee and its Terms of Reference

The Management Development and Remuneration Committee of the board comprises all the independent non-executive directors of the company as set out on pages 38 and 39 and the group Chairman. The Chairman of the Committee throughout the year was Mr R J W Walvis.

The Committee's terms of reference include determination on behalf of the board of fair remuneration for the Chief Executive, the other executive directors and the group Chairman (in which case the group Chairman does not participate), which, while set in the context of what the company can reasonably afford, recognises their individual contributions to the company's overall performance. In addition, the Committee assists the board in ensuring that the current and future senior management of the group are recruited, developed and remunerated in an appropriate fashion. The Director of Human Resources, Mr I F Stephenson, acts as secretary to the Committee. The full terms of reference of the Committee are available on the company's website at www.matthey.com.

Non-executive directors' remuneration is determined by the board, within the limits prescribed by the company's Articles of Association. The remuneration consists of fees, which are set following advice taken from independent consultants and are reviewed at regular intervals.

Executive Remuneration Policy

The Committee believes strongly that remuneration policy should be closely aligned with shareholder interests. The Committee recognises that, in order to maximise shareholder value, it is necessary to have a competitive pay and benefits structure.

The Committee also recognises that there is a highly competitive market for successful executives and that the provision of appropriate rewards for superior performance is vital to the continued growth of the business. To assist with this, the Committee appoints and receives advice from independent remuneration consultants on the pay and incentive arrangements prevailing in comparably sized industrial companies in each country in which Johnson Matthey has operations. During the year, such advice was received from the Hay Group, which also provided advice on job evaluation, and PricewaterhouseCoopers LLP. PricewaterhouseCoopers LLP also provided expatriate tax advice and other tax advice, tax audit work, completion of overseas tax returns, advice on set up of new overseas operations and some overseas payroll services. A statement regarding the use of remuneration consultants for the year ended 31st March 2010 is available on the company's website at www.matthey.com. The Committee also receives recommendations from the Chief Executive on the remuneration of those reporting to him as well as advice from the Director of Human Resources. Total potential rewards are earned through the achievement of demanding performance targets based on measures that represent the best interests of shareholders.

The remuneration policy is normally reviewed by the Committee annually and a formal review is undertaken every three years. A triennial review was due to be held in 2009 but was delayed due to the uncertain market conditions at the time. It will be carried out in 2010, with any recommendations being implemented in 2011 subject to shareholder approval where necessary. Remuneration consists of basic salary, annual bonus, long term incentives and other benefits. Salaries are based on median market rates with incentives providing the opportunity for upper quartile total remuneration, but only for achieving outstanding performance.

To ensure the interests of the executive directors remain aligned with those of the shareholders, they are encouraged to build up over time and hold a shareholding in the company equal to at least their basic salary.

Johnson Matthey and FTSE 100 Total Shareholder Return rebased to 100

The following graph charts total cumulative shareholder return of the company for the five year period from 31st March 2005 to 31st March 2010 against the FTSE 100 as the most appropriate comparator group, rebased to 100 at 1st April 2005. Johnson Matthey was ranked 70th by market capitalisation in the FTSE 100 as at 31st March 2010.

REMUNERATION REPORT

Executive Remuneration

Executive directors' remuneration consists of the following:

- **Basic Salary** – which is in line with the median market salary for each director's responsibilities as determined by independent surveys. The remuneration comparator used by the Committee for executive directors other than the Chief Executive is the industrial and service sectors (excluding the oil and financial services sectors). In the case of the Chief Executive, the remuneration comparator group used by the Committee is based on FTSE 100 and 250 industrial companies (excluding the oil and financial services sectors) with market capitalisation of around £3 billion and with over 45% of revenue coming from overseas. Basic salary is normally reviewed on 1st August each year and the Committee takes into account individual performance and promotion during the year. Where an internal promotion takes place, the median salary relative to the market would usually be reached over a period of a few years, which can give rise to higher than normal salary increases while this is being achieved.

- **Annual Bonus** – which is paid as a percentage of basic salary under the terms of the company's Executive Compensation Plan (which also applies to the group's 190 or so most senior executives). The executive directors' bonus award is based on consolidated underlying profit before tax (PBT) compared with the annual budget. The Board of Directors rigorously reviews the annual budget to ensure that the budgeted PBT is sufficiently stretching. An annual bonus payment of 50% of basic salary (prevailing at 31st March) is paid if the group meets the annual budget. This bonus may rise on a straight line basis to a maximum 100% of basic salary if 110% of budgeted PBT is achieved. PBT must reach 95% of budget for a minimum bonus of 15% to be payable. The Committee has discretion to vary the awards made. The Committee has discretion in awarding annual bonuses and is able to consider corporate performance on environmental, social and governance issues when awards are made to executive directors. The Committee ensures that the incentive structure for senior management does not raise environmental, social and governance risks by inadvertently motivating irresponsible behaviour. The bonus awarded to executive directors for 2009/10 was 100% of basic salary at 31st March 2010 based on achieved PBT levels.

- **Long Term Incentive Plan (LTIP)** – which is designed to achieve above average performance and growth.

  Share allocations made in 2007 and onwards – share allocations made in 2007 and onwards are made under the terms of the Johnson Matthey Long Term Incentive Plan 2007 (which also applies to the group's 850 senior and middle managers). Shares are released on the third anniversary of the allocation date and are subject to an earnings per share (EPS) performance target. Although the plan allows share allocations of up to a maximum of 200% of basic annual salary each year (to take account of evolution of market practice if required), it is the Committee's current intention that allocations will be no higher than 150% of basic salary each year, which is considered appropriate based on current market conditions. Whilst it is intended that this level of allocation should normally only be made to the Chief Executive, the Committee approved an allocation of 170% of basic annual salary to the newly appointed Group Finance Director in 2009 to ensure close alignment of his objectives with those of the shareholders.

  The allocations in 2007 and in 2008 were 150% of basic annual salary for the Chief Executive and 120% for executive directors. The release of the share allocation is subject to the achievement of a performance target measured over a three year performance period commencing in the year of allocation. The performance target is based on the compound annual growth in the company's underlying EPS. The minimum release, of 15% of the allocation, requires underlying EPS growth of 6% compound per annum over the three year period. For the maximum release of 100%

of the allocation, underlying EPS must have grown by at least 15% compound per annum over the three year performance period. The number of allocated shares released will vary on a straight line basis between these points. There is no retesting of the performance target and so allocations will lapse if underlying EPS growth is less than 6% compound per annum over the three year performance period.

In 2009 the Committee approved an adjustment to the performance targets for one year only to reflect the market conditions prevailing at the time of allocation. The top ten major shareholders were consulted regarding this adjustment. For the 2009 allocation only, the minimum release, of 15% of the allocation, requires underlying EPS growth of 3% compound per annum over the three year period, with no retesting of the performance target. For the maximum release of 100% of the allocation, underlying EPS must have grown by at least 10% compound per annum over the three year performance period. As a result of this adjustment, the level of award was reduced to 120% of basic annual salary for the Chief Executive and 100% for executive directors (except for the newly appointed Group Finance Director as explained above).

Although growth in underlying EPS is the primary financial measure, it is also a key objective of the company to achieve earnings growth only in the context of a good performance on return on invested capital (ROIC). As a result of this adjustment, the Committee is required to make an assessment of the group's ROIC over the performance period to ensure underlying EPS growth has been achieved with ROIC in line with the group's planned expectations. The Committee may scale back vesting to the extent that ROIC has not developed appropriately.

Share allocations made prior to 2007 – Share allocations made prior to 2007 were made under the Johnson Matthey Long Term Incentive Plan which was established in 1998. The last allocation of shares under this plan was made in 2006 and these shares were released in 2009. No further allocations will be made under this plan. The allocations under this plan were subject to a relative total shareholder return (TSR) performance target. This compared the company's TSR over a three year performance period commencing in the year of allocation with that of a comparator group which comprised those companies placed 51-150 in the FTSE Index. All of the allocated shares were released if the company ranked in the 76th percentile or above. None of the shares were released if the company ranked in the 50th percentile or below. If the company ranked between these percentiles, 35% to 100% of the shares were released on a straight line basis. In addition, the company's EPS had to be at least equal to the increase in UK RPI plus 2% per annum over the three year performance period before any release was made. Shares were released on the third anniversary of the allocation date.

- **Share Options** – the Johnson Matthey Long Term Incentive Plan 2007 is now the company's single means for the provision of long term awards and from 2007 replaced the granting of share options under the Johnson Matthey 2001 Share Option Scheme (the 2001 Scheme). From 2001 to 2006 options were granted each year under the 2001 Scheme. There have been no option grants since 2006. Options were granted at the market value of the company's shares at the time of grant and were subject to performance targets over a three year period. Options may be exercised upon satisfaction of the relevant performance targets. Approximately 800 employees were granted options under the 2001 Scheme each year.

  Options granted from 2004 to 2006 – Grants made in 2004, 2005 and 2006 were subject to a three year performance target of EPS growth of UK RPI plus 3% per annum. If the performance target was not met at the end of the three year performance period, the options lapsed as there was no retesting of the performance target. In addition, to reduce the cost calculated under the International Financial Reporting Standard 2 – 'Share-based Payment', gains made on the exercise of options are capped at 100% of the grant price.

REMUNERATION REPORT

Executive Remuneration (continued)

The Committee had the discretion to award grants greater than 100% of basic annual salary. Grants which were made above this threshold were, however, subject to increasingly stretching performance targets. Grants between 100% and 125% of basic annual salary were subject to EPS growth of UK RPI plus 4% per annum and grants between 125% and 150% of basic annual salary were subject to EPS growth of UK RPI plus 5% per annum. The executive directors were granted options equal to 150% of basic annual salary. All the options, other than those granted in 2006 which were subject to EPS growth of UK RPI plus 5% per annum, have met their performance targets. The 2006 options which did not meet their performance targets have lapsed.

Options granted prior to 2004 – Prior to 2004, options granted to the executive directors under the 2001 Scheme were up to a maximum of 100% of basic annual salary each year. Such options were subject to a performance target of EPS growth of UK RPI plus 4% per annum over any three consecutive years during the life of the option. The performance target was subject to annual retesting until the lapse of the options on the tenth anniversary of grant. All of these options have met their performance targets.

There were also options outstanding under the Johnson Matthey 1995 UK and Overseas Executive Share Option Scheme. The last option grant under this scheme was made in 2000. All options were granted in annual tranches up to the maximum permitted of four times earnings and were subject to a performance target of EPS growth of UK RPI plus 2% over the three year performance period. Option grants were not made to executive directors in the years 1998, 1999 and 2000.

- **Pensions** – all the executive directors are members of the Johnson Matthey Employees Pension Scheme (JMEPS) in the UK.

  Full disclosure of the pension arrangements are set out on pages 55 to 56.

- **Other Benefits** – Other benefits available to the executive directors are private medical insurance, a company car and membership of the group's employee share incentive plans which are open to all employees in the countries in which the group operates such schemes.

- **Service Contracts** – The executive directors are employed on contracts subject to one year's notice at any time. On early termination of their contracts the directors would normally be entitled to 12 months' salary and benefits. The contracts of service of the executive directors and the terms and conditions of appointment of the non-executive directors are available for inspection at the company's registered office during normal business hours and at the forthcoming Annual General Meeting.

Former Directors

Dr P N Hawker and Messrs D W Morgan and J N Sheldrick left during the year.

Dr Hawker stepped down from the board on 21st July 2009 and his employment ceased on 31st July 2009. He received compensation for loss of office in accordance with his service contract of £443,000 and statutory redundancy payment of £10,000. Of this amount, £205,860 was paid into the pension scheme.

Mr Morgan stepped down from the board on 21st July 2009 and his employment ceased on 31st July 2009. He received compensation for loss of office in accordance with his service contract of £359,000, accrued holiday pay of £13,000, statutory redundancy payment of £8,000 and an additional year's credit into the pension scheme. To account for the credit in respect of this additional year's service, the compensation for loss of office payment was reduced by £23,000.

Mr Sheldrick retired on 7th September 2009 at the normal retirement age for directors of 60.

Directors' Emoluments 2009/10

	Date of service agreement	Date of appointment	Base salary £'000	Payment in lieu of pension (1) £'000	Annual bonus £'000	Benefits £'000	Compensation for loss of office £'000	Total excluding pension £'000	Total prior year excluding pension £'000
Executive									
N A P Carson	1.8.99	1.8.99	700	175	700	21	–	1,596	979
R J MacLeod (2)	3.2.09	22.6.09	294	–	285	12	–	591	–
L C Pentz (3)	1.1.06	1.8.03	365	–	365	57	–	787	434
W F Sandford (4)	21.7.09	21.7.09	209	52	200	10		471	–
Total Continuing Directors			1,568	227	1,550	100	–	3,445	1,413
P N Hawker (5)	1.8.03	1.8.03	113	28	113	8	453	715	487
D W Morgan (6)	1.8.99	1.8.99	112	–	112	9	380	613	405
J N Sheldrick (7)	24.11.97	3.9.90	194	48	185	6	–	433	626
Total Former Directors			419	76	410	23	833	1,761	1,518
Total			1,987	303	1,960	123	833	5,206	2,931

REMUNERATION REPORT

Directors' Emoluments 2009/10 (continued)

	Date of letter of appointment	Date of appointment	Fees £'000	Total excluding pension £'000	Total prior year excluding pension [11] £'000
Non-Executive [8]					
Sir John Banham (Chairman)	10.12.05	1.1.06	280	280	270
Sir Thomas Harris	22.1.09	1.4.09	45	45	–
M J Roney	29.3.07	1.6.07	45	45	45
D C Thompson	22.5.07	1.9.07	45	45	45
A M Thomson	1.8.02	24.9.02	50[9]	50	50
R J W Walvis	1.8.02	24.9.02	50[10]	50	50
Total			**515**	**515**	**460**

The aggregate amount of remuneration paid or receivable to directors and non-executive directors totalled £5,721,000 (2009 £3,436,000).

Notes

[1] Messrs Carson and Sandford and Dr Hawker ceased to accrue pensionable service in the Johnson Matthey Employees Pension Scheme with effect from 31st March 2006 and Mr Sheldrick did so with effect from 31st March 2008. They received an annual cash payment in lieu of pension equal to 25% of basic salary. This is taxable under the PAYE system.

[2] Mr MacLeod's emoluments relate to the period from 22nd June 2009 to 31st March 2010. Mr MacLeod is a non-executive director of Aggreko plc. His fees for the period from 22nd June 2009 to 31st March 2010 in respect of this non-executive directorship were £37,200. This amount is excluded from the table above and retained by him.

[3] Mr Pentz is a non-executive director of Victrex plc. His fees for the year in respect of this non-executive directorship were £41,000. This amount is excluded from the table above and retained by him.

[4] Mr Sandford's emoluments relate to the period from 21st July 2009 to 31st March 2010.

[5] Dr Hawker stepped down from the board on 21st July 2009 and his employment ceased on 31st July 2009. Compensation for loss of office was in accordance with his service contract.

[6] Mr Morgan stepped down from the board on 21st July 2009 and his employment ceased on 31st July 2009. Compensation for loss of office was in accordance with his service contract.

[7] Mr Sheldrick retired on 7th September 2009 at normal retirement age for executive directors of 60.

[8] Non-executive fees (other than for the Chairman) were reviewed on 1st May 2007 for the period from 1st April 2007 to 31st March 2010. The fees are £45,000 per annum, with the fee for chairmanship of committees being £5,000 per annum. The Chairman and the non-executive directors do not receive any pension benefits, LTIP allocations, share option grants or bonus payments. The Chairman's fees include £25,000 per annum to cover his administrative and secretarial support costs.

[9] Includes £5,000 per annum for chairmanship of the Audit Committee.

[10] Includes £5,000 per annum for chairmanship of the Management Development and Remuneration Committee.

[11] Excludes the emoluments of Mr I C Strachan who retired on 31st March 2009. His emoluments were £45,000 bringing the total to £505,000.

Directors' Interests

The interests (in respect of which transactions are notifiable to the company under the Financial Services Authority's Disclosure and Transparency Rules) of the directors as at 31st March 2010 in the shares of the company were:

1. Ordinary Shares

	31st March 2010	31st March 2009
Sir John Banham	18,400	18,400
N A P Carson	174,027	143,258
Sir Thomas Harris	1,180	500[1]
R J MacLeod	3,400	400[1]
L C Pentz	24,968	19,464
M J Roney	3,000	3,000
W F Sandford	4,839	1,644[1]
D C Thompson	9,721	9,721
A M Thomson	2,383	2,323
R J W Walvis	1,000	1,000

[1] At date of appointment.

All of the above interests were beneficial. The executive directors are also deemed to be interested in shares held by an employee share ownership trust (see note 32 on page 100).

Directors' interests as at 31st May 2010 were unchanged from those listed above, other than that the trustees of the Johnson Matthey Share Incentive Plan have purchased on behalf of Messrs Carson, Pentz and Sandford a further 45 shares each. In addition, Mr Carson has acquired 1 share through his automatic quarterly PEP reinvestment.

REMUNERATION REPORT

Directors' Interests (continued)

2.   Share Options

As at 31st March 2010, individual holdings by the directors under the company's executive share option schemes were as set out below. Options are not granted to non-executive directors.

	Date of grant	Ordinary shares under option	Exercise price (pence)	Date from which exercisable	Expiry date	Total number of ordinary shares under option
Continuing Directors:						
N A P Carson	18.7.01	19,391	1,083.00	18.7.04	18.7.11	
	17.7.02	28,901	865.00	17.7.05	17.7.12	
	17.7.03	33,407	898.00	17.7.06	17.7.13	
	20.7.05	77,102	1,070.00	20.7.08	20.7.15	
	26.7.06	59,481	1,282.00	26.7.09	26.7.16	218,282 (2009 248,214)
L C Pentz	18.7.01	12,952	1,083.00	18.7.04	18.7.11	
	17.7.02	17,730	865.00	17.7.05	17.7.12	
	17.7.03	17,185	898.00	17.7.06	17.7.13	
	20.7.05	37,850	1,070.00	20.7.08	20.7.15	
	26.7.06	28,765	1,282.00	26.7.09	26.7.16	114,482 (2009 145,617)
W F Sandford	26.7.06	18,868	1,282.00	26.7.09	26.7.16	18,868 (2009 18,868) [1]
Former Directors:						
P N Hawker	20.7.05	37,850	1,070.00	20.7.08	20.7.15	
	26.7.06	34,518	1,282.00	26.7.09	26.7.16	72,368 [2] (2009 72,368)
D W Morgan	18.7.01	18,098	1,083.00	18.7.04	18.7.11	
	17.7.02	25,433	865.00	17.7.05	17.7.12	
	17.7.03	26,726	898.00	17.7.06	17.7.13	
	20.7.05	39,252	1,070.00	20.7.08	20.7.15	
	26.7.06	35,104	1,282.00	26.7.09	26.7.16	144,613 [3] (2009 144,613)
J N Sheldrick	18.7.01	25,854	1,083.00	18.7.04	18.7.11	
	17.7.02	34,682	865.00	17.7.05	17.7.12	
	17.7.03	36,191	898.00	17.7.06	17.7.13	
	20.7.05	52,570	1,070.00	20.7.08	20.7.15	
	26.7.06	39,003	1,282.00	26.7.09	26.7.16	188,300 [4] (2009 196,101)

Notes

[1]   At date of appointment.

[2]   At date ceased to be a director (21st July 2009). In accordance with the rules of the 2001 Scheme, Dr Hawker was permitted to retain his options upon cessation of his employment and was given six months from the date of his cessation of employment in which to exercise them, subject to the relevant performance targets being met. Dr Hawker has subsequently exercised all his remaining options (66,615 in total).

[3]   At date ceased to be a director (21st July 2009). In accordance with the rules of the 2001 Scheme, Mr Morgan was permitted to retain his options upon cessation of his employment and was given six months from the date of his cessation of employment in which to exercise them, subject to the relevant performance targets being met. Mr Morgan has subsequently exercised all his remaining options (138,762 in total).

[4]   At date of retirement as a director (7th September 2009). In accordance with the rules of the 2001 Scheme, Mr Sheldrick was permitted to retain his options upon his retirement and was given six months from the date of his retirement in which to exercise them. Mr Sheldrick has subsequently exercised all his remaining options.

REMUNERATION REPORT

Directors' Interests (continued)

2. **Share Options (continued)**

Between 1st April 2009 and 31st March 2010 the following options were exercised by directors and former directors:

	Date of grant	Date of exercise	Options exercised	Exercise price (pence)	Market price on exercise (pence)
Continuing Directors:					
N A P Carson	22.7.99	12.6.09	18,035	585.50	1,228.32
L C Pentz	22.7.99	5.6.09	12,158	585.50	1,224.00
	17.7.03	10.6.09	5,000	898.00	1,232.00
	19.7.00	1.12.09	8,224	942.00	1,500.00
Former Directors:					
P N Hawker	20.7.05	16.10.09	37,850	1,070.00	1,474.04
	26.7.06	16.10.09	28,765	1,282.00	1,474.04
D W Morgan	17.7.02	17.12.09	21,965	865.00	1,519.00
	17.7.03	18.12.09	26,726	898.00	1,504.30
	20.7.05	30.12.09	6,542	1,070.00	1,530.00
	20.7.05	5.1.10	6,542	1,070.00	1,579.00
	20.7.05	8.1.10	26,168	1,070.00	1,595.00
	18.7.01	15.1.10	18,098	1,083.00	1,620.25
	17.7.02	15.1.10	3,468	865.00	1,613.00
	26.7.06	19.1.10	15,000	1,282.00	1,623.70
	26.7.06	29.1.10	8,402	1,282.00	1,466.50
	26.7.06	29.1.10	5,851	1,282.00	1,460.00
J N Sheldrick	17.7.02	17.9.09	3,468	865.00	1,494.00
	17.7.02	17.9.09	31,214	865.00	1,486.05
	17.7.03	20.10.09	36,191	898.00	1,501.00
	20.7.05	11.11.09	8,761	1,070.00	1,525.00
	20.7.05	12.11.09	8,761	1,070.00	1,530.00
	20.7.05	13.11.09	10,000	1,070.00	1,550.00
	20.7.05	16.11.09	25,048	1,070.00	1,575.00
	18.7.01	18.11.09	10,000	1,083.00	1,620.00
	18.7.01	10.2.10	15,854	1,083.00	1,520.00
	26.7.06	11.2.10	16,202	1,282.00	1,573.00
	26.7.06	1.3.10	15,000	1,282.00	1,612.00
	26.7.06	2.3.10	7,801	1,282.00	1,635.00

Gains made on exercise of options by the directors (including amounts after they ceased to be directors) during the year totalled £2,106,852 (2009 £208,496).

The closing market price of the company's shares at 31st March 2010 was 1,746 pence. The highest and lowest closing market prices during the year ended 31st March 2010 were 1,761 pence and 1,070 pence respectively.

Between 1st April 2009 and 31st March 2010 the following options lapsed as the relevant performance target was not met:

	Date of grant	Date of lapse	Options lapsed
Continuing Directors:			
N A P Carson	26.7.06	26.7.09	11,897
L C Pentz	26.7.06	26.7.09	5,753
W F Sandford	26.7.06	26.7.09	3,774
Former Directors:			
P N Hawker	26.7.06	26.7.09	5,753
D W Morgan	26.7.06	26.7.09	5,851
J N Sheldrick	26.7.06	26.7.09	7,801

REPORT OF THE DIRECTORS - CORPORATE GOVERNANCE

REMUNERATION REPORT

Directors' Interests (continued)

3. **LTIP Allocations**
   Share allocations made prior to 2007
   Number of allocated shares:

	As at 31st March 2009	Shares released during the year	Allocations lapsed during the year	As at 31st March 2010
Continuing Directors:				
N A P Carson	56,148	42,112	14,036	–
L C Pentz	21,723	16,292	5,431	–
W F Sandford	12,665 [1]	9,499	3,166	–
Former Directors:				
P N Hawker	21,723	16,292	5,431	–
D W Morgan	22,091	16,568	5,523	–
J N Sheldrick	29,455	22,092	7,363	–

[1] At date of appointment.

On 3rd August 2009 shares allocated in 2006 (at an allocation price of 1,358 pence) under the LTIP were released to participants. The release of this allocation was subject to the achievement of a relative TSR performance target, further details of which can be found on page 49. The company's TSR performance relative to the comparator group qualified for a release of 75% of the allocated shares. This resulted in the following gains:

	Number of shares released	Share price when released (pence)	Gain £
Continuing Directors:			
N A P Carson	42,112	1,401.619	590,250
L C Pentz	16,292	1,401.619	228,352
W F Sandford	9,499	1,401.619	133,140
Former Directors:			
P N Hawker	16,292	1,401.619	228,352
D W Morgan	16,568	1,401.619	232,220
J N Sheldrick	22,092	1,401.619	309,646
Total			**1,721,960**

Share allocations made under the Johnson Matthey Long Term Incentive Plan 2007
Number of allocated shares:

	As at 31st March 2009	Allocations during the year	Market price at date of allocation (pence)	Lapsed during the year	As at 31st March 2010 [2]
Continuing Directors:					
N A P Carson	112,943	71,611	1,173.00	–	184,554
R J MacLeod	– [1]	55,072	1,173.00	–	55,072
L C Pentz	44,180	31,116	1,173.00	–	75,296
W F Sandford	30,586 [1]	25,575	1,173.00	–	56,161
Former Directors:					
P N Hawker	44,180	–	–	21,710	22,470
D W Morgan	43,858	–	–	21,497	22,361
J N Sheldrick	58,017	37,936	1,173.00	62,772	33,181

Notes
[1] At date of appointment.
[2] Under the rules of the Johnson Matthey Long Term Incentive Plan 2007, Dr Hawker, Mr Morgan and Mr Sheldrick have retained their share allocations. These will be released on the normal release dates (the third anniversary of the allocation dates) subject to the performance targets over the whole of the performance periods. The extent to which the allocations will be released is subject to pro rating based on the time which has elapsed from the allocation dates to the dates of cessation of employment / retirement.

REMUNERATION REPORT

Pensions

Pensions and life assurance benefits for the executive directors are currently provided through the company's occupational pension scheme for UK employees – the Johnson Matthey Employees Pension Scheme (JMEPS) – which is constituted under a separate Trust Deed. JMEPS is an exempt approved scheme under Chapter I of Part XIV of the Income & Corporation Taxes Act 1988. It is also a registered scheme for the purposes of the Finance Act 2004.

All pension accruals under the final salary sections of JMEPS ceased on 31st March 2010. From 1st April 2010, retirement benefits for UK employees are being provided through a defined benefit career average salary pension arrangement (called the Johnson Matthey Pension Plan – JMPP). This includes executive directors whose benefits do not exceed the Life Time Allowance. JMPP is a subsidiary section of JMEPS. Defined benefits based on career average salaries are non-contributory. Members may pay contributions to a defined contribution account and the company will match contributions up to 3% of pensionable pay contributed each year.

Executive directors whose retirement benefits are valued in excess of the Life Time Allowance may withdraw from pensionable service

and receive instead a supplemental payment of 25% of basic salary each year. Mr Carson, Dr Hawker and Mr Sandford withdrew from pensionable service and ceased paying member contributions on 31st March 2006 and Mr Sheldrick did so on 31st March 2008. No pensionable service in JMEPS has been accrued by these directors since those dates. The change in accrued pensions for these directors in the tables below is attributable solely to the increase in basic salary in 2009/10 and the effect of negative inflation. The supplemental payments received by Mr Carson, Dr Hawker, Mr Sandford and Mr Sheldrick are reflected in the table on page 50. The payments for Dr Hawker and Mr Sheldrick ceased when they left employment on 31st July 2009 and 7th September 2009 respectively.

Member contributions paid by executive directors to the final salary sections of JMEPS increased from 6% to 7% with effect from 1st April 2009.

Disclosure of directors' pension benefits has been made under the requirements of the United Kingdom Listing Authority Listing Rules and in accordance with the Directors' Remuneration Report Regulations 2002. The information below sets out the disclosures under the two sets of requirements.

a.   United Kingdom Listing Authority Listing Rules

	Age as at 31st March 2010	Years of JMEPS pensionable service at 31st March 2010	Directors' contributions to JMEPS during the year [1,2] £'000	Increase in accrued pension during the year (net of inflation) [3] £'000 pa	Total accrued pension as at 31st March 2010 [4] £'000 pa	Total accrued pension as at 31st March 2009 £'000 pa	Transfer value of increase in accrued pension (less directors' contributions) [5] £'000
Continuing Directors:							
N A P Carson	52	25	–	5	329	329	69
R J MacLeod [2]	45	1	–	4	4	–	27
L C Pentz [6]	54	25	26	11	83	76	148
W F Sandford	56	28	–	23	155	135	399
Former Directors:							
P N Hawker [7,9]	56	20	–	1	160	160	13
D W Morgan [8,9]	52	20	8	13	77	65	173
J N Sheldrick [10]	60	17	–	4	73	69	89

b.   Directors' Remuneration Report Regulations 2002

	Directors' contributions to JMEPS in the year [1,2] £'000	Increase in accrued pension in the year £'000 pa	Total accrued pension as at 31st March 2010 [4] £'000 pa	Transfer value of accrued pension as at 31st March 2010 [5] £'000	Transfer value of accrued pension as at 31st March 2009 [5] £'000	Increase in transfer value (net of directors' contributions) £'000
Continuing Directors:						
N A P Carson	–	–	329	4,952	3,921	1,031
R J MacLeod [2]	–	4	4	27	–	27
L C Pentz [6]	26	10	83	1,052	805	227
W F Sandford	–	20	155	2,734	2,005	729
Former Directors:						
P N Hawker [7,9]	–	–	160	2,712	2,421	291
D W Morgan [8,9]	8	12	77	1,090	730	352
J N Sheldrick [10]	–	4	73	1,503	1,310	193

REPORT OF THE DIRECTORS – CORPORATE GOVERNANCE

REMUNERATION REPORT

Pensions (continued)

Notes

(1) With the exception of Mr MacLeod who accrued benefits under JMPP, member contributions to the final salary section of JMEPS were paid at the general scheme rate of 7% of pensionable pay.

(2) Mr MacLeod joined JMPP when he was appointed to the board on 22nd June 2009 and has paid voluntary contributions of 3% of pensionable pay to the defined contribution arrangement. In accordance with JMPP rules, the company paid a matching contribution of £8,550 into his defined contribution account.

(3) The disclosure regulations require the pension accrued to the end of the previous year to be adjusted for inflation. In a period of negative inflation, this adjustment effectively reduces the previous year's accrued pension. For example, in the case of Mr Carson for whom there was no change in pensionable salary or service during the year, the increase in accrued pension is entirely due to the effect of negative inflation. Inflation was -1.4% for the year to 30th September 2009 as prescribed by the Revaluation Order (SI 2008 No. 3070) issued under the Pensions Schemes Act 1993.

(4) The entitlement shown under 'Total accrued pension at 31st March 2010' is the pension which would be paid annually from normal retirement, based on pensionable service to 31st March 2010 (except in the case of Messrs Carson and Sandford whose pensionable service ceased on 31st March 2006). The pension would be subject to an actuarial reduction for each month that retirement precedes age 60.

(5) The transfer values have been calculated on the basis of actuarial advice in accordance with the transfer value regulations. No allowance has been made in the transfer values for any discretionary benefits that have been or may be awarded under JMEPS. The transfer value in the United Kingdom Listing Authority Listing Rules is the value of the increase (net of inflation) in the accrued pension as at 31st March 2010. The transfer values in the Directors' Remuneration Report Regulations 2002 have been calculated at the start and the end of the year and, therefore, also take account of market movements.

(6) Mr Pentz is a US citizen but became a member of JMEPS on 1st January 2006. Prior to that he was a member of the Johnson Matthey Inc. Salaried Employees Pension Plan (a non-contributory defined benefit arrangement) and a US savings plan (401k). He also has benefits in a Senior Executive Retirement Plan. The pension values reported above are the aggregate for his separate membership of the UK and US pension schemes and the Senior Executive Retirement Plan. US entitlements have been converted to sterling by reference to exchange rates on 31st March 2009 and 31st March 2010. Mr Pentz's US pension was fixed on 31st December 2005. The sterling equivalent of it has fluctuated over the year as a result of exchange rate movements. This is reflected in the transfer values.

(7) Dr Hawker stepped down from the board on 21st July 2009 and his employment ceased on 31st July 2009. He chose to draw his retirement benefits immediately with effect from 1st August 2009 and his pension was reduced appropriately to take account of early retirement. Dr Hawker's pensionable service stopped on 31st March 2006 and the increase in pension is attributable only to an increase in basic salary. The company made an additional payment into JMEPS of £205,860 on a defined contribution basis.

(8) Mr Morgan stepped down from the board on 21st July 2009 and his employment ceased on 31st July 2009. He has not drawn his retirement benefits, but holds a deferred pension in the scheme. In lieu of a contractual bonus earned in 2008/09, the company made an additional payment into JMEPS of £50,250 on a defined contribution basis.

(9) Any tax liability arising out of regulations under the Finance Act 2009 that may become chargeable on the additional payments for Dr Hawker and Mr Morgan is the responsibility of these individuals.

(10) Mr Sheldrick retired from the board at his normal retirement date, age 60, on 7th September 2009 and payment of his pension started from that date. As his pensionable service stopped on 31st March 2008, the increase in pension is attributable only to an increase in basic salary.

The Remuneration Report was approved by the Board of Directors on 2nd June 2010 and signed on its behalf by:

Robert Walvis
Chairman of the Management Development and Remuneration Committee

RESPONSIBILITY OF DIRECTORS

Statement of Directors' Responsibilities in Respect of the Annual Report and Accounts

The directors are responsible for preparing the Annual Report and the group and parent company accounts in accordance with applicable law and regulations.

Company law requires the directors to prepare group and parent company accounts for each financial year. Under that law they are required to prepare the group accounts in accordance with International Financial Reporting Standards (IFRS) as adopted by the European Union (EU) and applicable law and have elected to prepare the parent company accounts on the same basis.

Under company law the directors must not approve the accounts unless they are satisfied that they give a true and fair view of the state of affairs of the group and parent company and of their profit or loss for that period. In preparing each of the group and parent company accounts, the directors are required to:

- select suitable accounting policies and then apply them consistently;
- make judgments and estimates that are reasonable and prudent;
- state whether they have been prepared in accordance with IFRS as adopted by the EU; and
- prepare the accounts on the going concern basis unless it is inappropriate to presume that the group and the parent company will continue in business.

The directors are responsible for keeping adequate accounting records that are sufficient to show and explain the parent company's transactions and disclose with reasonable accuracy at any time the financial position of the parent company and enable them to ensure that its accounts comply with the Companies Act 2006. They have general responsibility for taking such steps as are reasonably open to them to safeguard the assets of the group and to prevent and detect fraud and other irregularities.

Under applicable law and regulations the directors are also responsible for preparing a directors' report, directors' Remuneration Report and Corporate Governance statement that comply with that law and those regulations.

The directors are responsible for the maintenance and integrity of the corporate and financial information included on the company's website. Legislation in the UK governing the preparation and dissemination of accounts may differ from legislation in other jurisdictions.

Responsibility Statement of the Directors in Respect of the Annual Report and Accounts

Each of the directors as at the date of the Annual Report and Accounts, whose names and functions are set out on pages 38 and 39, confirms that to the best of their knowledge:

- the group and parent company accounts, prepared in accordance with the applicable set of accounting standards, give a true and fair view of the assets, liabilities, financial position and profit or loss of the company and the undertakings included in the consolidation taken as a whole; and
- the management report (which comprises the Report of the Directors) includes a fair review of the development and performance of the business and the position of the company and the undertakings included in the consolidation taken as a whole, together with a description of the principal risks and uncertainties that they face.

This responsibility statement was approved by the Board of Directors on 2nd June 2010 and is signed on its behalf by:

Sir John Banham
Chairman

ACCOUNTS

The audit and the role of auditors

As we have noted earlier, an annual audit of the accounts is a statutory requirement for all limited companies. In general, for accounting periods starting on or after 6 April 2008, companies having an annual sales revenue of less than £6.5 million and a balance sheet total of less than £3.26 million (refer to the Department for Business Innovation and Skills website *www.bis.gov.uk* for changes to these limits) are exempt from the annual audit requirement. The shareholders of a limited company are responsible for appointing suitably qualified, independent persons, either individually or as a firm, to act as auditors. The external auditors are not part of the company but are responsible to the shareholders, with a main duty of objectively reporting to shareholders and others as to whether, in their opinion, the financial statements show a true and fair view, and comply with statutory, regulatory and accounting standard requirements. Such an opinion is referred to as an unqualified opinion.

The report of the auditors is usually very short and additionally includes:

- reference to the directors' responsibility for preparation of the annual report and accounts
- reference to the responsibility as auditors being established by
  - UK statute
  - the **Auditing Practices Board (APB)**
  - the Listing Rules of the Financial Services Authority
  - the accountancy profession's ethical guidance.

The auditors are required to explain the basis of the audit, and report if in their opinion:

- the directors' report is not consistent with the accounts
- the company has not kept proper accounting records
- they have not received all the information and explanations required for the audit
- information specified by law, or the Listing Rules regarding directors' remuneration and transactions with the company, is not disclosed
- company policies are appropriate and consistently applied and adequately disclosed
- all information and explanations considered necessary provide sufficient evidence to give reasonable assurance that the accounts are free from material misstatement
- the overall presentation of information in the accounts is adequate.

There may very occasionally be circumstances when the financial statements may be affected by an inherent and fundamental uncertainty. In such cases the auditors are obliged to draw attention to the fundamental uncertainty. If the fundamental uncertainty is adequately accounted for and disclosed in the financial statements then the opinion of the auditors may remain unqualified. If there is inadequate disclosure about the fundamental uncertainty then the auditors must give what is termed a qualified opinion. A qualified **audit report** is something that may destroy company credibility and create uncertainty, and is obviously something to be avoided.

In addition to their reporting on the financial statements of the company, the auditors' reports now include a statement of the company's corporate governance compliance with the provisions of the UK Corporate Governance Code (prior to 29 June 2010 the Combined Code on Corporate Governance). This review is in accordance with guidelines issued by the Auditing Practices Board. The auditors are not required to:

- consider whether the statements by the directors on internal control cover all risks and controls
- form an opinion on the effectiveness of the company's corporate governance procedures or its risk management and internal control procedures
- form an opinion on the ability of the company to continue in operational existence.

The audit and the perceived role of auditors has been the subject of much criticism over the years. The responsibility of the auditors does not include guarantees that:

- the financial statements are correct
- the company will not fail
- there has been no fraud.

This gap, 'the expectations gap', between public expectation and what the audit actually provides is understandable in the light of the numerous examples of company failures and financial scandals from the 1980s to date. These have led to a lack of confidence of the business community in financial reporting, and in shareholders being unable to rely on safeguards they assumed would be provided by their auditors.

The problem is that 'correctness' of financial statements is an unachievable result. We have seen from our consideration of both the balance sheet and income statement the inconsistency in asset valuation and the level of subjective judgement required in their preparation. Directors are required to prepare, and auditors give an opinion on, accounts that give a true and fair view rather than accounts that are deemed 'correct'.

Companies increasingly face a greater diversity and level of risk:

- financial risk
- commercial risk
- operational risk

and the increasing possibility of corporate failure is very real. Although the financial statements of companies are based on the going concern concept, the directors and auditors cannot realistically give any assurance that those businesses will not fail.

An area of risk that is of increasing concern to companies is fraud. This is perhaps due to the:

- increasing pace of change
- widespread use of computer systems
- ease and speed of communications and transfer of funds
- use of the Internet
- increase in staff mobility
- increasing dependence on specific knowledge (for example, Nick Leeson and Barings, and dot.com companies' IT experts).

Fraud is perhaps something on which auditors may arguably be expected to give an opinion. This is not something that is currently required from an external audit. It is something for which an **internal audit** department may be responsible. In the same way, external auditors could be requested to report on the adequacy or otherwise of systems of internal control.

Most major corporate fraud is now associated with communications and information technology systems. The use of internal (or external) audit for the:

- detection of fraud
- minimisation of fraud
- elimination of fraud

therefore tends to be specialised and is something for which the costs and benefits must be carefully evaluated.

Progress check 6.4

What is the audit and to whom are the auditors responsible, and for what?

The report of the independent auditors to the shareholders of Johnson Matthey Plc, included in the report and accounts 2010, is illustrated on page 210. It can be seen to have complied with the standard audit reporting requirements outlined above. It may be interesting to compare the auditors' report for say 1990 with the same report for the year 2010, in which so many more areas are covered, and to appreciate the importance of corporate governance.

Worked example 6.3

The audit is the objective review (or sometimes the detailed examination) of business systems of internal control, risk management and corporate governance and the company's financial transactions. A business may employ internal and external auditors. The latter are considered the more independent, although both are paid by the business. External auditors are appointed by, and report to, the shareholders, whereas the internal auditors report to the company's audit committee.

(i) Why should the external auditors of a plc report direct to the shareholders and not to the chairman of the company?

(ii) Why should the internal auditors of a plc report to the audit committee and not to the finance director?

(iii) In what ways may the independence of a company's audit committee be demonstrated?

The answers to these questions are:

(i) The external auditors are appointed by and are responsible to the shareholders. The annual general meeting (AGM) is the formal meeting of directors, shareholders and auditors. Conceivably, the chairman could shelve the report, with shareholders unaware of the contents. The law is quite strict on auditors' right to communicate directly with shareholders.

(ii) The finance director is responsible for the system of recording transactions. The finance director could prevent vital information from the internal auditors being distributed to others in the organisation.

(iii) The audit committee may request the non-executive directors to review specific areas, for example, the output from the internal auditors. The audit committee meets many times during the year and it offers a degree of objectivity. The careers of its members do not depend on the continuance of their directorship.

The directors of a company may not be accountants and they very rarely have any hands-on involvement with the actual putting-together of a set of accounts for the company. However, directors of companies must make it their business to be fully conversant with the content of the accounts of their companies. Directors are responsible for ensuring that proper accounting records are maintained, and for ensuring reasonably accurate reporting of the financial position of their company, and ensuring their compliance with the Companies Act 2006. Immediately following the remuneration committee report, Johnson Matthey Plc's report and accounts 2010 includes on page 57 a section headed responsibility of directors (reproduced on page 206 of this book), which details the responsibilities of its directors in the preparation of its accounts.

We will now consider the role of directors and their responsibilities in more detail, and with regard to the UK Corporate Governance Code. We will also look at some of the circumstances in which directors of limited companies are particularly vulnerable, and how these may lead to disqualification of directors.

INDEPENDENT AUDITORS' REPORT

to the members of Johnson Matthey Public Limited Company

We have audited the group and parent company accounts of Johnson Matthey Plc for the year ended 31st March 2010 which comprise the Consolidated Income Statement, the Consolidated Statement of Total Comprehensive Income, the Consolidated and Parent Company Balance Sheets, the Consolidated and Parent Company Cash Flow Statements, the Consolidated Statement of Changes in Equity, the Parent Company Statement of Changes in Equity and the related notes. The financial reporting framework that has been applied in their preparation is applicable law and International Financial Reporting Standards (IFRS) as adopted by the EU and, as regards the parent company accounts, as applied in accordance with the provisions of the Companies Act 2006.

This report is made solely to the company's members, as a body, in accordance with Chapter 3 of Part 16 of the Companies Act 2006. Our audit work has been undertaken so that we might state to the company's members those matters we are required to state to them in an auditor's report and for no other purpose. To the fullest extent permitted by law, we do not accept or assume responsibility to anyone other than the company and the company's members as a body, for our audit work, for this report, or for the opinions we have formed.

Respective Responsibilities of Directors and Auditors

As explained more fully in the directors' responsibilities statement set out on page 57, the directors are responsible for the preparation of the accounts and for being satisfied that they give a true and fair view. Our responsibility is to audit the accounts in accordance with applicable law and International Standards on Auditing (UK and Ireland). Those standards require us to comply with the Auditing Practices Board's (APB's) Ethical Standards for Auditors.

Scope of the Audit of the Accounts

A description of the scope of an audit of accounts is provided on the APB's website at www.frc.org.uk/apb/scope/UKP.

Opinion on Accounts

In our opinion:

- the accounts give a true and fair view of the state of the group's and of the parent company's affairs as at 31st March 2010 and of the group's profit for the year then ended;
- the group accounts have been properly prepared in accordance with IFRS as adopted by the EU;
- the parent company accounts have been properly prepared in accordance with IFRS as adopted by the EU and as applied in accordance with the provisions of the Companies Act 2006; and
- the accounts have been prepared in accordance with the requirements of the Companies Act 2006 and, as regards the group accounts, Article 4 of the IAS Regulation.

Opinion on Other Matters Prescribed by the Companies Act 2006

In our opinion:

- the part of the directors' Remuneration Report to be audited has been properly prepared in accordance with the Companies Act 2006; and
- the information given in the Directors' Report for the financial year for which the accounts are prepared is consistent with the accounts.

Matters on Which we are Required to Report by Exception

We have nothing to report in respect of the following:

Under the Companies Act 2006 we are required to report to you if, in our opinion:

- adequate accounting records have not been kept by the parent company, or returns adequate for our audit have not been received from branches not visited by us; or
- the parent company accounts and the part of the directors' Remuneration Report to be audited are not in agreement with the accounting records and returns; or
- certain disclosures of directors' remuneration specified by law are not made; or
- we have not received all the information and explanations we require for our audit.

Under the Listing Rules we are required to review:

- the directors' statement, set out on page 23, in relation to going concern; and
- the part of the Corporate Governance statement on page 40 relating to the company's compliance with the nine provisions of the June 2008 Combined Code specified for our review.

D V Matthews (Senior Statutory Auditor)
for and on behalf of KPMG Audit Plc, Statutory Auditor
Chartered Accountants
8 Salisbury Square, London

2nd June 2010

The fact that a corporate governance code of practice exists or even that the appropriate corporate governance committees have been established is not necessarily a guarantee of effective corporate governance. There have been many examples of companies that have had corporate governance committees in place relating to directors and their remuneration, relations with shareholders, accountability and audit. Nevertheless, these companies have given cause for great concern from shareholders following much-publicised revelations about financial scandals and apparent loosely-adhered-to corporate governance practices.

Such examples have been by no means confined to the UK, as the press extract on page 212 illustrates. Bernie Madoff, founder and principal of Bernard L Madoff Investment Securities, had traded on Wall Street for 40 years, where he was described as a 'legend'. He seemed to epitomise probity and honesty in the sometimes murky world of financial dealings. Madoff's investment fund consistently outperformed similar funds and demonstrated remarkably little volatility of returns irrespective of market conditions. With his apparent astute financial skills and quiet authority there was no shortage of investors eager to increase their savings in Madoff's fund. The bad news was that Madoff's fund was a US$65bn fraud, a Ponzi scheme which paid returns to investors from their own investments or from the money from other investors.

The USA Securities and Exchange Commission (SEC) defines a Ponzi scheme as an investment fraud that involves the payment of purported returns to existing investors from funds contributed by new investors. Ponzi scheme organisers often solicit new investors by promising to invest funds in opportunities claimed to generate high returns with little or no risk. In many Ponzi schemes, the fraudsters focus on attracting new money to make promised payments to earlier-stage investors and to use for personal expenses, instead of engaging in any legitimate investment activity. The SEC further states that 'The schemes are named after Charles Ponzi, who duped thousands of New England residents into investing in a postage stamp speculation scheme back in the 1920s. At a time when the annual interest rate for bank accounts was five per cent per annum, Ponzi promised investors that he could provide a 50 per cent return in just 90 days.'

Bernie Madoff was sentenced to 150 years in prison in June 2009 for his part in what is probably the biggest financial fraud ever perpetrated. However, it is most unlikely that much of the investors' money embezzled will ever be recovered.

Directors' responsibilities

The responsibilities of directors, in terms of the UK Corporate Governance Code, can be seen to be important and far-reaching. It has been said that being a director is easy, but being a responsible director is not. It is important for all directors to develop an understanding and awareness of their ever-increasing legal obligations and responsibilities to avoid the potential personal liabilities, and even disqualification, which are imposed if those obligations are ignored.

It can be seen that the aims of most of the codes of practice and legislation have been to promote better standards of management in companies. This has also meant penalising irresponsible directors, the effect of which has been to create an increasingly heavy burden on directors regardless of the size or nature of the business they manage. The Government is actively banning offending directors.

Directors' duties are mainly embodied in the:

- Companies Act 2006
- Insolvency Act 1986 (as amended by the Enterprise Act 2002)
- Company Directors Disqualification Act 1986 (as amended by the Enterprise Act 2002)
- Enterprise Act 2002
- Health and Safety at Work Act 1974

Anything you can do I can do better

On Mar. 12, victims of Bernard Madoff's Ponzi scheme finally had one of their wishes come true. After a judge denied bail, Madoff is going directly to jail, and he isn't passing 'go'. But Madoff's victims still want answers.

They want to know where the money went. They want to know who else was involved. And they want to know how they got scammed.

At the courthouse, many victims said there were no warning signs and Madoff himself, in his courtroom statement, backed them up on at least one count. 'The clients receiving trade confirmations and account statements had no way of knowing by reviewing these documents that I had never engaged in the transactions', Madoff said during his guilty plea.

Maybe not. But to Harry Markopolos, the risk manager who alerted the SEC to Madoff's fraud in 1999 to no avail, the foul play seemed obvious. Madoff was supposedly using a complex trading system to generate returns, a strategy he dubbed the 'split-strike conversion strategy'. He would buy stocks in the Standard & Poor's 100 and sell options to reduce volatility. But Markopolos' firm was running a similar strategy and couldn't match the returns. A look at the returns was all it took for Markopolos to know something was up.

Preying on a Community

Markopolos had plenty of incentive to doubt Madoff; he was a competitor irked by Madoff's claims of too-good-to-be-true returns. For most of Madoff's clients, the math that Markopolos employed would have been out of their league. Some Madoff investors were sophisticated enough that they might have dug deeper into their statements and trade confirmations. A quick comparison of their returns with those of the actual markets might have been enough to tip them off that at least some of the trades were phony. Some of them might have realized that the average returns were too high and too constant, based on the mathematical probabilities. 'If the standard deviation is too low and the mean too high, something is wrong', says Utpal Bhattacharya, finance professor at the Indiana University Kelley School of Business. Still, 'the retail investor would need some help.'

Experts say investors can avoid Ponzi schemes and other scams without relying on math. The first step: Take a look around; who are your fellow investors? Often in a scam, a pattern emerges. There's a reason why many Madoff-like scams are called 'affinity crimes'. Charles Ponzi, for whom the scam is named, targeted Italians. Joseph Forte ripped off his friends. And before Madoff branched out into Europe in recent years, his clients were primarily Jews and Jewish foundations.

'Ponzis involve preying on people who have some association. The same clubs, religion, geographic location', says Tim Kochis, chief executive of financial advisory firm Aspiriant. 'Madoff's investors all trusted each other. They assumed that was good enough.' If investors get a sense that their adviser caters to a very narrow group, they should probably dig a little deeper.

Do Your Own Due Diligence

That starts with doing your own due diligence. Scamsters often make claims to bolster the confidence of investors that they're dealing with a heavyweight. Allen Stanford built an image of a successful businessman whose family's financial-services roots went back to 1932. In fact, his banking empire consisted of a Montserrat bank founded in 1986 that had its license revoked by the local government. Go back further, and Stanford filed for bankruptcy not once, but twice.

Victims of Tom Petters, the mastermind behind another recent Ponzi scheme in Minnesota that cost investors $2 billion, didn't check out basic claims, such as Petters' assertion that he was a major supplier to Sam's Club. He wasn't, which the investors could have figured out if they'd picked up the phone and made a call.

Madoff's investors might have been able to determine if their trades were legitimate if they'd checked how a stock or option traded on any given day. Even something as trivial as the accounting firm can be a tip-off. Both Madoff and Stanford used tiny accounting firms that would have been hard-pressed to handle the job. 'Investors have to do their own due diligence', says Gregory Hays, managing principal of Atlanta-based Hays Financial Consulting. 'They need to make sure what they're investing in is accurate.'

Investors also should dig into the firm and the background of its managers. A quick check on the Financial Industry Regulatory Authority, or FINRA, Web site could alert investors to a black mark on an adviser's record. Its Broker Check function alerts investors to any regulatory proceedings against an adviser, from bad record-keeping to misuse of client funds for firms and advisers. If the firm doesn't have a solid explanation, it could be time to look elsewhere.

The Defense of Skepticism

Even a quick search of Google can be revealing, yet it's a step few victims take. It would have revealed accusations from the 1990s that Madoff was front-running his customers, that is, buying or selling shares before filling their orders. The charges may amount to nothing. 'But', says Billy Procida, founder of William Procida Inc., a turnaround management firm for middle-market real estate companies, 'do I really want to take that chance?'

Still, the best defense may be a healthy dose of skepticism. Most people with money to invest with people like Madoff worked very hard for it. In business, they wouldn't have taken anybody's word for something. They'd have checked it out. But they didn't do the same with their advisers.

Richard Friedland, a CPA and Madoff investor, said on Mar. 12 that he could have recognized the scam if he had been looking for it. But he saw no reason to look for it. 'Madoff was the chairman of Nasdaq', Friedland said.

And that's what the Madoffs of the world depend on to build their webs of deception. They have fancy offices, fancy cars, and travel in private jets. They have pictures of governors, mayors, movie stars, and athletes.

'People love that', Procida says. 'They want to be with a star.'

Source: **Madoff: Lessons from a Disaster,** by Ben Levisohn
© *BusinessWeek Online*, 16 March 2009

- Health and Safety (Offences) Act 2008
- Financial Services Act 1986
- Corporate Manslaughter and Corporate Homicide Act 2007.

In addition, it should be noted that further statutory provisions giving rise to vicarious liability of directors for corporate offences are included in Acts of Parliament, which currently number well over 200! Directors can be:

- forced to pay a company's losses
- fined
- prevented from running businesses
- imprisoned.

The Directors' Remuneration Report Regulations 2002 (Statutory Instrument 2002 No. 1986) are now in force and require the directors of a company to prepare a remuneration report that is clear, transparent and understandable to shareholders. Many smaller companies without continuous legal advice are unaware about how much the rules have tightened. It is usually not until there is wide publicity surrounding high-profile business problems that boards of directors are alerted to the demands and penalties to which they may be subjected if things go wrong.

It was not only the 1980s and early 1990s that saw corporate scandals and irregularities (for example, Polly Peck and the Maxwell companies). At the end of 1999, accounting irregularities caused trading in engineering company TransTec shares to be suspended, with Arthur Andersen called in as administrative receiver. The case was fuelled by the revelation by former TransTec chief accountant Max Ayris that nearly £500,000 of a total of £1.3m in grants from the Department of Trade and Industry was obtained fraudulently. TransTec, founded by former Government minister Geoffrey Robinson, collapsed in December 1999, after the accounting irregularities were discovered, with debts of more than £70m. Following the collapse of the company the role of the auditors to the company, PricewaterhouseCoopers, was also to be examined by the Joint Disciplinary Scheme, the accountancy profession's senior watchdog.

Also during 1999, the trade finance group Versailles discovered that there had been some double counting of transactions, which prompted the Department of Trade and Industry to take a close interest in its affairs. Actual and apparent corporate misdemeanours continued, on an even larger scale, through the late 1990s and on into the twenty-first century (note the Barings debacle, Enron, World-Com and Tyco).

Non-executive directors are legally expected to know as much as executive directors about what is going on in the company. Ignorance is not a defence. Directors must be aware of what is going on and have knowledge of the law relating to their duties and responsibilities. Fundamentally, directors must:

- use their common sense
- be careful in what they do
- look after shareholders
- look after creditors
- look after employees.

Progress check 6.5

What are the main responsibilities of directors with regard to the accounting and financial reporting of their companies?

Duty of care

It is the duty of a director to exercise his or her powers in the best interests of the company, which includes not acting for his or her personal benefit, nor for an improper use. In the year 2000, Greg Hutchings, the chairman of a major plc, Tomkins, was criticised for alleged excessive perks, unauthorised donations, and inclusion of members of his family and household staff on the company payroll, without proper disclosure. Investors' concern over corporate governance practices at the group had been triggered by a fall in the share price of over 50% in two years. The resignation of the chairman followed an initial investigation. The new chairman very quickly launched a full inquiry into executive perks within the group, overseen by him personally.

Duty of care means doing the job with the skill and care that somebody with the necessary knowledge and experience would exercise if they were acting on their own behalf. Delegation of directors' power must be 'properly and sensibly done'. If a director of a company does not choose the right people or supervise them properly, all the directors may be liable for the misdeeds and mistakes of the people they have appointed.

When a company fails and is found to be insolvent, the **receiver** appointed will leave no stone unturned to identify whether any money may be recovered in order to pay off creditors. This will include checking for any oversights by directors for items they should have spotted 'if they had exercised their proper level of skill'.

Fiduciary duty

Directors must act in the best interests of the company. Courts will support directors who act honestly and in good faith. Acting in the best interests of the company includes not making personal profit at the company's expense, not letting personal interest interfere with the proper running of the business, or doing business which favours directors or their close associates. In the late 1990s and early 2000s there were several business failures within the dot.com sector, where directors did act in the best interests of the company although their business plans may not have been commercially successful (for example, *www.breathe.com*).

Corporate manslaughter

There is an offence of corporate manslaughter, which a company may be guilty of if a failure by its management is the cause of a person's death, and their failure is because their conduct is well below what can be reasonably expected. Before 1999 there were only five prosecutions in the UK for corporate manslaughter, resulting in two convictions. The risk for companies and their directors is remote but very real, and should therefore be managed in terms of awareness, training, preventative measures and liability insurance.

In earlier years companies were outside the criminal law. As one judge put it, 'a company had a soul to damn and no body to kick' – meaning that because a company did not have an actual existence it could not be guilty of a crime because it could not have a guilty will. In 1965 a case established the validity of the indictment of a company for manslaughter. Since then over 19,000 people have been killed as a result of corporate activity, but no company stood trial for manslaughter, apart from P&O European Ferries (Dover) Ltd after the capsize and sinking of the *Herald of Free Enterprise* off Zeebrugge in 1987. The directors of P&O Ferries did stand trial, but were acquitted because the trial collapsed halfway through. Currently, to succeed in a case of corporate manslaughter against a company there is a need to prove gross negligence and to prove that at least one sufficiently senior official was guilty of that same gross negligence.

Although each year hundreds of people are killed at work or in commercially related activity, if companies have been prosecuted at all they have been charged under the Health and Safety at Work Act (1974) and other regulatory legislation. Many of the companies implicated in work fatalities and public transport disasters operate with diffuse management systems and much delegated power. Such systems that appear to have no 'controlling mind' make it difficult to meet the requirement of the law because of the difficulty in identifying the individual(s) who may possess the mental element for the crime.

A case that was successfully prosecuted involved a small company, OLL Ltd, which organised a canoe expedition at Lyme Bay in 1993, in which four teenage schoolchildren died. In 1994 the jury in the case found OLL Ltd guilty of manslaughter – a historic decision. Peter Kite, the managing director of the activity centre responsible for the canoeing disaster, was jailed for three years for manslaughter, and OLL Ltd was fined £60,000. OLL Ltd was the first company in the UK ever to be found guilty of manslaughter, in a decision that swept away 400 years of legal history.

The Lyme Bay case was atypical of corporate homicide incidents. The company was small, so it was relatively easy to discover the 'controlling mind'; the risks to which pupils were exposed were serious and obvious and, critically, they were not technical or esoteric in any way. However, in the case of a large corporation with many levels of management it is virtually impossible to identify a controlling mind. The Corporate Manslaughter and Corporate Homicide Act (2007) replaces the concept of the controlling mind with a consideration of the way in which an organisation's activities were managed or organised. The Act puts emphasis on examining management systems and practices across the organisation to establish whether an adequate standard of care was applied to the fatal situation. At the time of writing this book the first attempted prosecution under the rules of the new Act was being tried in the courts, following several adjournments (the importance of this landmark case is illustrated in the press extract on the next page). The defendant was found guilty on 15 February 2011.

Great Western Trains was fined £1.5m over the Southall (1997) rail crash in which seven people were killed, following a Health and Safety Executive (HSE) prosecution. But no individual within the company was charged with manslaughter.

The Paddington (1999) rail crash case, again brought by the HSE, resulted in 31 people killed and over 400 injured. The company, Thames Trains, was fined £2m in April 2004, but even though the HSE said its enquiries had revealed 'serious failing in management', there was no prosecution for corporate manslaughter.

A few years ago the legal profession considered that the promised review of the Law Commission's recommendation for an involuntary homicide Act 'could result in company directors being made personally responsible for safety and therefore potentially liable in cases of avoidable accidents'. The Corporate Manslaughter and Corporate Homicide Act 2007 is now expected to dramatically increase the level of directors' accountability to ensure the provision of safe work environments for their employees.

Other responsibilities

Directors do not owe a direct duty to shareholders, but to the company itself. Directors have no contractual or fiduciary duty to outsiders and are generally not liable unless they have acted in breach of their authority. Directors must have regard to the interests of employees but this is enforceable against directors only by the company and not by the employees.

Progress check 6.6

What is meant by a duty of care and fiduciary duty with regard to company directors?

A new chapter in English law on corporate manslaughter?

In law, small cases often mark major milestones. When the prosecution of Cotswold Geotechnical Holdings begins next week at Stroud Magistrates' Court, a new chapter in English law will begin. It will be the first case brought under the Corporate Manslaughter and Corporate Homicide Act 2007 and it signifies a new approach to prosecuting companies for alleged crimes.

The case concerns the death of Alexander Wright, 27, a geologist, who was taking soil samples from a pit that had been excavated as part of a site survey when the sides collapsed, crushing him.

The first chapter of corporate manslaughter law began on February 2, 1965, but it was rather an empty one. The Times reported what was then an innovation in English law: a company had stood trial for manslaughter. Glanville Evans, a 27-year-old welder, had been killed when the bridge at Boughrood that he was demolishing collapsed and he fell into the River Wye. The company had evidently been reckless in instructing him to work in a perilous way but an attempt to convict it for manslaughter at Glamorgan Assizes failed on the evidence.

Nonetheless, the court accepted that a company could be prosecuted for manslaughter. A new crime was recognised. Since then more than 40,000 people have been killed at work or in commercial disasters, such as those involving ferries and trains, while prosecutions for corporate manslaughter have totalled just 38.

The old common law made it very difficult to prosecute companies because the doctrine of identification required the prosecution to pin all the blame on at least one director whose will was identified as the "mind" of the company. As companies commonly had responsibility for safety matters distributed across more than one directorial portfolio, pinning all the blame on one person was difficult. Various directors claimed to know only a fragment of the lethal danger that materialised. It was not permissible to incriminate the company by aggregating the fragmented faults of several directors.

The new law aims to criminalise corporate killing without the need to find all the blame in one individual. The offence is committed where an organisation owes a duty to take reasonable care for a person's safety but the way in which its business has been 'managed or organised' amounts to a gross breach of that duty and causes death.

The law says that, for a conviction, a 'substantial element' of the gross negligence must come from 'senior management' (as opposed to a maverick worker) but any company trying to evade the law by not making safety the responsibility of a senior manager would, by virtue of that very stratagem, be open to legal attack.

Companies convicted of manslaughter can be made to publicise their wrongdoing in the national press and are subject to an unlimited fine. The Sentencing Advisory Panel has suggested a level of fine of between 2.5 and 10 per cent of a convicted company's average annual turnover during the three years before the offence. This is a dramatic change. Most large companies convicted of fatal safety crimes are now fined at a level that is less than one 700th of annual turnover.

Directors can be prosecuted for safety offences alongside a corporate manslaughter prosecution and the Health and Safety (Offences) Act 2008 has widened the range of offences for which prison is a possible punishment.

The new corporate manslaughter law obliges the jury to consider whether a company is guilty by looking at what happened in the context of general safety law. Jurors are also invited to consider how far the evidence shows that there were 'attitudes, policies, systems or accepted practices within the organisation' that were likely to have encouraged the safety failures that resulted in death.

Historically, the law was chiselled to govern individuals accused of homicide and it could not properly be adapted to prosecute corporations. That became more problematic once companies became so powerful – of the world's 100 largest economic entities today, 49 are countries and 51 are companies. Having corporate citizens that are more powerful than governments is a challenge for good social governance.

Globally, more people are killed each year at work or through commercial enterprise – more than two million – than die in wars. If the Act works well in the United Kingdom it will be a good template to be adopted in other countries, and that would confer a substantial social benefit.

Source: **The small cases that will have a big influence on the way we work; Gary Slapper reflects on the deaths that have led to changes in corporate manslaughter law** © *The Times*, 11 July 2009

Insolvency

Insolvency, or when a company becomes insolvent, is when the company is unable to pay creditors' debts in full after realisation of all the assets of the business. The penalties imposed on directors of companies continuing to trade while insolvent may be disqualification and personal liability. Many directors have lost their houses (as well as their businesses) as a result of being successfully pursued by the receivers appointed to their insolvent companies.

The Insolvency Act 1986 (as amended by the Enterprise Act 2002) provides guidance on matters to be considered by liquidators and receivers in the reports that they are required to prepare on the conduct of directors. These matters include:

- breaches of fiduciary and other duties to the company
- misapplication or retention of monies or other property of the company
- causing the company to enter into transactions which defrauded the creditors
- failure to keep proper accounting and statutory records
- failure to make annual returns to the Registrar of Companies and prepare and file annual accounts.

If a company is insolvent, the courts assess the directors' responsibility for:

- the cause of the company becoming insolvent
- the company's failure to supply goods or services which had been paid for
- the company entering into fraudulent transactions or giving preference to particular creditors
- failure of the company to adhere to the rules regarding creditors' meetings in a creditors' **voluntary winding-up**
- failure to provide a **statement of affairs** or to deliver up any proper books or information regarding the company.

> ### Progress check 6.7
> How does insolvency impact on directors and what are their responsibilities in this regard?

Wrongful trading

A major innovation of the Insolvency Act 1986 was to create the statutory tort (civil wrong) of **wrongful trading**. It occurs where a director knows or ought to have known before the commencement of winding up that there was no reasonable prospect of the company avoiding insolvency and he or she does not take every step to minimise loss to creditors. If the court is satisfied of this it may:

- order the director to contribute to the assets of the business, and
- disqualify him or her from further involvement in corporate management for a specified period.

A director will not be liable for wrongful trading if he or she can show that from the relevant time he or she 'took every step with a view to minimising the potential loss to the company's creditors as (assuming him or her to have known that there was no reasonable prospect that the company would avoid going into insolvent liquidation) he or she ought to have taken'. A company goes into insolvent liquidation, for this purpose, if it does so at a time when its assets are insufficient for the payment of its debts and other liabilities and the expenses of winding-up.

Both subjective tests and objective tests are made with regard to directors. A director who is responsible, for example, for manufacturing, quality, purchasing, or human resources, is likely

to have less skill and knowledge regarding the financial affairs of the company than the **finance** ◀▥
director, unless otherwise fully briefed. Directors with financial or legal experience will certainly be expected to bear a greater responsibility than other directors because of their specialist knowledge.

Fraudulent trading

Fraudulent trading is an offence committed by persons who are knowingly party to the continu- ◀▥
ance of a company trading in circumstances where creditors are defrauded, or for other fraudulent purposes. Generally, this means that the company incurs more debts at a time when it is known that those debts will not be met. Persons responsible for acting in this way are personally liable without limitation for the debts of the company. The offence also carries criminal penalties.

The offence of fraudulent trading may apply at any time, not just in or after a winding-up. If a company is wound up and fraudulent trading has taken place, an additional civil liability arises in respect of any person who was knowingly a party to it.

> ### Progress check 6.8
>
> Are there any differences between wrongful trading and fraudulent trading? If so, what are they?

Disqualification of directors

Disqualification means that a person cannot be, for a specified period of time, a director or manager of any company without the permission of the courts. Disqualification is governed under the Company Directors (Disqualification) Act 1986, and may result from breaches under:

- the Companies Act 2006
  – from cases of fraud or other breaches of duty by a director
- the Insolvency Act 1986 (as amended by the Enterprise Act 2002)
  – if the courts consider that the conduct of a director makes him or her unfit to be concerned in the future management of a company.

Whilst there are serious implications for directors of companies under the Company Directors (Disqualification) Act 1986, it should be noted that the Act is not restricted to company directors. Over one half of the liabilities fall on 'any persons' as well as company directors. 'Any persons' in this context potentially includes any employee within the organisation.

The following offences, and their penalties, under the Act relate to any persons:

- being convicted of an indictable offence – disqualification from company directorships for up to five years, and possibly for up to 15 years
- fraud in a winding-up – disqualification from company directorships for up to 15 years
- participation in fraudulent or wrongful trading – disqualification from company directorships for up to 15 years
- acting as a director while an undischarged bankrupt, and failure to make payments under a county court administration order – imprisonment for up to two years, or a fine, or both
- personal liability for a company's debts where the person acts while disqualified – civil personal liability.

The following offences, and their penalties, under the Act relate to directors (but in some instances include other managers or officers of the company):

- persistent breaches of company legislation – disqualification from company directorships for up to five years
- convictions for not less than three default orders in respect of a failure to comply with any provisions of companies' legislation requiring a return, account or other document to be filed, delivered, sent, etc., to the Registrar of Companies (whether or not it is a failure of the company or the director) – disqualification from company directorships for up to five years
- finding of unfitness to run a company in the event of the company's insolvency – disqualification from company directorships for a period of between two years and 15 years
- if after investigation of a company the conduct of a director makes him or her unfit to manage a company – disqualification from company directorships for up to 15 years
- attribution of offences by the company to others if such persons consent, connive or are negligent – imprisonment for up to two years, or a fine, or both, or possibly imprisonment for not more than six months, or a fine.

Worked example 6.4

In February 2010 it was reported that five former directors of a timeshare firm Worldwide International UK Limited had been disqualified for a total of 32 years following an investigation by the Companies Investigation Branch (CIB). Mr Bruce Goss, the controlling director of the family firm, was disqualified for 8 years after the CIB investigation found that the company, which marketed timeshare and holiday products, was run with a 'serious lack of commercial probity', leading to several complaints to trading standards. The CIB suggested he caused the company to trade while insolvent and was responsible for 'intermingling' the accounts of several different companies. There was also a failure to keep proper accounts and failure to pay debts. In addition, it was claimed that the family had a 'propensity' to transfer surplus funds to their own accounts. In the judgement disqualifying Mr Goss, the High Court Registrar said, 'I am therefore satisfied that the allegations made against Mr Goss disclose persistent and serious dishonesty. Even when the company's financial situation was clearly hopeless he allowed it to continue to take money from customers and those customers who sought explanations were lied to and deceived.'

Let's look at the important implications of this case and the way in which the law protects society from the actions of unscrupulous directors.

There are some fundamental reasons why it is necessary for society to ban certain individuals from becoming directors of limited companies.

- The limited liability company is a very efficient means of conducting business, but if used by unscrupulous persons then innocent people can lose money, through no fault of their own.
- The limited liability company can offer a financial shield to protect employees and investors if things go wrong and the company ceases trading, and is unable to pays its creditors.

UK law is now quite strict and will attack an obviously unscrupulous person who takes advantage of the protection of the limited liability company and leaves various creditors out of pocket.

In recent times the UK government has banned an increasing number of persons from becoming directors, as well as publishing their names in the public domain (for example, on the Internet). Almost certainly the recently introduced regime is showing its teeth and punishing guilty directors in a most practical manner.

In some circumstances directors may be disqualified automatically. Automatic disqualification occurs in the case of an individual who revokes a county court administration order, and in the case of an undischarged bankrupt unless **leave of the court** is obtained. In all other situations the right to act as a director may be withdrawn only by an order of the court, unless a company through its Articles of Association provides for specific circumstances in which a director's appointment may be terminated. The City of London has seen a major toughening of the regime where persons have found themselves unemployable (for example, the fallout from the Baring Bank debacle in the mid-1990s).

Progress check 6.9

In what circumstances may a director be disqualified?

Summary of directors' obligations and responsibilities

In summary, the following may serve as a useful checklist of directors' obligations and responsibilities:

- both executive and non-executive directors must act with care, look after the finances and act within their powers, and look after employees
- directors are responsible for keeping proper books of account and presenting shareholders with accounts, and failure to do so can result in disqualification
- directors should understand the accounts and be able to interpret them
- the board of directors is responsible for filing accounts with the Registrar of Companies and must also notify changes to the board of directors and changes to the registered address
- shareholders must appoint auditors
- the directors are responsible for calling and holding annual general meetings, and ensuring minutes of all meetings are appropriately recorded
- directors are responsible for ensuring that the company complies with its memorandum and articles of association
- if a company continues to trade while technically insolvent and goes into receivership a director may be forced to contribute personally to repaying creditors
- a director trading fraudulently is liable to be called on for money
- any director who knew or ought to have known that insolvency was unavoidable without minimising loss to the creditors becomes liable
- directors can be disqualified for paying themselves too much
- inadequate attention paid to the financial affairs of the company can result in disqualification
- directors are required to prepare a remuneration report.

We have seen the onerous burden of responsibility placed on directors of limited companies in terms of compliance with guidelines and legislation. The obligations of directors continue to grow with the increase in government regulation and legislation. Sixteen new directives were introduced in the UK during the two years to 2001, relating to such issues as employee working conditions, health and safety and, for example, administration of a minimum wage policy.

How can directors make sure that they comply and cover themselves in the event of things going wrong?

Actions to ensure compliance

Directors of companies need to be aware of the dividing line between the commission of a criminal offence and the commission of technical offences of the Companies Act. Directors should take the necessary actions to ensure compliance with their obligations and responsibilities, and to protect themselves against possible non-compliance:

- directors may delegate their responsibilities within or outside the company and in such circumstances they must ensure that the work is being done by competent, able and honest people
- directors of small companies in particular should get professional help to ensure compliance with statutory responsibilities
- directors must ensure that they are kept fully informed about the affairs of the company by having regular meetings and recording minutes and material decisions
- directors should ensure they have service contracts that cover the company's duties, rights, obligations and directors' benefits
- directors must ensure that detailed, timely management accounts are prepared, and, if necessary, professional help sought to provide, for example, monthly reporting systems and assistance with interpretation of information produced and actions required.

It is essential that directors carefully watch for warning signs of any decline in the company's position, for example:

- falling sales or market share
- overdependence on one product or customer or supplier
- overtrading (see Chapter 16)
- pressure on bank borrowings
- increases in trade payables
- requirements for cash paid in advance
- increasing inventory levels
- poor financial controls.

The protection that directors may obtain is extremely limited. All directors should certainly take out individual professional liability insurance. But above all it is probably more important that all directors clearly understand their obligations and responsibilities, closely watch company performance, and take immediate, appropriate action as necessary, to ensure compliance and minimise their exposure to the type of personal risks we have discussed above.

Progress check 6.10

What actions should directors take to ensure they meet their obligations, and to protect themselves should things go wrong?

Summary of key points

- The framework for establishing good corporate governance and accountability has been established in a UK Corporate Governance Code, developed from the work of the Cadbury, Greenbury, Hampel, and Turnbull Committees.

- There is a statutory requirement for the audit of the accounts of limited companies, except for smaller limited companies.

- The election of suitably qualified, independent auditors is the responsibility of the shareholders, to whom they are responsible.

- Directors of limited companies have a specific responsibility to shareholders, and general responsibilities to all stakeholders and the community, for the management and conduct of companies. (Note the continued activities of pressure groups such as Greenpeace and Friends of the Earth.)

- Directors of limited companies have a fiduciary duty to act in the best interests of the company, and a duty of care to all stakeholders and to the community at large, particularly with regard to the Companies Act 2006, Health and Safety at Work Act 1974, Health and Safety (Offences) Act 2008, Financial Services Act 1986, Insolvency Act 1986, and Enterprise Act 2002.

- The risk for companies and their directors from the Corporate Manslaughter and Homicide Act 2007 has become very real, and should therefore be managed in terms of awareness, training, preventative measures and liability insurance.

- The implications for directors for wrongful trading may be to contribute to the assets of the business, and disqualification from further involvement in corporate management for a specified period.

- The implications for directors for fraudulent trading may be to contribute to the assets of the business without limit, disqualification, and possible criminal and civil penalties.

- The implications of the Company Directors (Disqualification) Act 1986 (as amended by the Enterprise Act 2002) apply not only to company directors, and over 50% of the provisions relate to any persons.

- Directors of limited companies, in addition to taking out individual professional liability insurance, must ensure that they clearly understand their obligations and responsibilities.

Assessment material

Questions

Q6.1 (i)   How was the UK Corporate Governance Code developed?

(ii) Why was it considered necessary?

Q6.2 Refer to the Johnson Matthey section on corporate governance in their annual report and accounts 2010, shown on pages 192–206, and illustrate their areas of compliance (or not) under the UK Corporate Governance Code (as distinct from the previous Combined Code of Practice).

Q6.3 (i)   Which areas of the business do auditors' opinions cover?

(ii) What happens if there is any fundamental uncertainty as to compliance?

Q6.4   Explain the implications of the 'expectation gap' with regard to external auditors.

Q6.5   Explain the obligations of directors of limited companies in terms of their duty of care, their fiduciary duty, and the Corporate Manslaughter and Corporate Homicide Act (2007).

Q6.6   If the severity of the penalty is determined by the seriousness of the offence, describe the half dozen or so most serious offences under the Company Directors (Disqualification) Act 1986 (as amended by the Enterprise Act 2002), which relate to directors of limited companies.

Q6.7   Outline the general responsibilities of a director of a limited company with regard to the company, its shareholders and other stakeholders.

Q6.8   What are the key actions that a director of a limited company may take to ensure compliance with his or her obligations and responsibilities?

Discussion points

D6.1   Discuss, and illustrate with some examples, how far you think the UK Corporate Governance Code goes to preventing the kind of corporate excesses we have seen in the recent past.

D6.2   'I pay my auditors a fortune in audit fees. I look upon this almost as another insurance premium to make sure that I'm protected against every kind of financial risk.' Discuss.

D6.3   'Everyone who embarks on a career in industry or commerce aspires to become a director of their organisation, because then all their troubles are over! Directors just make a few decisions, swan around in their company cars, and pick up a fat cheque at the end of each month for doing virtually nothing.' Discuss.

D6.4   In an age of increasingly sophisticated computer systems is the traditional role of the auditor coming to an end?

Exercises

Solutions are provided in Appendix 3 to all exercise numbers highlighted in colour.

Level I

E6.1   *Time allowed – 30 minutes*

> **Discuss why users of financial statements should have information on awards to directors of share options, allowing them to subscribe to shares at fixed prices in the future.**

E6.2   *Time allowed – 30 minutes*

> **Outline the basic reasons why there should be openness regarding directors' benefits and 'perks'.**

E6.3   *Time allowed – 30 minutes*

> **Can you think of any reasons why directors of UK plcs found that their contracts were no longer to be open-ended under the new regime of corporate governance?**

E6.4   *Time allowed – 60 minutes*

William Mason is the managing director of Classical Gas plc, a recently formed manufacturing company in the chemical industry, and he has asked you as finance director to prepare a report that covers the topics, together with a brief explanation, to be included in a section on corporate governance in their forthcoming annual report and accounts.

Level II

E6.5   *Time allowed – 60 minutes*

After the birth of her twins Vimla Shah decided to take a couple of years away from her career as a company lawyer. During one of her coffee mornings with Joan Turnbull, Joan confided in her that although she was delighted at her husband Ronnie's promotion to commercial director of his company, which was a large UK plc in the food industry, she had heard many horror stories about problems that company directors had encountered, seemingly through no fault of their own. She was worried about the implications of these obligations and responsibilities (whatever they were) that Ronnie had taken on. Vimla said she would write some notes about what being a director of a plc meant, and provide some guidelines as to the type of things that Ronnie should be aware of, and to include some ways in which Ronnie might protect himself, that may all offer some reassurance to Joan.

Prepare a draft of what you think Vimla's notes for Joan may have included.

E6.6   *Time allowed – 60 minutes*

Li Nan has recently been appointed managing director of Pingers plc, which is a company that supplies table tennis equipment to clubs and individuals throughout the UK and Europe. Li Nan is surprised at the high figure that appeared in last year's accounts under audit fees.

Li Nan is not completely familiar with UK business practices and has requested you to prepare a detailed report on what the audit fees cover, and to include the general responsibilities of directors in respect of the external audit.

E6.7   *Time allowed – 60 minutes*

Use the following information, extracted from Tomkins plc report and accounts for 2000, as a basis for discussing the users of financial information's need for information on directors' remuneration.

	Basic salary	Benefits in kind	Bonuses
G Hutchings, executive director	£975,000	£45,000	£443,000
G Gates (USA), non-executive director	nil, but has a 250,000 US$ consultancy agreement		
R Holland, non-executive director	£23,000	Nil	Nil

E6.8   *Time allowed – 60 minutes*

Explain what is meant by insolvency and outline the responsibilities of receivers appointed to insolvent companies.

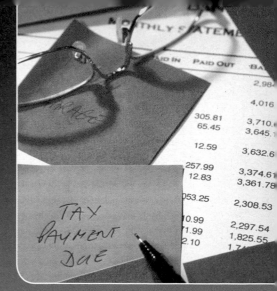

7

Financial statements analysis

Contents

Learning objectives

Completion of this chapter will enable you to:

- carry out a performance review of a business, including the use of SWOT analysis
- critically evaluate the limitations of the performance review process
- differentiate between divisional manager performance measurement and economic performance measurement
- analyse business performance through the use of ratio analysis of profitability; efficiency; liquidity; investment; financial structure
- use both profit and cash flow in the measurement of business performance
- critically compare the use of cash flow versus profit as the best measure in the evaluation of financial performance
- use earnings before interest, tax, depreciation and amortisation (EBITDA) as a close approximation of a cash flow performance measure.

Introduction

Chapters 2, 3, 4 and 5 introduced us to the financial statements of limited companies that are prepared with regard to the accountability we discussed in Chapter 6. This chapter is concerned with how the performance of a business may be reviewed through analysis and evaluation of the balance sheet, the income statement and the statement of cash flows. Business performance may be considered from outside or within the business for a variety of reasons. The performance review process provides an understanding of the business which, together with an analysis of all the relevant information, enables interpretation and evaluation of its financial performance during successive accounting periods and its financial position at the end of those accounting periods.

The chapter begins with an outline of the steps involved in the performance review process and also considers the limitations of such a process. The main body of this chapter is concerned with ratio analysis. Financial ratio analysis looks at the detailed use of profitability, efficiency, liquidity, investment and financial structure ratios in the evaluation of financial performance.

The chapter closes with a discussion about which is the best measure of performance – cash or profit. The use of earnings per share and cash flow in performance measurement are discussed along with the measurement of earnings before interest, tax, depreciation and amortisation (EBITDA) as an approximation of cash flow. The debate continues as to whether cash flow or profit represents the best basis for financial performance measurement.

In Chapter 8 we shall build on the knowledge gained from the current chapter when we examine the published report and accounts of a major UK plc, Johnson Matthey.

The performance review process

A performance review using financial statements may be undertaken for a number of reasons, for example:

- to assist in investment decisions
- to identify possible takeover targets
- to evaluate the financial strength of potential or existing customers or suppliers.

The main aim of a performance review is to provide an understanding of the business, and, together with an analysis of all the relevant information, provide an interpretation of the results. A performance review is generally undertaken using a standard format and methodology. The most effective performance review is provided from a balanced view of each of the activities of the organisation, which necessarily involves the close co-operation of each role: marketing; research and development; design; engineering; manufacturing; sales; logistics; finance; human resources management.

The performance review process begins with a **SWOT analysis** and works through a number of steps to the conclusions, as outlined in Figure 7.1. A SWOT analysis includes an internal analysis of the company and an analysis of the company's position with regard to its external environment.

1. SWOT analysis

SWOT is shorthand for strengths, weaknesses, opportunities and threats. The first look at a company's performance usually involves listing the key features of the company by looking internally at its particular strengths and weaknesses, and externally at risks or threats to the company and opportunities that it may be able to exploit. The SWOT analysis may give some indication of, for example, the strength of the company's management team, how well it is doing on product quality, and areas as yet untapped within its marketplace.

To keep the analysis focused, a cruciform chart may be used for SWOT analysis. An example is outlined in Figure 7.2, relating to the position in 2010 of the low-budget airline, Ryanair.

2. Consideration of major features

The increasing amount of information now provided in published financial statements enables the analyst to look in detail at the various industrial and geographical sectors of the business, the trends

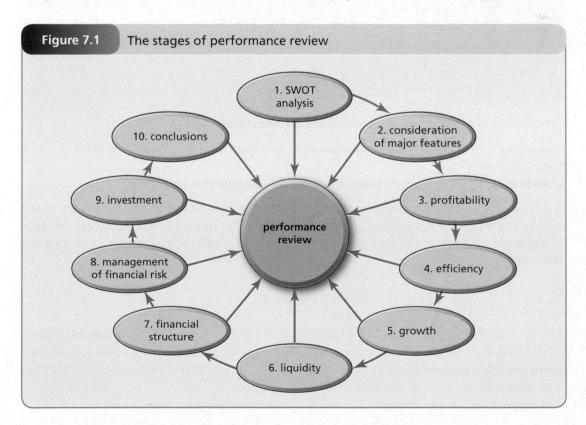

Figure 7.1   The stages of performance review

| Figure 7.2 | An example of a SWOT analysis |

Strengths	Weaknesses
Firm operating strategy	Declining profitability
Robust route network	Legal proceedings
Strong fleet operations	Unfunded employee post-retirement benefits

Opportunities	Threats
Accelerating UK airlines industry	Intense competition and price discounting
Positive outlook for the European online travel market	EU regulations on denied boarding compensation
Growing global travel and tourism industry	

within these and the business in general. Further background information may be extracted from the accounting policies, the auditors' report, chairman's report and details of any significant events that have been highlighted.

3. Profitability

A number of financial indicators and ratios may be considered to assess the profitability of the company, which may include:

- gross profit (or gross margin) to sales
- return on sales (ROS)
- **return on capital employed (ROCE)**, or **return on investment (ROI)**.

4. Efficiency

The efficiency of the company may be considered in terms of its:

- operating cycle – its receivables **collection days**, **payables days** and **inventories days**
- asset turnover
- **vertical analysis** of its income statement (which we will look at in Chapter 8).

In a vertical analysis of the income statement (which may also be applied to the balance sheet) each item is expressed as a percentage of the total sales. The vertical analysis provides evidence of structural changes in the accounts such as increased profitability through more efficient production.

5. Growth

Growth of the organisation may relate to sales growth and gross margin growth. **Horizontal analysis** (or common size analysis) of the income statement, which we will look at in Chapter 8, provides a line-by-line analysis of the numbers in the financial statements compared with those of the previous year. It may provide over a number of years a trend of changes showing either growth or decline in these numbers by calculation of annual percentage growth rates in profits, sales, inventories or any other item.

6. Liquidity

Liquidity is concerned with the short-term solvency of the company. It is assessed by looking at a number of key ratios, for example:

- **current ratio**
- **acid test**
- **defensive interval**
- cash ROCE
- **cash interest cover**.

7. Financial structure

How the company is financed is concerned with the long-term solvency of the company. It is assessed by looking at a number of other key ratios, for example:

- **gearing** – the proportion of capital employed financed by lenders rather than shareholders, expressed in a number of ways, for example the **debt/equity ratio** (long-term loans and preference shares/ordinary shareholders' funds)
- **dividend cover** (eps/dividend per share)
- **interest cover** (profit before interest and tax (PBIT)/interest payable)
- various forms of off balance sheet financing.

Off balance sheet financing is defined as the funding or refinancing of a company's operations in such a way that, under legal requirements and existing accounting conventions, some or all of the finance may not be disclosed in its balance sheet. The International Accounting Standards Board (IASB) has tried (and indeed continues to try) to introduce regulations forcing the exclusion of this type of financing.

8. Management of financial risk

The global market is here. Companies increasingly trade globally with greater levels of sophistication in products, operations and finance. Risk assessment and the management of risk are therefore now assuming increasing importance. The main areas of financial risk are in investment, foreign currency exchange rates and interest rates, and levels of trade credit.

9. Investment

Investment ratios examine whether or not the company is undertaking sufficient investment to ensure its future profitability. These ratios include, for example:

- earnings per share (eps)
- **price earnings ratio (P/E)**
- capital expenditure/sales revenue
- capital expenditure/gross non-current assets.

10. Conclusions

The conclusion of the performance review will include consideration of the company's SWOT analysis and the main performance features. It will consider growth and profitability and whether or not these are maintainable, as well as levels of finance and investment, and whether there is sufficient cash flow, and the future plans of the business.

All performance reviews must use some sort of benchmark. Comparisons may be made against past periods and against budget; they may also be made against other companies and using general data relating to the industry within which the company operates. Later in this chapter we will look in more detail at the use of profitability, efficiency, liquidity, and investment ratios, and ratios relating to financial structure.

Progress check 7.1

Describe each of the stages in a business performance review process.

Limitations of the performance review process

There are many obvious limitations to the above approach. In comparing performance against other companies (and sometimes within the company in comparing past periods), or looking at industrial data, it should be borne in mind that:

- there may be a lack of uniformity in accounting definitions and techniques
- the balance sheet is only a snapshot in time, and only represents a single estimate of the company's position
- there may actually be no standards for comparison
- changes in the environment and changes in money values, together with short-term fluctuations, may have a significant impact
- the past should really not be relied on as a good predictor of the future.

The speed of change in the computer peripherals market is well known to manufacturers. Some components may have been large revenue generators for many years yet even they finally cease to have a market. Sony had sold 3.5 inch floppy disks since 1983 and in 2002 sold 47 million of them in Japan. Inevitably, new technologies eventually superseded the floppy disk, leading to its decline in sales (see the press extract on the next page). Even a product which currently provides a strong income stream will not do so indefinitely.

Diversified companies present a different set of problems. Such companies by their very nature comprise companies engaged in various industrial sectors, each having different market conditions, financial structures and expectations of performance. The notes to the accounts, which appear in each company's annual report and accounts, invariably present a less than comprehensive picture of the company's position.

As time goes by, and accounting standards and legislation get tighter and tighter, the number of loopholes which allow any sort of window dressing of a company's results are reduced. Inevitably,

The past is not a good predictor of the future

They were once the stalwarts of the techno-logical era. But the humble floppy disk is about to bite the dust once and for all. The un-wieldy storage devices have been shown the door by their biggest manufacturer, Sony, which has announced that production will cease next year.

The plastic storage 'disks' have been usurped by smaller USB drives, which have more space for data and are far easier to transport. To tell the truth, we thought sales of floppy disks had nose-dived years ago. Yet, incredibly, Sony still sold 12 million floppy disks last year in Japan.

The first floppy was invented by IBM in 1971 and was eight wobbly inches wide. And while most people thought the floppiness of the whole thing gave the product its name, it was actually the circular magnetic disk inside that was technically the 'floppy' bit. This pioneering technology allowed information to be passed between computers – but heaven forbid you forgot to slap a brightly coloured sticky label on your anonymous-looking disk to remind you of the contents.

Later, the more common 3.5in disks weren't floppy at all, but the name stuck – though some show-offs called them 'diskettes'. Hundreds of millions of floppy disks have been sold since 1971 – until now.

But although computers don't have built in floppy drives any more, the floppy's legacy will live on – we still click on a little icon of one to save a document when we're using most computer software today.

Source: **Farewell then . . . floppy disks**, by Chris Beanland
© *Daily Mail*, 28 April 2010

however, there will always remain the possibility of the company's position being presented in ways that may not always represent the 'truth'. We will now look at the type of information that may be used and the important financial ratios and their meaning and relevance.

Progress check 7.2

What are the main limitations encountered in carrying out the performance review of a business?

Economic performance measurement

Most large organisations are divided into separate divisions in which their individual managers have autonomy and total responsibility for investment and profit. Within each division there is usually a functional structure comprising many departments. Divisionalisation is more appropriate for com-panies with diversified activities. The performance of the managers of each division may be measured in a number of ways, for example return on investment (ROI) and **residual income (RI)**.

The relationships between divisions should be regulated so that no division, by seeking to increase its own profit, can reduce the profitability of the company as a whole. Therefore, there are strong arguments for producing two broad types of performance measure. One type of measure is used to evaluate managerial performance and the other type of measure is used to evaluate economic performance.

Divisional performance measurement is discussed in Chapter 12. In the current chapter we are primarily concerned with the performance of the organisation as a whole. We will look at ratios that measure economic performance, which focus not only on profit and profitability, but on a range of other areas of performance that include, for example, cash and working capital.

Ratio analysis

The reasons for a performance review may be wide and varied. Generally, it is required to shed light on the extent to which the objectives of the company are being achieved. These objectives may be:

- to earn a satisfactory return on capital employed (ROCE)
- to maintain and enhance the financial position of the business with reference to the management of working capital, non-current assets and bank borrowings
- to achieve cost targets and other business targets such as improvements in labour productivity.

Ratio analysis is an important area of performance review. It is far more useful than merely considering absolute numbers, which on their own may have little meaning. Ratios may be used:

- for a subjective assessment of the company or its constituent parts
- for a more objective way to aid decision-making
- to provide **cross-sectional analysis** and **inter-company comparison**
- to establish models for loan and credit ratings
- to provide equity valuation models to value businesses
- to analyse and identify underpriced shares and takeover targets
- to predict company failure.

There are various models that may be used to predict company failure such as those developed by John Argenti (*Corporate Collapse: The Causes and Symptoms*, McGraw-Hill 1976), and Edward Altman (*Corporate Financial Distress: A Complete Guide to Predicting, Avoiding and Dealing with Bankruptcy*, John Wiley & Sons 1983). Altman's model is sometimes used for prediction of corporate failure by calculating what is called a *Z score* for each company. For a public industrial company, if the *Z score* is greater than 2.99 then it is unlikely to fail, and if the score is less than 1.81 then it is likely to fail. Statistical analyses of financial ratios may further assist in this area of prediction of corporate failure, using for example time series and line of business analyses.

As we saw in our examination of the performance review process, the key ratios include the following categories:

- profitability
- efficiency
- liquidity
- investment
- financial structure.

The financial structure, or gearing, of the business will also be considered in further detail in Chapters 14 and 15 when we look at sources of finance and the cost of capital. In the current chapter we will use the financial statements of Flatco plc, an engineering company, shown in Figures 7.3 to 7.8, to illustrate the calculation of the key financial ratios. The income statement and statement of cash flows are for the year ended 31 December 2010 and the balance sheet is as at 31 December 2010. Comparative figures are shown for 2009.

Profitability ratios

It is generally accepted that the primary objective for the managers of a business is to maximise the wealth of the owners of the business. To this end there are a number of other objectives, subsidiary to the main objective. These include:

- survival
- stability
- growth

- maximisation of market share
- maximisation of sales
- maximisation of profit
- maximisation of return on capital.

Each group of financial ratios is concerned to some extent with survival, stability, growth and maximisation of shareholder wealth. We will first consider ratios in the broad area of profitability (see Fig. 7.9), which give an indication of how successful the business has been in its achievement of the wealth maximisation objective.

$$\text{gross profit \%} = \frac{\text{gross profit}}{\text{revenue}} = \frac{\text{revenue} - \text{cost of sales (COS)}}{\text{revenue}}$$

Figure 7.3   Flatco plc balance sheets as at 31 December 2009 and 2010

Flatco plc
Balance sheet as at 31 December 2010

	2010 £000	2009 £000
Assets		
Non-current assets		
Tangible	1,884	1,921
Intangible	416	425
Investments	248	248
Total non-current assets	2,548	2,594
Current assets		
Inventories	311	268
Trade and other receivables	1,162	1,134
Cash and cash equivalents	327	17
Total current assets	1,800	1,419
Total assets	4,348	4,013
Liabilities		
Current liabilities		
Borrowings and finance leases	50	679
Trade and other payables	553	461
Current tax liabilities	50	44
Dividends payable	70	67
Provisions	82	49
Total current liabilities	805	1,300
Non-current liabilities		
Borrowings and finance leases	173	–
Trade and other payables	154	167
Deferred tax liabilities	–	–
Provisions	222	222
Total non-current liabilities	549	389
Total liabilities	1,354	1,689
Net assets	2,994	2,324
Equity		
Share capital	1,200	1,000
Share premium account	200	200
Retained earnings	1,594	1,124
Total equity	2,994	2,324

| Figure 7.4 | Flatco plc income statements for the years ended 31 December 2009 and 2010 |

Flatco plc
Income statement for the year ended 31 December 2010

	2010 £000	2009 £000
Revenue	3,500	3,250
Cost of sales	(2,500)	(2,400)
Gross profit	1,000	850
Distribution costs	(300)	(330)
Administrative expenses	(250)	(160)
Other income	100	90
Operating profit	550	450
Finance income	111	80
Finance costs	(71)	(100)
Profit before tax	590	430
Income tax expense	(50)	(44)
Profit for the year from continuing operations	540	386
Profit for the year from discontinued operations	–	–
Profit for the year	540	386

| Figure 7.5 | Flatco plc additional information to the financial statements 2010 |

Additional information

Administrative expenses for 2010 include an exceptional item of £95,000 redundancy costs.

Dividends were £70,000 for 2010 (2009: £67,000) and retained earnings were £470,000 (2009: £319,000).

Authorised and issued share capital 31 December 2010 was 1,200,000 £1 ordinary shares (2009: 1,000,000).

Total assets less current liabilities 31 December 2008 were £2,406,000. Trade receivables 31 December 2010 were £573,000 (2009: £517,000, 2008: £440,000).

The market value of ordinary shares in Flatco plc on 31 December 2010 was £2.75 (£3.00 2009).

Tangible non-current assets depreciation provision at 31 December 2010 was £1,102,000 (£779,000 2009).

Current liabilities: Provisions for 2010 include Accruals £82,000, and for 2009 include Accruals £49,000. Trade and other payables for 2010 include Trade payables £553,000 and other payables zero, and for 2009 include Trade payables £461,000 and other payables zero.

Figure 7.6   Flatco plc cash generated from operations for the years ended 31 December 2009 and 2010

Flatco plc
Cash generated from operations for the year ended 31 December 2010

	2010 £000	2009 £000
Profit before tax	590	430
Depreciation and amortisation charges	345	293
Adjust finance (income)/costs	(40)	20
Increase in inventories	(43)	(32)
Increase in trade and other receivables [1,134 − 1,162]	(28)	(25)
Increase in trade and other payables, and provisions		
[461 − 553 + 49 − 82 + 167 − 154]	112	97
Cash generated from operations	936	783

Figure 7.7   Flatco plc statement of cash flows for the years ended 31 December 2009 and 2010

Flatco plc
Statement of cash flows for the year ended 31 December 2010

	2010 £000	2009 £000
Cash flows from operating activities		
Cash generated from operations	936	783
Interest paid	(71)	(100)
Income tax paid	(44)	(40)
Net cash generated from operating activities	821	643
Cash flows from investing activities		
Purchases of tangible assets	(286)	(170)
Proceeds from sales of tangible assets	21	–
Purchases of intangible assets	(34)	–
Interest received	11	–
Dividends received	100	80
Net cash outflow from investing activities	(188)	(90)
Cash flows from financing activities		
Proceeds from issue of ordinary shares	200	290
Proceeds from borrowings	173	–
Dividends paid to equity shareholders	(67)	(56)
Net cash inflow from financing activities	306	234
Net increase in cash and cash equivalents in the year	939	787
Cash and cash equivalents and bank overdrafts at beginning of year	(662)	(1,449)
Cash and cash equivalents and bank overdrafts at end of year	277	(662)

Figure 7.8 Flatco plc analysis of cash and cash equivalents and bank overdrafts as at 31 December 2009 and 2010

Flatco plc
Analysis of cash and cash equivalents and bank overdrafts as at 31 December 2010

	At 1 January 2010 £000	At 31 December 2010 £000
Cash and cash equivalents	17	327
Bank overdrafts	(679)	(50)
Cash and cash equivalents and bank overdrafts	(662)	277

	At 1 January 2009 £000	At 31 December 2009 £000
Cash and cash equivalents	–	17
Bank overdrafts	(1,449)	(679)
Cash and cash equivalents and bank overdrafts	(1,449)	(662)

Figure 7.9 Profitability ratios

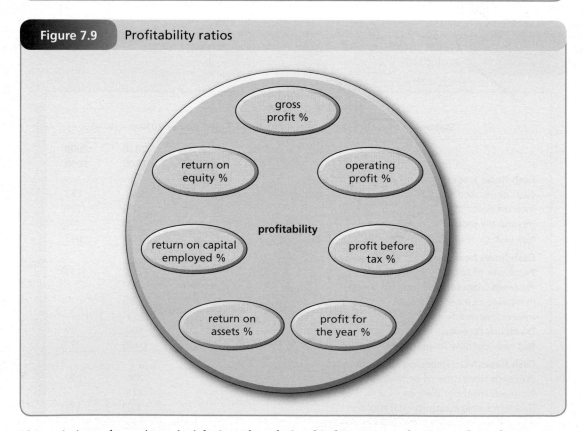

This ratio is used to gain an insight into the relationship between production and purchasing costs and sales revenue. The gross profit (or gross margin) needs to be high enough to cover all other costs incurred by the company, and leave an amount for profit. If the gross profit percentage is too low then sales prices may be too low, or the purchase costs of materials or production costs may be too high.

$$\text{operating profit \%} = \frac{\text{operating profit}}{\text{revenue}} = \frac{\text{revenue} - \text{COS} - \text{other operating expenses}}{\text{revenue}}$$

The operating profit (or profit before interest and tax (PBIT) excluding other operating income) ratio is a key ratio that shows the profitability of the business before incurring financing costs. If the numerator is not multiplied by 100 to give a percentage, it shows the profit generated by each £1 of sales revenue.

$$\text{profit before tax (PBT) \%} = \frac{\text{profit before tax}}{\text{revenue}} = \frac{\text{operating profit} +/- \text{ net interest}}{\text{revenue}}$$

This is the profit ratio that uses profit after financing costs, that is, having allowed for interest payable and interest receivable. It should be remembered that profit before tax (PBT) is a profit measure that goes further than dealing with the trading performance of the business, in allowing for net financing costs. It provides an indication of pre-tax profit-earning capability from the sales for the period.

$$\text{profit for the year \%} = \frac{\text{net profit}}{\text{revenue}} = \frac{\text{profit before tax (PBT)} - \text{corporate income tax}}{\text{revenue}}$$

This is the final profit ratio after allowing for financing costs and corporation tax. The net profit for the year (or profit after tax) or return on sales (ROS) ratio is the profit available for distribution to shareholders in the form of dividends and/or future investment in the business.

$$\text{return on assets (ROA) \%} = \frac{\text{operating profit}}{\text{total assets}}$$

Return on assets compares operational income with the total assets used to generate that income. Profit is calculated before net financing costs and tax.

$$\begin{array}{l}\text{return on capital employed (ROCE)}\\\text{or return on investment (ROI) \%}\end{array} = \frac{\text{operating profit}}{\substack{\text{total assets} - \text{ current liabilities}\\\text{(usually averaged)}}}$$

This is a form of return on capital employed (using pre-tax profit) which compares income with the net operational assets used to generate that income. Profit is calculated before net financing costs and tax. This is because the introduction of interest charges introduces the effect of financing decisions into an appraisal of operating performance, and tax levels are decided by external agencies (governments).

The average cost of a company's finance (equity, debentures, loans), weighted according to the proportion each element bears to the total pool of capital, is called the **weighted average cost of capital (WACC)**. The difference between a company's ROI and its WACC is an important measure of the extent to which the organisation is endeavouring to optimise its use of financial resources. In their 2009 annual report, Sainsbury's plc reported on the improvement in their ROCE versus WACC gap, stating that 'the pre-tax return on average capital employed continued to improve significantly, increasing by 85 basis points in the year to 11.0 per cent, around 70 basis points above the company's weighted average cost of capital'.

A company manages its ROCE through monitoring its operating profit as a percentage of its capital employed. A company manages its WACC by planning the proportions of its financing through either equity (ordinary shares) or debt (loans), with regard to the relative costs of each, based on dividends and interest.

WACC is an important measure when companies are considering acquisitions. This is emphasised by the Rio Tinto Group plc in their 2009 annual report, where the company identified how WACC is used in determining the potential future benefits that may be derived from investments: 'Forecast cash flows are discounted to present values using Rio Tinto's weighted average cost of capital with appropriate adjustment for the risks associated with the relevant cash flows, to the extent that such risks are not reflected in the forecast cash flows. For final feasibility studies and ore reserve estimation, internal hurdle rates are used which are generally higher than the weighted average cost of capital.' This refers to the importance of WACC as a factor used in the evaluation of investment in projects undertaken (or not) by a business (see Chapters 14 and 15).

$$\text{return on equity (ROE)} = \frac{\text{net profit}}{\text{equity}}$$

Another form of return on capital employed, ROE measures the return to the owners on the book value of their investment in a company. The return is measured as the residual profit after all expenses and charges have been made, and after corporate income tax has been deducted. The equity comprises share capital, retained earnings and reserves.

The profitability performance measures discussed above consider the general performance of organisations as a whole. It is important for managers also to be aware of particular areas of revenue or expenditure that may have a significant importance with regard to their own company and that have a critical impact on the net profit of the business. Companies may, for example:

■ suffer large warranty claim costs
■ have to pay high royalty fees
■ receive high volumes of customer debit notes (invoices) for a variety of product or service problems deemed to be their fault.

All managers should fully appreciate such key items of cost specific to their own company and be innovative and proactive in identifying ways that these costs may be reduced and minimised.

Managers should also be aware of the general range of costs for which they may have no direct responsibility, but nevertheless may be able to reduce significantly by:

■ improved communication
■ involvement
■ generation of ideas for waste reduction, increased effectiveness and cost reduction.

Such costs may include:

■ the cost of the operating cycle
■ costs of warehouse space
■ project costs
■ costs of holding inventories
■ depreciation (as a result of capital expenditure)
■ warranty costs
■ repairs and maintenance
■ stationery costs
■ telephone and fax costs
■ photocopy costs.

The relative importance of these costs through their impact on profitability will of course vary from company to company.

Worked example 7.1

We will calculate the profitability ratios for Flatco plc for 2010 and the comparative ratios for 2009, and comment on the profitability of Flatco plc.

Gross profit

$$\text{gross profit \% 2010} = \frac{\text{gross profit}}{\text{revenue}} = \frac{£1{,}000 \times 100\%}{£3{,}500} = 28.6\%$$

$$\text{gross profit \% 2009} = \frac{£850 \times 100\%}{£3{,}250} = 26.2\%$$

Profit before interest and tax, PBIT (PBIT is operating profit plus finance income)

$$\text{PBIT \% 2010} = \frac{\text{PBIT}}{\text{revenue}} = \frac{£661 \times 100\%}{£3{,}500} = 18.9\%$$

$$\text{PBIT \% 2009} = \frac{£530 \times 100\%}{£3{,}250} = 16.3\%$$

Profit for the year (or profit after tax PAT), or return on sales (ROS)

$$\text{PAT \% 2010} = \frac{\text{net profit}}{\text{revenue}} = \frac{£540 \times 100\%}{£3{,}500} = 15.4\%$$

$$\text{PAT \% 2009} = \frac{£386 \times 100\%}{£3{,}250} = 11.9\%$$

Return on assets, ROA

$$\text{ROA \% 2010} = \frac{\text{operating profit}}{\text{total assets}} = \frac{£550 \times 100\%}{£4{,}348} = 12.6\%$$

$$\text{ROA \% 2009} = \frac{£450 \times 100\%}{£4{,}013} = 11.2\%$$

Return on capital employed, ROCE (or return on investment, ROI)

$$\text{ROCE \% 2010} = \frac{\text{operating profit}}{\substack{\text{total assets} - \text{current liabilities} \\ \text{(average capital employed)}}}$$

$$= \frac{£550 \times 100\%}{(£3{,}543 + £2{,}713)/2} = \frac{£550 \times 100\%}{£3{,}128} = 17.6\%$$

$$\text{ROCE \% 2009} = \frac{£450 \times 100\%}{(£2{,}713 + £2{,}406)/2} = \frac{£450 \times 100\%}{£2{,}559.5} = 17.6\%$$

Return on equity, ROE

$$\text{ROE \% 2010} = \frac{\text{PAT}}{\text{equity}} = \frac{£540 \times 100\%}{£2{,}994} = 18.0\%$$

$$\text{ROE \% 2009} = \frac{£386 \times 100\%}{£2{,}324} = 16.6\%$$

Report on the profitability of Flatco plc

Sales revenue for the year 2010 increased by 7.7% over the previous year, partly through increased volumes and partly through higher selling prices.

Gross profit improved from 26.2% to 28.6% of sales, as a result of increased selling prices but also lower costs of production.

PBIT improved from 16.3% to 18.9% of sales (and operating profit, which is calculated as operating profit × 100/sales, improved from 13.8% to 15.7%). If the one-off costs of redundancy of £95,000 had not been incurred in the year 2010 operating profit would have been £645,000 (£550,000 + £95,000) and the operating profit ratio would have been 18.4% of sales, an increase of 4.6% over 2009. The underlying improvement in operating profit performance (excluding the one-off redundancy costs) was achieved from the improvement in gross profit and from the benefits of lower distribution costs and administrative expenses.

ROA increased from 11.2% to 12.6%. This was because although the total assets of the company had increased by 8.3%, operating profit had increased by 22.2% in 2010 compared with 2009.

ROCE was static at 17.6% because the increase in capital employed as a result of additional share capital of £200,000 and long-term loans of £173,000 was matched by a similar increase in operating profit.

Return on equity increased from 16.6% to 18%, despite the increase in ordinary share capital. This was because of improved profit after tax (up 3.5% to 15.4%) arising from increased income from non-current asset investments and lower costs of finance. Corporation tax was only marginally higher than the previous year despite higher pre-tax profits.

Progress check 7.3

How may financial ratio analysis be used as part of the process of review of business performance?

Efficiency ratios

The regular monitoring of efficiency ratios by companies is crucial because they relate directly to how effectively business transactions are being converted into cash. For example, if companies are not regularly paid in accordance with their terms of trading:

- their profit margins may be eroded by the financing costs of funding overdue accounts
- cash flow shortfalls may put pressure on their ability to meet their day-to-day obligations to pay employees, replenish inventory, etc.

Despite the introduction of legislation to combat slow payments to suppliers, the general situation in the UK still remains poor, although there are some signs of improvement, as can be seen from the extract on the next page from the *Daily Telegraph*.

The range of efficiency ratios is illustrated in Figure 7.10.

Efficiency generally relates to the maximisation of output from resources devoted to an activity or the output required from a minimum input of resources. Efficiency ratios measure the efficiency with which such resources have been used.

$$\text{collection days} = \frac{\text{trade receivables} \times 365}{\text{revenue}}$$

Companies that fail to pay suppliers on time

Small businesses are being forced to write off debt at a faster rate because they are struggling to reduce a near £63bn mountain of unpaid bills, say bankers.

Nearly three out of four **small and medium-sized enterprises (SMEs)** have been hit by late payments over the past year but less than half have taken steps to reduce the pressure, according to research among 500 companies by NatWest and its Royal Bank of Scotland parent. Invoices for £15.7bn are more than 120 days in arrears.

The banks estimate 235,000 SMEs have been wasting time chasing overdue invoices. The problem has been most acute among wholesalers where 93pc have suffered considerable delays, while retailers have fared better with 66pc troubled by late payments.

Other research from Barclays based on data from 1,000 companies suggests many businesses are taking active steps to reduce the pressure on cash flow with extensive debt write-offs.

Around 720,000 SMEs wrote off an average of £2,529 last year, double the 2008 figure of £1,133, according to Barclays.

NatWest and RBS estimate less than half of SMEs have taken action, with 11pc hiring an in-house credit controller, 9pc using invoice discounting and 8pc factoring to ease cashflow pressures.

Peter Ibbetson, chairman of NatWest and RBS small business operations, is concerned that so few SMEs are using banking services to alleviate the problem, but small business organisations believe companies are reluctant to incur extra charges after their bank borrowing experiences.

Barclays believes late payment pressures are easing with 18pc saying their survival is threatened compared with 32pc in 2008. The proportion worried about the impact on cash flow is down from 61pc to 26pc over the period.

Source: **Late payments mean bigger write-offs for small businesses**, by Roland Gribben © *Daily Telegraph*, 15 April 2010

Figure 7.10 Efficiency ratios

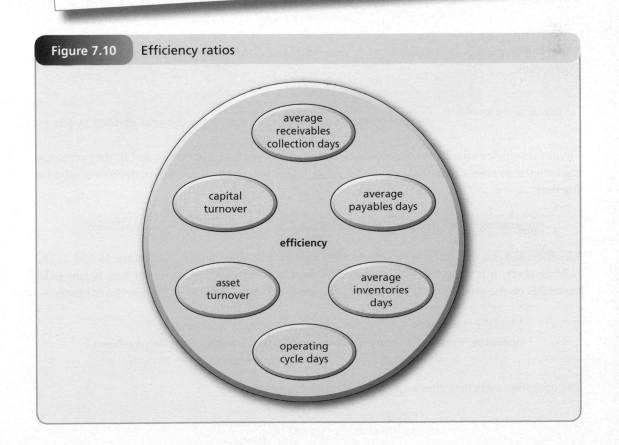

Collection days indicate the average time taken, in calendar days, to receive payment from credit customers. Adjustment is needed if the ratio is materially distorted by VAT (or other taxes). This is because sales invoices to customers, and therefore trade receivables, may include the net sales value plus VAT. However, sales revenue is reported net of VAT. To provide a more accurate ratio, VAT may be eliminated from the trade receivables numbers as appropriate. (Note: for example, export and zero-rated sales invoices, which may be included in trade receivables, do not include VAT and so an adjustment to total trade receivables by the standard percentage rate for VAT may not be accurate.)

$$\text{payables days} = \frac{\text{trade payables} \times 365}{\text{cost of sales (or purchases)}}$$

Payables days indicate the average time taken, in calendar days, to pay for supplies received on credit. For the same reason, as in the calculation of collection days, adjustment is needed if the ratio is materially distorted by VAT or other taxes.

$$\text{inventories days} = \frac{\text{inventories}}{\text{average daily cost of sales in period}} \quad \text{or} \quad \frac{\text{inventories} \times 365}{\text{cost of sales}}$$

Inventories days or inventory turnover is the number of days that inventories could last at the forecast or most recent usage rate. This may be applied to total inventory, finished goods, raw materials, or work in progress. The weekly internal efficiency of inventory utilisation is indicated by the following ratios:

$$\frac{\text{finished goods}}{\text{average weekly despatches}} \qquad \frac{\text{raw materials}}{\text{average weekly raw material usage}} \qquad \frac{\text{work in progress}}{\text{average weekly production}}$$

These ratios are usually calculated using values but may also be calculated using quantities where appropriate.

$$\text{inventories weeks} = \frac{\text{inventories}}{\text{average weekly cost of sales (total COS for the year divided by 52)}}$$

Financial analysts usually only have access to published reports and accounts and so they often use the inventories weeks ratio using the total closing inventories value in relation to the cost of sales for the year.

$$\text{operating cycle (days)} = \text{inventories days} + \text{collection days} - \text{payables days}$$

We discussed the operating cycle, or working capital cycle, in Chapter 3 when we looked at the balance sheet. It is the period of time which elapses between the point at which cash begins to be expended on the production of a product or service, and the collection of cash from the customer.

$$\text{operating cycle \%} = \frac{\text{working capital requirement}}{\text{(inventories + trade receivables - trade payables)}} \Big/ \text{revenue}$$

The operating cycle may alternatively be calculated as a percentage.

$$\text{asset turnover (times)} = \frac{\text{revenue}}{\text{total assets}}$$

Asset turnover measures the performance of the company in generating sales revenue from the assets under its control. The denominator may alternatively be average net total assets.

$$\text{capital turnover} = \frac{\text{revenue}}{\text{average capital employed in year}}$$

The capital turnover expresses the number of times that capital is turned over in the year, or alternatively the sales revenue generated by each £1 of capital employed. This ratio will be affected by capital additions that may have taken place throughout a period but have not impacted materially on the performance for that period. Further analysis may be required to determine the underlying performance.

Worked example 7.2

We will calculate the efficiency ratios for Flatco plc for 2010 and the comparative ratios for 2009, and comment on the efficiency of Flatco plc.

Receivables collection days

$$\text{collection days 2010} = \frac{\text{trade receivables} \times 365}{\text{revenue}} = \frac{£573 \times 365}{£3,500} = 60 \text{ days}$$

$$\text{collection days 2009} = \frac{£517 \times 365}{£3,250} = 58 \text{ days}$$

Payables days

$$\text{payables days 2010} = \frac{\text{trade payables} \times 365}{\text{cost of sales}} = \frac{£553 \times 365}{£2,500} = 81 \text{ days}$$

$$\text{payables days 2009} = \frac{£461 \times 365}{£2,400} = 70 \text{ days}$$

Inventories days (or inventory turnover)

$$\text{inventories days 2010} = \frac{\text{inventories}}{\text{average daily cost of sales in period}} = \frac{£311}{£2,500/365}$$

$$= 45 \text{ days (6.5 weeks)}$$

$$\text{inventories days 2009} = \frac{£268}{£2,400/365} = 41 \text{ days (5.9 weeks)}$$

Operating cycle days

$$\text{operating cycle 2010} = \text{inventories days} + \text{collection days} - \text{payables days}$$
$$= 45 + 60 - 81 = 24 \text{ days}$$

$$\text{operating cycle 2009} = 41 + 58 - 70 = 29 \text{ days}$$

Operating cycle %

$$\text{operating cycle \% 2010} = \frac{\text{working capital requirement}}{\text{revenue}}$$

$$= \frac{(£311 + £573 - £553) \times 100\%}{£3,500} = 9.5\%$$

$$\text{operating cycle \% 2009} = \frac{(£268 + £517 - £461) \times 100\%}{£3,250} = 10.0\%$$

Asset turnover

$$\text{asset turnover } 2010 = \frac{\text{revenue}}{\text{total assets}} = \frac{£3,500}{£4,348} = 0.80 \text{ times}$$

$$\text{asset turnover } 2009 = \frac{£3,250}{£4,013} = 0.81 \text{ times}$$

Capital turnover

$$\text{capital turnover } 2010 = \frac{\text{revenue}}{\text{average capital employed in year}} = \frac{£3,500}{£3,128} = 1.1 \text{ times}$$

$$\text{capital turnover } 2009 = \frac{£3,250}{£2,559.5} = 1.3 \text{ times}$$

Report on the efficiency of Flatco plc

A major cash improvement programme was introduced by the company late in the year 2010, which began with the implementation of new cash collection procedures and a reinforced credit control department. This was not introduced early enough to see an improvement in the collection days for the year 2010. Average receivables collection days actually worsened from 58 to 60 days.

The purchasing department negotiated terms of 90 days with a number of key large suppliers. This had the effect of improving the average payables period from 70 to 81 days.

A change in product mix during the latter part of the year 2010 resulted in a worsening of the average inventory turnover period from 41 to 45 days. This is expected to be a temporary situation. An improved **just in time (JIT)** system and the use of **vendor managed inventory (VMI)** with two main suppliers in the year 2011 are expected to generate significant improvements in inventory turnover.

Despite the poor inventory turnover, the operating cycle improved from 29 days to 24 days (operating cycle % from 10.0% to 9.5%). Operating cycle days are expected to be zero or better by the end of year 2011.

Asset turnover dropped from 0.81 in 2009 to 0.80 times in the year 2010. New capital was introduced into the company in 2010 to finance major new projects which are expected to result in significant increases in sales levels over the next few years which will result in improvements in asset turnover over and above 2009 levels.

Capital turnover for 2010 dropped to 1.1 times from 1.3 times in 2009. As with asset turnover, the new capital introduced into the company in the year 2010 to finance major new projects is expected to result in significant increases in sales revenue levels over the next few years, which will be reflected in improvements in capital turnover over and above 2009 levels.

> ### Progress check 7.4
>
> What do the profitability and efficiency ratios tell us about the performance of a business?

Liquidity ratios

The degree to which assets are held in a cash or near-cash form is determined by the level of obligations that need to be met by the business. Liquidity ratios (see Fig. 7.11) reflect the health or otherwise of the cash position of the business and its ability to meet its short-term obligations.

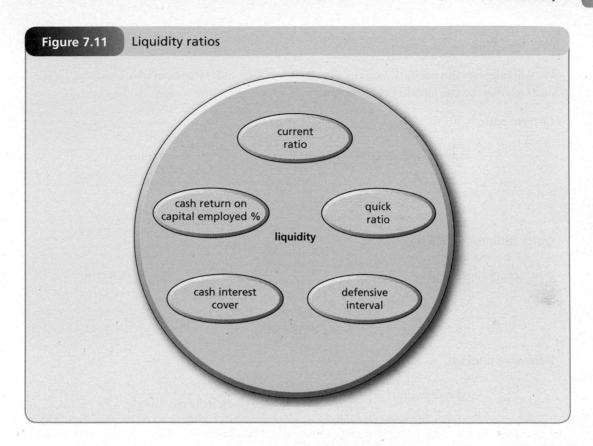

Figure 7.11   Liquidity ratios

$$\text{current ratio (times)} = \frac{\text{current assets}}{\text{current liabilities}}$$

The current ratio is an overall measure of the liquidity of the business. It should be appreciated that this ratio will be different for different types of business. For example, an automotive manufacturer may have a higher ratio because of its relatively high level of inventories (mainly work in progress) compared with a supermarket retailer which holds a very high percentage of fast-moving inventories.

$$\text{quick ratio (times)} = \frac{\text{current assets} - \text{inventories}}{\text{current liabilities}}$$

The **quick ratio** (or **acid test**) excludes inventories from current assets. While trade receivables and trade payables are just one step away from being converted into cash, inventories are two or more steps away from being converted into cash; they need to be worked on and processed to produce products which are then sold to customers. Therefore, the quick ratio indicates the ability of the company to pay its trade payables out of its trade receivables in the short term. This ratio may be particularly meaningful for supermarket retailers because of the speed with which their inventories are converted into cash.

$$\text{defensive interval (days)} = \frac{\text{quick assets (current assets} - \text{inventories)}}{\text{average daily cash from operations}}$$

The defensive interval shows how many days a company could survive at its present level of operating activity if no inflow of cash were received from sales revenue or other sources.

We will consider some of the other ratios outlined in Figure 7.11 later in this chapter.

Worked example 7.3

We will calculate the liquidity ratios for Flatco plc for 2010 and the comparative ratios for 2009, and comment on the liquidity of Flatco plc.

Current ratio

$$\text{current ratio 2010} = \frac{\text{current assets}}{\text{current liabilities}} = \frac{£1,800}{£805} = 2.2 \text{ times}$$

$$\text{current ratio 2009} = \frac{£1,419}{£1,300} = 1.1 \text{ times}$$

Quick ratio (or acid test)

$$\text{quick ratio 2010} = \frac{\text{current assets} - \text{inventories}}{\text{current liabilities}} = \frac{£1,800 - £311}{£805} = 1.8 \text{ times}$$

$$\text{quick ratio 2009} = \frac{£1,419 - £268}{£1,300} = 0.9 \text{ times}$$

Defensive interval

$$\text{defensive interval 2010} = \frac{\text{quick assets}}{\text{average daily cash from operations}}$$
$$\text{(opening trade receivables} + \text{sales revenue} - \text{closing trade receivables)}/365$$

$$= \frac{£1,800 - £311}{(£517 + £3,500 - £573)/365} = 158 \text{ days}$$

$$\text{defensive interval 2009} = \frac{£1,419 - £268}{(£440 + £3,250 - £517)/365} = 132 \text{ days}$$

Report on the liquidity of Flatco plc

From the statement of cash flows we can see that cash generated from operations improved from £783,000 in 2009 to £936,000 in 2010. Investments in non-current assets were more than covered by increases in long-term financing in both years. Operational cash flow improvement was reflected in the increase in net cash flow of £939,000 from £787,000 in 2009.

The improved cash flow is reflected in increases in the current ratio (1.1 to 2.2 times) and the quick ratio (0.9 to 1.8 times). The increase in the defensive interval from 132 to 158 days has strengthened the position of the company against the threat of a possible downturn in activity.

Although there has been a significant improvement in cash flow, the increase in investment in working capital is a cause for concern. Three key actions have already been taken since the year end 31 December 2010 to try and maximise the returns on investment: reduction in inventories levels (noted above); further reductions in trade receivables; investment of surplus cash in longer-term investments.

Progress check 7.5

What are liquidity ratios and why are they so important?

Figure 7.12 Investment ratios

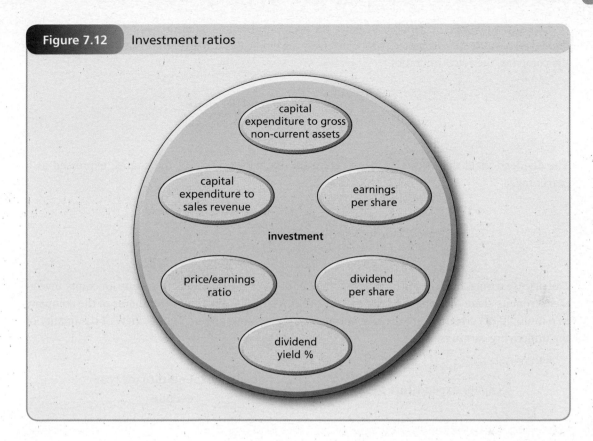

Investment ratios

Investment ratios (see Fig. 7.12) generally indicate the extent to which the business is undertaking capital expenditure to ensure its survival and stability, and its ability to sustain current revenue and generate future increased revenue.

$$\text{earnings per share (or eps)} = \frac{\text{profit for the year} - \text{preference share dividends}}{\text{number of ordinary shares in issue}}$$

Earnings per share, or eps, measures the return per share of earnings available to shareholders. The eps of companies may be found in the financial pages sections of the daily press.

$$\text{dividend per share} = \frac{\text{total dividends paid to ordinary shareholders}}{\text{number of ordinary shares in issue}}$$

Dividend per share is the total amount declared as dividends per each ordinary share in issue. It is the dividend per share actually paid in respect of the financial year. The amount must be adjusted if additional equity shares are issued during the financial year.

$$\text{dividend cover} = \frac{\text{earnings per share}}{\text{dividend per share}}$$

Dividend cover shows the number of times the profit attributable to equity shareholders covers the dividends payable for the period, and conversely also indicates the level of profit being retained by the company, the retention ratio.

$$\text{dividend yield \%} = \frac{\text{dividend per share}}{\text{current share price}}$$

The dividend yield shows the dividend return on the market value of the shares, expressed as a percentage.

$$\text{price/earnings (P/E) ratio} = \frac{\text{current share price}}{\text{eps}}$$

The price/earnings or P/E ratio shows the number of years it would take to recoup an equity investment from its share of the attributable equity profit. The P/E ratio values the shares of the company as a multiple of current or prospective earnings, and therefore gives a market view of the quality of the underlying earnings.

$$\text{capital expenditure to sales revenue \%} = \frac{\text{capital expenditure for year}}{\text{revenue}}$$

This ratio gives an indication of the level of capital expenditure incurred to sustain a particular level of sales revenue.

$$\text{capital expenditure to gross non-current assets \%} = \frac{\text{capital expenditure for year}}{\text{gross value of tangible non-current assets}}$$

This is a very good ratio for giving an indication of the replacement rate of new for old non-current assets.

Worked example 7.4

We will calculate the investment ratios for Flatco plc for 2010 and the comparative ratios for 2009, and comment on the investment performance of Flatco plc.

Earnings per share, eps

$$\text{eps } 2010 = \frac{\text{profit for the year} - \text{preference share dividends}}{\text{number of ordinary shares in issue}} = \frac{£540,000}{1,200,000} = 45\text{p}$$

$$\text{eps } 2009 = \frac{£386,000}{1,000,000} = 38.6\text{p}$$

Dividend per share

$$\text{dividend per share 2010} = \frac{\text{total dividends paid to ordinary shareholders}}{\text{number of ordinary shares in issue}}$$

$$= \frac{£70,000}{1,200,000} = 5.8\text{p per share}$$

$$\text{dividend per share 2009} = \frac{£67,000}{1,000,000} = 6.7\text{p per share}$$

Dividend cover

$$\text{dividend cover 2010} = \frac{\text{earnings per share}}{\text{dividend per share}}$$

$$= \frac{45\text{p}}{5.8\text{p}} = 7.8\text{ times}$$

$$\text{dividend cover 2009} = \frac{38.6\text{p}}{6.7\text{p}} = 5.8\text{ times}$$

Dividend yield %

$$\text{dividend yield 2010} = \frac{\text{dividend per share}}{\text{share price}}$$

$$= \frac{5.8\text{p} \times 100\%}{£2.75} = 2.11\%$$

$$\text{dividend yield 2009} = \frac{6.7\text{p} \times 100\%}{£3.00} = 2.23\%$$

Price/earnings ratio, P/E

$$\text{P/E ratio 2010} = \frac{\text{current share price}}{\text{eps}} = \frac{£2.75}{45\text{p}} = 6.1\text{ times}$$

$$\text{P/E ratio 2009} = \frac{£3.00}{38.6\text{p}} = 7.8\text{ times}$$

Capital expenditure to sales revenue %

$$\text{capital expenditure to sales revenue 2010} = \frac{\text{capital expenditure for year}}{\text{revenue}} = \frac{£286 \times 100\%}{£3,500} = 8.2\%$$

$$\text{capital expenditure to sales revenue 2009} = \frac{£170 \times 100\%}{£3,250} = 5.2\%$$

Capital expenditure to gross non-current assets %

$$\text{capital expenditure to gross non-current assets 2010} = \frac{\text{capital expenditure for year}}{\text{gross value of tangible non-current assets}}$$

$$= \frac{£286 \times 100\%}{(£1,884 + £1,102)} = 9.6\%$$

(net book value + cumulative depreciation provision)

$$\text{capital expenditure to gross non-current assets 2009} = \frac{£170 \times 100\%}{(£1,921 + £779)} = 6.3\%$$

Report on the investment performance of Flatco plc

The improved profit performance in 2010 compared to 2009 was reflected in improved earnings per share from 38.6p to 45p.

The price/earnings ratio dropped from 7.8 to 6.1 times, indicating that an investment in the company's shares may be recovered in 6.1 years from its current level of net profit.

The board of directors reduced the dividend for the year to 5.8p per share from 6.7p per share in 2009, establishing a dividend cover, or profit retention ratio, of 7.8 times. The increased profit retention provided internal financing in addition to its external financing to fund the company's increase in capital expenditure.

The increase in the capital expenditure to sales revenue ratio from 5.2% to 8.2% indicates the company's ability to both sustain and improve upon current sales revenue levels.

The increase in the capital expenditure to gross non-current assets ratio from 6.3% to 9.6% illustrates Flatco's policy of ongoing replacement of old assets for new in order to keep ahead of the technology in which the business is engaged.

Each of the above four ratios indicate that Flatco is a growth company, from which increased sales revenues and profits may be expected in future years.

The dividend yield reduced from 2.23% at 31 December 2009 to 2.11% at 31 December 2010.

Progress check 7.6

What are investment ratios and what is their purpose?

Financial ratios

Financial ratios (see Fig. 7.13) are generally concerned with the relationship between debt and equity capital, the financial structure of an organisation. This relationship is called gearing. Gearing is discussed in further detail in Chapter 14. The ratios that follow are the two most commonly used. Both ratios relate to financial gearing, which is the relationship between a company's borrowings, which includes both prior charge capital and long-term debt, and its shareholders' funds (share capital plus reserves).

$$\text{gearing} = \frac{\text{long-term debt}}{\text{equity} + \text{long-term debt}}$$

and

$$\text{debt/equity ratio (D/E or leverage)} = \frac{\text{long-term debt}}{\text{equity}}$$

These ratios are both equally acceptable in describing the relative proportions of debt and equity used to finance a business. Gearing calculations can be made in other ways, and in addition to those based on capital values may also be based on earnings/interest relationships, for example:

$$\text{dividend cover (times)} = \frac{\text{earnings per share (eps)}}{\text{dividend per share}}$$

Figure 7.13 Financial ratios

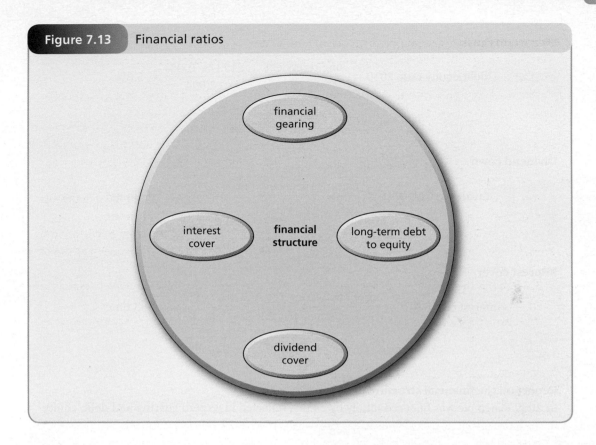

This ratio indicates the number of times the profits attributable to the equity shareholders covers the actual dividends paid and payable for the period. Financial analysts usually adjust their calculations for any exceptional or extraordinary items of which they may be aware.

$$\text{interest cover (times)} = \frac{\text{profit before interest and tax}}{\text{interest payable}}$$

This ratio calculates the number of times the interest payable is covered by profits available for such payments. It is particularly important for lenders to determine the vulnerability of interest payments to a fall in profit.

Worked example 7.5

We will calculate the financial ratios for Flatco plc for 2010 and the comparative ratios for 2009, and comment on the financial structure of Flatco plc.

Gearing

$$\text{gearing 2010} = \frac{\text{long-term debt}}{\text{equity} + \text{long-term debt}} = \frac{£173 \times 100\%}{(£2{,}994 + £173)} = 5.5\%$$

$$\text{gearing 2009} = \frac{£0 \times 100\%}{(£2{,}324 + £0)} = 0\%$$

Debt/equity ratio

$$\text{debt/equity ratio } 2010 = \frac{\text{long-term debt}}{\text{equity}} = \frac{£173 \times 100\%}{£2,994} = 5.8\%$$

$$\text{debt/equity ratio } 2009 = \frac{£0 \times 100\%}{£2,324} = 0\%$$

Dividend cover

$$\text{dividend cover } 2010 = \frac{\text{earnings per share (eps)}}{\text{dividend per share}} = \frac{45p}{5.8p} = 7.8 \text{ times}$$

$$\text{dividend cover } 2009 = \frac{38.6p}{6.7p} = 5.8 \text{ times}$$

Interest cover

$$\text{interest cover } 2010 = \frac{\text{profit before interest and tax}}{\text{interest payable}} = \frac{£661}{£71} = 9.3 \text{ times}$$

$$\text{interest cover } 2009 = \frac{£530}{£100} = 5.3 \text{ times}$$

Report on the financial structure of Flatco plc

In 2009 Flatco plc was financed totally by equity, reflected in its zero gearing and debt/equity ratios for that year. Flatco plc was still very low geared in 2010, with gearing of 5.5% and debt/equity of 5.8%. This was because the company's debt of £173,000 at 31 December 2010 was very small compared with its equity of £2,994,000 at the same date.

Earnings per share increased by 16.6% in 2010 compared with 2009. However, the board of directors reduced the dividend, at 5.8p per share for 2010, by 13.4% from 6.7p per share in 2009. This provided an increase in retained earnings (retained profit), shown by the increase in dividend cover from 5.8 times in 2009 to 7.8 times in 2010.

Interest payable was reduced by £29,000 in 2010 from the previous year, but PBIT was increased by £120,000 year on year. The result was that interest cover nearly doubled from 5.3 times in 2009 to 9.3 times in 2010. This ratio may drop again in 2011 as a result of an increase in interest payable in 2011 because of the loan taken by the company late in 2010.

Progress check 7.7

What are financial ratios and how may they be used to comment on the financial structure of an organisation?

In this chapter we have looked at most of the key ratios for review of company performance, and their meaning and relevance. However, the limitations we have already identified generally relating to performance review must always be borne in mind. In addition, it should be noted that the calculations used in business ratio analysis are based on past performance. These may not, therefore, reflect the current or future position of an organisation. Performance ratio analyses can also sometimes be misleading if their interpretation does not also consider other factors that may not always be easily quantifiable, and may include non-financial information, for example customer satisfaction, and delivery performance (see the section about non-financial performance indicators in Chapter 10). There may be inconsistencies in some of the measures used in ratio analysis; for example, sales revenue numbers being reported net of VAT, but trade receivable and trade payables numbers normally including VAT. Extreme care should therefore be taken with the conclusions used in any performance review to avoid reaching conclusions that may perhaps be ambiguous or erroneous.

If all the financial literature were thoroughly researched the number of different ratios that would be discovered may run into thousands. It is most helpful to use a limited set of ratios and to fully understand their meaning. The ratios will certainly help with an understanding of the company but do not in themselves represent the complete picture.

Calculation of the ratios for one company for one year is also very limited. It is more relevant to compare companies operating in the same market and to analyse how a company has changed over the years. However, difficulties inevitably arise because it is sometimes impossible to find another company that is strictly comparable with the company being analysed. In addition, the company itself may have changed so much over recent years as to render meaningless any conclusions drawn from changes in ratios.

The best performance measure – cash or profit?

The importance of cash flow versus profit (or earnings per share) as a measure of company performance has increased over the past few years. The advantages and disadvantages in the use of each are shown in Figures 7.14 and 7.15.

Cash flow has assumed increasing importance and has gained popularity as a measure of performance because the income statement has become somewhat discredited due to the unacceptable degree of subjectivity involved in its preparation. Some of the financial ratios that we have already looked at may be considered in cash terms, for example:

$$\text{cash ROCE \%} = \frac{\text{net cash flow from operations}}{\text{average capital employed}}$$

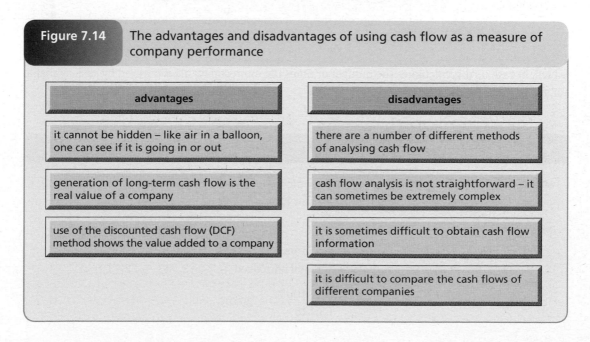

Figure 7.14 The advantages and disadvantages of using cash flow as a measure of company performance

advantages	disadvantages
it cannot be hidden – like air in a balloon, one can see if it is going in or out	there are a number of different methods of analysing cash flow
generation of long-term cash flow is the real value of a company	cash flow analysis is not straightforward – it can sometimes be extremely complex
use of the discounted cash flow (DCF) method shows the value added to a company	it is sometimes difficult to obtain cash flow information
	it is difficult to compare the cash flows of different companies

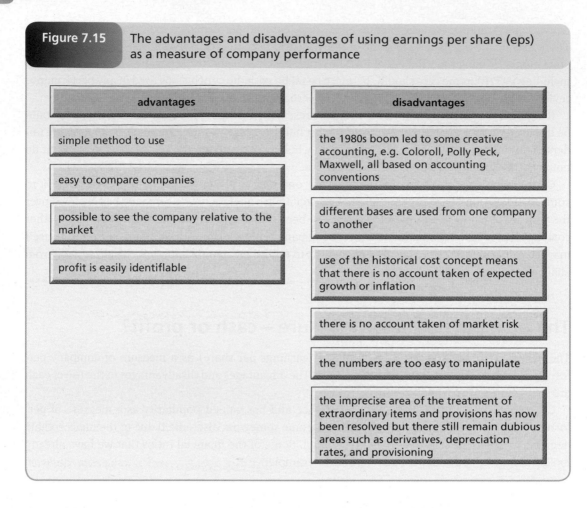

Figure 7.15   The advantages and disadvantages of using earnings per share (eps) as a measure of company performance

advantages	disadvantages
simple method to use	the 1980s boom led to some creative accounting, e.g. Coloroll, Polly Peck, Maxwell, all based on accounting conventions
easy to compare companies	
possible to see the company relative to the market	different bases are used from one company to another
profit is easily identiflable	use of the historical cost concept means that there is no account taken of expected growth or inflation
	there is no account taken of market risk
	the numbers are too easy to manipulate
	the imprecise area of the treatment of extraordinary items and provisions has now been resolved but there still remain dubious areas such as derivatives, depreciation rates, and provisioning

and

$$\text{cash interest cover} = \frac{\text{net cash inflow from operations} + \text{interest received}}{\text{interest paid}}$$

which, in cash terms, calculates the number of times the interest payable is covered by cash available for such payments.

Worked example 7.6

We will calculate the cash ROCE % for Flatco plc for 2010 and the comparative ratio for 2009, and compare with the equivalent profit ratio for Flatco plc.

Cash ROCE %

$$\text{cash ROCE \% 2010} = \frac{\text{net cash flow from operations}}{\text{average capital employed}} = \frac{£936 \times 100\%}{(£3,543 + £2,713)/2}$$

$$= \frac{£936 \times 100\%}{£3,128} = 29.9\%$$

$$\text{cash ROCE \% 2009} = \frac{£783 \times 100\%}{(£2,713 + £2,406)/2} = \frac{£783 \times 100\%}{£2,559.5} = 30.6\%$$

Report on the cash and profit ROCE of Flatco plc

While the profit ROCE % was static at 17.6% for 2009 and 2010, the cash ROCE % reduced from 30.6% to 29.9%. Operating cash flow for 2010 increased by only 19.5% over 2009, despite the fact that operating profit for 2010 increased by 22.2% over 2009.

Operating profit before depreciation (EBITDA) was £895,000 [£550,000 + £345,000] for 2010, which was an increase of 20.5% over 2009 [£450,000 + £293,000 = £743,000]. If pre-depreciation operating profit had been used to calculate ROCE, it would have been 28.6% for 2010 compared with 29.0% for 2009, a reduction of 0.4% and more in line with the picture shown by the cash ROCE.

The chairman of Flatco plc expects that ROCE will be improved in 2011 as a result of:

■ increased profitability resulting from higher sales revenues generated from the investments in new projects
■ reduction in levels of working capital, with more efficient use of company resources.

Progress check 7.8

What are the benefits of using cash flow instead of profit to measure financial performance? What are the disadvantages of using cash flow?

The increasing importance of cash flow as a measure of performance has led to new methods of measurement:

■ the Rappaport method uses DCF looking 10 years ahead as a method of valuing a company
■ the **economic value added (EVA™)** method, which we will discuss in Chapter 14 (pages 573 to 578) ◄⫶⫶
■ enterprise value, a very similar method to EVA, which excludes the peripheral activities of the company.

The profit-based measure of financial performance **EBITDA**, or earnings before interest, tax, depre- ◄⫶⫶
ciation and amortisation, has become widely used as an approximation to operational cash flow. Am-
ortisation, in the same way as depreciation applies to tangible non-current assets, is the systematic write-off of the cost of an intangible asset. The way in which EBITDA may be used has been illustrated in the Flatco plc Worked example 7.6.

Graphs showing BT plc's EBITDA and free cash flows cash flows derived from EDITDA for the years 2006 to 2010, which were included in the group's annual report for the year 2010, are shown in Figure 7.16.

In their 2010 annual report and accounts, BT plc commented on their use of EBITDA as a per-
formance measure: 'EBITDA is a common measure used by investors and analysts to evaluate the operating financial performance of companies, particularly in the telecommunications sector. We consider EBITDA to be a useful measure of our operating performance because it reflects the underlying operating cash costs, by eliminating depreciation and amortisation. EBITDA is not a direct measure of our liquidity, which is shown by our statement of cash flows, and it needs to be considered in the context of our financial commitments.'

We have seen that the method of performance measurement is not a clear-cut cash or profit choice. It is generally useful to use both. However, many analysts and the financial press in general continue to depend heavily on profit performance measures with a strong emphasis on earnings per share (eps) and the price/earnings ratio (P/E).

Figure 7.16   BT plc EBITDA and free cash flow for 2006 to 2010

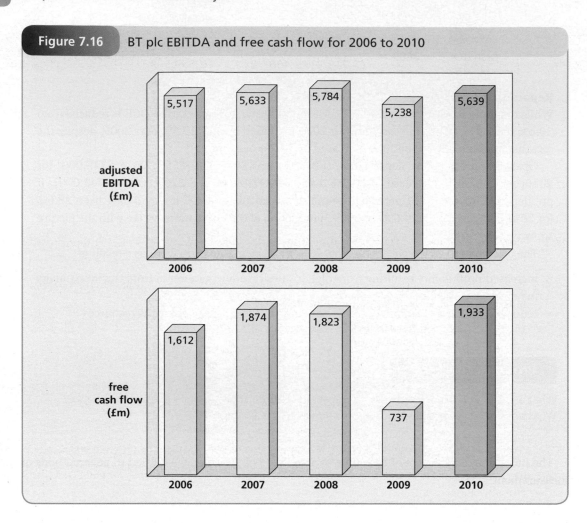

Summary of key points

■ The main aims of a business performance review are to provide an understanding of the business and provide an interpretation of results.

■ Care must be taken in reviewing business performance, primarily because of lack of consistency in definitions and changes in economic conditions.

■ An important area of business performance review is the use of ratio analysis looking at profitability, efficiency, liquidity, investment and growth, and financial structure.

■ Cash flow and cash ratios are becoming increasingly as important as profit and profitability ratios in the measurement of business performance.

■ There is no best way of evaluating financial performance and there are advantages and disadvantages in using earnings per share or cash flow as the basis of measurement.

■ Earnings before interest, tax, depreciation and amortisation (EBITDA) is sometimes used as an approximate measure of a cash flow performance.

Assessment material

Questions

Q7.1 (i) Who is likely to carry out a business performance review?

(ii) Describe what may be required from such reviews giving some examples from different industries and differing perspectives.

Q7.2 (i) Outline how the business performance review process may be used to evaluate the position of a dot.com company like Amazon UK.

(ii) What are the limitations to the approach that you have outlined?

Q7.3 How is ratio analysis, in terms of profitability ratios, efficiency ratios, liquidity ratios, investment ratios and financial structure ratios used to support the business review process?

Q7.4 Why should we be so careful when we try to compare the income statement of a limited company with a similar business in the same industry?

Q7.5 (i) Why does profit continue to be the preferred basis for evaluation of the financial performance of a business?

(ii) In what ways can cash flow provide a better basis for performance evaluation, and how may cash flow be approximated?

Discussion points

D7.1 In what ways may the performance review process be used to anticipate and react to change?

D7.2 'Lies, damned lies, and statistics.' In which of these categories do you think ratio analysis sits, if at all?

Exercises

Solutions are provided in Appendix 3 to all exercise numbers highlighted in colour.

Level I

E7.1 *Time allowed – 30 minutes*

The information below relates to Priory Products plc's actual results for 2009 and 2010 and their budget for the year 2011.

	2009 £000	2010 £000	2011 £000
Cash and cash equivalents	100	0	0
Overdraft	0	50	200
Loans	200	200	600
Ordinary share capital	100	200	400
Retained earnings	200	300	400

You are required to calculate the following financial ratios for Priory Products for 2009, 2010, and 2011:

(i)   debt/equity ratio (net debt to equity)

(ii) gearing (long-term loans to equity and long-term loans).

E7.2   *Time allowed – 60 minutes*

From the financial statements of Freshco plc, a Lancashire-based grocery and general supplies chain supplying hotels and caterers, for the year ended 30 June 2010, prepare a report on performance using appropriate profitability ratios for comparison with the previous year.

Freshco plc
Balance sheet as at 30 June 2010

	2010 £m	2009 £m
Non-current assets	146	149
Current assets		
Inventories	124	100
Trade receivables	70	80
Cash and cash equivalents	14	11
Total current assets	208	191
Total assets	354	340
Current liabilities		
Trade payables	76	74
Dividends payable	20	13
Income tax payable	25	20
Total current liabilities	121	107
Non-current liabilities		
Debenture loan	20	67
Total liabilities	141	174
Net assets	213	166
Equity		
Share capital	111	100
General reserve	14	9
Retained earnings	88	57
Total equity	213	166

Freshco plc
Income statement for the year ended 30 June 2010

	2010 £m	2009 £m
Revenue	894	747
Cost of sales	(690)	(581)
Gross profit	204	166
Distribution costs and administrative expenses	(121)	(84)

Operating profit	83	82
Net interest	(2)	(8)
Profit before tax	81	74
Income tax expense	(25)	(20)
Profit for the year	56	54
Retained profit brought forward	57	16
	113	70
Dividends for the year	(20)	(13)
	93	57
Transfer to general reserve	(5)	–
Retained profit carried forward	88	57

Additional information:

(i) Authorised and issued share capital 30 June 2010, £222m £0.50 ordinary shares (£200m, 2009).

(ii) Total assets less current liabilities 30 June 2008, £219m. Trade receivables 30 June 2008, £60m.

(iii) Market value of ordinary shares in Freshco plc 30 June 2010, £3.93 (£2.85, 2009).

(iv) Non-current assets depreciation provision 30 June 2010, £57m (£44m, 2009).

(v) Depreciation charge for the year to 30 June 2010, £13m (£10m, 2009).

Freshco plc
Cash generated from operations for the year ended 30 June 2010

	2010	2009
	£m	£m
Profit before tax	81	74
Depreciation charge	13	10
Adjust finance costs	2	8
Increase in inventories	(24)	(4)
Decrease/(increase) in trade receivables	10	(20)
Increase in trade payables	2	9
Cash generated from operations	84	77

Freshco plc
Statement of cash flows for the year ended 30 June 2010

	2010	2009
	£m	£m
Cash flows from operating activities		
Cash generated from operations	84	77
Interest paid	(2)	(8)
Income tax paid	(20)	(15)
Net cash generated from operating activities	62	54

Freshco plc
Statement of cash flows for the year ended 30 June 2010 (*continued*)

	2010 £m	2009 £m
Cash flows from investing activities		
Purchases of tangible assets	(10)	(40)
Net cash outflow from investing activities	(10)	(40)
Cash flows from financing activities		
Proceeds from issue of ordinary shares	11	0
Proceeds from borrowings	0	7
Repayments of borrowings	(47)	0
Dividends paid to equity shareholders	(13)	(11)
Net cash outflow from financing activities	(49)	(4)
Increase in cash and cash equivalents in the year	3	10

E7.3 *Time allowed – 60 minutes*

Using the financial statements of Freshco plc from Exercise E7.2, for the year ended 30 June 2010, prepare a report on performance using appropriate efficiency ratios for comparison with the previous year.

E7.4 *Time allowed – 60 minutes*

Using the financial statements of Freshco plc from Exercise E7.2, for the year ended 30 June 2010, prepare a report on performance using appropriate liquidity ratios for comparison with the previous year.

E7.5 *Time allowed – 60 minutes*

Using the financial statements of Freshco plc from Exercise E7.2, for the year ended 30 June 2010, prepare a report on performance using appropriate investment ratios for comparison with the previous year.

E7.6 *Time allowed – 60 minutes*

Using the financial statements of Freshco plc from Exercise E7.2, for the year ended 30 June 2010, prepare a report on performance using appropriate financial ratios for comparison with the previous year.

Level II

E7.7 *Time allowed – 60 minutes*

The summarised income statement for the years ended 31 March 2009 and 2010 and balance sheets as at 31 March 2009 and 31 March 2010 for Boxer plc are shown below:

Boxer plc
Income statement for the year ended 31 March

Figures in £000	2009	2010
Revenue	5,200	5,600
Cost of sales	(3,200)	(3,400)
Gross profit	2,000	2,200
Expenses	(1,480)	(1,560)
Profit before tax	520	640

Boxer plc
Balance sheet as at 31 March

	2009 £000	2010 £000
Non-current assets	4,520	5,840
Current assets		
Inventories	1,080	1,360
Trade receivables	680	960
Cash and cash equivalents	240	–
Total current assets	2,000	2,320
Total assets	6,520	8,160
Current liabilities		
Borrowings and finance leases	–	160
Trade payables	360	520
Income tax payable	240	120
Dividends payable	280	384
Total current liabilities	880	1,184
Non-current liabilities		
Debenture loan	1,200	1,200
Total liabilities	2,080	2,384
Net assets	4,440	5,776
Equity		
Ordinary share capital	4,000	5,200
Retained earnings	440	576
Total equity	4,440	5,776

Required:

(i) Calculate the following ratios for the years 2009 and 2010:
  (a) gross profit percentage of sales
  (b) profit before tax percentage of sales
  (c) return on capital employed
  (d) collection days
  (e) payables days
  (f) inventory turnover
  (g) current ratio
  (h) quick ratio.

(ii) Comment on Boxer plc's financial performance over the two years and explain the importance of effective management of working capital (net current assets).

E7.8   *Time allowed – 90 minutes*

The chief executive of Laurel plc, Al Chub, wants to know the strength of the financial position of Laurel's main competitor, Hardy plc. Using Hardy's financial statements for the past three years he has asked you to write a report that evaluates the financial performance of Hardy plc and to include:

(i) a ratio analysis that looks at profitability, efficiency and liquidity

(ii) an identification of the top five areas which should be investigated further

(iii) details of information that has not been provided, but if it were available would improve your analysis of Hardy's performance.

Hardy plc
Balance sheet as at 31 March 2010

	2008 £m	2009 £m	2010 £m
Non-current assets	106	123	132
Current assets			
Inventories	118	152	147
Trade receivables	53	70	80
Cash and cash equivalents	26	29	26
Total current assets	197	251	253
Total assets	303	374	385
Current liabilities			
Trade payables	26	38	38
Other payables	40	52	55
Total current liabilities	66	90	93
Non-current liabilities			
Debenture loan	38	69	69
Total non-current liabilities	38	69	69
Total liabilities	104	159	162
Net assets	199	215	223
Equity			
Share capital	50	50	50
Retained earnings	149	165	173
Total equity	199	215	223

Hardy plc
Income statement for the year ended 31 March 2010

	2008 £m	2009 £m	2010 £m
Revenue	420	491	456
Cost of sales	(277)	(323)	(295)
Gross profit	143	168	161
Distribution costs and administrative expenses	(93)	(107)	(109)
Operating profit	50	61	52
Net interest	(3)	(7)	(9)
Profit before tax	47	54	43
Income tax expense	(22)	(26)	(23)
Profit for the year	25	28	20
Dividends	(12)	(12)	(12)
Retained profit for the year	13	16	8

E7.9   *Time allowed – 120 minutes*

Locate the website for HSBC Bank plc on the Internet. Use their most recent annual report and accounts to prepare a report that evaluates their financial performance, financial position and future prospects. Your report should include calculations of the appropriate ratios for comparison with the previous year.

E7.10   *Time allowed – 120 minutes*

Locate the websites for Tesco plc and Morrisons plc on the Internet. Use their most recent annual report and accounts to prepare a report that evaluates and compares their financial performance and financial position. Your report should include calculations of the appropriate ratios for comparing the two groups, and an explanation of their differences and similarities.

8

Annual report and accounts

Value | Change %
3,006.62 | 38.97 ▲
2,649.71 | 33.35 ▲
807.90 | 2.93 ▲
10,744.54 | 96.03 ▲
1,367.40 | 13.28 ▲
626.42 | 4.70 ▲
61.33 | 0.49 ▼

Contents

Learning objectives

Completion of this chapter will enable you to:

■ explain why annual reports and accounts of limited companies are filed and published

■ recognise the key elements of the contents of the annual report and accounts of a typical public limited company

■ evaluate the information disclosed within the annual report and accounts

■ carry out a horizontal analysis of the income statement and the balance sheet

■ carry out a vertical analysis of the income statement and the balance sheet

■ interpret the information provided by segmental reporting

■ critically evaluate the quality of sustainability reporting within annual reports

■ appreciate the impact of inflation on the financial performance of companies

■ prepare and describe an alternative perception of the income statement illustrated by the value added statement.

Introduction

This chapter builds on the business performance analysis techniques we introduced in Chapter 7. It is concerned with the type of information, both financial and non-financial, that is included in a company's annual report and accounts. We will use the annual report and accounts of Johnson Matthey Plc for the year 2010 to illustrate the financial statements of a large UK plc. We will not consider the whole of the Johnson Matthey Plc annual report, a copy of which may be obtained from their head office at 40–42 Hatton Garden, London EC1N 8EE, UK. Further information about the company and copies of its report and accounts 2010 may be obtained from the Johnson Matthey website which is linked to the website accompanying this book at *www.pearsoned.co.uk/daviestony.*

We will look at extracts from Johnson Matthey Plc's report and accounts 2010, which are split into three main sections:

■ Report of the directors, which includes the business review and corporate governance (see Chapter 6)
■ Accounts
■ Other information.

Within the report of the directors we will look at the business review section that includes:

■ Financial highlights
■ Chairman's statement
■ Chief executive's statement
■ Financial review
■ Treasury policies
■ Liquidity and going concern
■ Sustainability.

An area of increasing importance appears in a section of the annual reports and accounts of UK plcs called sustainability. Corporate governance is an important area within this section, which is reported on and audited, and was discussed in Chapter 6.

Within the Accounts section we will look at the:

■ Accounting policies
■ Financial statements
■ Notes on the accounts
■ Segmental reporting.

Two further areas within this section: responsibility of directors and the independent auditors' report were included in Chapter 6.

We will use Johnson Matthey's five year record and other shareholder information, contained in the final section, other information, in Worked examples and Exercises later in this chapter.

The information disclosed in Johnson Matthey Plc's report and accounts 2010 provides us with a broad picture of what sort of company Johnson Matthey is. The report and accounts includes not only Johnson Matthey's historical financial performance, but also an indication of Johnson Matthey's prospects for the future. Included within the financial review is an example of how such a group manages risk.

In Chapter 7 we considered ratio analysis in our review of business performance. In this chapter we will look at some further tools of analysis. The first is horizontal analysis, or common size analysis, which provides a line-by-line comparison of the financial statements of a company (income statement and balance sheet) with those of the previous year. The second approach is the vertical analysis, where each item in the income statement and balance sheet is expressed as a percentage of the total.

The report and accounts of companies are now including more and more non-financial information, for example employee accident rates. Companies are also increasing generally their reporting on their sustainability performance. This includes areas such as health and safety, the environment, equal opportunities, employee development, and ethical issues. Johnson Matthey's report and accounts 2010 includes a comprehensive report on its sustainability performance, which is reproduced within this chapter.

The chapter closes with a look at the nature and purpose of the value added statement and its preparation. The value added statement is a variation on the income statement and is concerned with measuring the value added by a business rather than the profit earned by the business.

Why are annual accounts filed and published?

After each year end, companies prepare their annual report and accounts, which include the financial statements and the auditors' report, for their shareholders. Copies of the annual report and accounts must be filed with the Registrar of Companies (or Chambers of Commerce in some countries), and presented for approval by the shareholders at the company's annual general meeting (AGM). Further copies are usually made available to other interested parties such as financial institutions, major suppliers and other investors. The annual report and accounts of a plc usually take the form of a glossy booklet which includes photographs of the directors, products and activities and other promotional material, and many non-financial performance measures, as well as the statutory legal and financial information. Large companies also issue half-yearly, or interim reports, which include the standard financial information, but the whole report is on a much smaller scale than the annual report.

The following press extract includes comments on the interim financial report published by Johnson Matthey Plc for the six months to 30 September 2009, the first half of their 2009/10

Interim financial reporting

Profits at Johnson Matthey, the world's largest manufacturer of catalytic converters for cars, fell by a fifth in the first six months of the year, as vehicle production around the world was reined in.

The group was cautious about a recovery in the auto sector, arguing that the 'timing of a return in consumer confidence and the impact of the expiry of car scrappage schemes would be key factors in driving demand in the months ahead'.

The comments came as the group posted a 22pc fall in first-half profits to £109.5m pre-tax, on revenues down 18pc at £3.58bn.

The slide in revenues was caused by falling demand for catalysts and lower metals prices, the company said. Global car production fell 16pc in the period, despite Chinese car production increasing 42pc. The average platinum price was 33pc lower than the corresponding period last year. Sales excluding precious metals fell 5pc.

The group maintained its dividend at 11.1p, which will be paid on February 2. Most analysts had expected the pay-out to be trimmed. The group also said it expected to meet market forecasts for the full year.

Net debt increased by 8pc to £584.3m, but the company said its balance sheet remained strong and interest costs had fallen.

Rhian Tucker, an analyst at Credit Suisse, said that the results were 'steady' although given the recent share price run-up the group 'may not have done enough to excite'.

The shares fell 62p to £15.29.

Source: **Johnson Matthey cautious on recovery**, by Garry White © *Daily Telegraph*, 25 November 2009

financial year. Johnson Matthey Plc's pre-tax profits fell by 22% for the first six months of its financial year to 31 March 2010, as worldwide vehicle production contracted. Despite analysts' expectations that the dividend may be cut, the group maintained its dividend level at 11p per share. The share price fell by 62p to £15.29, but the group said that it expected to meet market forecasts for the financial year.

The publication of the annual report and accounts is always the time, of course, when forecasts may be seen to have been justified or not. There was uncertainty in 2010 following the end of the government scrappage schemes on new car sales, and the possible slowdown in China's industrial output. Pre-tax profit for the year ended 31 March 2010 for the Johnson Matthey group as a whole fell by 8% to £228.5m, and sales revenue was flat at £7.84bn. This represented a strong improvement in the second half of the year because profits for the first half of the year had fallen by 22% and sales revenue had declined by 18%. Johnson Matthey was also forecasting good progress in the first half of 2010/11, as industrial production gathered pace.

With governments around the world continuously tightening emissions levels, companies and individuals are seeking to live and work in a cleaner and more energy-efficient way. At the start of 2010 for example, the United States brought in far stricter rules on emissions for diesel used in large trucks. This meant that new models would have many more catalysts fitted, creating a big opportunity for Johnson Matthey.

Johnson Matthey also identified another opportunity for its catalysts in China. This would be as a result of China's desire to use its coal reserves to produce cleaner fuel rather than burning it in coal-fired power stations. Coal can be used to make methanol, a partial substitute for petrol, and about 5% to 10% of the fuel going into a car can be replaced with methanol without affecting the engine.

Platinum prices improved through 2009/10 as industrial production recovered. This precious metal is used in catalytic converters and other oil and gas processes, and Johnson Matthey's biggest business by sales is its precious metals products division (over two thirds of the total), which had sales revenue of £5.56bn in the year ended 31 March 2010.

Following publication of the year-end results, analysts felt that the long-term health of the Johnson Matthey business looked assured as a reduction in the impact of energy use on the environment becomes ever more important. But analysts and the company were both uncertain about the medium term. Johnson Matthey said that business would be harder to predict from autumn 2010 onwards, as the end of old car scrappage schemes revealed the true level of demand for new cars, which for Johnson Matthey means the catalytic converters that go into them. Johnson Matthey also currently derives just under one half of its sales revenue from Europe, which is the part of the world where economic growth looked most fragile in 2010.

Financial statements, whether for internal or external parties, are defined as summaries of accounts to provide information for interested parties. The key reports and statements within the published annual report and accounts are illustrated in Figure 8.1.

In 1993 the Accounting Standards Board (ASB) issued a statement of good practice that supported the earlier suggestion made in the report of the **Cadbury Committee** (1992) that companies should include in their annual reports an operating and financial review (OFR) of the business. The reason for this suggestion was that businesses had become increasingly diversified and complex, and it had

| Figure 8.1 | The key reports and statements within a company's annual report and accounts |

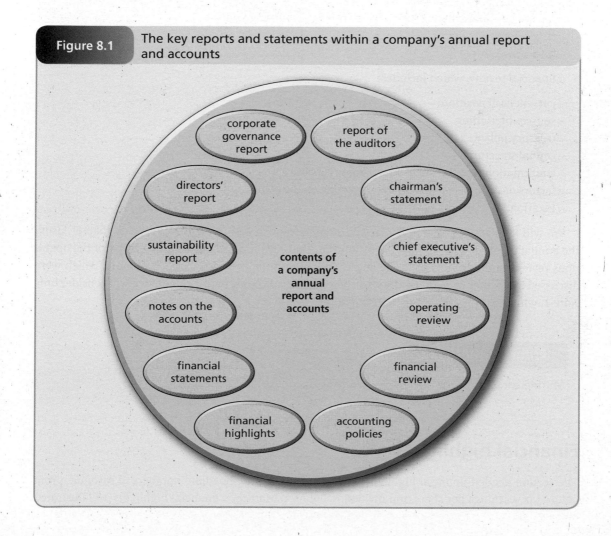

become increasingly difficult to understand information contained in financial reporting. Complex financial and organisational structures made it difficult to analyse and interpret financial information. It was felt that the OFR was needed to provide a greater insight into the affairs of the company, in addition to the information traditionally already provided by the chairman's statement and the directors' report.

The OFR was intended to cover the business as a whole for the year under review, and to include issues relevant to the assessment of future prospects. The OFR should include:

- brief reports that are easy to understand
- reports on each of the individual aspects of the business
- explanations of non-recurring aspects of the business
- discussion of matters that underpin the financial results for the period
- consideration of factors that might impact on the future performance of the business.

The OFR includes two separate reports which Johnson Matthey Plc includes within its business review:

- an operations review, which includes:
    - new product development information
    - details of shareholders' returns
    - sensitivities of the financial results to specific accounting policies
    - risks and uncertainties
    - future investment

- a financial review, which includes:

    - current cash position
    - sources of funding
    - treasury policy
    - capital structure
    - confirmation that the business is a going concern
    - factors outside the balance sheet impacting on the value of the business
    - taxation.

We will look at each of the reports and statements included in Figure 8.1 in this chapter, using the annual report and accounts 2010 of Johnson Matthey Plc as an illustration, except for the operations review, and also the corporate governance report and the report of the auditors, which were discussed in Chapter 6. With regard to the notes on the accounts, in this chapter we will consider only Note 1, which relates to **segmental reporting**.

Progress check 8.1

Why are annual accounts filed and published?

Financial highlights

The section headed financial highlights serves to focus on the headline numbers of revenue, profit before tax, earnings per share and dividends. Johnson Matthey's financial highlights are illustrated on page 269.

2009/10 WAS A CHALLENGING YEAR for Johnson Matthey but overall the group performed well. Despite the global economic downturn underlying profit before tax was only 5% down on our record performance in 2008/09.

FINANCIAL HIGHLIGHTS – 2010

	Year to 31st March		%
	2010	2009	change
Revenue	£7,839m	£7,848m	–
Sales excluding precious metals	£1,886m	£1,797m	+5
Profit before tax	£228.5m	£249.4m	-8
Total earnings per share	77.6p	82.6p	-6
Underlying*:			
Profit before tax	£254.1m	£267.9m	-5
Earnings per share	86.4p	89.6p	-4
Dividend per share	39.0p	37.1p	+5

* Before amortisation of acquired intangibles, major impairment and restructuring charges and profit or loss on disposal of businesses.

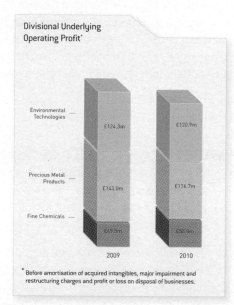

Divisional Underlying Operating Profit*

Environmental Technologies — £124.3m (2009) £120.9m (2010)
Precious Metal Products — £143.0m (2009) £116.7m (2010)
Fine Chemicals — £49.5m (2009) £55.8m (2010)

2009 2010

* Before amortisation of acquired intangibles, major impairment and restructuring charges and profit or loss on disposal of businesses.

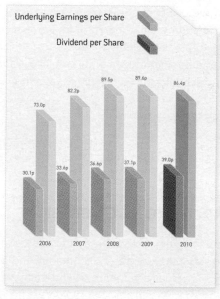

Underlying Earnings per Share

Dividend per Share

73.0p (2006), 82.2p (2007), 89.5p (2008), 89.6p (2009), 86.4p (2010)
30.1p (2006), 33.6p (2007), 36.6p (2008), 37.1p (2009), 39.0p (2010)

2006 2007 2008 2009 2010

Chairman's statement

In addition to the income statement and statement of cash flows for the year and the balance sheet as at the year-end date, the annual report and accounts includes much more financial and non-financial information such as:

- company policies
- financial indicators
- directors' remuneration
- employee numbers
- business analysis.

The annual report and accounts includes the chairman's statement. This offers an opportunity for the chairman of the company to report in unquantified and unaudited terms on the performance of the company during the past financial period and on likely future developments. Let's take a look at the Johnson Matthey chairman's statement from its chairman, Sir John Banham (see pages 271 to 272).

The Johnson Matthey chairman's statement can be seen to include his general comments about the performance of the company over the past year, its current position, and its outlook for the future. A couple of paragraphs describe the strategy of the group. As with most chairmen's statements, Johnson Matthey's statement includes comments about the board of directors, investments in research and development and in people, and the achievements of the management team and other employees over the preceding year. The Johnson Matthey statement devotes a large section to the importance of the company's employees and their training and development. It also includes reference to the importance of the company's full commitment to its reporting on its corporate social responsibility performance, including environmental issues (which we shall deal with later in this chapter). Sir John Banham's report concludes with a return to the company's goal of delivering superior shareholder value, and the importance of its employees and investment in research and development and manufacturing technology in achieving that goal.

> ### Progress check 8.2
>
> What is the purpose of a chairman's statement?

Chief executive's statement

Chief executives' statements generally include detail on the performance of the business particularly relating to products, markets, technology and the various geographical areas of activity. These statements include brief comments on the financial highlights of the preceding year and the recommended dividend payable to shareholders. The chief executive's statement includes a review of operations, which outlines the main factors underlying the business and identifies any changes or expected future changes which may impact on the business. It normally concludes with an outlook on the future prospects of the business.

The Johnson Matthey chief executive's statement for 2010, presented by Neil Carson (see pages 274 to 275), provides details about developments in the various divisions of the company including acquisitions. The report provides a great deal of information of particular interest to current and potential new shareholders relating to future growth opportunities, planned major investments, the development of new and existing technologies, new product development, and sustainability. This report includes some

CHAIRMAN'S STATEMENT

I am very pleased to report that, despite facing the most difficult economic conditions for many decades, Johnson Matthey performed well in 2009/10. The group produced underlying earnings per share that were only 4% lower than those in 2008/09, which, it should be remembered, was a record year for us.

Our strategy served us well during the downturn. The board, executive management team and employees at all levels of the company faced the challenges posed by extremely turbulent conditions in some of our key markets, especially in the western automotive markets, and took prompt and decisive action to reduce costs. However, this was done without sacrificing the future growth potential of our business. Whilst capital expenditure was significantly reduced, we continued our investment in new, highly efficient manufacturing capacity to make automotive emission control catalysts in Europe and the United States and a new plant in China to make catalysts to control emissions of oxides of nitrogen, or NOx, from coal fired power stations in that country. We also completed a facility in the UK to manufacture Apico, our revolutionary new methanol synthesis catalyst which was launched during the year and provides major performance benefits to customers worldwide.

The investment that we make in research and development is vital to the success of our company. It provides the high technology products and manufacturing processes that enable us to maintain market leadership and underpins the future growth of our businesses. Despite the difficult market conditions that we have faced over the last few years we have not cut our R&D spend, indeed we have continued to increase it. We are increasingly focusing our R&D efforts on developing new products that will help our customers to improve their resource efficiency, reduce energy consumption and waste and make their businesses more sustainable. Apico, which was developed in house by our world class scientists, will help to deliver many of these sustainability benefits to our customers in the methanol industry and is a great example of the crucial importance of R&D and innovation to our business.

As I visit Johnson Matthey businesses around the world I continue to be impressed by the commitment and enthusiasm of employees at all levels for Sustainability 2017, our group wide programme to make ours a more sustainable business by the year 2017, the two hundredth anniversary of the company's foundation. We have set ourselves some very challenging targets but given the commitment of our people and the spirit of innovation that is evident throughout the group, I feel confident that Sustainability 2017 will be a great success. Further details of our progress towards Sustainability 2017 are summarised on pages 29 to 37 and are presented in full in the group's Sustainability Report which will be published on our website in July.

Sir John Banham
Chairman

The last year has seen something of a changing of the guard among the executive directors of the company with the retirement from the board in July 2009 of David Morgan and Dr Pelham Hawker and the appointment of Bill Sandford as an executive director of the company. I marked these changes in my statement to you last year. As I also announced in my statement last year, John Sheldrick retired in September 2009 having served 19 years as Group Finance Director of Johnson Matthey. For the last few years John had the distinction of being the longest serving finance director of a FTSE 100 company. John had a long and distinguished career with Johnson Matthey since joining the company in 1990. He had a deep knowledge of all of the group's businesses and for several years had board level responsibility for our then Pharmaceutical Materials Division in addition to his role as Group Finance Director.

John Sheldrick played a key role in the evolution of the group into a world leading speciality chemicals company and in focusing it on its important opportunities for growth, especially those in its Environmental Technologies Division. On behalf of the board and indeed all of us at Johnson Matthey, I would like to thank John for the major contribution that he made to the development and success of the group and wish him all the very best for a well deserved, long and happy retirement. I am very pleased to welcome Robert MacLeod, who joined the board with effect from 22nd June 2009, as John Sheldrick's successor as Group Finance Director.

The most important investment that your company makes will always be the one that it makes in its people. This is very much brought home at times of difficult economic circumstances. We invest a great deal in the training and development of our staff and the last thing that we want to do is lose them. Unfortunately, as I mentioned earlier, this year saw us having to take action to reduce costs which inevitably led to a number of job losses. Even in these challenging times however, I never fail to be impressed by the enthusiasm, professionalism and dedication of our employees at all levels of the organisation. On your behalf, I would like to thank all of them around the world for their contribution to the success of the company in this difficult year. I would also like to take this opportunity to thank the senior management team for the excellent way that they responded to the challenges of the last year's difficult economic conditions.

Our investment in building our presence in the important Chinese market, which was the focus of our very successful investor presentation in January this year, has paid dividends during the recession and we are well positioned to continue to benefit from growth in China, India and other emerging economic powerhouses.

Johnson Matthey is in good shape and, despite the impact of the recession, continues to make progress towards delivering superior shareholder value. Whilst uncertainty remains about how quickly the world's economies will emerge from recession, all of the legislative, environmental and energy security drivers of our businesses remain very much in place. We are emerging from the recession stronger and more efficient than before it hit, when we were running flat out to keep pace with rapidly growing demand. I believe that your company has a terrific future ahead of it and I look forward to reporting on our progress in 2010/11.

Sir John Banham
Chairman

detail of the headline financial results, but its main focus is the operating review containing the sort of information referred to earlier, and an outlook for the business over the next few years. Further detail is provided in the reports that follow the chief executive's statement that cover group activities, strategy and objectives, group key performance indicators, group performance review, and operations review (see pages 276 to 288).

Financial review

The financial review goes into further financial detail than the chief executive's statement. It is normally prepared by the finance director. In the case of Johnson Matthey, the financial review has been prepared by its group finance director, Robert MacLeod. The purpose of the financial review is to review the results for the past year and to provide an overview of financial policy. Let's look at the Johnson Matthey financial review, included within the business review section, and its annual report and accounts for the year 2010 (see pages 289 to 291).

The Johnson Matthey financial review begins with a review of the results for the year to 31 March 2010, with an initial focus on sales, profit before tax and earnings per share. The review goes on to look in a little more detail at:

- dividends
- exchange rates
- return on invested capital
- profit before tax
- earnings per share
- cash flow
- return on sales
- interest
- taxation
- pensions
- capital structure.

We can see that the Financial Review includes many of the financial performance measures we have discussed in Chapter 7; for example return on sales and return on investment, which are analysed by each area of business activity.

Johnson Matthey has commented with regard to the greater stability but further weakness in £ sterling against most major currencies during 2009/10. Each one cent change in the average US$/£ exchange rate had an approximate £0.4m effect on the year's operating profit. The group benefited by £5.0m from the fall in sterling against the US$, and benefited by £2.8m from the fall in sterling against the **euro**. Sterling fell against the South African rand but any impact was mitigated because of operational factors. Exchange rate gains were responsible for increasing the group's operating profit for the year by £12.2m compared with 2008/09.

Further sections follow the financial review headed treasury policies, and liquidity and going concern, research and development, and risks and uncertainties (see pages 292 to 296). The treasury policies section explains the group's policies with regard to financial **risk management** and treasury policies. Risk management is a key strategic area for the type of business in which Johnson Matthey is involved. This section also covers the group's approach and policies relating to interest rate risk and foreign currency risk; it also includes the **financial instruments** that are used by Johnson Matthey to manage financial risks. Risk relating to fluctuations in precious metal prices, which have a significant impact on Johnson Matthey's results, is also outlined in terms of policy and the way in which that area of risk is managed. The group finance director indicated in an outline of its policy the extent to which the group is risk averse. The group hedges against future changes in precious metal prices where such hedging can be done at acceptable cost.

The liquidity and going concern section explains the group's policy on funding, its group borrowings, and future funding requirements. The group has undertaken a sensitivity analysis of the key factors which could affect cash flow and funding requirements to ensure adequate resources to fund its operations for the foreseeable future and to be able to prepare its accounts on a going concern basis.

Johnson Matthey has reported on its share price performance and other shareholder information on page 110 of its report and accounts for the year 2010 which is not reproduced in this book.

CHIEF EXECUTIVE'S STATEMENT

2009/10 was a challenging year for Johnson Matthey but I am pleased to say that we rose to those challenges and the group performed well. Revenue was flat at £7.8 billion and sales excluding precious metals were 5% up at £1.9 billion. Underlying profit before tax was 5% down at £254.1 million.

The year started in the depths of a global recession which certainly impacted our first half. However, the economic climate gradually improved throughout our second half aided by government efforts to stimulate the economy, particularly through various car scrappage schemes, and continued Chinese investment in the development of their energy resources and infrastructure. As a result, the year ended with a very creditable result, with underlying profit before tax only 5% down on 2008/09, which had been a record year for us. I would like to pay tribute to our management team who, despite being exposed to unprecedentedly volatile and difficult market conditions, stepped up to the many challenges that they faced in their businesses and produced such good results. We very quickly went from a situation where many of our businesses were running hard to keep up with strongly growing demand for their products to one of rapid and dramatic market contraction. It is to their great credit that they took the right decisions, quickly and efficiently. They did this without being told to do so, something that I believe reflects a great strength in Johnson Matthey.

Given the economic backdrop, our Environmental Technologies Division performed well in 2009/10. Its Emission Control Technologies (ECT) business was hit quite hard at a relatively early stage of the recession as a result of plummeting vehicle production, especially in North America, Europe and Japan. However, its light duty business came back steadily throughout the second half of the year aided by the scrappage schemes and also by dramatic growth of demand in China.

Neil Carson
Chief Executive

ECT is now well placed to continue to benefit from ongoing recovery with a lower cost base and two new highly efficient and low cost manufacturing facilities. The first of these is in Macedonia to supply catalysts for both light and heavy duty vehicles in Europe and the second in western Pennsylvania, USA to supply heavy duty diesel catalysts to meet the US 2010 legislation that came into force on 1st January this year. We now have a total of 14 emission control catalyst manufacturing facilities around the world.

Our Process Technologies business continued to perform well throughout 2009/10 with strong growth in its sales to ammonia and methanol markets which more than offset a decline in sales to oil refineries, which suffered a fall in demand for transportation fuels due to the economic downturn. During the year the business launched Apico, a new highly advanced methanol synthesis catalyst which brings a number of important benefits to our customers around the world. We are confident that it will make a major contribution to Process Technologies' growth in 2010/11 and for many years ahead.

Our Fuel Cells business continued to increase its sales despite the impact that the recession had on several of its smaller customers and the outlook for this year is encouraging.

Precious Metal Products Division was impacted by lower prices and subdued demand for platinum group metals, especially in the first half of the financial year. However the division's performance improved in the latter part of the year. Its manufacturing businesses, including our platinum group metals refining business, were slower to feel the effects of the recession than our ECT business and were also slower to begin to emerge from it. However, their performance showed signs of improvement towards the end of the year. By contrast, our gold and silver refining business had a very strong year driven by the high gold price and buoyant demand for investment bars.

Fine Chemicals Division had a mixed year. Its active pharmaceutical ingredients manufacturing businesses in the UK and the USA performed well and the division received the one-off US $12 million benefit from the launch of the first generic version of ADDERALL XR® by Teva Pharmaceutical Industries. However, its contract research business continued to feel the effects of the recession on venture capital funding for new drug development by many of its smaller customers. We have therefore taken action to restructure operations at its facility in Massachusetts, USA which has led to £1.6 million in redundancy and other costs and an £11.3 million impairment charge in respect of redundant assets in 2009/10.

Our investment in expanding our market presence and manufacturing infrastructure in Asia, particularly in China, has served us very well in this recession. We currently have four manufacturing plants in China with a fifth, to manufacture plate type catalysts to control NOx emissions from coal fired power stations, in the process of being commissioned. We are also pleased that we have a linked yet relatively diverse portfolio of businesses in catalysts, precious metals, fine chemicals and process technology that helped us to weather the storm of recession.

In last year's annual report we announced that in response to the market turmoil we intended to reduce our capital expenditure to around 1.2 times depreciation. This has still enabled us to pursue growth opportunities in our businesses, despite the recession. In 2009/10 we spent £134.4 million (1.2 times depreciation) on capex projects. These included the construction of our Chinese plate type catalyst manufacturing facility along with the completion of our emission control catalyst manufacturing plants in Macedonia and western Pennsylvania and our facility in Clitheroe, UK to manufacture our Apico methanol synthesis catalyst.

Sustainability

We have continued to focus on sustainability efforts across our business this year and sustainability remains a key element of our strategy for future growth. The group's Sustainability 2017 Vision sets out our aspirations and targets in this area. It is also directing our efforts for improving the resource efficiency of our operations and for designing the next generation of products to enable our customers to be more sustainable and competitive. We have continued to realise considerable savings through our sustainability programme and a significant proportion of profit this year was generated by environmentally beneficial products. However, growing our business through sustainability is not only about our operations and products. Protecting the health, safety and wellbeing of our employees has always been a key priority in Johnson Matthey and it is their contribution that will underpin the growth of our business in the years ahead. In 2008/09 we saw a disappointing increase in our lost time accident rate. We have taken action this year to revitalise our accident prevention processes and I am pleased to say that our rate of occupational accidents involving lost time has fallen to its lowest reported level.

We have continued to make steady progress towards the Sustainability 2017 aspirations in 2009/10 although much of the progress to date has been achieved by incremental improvements in operational and process efficiencies, the so called 'low hanging fruit'. We have recognised the need to focus further on the step change opportunities that will drive accelerated progress towards our 2017 targets and add real value to Johnson Matthey.

Outlook

This time last year, the group faced considerable uncertainty given the global economic turmoil that surrounded us. Whilst there is greater economic optimism today, substantial uncertainties still remain, as illustrated by the recent volatility in European markets. Quite how these will affect consumer confidence remains to be seen. The group continues to expect to make good progress in the first half of 2010/11, where underlying profit before tax should be significantly higher than the same period of 2009/10.

In the first six months of 2010/11, Environmental Technologies Division will benefit from relatively easy comparatives as it was particularly affected by the global slowdown in automotive demand in the first quarter of 2009/10.

Emission Control Technologies is expected to perform well in the early part of the year as the impact of government scrappage schemes coming to an end may take some time to feed through to our business. Its performance should also benefit from some stock building by our customers. Process Technologies is also expected to continue growing steadily. As a result, Environmental Technologies Division's operating profit in the first six months of 2010/11, particularly in the first quarter, should be significantly ahead of the first half of 2009/10.

Precious Metal Products Division supplies products and services to a wide range of industries, some of which have recovered from the recession more quickly than others. The division's results benefit in part from the strength of platinum group metal prices and the platinum price in the first two months of 2010/11 has averaged $1,677/oz, which is approximately 45% higher than in the same period last year. However, prices have been highly volatile, especially over the last few weeks. The performance of the division's manufacturing and refining businesses are also much stronger than this time last year. Taken together, the results for the division in the first half of 2010/11 should also be significantly ahead of the same period in 2009/10.

The performance of our Fine Chemicals Division is more predictable as its key markets are less impacted by volatility in the global economy. We expect that its businesses will continue to grow steadily but the division's results in the first half of 2010/11 will be impacted by the absence of the one-off benefit in 2009/10 associated with the launch of the generic version of ADDERALL XR®.

The group's performance in the second half of 2010/11 is harder to predict, not only because of the uncertainties surrounding the global economy, but also due to factors that more directly influence our business. These include uncertainties over the impact on vehicle sales as government vehicle scrappage schemes come to an end, when and how quickly the important North American heavy duty diesel market recovers and the strength of continued growth in demand for our products in China. Notwithstanding these uncertainties, we are confident that the group is well positioned to take advantage of a global economic recovery.

The longer term drivers for the group remain very much in place with ever tightening emissions standards around the world. The demand for energy security globally and the drive to reduce the environmental impact of chemical and industrial processes also plays to the strengths of Johnson Matthey. Together these give us confidence in the future. Over the last few turbulent years we have continued to invest in research and development and in expanding production capacity where we see opportunities for growth. This will continue. We have a strong balance sheet, a proven business model and are well placed to return to growth.

Neil Carson
Chief Executive

BUSINESS REVIEW

Group Activities

Johnson Matthey is a global speciality chemicals company. We serve our customer base from operations in over 30 countries and employ around 9,000 people worldwide. The group is organised into three global divisions: Environmental Technologies; Precious Metal Products and Fine Chemicals.

Environmental Technologies is a global supplier of catalysts and related technologies for applications which benefit the environment such as pollution control, cleaner fuel, more efficient use of hydrocarbons and the hydrogen economy. The division comprises three businesses:

- Emission Control Technologies is a global leader in catalytic systems for emissions control from vehicles and industrial processes.

- Process Technologies serves the world's chemical, oil, gas and refining industries. It manufactures catalysts, provides specialist services and designs and licenses chemical processes.

- Johnson Matthey Fuel Cells develops and manufactures catalysts and catalysed components for a wide range of clean energy fuel cell systems.

Precious Metal Products' activities comprise the marketing, distribution, refining and recycling of platinum group metals (pgms), fabrication of products using precious metals and related materials, pgm and base metal catalysts and pgm chemicals, and the refining of gold and silver.

Fine Chemicals is a global supplier of active pharmaceutical ingredients, fine chemicals and other speciality chemical products and services to a wide range of chemical and pharmaceutical industry customers and industrial and academic research organisations.

Strategy and Objectives

Johnson Matthey's strategic intent is to achieve consistent growth in earnings by concentrating on the development of high added value products and services in areas where our expertise provides a competitive edge, particularly in catalysis, precious metals, fine chemicals and process technology.

The group's financial objectives are:

- To continue to achieve consistent and above average growth in underlying earnings per share.

- To grow dividends in line with underlying earnings while maintaining dividend cover at about two and a half times to ensure sufficient funds are retained to support organic growth. Dividend cover may vary from the long term target to enable the group to maintain dividends at a consistent level.

- To deliver a return on investment above the group's cost of capital. We estimate Johnson Matthey's post tax cost of capital is currently about 7.8% (10.8% pre-tax). In addition we have a long run pre-tax target for the group of 20%.

The board's strategies to achieve these financial objectives are:

- Focus the business on the group's core skills in catalysis, precious metals, fine chemicals and process technology.

- Position the group in growth markets where our core skills are applicable. Catalysis is a key technology in many developing markets for the 21st century, particularly those concerned with protecting the environment such as in emission control, cleaner fuel, more efficient use of hydrocarbons and the hydrogen economy. Environmental Technologies Division, which combines our skills in catalysts and process technology, is well positioned to serve these emerging markets. Catalysis is also important in the manufacture of fine chemicals where Johnson Matthey has a number of strong niche market positions. Johnson Matthey's expertise and international strength in precious metals, particularly platinum group metals, was the starting point for many of our businesses. The market for platinum has grown steadily for many decades and demand is expected to grow significantly over the next ten years.

- Differentiate ourselves by using our world class technology. We will continue to invest significantly in research and development to develop new products and manufacturing processes. Technology is the key driver for most of our businesses and Johnson Matthey has a strong science base with technical centres located in all our major markets.

- Maintain strong relationships with our major customers, suppliers, government bodies and other stakeholders by investing resources on joint projects to ensure the group is well positioned for future market development.

- Continue to invest in Johnson Matthey's employees to ensure they are well trained, motivated and encouraged to meet the challenges of the future.

- Ensure the business is run in a sustainable way by using resources efficiently, minimising waste in our manufacturing processes and designing new products that help our customers to be more sustainable and competitive.

→ Research Chemicals' manufacturing joint venture, Alfa Aesar Synmax, in Yantai, China.

BUSINESS REVIEW

Group Key Performance Indicators

Johnson Matthey uses a range of key performance indicators (KPIs) to monitor the group's performance over time in line with the financial objectives and strategy summarised in the previous section. This year we have slightly refined our KPIs to better reflect the group's current priorities. These principal KPIs, together with the group's performance against them in 2009/10, are described below:

Sales Excluding Precious Metals
£ million

Monitoring sales provides a measure of the growth of the business. In measuring the growth of the group, we focus on sales excluding the value of precious metals because total revenue can be heavily distorted by year on year fluctuations in precious metal prices. Not only that, in many cases variations in the value of the precious metal contained within our products are passed directly on to our customers.

Underlying Earnings per Share
Pence

Underlying earnings per share is the principal measure used by the board to assess the overall profitability of the group. The following items are excluded from underlying earnings because they can distort the trend in measuring results:
- Amortisation of intangible assets arising on acquisition of businesses (acquired intangibles).
- Major impairment or restructuring charges.
- Profits and losses on disposal of businesses.
- Major tax items arising from changes in legislation.

Return on Invested Capital
%

In a business as capital intensive as Johnson Matthey's, profitability alone is a poor measure of performance; it is possible to generate good operating margins but poor value for shareholders if assets are not used efficiently. Return on invested capital (ROIC) is therefore used alongside profit measures to ensure focus upon the efficient use of the group's assets. ROIC is defined for the group as underlying operating profit divided by average capital employed (equity plus net debt). ROIC for individual divisions is calculated using average segmental net assets as the denominator.

Capital Expenditure
£ million

To enable the group to continue to grow, Johnson Matthey invests significant amounts in maintaining and improving our existing plants and in adding new facilities to provide additional capacity where necessary. All new capital expenditure is subject to detailed review to ensure that its investment case passes internal hurdles. Annual capital expenditure is measured as the cost of property, plant and equipment and intangible assets purchased during the year. The ratio of capital expenditure to depreciation gives an indication of the relative level of investment. For 2009/10 it was 1.2 times (2008/09 2.0).

Gross Research and Development Expenditure
£ million

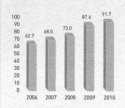

Johnson Matthey is fundamentally a technology company. To maintain our competitive position, we need to keep investing in research and development. Whilst absolute levels of research and development expenditure do not necessarily indicate how successful we are, that success rapidly feeds through to higher sales as lead times in our business can be quite short.

Sustainability – Global Warming Potential
Tonnes CO_2 equivalent ('000)

We measure our progress towards achieving carbon neutrality by looking at the group's total global warming potential (GWP). Total GWP is based on our direct and indirect energy usage and CO_2 equivalence which provide a strong platform for monitoring the impacts associated with energy use in our operations. We are working to broaden the scope of our GWP measurement to include all aspects of our business and to consider the beneficial impacts of our products and services. For further information on the group's GWP see pages 29, 30, 36 and 37.

* Calendar year.

Voluntary Employee Turnover
%

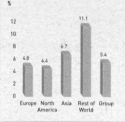

The success of Johnson Matthey is partly dependent upon the extent that we are able to attract and retain the most talented employees. This means that being an attractive employer is a prerequisite in a competitive environment. We monitor our success in retaining our staff using voluntary turnover statistics compared to those for UK manufacturing. In 2009, voluntary employee turnover for UK manufacturing was 7.7%*.

* Source: CIPD 2009 annual survey of recruitment, retention and turnover.

Safety – Annual Rate of >3 Day
Accidents per 1,000 Employees

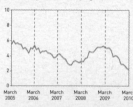

Johnson Matthey is a chemical manufacturing business and a significant proportion of our employees work in production environments with chemicals and process machinery. Rigorous safety systems apply across all facilities and are essential if the group is to avoid accidents which could cause injury to people or damage to our property, both of which can impact the group's performance. We actively manage our safety performance through monitoring the incidence of accidents that result in more than three days lost time.

Occupational Health – Annual Incidence of
Occupational Illness Cases per 1,000 Employees

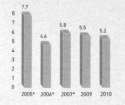

The health and wellbeing of our employees is a priority for Johnson Matthey and we are committed to minimising workplace related negative health effects. We manage our performance in this area by measuring the number of occupational illness cases arising as a result of exposure to workplace health hazards.

* Calendar year.

Case Study / Environmental Technologies Division

→ Process Technologies, Revolutionary New Catalyst

In June 2009 Process Technologies launched Apico, its new patented methanol synthesis catalyst. Developed in house by our world class scientists, Apico delivers huge value to our customers. Compared to other methanol synthesis catalysts, Apico has a much faster start up, produces fewer by products, increases methanol production and has a longer catalyst life. It is therefore a more sustainable product that enables customers to improve their plant efficiency and reduce their impact on the environment.

BUSINESS REVIEW

Group Performance Review

| | Year to 31st March | | |
	2010 **£ million**	2009 £ million	% change
Revenue	**7,839**	7,848	–
Sales excluding precious metals	**1,886**	1,797	+5
Operating profit	**250.6**	280.0	-11
Profit before tax	**228.5**	249.4	-8
Total earnings per share	**77.6p**	82.6p	-6
Underlying*:			
Operating profit	**271.8**	298.5	-9
Profit before tax	**254.1**	267.9	-5
Earnings per share	**86.4p**	89.6p	-4

* Before amortisation of acquired intangibles, major impairment and restructuring charges and profit or loss on disposal of businesses.

Sales

Revenue for the year ended 31st March 2010 was in line with last year at £7.8 billion, although performance was biased towards the second half of the year due to the increase in activity and precious metal prices; first half revenue was £3.6 billion and second half revenue was £4.2 billion. Despite the economic background, the group's sales excluding precious metals held up well and were 5% higher than last year at £1,886 million. Translated at constant exchange rates, revenue for the year fell by 3% and sales excluding precious metals grew by 1%.

→ Our new heavy duty diesel catalyst manufacturing facility in western Pennsylvania, USA.

Operating Profit

Underlying operating profit (before amortisation of acquired intangibles, major impairment and restructuring charges) was 9% lower than last year at £271.8 million. The group benefited from the weakness of sterling and at constant exchange rates underlying operating profit would have been 13% lower than last year.

This year we have taken an impairment charge in respect of redundant assets at our Pharmaceutical Materials and Services contract research business in Massachusetts, USA. This resulted in a charge of £11.3 million which has been excluded from underlying earnings per share.

The performance of the individual businesses is explained in more detail on pages 12 to 19 in the Operations Review.

BUSINESS REVIEW

Operations Review → Environmental Technologies Division

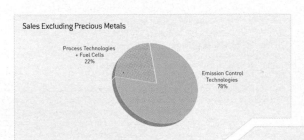

Sales Excluding Precious Metals

Process Technologies + Fuel Cells 22%

Emission Control Technologies 78%

Key Statistics

Return on sales excluding precious metals	9.7%
Return on invested capital (ROIC)	9.4%
Capital expenditure	£93.8m
Capex / depreciation	1.4
Average invested capital	£1,281m
Employees	4,985

	Year to 31st March		%	%
	2010 **£ million**	2009 £ million	% change	at constant rates
Revenue	**2,056**	2,226	-8	-11
Sales excluding precious metals	**1,247**	1,135	+10	+6
Underlying operating profit	**120.9**	124.3	-3	-6

Description of the Business

Emission Control Technologies (ECT)
ECT comprises Johnson Matthey's global autocatalyst, heavy duty diesel and stationary emissions control businesses. We are a world leading manufacturer of catalysts for vehicle exhaust emission control and a leader in catalyst systems for the reduction of emissions from industrial processes. Manufacturing plants are located in the UK, Germany, Belgium, Macedonia, Russia, USA, Mexico, Argentina, South Africa, Japan, Malaysia, India, China and South Korea. R&D facilities are in the USA, UK, Germany, Sweden, Japan, South Korea and Brazil.

Process Technologies
Process Technologies manufactures process catalysts for the syngas, methanol, ammonia, hydrogen, gas / coal to products, oil refineries and gas processing industries. Davy Process Technology develops chemical process technologies and licenses them to customers in the oil, gas and petrochemical industries. Our Tracerco business is an industrial leader in specialist technology for the diagnostics, measurement and analysis of process plant conditions across the hydrocarbon chain. Process Technologies serves customers around the world and has manufacturing sites in the UK, India and China, supported by several UK based technology centres and technical offices in key centres worldwide.

Fuel Cells
Johnson Matthey has a world leading position in the development and manufacture of catalysts and catalysed components for fuel cells.

Performance in 2009/10

In 2009/10 Environmental Technologies Division recovered from a weak first half with good growth in the second half of the year. ECT was significantly affected in the first half by the slowdown in demand across all areas but saw a strong recovery for autocatalysts in the second half. However, despite challenging economic conditions, Process Technologies continued to perform well supported by strong demand for its syngas products in China. For the year as a whole, Environmental Technologies Division's revenue fell by 8% to £2,056 million; sales excluding precious metals were 10% ahead at £1,247 million; however underlying operating profit fell by 3% to £120.9 million. Translated at constant exchange rates, sales excluding precious metals increased by 6% and underlying operating profit was 6% lower.

Emission Control Technologies

Emission Control Technologies' sales excluding precious metals grew by 12% to £974 million. Sales in the first half of the year were £440 million, but sales recovered strongly in the second half to £534 million. At constant exchange rates, sales excluding precious metals were up 7%.

In Johnson Matthey's financial year to 31st March 2010, global light duty vehicle sales grew by 7% to 66.7 million vehicles. Global production grew by 6% with a further small decrease in inventories. The effect of various government scrappage schemes around the world had a very positive effect on vehicle sales particularly in the second half. Johnson Matthey's light duty catalyst sales excluding precious metals grew by 17% to £754 million and

Estimated Light Vehicle Sales and Production

| | | Year to 31st March | | |
		2010 millions	2009 millions	change %
North America	Sales	**13.0**	14.4	-9.7%
	Production	**9.7**	10.8	-10.2%
Total Europe	Sales	**18.5**	19.9	-7.0%
	Production	**18.1**	18.8	-3.7%
Asia	Sales	**24.2**	17.2	+40.7%
	Production	**30.7**	25.5	+20.4%
Global	Sales	**66.7**	62.1	+7.4%
	Production	**65.2**	61.5	+6.0%

Source: IHS Global Insight

sales volumes of autocatalysts grew by more than 9% in the year, exceeding the growth in global car production as a result of increased fitment of diesel particulate filters (DPFs) in Europe and our strong performance in the growth markets of China and India.

Around 6.5 million diesel cars were sold in western Europe in the year (representing some 46% of total car sales, down from 51% last year) of which about 70% were fitted with DPFs. Over the next seven months the DPF market is set to grow further as all new diesel cars sold in the European Union will require fitment from January 2011.

In response to the fall in demand for our products in the second half of 2008/09 we took swift action to significantly reduce costs and, during this period of lower production, also took the opportunity to improve the efficiency of our manufacturing facilities and logistics. As a result, our ongoing production cost per unit reduced by approximately 7%. We, however, retained our flexibility and were able to react rapidly to increased customer orders from mid 2009/10. Since the low point in March 2009, our plant utilisation for light duty catalysts has almost doubled although we still have sufficient capacity to meet future growth in demand.

While the light duty catalyst business grew strongly in the year, sales excluding precious metals of our heavy duty diesel (HDD) catalysts fell by 5% to £173 million, a reduction of 10% on a constant currency basis. Our HDD business, which manufactures catalysts for trucks, buses and non-road vehicles, made a small loss in the year because, following our recent investment in HDD catalyst manufacturing infrastructure ahead of new legislation, we had surplus capacity given the downturn in truck production.

Sales of heavy duty trucks were depressed in the year in both Europe and the USA, falling in our financial year by 45% and 28% respectively, although in the year we enhanced our leading share of the HDD catalyst market. However our sales started to recover in the autumn and in March 2010 were nearly double those in the same month last year, albeit that the majority of our US sales were for trucks that still utilised pre-US 2010 HDD catalysts. Sales for the first quarter of 2010/11, the period for which we have greatest visibility, are expected to remain at around this level. Given current economic conditions it is difficult to predict when truck sales in Europe and the USA will recover fully. With HDD legislation now in place in South Korea, the introduction of tighter on road HDD emissions legislation in China, India and Brazil over the next few years and the phasing in of non-road legislation in the USA and European Union, the growth prospects for our HDD catalyst business remain very strong.

During the year we completed a significant, over £70 million, investment in new capacity and opened two new facilities, one in western Pennsylvania, USA with capacity to manufacture one million catalysts a year required to meet the new US 2010 HDD legislation in North America that came into effect from 1st January 2010, and the other in Macedonia with initial capacity to manufacture four million catalysts per annum for both light duty and heavy duty vehicles in Europe. Both of these facilities are now fully operational. We also completed a major expansion of our autocatalyst manufacturing capacity in Shanghai, China. This will enable us to meet the demands of the rapidly growing market in China where we continue to increase our market share, from around 17% five years ago to approximately 30% today. Construction of a new research and development facility in Shanghai is now underway and is expected to be operational in the autumn of 2010.

Our stationary emissions control (SEC) systems business for reducing emissions in a wide range of applications including power generation, industrial processes, coal fired power plants and marine applications suffered from the deferral of major energy projects due to the recession and uncertainty over carbon dioxide (CO_2) emissions standards in the USA and Europe. Despite this, sales were up by 6% to £47 million.

We have continued to build a new facility in Shanghai, China to supply plate type selective catalytic reduction (SCR) catalysts for controlling emissions of oxides of nitrogen (NOx) from coal fired power plants. This will serve a growing market in China where the State Environmental Protection Administration is expected to issue NOx control regulations that will come into effect in 2011. Our new facility is currently being commissioned and will begin supplying product during the first half of our 2010/11 financial year.

Process Technologies

Process Technologies continued to grow in 2009/10 despite the downturn in the global economy. Its sales excluding precious metals grew by 3% in the year to £268 million, an increase of 1% at constant exchange rates. The Ammonia, Methanol, Oil and Gas (AMOG) business, which represents approximately 60% of Process Technologies' sales, performed well with strong sales to both the ammonia and methanol markets, up 15% and 7% respectively. Demand for its gas purification products, used to remove contaminants such as mercury and chlorides, held up well throughout the year. However, sales of catalysts to produce hydrogen, which is used extensively in the hydrodesulphurisation process to remove sulphur from crude oil and to improve the quality of gasoline and diesel, were adversely impacted by the effect of the economic slowdown on demand for transportation fuels and by tight refinery margins and were down by more than 10%. Legislation requiring lower sulphur fuels continues to gain momentum around the world, particularly in South America, Asia and the Former Soviet Union, supporting continued demand for our hydrogen catalysts and purification products.

Process Technologies benefited from continued activity on projects to convert gas or coal into chemicals where some countries, particularly China, are seeking to enhance their energy security by utilising coal reserves to reduce their reliance on imported oil and gas. China continues to develop coal based technologies to manufacture methanol, ammonia and synthetic natural gas (SNG). Johnson Matthey has leading catalyst technology in these areas and is the number one supplier of catalysts for large scale methanol plants in China with a 40% market share.

REPORT OF THE DIRECTORS – BUSINESS REVIEW

BUSINESS REVIEW

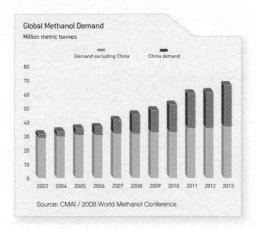

Global Methanol Demand
Million metric tonnes

Demand excluding China   China demand

Source: CMAI / 2008 World Methanol Conference

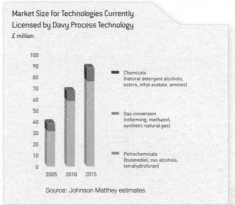

Market Size for Technologies Currently Licensed by Davy Process Technology
£ million

Chemicals (natural detergent alcohols, esters, ethyl acetate, amines)

Gas conversion (reforming, methanol, synthetic natural gas)

Petrochemicals (butanediol, oxo alcohols, tetrahydrofuran)

Source: Johnson Matthey estimates

Demand for methanol has continued to grow strongly in China, with consumption up by 35% to 17 million tonnes per annum, where it is increasingly being used as a substitute for petroleum based transportation fuels. As a result, our sales of methanol catalysts in China have increased by over 150% this year. The country is also investing in projects to manufacture SNG from coal that can be transported by existing pipelines and utilised for heating and industrial applications.

During the year Process Technologies commissioned a new state of the art methanol synthesis catalyst manufacturing facility at Clitheroe, UK. This plant produces Apico, our new patented methanol synthesis catalyst, which delivers a number of substantial performance benefits to customers, including the increase of methanol production from existing plants. Process Technologies remains a global leader in the licensing of methanol process technology and the sale of associated catalysts. The new Apico catalyst will further differentiate the business from its competitors.

Davy Process Technology (DPT) had another good year, with sales of £44 million, securing licence and engineering contracts for a further eight plants. The business was particularly successful in China, winning contracts for three methanol plants, an oxo alcohols plant and two speciality chemicals plants. In addition DPT won the contract for the first world scale SNG plant at Datang in China, including the supply of Johnson Matthey's catalysts.

DPT continues to invest in developing its technology portfolio. During the year it introduced the first world scale methylamine and dimethyl formamide process, dimethyl ether technology and a waste fat to diesel process. It is also in a position to license a gas to liquids process based on fixed bed Fischer Tropsch technology which has been jointly developed with BP.

Process Technologies continues to pursue other technology opportunities which have the potential to increase energy efficiency and reduce CO_2 emissions. Progress continues to be made in the development of technologies for high efficiency reforming, technology for the more cost effective capture of CO_2 prior to sequestration and in the area of gas to liquids technology, achieving a number of new milestones in catalyst development and increasing its sales of pilot scale catalysts this year. These are all areas that are coming into sharper focus as governments around the world strive to tackle CO_2 emissions.

Tracerco's sales were slightly up on last year with growth in its specialist measurements and taggants segments offsetting a poor year for its process diagnostics business, mainly due to reduced activity and investment by oil and gas companies. Vertec, which manufactures specialist organic titanates used in inks, paints and polymers, made an operating loss in 2009/10. The business has been facing stiff price competition from Asian manufacturers for a number of years. At the end of May 2010 we entered into consultation with its employees to look at the future options for the Vertec business.

Fuel Cells

The Fuel Cells business made further progress in 2009/10 despite the adverse economic conditions and as a result, the net expense fell by £0.3 million to £5.4 million. Several of our customers were impacted by the downturn and scaled back their growth plans but by year end they had recovered and had the confidence to start expanding again.

Direct methanol fuel cells are used in portable devices for leisure markets and sales of these were badly hit by the recession. However, our products are technically very competitive and we gained market share, mitigating the impact of a smaller market. Sales in this area have recovered, boosted by military applications starting to enter large scale trials. There also continues to be increasing interest in the use of natural gas fuelled systems to power buildings, an area where Johnson Matthey is a leading supplier of fuel cell components.

→ Chinese n-butanol plant based on DPT's chemical process technology. Reproduced with the kind permission of PetroChina Jilin Petrochemical Company.

Operations Review → Precious Metal Products Division

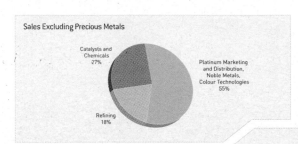

Sales Excluding Precious Metals

- Catalysts and Chemicals 27%
- Platinum Marketing and Distribution, Noble Metals, Colour Technologies 55%
- Refining 18%

Key Statistics

Return on sales excluding precious metals	27.8%
Return on invested capital (ROIC)	46.8%
Capital expenditure	£15.9m
Capex / depreciation	0.7
Average invested capital	£249m
Employees	2,594

	Year to 31st March		%	%
	2010	2009	%	at constant
	£ million	£ million	change	rates
Revenue	**5,562**	5,402	+3	–
Sales excluding precious metals	**420**	447	-6	-11
Underlying operating profit	**116.7**	143.0	-18	-22

Description of the Business

Precious Metal Products Division's activities comprise the marketing, distribution, refining and recycling of platinum group metals (pgms), fabrication of products using precious metals and related materials, pgm and base metal catalysts and pgm chemicals, and the refining of gold and silver. The division is organised into four businesses:

Platinum Marketing and Distribution

The business consists of our worldwide platinum marketing and distribution activities. Marketing is headquartered in Royston, UK with support facilities in Philadelphia, USA and Hong Kong. We are the world's leading distributor of pgms and the sole marketing agent for Anglo Platinum, the world's largest producer of platinum.

Noble Metals

Noble Metals produces a wide range of precious metal and other fabricated products for industrial and medical applications. Johnson Matthey is the market leader in pgm fabricated products for industrial applications. Manufacturing takes place in the UK and USA.

Catalysts, Chemicals and Refining

Catalysts, Chemicals and Refining manufactures precious and base metal catalysts, fine chemicals and electrochemical products. It also recovers pgms from spent catalysts and other secondary materials and refines primary pgms from global mining operations. The business also comprises our gold and silver refining and bullion manufacturing operations which serve the world's mining industries and recycle secondary scrap material.

Catalysts and chemicals manufacturing takes place in the UK, USA, Germany, India and China. Pgm refining facilities are in the UK and USA and gold and silver refining operations are located in the USA and Canada.

Colour Technologies

Headquartered in the Netherlands, our Colour Technologies business manufactures black obscuration enamels and silver conductive materials for automotive glass. It also makes colours, enamels and decorative precious metal products for other glass applications such as bottles and architectural glass as well as for tableware and other ceramic applications. Manufacturing takes place in the Netherlands, USA and South Korea.

Performance in 2009/10

Precious Metal Products Division's revenue increased by 3% to £5,562 million, boosted by higher platinum group metal prices in the second half of the year. Sales excluding the value of precious metals were 6% lower at £420 million with reductions across most of the division's businesses due to the effect of lower metal prices in the first half and the impact of the economic slowdown on its manufacturing businesses. Operating profit was also lower, down 18% at £116.7 million, following a difficult first half. Translated at constant exchange rates, sales excluding precious metals decreased by 11% and operating profit was 22% lower than last year.

BUSINESS REVIEW

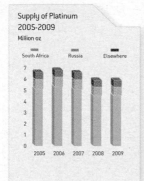

Supply of Platinum 2005-2009
Million oz

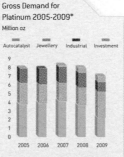

Gross Demand for Platinum 2005-2009*
Million oz

* Recycling of scrapped autocatalysts, electronics and jewellery contributed 1.83 million oz of platinum in 2008 and 1.41 million oz in 2009.

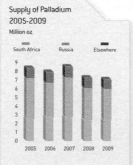

Supply of Palladium 2005-2009
Million oz

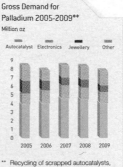

Gross Demand for Palladium 2005-2009**
Million oz

** Recycling of scrapped autocatalysts, electronics and jewellery contributed 1.62 million oz of palladium in 2008 and 1.43 million oz in 2009.

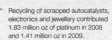

Platinum Marketing and Distribution

Profit in our Platinum Marketing and Distribution business fell in 2009/10 with performance improving in the second half of the financial year as precious metal prices increased.

Global demand for platinum fell by 11% in the calendar year 2009. Demand from the autocatalyst sector fell by 38% to a nine year low due to the global reduction in car production and a sharp decline in diesel market share in Europe. Jewellery demand increased in response to lower platinum prices, with a significant increase in stock rebuilding and retail sales in the key Chinese market. Buoyant jewellery demand was supported by an increase in physical investment through Exchange Traded Funds (ETFs). Supplies of platinum fell slightly with the output of new South African mines balanced by the closure of some existing production in the face of weaker platinum group metal prices in rand terms. The production environment in South Africa continued to be challenging with production interruptions due to safety closures and industrial action.

The substantial fall in platinum demand outweighed the more modest decline in production, moving the market into an oversupply position. The price of platinum nonetheless increased for much of the financial year with increasing investor positions having a more significant impact on the price than supply / demand fundamentals. After starting the year at $1,133/oz, platinum closed the financial year at a high point of $1,644/oz, averaging $1,343/oz for the year.

Palladium demand fell by 6% in 2009. Demand from the autocatalyst sector was 9% down, much less than for platinum, as car scrappage schemes in Europe favoured sales of small engined gasoline powered vehicles fitted with palladium catalysts. Although affected by the global fall in car production, palladium demand benefited from the rising production of cars in China which are mostly fitted with palladium catalysts. Physical investment in ETFs was also strong. Supplies of palladium declined slightly but the market remained in fundamental oversupply due to continuing sales of Russian state stocks.

Like platinum, the price of palladium increased for much of 2009/10. It also reached its high point of $479/oz at the end of the year, having averaged $325/oz which was 10% up on 2008/09.

The price of rhodium recovered slowly after a precipitous decline in 2008/09. Rhodium demand fell by around 20% in calendar year 2009 due to weak demand from the automotive sector. Although rhodium moved into a position of oversupply, the price more than doubled from $1,175/oz to $2,575/oz in thin trading. The average price of $1,936/oz was nonetheless only 40% of the level seen in 2008/09.

Noble Metals

Our Noble Metals business was affected by the general global downturn with sales excluding precious metals down by 5%. Demand for fabricated pgms was adversely impacted as the world economy slowed but we began to see recovery during the second half of the year. The year ended strongly for its European operations and whilst demand for products from its US business has been slower to pick up, industrial markets began to improve in the final quarter.

The business has established a market leading position in the supply of a nitrous oxide (N_2O) abatement catalyst to the nitric acid industry and last year saw continued good growth in demand for these products driven by incentives provided through the Kyoto agreement for plant operators to reduce their greenhouse gas emissions. N_2O is a powerful greenhouse gas with a global warming potential of 310 times that of CO_2. As western countries begin to introduce legislation to limit the emissions of greenhouse gases, we expect continued growth in demand for N_2O abatement technologies.

Whilst demand for our components for medical devices was mixed, our sophisticated machining capability in San Diego, USA has enabled us to become a leading supplier of high technology parts for several growing medical applications.

Catalysts, Chemicals and Refining

The Catalysts, Chemicals and Refining business was formed following the transfer of our Catalysts and Chemicals operations to Precious Metal Products Division on 1st April 2009. It also includes the division's Gold and Silver and Pgm Refining and Recycling activities. The business is organised into two businesses; Catalysts and Chemicals, and Refining.

Platinum and Palladium Prices
US$/oz

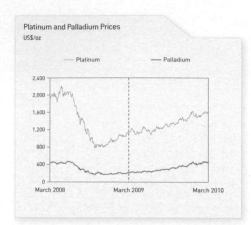

Rhodium Price
US$/oz

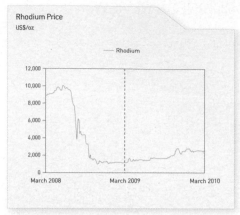

Catalysts and Chemicals

Catalysts and Chemicals had a difficult year with sales excluding precious metals falling by 14% to £114 million as a consequence of the global recession which impacted a number of end use markets, especially the automotive, construction and petrochemical sectors. The second half of the year saw some improvement, particularly in demand for precious metal salts for the automotive sector as car sales picked up driven by the government stimulus packages. Demand in China steadily improved throughout the year as a result of various government actions to stimulate the economy and in the year represented some 9% of the business' global sales. During the year we commissioned a new sponge nickel catalyst manufacturing facility in Shanghai, China to serve the local market. Further expansion is planned on the Shanghai site during 2010/11 to manufacture pgm catalysts for the growing pharmaceutical industry in China.

Refining

Our Refining business as a whole had a challenging year. Sales excluding precious metals fell by 6% to £77 million. The Pgm Refining and Recycling business was impacted, particularly in the first half, by reduced intakes as the result of lower pgm prices and a decline in the overall level of economic activity. Results improved in the second half as the effects of higher pgm prices and various automotive scrappage schemes around the world began to boost intakes of secondary material. During the year, the business continued to focus on capacity management and operational improvements at both its UK and US refineries to reduce the amount of metal in the refining circuit with improvements in the volume of residues processed through its arc furnaces.

In our Gold and Silver business, however, both our refineries had a very strong year with throughputs at record levels and improved margins. The gold price climbed steadily throughout the year, averaging over $1,000/oz, which had the effect of stimulating demand for the refining of secondary material, particularly jewellery scrap. Demand for gold investment bars was also very high. The business introduced a number of operational improvements in the year to reduce bottlenecks in the plant and improve metal throughput.

Colour Technologies

Colour Technologies performed well in difficult market conditions. Sales in our traditional businesses were flat but the acquisition of a small order book in March 2009 and good cost control resulted in profit being slightly higher than last year. Demand for our automotive glass enamel products continued to grow strongly in Asia throughout 2009/10. Sales in other parts of the world suffered in the first half in line with the downturn in vehicle production, however, we saw recovery in the second half as the European and North American automotive markets picked up. Colour Technologies increased its share of the automotive silver paste market, but demand for decorative precious metal products was impacted during the year by the high gold price.

The business opened a new technology centre in Maastricht, the Netherlands during the year to support the development of new products for its global markets.

→ Automotive glass enamel products manufactured by our Colour Technologies business.

BUSINESS REVIEW

Operations Review → Fine Chemicals Division

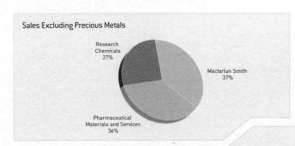

Sales Excluding Precious Metals

- Research Chemicals 27%
- Macfarlan Smith 37%
- Pharmaceutical Materials and Services 36%

Key Statistics

Return on sales excluding precious metals	25.5%
Return on invested capital (ROIC)	13.4%
Capital expenditure	£22.0m
Capex / depreciation	1.4
Average invested capital	£417m
Employees	1,026

	Year to 31st March			%
	2010	2009	%	at constant
	£ million	£ million	change	rates
Revenue	**221**	220	+1	-4
Sales excluding precious metals	**219**	215	+2	-2
Underlying operating profit	**55.8**	49.5	+13	+9

Description of the Business

Fine Chemicals Division is a global supplier of active pharmaceutical ingredients, fine chemicals and other speciality chemical products and services to a wide range of chemical and pharmaceutical industry customers and industrial and academic research organisations.

Macfarlan Smith

Macfarlan Smith manufactures active pharmaceutical ingredients (APIs) and intermediate products for the pharmaceutical and fine chemical industries. The business is the world's leading manufacturer of opiate alkaloids which are used for pain management and other pharmaceutical applications. It is headquartered in Edinburgh, UK.

Pharmaceutical Materials and Services

The Pharmaceutical Materials and Services business manufactures APIs and provides services to the pharmaceutical industry. The business specialises in the manufacture of APIs for controlled drugs and for platinum based anticancer treatments. It provides a full range of commercial scale manufacturing services for APIs to both generic and branded pharmaceutical companies. The business has operations in the USA.

Research Chemicals

The Research Chemicals business is a globally integrated catalogue based supplier of speciality inorganic and organic chemicals. It operates under the Alfa Aesar brand name and is based in the UK, USA, Germany, China and India.

Performance in 2009/10

Fine Chemicals Division achieved modest growth in the year in the face of challenging market conditions. The division's revenue increased by 1% to £221 million and sales excluding precious metals rose by 2% to £219 million. Operating profit was 13% ahead at £55.8 million. The division received a one-off benefit to sales and operating profit of US $12 million from the launch of the generic version of ADDERALL XR® in April 2009. However it also incurred £1.6 million in redundancy and other costs at its Pharmaceutical Materials and Services business in the USA. Excluding these items, the division's operating profit was 1% ahead at £49.9 million. On a constant currency basis sales excluding precious metals were 2% below and operating profit, excluding these items, was also 2% down.

Macfarlan Smith

Macfarlan Smith's sales of specialist opiate products, particularly buprenorphine, naloxone and naltrexone, continued to grow in 2009/10. However, its sales of bulk opiates, such as codeine phosphate, were impacted by reduced availability of raw material, and overall, sales of opiate based APIs were down on last year. As a result, sales excluding precious metals declined by 8% to £80 million. While the business took swift action to control costs and sales of non-opiate products, such as fentanyl and methylphenidate, saw continued growth, Macfarlan Smith's profit was a little down on last year.

Pharmaceutical Materials and Services

The division's Pharmaceutical Materials and Services business had a good year overall with sales excluding precious metals 14% ahead of 2008/09 at £79 million, benefiting from the income received as the result of the launch of the first generic version of ADDERALL XR® by Teva Pharmaceutical Industries. Excluding this one-off benefit, sales excluding precious metals still grew and were up by 3% at £71 million. Pharmaceutical Materials and Services' manufacturing business performed well with sales of amphetamine salts and opiate products continuing to show good growth, more than offsetting a decline in sales of platinum based anticancer APIs.

Our contract research business, however, continued to be adversely affected by a lack of venture capital funding for new drug development which has impacted many of our smaller customers. Sales excluding precious metals were down more than 30% in 2009/10 and the business generated an operating loss. Consequently a restructuring plan was implemented at its facility in Massachusetts, USA resulting, to date, in a 31% reduction in headcount compared to last year. In addition to the £1.6 million in redundancy and other costs, this plan resulted in an £11.3 million impairment charge in respect of redundant assets at the site. It will take some time for this business to recover, but we believe that its skills are necessary to assist our customers in the development of new APIs and hence feed growth in our manufacturing business.

Research Chemicals

The Research Chemicals business was impacted by a marked contraction in R&D spending in many parts of the world due to the global economic slowdown. Despite this, sales excluding precious metals were slightly up at £60 million. However, good cost control in North America and Europe offset, in part, additional costs incurred through the geographic expansion of the business in Asia, resulting in profits from the business being only marginally down on last year. Its European and North American markets were particularly badly hit in the first half of the year but saw some recovery in the second half, especially in North America. The business' Asian operations, however, were up on last year with good growth in sales in both China and Korea.

Research Chemicals continued to focus on geographic expansion with new warehouse facilities opening in both India and Germany during the course of the year. Its new manufacturing joint venture, Alfa Aesar Synmax in Yantai, China, in which we have a 51% shareholding, became operational with the commissioning of its pilot plant facility in March 2010. As well as serving the research chemicals needs of the rapidly growing market in China, Alfa Aesar Synmax has large scale capacity which allows Research Chemicals to bring the manufacturing of bulk and custom products in house and support the manufacturing activities at its facility in Heysham, UK.

→ Research Chemicals is a catalogue based supplier of speciality inorganic and organic chemicals. It operates under the Alfa Aesar brand name.

→ Manufacturing operations at our Pharmaceutical Materials and Services business in the USA.

REPORT OF THE DIRECTORS – BUSINESS REVIEW

BUSINESS REVIEW

Financial Review

Exchange Rates

The main impact of exchange rate movements on the group's results comes from the translation of foreign subsidiaries' profits into sterling. After last year's significant devaluation of sterling against most major currencies, this year sterling was more stable but continued to weaken further.

Around a quarter of the group's profits are made in North America, mainly in the USA. The average rate for the US dollar for the year was $1.595/£ compared with $1.719/£ for 2008/09. Each one cent change in the average rate for the dollar has approximately a £0.4 million effect on underlying operating profit in a full year. The reduction in the average exchange rate for the dollar in 2009/10 increased reported group underlying operating profit for the year by £5.0 million.

Sterling also fell against the euro averaging €1.129/£ compared with €1.205/£ in 2008/09, which increased reported underlying operating profit by £2.8 million. In addition, sterling also weakened against the South African rand, from R15.0/£ to R12.5/£. However, the catalysts manufactured by our South African business are ultimately for export and the impact of a stronger rand on margins offsets the translational effect.

Robert MacLeod
Group Finance Director

Overall, excluding the rand, exchange translation increased the group's underlying operating profit by £12.2 million compared with 2008/09.

Return on Sales

We measure return on sales as underlying operating profit divided by sales excluding precious metals. Return on sales for the group fell by 2.2% to 14.4% with the ratio improving in Fine Chemicals Division but declining in the other two divisions. The rise in return on sales in Fine Chemicals Division was primarily as a result of the one-off benefit associated with the launch of the generic version of ADDERALL XR®. If that benefit is excluded, the return on sales of Fine Chemicals Division would have been broadly in line with last year.

Environmental Technologies Division's return on sales for the year fell by 1.2% to 9.7%. While Emission Control Technologies' (ECT's) overall returns fell, the returns of our light duty vehicle catalyst business were ahead of last year as the business benefited from increased activity and lower costs. However, its heavy duty diesel catalyst business made a loss which reduced the returns for ECT as a whole. Process Technologies' return on sales was slightly lower than last year.

The fall in the return for Precious Metal Products Division from 32.0% to 27.8% reflected the more challenging market conditions for its Refining business. The return on sales for the rest of the division's businesses was broadly in line with last year.

Return on Invested Capital

The group's return on invested capital (ROIC) fell by 1.3% to 15.8%. Underlying operating profit was £26.7 million lower than last year at £271.8 million and average net assets were £24 million lower at £1,717 million. The group's ROIC of 15.8% was still well ahead of our pre-tax cost of capital, which we estimate to be 10.8%.

Our long term group target for ROIC remains at 20% on a pre-tax basis. Over the previous few years we had been making good progress towards that target but the global recession significantly impacted our performance. Demand reduced in a number of our markets, particularly the automotive market, and we now have spare capacity. However, the medium term outlook for the group remains encouraging with growth in catalyst demand underpinned by new emissions legislation which is already in place. Once global activity starts to recover, the group's ROIC should improve again as capacity utilisation increases.

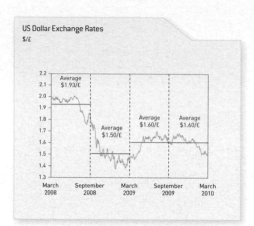

US Dollar Exchange Rates
$/£

	Sales excluding precious metals		Return on sales excluding precious metals [1]	
	2010 £ million	2009 £ million	2010 %	2009 %
Environmental Technologies	**1,247**	1,135	**9.7**	10.9
Precious Metal Products	**420**	447	**27.8**	32.0
Fine Chemicals	**219**	215	**25.5**	23.0
Total group	**1,886**	1,797	**14.4**	16.6

[1] Underlying operating profit divided by sales excluding precious metals.

Fine Chemicals Division improved its ROIC to 13.4%, up from 12.2% last year, once again due to the one-off benefit from the launch of the generic version of ADDERALL XR®. If that benefit is excluded, Fine Chemicals Division's ROIC would have been 11.6%. While Precious Metal Products Division's ROIC fell to 46.8%, its return was still well above the group's pre-tax cost of capital. Environmental Technologies Division's ROIC fell to 9.4%, 1.4% below the group's cost of capital, as a result of the impact of the global recession but it should return above the group's cost of capital as the business recovers.

Interest

The group's net finance costs decreased substantially, falling by £13.2 million to £19.4 million as a result of lower average borrowings and lower interest rates throughout the year. The group should continue to benefit from lower interest rates but around 65% of borrowings at 31st March 2010 have fixed interest rates averaging 5.1%.

The group also benefited in 2009/10 from interest receipts on tax rebates of £2.4 million.

Profit before Tax

Underlying profit before tax fell by 5% to £254.1 million. After amortisation of acquired intangibles, major impairment and restructuring charges and profit or loss on disposal of businesses, profit before tax was 8% down at £228.5 million.

Profit before tax included a £1.7 million profit from its associate, compared with a £2.0 million profit in 2008/09. This relates to AGR Matthey, the Australian gold refining business in which the group had a 20% stake and which performed well in the year with good demand for gold refining. An agreement between the partners of AGR Matthey to dissolve the partnership became effective on 29th March 2010 (see note 19 on page 90).

Taxation

The group's total tax charge for the year was £64.3 million, a tax rate of 28.1% on profit before tax (2008/09 30.8%). The effective tax rate on underlying profit before tax was 28.0% (2008/09 29.6%), reflecting the increased share of profit from lower tax jurisdictions such as China. This lower effective tax rate is likely to continue.

Earnings per Share

Underlying earnings per share decreased by 3.2 pence to 86.4 pence. Total earnings per share were 77.6 pence, 6% below last year.

This year we have taken an impairment charge in respect of redundant assets at our Pharmaceutical Materials and Services contract research business in Massachusetts, USA. This resulted in a charge of £11.3 million which has been excluded from underlying earnings per share.

Dividend

Despite the reduction in underlying earnings per share, as a demonstration of its confidence in the long term prospects of the group, the board is recommending to shareholders a final dividend of 27.9 pence, making a total dividend for the year of 39.0 pence, 5% up on last year. If approved, dividend cover for 2009/10 would be 2.2 times. Our long term policy remains to grow dividends in line with underlying earnings with dividend cover at about two and a half times.

Pensions

At 31st March 2010 the group's UK pension scheme was in deficit by £156.9 million (85% funded) on an IFRS basis compared with a deficit of £45.2 million at 31st March 2009. The £111.7 million increase in the deficit was principally due to a reduction in the discount rate used from 6.5% to 5.5%.

Worldwide, including provisions for the group's post-retirement healthcare schemes, the group had a net deficit of £245.7 million on employee benefit obligations at 31st March 2010 (2009 £151.6 million).

REPORT OF THE DIRECTORS – BUSINESS REVIEW

BUSINESS REVIEW

Return on Invested Capital

	Average invested capital [1]		Return on invested capital [2]	
	2010 £ million	2009 £ million	2010 %	2009 %
Environmental Technologies	1,281	1,179	9.4	10.5
Precious Metal Products	249	276	46.8	51.8
Fine Chemicals	417	404	13.4	12.2
Corporate / other	(230)	(118)	n/a	n/a
Total group	1,717	1,741	15.8	17.1

[1] Average of opening and closing segmental net assets as shown in note 1 on the accounts on pages 68 and 69. For the group, the average of opening and closing equity plus net debt.

[2] Underlying operating profit divided by average invested capital.

Underlying Operating Profit
(before amortisation of acquired intangibles, major impairment and restructuring charges and profit or loss on disposal of businesses)

	Year to 31st March			2009 at 2010 exchange rates	
	2010 £ million	2009 £ million	change %	£ million	change %
Environmental Technologies	120.9	124.3	-3	129.1	-6
Precious Metal Products	116.7	143.0	-18	148.9	-22
Fine Chemicals	55.8	49.5	+13	51.1	+9
Corporate	(21.6)	(18.3)		(18.4)	
Total group	271.8	298.5	-9	310.7	-13

The triennial revaluation of our UK scheme as at 1st April 2009 was completed by the scheme's actuaries during the year. They estimated that the scheme had an actuarial deficit of £173.4 million, which represented a funding level of 80%, and it is estimated to be broadly similar at 31st March 2010. This compares with an actuarial surplus of £21.0 million at 1st April 2006 and a funding level of 103%. As a result of the worsening of the scheme's funding position, the company, after a period of consultation, agreed with the Trustees that the final salary section of the UK defined benefit scheme would be closed to future accrual of benefits with effect from 1st April 2010. From that date, those employees affected accrue future benefits within the scheme's existing career average salary plan. This impacted approximately 2,000 employees.

The Trustees and the company also agreed a ten year recovery plan commencing on 1st April 2010, under which the company will make deficit funding contributions of £23.1 million per annum. In 2009/10 the group's normal ongoing contribution to the UK scheme was £23.1 million (2008/09 £22.1 million).

In December 2009 we made a one-off additional payment of US $30 million into our US schemes to reduce their deficits.

Cash Flow

During the year ended 31st March 2010 the group's cash generation was once again strong as the business generated a net cash inflow of £33.0 million.

Net cash flow from operating activities was £275.7 million (2008/09 £501.4 million). As demand for our products and precious metal prices picked up in the second half of the year, the group's working capital requirement increased, reversing the opposite effect in 2008/09. This increase is partly due to the impact of higher precious metal prices but we monitor our working capital excluding the element that relates to precious metals. On that basis, the group's working capital increased by £24.9 million, but the number of working capital days was 57 compared with 63 last year. Higher precious metal prices also increased working capital by £77.1 million however, this was lower than we had anticipated as a result of higher levels of customer funded metal within the business.

During the year our capital expenditure was £131.8 million which equated to approximately 1.2 times depreciation. In 2009/10 we completed the construction of our two new ECT facilities in Macedonia and western Pennsylvania, USA and the new production facility at Clitheroe, UK to manufacture methanol synthesis catalysts. We also commenced construction of a new plate type SCR catalyst manufacturing facility in Shanghai, China.

Having completed the majority of our recent investment programme, the group now has sufficient capacity to meet much of the growth forecast over the next few years. We therefore anticipate that capital expenditure will remain at around 1.0 to 1.2 times depreciation for the next few years. However, we retain the capacity to invest in further growth opportunities as they arise.

Capital Structure

In 2009/10 net debt fell by £61.0 million to £473.4 million and equity rose by £74.7 million to £1,250.8 million. Net debt / EBITDA for the year was 1.2 times and interest cover (underlying operating profit / net finance costs) was 14.0 times. If the post tax pension deficit of £148.2 million is included within net debt, the ratio would increase to 1.6 times. The board believes that it is important to maintain an appropriately efficient balance sheet with net debt (including the post tax pension deficit) / EBITDA between 1.5 and 2.0 times.

Gross borrowings (net of related swaps) amounted to £652.5 million offset by £179.1 million of cash and deposits. Included within gross borrowings at 31st March 2010 were drawings of £50.0 million out of total committed bank facilities, which are individually negotiated, of £280.0 million (see note 29c on page 94).

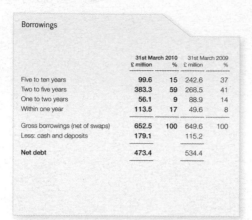

Borrowings

	31st March 2010 £ million	%	31st March 2009 £ million	%
Five to ten years	99.6	15	242.6	37
Two to five years	383.3	59	268.5	41
One to two years	56.1	9	88.9	14
Within one year	113.5	17	49.6	8
Gross borrowings (net of swaps)	652.5	100	649.6	100
Less: cash and deposits	179.1		115.2	
Net debt	473.4		534.4	

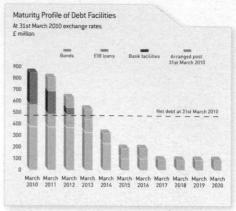

Maturity Profile of Debt Facilities
At 31st March 2010 exchange rates
£ million

Treasury Policies

Financial Risk Management and Treasury Policies

The group uses financial instruments, in particular forward currency contracts and currency swaps, to manage the financial risks associated with its underlying business activities and the financing of those activities. The group does not undertake any speculative trading activity in financial instruments. Our treasury department is run as a service centre rather than a profit centre.

Interest Rate Risk

At 31st March 2010 the group had net borrowings of £473.4 million. Some 65% of this debt was at fixed rates with an average interest rate of 5.1%. The remaining 35% of the group's net borrowings was funded on a floating rate basis. A 1% change in all interest rates would have a 0.7% impact on underlying profit before tax. This is within the range the board regards as acceptable.

Foreign Currency Risk

Johnson Matthey's operations are located in over 30 countries, providing global coverage. The majority of its profits are earned outside the UK. In order to protect the group's sterling balance sheet and reduce cash flow risk the group has financed most of its investment in the USA and Europe by borrowing US dollars and euros respectively. Although much of this funding is obtained by directly borrowing the relevant currency, a part is achieved through currency swaps which can be more efficient and reduce costs and credit exposure. To a lesser extent the group has also financed a portion of its investment in China, Japan and South Africa using currency borrowings and swaps. The group uses forward exchange contracts to hedge foreign exchange exposures arising on forecast receipts and payments in foreign currencies. Currency options are occasionally used to hedge foreign exchange exposures, usually when the forecast receipt or payment amounts are uncertain. Details of the contracts outstanding on 31st March 2010 are shown on pages 92 and 93.

Precious Metal Prices

Fluctuations in precious metal prices can have a significant impact on Johnson Matthey's financial results. Our policy for all manufacturing businesses is to limit this exposure by hedging against future price changes where such hedging can be done at acceptable cost. The group does not take material exposures on metal trading.

All the group's stocks of gold and silver are fully hedged by leasing or forward sales. Currently the majority of the group's platinum stocks are unhedged because of the lack of liquidity in the platinum market.

Liquidity and Going Concern

The group's policy on funding capacity is to ensure that we always have sufficient long term funding and committed bank facilities in place to meet foreseeable peak borrowing requirements. At 31st March 2010 the group had cash and deposits of £179.1 million and £230.0 million of undrawn committed bank facilities available to meet future funding requirements. The group also has a number of uncommitted facilities, including metal leases, and overdraft lines at its disposal.

Gross borrowings (net of related swaps) of £652.5 million at 31st March 2010 included £570.3 million of debt arranged under long term bond issues and long term funding from the European Investment Bank (EIB). Of this, £84.4 million falls due to be repaid in the 15 months to 30th June 2011 (the going concern period). This has been refinanced by a new ten year €100 million (£89.2 million) loan arranged since 31st March 2010. £200.0 million of the committed bank facilities have expiry dates after 30th June 2011. The maturity dates of the group's debt and borrowing facilities are illustrated in the table and chart above.

The directors have assessed the future funding requirements of the group and the company and compared it to the level of long term debt and committed bank facilities for the 15 months from the balance sheet date. The assessment included a sensitivity analysis on the key factors which could affect future cash flow and funding requirements. Having undertaken this work the directors are of the opinion that the group has adequate resources to fund its operations for the foreseeable future and so determine that it is appropriate to prepare the accounts on a going concern basis.

REPORT OF THE DIRECTORS – BUSINESS REVIEW

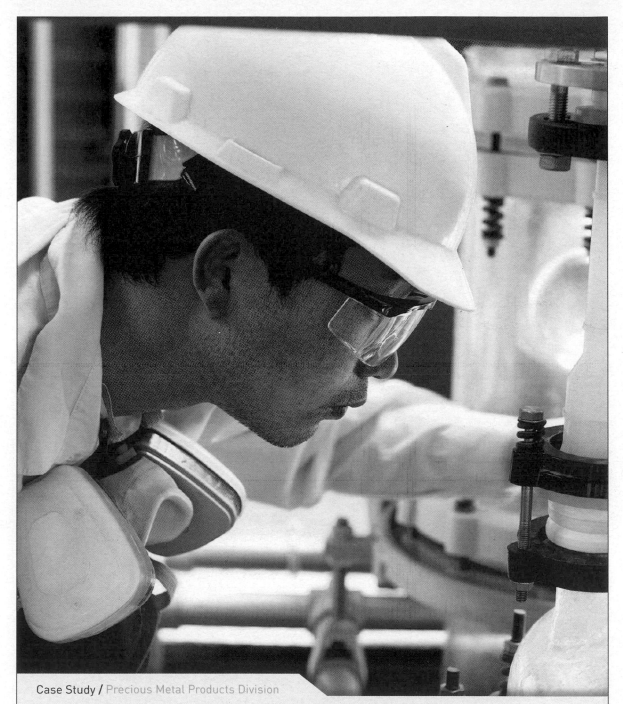

Case Study / Precious Metal Products Division

→ Catalysts and Chemicals, Shanghai, China

Sponge nickel catalysts are used as hydrogenation catalysts in a range of applications including the fine chemicals, pharmaceutical and polyols markets. With good growth expected in these markets in China over the coming years, Catalysts and Chemicals has recently completed construction of a brand new sponge nickel catalyst manufacturing facility in Shanghai. The new state of the art plant supports our existing facility in Tennessee, USA.

BUSINESS REVIEW

Research & Development

Investment in research and development (R&D) is an integral part of Johnson Matthey's growth strategy. It underpins the development of new products and manufacturing processes and enables the group to differentiate itself using its world class technology. In 2009/10 Johnson Matthey spent £91.7 million gross on R&D.

Our group technology centre is a central resource which conducts strategic R&D on behalf of all Johnson Matthey's businesses. It operates across three sites in the UK (Sonning Common, Billingham and Royston) and employs around 200 people. In addition, the group's businesses also have their own dedicated R&D and technical centres around the world which focus on the delivery of shorter term business specific projects.

In the group technology centre, R&D activities are broadly divided into four categories; core science, divisional projects, sponsored university programmes and collaborative external projects. This combination of internal research and collaboration ensures we have access to the very latest technology and develop relationships with leading scientists around the world.

Core Science

Some research skills are considered core to the company's technical expertise and are applicable across multiple businesses. In order to develop these skills the core science group develops fundamental knowledge about the science underpinning many of Johnson Matthey's technologies, transferring new products and processes to the divisions as appropriate.

Group R&D Activities

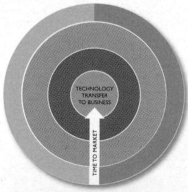

- Divisional projects – business funded R&D
- Core science
- Sponsored university programmes
- Collaborative external projects

An example of a core science technology area is advanced materials synthesis which has wide applications in our catalyst businesses. Johnson Matthey has a dedicated facility to produce a range of advanced materials using a state of the art technique called flame spray pyrolysis. This can be used to produce a wide array of materials ranging from metals, metal oxides and more complex mixed oxides or catalysts. Flame spray pyrolysis is a single step process where one or more precursor compounds are dissolved in a solvent and sprayed into a flame zone. The spray is combusted and the precursor is converted into extremely small metal or metal oxide particles. The technique is versatile and allows the use of a wide range of precursors, solvents and process conditions, thus providing control over particle size and composition.

Divisional Projects

The group technology centre undertakes a wide range of work for and directly funded by Johnson Matthey's divisions. One example is in the area of refining research where we are working to improve our platinum group metal (pgm) refining operations and services. By combining creative synthetic chemistry with cutting edge characterisation technology, we are developing faster and more efficient processes that separate pgms in very high yields. We are also able to draw on our international links with academia to build on our understanding of chemical transformations and to control more precisely the chemical behaviour of the precious metals. As with all divisional projects, we are working closely with development teams in Johnson Matthey's Refining business. Together we are delivering advances in process technology which will lower raw material consumption, minimise energy use and eliminate waste. We are also launching a modelling programme in which powerful simulations track and ultimately predict the behaviour of metals throughout the numerous complex processes within the refinery. Our range of R&D projects in this area all focus on delivering a streamlined and more sustainable refinery design.

Sponsored University Programmes

Developing our knowledge and expertise in advanced analytical and characterisation methods are a key component of our R&D programme. For a number of years we have worked closely with the University of Warwick in the UK to apply solid state nuclear magnetic resonance (NMR) spectroscopy to industrial R&D issues. The successful application of this method has led to major improvements in our understanding of the fundamental science of catalyst, glass and ceramic materials. We are now working to automate the technique which will allow for rapid screening and early identification of novel, highly tailored catalysts.

Collaborative External Projects

The continued development of new products or access to new markets requires the company to collaborate with both leading participants in these markets and with academic researchers who have an understanding of the latest developments. To support this, Johnson Matthey participates in a diverse range of UK and US government and European Union (EU) funded R&D programmes.

BUSINESS REVIEW

In one example, Johnson Matthey's researchers are engaged in a large EU collaboration that addresses some of the specific challenges around purifying bioderived synthesis gas. There is growing interest around the world in using non-food crops, such as wood and agricultural waste, to produce sustainable biofuels via bioderived synthesis gas. A range of biochemical and thermochemical processes are emerging, all of which offer opportunities for growth in the areas of catalysts, process technology and precious metals. Biofeedstocks are inherently variable and so fuel upgrading and purification of the bioderived synthesis gas are key issues. By engaging with a range of academic groups, Johnson Matthey is working to develop the purification materials, catalysts and processes for synthesis gas cleaning in the production of biofuels.

We maintain a close link between the four categories of our R&D activities and with the development work carried out directly by Johnson Matthey's businesses. This interaction is key in ensuring the rapid transfer of technology to support the continued development of new products and services for our customers.

Risks and Uncertainties

There are a number of potential risks and uncertainties which could have a material impact on the group's long term performance.

Technological Change and Patents

Much of the group's business is focused on selling products which are technologically advanced or employ technologically advanced processes in their manufacture. In most cases these products are subject to continuous improvement as new technology is developed. The group is exposed to the risk that if it does not keep up with changes in the market place its products will no longer be competitive. This is both a threat and an opportunity since Johnson Matthey can gain business as well as lose it. The group's strategy to meet this risk is to invest significantly in research and development to maintain or achieve leadership positions in those markets which offer sufficient added value to justify the long term investment required.

The group's results are also impacted by the status of patents. These include patents which the group itself registers and maintains, as well as the risks arising from new third party patents and the benefits that arise from the expiry of third party patents. All the group's divisions have significant registered intellectual property. The Fine Chemicals Division supplies active pharmaceutical ingredients to generic manufacturers and can benefit when third party patents expire. If actual patent lives differ from the expectations of the relevant group business, such as by being extended or successfully challenged, this can affect the group's results. The group has established policies both to monitor its existing patent portfolio and those of third parties, taking appropriate action as necessary in respect of infringement.

Legislation

Much of the stimulus for the development and growth of Johnson Matthey's products arises from new legislation governing the environmental or health impact of its customers' products in different jurisdictions worldwide. This is most significant for Emission Control Technologies where historic and future growth depends on global tightening of emissions limits.

Legislation is also relevant for some of the group's other businesses. Process Technologies and Catalysts and Chemicals manufacture products to remove contaminants or to produce particularly pure chemicals. Colour Technologies is supported by legislation phasing out lead, cadmium and other heavy metals from glass and ceramic glazes. The development of the fuel cells industry is also impacted by clean air regulations and the drive towards zero emissions within both local and national legislation.

Whilst the group has benefited considerably from the development of such legislation its growth could be adversely affected if the pace of legislative change slowed significantly. Johnson Matthey monitors the development of legislation globally and coordinates its development work to ensure it can achieve greatest advantage from each new requirement. Regular reviews are undertaken at the business and group level to monitor growth and to investigate other areas of potential if legislation slows.

Global, Political and Economic Conditions

Johnson Matthey operates in over 30 countries around the world including within Africa, Asia and Latin America. While benefiting from the opportunities and growth in these regions the group is exposed to the economic, political and business risks associated with such international operations. The group encounters different legal and regulatory requirements including those for taxation, environmental, operational and competitive matters. It is exposed to the effect of political risk which can include sudden changes in regulations, expropriation of assets, imposition of trade barriers and wage controls, limits on the export of currency and volatility of prices, taxes and currencies. The group is exposed to possible natural catastrophe risk, for example through major earthquake or flood, and possible terrorist action. Management monitors such risks, maintaining adequate insurance cover and amending business procedures as appropriate to mitigate any exposure while remaining in compliance with local and group requirements.

Environment, Health and Safety (EHS)

Johnson Matthey is committed to providing the highest level of protection to the environment and to safeguarding the health and safety of its employees, customers and communities. Shortcomings in any area of EHS can have devastating effects on people's lives and on the planet. In addition, the failure to maintain the required high standards in EHS could damage the group's reputation, result in financial penalties, cause disruption to the business and potentially result in temporary or permanent closure of sites.

The environmental laws of various jurisdictions impose actual and potential obligations on the group to remediate contaminated sites, both those currently owned and, also in some cases, those which have been sold. The group incurs costs annually in meeting these obligations and also maintains provisions for potential liabilities. If existing provisions are inadequate to cover any liabilities or the associated costs arising from environmental obligations this could materially impact the group's results.

All the group's manufacturing facilities are required to operate in accordance with the group's EHS policies which include comprehensive guidance on, inter alia, occupational safety, environmental protection and health management and are set out on the company's website at www.matthey.com. The group EHS management system supplements these policies and details additional guidance and requirements on matters including community relations, process risk management and product stewardship.

Commercial Relationships

Johnson Matthey benefits from close commercial relationships with a number of key customers and suppliers. The loss of any of these key customers or suppliers, or a significant worsening in commercial terms could have a material impact on the group's results.

Johnson Matthey devotes significant resources to supporting these relationships to ensure they continue to operate satisfactorily. From time to time the group undertakes customer satisfaction surveys which are reviewed by the board. Some of the relationships are supported by long term contracts, notably the group's relationship with Anglo Platinum.

While the group could be vulnerable to a global disruption in the supply of platinum group metals, it has access to world markets for these metals and is not dependent on any one source for obtaining supplies for operations. Appropriate sourcing arrangements are applied for other key raw materials to ensure that the group is not dependent on any one supplier.

Foreign Exchange

Johnson Matthey operates globally with the majority of the group's operating profit earned outside the UK. It has significant investments outside the UK with the single largest investment being in the USA. As such the group is exposed to movements in exchange rates between sterling and other world currencies, particularly the US dollar, which could adversely or positively impact results. The group's policies for managing its foreign currency exposures are set out in more detail on pages 23, 93 and 94.

Precious Metal Prices and Controls

A large proportion of the group's activities involve managing precious metals which has inherent risks associated with it in addition to bringing valuable business opportunities.

Precious metals have high prices which can fluctuate significantly and this can have an impact on Johnson Matthey's results. The group's policies for managing this risk are set out in more detail on page 23. The high value of precious metals means that any process losses could be material and there remains the possibility of theft or fraud. Johnson Matthey has extensive experience in operating with precious metals and employs strict security, assay and other process controls and reviews to minimise any exposure. Policies are reviewed regularly by the Chief Executive's Committee and reported to the Audit Committee.

Pensions

The group's defined benefit pension funds had a net deficit at 31st March 2010 of £201.0 million. This position is exposed to the risk of changes in interest rates and the market values of investments as well as inflation and increasing longevity of the members. The assumptions used in calculating the funding position of the pension funds are shown in detail on page 77. These risks are mitigated by paying appropriate contributions into the funds and through an investment asset allocation policy which has a high level of probability of avoiding a material deficit based on the results of an asset / liability matching study. From 1st April 2010 current employees in the group's UK pension scheme no longer accrue additional years' service based upon their final salary. From 1st April 2010 all UK employees who are members of the defined benefit pension scheme will accrue defined benefits based on their career average salary.

Customer Market Dynamics

The group sells products to manufacturers who in turn use these products to serve a diverse range of end markets. The group's performance is therefore impacted by the dynamics of its customers' end markets and their performance within these markets. A significant loss of market share at or by a major automotive customer could negatively impact the group's results. The group also has exposure to the wider automotive sector as a whole which is served by a number of the group's divisions. However, other factors such as tightening emissions legislation and the increasing technical demands from catalysts also play a significant role.

Risks are mitigated by monitoring both industry developments and market share at customers to prevent the group from becoming unduly dependent on any single customer.

Competitor Risk

The group operates in highly competitive markets. Significant product innovations, technical advances or the intensification of price competition could all adversely affect the group's results. Johnson Matthey invests significant resources in research and development in order to ensure the introduction of both new products and improved production processes to allow the group to be at the forefront of its chosen markets. The group also continually works to streamline its cost base to ensure it remains competitive.

Litigation and Investigations

The group is subject to a broad range of laws, regulations and standards in each of the jurisdictions in which it operates. Failure to comply properly with these laws, regulations and standards could significantly damage the reputation and performance of Johnson Matthey.

Regular internal reviews are undertaken to assess compliance with local and group policies, and provisions are made to rectify or compensate for any breaches. In the ordinary course of business, Johnson Matthey is subject to inspections and monitoring by certain regulatory or enforcement bodies and by the quality departments of some of its major customers. If existing provisions are inadequate to cover any liabilities arising from such investigations this could materially impact the group's results.

Credit Risk

The group derives a significant proportion of its revenue from sales to major customers, particularly in Emission Control Technologies. Sales to individual customers are frequently high if the value of precious metals is included in the price. The failure of any such company to honour its debts could materially impact the group's results.

Johnson Matthey derives significant benefit from trading with its large customers and manages the risk at many levels. Each business and division has a credit committee that regularly monitors its exposure. The Audit Committee receives a report every six months that details all significant credit limits, amounts due and amounts overdue within the group and the relevant actions being taken. As at 31st March 2010, no single outstanding balance exceeded 1% of the group's revenue. Further details of the group's credit control procedures are set out on page 96.

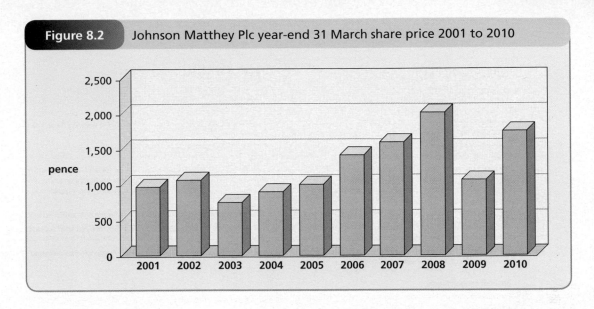

Figure 8.2   Johnson Matthey Plc year-end 31 March share price 2001 to 2010

Johnson Matthey's share price each 31 March from 2001 to 2010 is shown in the chart below and illustrated in Figure 8.2.

	Share price		Share price
2001	955.0	2006	1,396.0
2002	1,046.0	2007	1,576.0
2003	737.0	2008	2,005.0
2004	879.5	2009	1,053.0
2005	989.0	2010	1,746.0

Accounting policies

The statement of accounting policies informs readers of the policies the company has pursued in preparation of the report and accounts, and of any deviation from the generally accepted fundamental accounting concepts and conventions. Johnson Matthey devotes a large part of its statement of accounting policies to the management of risk, and its application of IFRSs and IASs (see pages 298 to 302).

Progress check 8.3

What information do the chief executive's statement and the financial review provide and how do these reports differ?

ACCOUNTING POLICIES
for the year ended 31st March 2010

The group's and parent company's significant accounting policies, together with the judgments made by management in applying those policies which have the most significant effect on the amounts recognised in the accounts, are:

Basis of accounting and preparation

The accounts are prepared in accordance with International Financial Reporting Standards (IFRS) and interpretations issued by the International Financial Reporting Interpretations Committee (IFRIC) or the Standing Interpretations Committee (SIC) as adopted by the European Union. For Johnson Matthey, there are no differences between IFRS as adopted by the European Union and full IFRS as published by the International Accounting Standards Board (IASB) and so the accounts comply with IFRS.

The accounts are prepared on the historical cost basis, except for certain assets and liabilities which are measured at fair value as explained below.

The parent company cash flow statement for the year ended 31st March 2009 has been restated to include dividends received from subsidiaries in profit before tax. This has no effect on net cash inflow from operating activities.

The parent company has not presented its own income statement, statement of total comprehensive income and related notes as permitted by section 408 of the Companies Act 2006.

Basis of consolidation

The consolidated accounts comprise the accounts of the parent company and all its subsidiaries, including the employee share ownership trust, and include the group's interest in its associate.

Entities over which the group has the ability to exercise control are accounted for as subsidiaries. Entities that are not subsidiaries or joint ventures but where the group has significant influence (i.e. the power to participate in the financial and operating policy decisions) are accounted for as associates.

The results and assets and liabilities of the associate are included in the consolidated accounts using the equity method of accounting.

The results of businesses acquired or disposed of in the year are consolidated from or up to the effective date of acquisition or disposal respectively. The net assets of businesses acquired are incorporated in the consolidated accounts at their fair values at the date of acquisition.

Transactions and balances between group companies are eliminated. No profit is taken on transactions between group companies and the group's share of profits on transactions with its associate is also eliminated.

In the parent company balance sheet, businesses acquired by the parent company from other group companies are incorporated at book value at the date of acquisition. Where the consideration given exceeds the book value of the net assets acquired this difference is accounted for as goodwill.

Revenue

Revenue comprises all sales of goods and rendering of services at the fair value of consideration received or receivable after the deduction of any trade discounts and excluding sales taxes. Revenue is recognised when it can be measured reliably and the significant risks and rewards of ownership are transferred to the customer. With the sale of goods, this occurs when the goods are despatched or made available to the customer, except for the sale of consignment products located at customers' premises where revenue is recognised on notification that the product has been used. With the rendering of services, revenue is recognised by reference to the stage of completion as measured by the proportion that costs incurred to date bear to the estimated total costs. With royalties and licence income, revenue is recognised in accordance with the substance of the relevant agreement.

Construction contracts

Where the outcome of a construction contract can be estimated reliably, revenue and costs are recognised by reference to the stage of completion. This is measured by the proportion that contract costs incurred to date bear to the estimated total contract costs.

Where the outcome of a construction contract cannot be estimated reliably, contract revenue is recognised to the extent of contract costs incurred that it is probable will be recoverable. Contract costs are recognised as expenses in the period in which they are incurred.

When it is probable that the total contract costs will exceed total contract revenue, the expected loss is recognised as an expense immediately.

Finance costs and finance income

Finance costs that are directly attributable to the construction of an asset that necessarily takes a substantial period of time to get ready for its intended use and for which construction was commenced after 1st April 2007 are capitalised as part of the cost of that asset. Other finance costs and finance income are recognised in the income statement in the year incurred.

Research and development

Research expenditure is charged to the income statement in the year incurred.

Development expenditure is charged to the income statement in the year incurred unless it meets the IFRS recognition criteria for capitalisation. When the recognition criteria have been met any further development expenditure is capitalised as an intangible asset.

ACCOUNTS

ACCOUNTING POLICIES

for the year ended 31st March 2010

Foreign currencies

Foreign currency transactions are recorded in the functional currency of the relevant subsidiary, associate or branch at the exchange rate at the date of transaction. Foreign currency monetary assets and liabilities are retranslated into the relevant functional currency at the exchange rate at the balance sheet date.

Income statements and cash flows of overseas subsidiaries, associates and branches are translated into sterling at the average rates for the year. Balance sheets of overseas subsidiaries, associates and branches, including any fair value adjustments and including related goodwill, are translated into sterling at the exchange rates at the balance sheet date.

Exchange differences arising on the translation of the net investment in overseas subsidiaries, associates and branches, less exchange differences arising on related foreign currency financial instruments which hedge the group's net investment in these operations, are taken to a separate component of equity. The group has taken advantage of the exemption allowed in IFRS 1 – 'First-time Adoption of International Reporting Standards' to deem the cumulative translation difference for all overseas subsidiaries, associates and branches to be zero at 1st April 2004.

Other exchange differences are taken to operating profit.

Property, plant and equipment

Property, plant and equipment are stated at cost less accumulated depreciation and any provisions for impairment. Finance costs that relate to an asset that takes a substantial period of time to construct and for which construction was started after 1st April 2007 are capitalised as part of the cost of that asset. Other finance costs are not capitalised.

Depreciation is provided at rates calculated to write off the cost less estimated residual value of each asset over its useful life. Certain freehold buildings and plant and equipment are depreciated using the units of production method, as this more closely reflects their expected consumption. All other assets are depreciated using the straight line method. The useful lives vary according to the class of the asset, but are typically: leasehold property 30 years (or the life of the lease if shorter); freehold buildings 30 years; and plant and equipment 4 to 10 years. Freehold land is not depreciated.

Goodwill

Goodwill arises on the acquisition of a business when the fair value of the consideration given exceeds the fair value attributed to the net assets acquired (including contingent liabilities). It is subject to annual impairment reviews.

The group and parent company have taken advantage of the exemption allowed under IFRS 1 and so goodwill arising on acquisitions made before 1st April 2004 is included at the carrying amount at that date less any subsequent impairments. Up to 31st March 1998 goodwill was eliminated against equity.

Intangible assets

Intangible assets are stated at cost less accumulated amortisation and any provisions for impairment. They are amortised in accordance with the relevant income stream or by using the straight line method over their useful lives from the time they are first available for use. The estimated useful lives vary according to the specific asset but are typically: 1 to 12 years for customer contracts and relationships; 3 to 8 years for capitalised software; 3 to 10 years for patents, trademarks and licences; and 3 to 8 years for capitalised development currently being amortised.

Intangible assets which are not yet being amortised are subject to annual impairment reviews.

Investments in subsidiaries

Investments in subsidiaries are stated in the parent company's balance sheet at cost less any provisions for impairment. If a distribution is received from a subsidiary then the investment in that subsidiary is assessed for an indication of impairment.

Leases

Leases are classified as finance leases whenever they transfer substantially all the risks and rewards of ownership to the group. The assets are included in property, plant and equipment and the capital elements of the leasing commitments are shown as obligations under finance leases. The assets are depreciated on a basis consistent with similar owned assets or the lease term if shorter. The interest element of the lease rental is included in the income statement.

All other leases are classified as operating leases and the lease costs are expensed on a straight line basis over the lease term.

Grants

Grants related to assets are included in deferred income and released to the income statement in equal instalments over the expected useful lives of the related assets.

Grants related to income are deducted in reporting the related expense.

Precious metal inventories

Inventories of gold, silver and platinum group metals are valued according to the source from which the metal is obtained. Metal which has been purchased and committed to future sales to customers or hedged in metal markets is valued at the price at which it is contractually committed or hedged, adjusted for unexpired contango and backwardation. Other precious metal inventories owned by the group, which are unhedged, are valued at the lower of cost and net realisable value using the weighted average cost formula.

ACCOUNTING POLICIES

for the year ended 31st March 2010

Other inventories

Non-precious metal inventories are valued at the lower of cost, including attributable overheads, and net realisable value. Except where costs are specifically identified, the first-in, first-out or weighted average cost formulae are used to value inventories.

Cash and cash equivalents

Cash and deposits comprise cash at bank and in hand, including short term deposits with a maturity date of three months or less from the date of acquisition. The group and parent company routinely use short term bank overdraft facilities, which are repayable on demand, as an integral part of their cash management policy. Therefore cash and cash equivalents in the cash flow statements are cash and deposits less bank overdrafts. Offset arrangements across group businesses have been applied to arrive at the net cash and overdraft figures.

Derivative financial instruments

The group and parent company use derivative financial instruments, in particular forward currency contracts and currency swaps, to manage the financial risks associated with their underlying business activities and the financing of those activities. The group and parent company do not undertake any trading activity in derivative financial instruments.

Derivative financial instruments are measured at their fair value. Derivative financial instruments may be designated at inception as fair value hedges, cash flow hedges or net investment hedges if appropriate. Derivative financial instruments which are not designated as hedging instruments are classified under IFRS as held for trading, but are used to manage financial risk.

Changes in the fair value of any derivative financial instruments that are not designated as or are not determined to be effective hedges are recognised immediately in the income statement.

Changes in the fair value of derivative financial instruments designated as fair value hedges are recognised in the income statement, together with the related changes in the fair value of the hedged asset or liability. Fair value hedge accounting is discontinued if the hedging instrument expires or is sold, terminated or exercised, the hedge no longer meets the criteria for hedge accounting or the designation is revoked.

Changes in the fair value of derivative financial instruments designated as cash flow hedges are recognised in equity, to the extent that the hedges are effective. Ineffective portions are recognised in the income statement immediately. If the hedged item results in the recognition of a non-financial asset or liability, the amount recognised in equity is transferred out of equity and included in the initial carrying amount of the asset or liability. Otherwise, the amount recognised in equity is transferred to the income statement in the same period that the hedged item is recognised in the income statement. If the hedging instrument expires or is sold, terminated or exercised, the hedge no longer meets the criteria for hedge accounting or the designation is revoked, amounts previously recognised in equity remain in equity until the forecast transaction occurs. If a forecast transaction is no longer expected to occur, the amounts previously recognised in equity are transferred to the income statement.

For hedges of net investments in foreign operations, the effective portion of the gain or loss on the hedging instrument is recognised in equity, while the ineffective portion is recognised in the income statement. Amounts taken to equity are transferred to the income statement when the foreign operations are sold.

Other financial instruments

All other financial instruments are initially recognised at fair value plus transaction costs. Subsequent measurement is as follows:

- Unhedged borrowings are measured at amortised cost.

- Available-for-sale investments are investments in equity instruments that do not have a quoted market price in an active market and whose fair value cannot be measured reliably and so are measured at cost.

- All other financial assets and liabilities, including short term receivables and payables, are measured at amortised cost less any impairment provision.

Taxation

Current and deferred tax are recognised in the income statement, except when they relate to items recognised directly in equity when the related tax is also recognised in equity.

Current tax is the amount of income tax expected to be paid in respect of taxable profits using the tax rates that have been enacted or substantively enacted at the balance sheet date.

Deferred tax is provided in full, using the liability method, on temporary differences arising between the tax bases of assets and liabilities and their carrying amount in the balance sheet. It is provided using the tax rates that are expected to apply in the period when the asset or liability is settled, based on tax rates that have been enacted or substantively enacted at the balance sheet date.

Deferred tax assets are recognised to the extent that it is probable that future taxable profits will be available against which the temporary differences can be utilised. No deferred tax asset or liability is recognised in respect of temporary differences associated with investments in subsidiaries, branches and associates where the group is able to control the timing of the reversal of the temporary difference and it is probable that the temporary difference will not reverse in the foreseeable future.

ACCOUNTS

ACCOUNTING POLICIES

for the year ended 31st March 2010

Provisions and contingencies

Provisions are recognised when the group has a present obligation as a result of a past event and a reliable estimate can be made of a probable adverse outcome, for example warranties, environmental claims and restructurings. Otherwise, material contingent liabilities are disclosed unless the transfer of economic benefits is remote. Contingent assets are only disclosed if an inflow of economic benefits is probable.

The group considers financial guarantees of its share of the borrowings and precious metal leases of its associate to be insurance contracts. The parent company considers financial guarantees of its subsidiaries' borrowings and precious metal leases to be insurance contracts. These are treated as contingent liabilities unless it becomes probable that it will be required to make a payment under the guarantee.

Share-based payments and employee share ownership trust (ESOT)

The fair value of outstanding share options granted to employees after 7th November 2002 was calculated using an adjusted Black-Scholes options valuation model and the fair value of outstanding shares allocated to employees under the long term incentive plans after 7th November 2002 is calculated by adjusting the share price on the date of allocation for the present value of the expected dividends that will not be received. The resulting cost is charged to the income statement over the relevant vesting periods, adjusted to reflect actual and expected levels of vesting where appropriate.

The group and parent company provide finance to the ESOT to purchase company shares in the open market. Costs of running the ESOT are charged to the income statement. The cost of shares held by the ESOT are deducted in arriving at equity until they vest unconditionally in employees.

Pensions and other post-employment benefits

The group operates a number of contributory and non-contributory plans, mainly of the defined benefit type, which require contributions to be made to separately administered funds.

The costs of the defined contribution plans are charged to the income statement as they fall due.

For defined benefit plans, the group and parent company recognise the net assets or liabilities of the schemes in their balance sheets. Obligations are measured at present value using the projected unit credit method and a discount rate reflecting yields on high quality corporate bonds. Assets are measured at their fair value at the balance sheet date. The changes in scheme assets and liabilities, based on actuarial advice, are recognised as follows:

- The current service cost is spread over the period during which benefit is expected to be derived from the employees' services based on the most recent actuarial valuation and is deducted in arriving at operating profit.

- The interest cost, based on the discount rate at the beginning of the year and the present value of the defined benefit obligation during the year, is included in operating profit.

- The expected return on plan assets, based on market expectations at the beginning of the year for returns over the entire life of the related obligation and amended for changes in the fair value of plan assets as a result of contributions paid in and benefits paid out, is included in operating profit.

- Actuarial gains and losses, representing differences between the expected return and actual return on plan assets and reimbursement rights, differences between actuarial assumptions underlying the plan liabilities and actual experience during the year, and changes in actuarial assumptions, are recognised in the statement of total comprehensive income in the year they occur.

- Past service costs are spread evenly over the period in which the increases in benefit vest and are deducted in arriving at operating profit. If an increase in benefits vests immediately, the cost is recognised immediately.

- Gains or losses arising from settlements or curtailments are included in operating profit.

Standards and interpretations adopted in the year

During the year, the following new and amendments to accounting standards and interpretations were adopted:

IFRS 8 – 'Operating Segments' has replaced International Accounting Standard (IAS) 14 – 'Segmental Reporting' and requires the identification of operating segments based on internal reporting to the chief operating decision maker and changes a number of disclosures. The business segments previously reported by the group have not changed as a result of adopting this standard and as such the adoption has not affected the reported results or financial position of the group and parent company.

The September 2007 revision to IAS 1 – 'Presentation of Financial Statements' resulted in a number of presentational changes to the primary statements of the group and parent company. The statements of changes in equity are now presented as primary statements rather than as notes on the accounts. The group has opted to continue presenting a separate income statement and statement of total comprehensive income (previously called statement of recognised income and expense). The revised standard has no impact on the reported results or financial position of the group and parent company.

Amendments to IFRS 7 – 'Improving Disclosures about Financial Instruments' has resulted in a number of changes to disclosures for the group and parent company about fair value measurement and liquidity risk but has no impact on the reported results or financial position of the group and parent company.

IFRIC 13 – 'Customer Loyalty Programmes', Amendment to IFRS 2 – 'Vesting Conditions and Cancellations', Amendments to IAS 32 and IAS 1 – 'Puttable Financial Instruments and Obligations Arising on Liquidation', Amendments to IFRS 1 and IAS 27 – 'Cost of an Investment in a Subsidiary, Jointly Controlled Entity or Associate', 'Improvements to IFRSs' issued May 2008, IFRIC 15 – 'Agreements for the Construction of Real Estate', IFRIC 16 – 'Hedges of a Net Investment in a Foreign Operation', IFRIC 18 – 'Transfers of Assets from Customers', IFRS 1 – 'First-time Adoption of International Financial Reporting Standards', Amendments to IFRIC 9 and IAS 39 – 'Embedded Derivatives' and the parts of 'Improvements to IFRSs' issued in April 2009 which were to be applied to annual periods beginning on or after 1st January 2009 or before have all been adopted during the year. There was no material impact on the reported results or financial position of the group and parent company.

ACCOUNTING POLICIES

for the year ended 31st March 2010

Standards and interpretations issued but not yet applied

IFRS 3 – 'Business Combinations' was revised and IAS 27 – 'Consolidated and Separate Financial Statements' was amended in January 2008 and are required to be applied for annual periods beginning on or after 1st July 2009. They require changes to the accounting for future business combinations and the accounting in the event of the loss of control over a subsidiary and so will not result in any restatement of reported results or net assets of the group and parent company.

Amendment to IAS 39 – 'Eligible Hedged Items' was issued in July 2008 and is required to be applied for annual periods beginning on or after 1st July 2009. This will not affect the reported results or net assets of the group and parent company.

IFRIC 17 – 'Distributions of Non-cash Assets to Owners' was issued in November 2008 and is required to be applied for annual periods beginning on or after 1st July 2009. This will not affect the reported results or net assets of the group and parent company.

'Improvements to IFRSs' was issued in April 2009 making minor amendments to a number of standards and is required to be applied mainly for annual periods beginning on or after 1st January 2010, with some amendments for annual periods beginning on or after 1st July 2009. The effect on the group and parent company is still being evaluated.

Amendment to IFRS 2 – 'Group Cash-settled Share-based Payment Transactions' was issued in June 2009 and is required to be applied for annual periods beginning on or after 1st January 2010. The amendment clarifies the scope of IFRS 2 and the accounting for group cash-settled share-based payments in the accounts of individual entities. The effect on the group and parent company is still being evaluated.

Amendments to IFRS 1 – 'Additional Exemptions for First-time Adopters' was issued in July 2009 and is applicable for annual periods beginning on or after 1st January 2010. This will not affect the reported results or net assets of the group and parent company.

Amendment to IAS 32 – 'Classification of Rights Issues' was issued in October 2009 and is applicable for annual periods beginning on or after 1st February 2010. This will not affect the reported results or net assets of the group and parent company.

IFRS 9 – 'Financial Instruments' was issued in November 2009 as the first stage of the IASB's project to review and replace IAS 39 – 'Financial Instruments: Recognition and Measurement', focusing on the classification and measurement of financial assets. The standard will be applicable for annual periods beginning on or after 1st January 2013. The effect on the group and parent company is still being evaluated.

IAS 24 – 'Related Party Disclosures' was issued in November 2009 and is applicable for annual periods beginning on or after 1st January 2011. The revision clarifies the definition of a related party for disclosure purposes and so will not result in any impact on the reported results or net assets of the group and parent company.

Amendments to IFRIC 14 – 'Prepayments of a Minimum Funding Requirement' was issued in November 2009 and is required to be applied for annual periods beginning on or after 1st January 2011. This will not affect the reported results or net assets of the group and parent company.

IFRIC 19 – 'Extinguishing Financial Liabilities with Equity Instruments' was issued in November 2009 and is applicable for annual periods beginning on or after 1st July 2010. This will not affect the reported results or net assets of the group and parent company.

Amendments to IFRS 1 – 'Limited Exemption from Comparative IFRS 7 Disclosures for First-time Adopters' was issued in January 2010 and is required to be applied for annual periods beginning on or after 1st January 2010. They will not affect the reported results or net assets of the group and parent company.

'Improvements to IFRSs' was issued in May 2010 making minor amendments to a number of standards and is required to be applied mainly for annual periods beginning on or after 1st January 2011, with some amendments for annual periods beginning on or after 1st July 2010. The effect on the group and parent company is still being evaluated.

ACCOUNTS

Worked example 8.1

We can use the Johnson Matthey Plc five-year record, which you will find on page 339 in the Exercises section at the end of this chapter, and the company's past years annual reports and accounts to present earnings per share and dividends per share for 2006 to 2010 in:

tabular form
   and
bar chart for comparison.

	Earnings per share (pence)	Dividend per share (pence)		Earnings per share (pence)	Dividend per share (pence)
2001	57.3	23.3	2006	70.8	30.1
2002	49.0	24.6	2007	96.9	33.6
2003	55.4	25.5	2008	88.5	36.6
2004	56.0	26.4	2009	82.6	37.1
2005	53.2	27.7	2010	77.6	39.0

Figure 8.3 Johnson Matthey Plc eps and dividend per share at each 31 March 2001 to 2010

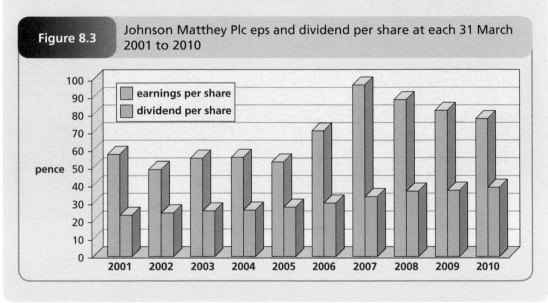

Income statement, balance sheet and statement of cash flows

The three financial statements that are shown on pages 304 to 308 illustrate Johnson Matthey Plc's consolidated income statement, statement of cash flows, and statement of changes in equity for the year to 31 March 2010, and its consolidated balance sheet as at 31 March 2010.

The income statement is consolidated to include the results of all the companies within the group, together with the parent company, Johnson Matthey Plc. The consolidated income statement also shows previous year comparative numbers.

The balance sheet is presented in consolidated form, also showing previous year comparative numbers.

CONSOLIDATED INCOME STATEMENT

for the year ended 31st March 2010

	Notes	2010 £ million	2009 £ million
Revenue	1,2	**7,839.4**	7,847.8
Cost of sales		**(7,325.4)**	(7,324.3)
Gross profit		**514.0**	523.5
Distribution costs		**(103.6)**	(101.2)
Administrative expenses		**(138.6)**	(123.8)
Major impairment and restructuring charges	3	**(11.3)**	(9.4)
Amortisation of acquired intangibles	4	**(9.9)**	(9.1)
Operating profit	1,6	**250.6**	280.0
Finance costs	7	**(30.5)**	(43.3)
Finance income	8	**11.1**	10.7
Share of profit of associate	19	**1.7**	2.0
Dissolution of associate	19	**(4.4)**	–
Profit before tax		**228.5**	249.4
Income tax expense	9	**(64.3)**	(76.7)
Profit for the year from continuing operations		**164.2**	172.7
Profit for the year from discontinued operations	41	**–**	1.2
Profit for the year		**164.2**	173.9
Attributable to:			
Equity holders of the parent company		**164.2**	174.1
Minority interests		**–**	(0.2)
		164.2	173.9

		pence	pence
Earnings per ordinary share attributable to the equity holders of the parent company			
Continuing operations			
Basic	11	**77.6**	82.0
Diluted	11	**77.3**	81.5
Total			
Basic	11	**77.6**	82.6
Diluted	11	**77.3**	82.1

CONSOLIDATED STATEMENT OF TOTAL COMPREHENSIVE INCOME

for the year ended 31st March 2010

	Notes	2010 £ million	2009 £ million
Profit for the year		**164.2**	173.9
Other comprehensive income:			
Currency translation differences	33	**(5.7)**	190.0
Cash flow hedges	33	**27.0**	(19.9)
Fair value gains / (losses) on net investment hedges		**32.8**	(146.9)
Actuarial loss on post-employment benefits assets and liabilities	14	**(124.6)**	(156.7)
Share of other comprehensive income of associate		**0.2**	(0.2)
Tax on above items taken directly to or transferred from equity	34	**34.1**	64.3
Other comprehensive expense for the year		**(36.2)**	(69.4)
Total comprehensive income for the year		**128.0**	104.5
Attributable to:			
Equity holders of the parent company		**127.9**	104.1
Minority interests		**0.1**	0.4
		128.0	104.5

The notes on pages 68 to 107 form an integral part of the accounts.

CONSOLIDATED AND PARENT COMPANY BALANCE SHEETS

as at 31st March 2010

	Notes	Group 2010 £ million	Group 2009 £ million	Parent company 2010 £ million	Parent company 2009 £ million
Assets					
Non-current assets					
Property, plant and equipment	15	921.6	924.7	245.3	258.0
Goodwill	16	513.8	516.0	110.5	132.4
Other intangible assets	17	131.6	135.8	6.3	6.3
Investments in subsidiaries	18	–	–	1,518.7	1,303.8
Investment in associate	19	3.4	5.8	–	–
Deferred income tax assets	31	57.1	27.5	49.1	18.2
Available-for-sale investments	20	7.5	6.3	–	–
Swaps related to borrowings	26	19.3	28.8	19.3	28.8
Other receivables	23	3.1	5.0	466.4	315.4
Post-employment benefits net assets	14	4.6	2.2	–	–
Total non-current assets		1,662.0	1,652.1	2,415.6	2,062.9
Current assets					
Inventories	21	390.1	371.7	101.2	114.0
Current income tax assets		12.9	41.5	–	27.5
Trade and other receivables	23	639.3	500.2	637.5	767.1
Cash and cash equivalents – cash and deposits	26	179.1	115.2	88.4	33.6
Swaps related to borrowings	26	–	1.9	–	1.9
Other financial assets	28	6.5	5.7	9.0	8.2
Assets classified as held for sale	25	–	6.0	–	6.0
Total current assets		1,227.9	1,042.2	836.1	958.3
Total assets		2,889.9	2,694.3	3,251.7	3,021.2
Liabilities					
Current liabilities					
Trade and other payables	24	(527.2)	(508.1)	(1,372.0)	(1,291.8)
Current income tax liabilities		(91.0)	(47.4)	(17.9)	–
Cash and cash equivalents – bank overdrafts	26	(14.7)	(15.4)	(10.3)	(38.6)
Other borrowings and finance leases	26	(98.8)	(36.1)	(84.7)	(21.2)
Other financial liabilities	27	(8.0)	(32.9)	(9.2)	(33.7)
Provisions	30	(8.7)	(8.8)	(0.4)	(2.2)
Total current liabilities		(748.4)	(648.7)	(1,494.5)	(1,387.5)
Non-current liabilities					
Borrowings and finance leases	26	(558.3)	(628.8)	(551.7)	(621.4)
Deferred income tax liabilities	31	(56.5)	(70.3)	–	–
Employee benefits obligations	14	(250.3)	(153.8)	(171.5)	(57.4)
Provisions	30	(19.6)	(14.3)	(9.5)	(6.6)
Other payables	24	(6.0)	(2.3)	–	(175.5)
Total non-current liabilities		(890.7)	(869.5)	(732.7)	(860.9)
Total liabilities		(1,639.1)	(1,518.2)	(2,227.2)	(2,248.4)
Net assets		1,250.8	1,176.1	1,024.5	772.8
Equity					
Share capital	32	220.7	220.7	220.7	220.7
Share premium account		148.3	148.3	148.3	148.3
Shares held in employee share ownership trust (ESOT)		(30.7)	(61.8)	(30.7)	(61.8)
Other reserves	35	73.4	18.5	0.2	(19.5)
Retained earnings		837.7	849.6	686.0	485.1
Total equity attributable to equity holders of the parent company		1,249.4	1,175.3	1,024.5	772.8
Minority interests		1.4	0.8	–	–
Total equity		1,250.8	1,176.1	1,024.5	772.8

The accounts were approved by the Board of Directors on 2nd June 2010 and signed on its behalf by:

N A P Carson
R J MacLeod   Directors

The notes on pages 68 to 107 form an integral part of the accounts.

ACCOUNTS

CONSOLIDATED AND PARENT COMPANY CASH FLOW STATEMENTS

for the year ended 31st March 2010

| | | Group | | Parent company | |
	Notes	2010 £ million	2009 £ million	2010 £ million	2009 restated £ million
Cash flows from operating activities					
Profit before tax		**228.5**	249.4	**376.9**	49.0
Adjustments for:					
Share of profit in associate	19	**(1.7)**	(2.0)	**–**	–
Dissolution of associate	19	**4.4**	–	**–**	–
Discontinued operations	41	**–**	0.9	**–**	–
Depreciation, amortisation, impairment losses and profit on sale of non-current assets and investments		**140.3**	110.3	**41.2**	69.1
Share-based payments		**4.7**	–	**4.2**	–
(Increase) / decrease in inventories		**(22.1)**	80.1	**12.0**	(54.2)
(Increase) / decrease in receivables		**(123.1)**	215.9	**(53.9)**	685.0
Increase / (decrease) in payables		**47.1**	(91.8)	**(90.7)**	198.1
Increase / (decrease) in provisions		**2.5**	6.3	**1.1**	(13.9)
Employee benefit obligations charge less contributions		**(24.9)**	(9.0)	**(7.9)**	(10.1)
Changes in fair value of financial instruments		**1.3**	(6.0)	**1.6**	(5.1)
Dividends received from subsidiaries		**–**	–	**(276.8)**	(56.0)
Net finance costs		**19.4**	32.6	**(11.5)**	14.9
Income tax (paid) / received		**(0.7)**	(85.3)	**41.1**	(25.8)
Net cash inflow from operating activities		**275.7**	501.4	**37.3**	851.0
Cash flows from investing activities					
Dividends received from associate	19	**0.6**	–	**–**	–
Dividends received from subsidiaries		**–**	–	**276.8**	56.0
Purchases of non-current assets and investments	36	**(131.8)**	(209.3)	**(239.8)**	(1,004.9)
Proceeds from sale of non-current assets and investments		**0.3**	0.2	**–**	–
Purchases of businesses and minority interests	36	**(5.7)**	(8.2)	**–**	–
Net proceeds from sale of businesses and minority interests	36	**–**	17.6	**56.3**	187.6
Net cash (outflow) / inflow from investing activities		**(136.6)**	(199.7)	**93.3**	(761.3)
Cash flows from financing activities					
Net proceeds on ESOT transactions in own shares	36	**18.4**	0.8	**18.4**	0.8
Proceeds from / (repayment of) borrowings and finance leases	36	**30.1**	(48.6)	**31.9**	(7.7)
Dividends paid to equity holders of the parent company	10	**(78.4)**	(78.1)	**(78.4)**	(78.1)
Settlement of currency swaps for net investment hedging		**(25.3)**	(93.9)	**(25.3)**	–
Proceeds from minority interest on share issue		**0.3**	–	**–**	–
Interest paid		**(31.5)**	(42.7)	**(46.7)**	(84.0)
Interest received		**10.4**	9.0	**52.6**	69.2
Net cash outflow from financing activities		**(76.0)**	(253.5)	**(47.5)**	(99.8)
Increase / (decrease) in cash and cash equivalents in the year		**63.1**	48.2	**83.1**	(10.1)
Exchange differences on cash and cash equivalents		**1.5**	13.1	**–**	–
Cash and cash equivalents at beginning of year		**99.8**	38.5	**(5.0)**	5.1
Cash and cash equivalents at end of year	37	**164.4**	99.8	**78.1**	(5.0)
Reconciliation to net debt					
Increase / (decrease) in cash and cash equivalents in the year		**63.1**	48.2	**83.1**	(10.1)
(Proceeds from) / repayment of borrowings and finance leases		**(30.1)**	48.6	**(31.9)**	7.7
Change in net debt resulting from cash flows		**33.0**	96.8	**51.2**	(2.4)
Exchange differences on net debt		**28.0**	(20.8)	**26.7**	(0.1)
Movement in net debt in year		**61.0**	76.0	**77.9**	(2.5)
Net debt at beginning of year		**(534.4)**	(610.4)	**(616.9)**	(614.4)
Net debt at end of year	26	**(473.4)**	(534.4)	**(539.0)**	(616.9)

The notes on pages 68 to 107 form an integral part of the accounts.

CONSOLIDATED STATEMENT OF CHANGES IN EQUITY

for the year ended 31st March 2010

	Share capital £ million	Share premium account £ million	Shares held in ESOT £ million	Other reserves (note 35) £ million	Retained earnings £ million	Total attributable to equity holders £ million	Minority interests £ million	Total equity £ million
At 1st April 2008	220.7	148.3	(68.6)	(20.6)	879.1	1,158.9	1.4	1,160.3
Profit / (loss) for the year	–	–	–	–	174.1	174.1	(0.2)	173.9
Actuarial loss on post-employment benefits	–	–	–	–	(156.7)	(156.7)	–	(156.7)
Cash flow hedges	–	–	–	(19.9)	–	(19.9)	–	(19.9)
Associate's cash flow hedges	–	–	–	(0.2)	–	(0.2)	–	(0.2)
Net investment hedges	–	–	–	(146.9)	–	(146.9)	–	(146.9)
Currency translation differences	–	–	–	189.4	–	189.4	0.6	190.0
Tax on other comprehensive income	–	–	–	16.7	47.6	64.3	–	64.3
Total comprehensive income	–	–	–	39.1	65.0	104.1	0.4	104.5
Dividends paid (note 10)	–	–	–	–	(78.1)	(78.1)	(0.4)	(78.5)
Purchase of shares for ESOT	–	–	(2.6)	–	–	(2.6)	–	(2.6)
Purchase of minority interest	–	–	–	–	(4.6)	(4.6)	(0.6)	(5.2)
Share-based payments	–	–	–	–	5.6	5.6	–	5.6
Cost of shares transferred to employees	–	–	9.4	–	(11.6)	(2.2)	–	(2.2)
Tax on share-based payments	–	–	–	–	(5.8)	(5.8)	–	(5.8)
At 31st March 2009	220.7	148.3	(61.8)	18.5	849.6	1,175.3	0.8	1,176.1
Profit for the year	–	–	–	–	164.2	164.2	–	164.2
Actuarial loss on post-employment benefits	–	–	–	–	(124.6)	(124.6)	–	(124.6)
Cash flow hedges	–	–	–	27.0	–	27.0	–	27.0
Associate's cash flow hedges	–	–	–	0.2	–	0.2	–	0.2
Net investment hedges	–	–	–	32.8	–	32.8	–	32.8
Currency translation differences	–	–	–	(5.8)	–	(5.8)	0.1	(5.7)
Tax on other comprehensive income	–	–	–	0.7	33.4	34.1	–	34.1
Total comprehensive income	–	–	–	54.9	73.0	127.9	0.1	128.0
Dividends paid (note 10)	–	–	–	–	(78.4)	(78.4)	(0.2)	(78.6)
Acquisition of minority interest	–	–	–	–	–	–	0.4	0.4
Share issue to minority interest	–	–	–	–	–	–	0.3	0.3
Share-based payments	–	–	–	–	10.4	10.4	–	10.4
Cost of shares transferred to employees	–	–	31.1	–	(18.4)	12.7	–	12.7
Tax on share-based payments	–	–	–	–	1.5	1.5	–	1.5
At 31st March 2010	220.7	148.3	(30.7)	73.4	837.7	1,249.4	1.4	1,250.8

The notes on pages 68 to 107 form an integral part of the accounts.

ACCOUNTS

PARENT COMPANY STATEMENT OF CHANGES IN EQUITY

for the year ended 31st March 2010

	Share capital £ million	Share premium account £ million	Shares held in ESOT £ million	Other reserves (note 35) £ million	Retained earnings £ million	Total equity £ million
At 1st April 2008	220.7	148.3	(68.4)	(0.4)	650.7	950.9
Profit for the year	–	–	–	–	12.7	12.7
Actuarial loss on post-employment benefits	–	–	–	–	(121.5)	(121.5)
Cash flow hedges	–	–	–	(18.0)	(0.6)	(18.6)
Currency translation differences	–	–	–	(6.6)	–	(6.6)
Tax on other comprehensive income	–	–	–	5.5	33.8	39.3
Total comprehensive income	–	–	–	(19.1)	(75.6)	(94.7)
Dividends paid (note 10)	–	–	–	–	(78.1)	(78.1)
Purchase of shares for ESOT	–	–	(2.6)	–	–	(2.6)
Share-based payments	–	–	–	–	3.4	3.4
Cost of shares transferred to employees	–	–	9.2	–	(9.2)	–
Tax on share-based payments	–	–	–	–	(6.1)	(6.1)
At 31st March 2009	220.7	148.3	(61.8)	(19.5)	485.1	772.8
Profit for the year	–	–	–	–	374.9	374.9
Actuarial loss on post-employment benefits	–	–	–	–	(122.0)	(122.0)
Cash flow hedges	–	–	–	26.6	(0.2)	26.4
Currency translation differences	–	–	–	0.5	–	0.5
Tax on other comprehensive income	–	–	–	(7.4)	33.6	26.2
Total comprehensive income	–	–	–	19.7	286.3	306.0
Dividends paid (note 10)	–	–	–	–	(78.4)	(78.4)
Share-based payments	–	–	–	–	8.0	8.0
Cost of shares transferred to employees	–	–	31.1	–	(16.0)	15.1
Tax on share-based payments	–	–	–	–	1.0	1.0
At 31st March 2010	**220.7**	**148.3**	**(30.7)**	**0.2**	**686.0**	**1,024.5**

The notes on pages 68 to 107 form an integral part of the accounts.

The statement of cash flows is consolidated to include the cash flows of all the companies within the group, and includes the parent company, Johnson Matthey Plc.

We will look at the financial performance of Johnson Matthey in Worked examples 8.2 and 8.3 using the two approaches to ratio analysis that were mentioned in the introduction to this chapter:

- horizontal analysis, or common size analysis, which provides a line-by-line comparison of the income statement (and balance sheet) with those of the previous year
- vertical analysis, where each item in the income statement (and balance sheet) is expressed as a percentage of the total sales (and total assets).

Horizontal analysis

We introduced the technique of horizontal analysis in Chapter 7. The following example illustrates the technique applied to a summary of the Johnson Matthey Plc income statement for the years to 31 March 2009 and 31 March 2010.

Worked example 8.2

We can prepare a horizontal analysis using a summary of the income statement results for Johnson Matthey Plc for 2009 and 2010, using 2009 as the base year.

(You may note that a part of the income statement refers to profit for the year from **continuing operations**, as distinct from **discontinued operations,** which are defined in the glossary at the end of this book.)

Johnson Matthey Plc
Consolidated income statement for the year ended 31 March 2010

	2010 £m	2009 £m
Revenue	7,839.4	7,847.8
Cost of sales	(7,325.4)	(7,324.3)
Gross profit	514.0	523.5
Distribution costs	(103.6)	(101.2)
Administrative expenses	(138.6)	(123.8)
Restructuring charge	(11.3)	(9.4)
Amortisation of acquired intangibles	(9.9)	(9.1)
Operating profit	250.6	280.0
Finance costs	(30.5)	(43.3)
Finance income	11.1	10.7
Share of profit/(loss) of associate	1.7	2.0
Dissolution of associate	(4.4)	–
Profit before tax	228.5	249.4
Income tax expense	(64.3)	(76.7)
Profit for the year from continuing operations	164.2	172.7
Profit for the year from discontinued operations	–	1.2
Profit for the year	164.2	173.9
Attributable to:		
Equity holders of the parent company	164.2	174.1
Minority interests	–	(0.2)
	164.2	173.9

Worked example 8.2 considers only two years, and has used 2009 as the base year 100. This means, for example:

If

$$\text{revenue for 2009 of } £7{,}847.8\,m = 100$$

Then

$$\text{revenue for 2010 of } £7{,}839.4\,m = \frac{£7{,}839.4\,m \times 100}{£7{,}847.8\,m} = 99.9$$

Subsequent years may similarly be compared with 2009 as base 100, using the same sort of calculation.

Johnson Matthey Plc
Consolidated income statement for the year ended 31 March 2010

Horizontal analysis	2009	2010
Revenue	100.0	99.9
Cost of sales	100.0	100.0
Gross profit	100.0	98.2
Distribution costs	100.0	102.4
Administrative expenses	100.0	111.9
Restructuring charge	100.0	120.2
Amortisation of acquired intangibles	100.0	108.8
Operating profit	100.0	89.5
Finance costs	100.0	70.4
Finance income	100.0	103.7
Share of profit/(loss) of associate	100.0	85.0
Dissolution of associate	100.0	–
Profit before tax	100.0	91.6
Income tax expense	100.0	83.8
Profit for the year from continuing operations	100.0	95.1
Profit for the year from discontinued operations	100.0	–
Profit for the year	100.0	94.4
Attributable to:		
Equity holders of the parent company	100.0	94.3
Minority interests	100.0	94.4

The horizontal analysis technique is particularly useful to make a line-by-line comparison of a company's accounts for each accounting period over say five or 10 years, using the first year as the base year. When we look at a set of accounts we may by observation automatically carry out this process of assessing percentage changes in performance over time. However, presentation of the information in tabular form, for a number of years, gives a very clear picture of trends in performance in each area of activity and may provide the basis for further analysis.

We can easily see from the above horizontal analysis how the profit for 2010 compares with that for 2009. Sales decreased by 0.1% in 2010 compared to 2009, and operating profit was 89.5% of the 2009 level. However, profit for the year was 94.4% of the previous year's.

Progress check 8.4

What can a horizontal analysis of the information contained in the financial statements of a company add to that provided from ratio analysis?

Vertical analysis

Worked example 8.3 uses total turnover as the basis for calculation. The following analysis confirms the conclusions drawn from the horizontal analysis.

Worked example 8.3

We can prepare a vertical analysis using a summary of the consolidated income statement results for Johnson Matthey Plc for 2009 and 2010.

Johnson Matthey Plc
Consolidated income statement for the year ended 31 March 2010

Vertical analysis	2009	2010
Revenue	100.0	100.0
Cost of sales	(93.3)	(93.5)
Gross profit	6.7	6.5
Distribution costs	(1.3)	(1.3)
Administrative expenses	(1.6)	(1.8)
Restructuring charge	(0.1)	(0.1)
Amortisation of acquired intangibles	(0.1)	(0.1)
Operating profit	3.6	3.2
Finance costs	(0.5)	(0.4)
Finance income	0.1	0.1
Share of profit/(loss) of associate	–	–
Dissolution of associate	–	–
Profit before tax	3.2	2.9
Income tax expense	(1.0)	(0.8)
Profit for the year from continuing operations	2.2	2.1
Profit for the year from discontinued operations	–	–
Profit for the year	2.2	2.1
Attributable to:		
Equity holders of the parent company	2.2	2.1
Minority interests	–	–

Operating profit fell from 3.6% of sales revenue in 2009 to 3.2% in 2010. Profit before tax fell from 3.2% of sales revenue in 2009 to 2.9% in 2010. Profit for the year fell from 2.2% of sales revenue in 2009 to 2.1% in 2010.

Progress check 8.5

What can a vertical analysis of the information contained in the financial statements of a company add to the information provided from a horizontal analysis and a ratio analysis?

Notes on the accounts

The section headed notes on the accounts in the annual report and accounts contains information that must be reported additional to, and in support of, the financial statements. This may be used to comment on financial performance. Generally, the information disclosed in notes to the accounts includes:

- segmental information – analysis by business and geographical area relating to revenue and net assets
- revenue
- exceptional items
- fees payable to auditors
- operating profit
- finance costs
- finance income
- taxation
- dividends
- earnings per share
- employee numbers
- employee costs
- post-employment benefits
- incentive schemes
- non-current assets
- goodwill
- other intangible assets
- investments in subsidiaries
- investments in associates
- other investments
- inventories
- construction contracts
- trade and other receivables
- trade and other payables
- other liabilities and assets held for sale
- net debt
- other financial assets
- other financial liabilities
- financial risk management: interest rate; foreign currency; liquidity; trade credit; capital management
- provisions
- **contingent liabilities**
- deferred taxation
- share capital
- reserves
- minority interests
- cash flow
- commitments
- acquisitions
- discontinued operations
- related parties transactions
- **post balance sheet events**
- estimation uncertainty.

NOTES ON THE ACCOUNTS
for the year ended 31st March 2010

1   Segmental information

As described in the Annual Report and Accounts for the year ended 31st March 2009, the group reorganised its divisional structure on 1st April 2009. The Catalysts and Chemicals business, which makes precious metal and some base metal catalysts and precious metal chemicals, has been transferred into the Precious Metal Products Division. The remaining businesses in the Fine Chemicals & Catalysts Division have been renamed as the Fine Chemicals Division. The segmental information below reflects the new divisional structure and comparative information has been restated to reflect the change.

For management purposes, the group is organised into three operating divisions – Environmental Technologies, Precious Metal Products and Fine Chemicals and each division is represented by a director on the Board of Directors. These operating divisions represent the group's segments. Their principal activities are described on pages 12 to 19. The performance of the divisions is assessed by the Board of Directors on underlying operating profit, which is before amortisation of acquired intangibles, major impairment and restructuring charges and profit or loss on disposal of businesses. Sales between segments are made at market prices, taking into account the volumes involved.

Year ended 31st March 2010	Environmental Technologies £ million	Precious Metal Products £ million	Fine Chemicals £ million	Eliminations £ million	Total £ million
Sales to external customers	2,056.4	5,561.8	221.2	–	7,839.4
Inter-segment sales	5.2	636.5	1.8	(643.5)	–
Total revenue	2,061.6	6,198.3	223.0	(643.5)	7,839.4
External sales excluding the value of precious metals	1,246.5	419.9	219.1	–	1,885.5
Segmental underlying operating profit	120.9	116.7	55.8	–	293.4
Unallocated corporate expenses					(21.6)
Underlying operating profit					271.8
Major impairment and restructuring charges (note 3)					(11.3)
Amortisation of acquired intangibles (note 4)					(9.9)
Operating profit					250.6
Net finance costs					(19.4)
Share of profit of associate					1.7
Dissolution of associate (note 19)					(4.4)
Profit before tax					228.5
Segmental assets	1,710.6	452.8	433.0	(80.6)	2,515.8
Investment in associate	–	3.4	–	–	3.4
Segmental total assets	1,710.6	456.2	433.0	(80.6)	2,519.2
Cash, deposits and swaps related to borrowings					198.4
Current and deferred income tax assets					70.0
Post-employment benefits net assets					4.6
Unallocated corporate assets					97.7
Total assets					2,889.9
Segmental net assets	1,333.7	261.2	400.8	–	1,995.7
Net debt					(473.4)
Post-employment benefits net assets and liabilities					(245.7)
Deferred income tax assets and liabilities					0.6
Provisions and non-current other payables					(34.3)
Unallocated corporate net assets					7.9
Total net assets					1,250.8
Segmental capital expenditure	93.8	15.9	22.0	–	131.7
Other additions to non-current assets (excluding financial assets, deferred tax assets and post-employment benefits net assets)	3.5	1.0	0.3	(0.3)	4.5
Segmental total additions to non-current assets	97.3	16.9	22.3	(0.3)	136.2
Corporate capital expenditure					2.7
Total additions to non-current assets					138.9
Segmental depreciation and amortisation	69.3	23.1	15.8	–	108.2
Corporate depreciation					2.7
Amortisation of acquired intangibles					9.9
Total depreciation and amortisation					120.8

NOTES ON THE ACCOUNTS
for the year ended 31st March 2010

1   Segmental information (continued)

Year ended 31st March 2009 (restated)	Environmental Technologies £ million	Precious Metal Products £ million	Fine Chemicals £ million	Eliminations £ million	Total £ million
Sales to external customers	2,226.1	5,401.7	220.0	–	7,847.8
Inter-segment sales	7.4	933.0	2.6	(943.0)	–
Total revenue	2,233.5	6,334.7	222.6	(943.0)	7,847.8
External sales excluding the value of precious metals	1,135.2	446.5	215.2	–	1,796.9
Segmental underlying operating profit	124.3	143.0	49.5	–	316.8
Unallocated corporate expenses					(18.3)
Underlying operating profit					298.5
Major impairment and restructuring charges (note 3)					(9.4)
Amortisation of acquired intangibles (note 4)					(9.1)
Operating profit					280.0
Net finance costs					(32.6)
Share of profit of associate					2.0
Profit before tax					249.4
Segmental assets	1,571.8	399.4	466.0	(59.4)	2,377.8
Investment in associate	–	5.8	–	–	5.8
Segmental total assets	1,571.8	405.2	466.0	(59.4)	2,383.6
Cash, deposits and swaps related to borrowings					145.9
Current and deferred income tax assets					69.0
Post-employment benefits net assets					2.2
Unallocated corporate assets					93.6
Total assets					2,694.3
Segmental net assets	1,228.2	237.7	432.9	–	1,898.8
Net debt					(534.4)
Post-employment benefits net assets and liabilities					(151.6)
Deferred income tax assets and liabilities					(42.8)
Provisions and non-current other payables					(25.4)
Unallocated corporate net assets					31.5
Total net assets					1,176.1
Segmental capital expenditure	160.2	24.5	13.6	–	198.3
Other additions to non-current assets (excluding financial assets, deferred tax assets and post-employment benefits net assets)	2.3	0.3	–	(0.4)	2.2
Segmental total additions to non-current assets	162.5	24.8	13.6	(0.4)	200.5
Corporate capital expenditure					5.2
Total additions to non-current assets					205.7
Segment depreciation and amortisation	57.2	22.6	17.3	–	97.1
Corporate depreciation					2.5
Amortisation of acquired intangibles					9.1
Total depreciation and amortisation					108.7

The group received £1,030.5 million of revenue from one external customer (2009 £856.4 million) which is 13% (2009 11%) of the group's sales to external customers. The revenue is reported in Precious Metal Products as it is generated by the group's platinum marketing and distribution activities and so has a very low return on sales.

ACCOUNTS

NOTES ON THE ACCOUNTS

for the year ended 31st March 2010

1 Segmental information (continued)

The group's country of domicile is the UK. Sales to external customers are based on the customer's location. Non-current assets are based on the location of the assets and excludes financial instruments, deferred tax assets and post-employment benefits net assets.

| | Sales to external customers | | Non-current assets | |
	2010 £ million	2009 £ million	2010 £ million	2009 £ million
UK	2,192.6	1,940.3	676.7	686.4
Germany	659.5	739.9	250.9	268.0
Rest of Europe	713.4	886.2	122.2	110.2
USA	1,928.1	1,835.3	309.8	343.0
Rest of North America	122.6	96.2	14.3	13.5
China (including Hong Kong)	1,138.5	1,031.0	42.9	25.3
Rest of Asia	547.3	802.0	105.2	96.0
Rest of World	537.4	516.9	51.3	42.9
Total	7,839.4	7,847.8	1,573.3	1,585.3

Segmental reporting

The first note in the notes on the accounts in Johnson Matthey's report and accounts for 2010 is headed segmental information. International Financial Reporting Standard IFRS 8, Operating Segments, requires large companies to disclose segmental information by each operating segment, which could be a type of activity, a class of product or service or a geographical region. This analysis is required in order that users of financial information may carry out more meaningful financial analysis.

Most large companies usually comprise diverse businesses supplying different products and services, rather than being engaged in a single type of business. Each type of business activity may have:

- a different structure
- different levels of profitability
- different levels of growth potential
- different levels of risk exposure.

The financial statements of such diversified companies are consolidated to include all business activities, which is a potential problem for the users of financial information. For analysis and interpretation of financial performance, aggregate figures are not particularly useful for the following reasons:

- difficulties in evaluation of performance of a business which has interests that are diverse from the aggregated financial information
- difficulties of comparison of trends over time and comparison between companies because the various activities undertaken by the company are likely to differ in size and range in comparison with other businesses
- differences in conditions between different geographical markets, in terms of levels of risk, profitability and growth
- differences in conditions between different geographical markets, in terms of political and social factors, environmental factors, currencies and **inflation** rates.

Segmental reporting analysis enables:

- the further analysis of segmental performance to determine more accurately the likely growth prospects for the business as a whole
- evaluation of the impact on the company of changes in conditions relating to particular activities
- improvements in internal management performance, because it may be monitored through disclosure of segmental information to shareholders
- evaluation of the acquisition and disposal performance of the company.

Worked example 8.4

The information in the table below relates to global sales by Nestlé SA, the Swiss nutrition and foods giant, for the years 2009 and 2008.

Figures in Swiss francs (CHF) millions

	Europe 2009	Americas 2009	Asia and Africa 2009	Europe 2008	Americas 2008	Asia and Africa 2008
Beverages	5,362	3,746	5,331	5,072	3,830	5,576
Milk products	3,147	9,884	5,228	2,708	9,698	5,013
Prepared dishes	7,243	5,291	2,565	6,288	5,414	2,680
Confectionery	5,416	4,632	1,850	4,686	4,831	1,852
Pet care	3,930	7,804	733	3,774	8,395	770
Total sales	25,098	31,357	15,707	22,528	32,168	15,891

(i) Using the information provided we may prepare a simple table that compares the sales for 2009 with the sales for the year 2008.

(ii) We can also consider how a simple sales analysis can provide an investor with information that is more useful than just global sales for the year.

(i)

	Europe			Americas			Asia and Africa		
	2009		2008	2009		2008	2009		2008
Beverages	5,362	+5.72%	5,072	3,746	−2.19%	3,830	5,331	−4.39%	5,576
Milk products	3,147	+16.21%	2,708	9,884	+1.92%	9,698	5,228	+4.29%	5,013
Prepared dishes	7,243	+15.19%	6,288	5,291	−2.27%	5,414	2,565	−4.29%	2,680
Confectionery	5,416	+15.58%	4,686	4,632	−4.12%	4,831	1,850	−0.01%	1,852
Pet care	3,930	+4.13%	3,774	7,804	−7.04%	8,395	733	−4.81%	770
Total sales	25,098	+11.41%	22,528	31,357	−2.52%	32,168	15,707	−1.16%	15,891

(ii) Numbers that are blandly presented in a global format do not usually reveal trends. Analysis of information year on year by area and by percentage, for example, may reveal trends and may illustrate the impact of new policies or the changes in specific economic environments. The analysis of the Nestlé SA sales for the two years shows:
- in which geographical area sales have increased or decreased
- which products' sales have increased or decreased.

Analysis of the results over several years is usually needed to provide meaningful trend information as a basis for investigation into the reasons for increases and decreases.

An operating segment is a component of a company that engages in business activities from which it earns revenues and incurs expenses and for which discrete financial information is available.

For each operating segment of a company IFRS 8 requires information to be provided about

- how the business identifies its operating segments
- the types of products and services from which it earns revenues in each operating segment
- the reported profit or loss of each segment.

Also required is an analysis of revenues and non-current assets by geographical area irrespective of the identification of operating segments and a requirement to disclose information about transactions with major customers.

Let's take a look at Johnson Matthey's segmental reporting (see pages 313 to 315). This may be used to provide even more useful information through horizontal and vertical analysis of the numbers. Such an analysis over a five- or 10-year period would be particularly useful to identify trends in performance, and changes that may have taken place in the activities of the business and the areas of the world in which the company has operated.

Worked example 8.5

If we refer to note 1 in the Johnson Matthey Plc notes on the accounts in their annual report and accounts 2010 we can identify total sales revenue for each global division for 2010 and 2009. We can use this to present the data in both pie chart format (see Fig. 8.4 and Fig. 8.5) and bar chart format (see Fig. 8.6) and more clearly explain JM's sales results for 2010 and 2009.

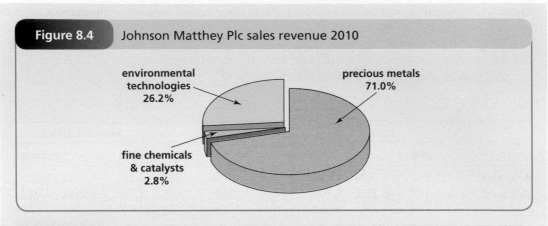

Figure 8.4   Johnson Matthey Plc sales revenue 2010

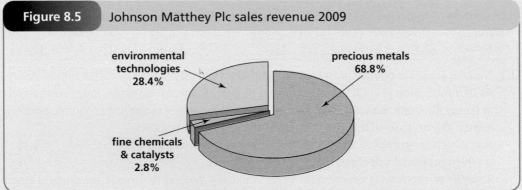

Figure 8.5   Johnson Matthey Plc sales revenue 2009

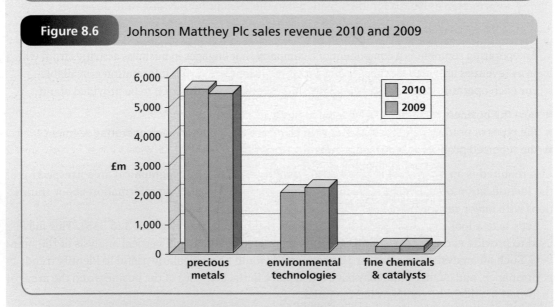

Figure 8.6   Johnson Matthey Plc sales revenue 2010 and 2009

The pie charts give a broad indication of sales revenue by type of business, and show that for both years precious metals provide over two thirds of the sales revenue and is increasing, and environmental technologies provide over one quarter of sales revenue. Fine chemicals and catalysts is the smallest sector that provides the balance.

The bar chart is probably more useful in showing more clearly that sales revenue from the largest sector has increased in 2010 over 2009, that the next largest sector has decreased, and the smallest sector has remained at around the same volume.

There are many problems relating to the principle of disclosure of segmental information, some of which we have already identified:

■ directors may be reluctant to disclose information that may damage the competitive position of the company – foreign competitors may not have to disclose similar data
■ segmental information may not be useful since the total company results are what should be relevant to shareholders
■ some users of information may not be sufficiently financially expert to avoid being confused by the segmental information
■ conglomerates may choose not to disclose segmental information, whereas a single activity company by definition is unable to hide anything.

There are, in addition, some accounting problems concerned with the preparation of segmental reports:

■ identification of operating segments is not defined in IFRS 8, but is left to the judgement of the directors of the company
■ lack of definition of segments results in difficulty in comparison of companies
■ difficulties in analysis and apportionment of costs that are common between operating segments
■ difficulties in the treatment of costs of transfers of goods and services between segments.

Progress check 8.6

Describe what is meant by segmental reporting and to whom it is useful.

Sustainability reporting

An inspection of Johnson Matthey's report and accounts 2010 will reveal that sustainability, and health and safety issues with regard to its employees, customers and the community, rank highly amongst the company's priorities. This is demonstrated in the coverage given to such issues in the section of the business review headed sustainability (see pages 320 to 329).

Throughout the past 10 years or so companies have started to show greater interest in their position with regard to environmental and social issues. General corporate awareness has increased as to how the adoption of particular policies may have adverse social and environmental effects. Environmental issues naturally focus on our inability to sustain our use of non-renewable resources, the disappearance of the ozone layer and forestation, pollution and waste treatment. Social issues may include problems associated with race, gender, disability, sexual orientation and age, and the way that companies manage bullying, the incidence of accidents, employee welfare, training and development.

The increase in awareness of environmental and social issues has followed the concern that the focus of traditional reporting has been weighted too heavily towards the requirements of shareholders, with too little regard for the other stakeholders. That led to an over-emphasis on the financial performance, particularly the profitability, of the business. The accountancy profession and other interested parties have given thought to the widening of the annual report and accounts to meet the requirements of all stakeholders, and not just the shareholders of the business.

In March 2000, the UK Government appointed a Minister for Corporate Social Responsibility, and produced two reports on CSR:

■ Business and Society, developing corporate social responsibility in the UK (2001)
■ Business and Society – corporate social responsibility report (2002).

Case Study / Sustainability

→ A Picture is Worth a Thousand Words…

Everyone in Johnson Matthey is working towards Sustainability 2017 – employee engagement is at the very heart of this long term vision to support business growth. Our Emission Control Technologies (ECT) business has created a 'Visual Plant' concept to help employees put sustainability into practice. Visual Plant is being adopted across ECT and other group businesses and exemplifies how clear, effective visual communication, teamwork and sharing best practice can drive improved performance and deliver real benefits for Johnson Matthey.

28 - Johnson Matthey

BUSINESS REVIEW

Sustainability

Sustainability is a key element of our strategy for the future growth of the business. The group's Sustainability 2017 Vision, launched in December 2007, sets out our aspirations for building a more sustainable business and includes challenging targets to support business growth. Our aims are to at least double our underlying earnings per share whilst achieving carbon neutrality, zero waste to landfill and halving the key resources that we consume per unit of output by 2017, the 200th anniversary of the founding of the company. The full statement is available on the company's website at www.matthey.com.

There are two key drivers for our vision. The first is to be more efficient with the resources we use as a business and the second is to design new products and services that help our customers to be more sustainable and competitive. However, growing our business through sustainability is not only about our operations and products. We are also committed to best practice in governance, to creating a positive working environment for employees and to being a responsible partner for our customers, suppliers and communities. Some of the progress we have made towards achieving the vision is presented in summary in this report. Further details can be found in Johnson Matthey's Sustainability Report 2009/10 which will be published on the company's website in July 2010.

Sustainability is embedded into our routine management processes. All of the group's businesses are required to develop, implement and report progress on their own sustainability plans as part of the group's annual financial budgeting processes. These plans have the common corporate objectives as their foundation and are tailored to the businesses' own specific operations. This approach encourages commitment at a local level and takes advantage of Johnson Matthey's culture and methods of working.

Progress towards our Sustainability 2017 targets and the group's other social, environmental and ethical targets is summarised in the table on page 30. We have developed appropriate key performance indicators (KPIs) to enable us to monitor performance and data is reported relative to a baseline year which, unless stated, is taken as our performance in 2006/07.

In 2009/10 performance against our targets has improved relative to the baseline year. Year on year progress (2009/10 versus 2008/09) has also been steady with improvement against all but three targets; earnings per share (EPS), carbon neutrality and natural gas consumption. During 2009/10, EPS growth has been held back by the impact of the global economic downturn on our business. The group's natural gas consumption and global warming potential (GWP) both increased this year resulting from the inclusion of data from three major new manufacturing facilities. The increase in GWP was also due in part to the geographical mix of production where this year, a greater proportion of our total output originated in countries where the carbon intensity from grid electricity is high.

Much of our progress to date has been achieved by incremental improvements in operational and process efficiencies, the so called 'low hanging fruit'. We have recognised the need to focus further on the step change opportunities that will drive accelerated progress towards our 2017 targets and add real value to Johnson Matthey.

During the year we have continued to develop our strategy to achieve carbon neutrality. We have also introduced a more formal system of site and functional reviews to drive improved performance. Conducted by members of the Group Sustainability team, the reviews aim to raise awareness of sustainability, provide help and support with initiatives, identify and share examples of good practice and ensure that the principles of sustainability are fully embedded across Johnson Matthey.

The site and functional reviews also focus on the progress being made against local plans and on the alignment of local targets with the 2017 goals. This includes examination of the tools and metrics which can be used to understand the sustainability impacts and benefits of our operations and products.

Sharing information on successes, ideas and challenges across the whole group is also important to support continued progress. Employee engagement has remained a key priority to ensure all staff have a clear view of the importance of sustainability to the overall business strategy and to equip them with the information they need to take forward their own ideas. A dedicated intranet site has recently been launched to provide a means for everyone in the group to share good practice on sustainability and to offer a central source of information which employees can draw upon to support their initiatives.

During the year the Johnson Matthey Sustainability Awards were introduced to recognise and share best practice across the group. The awards, which will be made each year, span five categories which were carefully chosen to reflect the breadth of our Sustainability 2017 Vision. Last year a very strong set of around 90 entries was received, demonstrating the way in which everyone in the group continues to embrace sustainability and embed it as part of the way of doing business. Details of the seven winners can be found in the 2008/09 Sustainability Report.

Going forward the group will focus on accelerating performance towards the Sustainability 2017 targets through identifying and implementing operational / process improvements and by developing new sustainable products for our customers. The global sustainability agenda continues to evolve at a considerable pace presenting new challenges and opportunities for our industry. Johnson Matthey will continue its ongoing assessment of the current and likely future impacts on its business and the identification of new markets to ensure the group is well positioned to respond and benefit over the years ahead.

Managing Sustainability

Johnson Matthey has adopted the principles of corporate social responsibility and embedded them into its risk management processes. Since 2003 we have reported annually on our social, environmental and ethical performance in a separate report. Through the launch of Sustainability 2017 we have defined our own vision and direction to manage our impacts and opportunities with increasing efficiency.

Sustainability is managed across the group according to five elements: financial; governance; social; health and safety; and environment.

BUSINESS REVIEW

Progress Towards Sustainability 2017

Sustainability 2017 Aspiration	KPI	Baseline 2006/07	2009/10 [1]	2017 Target
At least double earnings per share	Underlying earnings per share (pence)	82.2 [2]	86.4	≥ 164.4
Achieve carbon neutrality	Total global warming potential (tonnes CO_2 equivalent)	401,119 [3,4]	390,389	0
Achieve zero waste to landfill	Amount of waste to landfill (tonnes)	16,555 [4]	4,998	0
Halve key resources per unit of output [5]	Electricity consumption (GJ '000)	1,469 [4]	1,389	735
	Natural gas consumption (GJ '000)	2,146 [4]	2,084	1,073
	Water consumption (m³ '000)	1,909 [4]	1,734	955

Other Targets	KPI	Baseline	2009/10 [1]	Target
Zero greater than three day accidents	Annual accident rate per 1,000 employees	n/a	2.14 [6]	0
ISO 14001 implemented by all manufacturing sites in 2010	Number of manufacturing sites with ISO 14001 registration	n/a	41	45 [7]
Incidence of occupational illness cases reduced by at least 30% by 2013/14	Annual incidence of occupational illness cases per 1,000 employees	5.3 [8]	5.2	≤ 3.7 [9]

[1] Data presented is for the period 1st April 2009 to 31st March 2010.
[2] Data presented is for the period 1st April 2006 to 31st March 2007.
[3] Restated.
[4] Data presented is for the period 1st January 2006 to 31st December 2006.
[5] The top three target resources were identified for each facility and from this electricity consumption, natural gas consumption and water use were most significant for the majority of the group.
[6] At March 2010.
[7] Target to be achieved in 2010.
[8] Baseline is incidence of occupational illness cases per 1,000 employees in calendar year 2008.
[9] Target to be achieved by 2013/14.

Financial

Financial viability is a key element of sustainability. Continued growth in profit is an important aspiration of our Sustainability 2017 Vision and we have set a target to more than double our underlying earnings per share by 2017. Details of our progress are outlined in the Financial Review on pages 20 to 22, in the Group Key Performance Indicators section on pages 8 and 9 and in the Five Year Record on page 109.

The two major thrusts of our vision are about being more efficient with the resources we use and designing new products that help our customers to be more sustainable. Using fewer resources as a business will save us money. It will enable us to maintain or improve our margins and allow us to invest more in R&D and infrastructure. We have started to evaluate the monetary savings realised by our businesses through implementation of their Sustainability 2017 plans and estimate that savings of up to £12 million have been achieved in 2009/10. These savings have been achieved as a result of a large number of initiatives across all our businesses. For example, energy reduction projects in Emission Control Technologies have saved around £170,000, solvent reduction programmes at Macfarlan Smith have delivered around £200,000 in savings and Catalysts and Chemicals in Shanghai, China has saved over £140,000 through initiatives to deliver reductions across its five key resources.

Designing innovative new products for our customers will allow us to maintain or strengthen our competitive position in the markets we serve today and benefit from the growth opportunities in emerging markets within the sustainability sector. In 2009/10 a significant proportion of profit was generated by products that directly benefit the environment.

We continue to work towards obtaining more robust evaluations of the financial benefits of our sustainability programme and on establishing further metrics to monitor the financial impact of sustainability initiatives on business performance.

Governance

Good governance is a cornerstone of sustainability and the group has well established policies and management systems to support this which apply to all operations worldwide. Legal requirements are a minimum standard and in many cases our policies and systems are in advance of these. Johnson Matthey has policies in the areas of Environment, Health and Safety (EHS); Employment; and Business Integrity and Ethics which provide the framework for managing environmental, social and governance matters. These are presented on the company's website at www.matthey.com. Further details of our policies, initiatives and progress can be found in the Sustainability Report on our website and are presented here in summary.

As outlined in the Corporate Governance section (page 42) the board has embedded environmental, social and governance matters into its risk management processes and formally reviews the area once a year. These matters are monitored by the CSR Compliance Committee, a sub-committee of the Chief Executive's Committee. A description of the role of the Committee can be found on page 42.

Policies and Management Systems – Environment, Health and Safety
Johnson Matthey is committed to providing the highest level of protection to the environment and to safeguarding the health and safety of its employees, customers and communities. This is supported by policies, a comprehensive management system, governance, careful risk assessment, auditing and training which promote continuous improvement and ensure that high standards are achieved at sites worldwide. In addition, all facilities have developed local policies to meet corporate requirements.

The EHS policy is a written statement, formulated and agreed by the Chief Executive's Committee and approved by the board. Signed by the Chief Executive, it is available at all sites, is published on the website and forms the basis of the group EHS management system.

The group EHS management system is available to all employees via the group intranet. It is regularly reviewed and, together with the corporate policies and objectives, it defines accountability and sets the standards against which conformance audits are assessed.

EHS compliance audits are vital to maintain continuous improvement and all Johnson Matthey operated manufacturing and research and development facilities are included in the audit programme. Audit frequency for each facility is determined by the scale, inherent risk and past performance of the operation. Audits are carried out by experienced ISO qualified EHS professionals and controlled by the Group EHS Assurance Director. Health management reviews are undertaken every three to four years at all operational sites. They are conducted by the Director of Group Health who provides consulting advice to support the prioritisation and planning of programmes to optimise workplace health and promote workforce sustainability. In addition, all businesses undertake annual health management improvement planning to adjust health programmes to meet changing business needs.

All audit reports, including health management reviews, are reviewed by the CSR Compliance Committee and appropriate follow up actions are taken on outstanding issues. During 2009/10 30 detailed compliance audits and six one day audit action reviews were completed. Health management reviews were conducted at 14 facilities.

Training is a vital element in ensuring continuous improvement in EHS performance and a variety of programmes are in place. Regular meetings are held in Europe and North America to enable EHS professionals across the group to network, share best practice and discuss the impact of future EHS legislation. Meetings have been extended to include the Asia region and its first meeting was held in May 2010.

Regulatory Matters and Product Stewardship
Johnson Matthey's corporate REACH compliance programme is well advanced. Projects to support substances subject to registration in 2010 are on track and it is anticipated that all dossier submissions will be made on time. We continue to participate in industry consortia collaborations as an efficient and cost effective method of managing current and future registration requirements. Our businesses are now engaged in the transition to the Globally Harmonised System (GHS) for chemical classification and hazard communication and work is underway to ensure compliance with the European Union Classification Regulation. As part of our continuous improvement programme for product stewardship, a comprehensive training update programme on the US Toxic Substances Control Act (TSCA) is being delivered across the group and is over 80% complete. A further three product regulatory specialists have been recruited during 2009/10 to support our global efforts.

No notifications of significant health effects at end user level involving our products and no major incidents or environmental releases during product transportation and distribution were recorded in 2009/10. During the year, there were no major product related regulatory penalties or non-compliances.

Policies and Management Systems – Human Resources
The group's human resources standards are progressive, consistent and aimed at bringing out the best in our people. Group policies are supported by detailed regional and individual business procedures which are regularly updated to reflect both regional best practice and local legislation. Site specific human resources policies and procedures are communicated to staff at inductions and through staff handbooks. Human resources policies and risks are examined by the Chief Executive's Committee and the CSR Compliance Committee.

REPORT OF THE DIRECTORS – BUSINESS REVIEW

Managing Sustainability

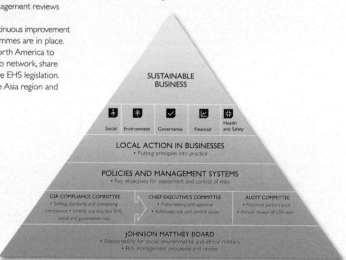

SUSTAINABLE BUSINESS

Social | Environment | Governance | Financial | Health and Safety

LOCAL ACTION IN BUSINESSES
• Putting principles into practice

POLICIES AND MANAGEMENT SYSTEMS
• Key objectives for assessment and control of risks

CSR COMPLIANCE COMMITTEE
• Setting standards and overseeing compliance • Identify and monitor EHS, social and governance risks

CHIEF EXECUTIVE'S COMMITTEE
• Policy setting and approval • Addresses risk and control issues

AUDIT COMMITTEE
• Monitors performance • Annual review of CSR risks

JOHNSON MATTHEY BOARD
• Responsibility for social, environmental and ethical matters
• Risk management processes and review

BUSINESS REVIEW

The group's policies on equal opportunities and training are published in full on the website and are detailed below.

Our Equal Opportunities Policy is to recruit, train and develop employees who meet the requirements of the job role, regardless of gender, ethnic origin, age, religion, sexual orientation or disability. The policy recognises that people with disabilities can often be denied a fair chance at work because of misconceptions about their capabilities and seeks to enhance the opportunities available by attempting, wherever possible, to overcome obstacles, such as the need to modify equipment, restructure jobs or to improve access to premises, provided such action does not compromise health and safety standards. Similarly, employees who become disabled during their employment will be offered employment opportunities consistent with their capabilities. We value the diversity of our people as a core component of a sustainable business and employment applications are welcomed and encouraged from all sections of the community including minority groups.

The Management Development and Remuneration Committee of the board takes a special interest in ensuring compliance with the Training and Development Policy objectives in order to:

- Ensure highest standards in the recruitment of employees.
- Assess training needs in the light of job requirements.
- Ensure relevance of training and link with business goals.
- Employ and evaluate effective and efficient training methods.
- Promote from within, from high potential pools of talent.
- Understand employees' aspirations.
- Provide development opportunities to meet employees' potential and aspirations.

Policies and Management Systems – Business Integrity and Ethics
Johnson Matthey strives to maintain the highest standards of ethical conduct and corporate responsibility worldwide to ensure we act with integrity, transparency and with care for the rights of the individual. The group's principles are set out in the Business Integrity and Ethics Policy and issues are further safeguarded through corporate governance processes and monitoring by the board and its committees. The policy applies to all the group's employees and is presented on the website.

Compliance training is provided to employees to support their understanding of and commitment to group policies in order to protect and enhance the company's reputation. The training educates managers in their responsibilities for employees, commercial contracts and company assets and is delivered globally via online learning programmes and seminars.

All facilities have established policies and procedures for employees to raise employment related issues for consideration and resolution. A confidential and secure 'whistleblowing' website and telephone helpline are also in place to give all employees additional means to raise any issue of personal concern.

Management of supply chain and contractor activities is a core component of the ISO 9000 and ISO 14000 series of standards. Supply chain and contractor management questionnaires are a requirement of achieving and maintaining registration and as such, ISO registered Johnson Matthey operations require the completion of appropriate questionnaires. For those operations without ISO registration, the group EHS management system provides policy and guidance on supply chain management and contractor control.

During the year, procurement professionals from across Johnson Matthey have been working together to develop an Ethical and Sustainable Procurement Policy. The policy provides clear guidance on various topics including those relating to the selection of suppliers, auditing against standards and ethical conduct with suppliers. It was published in May 2010.

Johnson Matthey is confident of the human rights performance of its own operations but recognises that business practices in the supply chain are not always transparent and represent a risk that must be managed. Every effort is made to ensure the issues are managed effectively. We support the principles defined within the United Nations Universal Declaration of Human Rights and the International Labour Organisation Core Conventions including the conventions in relation to child labour, forced labour, non-discrimination, freedom of association and collective bargaining. Compliance with and respect for these core principles are integrated within the risk assessment procedures and impact assessments which are undertaken when entering into business in a new territory and within the due diligence processes when making an acquisition or entering a joint venture.

→ Employees at Johnson Matthey Mexico joined children at a local kindergarten in planting trees. The site also donated hoses, sprinklers and soccer equipment.

→ Apprentice at Johnson Matthey's Redwitz site in Germany. The site's apprentice scheme combines company training with formal education at an occupational college.

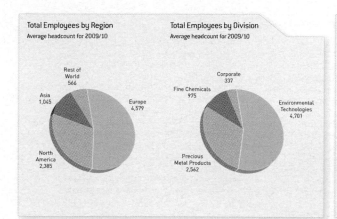

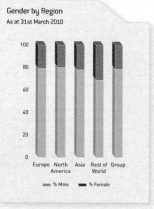

REPORT OF THE DIRECTORS – BUSINESS REVIEW

Social

Recruitment, Training, Development and Diversity

Johnson Matthey's employees are respected as the group's most valuable resource and play a vital role in building a sustainable business. We are committed to recruiting high calibre employees and providing them with the information, training and working environment they need to perform to the highest standards. All employees are encouraged to develop to their maximum potential, supported by human resources policies and practices that are strategically linked to the needs of the business and our customers.

The skills, qualities and wellbeing of employees underpin the company's success. An effective, streamlined recruitment procedure supports the steady requirement for high calibre graduates and career foundation training programmes are in place to engage new recruits. We also offer training and development programmes at middle and senior manager levels. Employees from acquired businesses are actively encouraged to attend programmes to expose them to the wider group culture and help them integrate. Our extensive portfolio of training is provided at our facilities around the world and programmes include presentations from senior executives to anchor the course content to the company's strategies and progress.

Our aim is to retain high potential and high performing staff. Providing career development opportunities for employees assists in staff retention and in turn, succession planning and the sustainability of management. Recruiting well qualified staff is vital to support business development, particularly in new and emerging markets such as in Asia, and this is achieved by appropriate manpower planning, local recruitment and the encouragement of international and cross divisional mobility. The group has a management skills inventory database to help to identify and match suitably qualified internal candidates to promotional and development opportunities globally and / or across our divisions as we strive to place the right people with the right skills in the right places. Beyond satisfying the immediate business needs, the company is committed to developing a more internationally diverse workforce to support its global business.

The group's gender balance remains almost unchanged this year at 79% male and 21% female. The group recognises the importance of creating an enhanced environment for the development of women in management and during the year has introduced an initiative to increase awareness of this issue. As part of this, managers have been encouraged to use the annual appraisal with their female staff as an opportunity to understand aspirations, identify any perceived obstacles to progression, discuss opportunities for career development and highlight details of the group's family friendly policies.

Employee Relations and Communication

The quality of our employee relations is a priority for the company and Johnson Matthey is proud of the high level of commitment and loyalty from its employees. We have a low voluntary staff turnover (5.4% in 2009/10, see page 9) with many employees staying with the company for their whole careers.

Effective communication with employees is important and in particular, face to face dialogue. Communication is exchanged through the in house magazines, attitude surveys, regular news bulletins, presentations to staff and team briefings. Employees are also encouraged to access the group's corporate intranet, sustainability intranet and website.

The company supports employee share ownership and employees have the opportunity to participate in share ownership plans, where practicable. Under these plans, employees can buy shares in the company which are matched by a company funded component. Employees in six countries are able to contribute to a company share ownership plan or a 401k approved savings investment plan. Through these ownership plans Johnson Matthey's current and former employees collectively held 1.83% of the company's shares at 31st March 2010.

Johnson Matthey also sponsors pension plans for its employees worldwide. These pension plans are a combination of defined benefit and defined contribution pension arrangements, savings schemes and provident funds designed to provide appropriate retirement benefits based on local laws, custom and market practice. In 2009/10 there was a major change to the Johnson Matthey Employees Pension Scheme in the UK (JMEPS).

BUSINESS REVIEW

Following a full consultation exercise with around 2,000 employees who were affected by the change, from 31st March 2010 those employees ceased to accrue further benefits based upon their final salary. From 1st April 2010 those employees will accrue benefits based upon their career average salary and may also make defined contributions to their pension which are matched by the company up to 3% of pensionable pay. This is in line with the pension arrangements for UK employees who joined JMEPS since 2006. These actions were deemed necessary to preserve the long term strength and integrity of the pension funds and of the company itself. Further details are provided on page 22. The design of the career average section of the scheme is geared to providing overall benefits of a similar level to the previous final salary section but has removed or reduced some of the liabilities that the company could potentially face in the future. The changes only affected UK based employees.

In 2008/09 the global economic slowdown had made it necessary to reduce employee numbers at some of our manufacturing sites and our monthly employee numbers continued to fall during the early part of 2009/10. A minimum point was reached in June 2009 and since then, employee numbers have increased by around 7%, as we have seen a recovery in demand for our products.

Johnson Matthey continues to maintain good and constructive relations with all recognised trade unions which collectively represent 33% of all group employees worldwide. During 2009/10 no working time was lost within the group due to employee action.

The corporate sickness absence rate during 2009/10 was 2.1% compared to 2.2% (restated) for 2008/09. We continue to increase investment in sustainable health and wellness programmes to support the longer term health, wellbeing and performance of our employees.

Community Investment

Johnson Matthey has a strong tradition for good community relations and the company and its employees are actively involved in programmes worldwide. We have an important contribution to make to the economic development of our local communities, not only as an employer but also through collaboration and investment, both financial and in kind. Johnson Matthey is a member of the London Benchmarking Group (LBG).

Guidance on site requirements is detailed in the group EHS management system and a review of community investment activities across the group is carried out each year. In 2009/10, the review indicates that 98% of Johnson Matthey's operations with over 50 employees participated in activities within their local communities. These activities are wide ranging and include charitable giving, support for educational projects, the advancement of science and economic regeneration projects. Employees also participate in activities or hold community related roles outside of the work environment. The company is supportive of this broader community engagement, allowing employees time off during working hours as appropriate. The review also demonstrates that a higher proportion of sites have specific budgets for community investment and are setting objectives for their activities.

Johnson Matthey's long history of support for charitable causes continues today through group and business programmes. The causes we support reflect the areas in which the group's technologies have a benefit and the issues which strike a chord with our employees. At a group level, Johnson Matthey operates a charitable donations programme which includes support for organisations working in the areas of environment, medical and health, science and education, social welfare and international development. The programme includes an annual donations scheme where a number of charities are selected triennially and receive a donation from the company each year for a three year period. In 2009/10 48 charitable causes received an annual donation through this scheme. The group's programme also considers individual requests for support throughout the year and a further 44 charitable organisations received donations on this basis in 2009/10.

The group also has a specific programme of support focused on promoting the understanding and awareness of science among children and young people. During the year we have worked with StemNet, a UK organisation that creates opportunities for young people in science, technology, engineering and mathematics (STEM), to develop practical materials for use in school STEM clubs. The programme we have devised, called 'Sustainability is Precious', has been trialled by several schools and will be rolled out nationally later this year.

Johnson Matthey continues to operate its annual charity of the year programme and employee views are considered when deciding on the charity. The group is supporting Alzheimer's Society in 2009/10 and further details on the partnership are available in the Sustainability Report. Johnson Matthey's sites around the world also lend support to many other charities locally and nationally through donations, employee time or loans of company facilities.

Royston, UK is home to Johnson Matthey's global headquarters and is the company's largest site. For several years the company has supported the town's initiative to become a Business Improvement District (BID) and has provided management time and £50,000 of financial support. Achieving BID status requires local businesses to vote in favour of making a small increase in their business rate payments. These are then directly reinvested to provide funds for the improvement of the town's facilities with the aim of creating a better place to live and work. Royston successfully gained its BID status in April 2009 and Johnson Matthey continues to be involved in the implementation of the improvement plans.

→ Johnson Matthey is supporting Royston's BID initiative. John Gourd of Johnson Matthey (centre) with Oliver Heald, MP for Hertfordshire North East (left) and Geraint Burnell of Royston First (right).

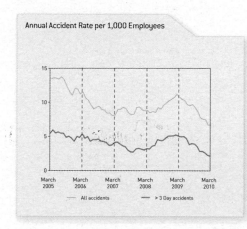

Annual Accident Rate per 1,000 Employees

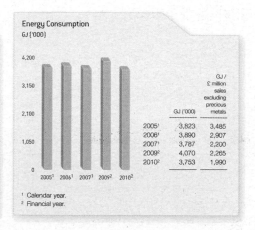

Energy Consumption
GJ ('000)

	GJ ('000)	GJ / £ million sales excluding precious metals
2005[1]	3,823	3,485
2006[1]	3,890	2,907
2007[1]	3,787	2,200
2009[2]	4,070	2,265
2010[2]	3,753	1,990

[1] Calendar year.
[2] Financial year.

REPORT OF THE DIRECTORS – BUSINESS REVIEW

In the financial year to 31st March 2010 Johnson Matthey donated £458,000 to charitable organisations. This figure only includes donations made by Johnson Matthey and does not include payroll giving, donations made by staff or employee time. The company made no political donations in the year. We will continue to support a wide range of charitable causes in 2010/11.

Stakeholder Engagement
Johnson Matthey has a wide range of stakeholders with an interest in hearing from or working with the company. These include customers, employees, fund managers, shareholders, communities, governments, non-governmental organisations (NGOs) and national and international trade associations. We aim to provide meaningful and transparent communications to meet the needs of all stakeholder groups and deliver information to them in the most appropriate format. These formats may include annual performance reports, participation in performance indices (Carbon Disclosure Project, FTSE4Good, Dow Jones Sustainability Index, for example) or one to one discussions on specific topics. We communicate with our stakeholders throughout the year and engagement is integrated into business decision making processes.

The company is actively involved with the Chemical Industries Association (CIA), the European Precious Metals Federation (EPMF) and plays a leading advisory role through participation in a number of sector trade associations and government bodies. The company is also engaged with national and local government to inform the development of policy in areas where Johnson Matthey's technology and products can play a pivotal role.

Neil Carson, Chief Executive of Johnson Matthey, is a prominent member of the Corporate Leaders Group and is a member of the Advisory Board for the Cambridge Programme for Sustainability Leadership. A number of the company's senior management are involved in the UK government's sustainability and climate change initiatives. Johnson Matthey's executives have also made a contribution to a range of organisations and committees during the year, such as the Carbon Trust, and the company continues to participate in numerous government consultations. We have also continued to support the activities of Forum for the Future and the Green Alliance.

At regular meetings with the company's major shareholders, matters relating to sustainability and corporate social responsibility may be discussed together with the performance and development of the group's businesses.

During the year Johnson Matthey was awarded the Chemical Industries Association 2009 Award for Environmental Leadership. It also received two awards at the inaugural Institute of Chartered Secretaries and Administrators (ICSA) Hermes Transparency in Governance Awards, one for Best Practice Disclosure on Sustainability and a second for Best Practice Disclosure on Stakeholder Engagement. The company is committed to achieving high standards of reporting and disclosure to enhance openness and dialogue between the company's board and its investors and other stakeholders. Winning these two awards recognises our commitment to maintaining a well run company and to achieving best practice in our corporate governance reporting.

Throughout the year the company has sought to engage with its stakeholders to garner views on how we report our sustainability performance and the level of confidence it provides. A structured survey was devised and input was received from suppliers, customers, NGOs and institutional investors. This is being used to direct the structure of our reports going forward.

Health and Safety
We are committed to minimising the health and safety related impacts for employees, customers and communities and of our products in use. In addition, many of our products and services make a contribution to enhancing general health and wellbeing or provide safety benefits.

For Johnson Matthey, any accident is unacceptable and our target is zero greater than three day accidents. In July 2009 however, an employee of a contractor company who was engaged in work at Johnson Matthey's catalyst manufacturing site in Taloja, India received a severe electric shock whilst carrying out work at the site. Regrettably, despite hospital treatment, his life could not be saved. Investigations have been carried out by site personnel, supported by Group EHS department staff. A police investigation has also been conducted.

BUSINESS REVIEW

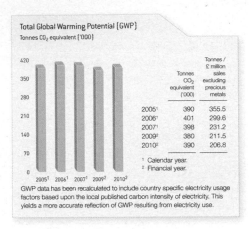

Total Global Warming Potential [GWP]
Tonnes CO₂ equivalent ['000]

	Tonnes CO₂ equivalent ('000)	Tonnes / £ million sales excluding precious metals
2005[1]	390	355.5
2006[1]	401	299.6
2007[1]	398	231.2
2009[2]	380	211.5
2010[2]	390	206.8

[1] Calendar year.
[2] Financial year.

GWP data has been recalculated to include country specific electricity usage factors based upon the local published carbon intensity of electricity. This yields a more accurate reflection of GWP resulting from electricity use.

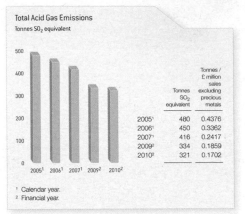

Total Acid Gas Emissions
Tonnes SO₂ equivalent

	Tonnes SO₂ equivalent	Tonnes / £ million sales excluding precious metals
2005[1]	480	0.4376
2006[1]	450	0.3362
2007[1]	416	0.2417
2009[2]	334	0.1859
2010[2]	321	0.1702

[1] Calendar year.
[2] Financial year.

Accident Statistics

	2010	2009	Change %
Incidence of greater than three day accidents per 1,000 employees	2.14	5.03[1]	-57
Total number of accidents that resulted in lost time	60	106[1]	-43
Total accident rate per 1,000 employees	6.77	10.83[1]	-37
Total lost time accident incident rate per 100,000 hours worked	0.34	0.53	-36
Total number of days lost per 1,000 employees	64	124[1]	-48

[1] Restated.

Accidents are actively monitored and detailed statistics are compiled monthly at group level. Any accident is thoroughly investigated to determine root causes and appropriate preventative and corrective actions are assigned. The group's five year performance is shown in the graph on page 35. In 2009/10 Johnson Matthey's rate of occupational accidents involving lost time, shown in the table above, has fallen to its lowest reported level. Following our disappointing performance in 2008/09 the company took action to revitalise its accident prevention processes, introducing an EHS Learning Events programme. This group wide programme has already led to improvements in safety performance and a sharpened awareness and understanding of workplace risks. The EHS Learning Events programme will be updated and expanded in 2010/11 to incorporate the learning acquired during its first year.

Johnson Matthey has a mature system for reporting accidents and incidents that involve the group's employees. However, it is not currently possible to determine the safety performance of all contractors working at our facilities. The company engages temporary workers typically to cover periods of long term sickness absence, maternity leave or to manage seasonal variations in workload. During 2010/11, new safety performance metrics specifically for contractors will be introduced which are similar to those already in place for group employees.

A corporate reporting system is used to report and investigate occupational illness cases arising as a result of exposure to workplace health hazards. In 2009/10 the incidence of cases reported was 5.2 cases per 1,000 employees (0.26 cases per 100,000 employee work hours) compared to 5.5 cases per 1,000 employees (restated) in 2008/09.

The group has introduced a target to reduce the annual incidence of occupational illness cases by at least 30% by 2013/14 from a baseline incidence of 5.3 cases per 1,000 employees in calendar year 2008 (to 3.7 cases or less per 1,000 employees by 2013/14). To help achieve this target, a new corporate chemical exposure management programme has been developed during 2009/10 which is now being implemented globally at all facilities. This aims to reduce the risk of chemical exposure related health effects to as low a level as is reasonably achievable. During 2010/11 training will be provided at all facilities to assist with implementation of the programme. In addition, a programme to promote effective ergonomic risk management will be developed.

Plans are also underway to pilot a sustainable health leading metrics scorecard in 2010/11 which will enable facilities to continually improve the performance of preventive health initiatives.

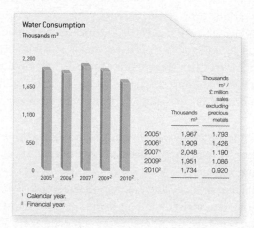

Water Consumption
Thousands m³

	Thousands m³	Thousands m³ / £ million sales excluding precious metals
2005[1]	1,967	1.793
2006[1]	1,909	1.426
2007[1]	2,048	1.190
2009[2]	1,951	1.086
2010[2]	1,734	0.920

[1] Calendar year.
[2] Financial year.

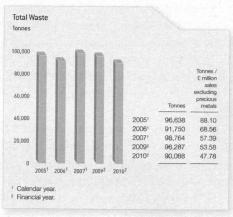

Total Waste
Tonnes

	Tonnes	Tonnes / £ million sales excluding precious metals
2005[1]	96,638	88.10
2006[1]	91,750	68.56
2007[1]	98,764	57.39
2009[2]	96,287	53.58
2010[2]	90,088	47.78

[1] Calendar year.
[2] Financial year.

Environment

Johnson Matthey has an impact on the environment in many ways; through the resources we use, the way we operate our processes and the action of our products and services on enhancing the environment for others.

We undertake a comprehensive annual review of group environmental performance which covers all manufacturing and research and development facilities. Five key performance metrics (energy consumption, global warming potential, acid gas emissions, water use and waste produced) are reported here and are shown in the tables on pages 35 to 37. Where necessary, past environmental data has been restated to reflect changes in the business, for example divestments and site closures. Additional environmental performance metrics are presented in the company's Sustainability Report.

2009/10 saw steady progress with reductions in energy and water use, acid gas emissions and waste produced, despite the inclusion of data this year from three major new manufacturing facilities. Manufacturing sites across the group continued to make progress against their individual environmental improvement targets in 2009/10 which has had a positive impact on overall group performance.

The group's total global warming potential (GWP) is based on our Scope 1 and Scope 2 emissions. Data relating to the group's GWP has been recalculated to include country specific electricity usage factors based upon the local published carbon intensity of electricity. This yields a more accurate reflection of Johnson Matthey's GWP resulting from electricity use. The group's GWP increased by 3% in 2009/10. This increase is due in part to increased production (including that from the three new manufacturing facilities) but also due to the geographical mix of production where this year, a greater proportion of our total output originated in countries where the carbon intensity from grid electricity is high.

Continued progress has been made to implement ISO 14001, in line with our target of achieving registration at all major manufacturing sites in 2010. By the end of March 2010, 41 sites had achieved ISO 14001 registration representing around 93% of the group's manufacturing workforce. The remaining four manufacturing sites have plans in place to achieve registration during 2010/11.

Johnson Matthey's EHS Learning Events initiative (see page 36) is the group's flagship occupational safety programme which has delivered improved performance in its first year. In 2010/11, the programme will be extended beyond occupational safety matters and facilities will be encouraged to report environmental and health related issues as well as those involving at-risk safety behaviour.

Verification and Assurance

The Board of Directors, Audit Committee, Chief Executive's Committee and CSR Compliance Committee review sustainability issues as part of the company's risk management processes. The board believes that the internal measures taken to review the sustainability information provide a high level of confidence. Third party assurance of our full Sustainability Report has also been commissioned. The Sustainability Report 2009/10 will be published on the company's website at www.matthey.com in July 2010.

REPORT OF THE DIRECTORS – BUSINESS REVIEW

The UK Government, prior to May 2010, viewed CSR as the business contribution to sustainable development goals. They regarded CSR as essentially about how business takes account of its economic, social and environmental impacts in the way it operates – maximising the benefits and minimising the downsides. Indeed, the role played by businesses was clearly put at the centre of the Government's vision for the development of sustainable CSR, which saw 'UK businesses taking account of their economic, social and environmental impacts, and acting to address the key sustainable development challenges based on their core competences wherever they operate – locally, regionally and internationally'. However, following the general election of May 2010, the UK has been without a minister for CSR, thus putting the responsibility to continue its development firmly with businesses in the private sector.

CSR is about companies moving beyond a base of legal compliance to integrating socially responsible behaviour into their core values, and in recognition of the sound business benefits in doing so. In principle, CSR applies to SMEs as well as to large companies.

There is currently no consensus of 'best practice' in the area of social and **environmental reporting**. Nor is there a compulsory requirement for companies to include such statements in their annual reports and accounts. The Government's approach has been to encourage the adoption and reporting of CSR through best practice guidance, including development of a Corporate Responsibility Index and, where appropriate, intelligent regulation and fiscal incentives. Most large companies have reacted positively to the need for such reporting, although the quality, style and content, and the motives for inclusion, may vary from company to company. Motives may range from a genuine wish to contribute to the goal of sustainable development to simple reassurance, or attempts to mould and change opinion, and political lobbying.

While CSR does not currently appear one of the UK Government's top priorities, the European Union remains strongly supportive of CSR initiatives. The EU defines CSR as 'a concept whereby companies integrate social and environmental concerns in their business operations and in their interaction with their stakeholders on a voluntary basis'. The EU material on CSR may be viewed on its website at: *http://ec.europa.eu/enterprise/policies/sustainable-business/corporate-social-responsibility*.

Companies that include CSR reporting in their annual reports and accounts now endeavour to go beyond a simple outline of their environmental and social policies. Many companies include reports expanding on these policies in qualitative ways that explain the performance of the business in its compliance with national and international standards. Some companies (for example, Johnson Matthey Plc) have taken the next step to provide detailed quantitative reports of targets, performance, and the financial impact of social and environmental issues.

CSR performance reporting is still in its infancy. Although there has not been a great deal of work on what really constitutes best practice in CSR reporting, some research has suggested that the higher standards of quality in CSR reporting are to be found in large companies which have the potential for greater impacts on the environment. Companies engaged in CSR may benefit from improvements in their image and reputation, and in the longer term perhaps their profitability. As the focus on standardisation of targets, indicators and audit of social and environmental performance increases, then the pressure for wider reporting may increase, and perhaps may be supported by a CSR financial reporting standard.

Progress check 8.7

What is sustainability reporting and why is it becoming increasingly important to companies?

Responsibility of directors report

The responsibility of directors report included in Johnson Matthey's report and accounts 2010 (see page 206 in Chapter 6) emphasises the responsibility that directors of companies have for the preparation of the annual report and accounts. The report states that the directors are responsible for preparing the annual report and the group and parent company accounts in accordance with company law requirements for each financial year. Under that law they are required to prepare the group accounts in accordance with International Financial Reporting Standards (IFRSs) as adopted by the European Union (EU) and applicable law and have elected to prepare the parent company accounts on the same basis. The group and parent company accounts are required by law and IFRSs as adopted by the EU to present fairly the financial position of the group and the parent company and the performance for that period; the Companies Act 2006 provides in relation to such accounts that references in the relevant part of that Act to accounts giving a true and fair view are references to their achieving a fair presentation.

The directors are required to:

- select suitable accounting policies and apply them consistently
- make judgements and estimates that are reasonable and prudent
- state whether they have been prepared in accordance with IFRSs as adopted by the EU
- prepare the accounts on the going concern basis unless it is inappropriate to presume that the group and parent company will continue in business.

Each of the directors of a company whose names and functions are listed within the annual report and accounts, are required to confirm that:

- they have complied with applicable UK law and in conformity with IFRSs in preparation of their financial statements
- the financial statements give a true and fair view of the assets, liabilities, financial position and profit or loss of the company and all companies included within their consolidated group accounts as a whole
- they have provided a fair review of the development and performance of the business and the position of the company and all companies included within their consolidated group accounts as a whole, together with a description of the principal risks and uncertainties they face.

Progress check 8.8

What purpose does the responsibility of directors report serve and what information does it usually include?

Inflation and reporting

Inflation is a general increase in the price level over time. We will consider the impact of inflation on the financial statements prepared under the traditional, historical cost convention. In this book we will not cover in detail the alternative approaches to reporting the effect of inflation, other than to highlight the level of awareness of the problem. The accountancy profession has, over the years, considered many proposals for methods to try and deal with inflation-related problems requiring financial reports to reflect the effects of inflation. The proposals relating to the treatment of inflation in financial reporting have revolved around two schools of thought:

- the purchasing power approach, using a price index like the Retail Price Index (RPI), to adjust the historical costs of transactions
- the current cost accounting approach, which requires non-current assets and inventories to be included in the accounts at their current value rather than their historical cost.

We have previously discussed the reasons for using money as the unit of measurement, which include its properties as a medium of exchange and a store of value. Its use implies some stability in its value, which in the real world is patently not the case. One £ held today does not have the same value as one £ held in a year's time; it will purchase less in a year's time despite the relatively low levels of inflation prevailing in the UK over recent years – but note how in the mid-1970s the inflation level reached nearly 25% per annum!

The basic problem of inflation in financial reporting is that it tends to overstate profit calculated using traditional historical costs. In periods of inflation the impact on profit is seen in four key areas:

- borrowing and extended credit received are worth less in real terms when settled compared to when the borrowing took place or the credit was received, which is a gain for the business
- financial investments made and extended credit allowed are worth less in real terms when settled compared to when the investments took place or the credit was granted, which is a loss for the business
- depreciation of non-current assets is understated, being based on non-current assets' historical costs and so when assets eventually have to be replaced the replacement cost will be higher, for which the company may have provided insufficient cash resources
- closing inventories will be more likely to have higher values, on a like-for-like basis, compared with opening inventories and so profit may be overstated, but the pressure on cash resources will be felt when inventories have been sold and then need to be replaced at higher prices.

It is important for the non-accounting specialist to be aware that the published financial statements of UK limited companies have not been adjusted to allow for the effects of inflation. Over extended periods there is therefore significant distortion in the accounting information that has been presented based on historical costs. However, the non-specialist may be assured that the accountancy profession continues to grapple with the problem of inflation in financial reporting.

Progress check 8.9

Why should users of financial information be aware of the effects of inflation on financial reporting?

Value added statements

Value added is a measure of the wealth created by a company through its activities. It is the difference between the value of its sales and the cost of the materials and services that it has bought in.

The **value added statement** is effectively a rearrangement of the income statement. It shows how value added is distributed among the relevant parties:

- employees
- lenders
- shareholders
- government

and the amount to provide maintenance and expansion of the business.

The value added statement has often been compared with a cake or a pie, with interested parties asking 'are we getting our fair share of the cake?' This question is often the basis of trades union employee wage negotiations with companies.

The Accounting Standards Committee in 1975 published *The Corporate Report*, which described the value added statement as 'the simplest and most immediate way of putting profit into a proper perspective *vis à vis* the whole enterprise as a collective effort of capital, management and employees'. The value added statement has certain advantages as a business performance measure as it:

- is simple to calculate
- enables comparison between companies with different activities
- improves relationships between shareholders, managers and employees
- cannot be manipulated to the same extent as accounting profit
- enables further analysis, for example vertical analysis against revenue
- lends itself to integration with employee incentive schemes.

The value added statement for Johnson Matthey Plc shown in Worked example 8.6 illustrates how value added has been derived and how it has been applied in absolute terms for the years 2009 and 2010. A vertical analysis of the numbers perhaps provides a better basis for comparison, which is illustrated in Worked example 8.7.

Worked example 8.6

We can prepare a value added statement for Johnson Matthey Plc using the consolidated income statements, and consolidated statement of cash flows for 2010 and 2009. Employee costs for 2010 were £403.9m (2009, £361.8m).

Johnson Matthey Plc
Consolidated value added statement for the year ended 31 March 2010

Figures in £m	2010	2009
Sales revenue (from the consolidated income statement)	7,839.4	7,847.8
Bought in materials and services (balancing number)	7,185.7	7,123.5
Value added	653.7	724.3
Applied as follows:		
To pay employees	403.9	361.8
To pay providers of capital (from the consolidated income statement)		
Net interest on loans (from the consolidated statement of cash flows)	21.1	33.7
Dividends to shareholders (from the consolidated statement of changes in equity)	78.4	78.1
To pay Government		
Income tax (from the consolidated income statement)	64.3	76.7
To provide maintenance and expansion		
Depreciation, amortisation and impairment (from the notes on the accounts)	97.9	203.5
Retained earnings (from the five-year record)	(11.9)	(29.5)
	653.7	724.3

Worked example 8.7

We can use the value added statement from Worked example 8.6 to:

prepare a vertical analysis of the data, and
present the results in a pie chart format (see Figs 8.7 and 8.8).

Johnson Matthey Plc
Consolidated vertical analysis value added statement
for the year ended 31 March 2010

	2010	2009
Value added	100.0	100.0
Applied as follows:		
To pay employees	61.8	50.0
To pay providers of capital		
Net interest on loans	3.2	4.6
Dividends to shareholders	12.0	10.8
To pay Government		
Income tax	9.8	10.6
To provide maintenance and expansion		
Depreciation	15.0	28.1
Retained earnings	(1.8)	(4.1)

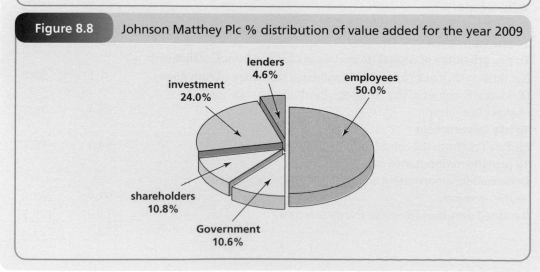

Figure 8.7 Johnson Matthey Plc % distribution of value added for the year 2010

investment 13.2%
lenders 3.2%
employees 61.8%
shareholders 12.0%
Government 9.8%

Figure 8.8 Johnson Matthey Plc % distribution of value added for the year 2009

lenders 4.6%
employees 50.0%
investment 24.0%
shareholders 10.8%
Government 10.6%

The vertical analysis of the value added statement for Johnson Matthey Plc shows us that over one half of the value generated by the business is distributed to employees in the form of salaries, wages and benefits (50.0% for 2009 up to 61.8% for 2010). The proportion of value added distributed to the providers of capital (lenders and shareholders) was 15.2% for 2010 (15.4% for 2009), and the proportion paid to lenders was lower in 2010 than 2009 (3.2% compared with 4.6%). Corporation tax fell from 10.6% in 2009 to 9.8% in 2010.

The remainder of value added is retained for maintenance and expansion of assets. This fell from 24.0% in 2009 to 13.2% in 2010, indicating a decrease in the financing of growth of the business through internally generated sources. Retained profits and depreciation were both lower in 2010 than in 2009.

The value added statement provides a great deal of clarification on company performance, but, of course, also has disadvantages:

- some difficulty encountered in measurement and reporting
- classification of items – for example taxation, which normally excludes employee tax and National Insurance, and business rates
- unstandardised format with varying treatment of items in the value added statement
- current lack of popularity among companies, despite the inclusion of a value added statement by a large percentage of large companies up to the early 1980s in their annual reports and accounts.

The value added statement seems unlikely to replace the conventional income statement or statement of cash flows as a decision-making tool or as a measure of business performance. However, it may continue to be useful for internal communication of company financial performance to employees, and in support of employee incentive schemes.

Progress check 8.10

What is a value added statement and what does it tell us?

Summary of key points

- Limited companies prepare their annual reports and accounts to keep shareholders informed about financial performance and the financial position of the business.

- The annual report and accounts of a public limited company requires disclosure of a great deal of both financial and non-financial information in addition to the financial statements.

- The annual report and accounts allows evaluation of a public limited company in a wider context than was possible from the sort of financial information traditionally required by the shareholders.

- Horizontal analysis of the income statement (which may also be applied to the balance sheet) for two or more years starts with a base year 100 and shows each item, line-by-line, indexed against the base year, and is particularly useful in looking at performance trends over a number of years.

- Vertical analysis of the income statement (which may also be applied to the balance sheet) shows every item as a percentage of revenue (or in the balance sheet – total assets), and is also particularly useful in looking at performance trends over a number of years.

- Segmental reporting provides a further dimension to the financial statements through analysis of revenues and expenses by operating segment and analysis of geographical results.

- The quality and depth of sustainability reporting, in both qualitative and quantitative terms, is becoming increasingly important as annual reports and accounts are required to meet the needs of all stakeholders, not just the shareholders.

- Although the financial statements of limited companies are not adjusted for the effects of inflation, the impact of inflation is a factor that must be considered in evaluation of business performance.

- The value added statement, which is an alternative presentation of the traditional income statement, measures wealth as the value added by the business rather than the profit earned by the business.

Assessment material

Questions

Q8.1 (i) Why, and for whom, do the annual reports and accounts of limited companies have to be prepared?

(ii) Where do they have to be filed?

(iii) Who are the main users of the information contained in the annual report and accounts?

(iv) How do they use the information?

Q8.2 (i) Why do you think that the directors, chairman, chief executive and finance director of a plc each need to provide a statement or report for inclusion in the annual report and accounts?

(ii) What purpose do these reports serve and in what ways do they differ?

Q8.3 (i) Describe the key elements of Johnson Matthey's financial review that are included in their report and accounts for 2010, and what these indicate about the performance of the business.

(ii) Why do you think that about a third of this report is devoted to financial risk management?

(iii) What does risk management mean?

(iv) What are the financial risks faced by Johnson Matthey?

Q8.4   Describe the technique of horizontal analysis and how it may be used to evaluate, explain and compare company performance.

Q8.5   Describe the technique of vertical analysis and how it may be used to evaluate, explain and compare company performance.

Q8.6   (i) What were the inadequacies in financial statement reporting that IFRS 8, Operating Segments, sought to address and how did it do this?

   (ii) What are the practical problems that companies face associated with their compliance with IFRS 8?

Q8.7   (i) Why do you think that sustainability reporting has become increasingly important in terms of corporate awareness, and with regard to the awareness of the non-business community?

   (ii) Examine the annual reports and accounts of a number of large UK plcs to critically evaluate and compare their sustainability reporting with that provided by Johnson Matthey in its 2010 report and accounts.

Q8.8   (i) How does inflation distort accounting information that has been prepared under the historical cost convention?

   (ii) In what ways has the accountancy profession considered some alternative approaches to try and deal with the problem of inflation?

Q8.9   (i) Explain what is meant by a value added statement.

   (ii) In what ways may a value added statement be used to measure financial performance?

   (iii) What are the disadvantages in using value added statements?

   (iv) Why do you think the levels of popularity they enjoyed in the 1980s have not been maintained?

Q8.10   What information included in the annual report and accounts of UK public listed companies (plcs) may influence prospective investors and in what ways? How impartial do you think this information is?

Discussion points

D8.1   'The annual reports and accounts prepared by the majority of UK plcs serve to ensure that shareholders, and other stakeholders, are kept very well informed about the affairs of their businesses.' Discuss.

D8.2   'In the global competitive world in which we live, company directors should be able to exercise their full discretion as to the amount of information they disclose in their annual reports and accounts. If they are not allowed this discretion in disclosure, their companies may be driven out of business by their competitors, particularly foreign competitors who may not have the restriction of such extensive reporting requirements.' Discuss.

D8.3   'The main reason that companies increasingly include sustainability reports in their annual reports and accounts is to change the views of users and regulators about the activities in which their businesses are engaged, in order to pre-empt and avoid any negative or harmful reactions.' Discuss this statement by drawing on examples of the type of businesses to which this might apply.

   (Hint: You may wish to research British Gas, as well as Johnson Matthey Plc, to provide material for this discussion.)

Exercises

Solutions are provided in Appendix 3 to all exercise numbers highlighted in colour.

Level I

E8.1   *Time allowed – 60 minutes*

Refer to note 1 in Johnson Matthey Plc's notes on the accounts in their annual report and accounts 2010 and identify the geographical analysis by origin for 2010 and 2009 for:

(a) total revenue
(b) non-current assets.

> (i)   Present each of the data from (a) and (b) in both pie chart and bar chart format.
> (ii) What do the charts you have prepared tell you about Johnson Matthey's revenue and non-current assets for 2010 and 2009?

E8.2   *Time allowed – 60 minutes*

> (i)   Use the five-year record of Johnson Matthey (see page 339) to prepare a horizontal analysis of the income statement for the five years 2006 to 2010, using 2006 as the base year.
> (ii) What does this analysis tell us about Johnson Matthey's financial performance over that period?

E8.3   *Time allowed – 60 minutes*

> (i)   Use the five-year record of Johnson Matthey (see page 339) to prepare a horizontal analysis of the balance sheet for the five years 2006 to 2010, using 2006 as the base year.
> (ii) What does this analysis tell us about Johnson Matthey's financial position over that period?

Level II

E8.4   *Time allowed – 60 minutes*

> (i)   Use the five-year record of Johnson Matthey (see page 339) to prepare a vertical analysis of the income statement for the five years 2006 to 2010.
> (ii) What does this analysis tell us about Johnson Matthey's financial performance over that period?

E8.5   *Time allowed – 60 minutes*

Note 1 in the Johnson Matthey Plc notes on the accounts in their annual report and accounts 2010 provides a segmental analysis for the years 2010 and 2009.

> Prepare a horizontal analysis from this information, with 2009 as the base year, and use it to explain the appropriate elements of financial performance and the changes in the financial position of the business.

FIVE YEAR RECORD

	2006 £ million	2007 £ million	2008 £ million	2009 £ million	2010 £ million
Revenue	4,755.9	6,151.7	7,498.7	7,847.8	7,839.4
Sales excluding the value of precious metals	1,341.2	1,454.2	1,750.2	1,796.9	1,885.5
EBITDA	305.5	329.9	374.1	398.1	382.7
Depreciation	(64.7)	(68.6)	(68.3)	(88.7)	(97.3)
Amortisation	(5.3)	(6.1)	(9.0)	(10.9)	(13.6)
Underlying operating profit	235.5	255.2	296.8	298.5	271.8
Amortisation of acquired intangibles	(0.8)	(2.8)	(3.1)	(9.1)	(9.9)
Major impairment and restructuring charges	(6.0)	–	–	(9.4)	(11.3)
Operating profit	228.7	252.4	293.7	280.0	250.6
Net finance costs	(14.7)	(26.8)	(30.3)	(32.6)	(19.4)
Share of (loss) / profit of associates	(0.2)	0.9	(1.1)	2.0	1.7
Dissolution of associate	–	–	–	–	(4.4)
Profit before tax	213.8	226.5	262.3	249.4	228.5
Income tax expense	(62.5)	(64.7)	(77.2)	(76.7)	(64.3)
Profit after taxation	151.3	161.8	185.1	172.7	164.2
Profit for the year from discontinued operations	–	43.7	0.3	1.2	–
Minority interests	0.8	1.0	0.8	0.2	–
Profit attributable to equity holders of the parent company	152.1	206.5	186.2	174.1	164.2
Underlying earnings per ordinary share	73.0p	82.2p	89.5p	89.6p	86.4p
Earnings per ordinary share	70.8p	96.9p	88.5p	82.6p	77.6p
Dividend per ordinary share	30.1p	33.6p	36.6p	37.1p	39.0p
Summary Balance Sheet					
Assets employed:					
Goodwill	402.4	399.2	480.4	516.0	513.8
Property, plant and equipment / other intangible assets	702.4	640.8	827.9	1,060.5	1,053.2
Non-current investments / associates	10.2	9.6	8.9	12.1	10.9
Inventories	345.8	362.7	380.4	371.7	390.1
Receivables / current investments / tax assets / financial assets	497.1	549.2	712.4	585.9	718.9
Payables / provisions / tax liabilities / financial liabilities	(520.2)	(519.5)	(655.7)	(684.1)	(717.0)
Post-employment benefits net assets / employee benefits obligations	18.8	0.9	16.4	(151.6)	(245.7)
	1,456.5	1,442.9	1,770.7	1,710.5	1,724.2
Financed by:					
Net debt	412.0	364.8	610.4	534.4	473.4
Retained earnings	708.0	783.7	879.1	849.6	837.7
Share capital, share premium, shares held in ESOTs and other reserves	330.1	292.0	279.8	325.7	411.7
Minority interests	6.4	2.4	1.4	0.8	1.4
Capital employed	1,456.5	1,442.9	1,770.7	1,710.5	1,724.2
Return on invested capital	17.1%	17.6%	18.5%	17.1%	15.8%

(Underlying operating profit / average capital employed)

The balance sheet for 2008 has been restated for the changes to Argillon Group's fair value at acquisition and goodwill on acquisition.

OTHER INFORMATION

E8.6 *Time allowed – 60 minutes*

Refer to the financial statements included in Johnson Matthey's report and accounts 2010 to calculate the appropriate ratios for comparison with the previous year, and include them in a report on the profitability of the group (see Chapter 7).

E8.7 *Time allowed – 60 minutes*

Refer to the financial statements included in Johnson Matthey's report and accounts 2010 to calculate the appropriate ratios for comparison with the previous year, and to give your assessment of the company's sources and uses of cash, and include them in a report on the group's cash position (see Chapter 7).

E8.8 *Time allowed – 60 minutes*

Refer to the financial statements included in Johnson Matthey's report and accounts 2010 to calculate the appropriate ratios for comparison with the previous year, and include them in a report on the working capital of the group (see Chapter 7).

E8.9 *Time allowed – 60 minutes*

Refer to the financial statements included in Johnson Matthey's report and accounts 2010 to calculate the appropriate ratios for comparison with the previous year, and include them in a report on the investment performance of the group (see Chapter 7).

E8.10 *Time allowed – 60 minutes*

Refer to the financial statements included in Johnson Matthey's report and accounts 2010 to calculate the appropriate ratios for comparison with the previous year, and include them in a report on the financial structure of the group (see Chapter 7).

E8.11 *Time allowed – 90 minutes*

The notes and five-year income statement extracts from the financial statements of an alcoholic drinks group are shown below.

You are required to use these to carry out an appropriate analysis and provide a report on the likely explanations of differences in performance over the five years.

Notes:

■ The group sells alcohol-based products to consumers and operates in nearly every major country throughout the world.
■ Local and global competition is intense in many markets.
■ Brands have been sold during the five years.
■ New products are invariably variants on the group's basic products of beers, wines and spirits.
■ The group share price had been relatively static due to the maturity of the market and the pattern of profits.

- Other investment income shown in the five-year analysis related to an investment in a French luxury goods group.
- Soon after year six the group merged with another international food and drinks business, which also had an extensive portfolio of own and purchased brands.
- After the merger several brands were sold to competitors.
- After the merger many of the directors left the group's management team.
- Exchange rates over the five-year period in several of the group's markets were quite volatile.
- The group had £1.4 billion of brands in its balance sheet.

Five-year income statement

	Year 5 £m	Year 4 £m	Year 3 £m	Year 2 £m	Year 1 £m
Sales revenue	4,730	4,681	4,690	4,663	4,363
Gross profit	961	943	956	938	1,023
Other investment income	113	47	89	(48)	(24)
Operating profit	1,074	990	1,045	890	999
Finance cost	(99)	(114)	(130)	(188)	(204)
Profit before tax	975	876	915	702	795
Income tax expense	(259)	(251)	(243)	(247)	(242)
Profit after tax	716	625	672	455	553
Minority interests	(31)	(30)	(31)	(22)	(29)
Profit for the year	685	595	641	433	524
Dividends	(295)	(302)	(279)	(258)	(237)
Retained earnings	390	293	362	175	287
Earnings per share	35.1p	29.4p	31.8p	22.9p	28.1p
Interest cover	10.8	8.7	8.0	4.7	4.9
Dividend cover	2.2	2.0	2.3	1.8	2.3

E8.12 *Time allowed – 90 minutes*

The BOC Group is a company in the chemical industry, and is in the same industrial sector as Johnson Matthey Plc. Locate the website for BOC Group plc on the Internet. Review their most recent annual report and accounts and prepare a report that compares it with Johnson Matthey Plc's report and accounts for the same year. Your report should include comments that relate to specific points that have been covered in Chapter 8, and also the differences and the similarities between the two companies.

Case Study I
BUZZARD LTD

The Buzzard Group is a first-tier global supplier to major passenger car and commercial vehicle manufacturers. As a first-tier supplier Buzzard provides systems that fit directly into motor vehicles, which they have manufactured from materials and components acquired from second, third, fourth-tier, etc., suppliers. During the 2000s, through investment in R&D and technology, Buzzard became regarded as one of the world's leaders in design, manufacture and supply of innovative automotive systems.

In the mid-2000s Buzzard started business in one of the UK's many development areas. It was established through acquisition of the business of Firefly from the Stonehead Group by a Buzzard subsidiary, Buzzard Ltd. Firefly was a traditional, mass production automotive component manufacturer, located on a brownfield site in Gentbridge, once a fairly prosperous mining area. Firefly had pursued short-term profit rather than longer-term development strategies, and had a poor image with both its customers and suppliers. This represented a challenge but also an opportunity for Buzzard Ltd to establish a world class manufacturing facility.

A major part of Buzzard's strategic plan was the commitment to investing £30m to relocate from Gentbridge to a new fully equipped 15,000 square metre purpose-built factory on a 20-acre greenfield site in Bramblecote, which was finally completed during the year 2010. At the same time, it introduced the changes required to transform its culture and implement the operating strategies required to achieve the highest level of industrial performance. By the year 2010 Buzzard Ltd had become an established supplier of high quality and was close to achieving its aim of being a world class supplier of innovative automotive systems.

In December 2010 a seven-year bank loan was agreed with interest payable half yearly at a fixed rate of 5% per annum. The loan was secured with a floating charge over the assets of Buzzard Ltd.

The financial statements of Buzzard Ltd, its accounting policies and extracts from its notes to the accounts, for the year ended 31 December 2010 are shown below, prior to the payment of any proposed dividend. It should be noted that note 3 to the accounts – profit for the year – reports on some of the key items included in the income statement for the year and is not a complete analysis of the income statement.

Required

(i) Prepare a SWOT analysis for Buzzard Ltd based on the limited information available.

(ii) What do you consider to be the main risks faced by Buzzard Ltd, both internally and external to the business, based on your SWOT analysis and your own research about the automotive industry in the UK?

(iii) Prepare a report for shareholders that describes Buzzard Ltd's performance, supported by the appropriate profitability, efficiency, liquidity and investment ratios required to present as complete a picture as possible from the information that has been provided.

(iv) The company has demonstrated its achievement of high levels of quality and customer satisfaction but would you, as a shareholder, be satisfied with the financial performance of Buzzard Ltd?

**Income statement
for the year ended 31 December 2010**

	Notes	2010 £000	2009 £000
Revenue	1	115,554	95,766
Cost of sales		(100,444)	(80,632)
Gross profit		15,110	15,134
Distribution costs		(724)	(324)
Administrative expenses		(12,348)	(10,894)
Operating profit		2,038	3,916
Finance costs	2	(1,182)	(1,048)
Finance income	2	314	76
Profit for the year from continuing operations	3	1,170	2,944
Income tax expense		–	–
Profit for the year		1,170	2,944

The company has no recognised gains and losses other than those included above.

**Balance sheet
as at 31 December 2010**

	Notes	2010 £000	2009 £000
Non-current assets			
Tangible assets	8	42,200	29,522
Total non-current assets		42,200	29,522
Current assets			
Inventories	9	5,702	4,144
Trade and other receivables	10	18,202	16,634
Cash and cash equivalents		4	12
Total current assets		23,908	20,790
Total assets		66,108	50,312
Current liabilities	11	23,274	14,380
Non-current liabilities			
Borrowings and finance leases	12	6,000	–
Provisions	13	1,356	1,508
Accruals and deferred income	14	1,264	1,380
Total non-current liabilities		8,620	2,888
Total liabilities		31,894	17,268
Net assets		34,214	33,044
Equity			
Share capital	15	22,714	22,714
Retained earnings		11,500	10,330
Total equity	16	34,214	33,044

**Statement of cash flows
for the year ended 31 December 2010**

	2010 £000	2009 £000
Cash flows from operating activities		
Net cash generated from operating activities	11,742	2,578
Cash flows from investing activities		
Purchases of non-current assets	(20,490)	(14,006)
Proceeds from sales of non-current assets	12	30
Interest received	314	76
Proceeds from Government grants	1,060	1,900
Net cash outflow from investing activities	(19,104)	(12,000)
Cash flows from financing activities		
Proceeds from issue of ordinary shares	–	8,000
Proceeds from borrowings	6,000	–
Net cash inflow from financing activities	6,000	8,000
Decrease in cash and cash equivalents in the year	(1,362)	(1,422)
Cash and cash equivalents and bank overdrafts at beginning of year	(1,974)	(552)
Cash and cash equivalents and bank overdrafts at end of year	(3,336)	(1,974)

Accounting policies

The financial statements have been prepared in accordance with applicable financial reporting standards. A summary of the more important accounting policies which have been applied consistently is set out below.

Basis of accounting The accounts are prepared under the historical cost convention.

Research and development Expenditure on research and development is written off as it is incurred.

Tangible non-current assets Tangible non-current assets are stated at their purchase price together with any incidental costs of acquisition.

Depreciation is calculated so as to write off the cost of tangible non-current assets on a straight line basis over the expected useful economic lives of the assets concerned. The principal annual rates used for this purpose are:

Freehold buildings	20 years
Plant and machinery (including capitalised tooling)	4–8 years
Office equipment and fixtures and fittings	5–8 years
Motor vehicles	4 years
Freehold land is not depreciated.	

Government grants Grants received on qualifying expenditure or projects are credited to deferred income and amortised in the income statement over the estimated useful lives of the qualifying assets or over the project life as appropriate.

Inventories and work in progress Inventories and work in progress are stated at the lower of cost and net realisable value. In general, cost is determined on a first in first out basis; in the case of manufactured products cost includes all direct expenditure and production overheads based on the normal level of activity. Net realisable value is the price at which inventories can be sold in the normal course of business after allowing for the costs of realisation and, where appropriate, the cost of conversion from their existing state to a finished condition. Provision is made where necessary for obsolescent, slow moving and defective inventories.

Foreign currencies Assets, liabilities, revenues and costs denominated in foreign currencies are recorded at the rate of exchange ruling at the date of the transaction; monetary assets and liabilities at the balance sheet date are translated at the year-end rate of exchange or where there are related forward foreign exchange contracts, at contract rates. All exchange differences thus arising are reported as part of the results for the period.

Revenue Sales revenue represents the invoiced value of goods supplied, excluding value added tax.

Warranties for products Provision is made for the estimated liability arising on all known warranty claims. Provision is also made, using past experience, for potential warranty claims on all sales up to the balance sheet date.

Notes to the accounts
1 Segmental analysis

	Revenue		Profit before tax	
	2010 £000	2009 £000	2010 £000	2009 £000
Class of business				
Automotive components	115,554	95,766	1,170	2,944
Geographical segment				
United Kingdom	109,566	92,020		
Rest of Europe	5,290	3,746		
Japan	698	–		
	115,554	95,766		

2 Finance costs/income

	2010 £000	2009 £000
Interest payable on bank loans and overdrafts	(1,182)	(1,048)
Interest receivable	314	76
	(868)	(972)

3 Profit for the year from continuing operations

	2010 £000	2009 £000
Profit for the year is stated after crediting:		
Amortisation of government grant	1,176	796
(Loss)/profit on disposal of non-current assets	(18)	10
and after charging:		
Depreciation charge for the year:		
Tangible non-current assets	7,782	4,742
Research and development expenditure	7,694	6,418
Auditors' remuneration for:		
Audit	58	58
Other services	40	52
Hire of plant and machinery – operating leases	376	346
Hire of other assets – operating leases	260	314
Foreign exchange losses	40	20

4 Directors and employees

The average weekly number of persons (including executive directors) employed during the year was:

	2010 number	2009 number
Production	298	303
Engineering, quality control and development	49	52
Sales and administration	56	45
	403	400

Staff costs (for the above persons):	2010 £000	2009 £000
Wages and salaries	6,632	5,837
Social security costs	562	483
Other pension costs	286	218
	7,480	6,538

8 Tangible non-current assets

	Freehold land and buildings £000	Motor vehicles £000	Plant, machinery and tooling £000	Office equipment, fixtures and fittings £000	Total £000
Cost					
At 1 January 2010	15,450	114	20,648	4,600	40,812
Additions	20	28	19,808	634	20,490
Disposals	–	–	(80)	(10)	(90)
At 31 December 2010	15,470	142	40,376	5,224	61,212
Depreciation					
At 1 January 2010	834	54	7,932	2,470	11,290
Charge for year	734	22	6,226	800	7,782
Eliminated in respect of disposals	–	–	(58)	(2)	(60)
At 31 December 2010	1,568	76	14,100	3,268	19,012
Net book value at 31 December 2010	13,902	66	26,276	1,956	42,200
Net book value at 31 December 2009	14,616	60	12,716	2,130	29,522

9 Inventories

	2010 £000	2009 £000
Raw materials and consumables	4,572	3,274
Work in progress	528	360
Finished goods and goods for resale	602	510
	5,702	4,144

10 Trade and other receivables

	2010 £000	2009 £000
Trade receivables	13,364	8,302
Other receivables	4,276	7,678
Prepayments and accrued income	562	654
	18,202	16,634

11 Current liabilities

	2010 £000	2009 £000
Bank overdraft	3,340	1,986
Trade payables	13,806	8,646
Other taxation and social security payable	2,334	1,412
Other payables	122	350
Accruals and deferred income	3,672	1,986
	23,274	14,380

12 Borrowings and finance leases

	2010 £000	2009 £000
Bank and other loans repayable otherwise than by instalments		
Over five years	6,000	–

13 Provisions

	Pensions £000	Warranties for products £000	Total £000
At 1 January 2010	732	776	1,508
Expended in the year	(572)	(494)	(1,066)
Charge to profit and loss account	562	352	914
At 31 December 2010	722	634	1,356

14 Accruals and deferred income

	2010 £000	2009 £000
Government grants		
At 1 January 2010	1,380	2,176
Amount receivable	1,060	–
Amortisation in year	(1,176)	(796)
At 31 December 2010	1,264	1,380

15 Equity

	2010 £000	2009 £000
Authorised share capital		
28,000,000 (2009: 28,000,000) ordinary shares of £1 each	28,000	28,000
Issued and fully paid share capital		
22,714,000 (2009: 22,714,000) ordinary shares of £1 each	22,714	22,714

16 Reconciliation of movement in shareholders' funds

	2010 £000	2009 £000
Opening shareholders' funds	33,044	22,100
Issue of ordinary share capital	–	8,000
Profit for the year	1,170	2,944
Closing shareholders' funds	34,214	33,044

17 Capital commitments

	2010 £000	2009 £000
Capital expenditure that has been contracted for but has not been provided for in the financial statements	1,506	162
Capital expenditure that has been authorised by the directors but has not yet been contracted for	6,768	5,404

18 Financial commitments

At 31 December 2010 the company had annual commitments under non-cancellable operating leases as follows:

	Land and buildings 2010 £000	Other 2010 £000	Land and buildings 2009 £000	Other 2009 £000
Expiring within one year	–	96	112	210
Expiring within two to five years	–	254	–	360
Expiring after five years	–	120	–	90
	–	470	112	660

Case Study II
DESIGN PIERRE LTD

Design Pierre Ltd is a designer and manufacturer of gift and presentation packaging, aimed particularly at the mass market, via jewellery shops, large retail chains and mail order companies. The company was founded many years ago by Pierre Girault, who was the managing director and was involved in the sales and marketing side of the business.

Towards the end of 2007 when Pierre was due to retire, Marie Girault, Pierre's daughter, joined the company as managing director, along with Erik Olsen as marketing director. Marie had worked as a senior manager with Saturn Gifts plc, a large UK designer and manufacturer of giftware, of which Erik had been a director. Marie and Erik capitalised on their experience with Saturn to present some very innovative ideas for developing a new product range for Design Pierre. However, Marie and Erik's ideas for expanding the business required additional investment, the majority of which was spent during the financial year just ended on 31 March 2010.

The share capital of Design Pierre Ltd, 800,000 £1 ordinary shares, had all been owned by Pierre himself. On retirement he decided to transfer 390,000 of his shares to his daughter Marie, and to sell 390,000 shares to Erik Olsen (to help fund his pension). Pierre gifted his remaining 20,000 shares to Nigel Finch, who was the production director and had given the company many years of loyal service. Although Marie had received her share in the company from her father, Erik had used a large part of his personal savings and had taken out an additional mortgage on his house to help finance his investment in the business. This was, of course, paid to Pierre Girault and did not provide any additional capital for the business.

In order to raise additional share capital, Marie and Erik asked Pierre's advice about friends, family and business contacts who may be approached. Pierre suggested approaching a venture capital company, Fishtale Ltd, which was run by a friend of his, Paul Fish. Fishtale already had a wide portfolio of investments in dot.com and service businesses, and Paul was interested in investing in this type of growing manufacturing business. He had known Pierre and the Girault family for many years, and was confident that Marie and Erik would make a success of the new ideas that they presented for the business. Additional capital was therefore provided from the issue of 800,000 new £1 shares at par to Fishtale Ltd, to become the largest shareholder of Design Pierre Ltd. Design Pierre Ltd also had a bank loan, which it increased during 2009/10, and had a bank overdraft facility.

The directors of the newly structured Design Pierre Ltd, and its shareholders were as follows:

Marie Girault	Managing director	390,000 shares
Erik Olsen	Marketing director	390,000 shares
Nigel Finch	Production director	20,000 shares
Paul Fish	Non-executive director	800,000 shares
Fishtale Ltd		

As a non-executive director of Design Pierre Ltd, Paul Fish attended the annual general meetings, and review meetings that were held every six months. He didn't have any involvement with the day-to-day management of the business.

The new range at Design Pierre did quite well and the company also began to export in a small way to the USA and Canada. Marie and Erik were pleased by the way in which the sales of the business had grown, and in the growth of their customer base. They had just received a large order from Norbox, a Swedish company, which was regarded as an important inroad into the Scandinavian market. If Norbox became a regular customer, the sales of the company were likely to increase rapidly over the next few years and would establish Design Pierre as a major player in the market.

In the first week of May 2010, the day that Design Pierre received the order from Norbox, Marie also received a letter from the bank manager. The bank manager requested that Design Pierre Ltd immediately and considerably reduce its overdraft, which he felt was running at a level which exposed the bank and the company to a higher level of risk then he was prepared to accept. Marie Girault was very angry and felt very frustrated. Marie, Erik and Nigel agreed that since they had just had such a good year's trading and the current year looked even better, the reduction in the overdraft facility was going to seriously jeopardise their ability to meet the commitments they had to supply their customers.

When they joined the company, Marie and Erik decided that Design Pierre, which had always been production led, would become a design- and marketing-led business. Therefore, a great deal of the strategic planning was concerned with integrating the product design and development with the sales and marketing operations of the business. Over the past three years Marie and Erik had invested in employing and training a young design team to help continue to develop the Design Pierre brand. The marketing team led by Erik had ensured that the enthusiasm of their key customers was converted into new firm orders, and that new orders were received from customers like Norbox. The order book grew until it had now reached the highest level ever for the company.

In addition to his role as production director, Nigel had always tended to look after the books and any financial matters. Nigel wasn't an accountant and he hadn't had any formal financial training. But, as he said, he had a small and experienced accounts team who dealt with the day-to-day transactions; if ever there had been a problem, they would ask Design Pierre's auditors for some advice.

As soon as she received the letter from the bank, Marie called the bank manager to try and persuade him to continue to support the overdraft facility at the current level, but with no success. Marie also convened an urgent meeting of the directors, including Paul Fish, to talk about the letter and the draft accounts of the business for the year ended 31 March 2010. The letter from the bank was distributed to all the directors before the meeting.

Erik Olsen was very worried about his investment in the company. He admitted that his accounting knowledge was fairly limited. He thought that the company was doing very well, and said that the draft accounts for the year to 31 March 2010 seemed to confirm their success. Profit before tax was more than double the profit for 2009. He couldn't understand why the cash flow was so bad. He appreciated that they had spent a great deal of money on the additional plant and equipment, but they had already had a bank loan to help with that. He thought that the cash situation should really be even better than the profit because the expenses included £1.5m for depreciation, which doesn't involve any cash at all.

Marie Girault still appeared very angry at the lack of support being given by the bank. She outlined the impact that the overdraft reduction would have on their ability to meet their commitments over the next year. She said that the bank's demand to cut their overdraft by 50% over the next three months put them in an impossible position with regard to being able to meet customer orders. Design Pierre Ltd couldn't find an alternative source of such a large amount of money in such a short time.

Erik, Marie and Nigel had, before the meeting, hoped that Paul Fish would be prepared to help out by purchasing further additional new shares in the company or by making a loan to the company. However, it was soon made clear by Paul that further investment was not a possible option. Fishtale Ltd had made a couple of new investments over the past few months and so did not have the money to invest further in Design Pierre. As a venture capitalist, Fishtale had actually been discussing the possible exit from Design Pierre by selling and trying to realise a profit on the shares. Finding a prospective buyer for their shares, or floating Design Pierre on the alternative investment market (AIM), did not currently appear to be a realistic option.

Paul Fish had been so much involved in running his own business, Fishtale Ltd, that he had neglected to monitor the financial position of Design Pierre Ltd as often and as closely as he should have done. At the directors' meeting he realised that he should have been much more attentive and there was now a possibility that Design Pierre would not provide the returns his company expected, unless things could be drastically improved.

The accounts of Design Pierre Ltd for the past two years are shown below:

Income statement for the year ended 31 March

	2009	2010
	£000	£000
Revenue	7,000	11,500
Cost of sales	3,700	5,800
Gross profit	3,300	5,700
Operating expenses	2,200	3,100
Operating profit	1,100	2,600
Interest paid	200	500
Profit before tax	900	2,100
Income tax expense	200	400
Profit for the year	700	1,700
Dividend	200	300
Retained earnings for the year	500	1,400
Retained earnings brought forward	1,100	1,600
Retained earnings carried forward	1,600	3,000

Balance sheet as at 31 March

	2009	2010
	£000	£000
Non-current assets	4,300	7,200
Current assets		
Inventories	1,200	2,900
Trade receivables	800	1,900
Other receivables	100	200
Cash and cash equivalents	100	–
Total current assets	2,200	5,000
Total assets	6,500	12,200
Current liabilities		
Borrowings and finance leases	–	2,100
Trade payables	600	1,300
Other payables	100	200
Income tax payable	200	400
Dividends payable	200	300
Total current liabilities	1,100	4,300
Non-current liabilities		
Loan	2,200	3,300
Total liabilities	3,300	7,600
Net assets	3,200	4,600

Equity

Ordinary shares (£1)	1,600	1,600
Retained earnings	1,600	3,000
Total equity	3,200	4,600

The directors of Design Pierre Ltd were unable to agree on a way of dealing with the financial problem faced by the company. Marie thought it best that she continue to try and negotiate with the bank manager, and believed that she could change the bank manager's mind if she:

- presented him with the accounts for 31 March 2010, which showed such good results, and
- made him fully aware of the implications of the reduction in the overdraft facility on the future of Design Pierre.

However, Erik and Nigel said that they were aware that Design Pierre Ltd had exceeded its agreed overdraft limit a few times over the past two years and so they were not confident that Marie could persuade the bank to change its mind. They suggested that they should try and find another investor prepared to provide additional funds for the business, to keep the business going. They really believed that the year-end accounts showed how successful Design Pierre had been over the past two years and that their track record was sufficient to attract a potential new investor in the business. Paul didn't agree. He felt that this would not be a practical solution. More importantly, Fishtale didn't want to have another large shareholder in the company because it would dilute its shareholding, and also reduce its influence over the future direction of the business. However, Paul agreed that immediate and radical action was necessary to be taken by the company.

After hours of argument and discussion, it became apparent that the problem would not be resolved at the meeting. Therefore, it was agreed by all present that expertise from outside the company should be sought to help the company find an acceptable and viable solution to the problem. The directors decided to approach Lucis Consulting, which specialises in helping businesses with financial problems, and to ask them to produce a plan of action for their consideration.

Required

As a member of the Lucis team, prepare a report for the board of directors of Design Pierre Ltd which analyses the problems faced by the company and which sets out a detailed plan of action for dealing with its financing problem.

Your report should be supported by the appropriate analyses, and a full statement of cash flows for the year ended 31 March 2010.

Part II

FINANCIAL MANAGEMENT

Outline of Part II

Part II is about financial management, which is broadly defined as the management of all the processes associated with the efficient acquisition and deployment of both short- and long-term financial resources. Businesses raise money from shareholders and lenders to invest in assets, which are used to increase the wealth of the business and its owners. The underlying fundamental economic objective of a company is to maximise shareholder wealth. Financial management includes management accounting which is concerned with looking at current issues and the future in terms of providing information to assist managers in decision-making, forecasting, planning and achievement of plans.

Chapter 9 provides an introduction to management accounting and the framework in which it operates. It looks at the nature and behaviour of costs and how they change in response to changes in levels of activity.

Chapter 10 takes a broad approach to the management of costs, and the relationships between costs, activity volumes and profit. This chapter introduces the topic of break-even analysis, and various approaches to the treatment of costs, and goes on to consider some of the more recently developed techniques of cost management, such as activity based costing (ABC), and includes non-financial performance measurement and the balanced scorecard.

Chapter 11 considers how some of the techniques of management accounting may be used in the decision-making process. Decision-making is looked at in the context of both costs and sales pricing.

Chapter 12 deals with the way in which businesses, as part of their strategic management process, translate their long-term objectives and plans into forecasts, short-term plans and budgets.

Chapter 13 deals with budgetary control. This is concerned with the periods after the budgeting process has been completed, in which actual performance may be compared with the budget. This chapter looks at how actual performance comparisons with budget may be made and analysed to explain deviations from budget, and to identify appropriate remedial actions.

Chapter 14 deals primarily with long-term, external sources of business finance for investment in businesses. This relates to the various types of funding available to business, including the raising of funds from the owners of the business (the shareholders) and from lenders external to the business. This chapter includes evaluation of the costs of the alternative sources of capital, which may be used in the calculation of the overall cost of capital that may be used by companies as the discount rate to evaluate proposed investments in capital projects, and in the calculation of economic value added (EVA).

Chapter 15 considers how businesses make decisions about potential investments that may be made, in order to ensure that the wealth of the business will be increased. This is an important area of decision-making that usually involves a great deal of money and relatively long-term commitments that therefore require techniques to ensure that the financial objectives of the company are in line with the interests of the shareholders.

In **Chapter 16** we look at one of the areas of funds management internal to the business, the management of working capital. Working capital comprises the short-term assets of the business, inventories, trade and other receivables, cash and cash equivalents, and claims on the business, trade and other payables. This chapter deals with how these important items may be effectively managed.

9

The nature of costs

Contents

Learning objectives

Completion of this chapter will enable you to:

■ outline the additional accounting concepts that relate to management accounting

■ explain what is meant by the term cost, and explain its nature and limitations

■ identify the bases for allocation and apportionment of costs

■ determine the costs of products, services and activities using the techniques of absorption costing and marginal costing

■ critically compare the techniques of absorption costing and marginal costing.

Introduction

The chapters included in Part I of this book were concerned with financial accounting, with particular emphasis on the three key financial statements: balance sheet; income statement; statement of cash flows. This has necessarily focused on the historical aspect of accounting. To use a car-driving analogy, we have made far more use of the rear view mirror than the view through the windscreen. We have concentrated on the accumulation of data and the reporting of past events, rather than the consideration of current and future activities.

We have previously identified accounting as having the three roles of maintaining the scorecard, problem-solving and attention-directing. The scorecard role, although primarily a financial accounting role, remains part of the responsibility of management accounting. However, its more important roles are those of problem-solving and attention-directing. These roles focus on current and future activities, with regard to the techniques involved in decision-making, planning and control that will be covered in this and subsequent chapters.

This chapter introduces management accounting by looking at some further concepts to those that were covered in Chapter 1. Management accounting is concerned with costs. We will look at what cost is, how costs behave and how costs are ascertained. This will include some of the approaches used to determine the costs of products and services.

Management accounting concepts

Management accountants are frequently involved in the preparation of financial information that relates to issues requiring senior management decisions. The outcomes of these are not always popular, for example the downsizing of businesses. Management accountants may also be involved in many more positive ways, for example in the development of businesses, as illustrated in the extract on the next page from the *Huddersfield Daily Examiner*.

We can see from the AS Fabrications example in the press extract that the management accounting function is extremely important in adding value to the business through its involvement in providing a sound reporting system upon which to base planning and control activities.

The management accounting function is extremely important in adding value to the business through its involvement in:

■ investment decision-making

■ scorecard design

■ development of budgetary control systems

■ capacity planning.

The importance of management accounting

A metalworking firm which rose from the wreckage of a devastating collapse has been recognised with a top award.

Liversedge-based AS Fabrications (UK) Ltd was formed just 12 months ago by managers who had been left high and dry when their company went into liquidation in May last year.

Although Glentworth Architectural Metalwork was trading profitably, the firm had to close because of financial problems in its parent group.

The shock collapse left the firm's directors and 40 staff out of work.

But instead of giving up, the management team took over the business just four weeks after being made redundant – and by obtaining financial support from HSBC and Yorkshire Forward were able to re-employ 18 of the axed workers.

Now the company has increased staffing levels to 39, introduced its own training schemes and is going from strength to strength with the backing of customers and suppliers.

Managing director Mick Fortune took the plaudits yesterday when he stepped up to receive the Business of the Year Award at a ceremony hosted by Huddersfield law firm Eaton Smith and its award partners Mid Yorkshire Chamber of Commerce and Business Link.

He said: 'As managers of the previous company, we picked up the pieces and established the new business under a new structure.

'We found financial support and we have based the business on a few fundamental values which should apply to every business – strict financial control, monthly management accounting, looking after our team and providing high quality customer service.

'We have tried to stick to these principles and it is paying dividends.'

Mr Fortune said winning the award had been a team effort by all the staff, adding: 'It shows that if you put the effort in you will get something out.'

Source: **Firm shows iron will to net major award,** by Henryk Zientek © *Huddersfield Daily Examiner*, 3 July 2010

The management accounting function may also be involved in many more important areas of business activity, for example:

- planning and preparation of business plans
- directing attention to specific areas and providing proposed solutions to actual and anticipated problems
- formulation of cost-cutting proposals and the evaluation of their impact on current and future operations
- preparation of forecasts
- negotiation with bankers for funding
- analysis and interpretation of internal and external factors in support of strategic decision-making.

Management accounting is an integral part of management, requiring the identification, generation, presentation, interpretation and use of information relevant to the activities outlined in Figure 9.1:

- formulating business strategy involves setting the long-term objectives of the business
- planning and controlling activities deal with short-term objectives and investigations into the differences that may arise from actual outcomes against the plan and the recommendation and implementation of remedial actions
- decision-making includes identification of those items of information relevant to a particular decision and those items that may be ignored

> **Figure 9.1**   The areas of business activity supported by management accounting
>
>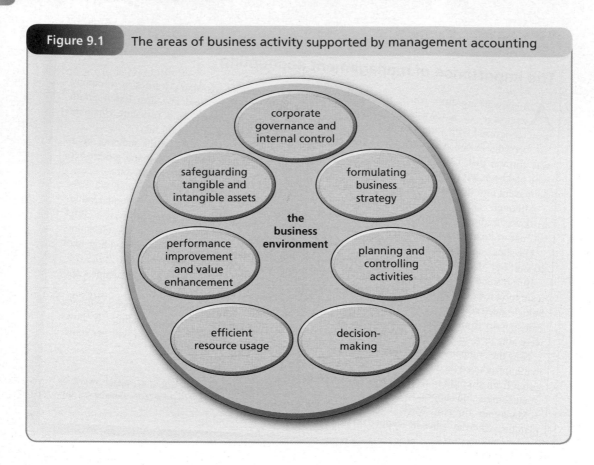

- efficient resource usage may be determined from the process of setting short-term budget plans and in their implementation
- performance improvement and value enhancement includes cost reduction and profit improvement exercises and the implementation of improvement initiatives such as quality costing, continuous improvement and **benchmarking**
- safeguarding tangible and intangible assets – the management of non-current assets, and working capital (which we shall look at in more detail in Chapter 16) are key financial management responsibilities in ensuring that there is no undue diminution in the value of assets such as buildings, machinery, inventories, and trade receivables, as a result, for example, of poor management and weak physical controls, and to ensure that every endeavour is made to maximise returns from the use of those assets
- corporate governance and internal control were considered in Chapter 6 and are concerned with the ways in which companies are controlled, the behaviour and accountability of directors and their levels of remuneration, and disclosure of information.

Therefore, it can be seen that management accounting, although providing information for external reporting, is primarily concerned with the provision of information to people within the organisation for:

- product costing
- forecasting, planning and control
- decision-making.

Outline what is meant by management accounting and give examples of areas of business activity in which it may be involved.

In addition to the fundamental accounting concepts that were discussed in Chapter 1, there are further fundamental management accounting concepts (see Fig. 9.2). These do not represent any form of external regulation but are fundamental principles for the preparation of internal management accounting information. A brief outline of these principles is as follows.

The accountability concept

Management accounting presents information measuring the achievement of the objectives of an organisation and appraising the conduct of its internal affairs in that process. In order that further action can be taken, based on this information, the **accountability concept** makes it necessary at all times to identify the responsibilities and key results of individuals within the organisation.

The controllability concept

The **controllability concept** requires that management accounting identifies the elements or activities which management can or cannot influence, and seeks to assess risk and sensitivity factors. This facilitates the proper monitoring, analysis, comparison and interpretation of information which can be used constructively in the control, evaluation, and corrective functions of management.

Figure 9.2   Management accounting concepts

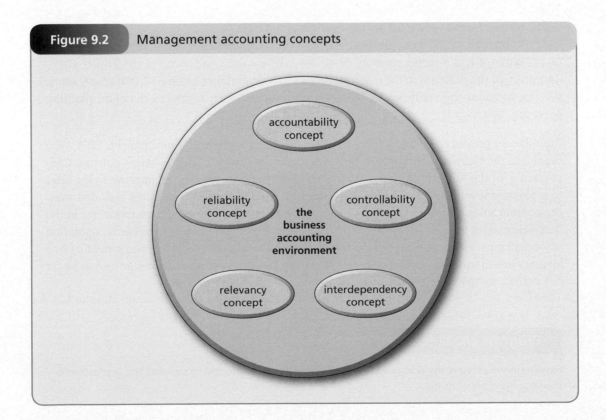

The interdependency concept

⫸ The **interdependency concept** requires that management accounting, in recognition of the increasing complexity of business, must access both internal and external information sources from interactive functions such as marketing, production, human resources, procurement and finance. This assists in ensuring that the information is adequately balanced.

The relevancy concept

⫸ The **relevancy concept** ensures that flexibility in management accounting is maintained in assembling and interpreting information. This facilitates the exploration and presentation, in a clear, understandable and timely manner, of as many alternatives as are necessary for impartial and confident decisions to be taken. This process is essentially forward-looking and dynamic. Therefore, the information must satisfy the criteria of being applicable and appropriate.

The reliability concept

⫸ The **reliability concept** requires that management accounting information must be of such quality that confidence can be placed on it. Its reliability to the user is dependent on its source, integrity and comprehensiveness.

Worked example 9.1

The Nelson Mandela Bay stadium in Port Elizabeth, South Africa, was built between 2007 and 2009 at a cost of over US$159 million as one of five new stadia constructed in preparation for South Africa's hosting of the 2010 FIFA Football World Cup.

It was opened in 2009 and the first of eight World Cup matches was played there in June 2010. While it had a target capacity of 42,486, the stadium had some of the lowest attendances of all the matches in the tournament, with some matches having 12,000 empty seats. We can consider the stadium and its attendance targets with regard to the controllability concept.

Attendances proved to be a problem across all the stadia used for the tournament. FIFA, who organised the tournament, admitted that they had made errors in their ticketing policies. Consequently, in the month before the first match FIFA tried various ways to improve ticket sales to a planned level of 95% capacity. Their ticket sales improvement initiatives included over-the-counter sales as previously all sales had been online, which had not been successful in the domestic market because of the lack of Internet access among the largely poor black population of football fans. FIFA also tried to boost attendances by reducing ticket prices and providing free bus services to transport fans to games. Ultimately, however, the attendances proved to be far below the anticipated levels.

Progress check 9.2

Explain in what ways the additional concepts have been developed to support the profession of management accounting.

The nature of costs

Costs and revenues are terms that are inextricably linked to accounting. Revenues relate to inflows of assets such as cash and accounts receivable from customers, or reductions in liabilities, resulting from trading operations. Costs generally relate to what was paid for a product or a service. It may be a past cost:

- a particular use of resources forgone to achieve a specific objective
- a resource used to provide a product or a service
- a resource used to retain a product or a service.

A cost may be a future cost in which case the alternative uses of resources other than to meet a specific objective may be more important, or relevant, to the decision whether or not to pursue that objective.

Cost is not a word that is usually used without a qualification as to its nature and limitations. On the face of it cost may obviously be described as what was paid for something. Cost may, of course, be used as a noun or a verb. As a noun it is an amount of expenditure (actual or notional) incurred on, or attributable to, a specified thing or activity; it relates to a resource sacrificed or forgone, expressed in a monetary value. As a verb, we may say that to cost something is to ascertain the cost of a specified thing or activity.

A number of terms relating to cost are regularly used within management accounting. A comprehensive glossary of key terms appears at the end of this book. These terms will be explained as we go on to discuss each of the various topics and techniques.

Progress check 9.3

What does 'cost' mean?

Cost accumulation relates to the collection of cost data. Cost data may be concerned with past costs or future costs. Past costs, or historical costs, are the costs that we have dealt with in Chapters 2, 3, 4 and 5, in the preparation of financial statements.

Costs are dependent on, and generally change with, the level of activity. The greater the volume or complexity of the activity, then normally the greater is the cost. We can see from Figure 9.3 that there are three main elements of cost:

- **fixed cost**
- **variable cost**
- **semi-variable cost**.

Fixed cost is a cost which is incurred for an accounting period, and which, within certain manufacturing output or sales revenue limits, tends to be unaffected by fluctuations in the level of activity (output or revenue). An example of a fixed cost is rent of premises that will allow activities up to a particular volume, but which is fixed regardless of volume, for example a car production plant. In the longer term, when volumes may have increased, the fixed cost of rent may also increase from the need to provide a larger factory. Discussion on fixed costs invariably focuses on: when should the fixed costs no longer be considered 'fixed'? Since most businesses these days need to be dynamic and constantly changing, changes to fixed costs inevitably follow changes in their levels of activity.

A variable cost varies in direct proportion to the level, or volume, of activity, and again strictly speaking, within certain output or sales limits. The variable costs incurred in production of a

Figure 9.3   The elements of total costs

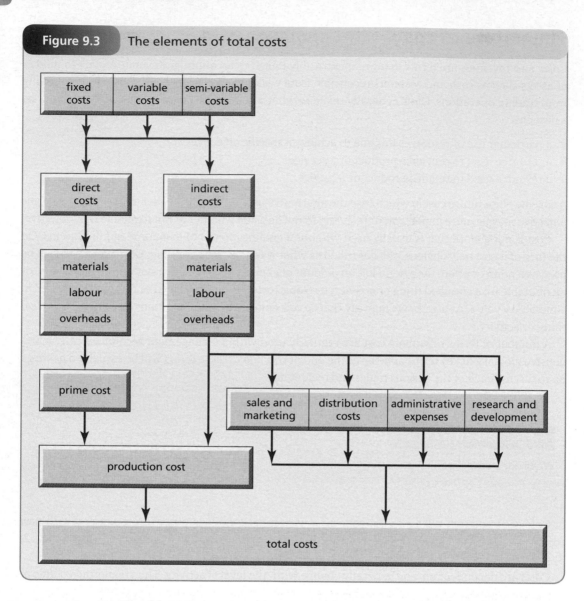

car: materials; labour costs; electricity costs; and so on, are the same for each car produced and so the total of these costs varies as volume varies. The relationship holds until, for example, the cost prices of materials or labour change.

Progress check 9.4

Discuss whether or not knowledge of labour costs can assist management in setting prices for products or services.

A semi-variable cost is a cost containing both fixed and variable components and which is thus partly affected by a change in the level of activity, but not in direct proportion. Examples of semi-variable costs are maintenance costs comprising regular weekly maintenance and also breakdown costs, and telephone expenses that include line and equipment rental in addition to call charges.

Worked example 9.2

Quarterly telephone charges that may be incurred by a business at various levels of call usage are shown in the table below, and in the chart in Figure 9.4. If the business makes no calls at all during the quarter it will incur costs of £200, which cover line rentals and rental of equipment.

Calls (units)	1,000	2,000	3,000
Call charges	£700	£1,400	£2,100

Figure 9.4	An example of how a quarterly semi-variable telephone cost comprises both fixed and variable elements

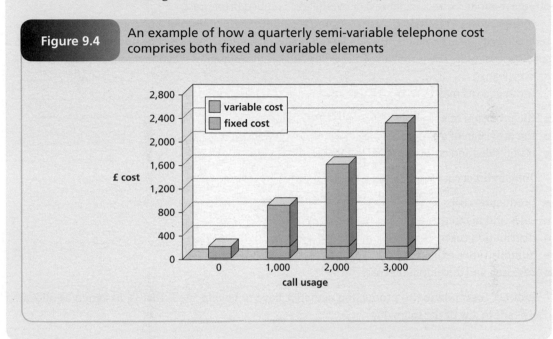

The total costs of an entity comprise three categories:

■ labour costs, the costs of employment which include
  – gross pay
  – paid holidays
  – employer's contributions to National Insurance
  – pension schemes
  – sickness benefit schemes
  – other benefits, for example protective clothing and canteen subsidies
■ materials, which include
  – raw materials purchased for incorporation into products for sale
  – consumable items
  – packaging
■ overheads, relating to all costs other than materials and labour costs.

Each of the above three categories may be further analysed into:

■ **direct costs**
■ **indirect costs**.

> ### Progress check 9.5
>
> Are managers really interested in whether a cost is fixed or variable when assessing cost behaviour within an organisation?

Direct costs are those costs that can be traced and identified with, and specifically measured with respect to a relevant cost object. A **cost object** is the thing we wish to determine the cost of. Direct costs include **direct labour**, **direct materials** and direct overheads. The total cost of direct materials, direct labour and direct expenses, or overheads, is called prime cost.

Indirect costs, or overheads, are costs untraceable to particular units (compared with direct costs). Indirect costs include expenditure on labour, materials or services, which cannot be identified with a saleable cost unit. The term 'burden' used by American companies is synonymous with indirect costs or overheads.

Indirect costs may relate to:

- the provision of a product
- the provision of a service
- other 'sales and administrative' activities.

Total indirect costs may therefore be generally categorised as:

- production costs
- sales and marketing costs
- distribution costs
- administrative expenses
- research and development costs.

Indirect costs relating to production activities have to be allocated, that is, assigned as allocated overheads to any of the following:

- a single **cost unit**
- a unit of product or service in relation to which costs are ascertained
- a **cost centre**
- a production or service location, function, activity or item of equipment for which costs are accumulated
- a cost account
- a record of the expenditure of a cost centre or cost unit
- a time period.

> ### Worked example 9.3
>
> Are managers are really interested in whether a cost is fixed or variable when assessing cost behaviour within their departments?
>
> A manager should know how a cost will behave when setting a departmental budget. As time goes by and the manager routinely reports actual compared to budget, several differences will be caused by the behaviour of the cost. For example, certain wage costs may be greater per hour for hours worked after 6 pm each day.

Progress check 9.6

Explain costs in terms of the hierarchy of costs that make up the total costs of a business.

Cost allocation and cost apportionment

The indirect costs of service departments may be allocated both to other service departments and to production departments. An idea of the range of departments existing in most large businesses can be gained by simply looking at the newspaper job advertisements of major companies, where each department may represent an 'allocation of costs' problem.

Allocation of overheads is the charging to a cost centre of those overheads that result solely from the existence of that cost centre. Cost assignment defines the process of tracing and allocating costs to the cost object. Overheads are allocated where possible, but allocation can only be done if the exact amount incurred is known without having to carry out any sort of sharing. For example, a department in a factory may have a specific machine or a type of skilled labour that is only used in that department. The depreciation cost of the specific machine and the cost of the skilled labour would be allocated to that department. If the amount is not known and it is not possible to allocate costs then the total amount must be apportioned.

Worked example 9.4

A degree of subjectivity is involved in the allocation of expenses to a department, or cost centre, which can frequently cause problems. However, the allocation of wages and salaries costs to the Nelson Mandela Bay Stadium project should have been fairly straightforward.

Although some events had been staged at the stadium prior to the World Cup football tournament there were considerable questions over its continued use after the tournament. This made the stadium a very large and expensive capital project with a very short projected active life, starting in 2009 and finishing with the third-place play-off match on 10 July 2010. The ticket office would also have a very short life – it would have no tickets to sell after 10 July 2010. The costs of staff working in the ticket office would also be easy to identify.

Apportionment is the charging to a cost centre of a fair share of an overhead on the basis of the benefit received by the cost centre in respect of the facilities provided by the overhead. For example, a factory may consist of two or more departments that occupy different amounts of floor space. The total factory rent cost may then be apportioned between the departments on the basis of floor space occupied.

Therefore, if an overhead cannot be allocated then it must be apportioned, involving use of a basis of apportionment, a physical or financial unit, so that the overhead will be equitably shared between the cost centres. Bases of apportionment, for example, that may be used are:

- area – for rent, heating and lighting, building depreciation
- number of employees – for personnel and welfare costs, safety costs
- weights or sizes – for materials handling costs, warehousing costs.

The basis chosen will use the factor most closely related to the benefit received by the cost centres.

Worked example 9.5

For the FIFA World Cup football tournament the Nelson Mandela Bay Stadium in Port Elizabeth, South Africa had many areas that were financed by outside companies, which had signed contracts for the duration of the tournament. The contracts would have included clauses regarding recovery of certain costs from them by the operator Access Facilities and Leisure Management (Pty) Limited. It is likely that different bases of apportionment would need to have been chosen for the costs of cleaning and security.

The cleaning costs would have been fairly straightforward to apportion, probably on a surface area basis (square metres).

The security costs may have been more problematical. They may have used, for example, a basis of apportionment such as the number of people screened on entering the stadium or the number of cars checked in the car parks. Alternatively, they may have used the number of steward activities in the ground, or the number of specialist activities such as personal protection for teams, match officials and distinguished guests.

Once overheads have been allocated and apportioned, perhaps via some service cost centres, ultimately to production cost centres, they can be charged to cost units. For example, in a factory with three departments the total rent may have been apportioned to the manufacturing department, the assembly department, and the goods inwards department. The total overhead costs of the goods inwards department may then be apportioned between the manufacturing department and the assembly department. The total costs of the manufacturing department and the assembly department may then be charged to the units being produced in those departments, for example television sets or cars. The same process may be used in the service sector, for example theatre seats and hospital beds. A cost unit is a unit of product or service in relation to which costs are ascertained. A **unit cost** is the average cost of a product or service unit based on total costs and the number of units.

Worked example 9.6

The unit cost ascertainment process illustrated in Figure 9.5 involves taking each cost centre and sharing its overheads among all the cost units passing through that centre.

This example considers one cost centre, the manufacturing department, which is involved with the production of three different products, A, B and C. The process is similar to apportionment but in this case cost units (which in this case are products) are charged instead of cost centres. This process of charging costs to cost units is called absorption and is defined as the charging of overheads to cost units.

Figure 9.5   An example of unit cost ascertainment

	Number of units	Production time	Rate per hour	Total charge on the basis of hours		Charge per unit
Overhead costs	3,000 product A	1,000 hours	£5	£5,000	[£5,000/3,000]	£1.67
for January	2,000 product B	4,000 hours	£5	£20,000	[£20,000/2,000]	£10.00
£50,000	5,000 product C	5,000 hours	£5	£25,000	[£25,000/5,000]	£5.00
	10,000 units	10,000 hours		£50,000		

Manufacturing department

The cost of converting material into finished products, that is, direct labour, direct expense and production overhead, is called the conversion cost. An example of this may be seen in the manufacture of a car bumper, which may have started out as granules of plastic and 'cans of paint'. After the completion of carefully controlled processes that may use some labour and incur overhead costs, the granules and paint are converted into a highly useful product.

Progress check 9.7

What are cost allocation and cost apportionment? Give some examples of bases of cost apportionment.

Within the various areas of management accounting there is greater interest in future costs. The future costs that result from management decisions are concerned with **relevant costs** and **opportunity costs**, which are described briefly below but which will be illustrated in greater detail when we consider the techniques of decision-making in Chapter 11.

Relevant costs (and revenues) are the costs (and revenues) appropriate to a specific management decision. They are represented by future cash flows whose magnitude will vary depending upon the outcome of the management decision made. If inventory is sold to a retailer, the relevant cost, used in the determination of the profitability of the transaction, would be the cost of replacing the inventory, not its original purchase price, which is a sunk cost. **Sunk costs**, or irrecoverable costs, are costs that have been irreversibly incurred or committed to prior to a decision point and which cannot therefore be considered relevant to subsequent decisions.

An opportunity cost is the value of the benefit sacrificed when one course of action is chosen in preference to an alternative. The opportunity cost is represented by the forgone potential benefit from the best of the alternative courses of action that have been rejected.

Worked example 9.7

A student may have a weekend job that pays £7 per hour. If the student gave up one hour on a weekend to clean his car instead of paying someone £5 to clean it for him, the opportunity cost would be:

One hour of the student's lost wages	£7
less: **Cost of car cleaning**	£5
Opportunity cost	£2

Absorption costing

In this section we are looking at profit considered at the level of total revenue less total cost. If a CD retailer, for example, uses absorption costing it includes a proportion of the costs of its premises, such as rent and utilities costs, in the total unit cost of selling each CD. The allocation and apportionment process that has been outlined in the past few paragraphs is termed **absorption costing**, or full costing. This process looks at costing in terms of the total costs of running a facility like a hospital, restaurant, retail shop, or factory, being part of the output from that facility. This is one method of costing that, in addition to direct costs, assigns all, or a proportion of, production overhead costs to cost units by means of one or a number of **overhead absorption rates**. There are two steps involved in this process:

- computation of an overhead absorption rate
- application of the overhead absorption rate to cost units.

The basis of absorption is chosen in a similar way to choosing an apportionment base. The overhead rate is calculated using:

$$\text{overhead absorption rate} = \frac{\text{total cost centre overheads}}{\text{total units of base used}}$$

Worked example 9.8

Albatross Ltd budgeted to produce 44,000 dining chairs in the month of January, but actually produced 48,800 dining chairs (units). It sold 40,800 units at a price of £100 per unit.

Budgeted costs for January:

Direct material	£36 per unit
Direct labour	£8 per unit
Variable production overheads	£6 per unit
Fixed costs:	
Production overheads	£792,000
Administrative expenses	£208,000
Selling costs	£112,000

Sales commission is paid at 10% of sales revenue. There were no opening inventories and budgeted costs were the same as actual costs.

We can prepare the income statement for January using absorption costing techniques, on the basis of the number of budgeted units of production.

$$\text{Overhead absorption rate} = \frac{\text{budgeted fixed production cost}}{\text{budgeted units of production}} = \frac{£792,000}{44,000} = £18 \text{ per unit}$$

Over-absorption of fixed production overheads
= (actual production − budgeted production) × fixed production overhead rate per unit
= (48,800 − 44,000) × £18 per unit = £86,400

Production costs per unit

	£	
Direct material	36	
Direct labour	8	
Variable production overhead	6	
Variable production cost	50	
Fixed production overhead	18	see above
Full production cost per unit	68	

Income statement

	£
Revenue (40,800 × £100)	4,080,000
Full production costs (48,800 × £68)	3,318,400
plus Opening inventories	–
less Closing inventories (8,000 units × £68)	544,000
Cost of sales	2,774,400
Gross profit	1,305,600
less Other expenses	
Sales commission (£4,080,000 × 10%)	408,000
Administrative expenses	208,000
Selling costs	112,000
Total other expenses	728,000
Revenue less total costs	577,600
plus Over-absorption	
Fixed production overheads	86,400 see above
Profit for January before tax	664,000

Under or over-absorbed overheads represent the difference between overheads incurred and overheads absorbed. Over-absorbed overheads are credited to the profit and loss account, increasing the profit, as in the above example (refer to Chapter 2 to refresh your knowledge of debits and credits). Under-absorbed overheads are debited to the profit and loss account, reducing the profit. In this example, the over-absorption of overheads was caused by the actual production level deviating from the budgeted level of production. Deviations, or variances, can occur due to differences between actual and budgeted volumes and/or differences between actual and budgeted expenditure.

There are many bases that may be used for calculation of the overhead absorption rate, for example:

- units of output
- direct labour hours
- machine hours.

Computerised models can assist in these calculations and provide many solutions to the problem of the 'overhead absorption rate', allowing consideration of a number of 'what-if' scenarios before making a final decision.

It can be seen that absorption costing is a costing technique whereby each unit of output is charged with both fixed and variable production costs. The unit cost is called the product cost. The fixed production costs are treated as part of the actual production costs. Inventories of product, in accordance with IAS 2, are therefore valued on a full production cost basis and 'held' within the balance sheet until the inventories have been used in production or sold, rather than charged to the profit and loss account in the period in which the costs of the inventories are incurred. The accounting treatment is different from that applied to a **period cost**, which relates to a time period and is charged to the profit and loss account when it is incurred rather than when a product is sold. When the inventories of product are sold in a subsequent accounting period their product costs are matched with the sales revenue of that period and charged to the profit and loss account in the same period. The objective of absorption costing is to obtain an overall average economic cost of carrying out whatever activity is being costed.

In order for costings to be carried out from the first day of operations, overhead rates are invariably calculated on the basis of expected future, or budgeted, overheads and the number of units of manufacturing capacity. Actual overheads and levels of production are unlikely to exactly equal budgeted amounts and so the use of budgeted overhead absorption rates will inevitably lead to an **overhead over- or under-absorption** (as we have seen in Worked example 9.8), which is transferred (usually) monthly to the profit and loss account, for internal management accounting reporting.

Progress check 9.8

What is absorption costing and how is it used? Give some examples of bases that may be used for the calculation of overhead absorption rates applied to cost units.

Worked example 9.9

The total costs for one specific manufacturing process have been incurred at various levels of output as shown in the table below. We can assume that the fixed costs and the variable cost per unit remain constant over this range of output, that is to say there is a linear relationship between total costs and output.

Output units	Total cost £
28,750	256,190
30,000	261,815
31,250	267,440
32,500	273,065
33,750	278,690
35,000	284,315

From the table above we can use a high-low analysis to determine:

(i) the variable cost per unit for the process
(ii) the fixed cost of the process.

(i)

	Units output	Total cost £
High	35,000	284,315
Low	28,750	256,190
Difference	6,250	28,125

Variable cost per unit:

$$\frac{£28,125}{6,250} = £4.50$$

(ii) Using the answer from (i) we can calculate the total variable costs at any level of output, for example at 30,000 units we have:

$$\text{Variable costs} = 30,000 \text{ units} \times £4.50 = £135,000$$

We can now use this to determine fixed costs:

Total costs at an output level of 30,000 units = £261,815
Less: variable cost element   = £135,000
Therefore fixed cost   = £126,815

Alternatively, you may like to try and achieve the same result for Worked example 9.9 using a graphical approach. If you plot the data in the table you should find that at the point where the graph crosses the *y*-axis (total costs) output (the *x*-axis) is zero. At that point total costs are £126,815, which is the fixed cost – the cost incurred even when no output takes place. The slope of the graph represents the variable cost of £4.50 per unit.

We shall now consider another costing technique, **marginal costing**, which is also known as variable costing. We will return to Worked Example 9.8 later, using the marginal costing technique and compare it with the absorption costing technique.

Marginal costing

We have considered above a costing method that looks at profit considered at the level of total sales revenue less total cost. We will now look at another way of considering profit, called **contribution**, and its corresponding costing system called marginal costing (see Fig. 9.6).

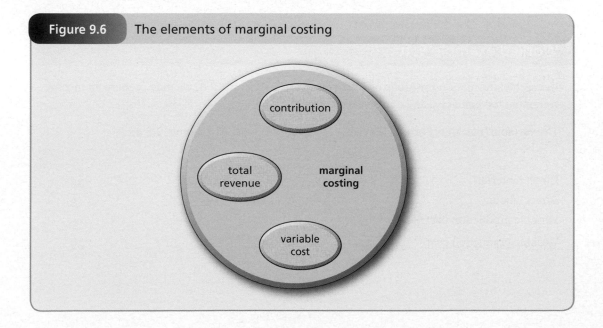

Figure 9.6   The elements of marginal costing

contribution

total revenue

marginal costing

variable cost

$$\text{total contribution} = \text{total revenue} - \text{total variable costs}$$

Marginal costing, or variable costing, is a costing technique whereby each unit of output is charged only with variable production costs. The costs which are generated solely by a given cost unit are the variable costs associated with that unit, including the variable cost elements of any associated semi-variable costs. Marginal cost ascertainment includes all unit direct costs plus the variable overhead cost per unit incurred by the cost unit. The marginal cost of a unit may be defined as the additional cost of producing one such unit. The marginal cost of a number of units is the sum of all the unit marginal costs. Whereas absorption costing deals with total costs and profits, marginal costing deals with variable costs and contribution. Contribution is defined as the sales value, or revenue, less the variable cost of sales. Contribution may be expressed as:

- total contribution
- contribution per unit
- contribution as a percentage of sales.

If a business provides a series of products that all provide some contribution, the business may avoid being severely damaged by the downturn in demand of just one of the products. Fixed production costs are not considered to be the real costs of production, but costs which provide the facilities, for an accounting period, that enable production to take place. They are therefore treated as costs of the period and charged to the period in which they are incurred against the aggregate contribution. Inventories are valued on a variable production cost basis that excludes fixed production costs.

Marginal cost ascertainment assumes that the cost of any given activity is only the cost that that activity generates; it is the difference between carrying out and not carrying out that activity. Each cost unit and each cost centre is charged with only those costs that are generated as a consequence of that cost unit and that cost centre being a part of the company's activities.

We will now return to Worked example 9.8 and consider the results using marginal costing, and contrast them with those achieved using absorption costing in Worked example 9.10.

Worked example 9.10

Using the information for Albatross Ltd from Worked example 9.8, we may prepare an income statement for January using marginal costing.

The variable (marginal) production costs per unit from Worked example 9.8 are:

	£
Direct material	36
Direct labour	8
Variable production overhead	6
Variable production cost	50

Income statement

	£
Revenue (40,800 × £100)	4,080,000
Variable production costs (48,800 × £50)	2,440,000
plus Opening inventories	–
less Closing inventories (8,000 units × £50)	400,000
Cost of sales	2,040,000
Gross contribution	2,040,000
less Sales commission (£4,080,000 × 10%)	408,000
Net contribution	1,632,000
less Fixed costs	
Production overheads	792,000
Administrative expenses	208,000
Selling costs	112,000
Total fixed costs	1,112,000
Profit for January before tax	520,000

It can be seen that profit calculated using the marginal costing technique is £144,000 less than that using the absorption costing technique: under absorption costing, inventories are valued at full production cost, the fixed production overheads being carried forward in inventories to the next period instead of being charged to the current period as it is under marginal costing.

Note: The activity is the same regardless of the costing technique that has been used. It is only the method of reporting that has caused a difference in the profit.

Inventory valuation difference

Closing inventory units × (absorption cost per unit − marginal cost per unit) = profit difference

8,000 units × (£68 − £50) = £144,000

Some specific features of the marginal costing technique are:

- its recognition of cost behaviour, providing better support for sales pricing and decision-making, which we shall explore further in Chapter 11
- it allows better control reports to be prepared because contribution is based on, and varies with, the sales level, which we shall examine when we look at cost and overhead relationships in Chapter 10
- fixed costs may be addressed within the period that gives rise to them.

However, marginal costing is not suitable for inventory valuation in line with accounting standard IAS 2, because there is no fixed cost element included. IAS 2 requires closing inventories to include direct materials, direct labour and appropriate overheads. A great many companies, large and small, adopt marginal costing for monthly management reporting and inventory valuation for each of their accounting periods throughout their financial year. Such companies overcome the problems of non-compliance with IAS 2 by making an adjustment to their inventory valuation and their reported profit to include an allowance for fixed production overheads, in the final accounting period at their year end.

Absorption costing versus marginal costing

A more comprehensive list of the advantages and disadvantages of both techniques is summarised in Figures 9.7 and 9.8.

Figure 9.7	Advantages and disadvantages of absorption costing

advantages	disadvantages
it is simple to use, and based on a formula that uses an estimated or planned fixed overhead rate included in the calculation of unit costs of products and services	fixed costs are not necessarily avoidable and they have to be paid regardless of whether sales and production volumes are high, low or zero
it is easy to apply using cost or a percentage mark-up to achieve a reasonable profit	fixed costs are not variable in the short run
apportionment and allocation of fixed costs to cost centres makes managers aware of costs and services provided and ensures that they remember that all costs need to be covered for the company to be profitable	there are different alternative bases of overhead allocation which therefore result in different interpretations
cost price or full cost pricing ensures that all costs are covered	the capacity levels chosen for overhead absorption rates are based on historical information and are therefore open to debate
it conforms with the accrual concept by matching costs with revenues for a particular accounting period, as in the full costing of inventories	activity must be equal to or greater than the budgeted level of activity or else fixed costs will be under-absorbed
inventories valuation complies with IAS 2, as an element of fixed production cost is absorbed into inventories	if sales revenues are depressed then profits can be artificially increased by increasing production thus increasing inventories
it avoids the separation of costs into fixed and variable elements, which are not easily and accurately identified	
analysis of over- and under-absorbed overheads highlights any inefficient utilisation of production resources	

| Figure 9.8 | Advantages and disadvantages of marginal costing |

advantages	disadvantages
it is market based not cost based; exclusion of fixed production costs on a marginal basis enables the company to be more competitive	pricing at the margin may lead to underpricing with too little contribution and non-recovery of fixed costs, particularly in periods of economic downturn
it covers all incremental costs associated with the product, production and sales revenues	inventory valuation does not comply with IAS 2, as no element of fixed production costs is absorbed into inventories
it enables the analysis of different market price and volume levels to allow selection of optimal contributions	
it enables the company to determine break-even points and plan profit, and to use of the opportunity cost approach	
it avoids the arbitrary apportionment of fixed costs and avoids the problem of determining a suitable basis for the overhead absorption rate, e.g. units, labour hours, machine hours etc.	
most fixed production overheads are periodic, or time-based, and incurred regardless of levels of production, and so should be charged to the period in which they are incurred, e.g. factory rent, salaries, and depreciation	
fixed production costs may not be controllable at the departmental level and so should not be included in production costs at the cost centre level – control should be matched with responsibility	
profits cannot be manipulated by increasing inventories in times of low sales revenues because inventories exclude fixed costs and profits therefore vary directly with sales revenues	
it facilitates control through easier pooling of separate fixed costs and variable costs totals, and preparation of flexible budgets to provide comparisons for actual levels of activity	
inventories valued on a variable cost basis supports the view that the additional cost of inventories is limited to its variable costs	
marginal costing is prudent because fixed costs are charged to the period in which they are incurred, not carried forward in inventories which may prove to be unsaleable and result in earlier profits having been overstated	

Progress check 9.9

Should managers participate in the accounting exercise of allocation of fixed costs? (Hint: You may wish to consider the cyclical nature of the construction industry as an example that illustrates the difficulty of allocating fixed costs.)

In the long run, over several accounting periods, the total recorded profit of an entity is the same regardless of whether absorption costing or marginal costing techniques are used. The difference is one of timing. The actual amounts of the costs do not differ, only the period in which they are charged against profits. Thus, differences in profit occur from one period to the next depending on which method is adopted.

Figure 9.9 illustrates and compares the formats of an income statement using absorption costing and marginal costing.

Figure 9.9   Income statement absorption costing and marginal costing formats

Absorption costing	Marginal costing
Revenue	Revenue
less production costs:	less variable costs:
Direct materials	Direct materials
Direct labour	Direct labour
Production overhead	Variable production overhead
	Variable selling and distribution costs
Production cost of sales	Production cost of sales
Gross profit	Contribution
less non-production costs:	less fixed costs:
	Fixed production overheads
Selling costs	Selling costs
Distribution costs	Distribution costs
Administrative expenses	Administrative expenses
Research and development costs	Research and development costs
Non-production costs	Total fixed costs
Profit before tax	Profit before tax

Marginal costing is a powerful technique since it focuses attention on those costs which are affected by, or associated with, an activity. We will return to marginal costing in Chapter 10, with regard to cost/volume/profit (CVP) relationships and break-even analysis. It is also particularly useful in the areas of decision-making and relevant costs, and sales pricing which we shall be looking at in Chapter 11.

Worked example 9.11

Management accounting provides information to various departments within a business. Fast-moving businesses need this information very quickly. Hotel groups have invested in central booking systems and these systems are used to reveal times of the year when reservations are down because of national and local trends. Let's consider how the marketing department and the management accounting function might work together to generate extra bookings.

The marketing department may assess the periods and times in which each hotel has gaps in its reservations. The management accountant may assess the direct costs associated with each reservation, for example the costs of cleaning and food. The two departments may then suggest a special offer for a fixed period of time. For example, Travelodge ran a special offer for May 2010 whereby customers could book a room in specified locations for only £19 per night in May 2010, but the booking had to be made during the first week of April 2010. The special offer may, therefore, allow for local conditions by varying the price within a range, for example £20 to £30 per night.

Management accounting continues to change and develop as it meets the needs presented by:

- changing economic climates
- globalisation
- information technology
- increasing competition.

Marginal costing developed from absorption costing in recognition of the differences in behaviour between fixed costs and variable costs. In most industries, as labour costs continue to become a smaller and smaller percentage of total costs, traditional costing methods, which usually absorb costs on the basis of direct labour hours, have been seen to be increasingly inappropriate.

In Chapter 10 we will look at some management accounting techniques that have been developed more recently in response to some of the criticisms of traditional costing methods:

- **activity based costing (ABC)**
- **throughput accounting (TA)**
- **life cycle costing**
- target costing
- benchmarking
- *kaizen*.

Progress check 9.10

What is marginal costing and in what ways is it different from absorption costing?

Summary of key points

- There are a number of additional accounting concepts that relate to management accounting.

- Cost (as a noun) is an amount of expenditure attributable to a specified thing or activity, but also relates to a resource sacrificed or forgone, expressed in a monetary value.

- Cost (as a verb) may be used to say that to cost something is to ascertain the cost of a specified thing or activity, but cost is not a word that is usually used without a qualification as to its nature and limitations.

- Direct costs are directly identified with and traceable to cost objects.

- Indirect costs have to be allocated or apportioned to cost units, cost centres or cost accounts using appropriate bases for allocation and apportionment.

- Unit costs of products, services or activities may be determined using the traditional costing techniques of absorption costing and marginal costing.

- There are many arguments for and against the use of the techniques of both absorption costing and marginal costing, revolving mainly around the basis chosen for allocation and apportionment of overheads.

Assessment material

Questions

Q9.1 (i) What are the main roles of the management accountant?
(ii) How does management accounting support the effective management of a business?

Q9.2 (i) What are the differences between fixed costs, variable costs and semi-variable costs?
(ii) Give some examples of each.

Q9.3 (i) Why do production overheads need to be allocated and apportioned, and to what?
(ii) Describe the processes of allocation and apportionment.

Q9.4 (i) Which costing system complies with the provisions outlined in IAS 2?
(ii) Describe the process used in this technique.

Q9.5 What is marginal costing and how does it differ from absorption costing?

Q9.6 What are the main benefits to be gained from using a system of marginal costing?

Discussion points

D9.1 'Surely an accountant is an accountant! Why does the function of management accounting need to be separated from financial accounting and why is it seen as such an integral part of the management of the business?' Discuss.

D9.2 'Do the benefits from using marginal costing outweigh the benefits from using absorption costing sufficiently to replace absorption costing in IAS 2 as the basis for inventory valuation and the preparation of financial statements?' Discuss.

Exercises

Solutions are provided in Appendix 3 to all exercise numbers highlighted in colour.

Level I

E9.1   *Time allowed – 45 minutes*

Bluebell Woods Ltd produces a product for which the following standard cost details have been provided based on production and sales volumes of 4,300 units in a four-week period:

Direct material cost	£0.85 per kg
Direct material usage	2 kg per unit
Direct labour rate	£4.20 per hour
Direct labour time per unit	42 minutes
Selling price	£5.84 per unit
Variable production overheads	£0.12 per unit
Fixed production overheads	£3,526 per four-week period

Prepare an income statement for the four-week period using:

(i)   absorption costing

(ii) marginal costing.

E9.2   *Time allowed – 45 minutes*

A manufacturing company, Duane Pipes Ltd, uses predetermined rates for absorbing manufacturing overheads based on the budgeted level of activity. A total rate of £35 per direct labour hour has been calculated for the Assembly Department for March 2011, for which the following overhead expenditure at various different levels of activity have been estimated:

Total manufacturing overheads

£	Number of direct labour hours
465,500	12,000
483,875	13,500
502,250	15,000

You are required to calculate the following:

(i)   the variable overhead absorption rate per direct labour hour

(ii)   the estimated total fixed overheads

(iii) the budgeted level of activity for March 2011 in direct labour hours

(iv)   the amount of under- or over-recovery of overheads, and state which, if the actual direct labour hours were 13,850 and actual overheads were £509,250

and

(v)   outline the reasons for and against using departmental absorption rates as opposed to a single blanket factory-wide rate.

Level II

E9.3   *Time allowed – 75 minutes*

Square Gift Ltd is located in Wales, where the national sales manager is also based, and has a sales force of 15 salesmen covering the whole of the UK. The sales force, including the national sales manager all have the same make and model of company car. A new car costs £16,000, and all cars are traded in for a guaranteed £6,000 when they are two years old.

The salesman with the lowest annual mileage of 18,000 miles operates in the South East of England. The salesman with the highest annual mileage of 40,000 miles operates throughout Scotland. The annual average mileage of the complete sales team works out at 30,000 miles per car.

The average salesman's annual vehicle running cost is:

	£
Petrol and oil	3,000
Road tax	155
Insurance	450
Repairs	700
Miscellaneous	300
Total	4,605

Annual vehicle repair costs include £250 for regular maintenance.
Tyre life is around 30,000 miles and replacement sets cost £350.

No additional repair costs are incurred during the first year of vehicle life because a special warranty agreement exists with the supplying garage to cover these, but on average £200 is paid for repairs in the second year – repair costs are averaged over the two years with regular maintenance and repairs being variable with mileage rather than time.

Miscellaneous vehicle costs include subscriptions to motoring organisations, vehicle cleaning costs, parking, and garaging allowances.

> **Analyse the total vehicle costs into fixed costs and variable costs separately to give total annual costs for:**
>
> **(i) the lowest mileage per annum salesman**
> **(ii) the highest mileage per annum salesman.**
>
> **You may ignore the cost of capital and any possible impacts of tax and inflation.**

(Hints:

– Assume that insurance costs are the same for each area.

– Assume that miscellaneous operating costs are fixed.

– Repairs are based on amount of mileage.)

E9.4   *Time allowed – 75 minutes*

Rocky Ltd manufactures a single product, the budget for which was as follows for each of the months July and August 2010:

	Total	Per unit
	£	£
Revenue (6,000 units)	60,000	10.00
Production cost of sales:		
Variable overhead	45,000	7.50
Fixed overhead	3,000	0.50
	48,000	8.00
Revenue less production cost	12,000	2.00
Selling and distribution costs (fixed)	4,200	0.70
Administrative expenses (fixed)	3,000	0.50
Profit	4,800	0.80

Actual units produced, sold, and levels of inventories in July and August were:

	July	August
Opening inventories	–	900
Production	5,300	4,400
Sales	4,400	5,000
Closing inventories	900	300

Prepare income statements for each of the months July and August, assuming that fixed production overhead is absorbed into the cost of the product at the normal level shown in the monthly budget.

(Hint: This is the absorption costing approach.)

E9.5   *Time allowed – 75 minutes*

Using the data for Rocky Ltd from Exercise E9.4, prepare income statements for each of the months July and August, assuming that fixed production overhead is not absorbed into the cost of the product, but is treated as a cost of the period and charged against sales.

(Hint: This is the marginal costing approach.)

E9.6   *Time allowed – 75 minutes*

Using your answers to Exercises E9.4 and E9.5, explain why the profit for July and August is different using the two costing methods, and support your explanation with an appropriate reconciliation of the results.

10

Managing costs

Contents

Learning objectives

Completion of this chapter will enable you to:

- explain cost/volume/profit (CVP) relationships and break-even analysis
- identify the limitations of CVP analysis
- outline the more recently developed techniques of activity based costing (ABC) and throughput accounting (TA)
- identify the conditions appropriate to the use of life cycle costing
- apply the principles of target costing
- consider benchmarking as a technique to identify best practice and enable the introduction of appropriate performance improvement targets
- outline *kaizen* as a technique for continuous improvement of all aspects of business performance
- explain the types of information and measurements used in lean accounting systems
- use cost of quality (COQ) to identify areas for improvement and cost reduction within each of the processes throughout the business
- appreciate the importance of both financial and non-financial indicators in the evaluation of business performance
- consider the use of both financial and non-financial measures incorporated into performance measurement systems such as the balanced scorecard.

Introduction

In Chapter 9 we introduced costs, contribution and profit. This chapter develops the importance of contribution as a measure of profitability and begins with an examination of the relationship between costs, volumes of activity and profit, or CVP analysis. We will look at a particular application of CVP analysis in break-even analysis, and consider some of the advantages and limitations of its use.

This chapter looks at some of the more recently developed management accounting techniques, some of which have been developed in response to the criticisms of traditional costing methods, for example: activity based costing; throughput accounting; life cycle costing; target costing; benchmarking; *kaizen*; quality costing; non-financial performance indicators; and the balanced scorecard.

The broadening of the range of activities supported by management accounting has resulted in a gradual disappearance of the boundaries between itself and financial management. Management accounting continues to develop with an emphasis on decision-making and strategic management, and financial management. Financial management is usually defined as the management of the processes that deal with the efficient acquisition and deployment of short- and long-term financial resources. It was interesting to note in September 2000 that CIMA renamed its monthly journal from *Management Accounting* to *Financial Management*.

This chapter provides an introduction to the development of lean accounting systems, and closes with an examination of the important area of non-financial indicators in the evaluation of business performance. The contribution of financial and non-financial measures is examined in their incorporation into performance measurement systems such as the balanced scorecard, developed by David Norton and Robert Kaplan in the early 1990s.

Cost/volume/profit (CVP) relationships and break-even analysis

It is sometimes said that accountants think in straight lines whereas economists think in curves. We can see this in the way that economists view costs and revenues. Generally, economists are looking at the longer term when they consider a company's total costs and total revenues.

We can see from Figure 10.1 that the total revenue curve starts where the volume is zero and therefore the total revenue is zero (nothing is sold and so there is no sales value). The economist says that as the selling price (which the economist calls marginal revenue) is increased then total revenue will continue to increase, but by proportionately less and less. This continues up to a point where the decrease in selling price starts to have less and less impact on volume and so total revenue starts to decline. The result of this is a total revenue curve that increases but which becomes gradually less steep until it eventually flattens out and then falls away.

The total cost curve starts some way up the y axis (£) because fixed costs are incurred even when sales are zero. Total costs comprise fixed costs and variable costs (or marginal costs). As volumes increase then total costs increase. The economist assumes that fixed costs continue to be unchanged, and when volumes increase unit costs decrease because the fixed cost is spread amongst a greater number of products. Therefore, the total costs increase but by proportionately less and less. In addition, the economist says that the total costs further benefit from decreases in variable costs as volume increases. This happens as a result of economies of scale:

- as labour becomes more experienced then less is required for a given level of output
- materials cost prices reduce as purchasing power increases from greater volumes.

Economies of scale continue until further economies are not possible, and we begin to see diminishing returns. This happens when variable costs start to increase, which may be due to the overloading of processes at high volumes, leading to possible malfunctions, breakdowns and bottlenecks.

Initially the total cost curve does not rise steeply because of the fixed costs effect and the positive impact of economies of scale on variable costs. As the business reaches its most efficient volume level further economies of scale are not possible and the total cost curve quickly becomes very steep as a result of the adverse impact of diminishing returns on variable costs.

It can be seen from Figure 10.1 that profit is maximised at a specific point shown where the gap between the two curves is greatest. Also, because of the shapes of the economist's longer-term total

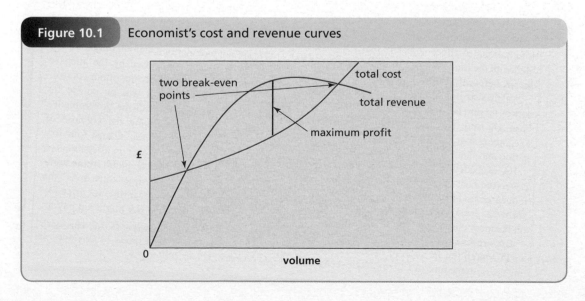

Figure 10.1 Economist's cost and revenue curves

cost and total revenue curves, it can be seen that they cross at two points. At these points total costs are equal to total revenues and so for the economist there are two break-even points. This contrasts with the accountant's view of costs, volumes and break-even, which is explained below. This chapter will focus on the accountant's view of CVP analysis and break-even.

The break-even point was seen as an important measure in 2010 for British Airways (see the press extract below):

■ 2009 had seen the company's worst financial performance and the confidence which a year without reporting losses would give to shareholders, potential lenders and the financial markets was seen by BA as imperative

■ BA implemented measures to try to break even, but the effect of these cost-cutting measures on BA staff along with disruptions caused by a volcanic ash cloud originating in Iceland threatened to upset BA's carefully structured plan.

The importance of breaking-even, and the ways and means to do it

British Airways vowed to press ahead with cost-cutting plans yesterday as the strike-hit airline reported its worst-ever annual loss of £531m.

Tough action on overheads, including a controversial reduction in cabin crew staffing levels, allowed BA to report a pre-tax loss that beat market expectations. The deficit included the estimated £43m loss from seven days of strikes in March which will be followed by the three waves of five-day walkouts from Monday unless BA and the Unite trade union reach a last-ditch compromise.

However, BA's ambition to break even this year could be threatened by the industrial row over staffing reductions and the airline's reaction to the March walkouts. Asked if his own position might be at risk because of the long-running dispute and its effect on morale among BA's 38,000 staff, Walsh said: 'It is absolute nonsense.' In an entrepreneurial attempt to cash in on BA's difficulties, Ladbrokes yesterday put odds of 11/10 on Walsh leaving the carrier including the new International Airlines company that will be created with the imminent merger of BA and Spain's Iberia, before the end of the year.

Walsh also implicitly criticised his predecessors as he said BA could no longer sustain its cost base. He said: 'I am doing what previous chief executives should have done with great determination and fantastic support from BA staff.'

BA exceeded last year's £401m loss despite a concerted cost-cutting drive that saw the airline reduce costs by £1bn, which meant it fully absorbed a revenue loss of £1bn, caused by pressure on business class fares from the downturn.

BA's revenues of just under £8bn for the year to 31 March fell far short of the carrier's operating costs, to the tune of £231m. Interest payments and pension costs pushed the pre-tax deficit to £531m.

BA withheld a dividend for the second consecutive year. The pre-tax loss beat analysts' expectations of a deficit of more than £600m, although yesterday's result takes the carrier's two-year pre-tax loss to nearly £1bn. BA also indicated that it would break even this year, provided it meets a revenue growth target of 6%.

BA reported a recent improvement in yields, or average fares, and added that the airline's all-important transatlantic business class traffic, its main profit driver, was also showing signs of recovery.

'Market conditions are showing improvement from the depressed levels in 2009-10', said BA, adding that some of the numbers that could dent next year's performance would be challenged by the airline. It has lost £100m from the volcanic ash cloud that shut down British airspace for an unprecedented six days last month and Walsh noted that the government is considering paying compensation to carriers.

'We are not looking for a bailout, only for compensation for the losses caused by the airspace closure which was completely out of our control.'

BA also signalled that it was on course for another legal showdown with the government's consumer watchdog following the collapse of an Office of Fair Trading case against four former and current BA employees on allegations of price fixing. Walsh said the acquittal of the high-ranking managers raised questions over the £121.5m fine imposed on the airline for price fixing in 2007 and hinted that BA might not pay it.

Source: **BA reports worst ever loss of £531m: This year's break-even hopes hit by strike threat,** by Dan Milmo © *The Guardian*, 22 May 2010

For the accountant the total cost and total revenue functions are not represented as curves, but as straight lines. There are a number of assumptions made by the accountant that support this, as follows:

- fixed costs may remain unchanged over a specific range of volumes but they increase in steps over higher ranges of volumes, because when volumes are significantly increased additional fixed costs are incurred on items like new plant and machinery, factories, etc. – the accountant considers a short-term relevant range of volumes over which fixed costs remain unchanged
- over the short term the selling price may be considered to be constant
- over the short term the unit variable cost may be considered to be constant.

The result of these assumptions is that, unlike the economist, the accountant views income from sales (total revenue) and total cost as straight lines over the relevant short-term period. This means that profit continues to increase as volume increases. Profit is maximised at the volume where maximum capacity is reached. Also, there is only one point where the total revenue and total cost lines cross and so for the accountant there is only one break-even point.

Cost/volume/profit (CVP) analysis studies the effects on future profit of changes in fixed costs, variable costs, volume, sales mix, and selling price. The relationship between fixed costs and total costs is called **operating gearing**. Break-even (B/E) analysis is one application of CVP, which can be useful for profit planning, sales mix decisions, production capacity decisions and pricing decisions.

There are three fundamental cost/revenue relationships which form the basis of CVP analysis:

$$\text{total costs} = \text{total variable costs} + \text{total fixed costs}$$

$$\text{total contribution} = \text{total revenue} - \text{total variable costs}$$

$$\text{profit} = \text{total revenue} - \text{total costs}$$

The **break-even point** is the level of activity at which there is neither profit nor loss. It can be ascertained by using a break-even chart or by calculation. The break-even chart indicates approximate profit or loss at different levels of sales volume within a limited range. Break-even charts may be used to represent different cost structures and also to show contribution break-even positions and profit/volume relationships (see Figs 10.2, 10.3, 10.4 and 10.5). Computerised spreadsheets can be

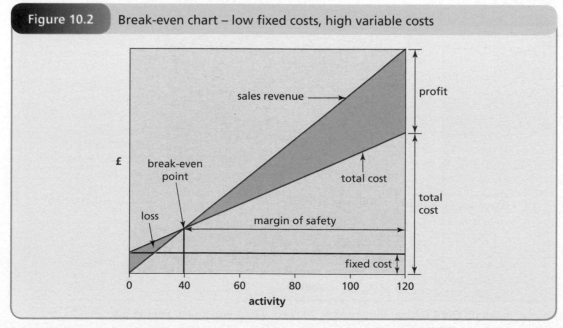

Figure 10.2   Break-even chart – low fixed costs, high variable costs

Source: Based on *CIMA Official Terminology*, 2005 ed., CIMA Publishing, Elsevier p.4.

Figure 10.3   Break-even chart – high fixed costs, low variable costs

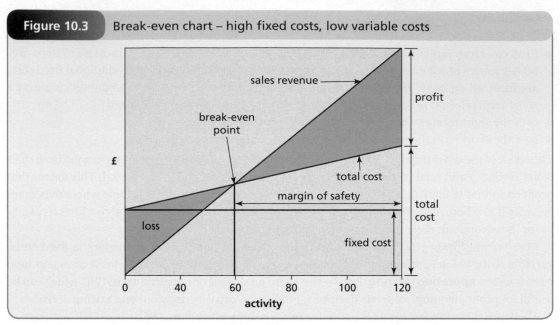

Source: Based on *CIMA Official Terminology*, 2005 ed., CIMA Publishing, Elsevier p.4.

used to convert profit/volume relationship 'what-ifs' into either charts or tables that may be used for presentation or decision-making purposes. They provide the means of exploring any area within fixed costs, variable costs, semi-variable costs, and sales, in terms of values and volumes.

The slopes of the total cost lines in Figure 10.2 and Figure 10.3 represent the unit variable costs. The break-even chart shown in Figure 10.2 shows a relatively low level of fixed costs with variable costs rising quite steeply as the level of activity increases. Where the total revenue line intersects the total cost line is the point at which total revenue equals total cost. This activity of 40 units is the break-even point.

The break-even chart shown in Figure 10.3 shows the impact of a higher level of fixed costs with a higher break-even point at around 60 units, even though variable costs are lower than the cost

Figure 10.4   Contribution break-even chart

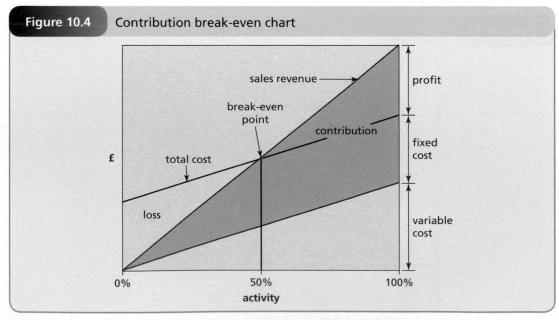

Source: Based on *CIMA Official Terminology*, 2005 ed., CIMA Publishing, Elsevier p.5.

| Figure 10.5 | Profit/volume (PV) chart |

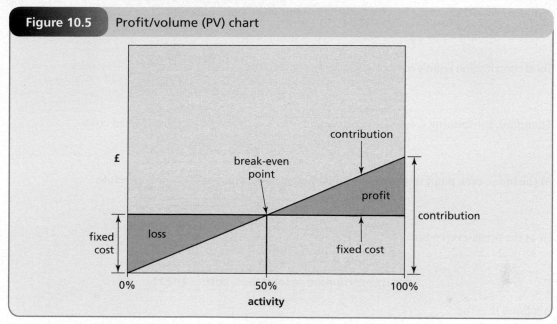

Source: Based on *CIMA Official Terminology*, 2005 ed., CIMA Publishing, Elsevier p.5.

structure shown in Figure 10.2. If variable costs had stayed the same, the break-even point would be even higher at over 80 units of activity.

The **margin of safety** shown in each of these charts will be explained when we look a little further at some break-even relationships.

Progress check 10.1

Explain how a break-even analysis could be used within the planning of a 'one-off' event that involves:

■ the sales of tickets
■ provision of hotel accommodation
■ live music.

Figure 10.4 shows a contribution break-even chart, which is just a variation of the previous charts. In this chart, variable costs are shown starting from the zero on the *x* and *y* axes in the same way as sales. The effect of adding fixed costs to variable costs (or marginal costs) is shown in the total cost line. Where the sales line intersects the total cost line there is zero profit. This is the break-even point.

Figure 10.5 shows a profit volume chart. The horizontal line represents fixed costs and the diagonal line represents the total contribution at each level of activity. The break-even point, where total sales equals total costs, is also where total contribution equals fixed costs.

We will look at why the break-even point is where total contribution equals fixed costs and also consider some further break-even relationships.

Consider
Total revenue = R
Total variable costs = V
Total fixed costs = F
Profit = P
Total contribution = C

Profit equals total revenue less total costs (variable costs and fixed costs)

$$P = R - V - F$$

Total contribution equals total revenue less total variable costs

$$C = R - V$$

Therefore, substituting C for R − V, profit equals total contribution less total fixed costs

$$P = C - F$$

At the break-even point total revenue equals totals costs, and profit is zero, therefore

$$0 = C - F$$

Or at the break-even point

$$C = F$$
total contribution = total fixed costs   (BE1)

It follows that the:

number of units at the break-even point × contribution per unit = fixed costs, or

$$\text{number of units at break-even point} = \frac{\text{fixed costs}}{\text{contribution per unit}} \quad \text{(BE2)}$$

Therefore the break-even in £ sales value is:

number of units at the break even point × selling price per unit or

$$\text{£ sales value at break-even point} = \frac{\text{fixed costs}}{\text{contribution per unit}} \times \text{selling price per unit}$$

But the selling price per unit divided by contribution per unit is the same as total sales revenue divided by total contribution, which is the reciprocal of the contribution to sales ratio percentage.

So, an alternative expression is:

$$\text{£ sales value at break-even point} = \frac{\text{fixed costs}}{\text{contribution to sales ratio \%}} \quad \text{(BE3)}$$

The term 'margin of safety' is used to define the difference between the break-even point and an anticipated or existing level of activity above that point.   (BE4)

In other words, the margin of safety measures the extent to which anticipated or existing activity can fall before a profitable operation turns into a loss-making one (see Figs 10.2 and 10.3).

Progress check 10.2

Discuss how department stores might use the concept of contribution and break-even analysis when analysing their financial performance.

The following worked example uses the relationships we have discussed to illustrate the calculation of a break-even point.

Worked example 10.1

	£
Revenue (1,000 units)	10,000
Variable costs (direct materials and direct labour)	6,000
Contribution	4,000
Fixed costs	2,000
Profit	2,000

From the above table of sales revenue and cost data we can find the break-even point in number of units and the sales value at that point.

Number of units sold $\qquad$ 1,000

Therefore, contribution/unit $= \dfrac{£4,000}{1,000} = £4$ per unit

And, the contribution to sales ratio % $= \dfrac{£4,000}{£10,000} \times 100\% = 40\%$

Using BE2 number of units at break-even point
$$= \frac{\text{fixed costs}}{\text{contribution per unit}}$$
$$= £2,000/£4$$
$$= 500 \text{ units}$$

Using BE3 £ sales value at break-even point
$$= \frac{\text{fixed costs}}{\text{contribution to sales ratio \%}}$$
$$= £2,000/40\%$$
$$= £5,000$$

The CVP technique may also be used to derive a **target cost** estimate, by subtracting a desired margin or target profit from a competitive market price. This cost may be less than the planned initial product cost, but will be a cost that is expected to be achieved by the time the product reaches the mass production stage. Sales volumes or sales revenues may be calculated that are required to achieve a range of profit targets.

Worked example 10.2

Bill Jones, who had worked for many years as an engineer in the automotive industry, had recently been made redundant. Bill, together with a number of colleagues, now had the opportunity to set up a business to make and sell a specialised part for motor vehicle air-conditioning units. Bill had already decided on a name for the company. It would be called Wilcon Ltd. Bill had some good contacts in the industry and two automotive components manufacturers had promised him contracts that he estimated would provide sales of 15,000 units per month, for the foreseeable future.

The business plan was based on the following data:

Selling price per unit   £17.50
Variable costs per unit   £13.00
Fixed costs for month   £54,000 including salaries for 5 managers @ £1,500 each

Bill and his colleagues are very interested in determining the break-even volume and sales revenue for Wilcon Ltd.

Contribution/unit

	£
Selling price	17.50
Variable cost	13.00
	4.50

Break-even volume

If the number of units sold is n

Total contribution $= n \times £4.50$

At the break-even point fixed costs equal total contribution (see BE1)

$$£54,000 = £4.50 \times n$$

Therefore $n = £54,000/£4.50 = 12,000$ units

Sales revenue at break-even point   = number of units at break-even point $\times$ selling price per unit

= $12,000 \times £17.50$

= £210,000

Bill and his colleagues are also interested in looking at the break-even points at different levels of sales, costs and profit expectation, which are considered in Worked examples 10.3 to 10.7.

Worked example 10.3

The data from Worked example 10.2 can be used to find the margin of safety (volume and value) for Wilcon Ltd if the predicted sales volume is 12,500 units per month.

Margin of safety (volume and value) if the predicted sales volume is 12,500 units per month

The predicted or forecast volume is 12,500 units, with a sales value of $12,500 \times £17.50$

= £218,750

The margin of safety is predicted volume − break-even volume (see BE4)

= 12,500 − 12,000

= 500 units

Margin of safety sales revenue   = £218,750 − £210,000

= £8,750

Worked example 10.4

The data from Worked example 10.2 can be used to find the reduction in break-even volume if one less manager were employed by Wilcon Ltd.

Reduction in break-even volume if one less manager were employed

Fixed costs become £54,000 − £1,500

$$= £52,500$$

If the number of units sold is n

$$£52,500 = £4.50 \times n$$

Therefore, $n = £52,500/£4.50 = 11,667$ units

Therefore reduction in volume from break-even is 12,000 − 11,667, or 333 units

Worked example 10.5

The data from Worked example 10.2 can be used to find the volume of units to be sold by Wilcon Ltd to make £9,000 profit per month.

Volume of units to be sold to make £9,000 profit

Profit = contribution − fixed costs

If n equals the number of units, then for a profit of £9,000

$$£9,000 = (n \times £4.50) − £52,500 \quad [54,000 − 1,500]$$

Or, $n = £61,500/£4.50$

Volume of sales $= 13,667$ units

Worked example 10.6

The data from Worked example 10.2 can be used to find the revised break-even volume if fixed costs are reduced by 10% and variable costs are increased by 10% by Wilcon Ltd.

Revised break-even volume if fixed costs are reduced by 10% and variable costs are increased by 10%

If fixed costs are   90% × £54,000 = £48,600
And variable costs are   110% × £13 = £14.30
Then unit contribution becomes

$$£17.50 − £14.30 = £3.20$$

At break-even $£48,600 = £3.20 \times n$

Therefore, $n = £48,600/£3.20$

Revised break-even volume $= 15,188$ units

Worked example 10.7

The data from Worked example 10.2 can be used to find the revised selling price that must be charged by Wilcon Ltd to show a profit of £6,000 on sales of 10,000 units.

Revised selling price that must be charged to show a profit of £6,000 on sales of 10,000 units

Profit = contribution − fixed costs
If total contribution is TC

$$£6,000 = TC - £54,000$$
$$TC = £60,000$$

Therefore
  Contribution/unit   £60,000/10,000 = £6 per unit
Variable cost is £13 per unit
  Therefore revised selling price is £13 + £6 = £19 per unit

Worked examples 10.3 to 10.7 have used the technique of **sensitivity analysis**. We have considered the sensitivity of the break-even point against expected volumes of activity. We have also considered the impact on the break-even point of changes to fixed costs and variable costs, and how costs and price levels need to change to achieve a planned level of profit. Sales price sensitivity may be considered in terms of volume through analysis of fixed labour and overhead costs, and variable material, labour and overhead costs.

CVP analysis may therefore be used in:

- profit planning
- project planning
- establishing points of indifference between projects
- make-or-buy decision-making
- shut-down or continuation decisions
- product mix decisions
- sales pricing.

We shall consider many of these applications of CVP analysis in Chapter 11 when we look at decision-making.

Progress check 10.3

What is a break-even point? Why is it important for a business to know its break-even point, and what types of sensitivity can it be used to analyse?

Limitations of CVP analysis

We have seen that break-even analysis is just one of the applications of CVP analysis that may be viewed differently by the economist and the accountant. The many assumptions made by the accountant, on which CVP analysis relies, include:

- that output is the only factor affecting costs – there may be others including inflation, efficiency, and economic and political factors
- the simplistic approach to cost relationships: that total costs are divided into fixed and variable costs – in reality costs cannot be split easily, even into variable and fixed costs
- the likelihood that fixed costs do not remain constant beyond certain ranges
- the behaviour of both costs and revenue is linear – linearity is rare with regard to costs and revenue
- there is no uncertainty – there is much uncertainty involved in the prediction of costs and sales revenues
- there is a single product – businesses usually produce more than one product and sales mix is not constant but continually changes due to changes in demand
- that inventory levels do not change
- the time value of money is ignored (see Chapter 14)
- that these assumptions hold over the relevant range (the activity levels within which assumptions about cost behaviour in break-even analysis remain valid; it is used to mitigate the impact of some of the limitations of CVP analysis mentioned above).

In real-life situations the above assumptions clearly do not hold because, as has been noted previously, cost relationships are not simple and straightforward. Factors affecting the costs and volumes of products and services do change frequently. Such factors do not usually change just one at a time but more usually change all at once. The above limitations to CVP analysis are very real and should be borne in mind when using the technique, for example, to consider alternative pricing options that use both the marginal and full absorption costing approaches. Nevertheless, the principles of CVP analysis continue to hold true, and some of the above limitations may be overcome.

Multiple product break-even analysis

The break-even analyses that we have considered thus far have assumed that only one product or service is being provided. In practice, however, this is rarely the case. Businesses usually offer a range of products or services.

In the same way as we have calculated for a single product, the weighted average contribution may be used for two or more products to calculate the selling prices required to achieve targeted profit levels, and revised break-even volumes and sales revenues resulting from changes to variable costs and fixed costs.

Worked example 10.8

Curtis E. Carr & Co provides a range of three limousines for hire. The proprietor, Edna Cloud, has prepared the following details of estimated activity for 2010.

Limousine	Elvis	Jackson	Madonna
Estimated number of hours of hire	600	900	500
Hire price per hour	£25	£20	£24
Variable costs per hour of hire	£5	£3	£4

Fixed costs for the year £5,595

Edna would like to know the break-even position for the firm in total hours of hire and sales revenue.

We can summarise the estimated sales revenue, contribution and profit from the information given by Edna, as follows:

Limousine	Elvis	Jackson	Madonna	Total
Contribution per hour of hire	£20 (£25−£5)	£17 (£20−£3)	£20 (£24–£4)	
Estimated number of hours of hire	600	900	500	2,000
Total sales revenue	£15,000	£18,000	£12,000	£45,000
Total contribution	£12,000	£15,300	£10,000	£37,300
Fixed costs for 2010				£5,595
Estimated profit for 2010				£31,705

To calculate the break-even position we need to weight the level of activity of each of the products, the hours of hire of each of the limousines:

	Hours	% of total hours
Elvis	600	30
Jackson	900	45
Madonna	500	25
	2,000	100

The weighting percentages of each product may then be used to calculate a weighted average contribution per hour:

	Contribution per hour	Weighting %	Weighted contribution
Elvis	£20	30	£6.00
Jackson	£17	45	£7.65
Madonna	£20	25	£5.00
Weighted average contribution per hour			£18.65

The multiple product break-even point is derived from:

$$\frac{\text{total fixed costs}}{\text{weighted average contribution}} = \frac{£5,595}{£18.65} = 300 \text{ hours}$$

The break-even level of activity (300 hours) may then be used to calculate the proportion of total hours for each product and the contribution for each product and the business.

		Break-even hours	Contribution per hour	Total contribution
Elvis	30% × 300 hours	90	£20	£1,800
Jackson	45% × 300 hours	135	£17	£2,295
Madonna	25% × 300 hours	75	£20	£1,500
		300		£5,595

The total contribution can be seen to equal total fixed costs at the break-even point.

Break-even sales revenue may be calculated by first calculating the:

$$\text{weighted average contribution to sales ratio \%} = \frac{\text{total contribution}}{\text{total sales}} = \frac{£37,300}{£45,000}$$

$$= 0.8289$$

$$£ \text{ sales revenue at the break-even point} = \frac{\text{total fixed costs}}{\text{contribution to sales ratio \%}}$$

$$= \frac{£5,595}{0.8289}$$

$$= £6,750$$

for the total 300 hours of hire.

A greater degree of sophistication may be achieved from more dynamic and complex models, and using computerised simulation models. Uncertainty will always remain, but the impact of the results of the occurrence of uncertain events, within given constraints, may be evaluated using sensitivity analysis. Spreadsheets like Excel can provide very sensitive 'what-if' solutions, and the linking features in modelling systems can speedily provide a range of alternative values.

Progress check 10.4

Discuss the usefulness of a sensitivity analysis of the factors used in calculation of the break-even point of a national fast food chain outlet that uses television advertising campaigns.

In addition to break-even analysis, cost/volume/profit (CVP) analysis techniques may be used in a number of decision-making scenarios, some of which we will look at in Chapter 11. Very often, for example, in a decision-making scenario there are two or more **limiting factors**, in which case a linear programming model would need to be used to determine optimum solutions. **Linear programming** is not covered in this book.

Progress check 10.5

What is CVP analysis and on what assumptions is it based?

Activity based costing (ABC)

The activities of businesses across the entire chain of value-adding organisational processes have a considerable impact on costs and therefore profit. A recently developed management accounting approach to evaluating the extent of this impact and to dealing with the root causes of costs is activity based costing (ABC).

Activity based costing (ABC) provides an alternative approach to the costing of products in response to some of the criticisms that have been aimed at the more traditional approaches. Before we examine the concept of ABC let's look at a simple example, which puts these criticisms in context.

Worked example 10.9

Traditional Moulding Ltd manufactures two plastic fittings, the RX-L and the RX-R. Both products are produced in the Moulding2 department, which has total overheads of £5,000 for the month of March. Moulding2 uses 4,000 hours of direct labour to produce the RX-L (2,000 hours) and RX-R (2,000 hours). The other activities within the Moulding2 department are ten machine set-ups (eight to produce the RX-L and two to produce the RX-R) which cost £3,200, and the processing of 90 sales orders (50 for the RX-L and 40 for the RX-R) costing £1,800.

The costs charged to each product may be determined using absorption costing on a direct labour hours basis, and alternatively they may be determined on the basis of the other activities within the department.

Absorption costing basis
Cost per labour hour = £5,000/4,000 hours = £1.25 per direct labour hour

	RX-L	RX-R	Total
	£	£	£
2,000 hours at £1.25	2,500		2,500
2,000 hours at £1.25		2,500	2,500
	2,500	2,500	5,000

Alternative activities basis

	RX-L	RX-R	Total	
Machine set-ups	8	2	10	(cost £3,200)
Sales orders	50	40	90	(cost £1,800)
				(total cost £5,000)

	RX-L	RX-R	Total
	£	£	£
Machine set-ups, 8 and 2 at £320 each	2,560	640	3,200
Sales orders, 50 and 40 at £20 each	1,000	800	1,800
	3,560	1,440	5,000

There is obviously a considerable difference between the overhead costs attributed to each of the products, depending on which basis we have used. We may question whether or not the absorption basis is fair and whether or not the activity basis provides a fairer method.

Increasing competition is a fact of life within any industry, public or private, and whatever product or service is being offered to customers in the marketplace. Globalisation has brought increased pressures of competition. Pressures on a company's profit margins inevitably follow from the increasing pace of technological change, which results in shortened life cycles of products that have been manufactured by the company as they are replaced by completely new models. Thus, the obsolescence of capital equipment is accelerated. This all means that the basis of competition has changed.

The effects on businesses are significant, and those that do not respond successfully may fail, or be acquired by other companies. Costs such as development costs and costs of capital equipment must be recovered over a shorter time period. The phases within the product life cycle must be managed more effectively and efficiently. The faster pace of business and the need for quick decisions and action mean that effective computerised information systems are required to provide relevant and timely information.

The above changes in the manufacturing business environment have led to changes in the patterns of cost behaviour. Technological and other changes have meant a lowering of the percentage of direct labour costs as a proportion of total manufacturing costs. An indication of the trend and the scale of this reduction in percentage of direct labour cost are shown in Figure 10.6. In many industries materials and components costs have become an increasingly large proportion of total manufacturing costs. Automation and decreasing equipment life spans have led to capital equipment costs forming a higher percentage of total costs. The costs of information technology and other overhead and indirect costs have also increased as a percentage of total cost. There has therefore been increasing dissatisfaction with traditional costing and decision-making techniques and the search for other, perhaps more relevant and meaningful methods.

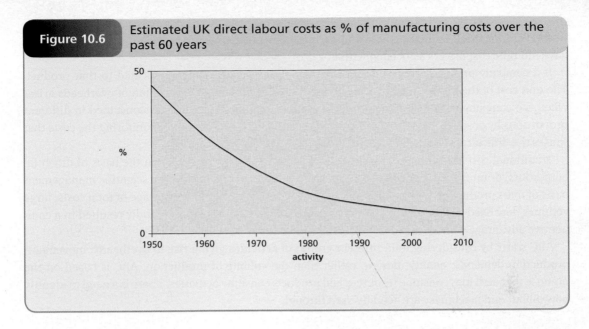

Figure 10.6   Estimated UK direct labour costs as % of manufacturing costs over the past 60 years

Traditional decision-making and control have looked at cost/volume relationships and the splitting of fixed and variable costs. The consideration of 'other characteristics' has not been emphasised. Activity based costing (ABC) was developed by Kaplan and Cooper in 1984 (see Kaplan, R. S. 1983. Measuring manufacturing performance: A new challenge for managerial accounting research. *The Accounting Review* (October): 686–705 and Kaplan, R. S. 1984. The evolution of management accounting. *The Accounting Review* (July): 390–418) and was aimed to get accountants to consider 'other characteristics' in terms of the causes of cost, or what are defined as the **cost drivers**.

Kaplan and Cooper said that one cost system was not enough, and that three were needed:

- for inventory valuation
- for operational control
- for product cost measurement.

Together with Cooper, Kaplan proposed ABC as a method for dealing with the latter two requirements. ABC involves the examination of activities across the entire chain of value-adding organisational processes underlying the causes, or drivers, of cost and profit. Kaplan and Cooper have defined ABC as an approach to costing and monitoring of activities which involves tracing resource consumption and costing final outputs. Resources are assigned to activities and activities to cost objects based on consumption estimates. The latter utilise cost drivers to attach activity costs to outputs.

Progress check 10.6

Why does traditional analysis of fixed and variable costs within a fast moving company (for example, a company that supplies computer hardware, software and helpline services) not appear to provide managers with enough information?

An activity driver is defined as a measure of the frequency and intensity of the demands placed on activities by cost objects. An example is the number of customer orders which measures the consumption of order entries by each customer. A cost driver is defined as any factor which causes a change in the cost of an activity. For example, the quality of parts received by an activity is a determining factor in the work required by that activity and therefore affects the resources required. An activity may have multiple cost drivers associated with it.

If a company produces only one product then all overheads may be allocated to that product. The unit cost of the product is then the average cost. The difficulty of allocation of overheads arises when the company produces many products using many different resources consumed in different proportions by products. It is the sharing of overheads and the feasibility of monitoring the costs that causes the difficulty.

Traditional cost allocation approaches allocate overheads, for example, on the basis of direct labour hours, or units produced. They are therefore volume driven, based on a scientific management basis of mass production with standard design, a high labour content percentage of total costs, large volumes, low fixed costs, and with demand greater than supply. This incidentally resulted in a competitive advantage gained from cost leadership.

ABC starts by considering four different groups of activities giving rise to overheads: movement; production demands; quality; design, rather than the volume of production. ABC is based on the premise that activities consume resources and products consume activities. There is a need to identify how labour and machinery are actually used through:

■ interview
■ questionnaire
■ observation
■ process activity mapping.

Activities are often cross-functional, for example a company buying function that involves purchasing, finance, administration and human resources departments in the whole procurement process. This speeds up and improves communication and may avoid a great deal of unnecessary and duplicate clerical and administrative tasks.

ABC requires the analysis of total overhead costs into variable costs and fixed costs, with variable costs split into short-term and long-term variable costs. Within an ABC system it is assumed that fixed costs do not vary with any measure of activity volume for a given time period. Short-term variable costs – volume-based costs – are defined in the same way as traditional volume-driven variable costs – materials and direct labour. Long-term variable costs – activity based costs – are defined as those costs which vary with the level of activity, which may be non-productive, and the variation may not be instant. Examples of these are machine set-up costs, and goods receiving costs, which are driven by the activities of the number of production runs and number of customer orders, respectively.

The diagram in Figure 10.7 represents an example of the framework of ABC. The bases of ABC are:

■ it is activities that cause costs, not products
■ it is activities and not costs that can be managed
■ control of costs is best achieved through the management of activities
■ each cost driver, or activity, is evaluated by setting up its own individual cost centre, to see if it is worth undertaking or buying in, and to see how it may be managed, reported on and evaluated.

Progress check 10.7

Use an example of a media group to provide the basis for a discussion on how ABC analysis considers departmental activities as the causes of costs rather than the products that are being produced.

Figure 10.7   Framework of activity based costing (ABC)

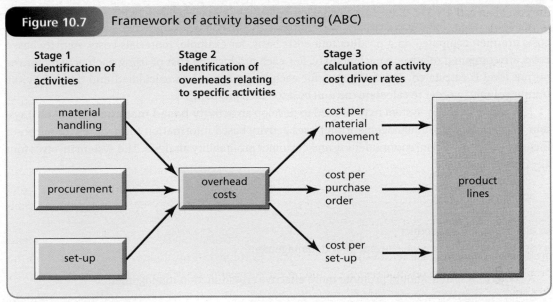

Source: Based on *CIMA Official Terminology*, 2005 ed., CIMA Publishing, Elsevier p.3, (Figure based on Kaplan and Cooper).

The search for alternative methods such as ABC also highlights many weaknesses in traditional cost accounting methods. Indiscriminate use of a single performance measure can lead to misleading conclusions about profit and cost performance. Traditional cost accounting methods can lead to a failure to understand the activities that are causing costs, and a compartmentalised approach to costing which does not look at the processes and activities that cross departmental boundaries. These weaknesses result in:

- pricing and profitability errors
- misidentified cause and effect relationships
- inappropriate make or buy decisions
- inappropriate design initiatives
- irrelevant and untimely variance analysis
- misallocations of capital and resources
- non-productive activities.

Worked example 10.10

Let's consider how the costs of a wine-bottling process, for example, for supply to one large customer, may be classified into those that are volume based, activity based, or on some other basis.

The bottle-filling process costs may be totally volume related. The labelling and corking processes may be related to stocking and handling of materials and the set-up of the processes required to align labels and corks. Alternatively, costs may in some way be related to the different grades of product, perhaps the perceived quality of the wine as cheap 'plonk' or fine wine.

The ABC methodology requires all cost types to be identified and classified into those that are volume based, those that are activity based, and those that may have some other basis. Volume-based costs are then computed on a product unit costs basis, for example, materials costs. Activity based costs are computed relative to each activity. For each product the cost of using each activity for the output level is calculated. The total costs for each product are then calculated and divided by the output volume in order to calculate the unit cost for each product.

The ABC accounting system may be used to develop an **activity based management (ABM)** system. This is a system of management that uses activity based information for a variety of purposes including cost reduction, cost modelling and customer profitability analysis. The system involves four key operations:

- activity analysis
- activity costings
- activity costs per product
- activity performance measurement and management.

A good ABM system should promote more effective cross-function management.

Major companies involved with providing consumers with customer service and advice found the resources required on site were quite expensive, both in capital and management time. As a result of various experiments during the latter part of the 1990s, the UK has seen a major move towards the outsourcing of these services to specialist call centres located in 'low-cost' areas, away from 'high-cost' city centres. This illustrates the ABM process applied to the customer service activity. Decisions are taken following analyses of activities and their costs, followed by the evaluation of various alternative options that might be available, their implementation and subsequent management. In a similar way, many companies have investigated the outsourcing of a number of routine accounting functions to specialist contractors.

The activity analysis identifies all activities and analyses all inputs and outputs of each activity. Activity costings identify all relevant and important costs of all activities. The activity volume that is chosen is the one that most directly influences costs, and the total costs are expressed in terms of activity per unit of activity volume.

Next, the activity costs per product are calculated by identifying the activity that each product consumes, and measuring the consumption rates of activities per product. Using the unit activity cost consumption rates, costs are then allocated to each product.

The final step is activity performance measurement and management. This involves evaluation of the major elements in the performance of an activity. Changes in activity levels are then evaluated and performance reviewed which may then result in the re-engineering of the methods used in that activity. The results are evaluated by:

- measuring
- monitoring
- controlling.

the re-engineered activity.

Worked example 10.11

Let's assume that Traditional Moulding Ltd (from Worked example 10.9) had achieved improvements in the processes, which resulted in a reduction in the costs and number of machine set-ups required. We can calculate the revised costs that would result if the RX-L and the RX-R each required only one set-up and the total cost of set-ups was only £640.

	RX-L	RX-R	Total	
Machine set-ups	1	1	2	(cost £640)
Sales orders	50	40	90	(cost £1,800)
				(total cost £2,440)

	RX-L	RX-R	Total
	£	£	£
Machine set-ups, 1 and 1 at £320 each	320	320	640
Sales orders, 50 and 40 at £20 each	1,000	800	1,800
	1,320	1,120	2,440

There is another considerable difference between the overhead costs attributed to each of the products. We have used the same basis as previously, but an improvement in one of the processes has brought the costs attributed to each product virtually in line with each other whereas previously one product bore almost three times the cost of the other product.

A full worked example will clarify the ABC accounting concepts we have discussed and show the results obtained using ABC compared with those using the alternative traditional absorption costing method.

Worked example 10.12

A clothing manufacturer, Brief Encounter Ltd, manufactures two products, the Rose and the Rouge, using the same equipment and similar processes. Activities have been examined to identify the relevant cost drivers as machine hours, set-ups and customer orders. August budget data have been provided relating to the cost drivers, in addition to material, labour and overhead costs, and quantities produced.

August budget ABC data	Rose	Rouge
Budgeted number of units manufactured	20,000	10,000
Direct material cost per unit	£5	£20
Direct labour hours per unit	0.5	0.5
Direct labour cost per hour	£8	£8
Machine hours per unit	2	4
Set-ups during the month	30	70
Customer orders handled in the month	40	160

Overhead costs for the month:		
relating to machine activity	£300,000
relating to set-ups of production runs	£50,000
relating to order handling	£70,000

We can use the above data to illustrate ABC and to provide a comparison with traditional costing methods. The full production cost of each unit of the Rose and the Rouge using both a traditional absorption costing approach and an ABC costing approach may be compared and illustrated in both tabular and graphical form.

Absorption costing

Using a traditional absorption costing approach, the full production cost of each unit of a Rose and Rouge may be calculated:

budget direct labour hours (20,000 units × 0.5 hours) + (10,000 units × 0.5 hours)
$$= 15,000 \text{ hours}$$

overhead absorption rate per direct labour hour

$$= \frac{\text{machine activity costs + set-up costs + order handling costs}}{\text{direct labour hours}}$$

$$= \frac{(£300,000 + £50,000 + £70,000)}{15,000 \text{ hours}}$$

$$= £28 \text{ per direct labour hour}$$

Absorption cost full unit production costs of the Rose and the Rouge:

		Rose £		Rouge £
Direct materials		5.00		20.00
Direct labour	(0.5 hours × £8)	4.00	(0.5 hours × £8)	4.00
Factory overhead	(0.5 hours × £28)	14.00	(0.5 hours × £28)	14.00
Unit production costs		23.00		38.00

Total costs (20,000 × £23) + (10,000 × £38) = £840,000

Activity based costing (ABC)

Using an ABC costing approach the full production cost of each unit of the Rose and the Rouge may be calculated:

Planned for the month of August:

Machine hours (20,000 units × 2 hours) + (10,000 × 4 hours)		= 80,000 hours
Machine costs		= £300,000
Machine rate per hour		= £3.75
Number of set-ups	(30 + 70)	= 100 set-ups
Set-up costs		= £50,000
Cost per set-up		= £500
Number of orders handled	(40 + 160)	= 200 orders
Order handling costs		= £70,000
Cost per order handled		= £350

Overhead costs per unit of the Rose and the Rouge on an ABC basis:

		Rose £		Rouge £
Machine activity	(2 hours × £3.75)	7.50	(4 hours × £3.75)	15.00
Set-ups	(30 × £500)/20,000	0.75	(70 × £500)/10,000	3.50
Order handling	(40 × £350)/20,000	0.70	(160 × £350)/10,000	5.60
Unit overhead costs		8.95		24.10

ABC unit production costs of the Rose and the Rouge:

		Rose		Rouge
		£		£
Direct materials		5.00		20.00
Direct labour	(0.5 hours × £8)	4.00	(0.5 hours × £8)	4.00
Factory overhead		8.95		24.10
Unit production costs		17.95		48.10

Total costs (20,000 × £17.95) + (10,000 × £48.10) = £840,000

Summary of unit product costs:

	Rose	Rouge
	£	£
Absorption cost per unit	23.00	38.00
ABC cost per unit	17.95	48.10

Figure 10.8	Unit costs for the Rose and the Rouge using absorption costing and ABC

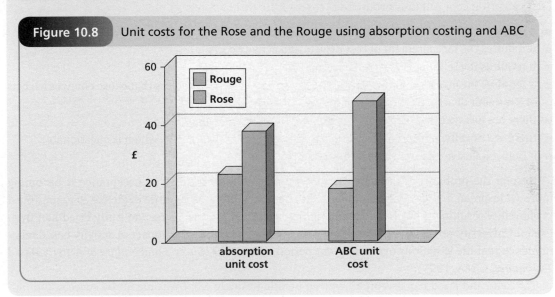

There are large differences between the two alternative calculations of unit costs. In practice, this can have a significant impact on pricing policies adopted by companies, and on other decision-making, for example with regard to continuation of apparently unprofitable products.

It can be seen from Worked example 10.12 that all costs have been accounted for and included in the unit costs for the Rose and the Rouge using both the absorption costing and ABC methods. However, using absorption costing, the Rose has been shown to be far less profitable, and the Rouge shown to be far more profitable than by using the ABC approach. In this brief example, the ABC approach has probably shown the more correct and realistic unit costs applying to the Rose and the Rouge because it has identified the activities, the causes of costs, directly related to the manufacture of each product. The identification of the costs associated with each activity has enabled costs to be attributed directly to each product, rather than using an estimate based on direct labour hours. Therefore, a more informed approach may be taken to improving machine set-up, and order-handling performance, and their cost reduction, and better pricing decisions may be made regarding both the Rose and the Rouge.

The benefits to be gained from the use of ABC are that it:

- facilitates improved understanding of costs
- enables improvements and overhead savings to be made
- focuses on activities and not production volumes
- examines the profitability of products
- identifies loss-making products
- leads to development of activity based management systems.

However, there are also many problems associated with the implementation and use of an ABC system:

- it does not comply with inventory valuation requirement standards
- it is as subjective as absorption costing
- it is historical
- it uses cost pooling (points of focus for the costs relating to particular activities), but also requires the use of apportionment, which involves the same problems of subjectivity identified in the use of absorption costing
- it requires identification of appropriate cost drivers
- it requires the measurement of cost drivers and activity costs
- it requires the relating of activities to products
- it requires the measurement of cross-product drivers, which are factors that cause changes in costs of a number of activities and products
- there are always other consequences that ABC does not address
- there is a novelty, or flavour of the month, factor associated with ABC which is questionable
- it is an expensive and time-consuming exercise.

Despite the problems associated with the implementation of ABC, its acceptance is becoming more widespread in the UK and globally. Nevertheless, there is as yet little evidence as to improved profitability resulting from the implementation of ABC. Dr Stephen Lyne and Andy Friedman from Bristol University carried out research into 11 companies to study the impact of activity based techniques in real-life situations over a six-year period up to 1999 (*Success and Failure of Activity Based Techniques*, CIMA, 1999).

The Lyne and Friedman research involved defining exactly what was meant by success and failure, and using the researchers' criteria, five companies failed and six were deemed a partial success. Interestingly, the research highlighted some key factors that influenced the success or otherwise of implementing ABC:

- the positive and negative roles of individuals
- the degree to which ABC was an embedded system
- the degree of integration with information technology systems
- the use of consultants
- relations between accountants and operational managers.

ABC should perhaps not be regarded totally as the panacea, the answer to all the problems associated with cost accounting. ABC, no doubt, represents an enlightened approach and adds something more meaningful than traditional costing methods. Its implementation requires very large and complex data-collection exercises in which involvement of all activities throughout the whole organisation is necessary. ABC is very time-consuming and costly. Care needs to be taken in evaluation of the results of ABC. It is very useful for identification and management of the activities that cause costs. It is a useful tool to assist in product pricing decisions. It is not yet a costing method which may replace absorption costing for use in financial statements reporting.

Describe the activity based costing (ABC) process and in what ways it may be most effectively used.

Throughput accounting (TA)

Another recent development in management accounting has been the introduction of throughput accounting (TA). It has its roots in the development of the production scheduling software, **optimised production technology (OPT)**, from the mid-1970s. Through the 1980s and 1990s Eli Goldratt further developed and refined these ideas to construct the **theory of constraints (TOC)**, which was outlined in 1984 by Goldratt and Cox in their book *The Goal* (Gower, 1984).

As part of the OPT approach, TA, developed from Goldratt's TOC, provides a new measurement system. This approach takes labour and overhead costs as given and concentrates on the flow of production through the factory. TA recognises that maybe only one or two variables limit the ability of the organisation to achieve its goal to make money. Concentration only on those specific variables, and putting the efforts where the problems are, can result in huge overall gains.

A simple definition of TA was provided by Takeo Yoshikawa in *Contemporary Cost Management* (Chapman and Hall, 1993). Throughput accounting (TA) is an approach to accounting which is to a large extent aligned with the just in time (JIT) philosophy. In essence, TA assumes that a manager has a given set of resources available. These (fixed resources) comprise existing buildings, capital equipment and a labour force. Using these resources, purchased materials and parts must be processed to generate sales revenue. Given this scenario the most appropriate financial objective to set for doing this is the maximisation of **throughput**.

Just in time (JIT) is a management philosophy with an objective to produce or to procure products or components as they are required by a customer or for use, rather than for inventory. A JIT system is a 'pull' system, which responds to demand, in contrast to a 'push' system, in which inventories act as buffers between the different elements of the system, such as purchasing, production and sales.

There is a link between TA and JIT in that throughput is not directly generated by producing for inventory but only by effecting sales from finished output. TA is probably more usefully regarded as a new general approach within which a number of different measures can be constructed, rather than a new set of accounting techniques. This then needs to be supported by a change from traditional cost thinking to throughput thinking as a means of improving profitability.

TA is similar to the approach of contribution per unit of scarce resource (see Chapter 11), but whereas

$$\text{total contribution} = \text{total revenue} - \text{total variable costs}$$

Throughput is defined as:

$$\text{throughput} = \text{total revenue} - \text{total direct materials cost}$$

An advantage of TA over traditional methods is that decisions made on standard costing 'efficiencies' are thus avoided. Examples of such decisions are those based on apparent improvements in labour productivity gained from manufacturing increased volumes (and build-ups of unnecessary inventories), not supported by increased customer orders. TA concentrates on identification and management of **bottlenecks** (which is in itself a process of continuous improvement) and so priority may be given to investment to reduce bottlenecks. The concentration on throughput highlights the critical profit improvement areas of sales prices, volume, and materials costs.

Figure 10.9	Throughput report

	£
Revenue	x
Direct materials	(x)
Throughput	x
Direct labour	(x)
Production overhead	(x)
Administration expenses	(x)
Selling costs	(x)
Operating profit	x

TA is a method of performance measurement that relates production and other costs to throughput. The product costs calculated using TA relate to the usage of key resources by various products. As the costs of all factors other than materials are deemed fixed, the objective of maximisation of throughput will motivate management to generate the greatest profit for the business. TA is therefore an extreme form of marginal costing. The similarity can be seen in Figure 10.9 from the example of a throughput report developed by Yoshikawa.

In *The Goal*, Goldratt defines:

- throughput as the rate at which the system generates money through sales
- inventory is all the money that the system invests in purchasing things which it intends to sell (not to be confused with inventories of stock items)
- operational expense is all the money the system spends in order to turn inventory into throughput.

Goldratt's three measures are operationalised through a number of simple calculations:

- throughput = sales revenue − outside purchases of product-related materials and services
- inventory (in Goldratt's terminology) includes materials inventories plus machines and buildings
- operational expense covers conversion cost, including direct and indirect employee costs, and operating, or idle time.

From these three measures Goldratt defines two important relationships:

$$\text{net profit} = \text{throughput} - \text{operational expense}$$

$$\text{return on investment (ROI)} \atop \text{(in the TA world)} = \frac{\text{throughput operational expense}}{\text{inventory}}$$

(Note the difference between this definition of ROI and the financial accounting definition that we looked at in Chapter 7.)

The three elements of the throughput accounting ROI ratio belong to three different 'worlds':

- throughput – the throughput world
- operational expense – the cost world, which is obsessed and involved with cost cutting
- inventories – the just in time (JIT) world, concentrating on reducing inventories and the costs of holding inventories and with the aim of reducing waste.

Goldratt sees throughput as the priority, with inventory second, and operational expense last. This is a big change in managers' mindsets in which it is crucial for cost accounting not to interfere with the improvement of manufacturing performance. Traditional cost accounting methods may be criticised for reporting efficiency gains from longer production runs and increased volumes of production. Such efficiencies may be illusory if the result is high levels of unsold inventories.

Progress check 10.9

Discuss the relationship between throughput and the traditional ratio of return on capital employed (ROCE) or return on investment (ROI).

Goldratt's approach broadened from a concentration on 'bottlenecks' (in production) to a general concern with constraints. A constraint may be defined as anything that prevents a system from achieving a higher performance relative to its goal. Constraints do not necessarily have to be within the production processes, but may, for example, be concerned with

- demand
- skills
- accounting systems.

Note how in 2009 and 2010, the UK general public saw the Government attempting to solve constraint problems by allocating further funds to the health service and schools.

There are four key influences on throughput, and therefore profitability:

- selling prices
- direct materials purchase costs
- direct material usage
- volume of throughput.

Progress check 10.10

Discuss the connection between TA and the electronic point of sale (EPOS) systems used by all the major supermarket chains.

Hint: Start the discussion by considering just in time (JIT).

To maximise throughput it is first necessary to identify the constraints, the factors that currently limit the expansion of throughput. Constraints may be:

- the existence of uncompetitive selling prices
- the need for on-time deliveries
- the lack of product quality and reliability
- the lack of reliable materials supplies
- shortages of production resources.

Attention may then be given by managers to minimisation or elimination of these constraints.

TA then focuses on some key activities:

- identification of bottlenecks and constraints, through profiling of processes and identification of buffer stocks
- close attention to decision-making on new capital equipment investments
- project teams investigating and implementing reductions in lead times, set-up times and waiting times.

Along with its inventive approach to performance measurement and control, the overriding benefit of TA is that it forces everyone, and management in particular, to get back to understanding what is actually happening where the products and services are being provided, and to appreciate the critical need for adherence to customer schedules.

Worked example 10.13

An aim of throughput accounting (TA) is maximisation of throughput, defined as sales revenue less direct material cost. Purchased materials and parts must be processed to generate this sales revenue.

We may discuss how the contemporary scenario of manufacturing clothing in the Far East and selling in London's West End may generate stress within the UK managers of such a business.

Throughput as defined by Goldratt and Cox is sales (and money) driven. Competition between the clothing retailers is intense. There is no guarantee that what is on the racks of the UK retailers will sell out, ready for the next range. Anything not sold by a certain date must be discounted for a short time or sold at a greatly reduced price to other specialist retailers. Time is of the essence as the selling seasons are fashion, weather and temperature driven. There must be careful monitoring of sales and inventory levels, and continuous contact by the UK retailer managers with their Far East factories to boost production of fast sellers and reduce excess inventories and production of the slow sellers to the minimum.

(You may also like to consider the cost impact on the industry as a whole, and of society in general, of clothing products that eventually remain completely unsold.)

Progress check 10.11

What is throughput and what do we mean by throughput accounting (TA)? In what ways can TA be used to improve productivity?

Life cycle costing

Life cycle costing has an ultimate aim of minimising total expenditure over the lifetime of a product, or over the lifetime of a non-current asset. Life cycle costing involves the maintenance of physical asset records over the entire asset life, so that decisions concerning the acquisition, use or disposal of the asset can be made in a way that achieves the optimum assets usage at the lowest possible cost to the business.

With a focus on maximising reliability and minimising maintenance and repair costs, acquisition of machinery or equipment involves an examination of the original cost and the support cost of the asset over the number of years of its expected lifetime. Depending on the type of equipment, support costs may range from 10 to 100 times the cost of acquisition. The approach may be applied to smaller items such as computer hardware and software, and vehicles, to very large equipment like buildings and aircraft. The construction industry has become increasingly aware of the need to adopt a holistic approach to the design, building and disposal of structures. It has been estimated that around 60% of a typical total construction budget is spent on repairs and maintenance and so there is an obvious need to design for reliability and durability, with more carefully planned maintenance and repair schedules.

As distinct from the service sector, the manufacturing environment has become more advanced in response to customer requirements for higher and higher levels of quality, durability, and reliability. Such factors have to be designed into the product at the planning stage in addition to design for ease and speed of manufacture. Prototype and pre-production stages of a product's development have a significant impact on the product, and its cost over the entire life of the product. Life cycle costing may be applied to the profiling of cost over a product's life, including the prototyping and pre-production stages and in terms of the life cycles of both the business and the industry.

Worked example 10.14

Powerful IT resources are now widely available, and all types of business may benefit from their acquisition and use. Non-current asset registers used to be maintained by businesses manually or in many cases not at all. Now they can be maintained with ease on a computer.

A large plc, for example, can benefit from maintaining its fleet of company cars (say 100 vehicles) on a computer system, using a spreadsheet that may cost no more than £100. Any spreadsheet can easily hold all the records relating to 100 cars.

The records should include acquisition cost, date of acquisition, supplier, specification, insurance, maintenance, mileages, market values (from external sources), and depreciation.

The spreadsheet should be robust enough to last several years and be able to be exported to other IT packages for reporting and updating purposes.

Managers should be able to interrogate the data to make decisions on the future management of their fleet, and expansion of the system and retrieval of data should be available at all times.

Progress check 10.12

How can life cycle costing achieve its aims of improving reliability and minimising costs?

Target costing

Management accounting traditionally supported pricing decisions based on, for example, the calculation of the selling price required to be charged for a product or service that covered total costs plus a margin for profit for the business. Such an approach took no account of the price which the market might accept for the particular product or service. Neither did this approach encourage the objective of total cost minimisation. In fact, one could argue that such an approach encouraged costs to be increased since the higher the cost, the higher was the level of total profit. Increased pressures on businesses to provide higher and higher specifications and levels of quality at more competitive prices has prompted changes to traditional approaches to the costing of products and services.

Target costing policies have been developed from wide usage in Japan based on the principle that a product must have a target price that will succeed in winning a share of the market. A target cost is a product cost estimate (for example a car at £12,000) derived by subtracting a desired profit margin (for example £2,000) from a competitive market price (for example £14,000), determined through customer analysis and market research. The target cost may be less than the planned initial product cost (which may have been say £13,500). The cost reduction (in this case £1,500) will be expected to be achieved by the time the product reaches the mass production stage, through continuous improvement and replacement of outdated and inefficient technologies and processes.

Target costing has also been described as a structured approach to determining the cost at which a proposed product with specified functionality and quality must be produced in order to generate the desired level of profitability at the product's anticipated selling price. Target costing focuses on reducing the cost of a product through design changes.

The traditional Western approach of 'cost-plus' involves the setting of a target selling price by adding an expected profit margin to expected costs. If actual costs are more than expected then the selling price would be higher. Using target costing, in the long run costs must come down to below the target price for the product to be worth manufacturing. This is saying that market prices determine product costs and not *vice versa*.

Target costs are determined by setting specific goals. Better performance then emerges from specific, challenging goals rather than a company's general goal of merely doing its best. Over many years, car manufacturers have been replacing metal with composites and upgrading vehicle specifications without increasing prices. Many examples of this can now be seen from car advertisements appearing in the UK press.

Worked example 10.15

UK mobile phone buyers continue to see major improvements to the specifications of handsets. We may consider how the marketplace needs to react regarding the functionality of a mobile phone.

Mobile phone technology changes very quickly indeed. Products using the latest technology command very high prices (Nokia, for example, advertised five phones with a price in excess of £440 during June 2010). A high volume of demand for older models (over 6 months old!) may be stimulated by offering consumers competitive target selling prices. High throughput then enables the suppliers of mobile phones, and add-ons, to meet such target prices by using economies of scale to drive down unit prices. The majority of mobiles that are sold for around £60 or less in the UK usually include, as standard, Internet access, Bluetooth, camera and radio. Most retailers and dealers also include free texts, warranties and free delivery in their promotional deals. The consumer normally prefers to buy this type of package off the shelf from one source at the lowest price. The mobile phone dealer aims to maintain the unit price as high as possible.

There are three factors that affect the structure of a target costing system:

- type of product – complex, capital-intensive products that have a long development time tend to require more sophisticated target costing systems that are closely linked to the use of **value engineering** techniques
- the market – where goods are supplied to the general public, the target costing system is based on a heavier bias towards consumer analysis and a focus on functionality; examples were apparent in UK press advertisements during 2010, where mobile phones were being marketed with increased ranges of functionality. In January 2010 Nokia announced it was providing satellite navigation software free to current and future owners of its smartphones to combat the increasing functionality of Apple's iPhone handsets using Google's Android platform.
- influence over suppliers – the target costing system creates a downward pressure on supplier prices, assuming that the customer company has greater power and is more important than the supplier company; in the UK, for example, many manufacturers find themselves continually being pressurised by the major retailers to hold or reduce their prices in the electrical goods sector, for example, which reflects 'target costing' by those retailers.

Worked example 10.16

Each summer brings an international sporting event to televisions in the UK, be it Wimbledon, cricket test matches, Ascot racing, the Olympics, or European or World football championships. Just prior to the event there is an inevitable competitive struggle between the major TV retailers.

The summer of 2010 saw a range of promotions being advertised in newspapers and on websites. While Currys was selling half-price Xbox 360 computer game consoles to customers on selected new sets, Marks & Spencer and John Lewis were both offering free Blu-ray players on selected new TV sets. The buying power of Marks & Spencer and John Lewis enables them to exert some pressure on suppliers of Blu-ray players.

Neither company should let the other company drive down prices unilaterally. One of the key ways of remaining competitive is to examine 'ways and means' of reducing the number of constituent parts of the package and unit costs from various individual sources. Almost certainly both companies may have had alternative sources, to enable them to play one off against the other, which is really standard buyer practice.

Worked example 10.17

Since 2002 supermarkets in the UK have been expected to comply with the Supermarket Code of Practice.

While supermarkets continue to report that they work in partnership with their suppliers and provide help, support and training to them to deliver the highest standards of quality, these suppliers are all aware of other suppliers providing the same products for the same outlets. As a result, supermarkets are still able to put pressure on their suppliers. For example, the press reported in April 2009 that, following duty increases on alcohol implemented in the Government's budget for that year, Sainsbury's had contacted suppliers to inform them they would be replacing any lines they could not maintain margins on. The implication was that the suppliers had to absorb the increases or they would be removed from Sainsbury's supplier lists.

There may always be several potential manufacturers that can supply a garment or a food product, for example, to a retailer. The national retailers are aware of this and may use these circumstances to negotiate volumes, prices, quality and deliveries. There will always be such a 'tension' between the retailer and manufacturer.

Target costs may be used to exert pressure on suppliers to reduce costs. However, target costing creates a great deal of pressure within the organisation and the targets set must be achievable. It is not a method of cost control in the traditional sense, but rather provides a goal and a focus for cost reduction. Target costing is something that must be applied at the design stage of new product development, and cross-functional support and co-operation are absolute requirements for its success. The cross-functional support might involve:

- the designer wanting to change from one material used in manufacture to another
- the buyer sourcing materials or components from a new supplier
- the factory floor agreeing that the new product will cause no problems during assembly.

Worked example 10.18

Nissan operates in the automotive market where functionality continues to increase at a quite rapid pace. Nissan also uses a target costing system.

Nissan's target costing system would tend to be determined by market factors, using the following process:

- identification of the major characteristics of the car model, its engine, air conditioning system, etc.
- determination of current costs
- calculation of the 'allowable cost' of each function
- assessment of the level of cost reductions required
- use of an iterative process looking at costs and possible reductions in levels of functionality, in consultation with the marketing department
- assessment of first draft target costs achievable using value engineering
- detailed review of target costs to assess feasibility
- acceptance of draft target costs to be implemented in product development
- implementation of target costs using value engineering as appropriate.

After products are in production, costs are constantly monitored against targets. If costs are not in line with target costs then further cost reduction exercises are introduced to achieve targets.

Progress check 10.13

Outline what is meant by target costing and why it has become increasingly used by large manufacturers of consumer products.

Benchmarking

Benchmarking is the establishment, through data gathering, of targets and comparators, through whose use relative levels of performance (and particularly areas of under-performance) can be identified. Through the adoption of identified best practices it is hoped that performance will improve.

The performance of other companies should be continually benchmarked. This should look at, for example, design, quality, cost, and delivery, and it is known as internal benchmarking, which is a method of comparing one operating unit or function with another within the same industry.

Benchmarking need not be restricted to companies with similar products, or to companies in the same industry. Lessons may be learned and costs reduced by comparing the company's processes with processes in other non-related companies or industries. Functional benchmarking (also known as operational, or generic benchmarking), compares internal functions with those of the best external practitioners of those functions, regardless of the industry they are in. A well-known airline achieved such improvements from benchmarking a photocopier manufacturer.

Competitive benchmarking compares performance from information gathered about direct competitors, through techniques such as **reverse engineering**. Reverse engineering relates to the decomposition and analysis of competitors' products in order to determine how they are made, their costs of production and the way in which future development may proceed. This is a technique favoured by Japanese manufacturers who have used it to advantage to copy and improve on quality and reliability of competing products and to manufacture at lower cost. Another type of competitive benchmarking is strategic benchmarking, which is aimed at strategic action and organisational change.

Benchmarking is a very useful tool that companies may use to develop suitable performance measures and also targets for improvement in each part of their business. A number of further techniques and concepts may be adopted to achieve such improvements, for example:

- **value analysis** and value engineering
- **concurrent engineering**
- **cost of quality**
- *kaizen*.

We will look at two of most important of these concepts and techniques, *kaizen* and cost of quality (COQ), in the sections that follow.

> ### Progress check 10.14
>
> What is benchmarking and how can it be used in support of business performance improvement?

Kaizen

Change management is sometimes considered an oxymoron by many people, who say that change is usually, by its very nature, unplanned and independent of human purpose and is therefore unmanageable. However, the management of change was for many years one of the fundamental sources of competitive advantage that Japanese businesses had over their Western counterparts. The management of change is the basis of the concept of *kaizen*, which simply means improvement. It was a concept so natural and obvious to most Japanese managers that they often did not realise they possessed it.

The tools of *kaizen* were introduced to Japan in the 1950s by two management gurus from the USA, Deming and Juran. However, the concept continued to be rejected for a long time in the West until the Japanese postwar 'economic miracle' began to be studied more seriously and the techniques applied to achieve the same improvements in productivity.

Kaizen means continuous improvement involving everyone, including both managers and operators – the people actually making products or providing services. The *kaizen* philosophy assumes that everyone's way of life, whether it is working life, social life, or home life, deserves to be constantly improved. *Kaizen* signifies small continuous improvements to the *status quo* as a result of constant efforts rather than drastic investment and improvement programmes.

In his book *Kaizen* (McGraw-Hill, 1986), Masaaki Imai described *kaizen* as an umbrella concept (see Fig. 10.10), covering most of those 'uniquely Japanese' practices that have achieved such world-wide fame.

Kaizen teams are small multi-disciplined groups that are brought together to brainstorm and develop improvement ideas. A prerequisite for *kaizen* is a culture within the organisation that is conducive to change – from top to bottom. Two of the fundamentals of **total quality control (TQC)**, **policy deployment** and **cross-function management**, provide an important framework in which *kaizen* may operate. Policy deployment is a process of internalising improvement policies throughout the company from translation of customer requirements, through each process of specification, design, etc. to final manufacturing and delivery. *Kaizen* usually involves first line maintenance becoming the responsibility of operators in what is termed **total productive maintenance (TPM)**.

An organisation that has a cross-functional structure has a horizontal, cross-departmental organisation as opposed to the traditional vertical, functional, chimney organisation of separate

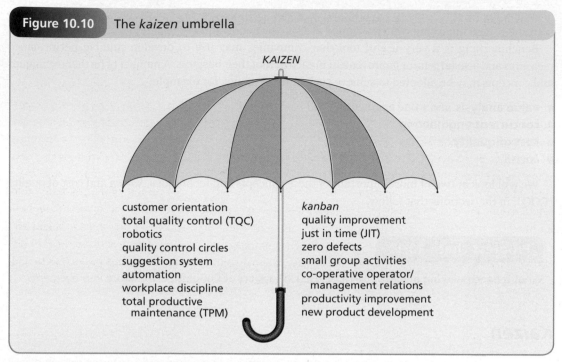

Figure 10.10 The *kaizen* umbrella

KAIZEN

customer orientation
total quality control (TQC)
robotics
quality control circles
suggestion system
automation
workplace discipline
total productive
   maintenance (TPM)

kanban
quality improvement
just in time (JIT)
zero defects
small group activities
co-operative operator/
   management relations
productivity improvement
new product development

Source: *Kaizen*, McGraw-Hill (Masaaki Imai 1986) © The McGraw-Hill Companies, Inc.

departments or functions. This allows for improved communication and team-working, and develops better relationships and quicker decision-making.

It is always beneficial for a business to have at least one continuous improvement team running at any one time to look at:

- products
- materials
- processes
- purchasing
- logistics
- any of the support functions.

The members of the *kaizen* teams should be changed frequently and the process should ensure that employees are involved in assessing, and auditing, departments and tasks other than their own departments.

Progress check 10.15

What does *kaizen* mean in terms of business performance?

Lean accounting

In 1990 we were introduced for the first time to the terms 'lean production' and 'lean enterprise', which were coined by Dan Jones in his landmark business book *The Machine That Changed The World* (Macmillan, 1990). Since that time the term 'lean' has become a generally accepted part of business-speak: lean design; lean organisation; lean management; lean supply; lean customer relations, etc. Lean anything means using less of everything to provide more, and in greater variety. Getting more from less is very much about the control and elimination of waste in all its forms (see more about this in the section about inventory management in Chapter 16); **lean accounting** provides the relevant information and measurements to support this and to encourage lean thinking throughout the organisation.

The introduction of lean techniques is now well established, particularly in the automotive, aerospace and construction industries, and they have had an impressive impact on company financial performance. It is crucial that the implementation of lean techniques has the total ongoing commitment of management (from board level down), and is supported by the introduction of monitoring mechanisms to ensure that the optimum benefits are being gained from the adoption of these techniques.

Weir plc, the Scottish mining, oil and gas, power and industrial company, introduced a lean production system in 2002, as reported in their 2008 annual report and accounts. The Weir group's goal is to consistently meet customer demand, on time, and at the minimum cost, which it aims to achieve through implementation of the Weir Production System, which is an adaptation of the Toyota Production System. Their key objective is to ensure that appropriate best practices are adopted throughout all business processes to produce just what is needed, when it is needed, in the most efficient and effective way. The Weir group has adopted a lean management philosophy that focuses on reduction of the seven wastes, identified by the Japanese quality guru Taiichi Ohno (see pages 633 to 634, Chapter 16), to improve overall customer value. The seven wastes are:

- overproduction
- waiting
- transportation
- inappropriate processing
- unnecessary inventory
- unnecessary motion
- product defects.

Elimination of waste leads to higher levels of quality, shorter production lead times, and reduced costs.

Ownership of each process is of paramount importance, and the measurement of management performance is made by an evaluation across all Weir group companies that compares their current plant practice against world-class practice and performance. The evaluation involves an audit of each manufacturing and service site, which results in the site being awarded a lean score. The lean scores for each site are then totalled and expressed as a group lean score; the results are audited annually by internal peer groups. The Weir group lean scores for 2006, 2007 and 2008 are shown in Figure 10.11.

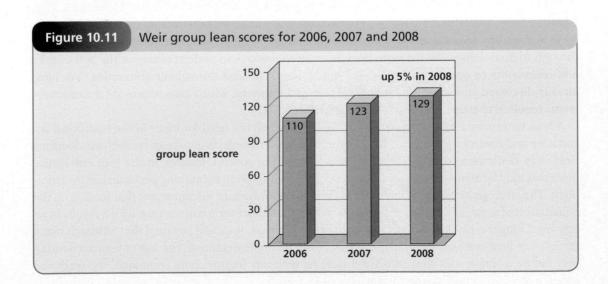

Figure 10.11   Weir group lean scores for 2006, 2007 and 2008

The prior year comparative results shown in Figure 10.11 have been restated to take account of disposals of companies by the group. The lean score may be interpreted as follows:

- 0–60 means the site needs significant improvement – action is required
- 61–99 means relatively good practice – regular follow-up and further improvements are required
- 100–150 is world class practice – the process has taken root and needs to be maintained and further improved.

The scores awarded to individual businesses within the Weir group are analysed to identify improvement actions and set future targets, aligned with the overall business objectives. The Weir Production System is continually reviewed to identify improvements; the recent introduction of a new scoring system has included five additional factors:

- on-time delivery
- inventory turnover
- lost time due to accidents
- direct labour utilisation
- policy deployment.

A recent example of a UK business that has used a lean approach to gain a competitive advantage is Leyland Trucks, the only surviving large-scale lorry manufacturer in Britain. In 2010, Leyland Trucks received the MX award, a manufacturing industry award celebrating achievement awarded by the Institution of Mechanical Engineers (IMechE). Leyland Trucks focused on coming out of the recession and managing the upturn with a commitment to continuous improvement, lean manufacturing, team working, strong financial control, and the use of zero-based budgeting. The company demonstrated its commitment to sustainability through the setting up of a re-engineering centre where unsold trucks can be converted into more saleable vehicles and their components recycled. The company sends no waste to landfill. Leyland Trucks' lean manufacturing capacity means that the company can now build different truck models individually on the same production line specifically to customers' needs. Each of its models can be produced in any order and Leyland's manufacturing systems are able to cope with the complexity of manufacturing different vehicles on the same line.

However, as the press extract on the next page reports, not all manufacturers have yet appreciated the benefits that may be gained from the implementation of lean techniques.

Lean accounting includes the use of target costing (as we have seen) to drive the business from customer value rather than from a cost perspective. It also includes value stream cost analysis, which looks at costs and capacity in every process (from the basic supply of materials and other resources through to final delivery to the customer), in order to provide an understanding of the bottlenecks and constraints to operations, as we saw when we considered throughput accounting. We have already discussed *kaizen*, one of the tools of lean management, which aims to provide the improvements required to create customer value at the lowest cost.

A lean enterprise should be operating at a level at which the need for many of the traditional accounting and control mechanisms, for example inventory records, is unnecessary. Such mechanisms were only really necessary because processes were out of control. Instead, in the lean enterprise, processes may be managed and controlled primarily through lean accounting performance measurement. The strategic emphasis of lean accounting is on performance measurement that focuses on the elimination of waste and creation of capacity, rather than short-term cost-cutting, which results in an improved longer-term financial performance of the business. It should be noted that although many disciples of lean methods claim major savings from its implementation, the use of lean accounting may not be a simple and straightforward task. As with any improvement technique, the costs and benefits of its use should be carefully evaluated.

Lean pickings for management accountants

Just 14 per cent of UK manufacturing companies have adopted the principles of lean accounting, according to new research by accountants and business advisers BDO Stoy Hayward.

BDO Stoy Hayward's head of manufacturing Tom Lawton, who is based in Birmingham, said: 'UK manufacturing continues to make great strides in adopting ideas around lean manufacturing, and we believe that this has been one of the reasons that the sector has been so successful in recent years.

'However, lean accounting, which provides strong support to the lean manufacturing process, has not been widely adopted, meaning that manufacturers are not using the right financial metrics in measuring and monitoring their improvements under lean manufacturing.

As a result, it could be reducing the benefits available under continuous improvement processes.'

The survey shows that the principles of lean accounting are not well understood by most UK manufacturers and this may be the reason for the low take up.

'But at its heart lean accounting is about establishing a financial reporting system that supports, complements and enhances lean manufacturing – and therefore helps improve a company's profitability and working capital management', added Mr Lawton.

'In the current difficult times this focus on profit and working capital management, particularly the reduction of inventories, is fundamental to the well managed manufacturing business.'

The research canvassed 101 UK manufacturers across the automotive, electrical/electronic, aerospace & defence, food & beverage and petrochemical & pharmaceutical sectors on their opinions of lean accounting.

The study found the biggest barriers to implementation were a lack of understanding of the approach (60 per cent) and a lack of understanding of the benefits (51 per cent).

On a more positive note, a near quarter (24 per cent) of manufacturers planned on introducing lean accounting into their businesses within two years.

Source: **Why lean accounting stands fat chance in UK**
© *Birmingham Post*, 21 October 2008

In the next two sections we will discuss some aspects of lean accounting that deal with the management of quality costs, and the increasingly important area of non-financial performance measurement.

Cost of quality (COQ)

Quality, once a deviation from the 'normal' product by providing extra 'luxury' and more features, is now a given. Quality means doing what the customer wants every time at the lowest internal cost. It involves:

- getting it right
- getting it right first time
- only doing the right things and doing them right
- doing the right things better.

In many businesses that have no quality systems, or have neglected quality systems, the cost of quality is usually in excess of 20% of sales revenue. Within service industries this cost may be 40% or more! Organisations that have implemented well-developed quality systems may be able to reduce the cost of quality down to below 20% and perhaps as low as 2% of sales revenue.

Cost of quality (COQ) is a technique that is used to measure the difference between the actual costs incurred within each of the processes of manufacture and supply of goods and services, and the equivalent costs if there were no failures within each of those processes. It may be defined as the additional cost incurred in non-added-value activities and events in a business in fully satisfying customers' agreed requirements for products and services delivered. It is the cost of both not doing the right things and not doing things right first time.

Worked example 10.19

Amazon.com was set up to be able to take orders in the UK for books and CDs through the Internet. If a customer complained regarding poor delivery, the order would be re-sent by courier, even if Amazon was sure that the original had been despatched, if there was an acceptable reason for the delay.

A simple internal report could have been used to reveal to the managers of Amazon whether or not they were delivering a quality service.

The managers of Amazon could obtain, at any time, reports in detail or summary of deliveries by courier, because of the availability of their powerful IT resources. The reports should identify causes of delay and identify whether these are within or outside the control of Amazon. The managers may then accept the reasonable causes of delay to customers (snow or earthquake?), or take the appropriate corrective action regarding their operations.

In the UK, the British Standards Institute (BSI) quality standard BS6143 (1990) defines quality costs using four categories:

- two types of cost of achieving quality
  - prevention costs
  - appraisal costs
- two costs of not achieving quality
  - internal failure costs
  - external failure costs.

In addition, there are two further important categories, which are the costs of exceeding requirements, and the cost of lost opportunities.

These six costs of quality are fertile areas for cost reduction and performance improvement.

Quality costs

- Prevention costs – costs of activities that prevent failure from occurring
  - training employees
  - quality awareness programmes
  - planning and continuous improvement teams
  - costs of supplier assurance
  - costs of calibration, test and control equipment.
- Appraisal costs – costs incurred to determine conformance with quality standards
  - inspection
  - checking
  - auditing or expediting parts or documentation
  - performance testing
  - costs of inventory evaluation and storage records (e.g. traceability).

Non-quality costs

■ Internal failure costs – costs of correcting products or services which do not meet quality standards prior to delivery to customers
  – scrap
  – rework
  – design changes after process implementation
  – obsolete inventories
  – absenteeism
  – costs of downtime.
■ External failure costs – costs incurred to correct products and services after delivery to customers
  – customer credits
  – replaced products
  – customer invoice errors and adjustments
  – unplanned field service costs
  – costs of complaints
  – warranty claims
  – concessions (deviations from specification)
  – product liability.
■ Cost of exceeding requirements – costs incurred providing information or services or product features which are unnecessary or unimportant, or for which no known requirement has been established
  – excess inventories
  – redundant copies of documents
  – reports which are not read
  – detailed analytical effort when simple estimates would suffice.
■ Cost of lost opportunities – lost revenues resulting from the loss of existing customers, the loss of potential customers, and the loss of business growth arising from the failure to deliver products and services at the required quality standards.
  – cancellations due to inadequate service response times
  – ordering of competitors' products because the company's products are not available
  – wrong products offered for the specific customer's application.

Worked example 10.20

We will use Flatco plc as an example and look at its cost of quality for the year 2010. In the year 2010 Flatco plc's sales revenue was £3.5m, and its profit before tax was £590,000. Flatco plc has calculated the following costs of quality for 2010, which have been categorised as:

PR = prevention   AP = appraisal   ER = exceeding requirements
IF = internal failure   EF = external failure

Flatco plc
Costs of quality

Department	Description	Cost £000	Category
Logistics	Unnecessary storage space	12	IF
Management	Ineffective meetings	10	IF
Production	Scrap	10	IF

Flatco plc
Costs of quality (*continued*)

Department	Description	Cost £000	Category
Finance	Computer maintenance records	15	PR
Purchasing	Order errors	13	IF
Human resources	Health and Safety and environmental costs	20	PR
Human resources	Unplanned absenteeism	30	IF
Quality	Customer warranty returns	55	EF
Logistics	Excess inventories	14	ER
Quality	Costs of inspection equipment	14	AP
Management	Training in problem solving	7	PR
Production	Unused production floor space	9	ER
Human resources	Training in skill improvement	32	PR
Purchasing	Inefficient scheduling	19	IF
Design and development	Design changes	21	IF
Design and development	Project overruns	31	IF
Total		312	

The costs of quality were first identified in each of the departments in the company and then a cost and a category allocated to them. Excess inventories of £14,000, for example, were calculated from an average of £35,000 surplus inventories through the year, which were unusable inventories with no value, multiplied by 40%, its carrying costs (space, handling, funding, etc.). The purchasing department employed a person, costing £20,000 per annum, who was employed for two thirds of her time on correction of purchase orders, therefore costing £13,000. The total cost of quality at £312,000 can be seen to be 8.9% of sales revenue of £3.5m. Whilst not perhaps at disastrous levels this is nevertheless a big number at 53% of profit before tax. The analysis of costs of quality shows prevention costs £74,000, and appraisal costs £14,000. The analysis of costs of non-quality shows internal failure costs £146,000, external failure costs £55,000, and costs of exceeding requirements £23,000. The total quality costs of £88,000 are incurred to maintain a high level of quality. The balance of £224,000 non-quality costs is incurred as a result of low quality. These costs should be prioritised for inclusion in a cost-reduction plan to minimise or eliminate. This may involve spending on additional quality costs but would result in significant profit improvement.

The traditional view of quality was to consider it as an inevitable cost (see Fig. 10.12). Improvements in quality were considered as expensive and the increased cost was reflected in higher-priced products having greater levels of quality than 'standard' products, for example 'luxury' or 'gold-plated' models. The culture within businesses having a traditional approach to quality was reactive to problems rather than trying to anticipate and prevent them. Quality problems were usually considered as being the fault of operatives. 'Acceptable' levels of quality costs were established as the norm. Resources were committed to the checking and detection of faults and defects as 'acceptable' levels of costs of quality.

The total quality approach to quality costs is illustrated in Figure 10.13. It considers that quality will pay for itself. There are no 'standard' and 'luxury' products. The highest quality at the

Figure 10.12   The traditional view of quality costs

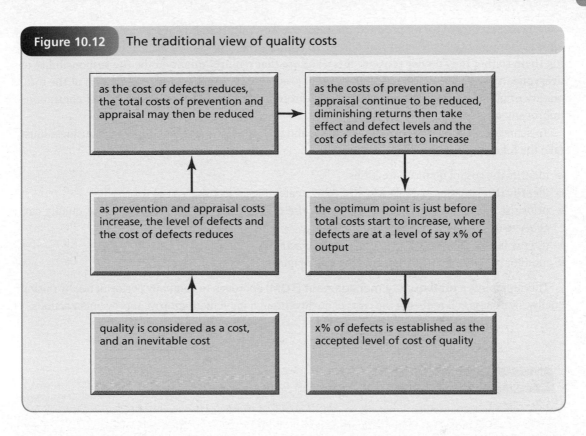

Figure 10.13   The total quality view of quality costs

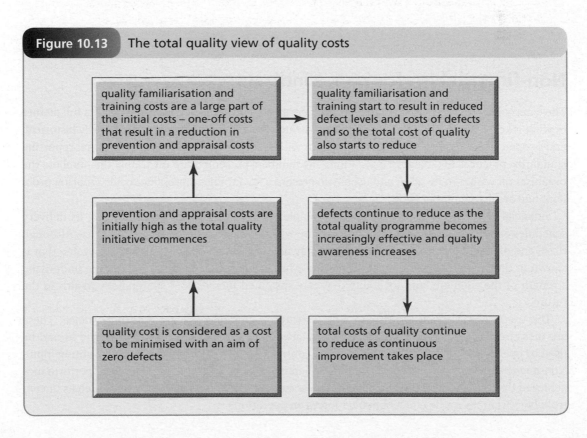

lowest cost is required for all products and services. The culture of businesses having a total quality approach to quality is pre-emptive, aiming to identify the root causes of problems and eliminating them so that they do not reoccur. It is a culture that requires quality to be the responsibility of everyone in the organisation to ensure that all processes are 'right first time'. The aim of the total quality organisation is to become defect-free through the effective implementation of continuous improvement.

To achieve an improvement in performance, and therefore an increase in profit, the business must take the following approach:

- identify the cost of quality categories
- identify the activities and events within these categories that result in cost of quality
- prioritise as high, medium, or low to categorise each activity and specify the cost of quality category to determine areas of high opportunity
- use the information to focus on improvement actions
- monitor progress towards reducing the cost of quality.

This represents a **total quality management (TQM)** approach to company performance by raising quality awareness and reducing the costs of quality through implementation of improvement actions.

Progress check 10.16

How does the total quality approach to cost of quality differ from the traditional approach to quality and how may this result in improved profitability?

Non-financial performance indicators

The externally published financial reports and internal financial information do not give a full picture of what is actually happening in an organisation. Such financial information is necessarily historical, and is open to manipulation and interpretation within the scope of the various financial reporting standards, practices and current legislation. The numbers presented are invariably the numbers the organisation wishes to be seen, and usually to present a favourable impression, while ignoring problems and areas for improvement.

Financial reporting does not tell us, for example, how well the company is meeting its delivery schedules or how satisfied its customers really are with its products and after-sales service. Although these and other such performance indicators may not necessarily be given a monetary value that is shown in the financial statements, they certainly have significant value in terms of the underlying strength of the company and its ability to create sustained increases in shareholder wealth in the future.

The use of **non-financial performance indicators** is assuming increasing importance. These are measures of performance based on non-financial information, which may originate in and be used by operating departments to monitor and control their activities without any accounting input. Non-financial performance measures may give a more timely indication of the levels of performance achieved than do financial ratios, and may be less susceptible to distortion by factors such as uncontrollable variations in the effect of market forces on operations.

Some examples of non-financial performance indicators are:

Customer service quality	<ul><li>number of customer complaints</li><li>% of repeat orders</li><li>customer waiting time</li><li>number of on-time deliveries</li><li>% customer satisfaction index</li><li>number of cut orders</li></ul>
Manufacturing performance	<ul><li>% waste</li><li>number of rejects</li><li>set-up times</li><li>output per employee</li><li>material yield %</li><li>adherence to production schedules</li><li>% of rework</li><li>manufacturing lead times</li></ul>
Purchasing and logistics	<ul><li>number of suppliers</li><li>number of days inventories held</li><li>purchase price index</li></ul>
Customer development	<ul><li>number of new accounts</li><li>number of new sales orders</li><li>% annual sales increase</li><li>% level of promotional activity</li><li>% level of product awareness within company</li></ul>
Marketing	<ul><li>market share trends</li><li>growth in sales volume</li><li>sales volume actual versus forecast</li><li>number of customers</li><li>customer survey response information</li></ul>
New product development	<ul><li>number of new products developed</li><li>number of on-time new product launches</li><li>% new product order fulfilment</li></ul>
Human resources, communications and employee involvement	<ul><li>staff turnover</li><li>absenteeism days and %</li><li>accident and sickness days lost</li><li>training days per employee</li><li>training spend % to sales</li><li>% of employees having multi-competence</li><li>% of employees attending daily team briefings</li></ul>
Information technology	<ul><li>number of computer breakdowns</li><li>number of IT training days per employee</li><li>% system availability</li><li>number of hours lead time for queries and problem-solving</li></ul>

The balanced scorecard

In 1990 David Norton and Robert Kaplan were involved in a study of a dozen companies that covered manufacturing and service, heavy industry and high technology to develop a new performance measurement model. The findings of this study were published in the *Harvard Business Review* in January 1992 and gave birth to an improved measurement system, the **balanced scorecard**.

The balanced scorecard concept had evolved by 1996 from a measurement system to a core management system. *The Balanced Scorecard* (Harvard Business Press, 1996), written by Kaplan and Norton, illustrates the importance of both financial and non-financial measures incorporated into performance measurement systems; these are included not on an *ad hoc* basis but are derived from a **top-down process** driven by the company's **mission** and strategy.

An example of a balanced scorecard is shown in Figure 10.14. It provides a framework for translating a strategy into operational terms.

The balanced scorecard includes headings covering the following four key elements:

- financial
- internal business processes
- learning and growth
- customer.

Figure 10.14 An example of a balanced scorecard

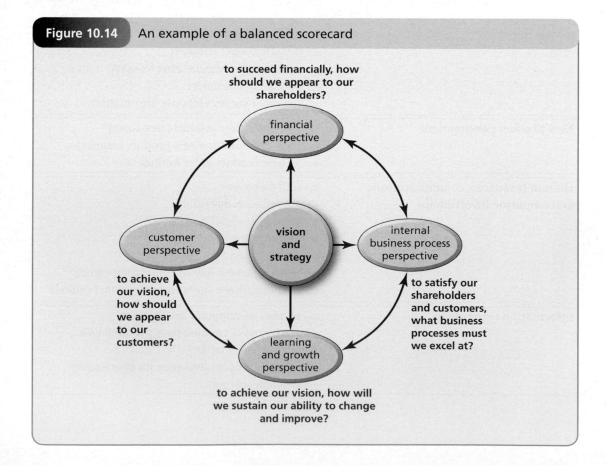

From Figure 10.14 it can be seen that although

- objectives
- measures
- targets
- initiatives

are implied within each of the elements, the financial element represents only one quarter of the total.

How the company appears to its shareholders is an important underlying factor of the balanced scorecard approach. But it is interesting to see that the measures that are considered by the company in satisfying shareholders go much further than just financial ones:

- to satisfy our shareholders and customers, what business processes must we excel at?
- to achieve our vision, how will we sustain our ability to change and improve?
- to achieve our vision, how should we appear to our customers?

Norton and Kaplan comment on the dissatisfaction of investors who may see only financial reports of past performance. Investors increasingly want information that will help them forecast future performance of companies in which they have invested their capital. In 1994 the American Certified Public Accountants (CPA) Special Committee on Financial Reporting in New York reinforced this concern with reliance on financial reporting for measuring business performance. 'Users focus on the future while today's business reporting focuses on the past. Although information about the past is a useful indicator of future performance, users also need forward-looking information.'

The CPA committee was concerned with how well companies are creating value for the future and how non-financial performance measurement must play a key role. 'Many users want to see a company through the eyes of management to help them understand management's perspective and predict where management will lead the company. Management should disclose the financial and non-financial measurements it uses in managing the business that quantify the effects of key activities and events.'

The subject of non-financial performance measures and techniques like the balanced scorecard have been introduced in this book as an illustration and to provide some balance against the dominance of financial measures that are used to measure and evaluate performance in most businesses. It also serves to highlight the recognition that the accountancy profession itself has given to these wider business issues and the way in which the professional accounting bodies in particular have led the thinking away from their narrowly focused beginnings.

Progress check 10.18

Describe the framework of the balanced scorecard approach and explain what you think it tries to achieve.

Summary of key points

- Cost/volume/profit (CVP) analysis may be used to determine the break-even position of a business and provide sensitivity analyses on the impact on the business of changes to any of the variables used to calculate break-even.
- There are a great many limitations to CVP analysis, whether it is used to consider break-even relationships, decision-making or sales pricing.

- The more recently developed techniques of activity based costing (ABC) and throughput accounting (TA) are approaches that attempt to overcome the problem of allocation and apportionment of overheads.

- Life cycle costing uses maintenance of cost records over entire asset lives so that decisions regarding acquisition or disposal may be made in a way that optimises asset usage at the lowest cost to the business.

- A target cost is a product cost estimate (which may be less than the planned initial product cost but which will be expected to be achieved by the time the product reaches the mass production stage through continuous improvement and replacement of technologies and processes), derived by subtracting a desired profit margin from a competitive market price, determined through customer analysis and market research.

- Benchmarking processes of the best performing organisations within the industry, or within any other industry, can identify best practice, the adoption of which may improve performance.

- *Kaizen*, an 'umbrella' concept covering most of the 'uniquely Japanese' practices, is a technique used for continuous improvement of all aspects of business performance.

- Cost of quality (COQ) is used to identify areas for improvement and cost reduction within each of the processes throughout the business.

- The use of non-financial indicators is important in the evaluation of business performance.

- Both financial and non-financial measures are now incorporated into performance measurement systems such as the balanced scorecard.

Assessment material

Questions

Q10.1 How may cost/volume/profit (CVP) analysis be used to determine the break-even point of a business?

Q10.2 Are the assumptions on which CVP analysis is based so unrealistic that the technique should be abandoned?

Q10.3 (i) What are the principles on which activity based costing (ABC) is based?
(ii) How does ABC differ from traditional costing methods?

Q10.4 (i) Is throughput accounting (TA) an alternative to traditional costing methods?
(ii) What may be some of the real benefits from the use of TA?

Q10.5 Describe the process of life cycle costing, together with some examples that illustrate its aims and benefits.

Q10.6 (i) Describe the various approaches to target costing.
(ii) Critically evaluate the differences between target costing approaches and traditional cost-plus pricing.

Q10.7 The *kaizen* philosophy includes a wide range of practices and techniques concerned with achievement of continuous improvement. Describe the role of three of these and how you think they may support the implementation of *kaizen* in a business within a service industry.

Q10.8 How may benchmarking be used to add value to a business?

Q10.9 **(i)** Describe what is meant by cost of quality, giving examples within each of the categories of cost of quality you have outlined.

(ii) Explain how quality costing may be used to achieve business performance improvement.

Q10.10 (i) What does financial performance not tell us about the health of a business?
(ii) Give examples, from each of the key areas of business activity, of non-financial measures that may fill these gaps.

Q10.11 (i) Why has the balanced scorecard become such an essential part of so many business management toolkits in recent years?
(ii) How can the balanced scorecard be used to achieve improved business performance?

Discussion points

D10.1 Is activity based costing (ABC) a serious contender to replace the traditional costing methods? What are some of the drawbacks in implementing this?

D10.2 'Many companies benchmark every element of every process, at great cost, but seem to lose sight of what they are trying to achieve.' Discuss.

D10.3 '*Kaizen* is probably the Japanese business tool that has had the most significant impact on performance improvement in the West.' Why should that be so?

D10.4 The balanced scorecard is a recently developed technique, but it also appears to be the grouping together of a number of well-established principles and techniques. In what ways does it represent a new technique?

Exercises

Solutions are provided in Appendix 3 to all exercise numbers highlighted in colour.

Level I

E10.1 *Time allowed – 15 minutes*

Break-even sales revenue	£240,000
Marginal cost of sales	£240,000
Sales revenue for January	£320,000

What is the profit?

E10.2 *Time allowed – 15 minutes*

Sales revenue for January	£120,000, on which profit is £10,000
Fixed cost for January	£30,000

What is the sales revenue at the break-even point?

E10.3 *Time allowed – 15 minutes*

Selling price	£15
Marginal cost	£9
Fixed cost for January	£30,000
Sales revenue for January	£120,000

What is the sales revenue at the break-even point and what is the profit for January?

E10.4 *Time allowed – 30 minutes*

Seivad Ltd plans to assemble and sell 20,000 novelty phones in 2010 at £30 each. Seivad's costs are as follows:

Variable costs:

materials	£10	per phone
labour	£7	per phone
overheads	£8	per phone

Fixed costs: £70,000 for the year

You are required to calculate:

(i)   Seivad Ltd's planned contribution for 2010.
(ii) Seivad Ltd's planned profit for 2010.
(iii) The break-even sales revenue value.
(iv) The break-even number of phones sold.
(v)   The margin of safety for 2010 in sales revenue value.
(vi) The margin of safety for 2010 in number of phones sold.

and

(vii) If fixed costs were increased by 20% what price should be charged to customers for each phone to enable Seivad Ltd to increase the profit calculated in (ii) above by 10%, assuming no change in the level of demand?

E10.5 *Time allowed – 60 minutes*

Atlas plc, a large UK manufacturer and supplier of business equipment, had total sales revenue for 2010 of £50m. Its profitability has suffered over the past couple of years through competition, lack of innovation, high inventories levels, slow introduction of new products, and high levels of rework in production. The managing director has proposed the implementation of a quality costing system to identify the problems in each department and to develop action plans for improvement.

In the sales and marketing department a number of areas have been identified for action. A reduction in the volume of sales orders has revealed that £4m of sales revenue has been lost to competitors' products. The budget for the year had been based on earning a profit before tax of 12% of sales revenue, but the actual profit for the past year was 4% of sales revenue, due to higher costs. The marketing department has discovered that the company's competitors on average have been able to price products at an average premium of 10% over Atlas due to superior quality and the fact that Atlas has been forced to reduce prices to maintain sales levels. 15% of sales orders completed by Atlas salesmen have errors (which does not please the customers at all), resulting in delivery delays, invoicing, pricing and quantity errors. Delays in payments from customers have resulted in accounts receivable levels increasing by £2.5m mainly because of invoicing errors resulting from incorrect sales orders.

We are told that costs of production are 65% of sales revenue, and the number of people in the sales team is 84 and the average annual gross cost per person is £27,000. Rework and error correction costs have been estimated at 25% of original costs, and Atlas's borrowing costs are 9% per annum.

> (i)   Based on the information provided, what is the total cost of quality for the sales and marketing department in value and as a percentage of total sales revenue, and
> (ii) in which quality cost categories should they be categorised?
> (iii) What actions would you recommend to provide a significant reduction to these costs?

Level II

E10.6   *Time allowed – 45 minutes*

It is a morning in February and Marsha Ighodaro picks up the keys of her brand new Mini Cooper from the BMW dealer in a town situated some 29 miles from the village in which she lives. She drives away in the car she has dreamt about since finally choosing and ordering it five weeks earlier (she has very quickly rationalised her acceptance of the red model instead of the British racing green she originally wanted). It's a cold morning and so she turns on the heater control. Alas, nothing happens! The heater doesn't work.

> Fortunately, these days, such failures rarely occur. But how may a manufacturing company ensure that the complete product offering, such as a Mini Cooper, provides the required level of quality and delivery on each of the assemblies making up the product to meet the expectations of the customer, at a cost he or she is willing to pay?

E10.7   *Time allowed – 45 minutes*

The managing director of Flatco plc has agreed with his budget committee that a profit before tax of 20% of sales revenue should be achievable for 2011. The sales and marketing department have already agreed to a target of 10% increase in sales revenue for 2011 over 2010. The managing director has suggested that a percentage improvement should be targeted for costs in all areas of the company that will provide a 20% profit before tax. (The Flatco plc income statement for the year 2010 is shown in Fig. 4.4 in Chapter 4, page 122.)

> (i)   Calculate the required percentage cost reduction on the assumption that same percentage is applied throughout the company.
> (ii) How fair do you think this is as a method of target setting?
> (iii) How may each department assess whether such targets are achievable or not?
> (iv) What impacts may such targets have on the effectiveness of each of the departments within Flatco?

E10.8   *Time allowed – 60 minutes*

Abem Ltd produces three products, using the same production methods and equipment for each. The company currently uses a traditional product costing system. Direct labour costs £8 per hour.

Production overheads are absorbed on a machine hour basis and the rate for the period is £25 per machine hour. Estimated cost details for the next month for the three products are:

	Hours per unit		Materials per unit £	Volumes (units)
	Labour hours	Machine hours		
Product A	½	1½	20	750
Product B	1½	1	10	1,975
Product C	1	3	25	7,900

An ABC system is being considered by Abem Ltd, and it has been established that the total production overhead costs may be divided as follows:

	%
Costs relating to set-ups	35
Costs relating to machinery	20
Costs relating to materials handling	15
Costs relating to inspection	30
	100

The following activity volumes are associated with the production for the period.

	Number of set-ups	Number of movements of materials	Number of inspections
Product A	70	10	150
Product B	120	20	180
Product C	480	90	670
	670	120	1,000

Required:

(i) Calculate the cost per unit for each product using the traditional method of absorption costing.

(ii) Calculate the cost per unit for each product using ABC principles.

(iii) Comment on any differences in the costs in your answers to (i) and (ii).

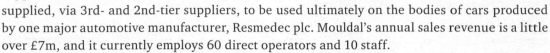

Case Study III
MOULDAL LTD

Mouldal Ltd is a 4th-tier automotive components supplier. All of its aluminium casting output is supplied, via 3rd- and 2nd-tier suppliers, to be used ultimately on the bodies of cars produced by one major automotive manufacturer, Resmedec plc. Mouldal's annual sales revenue is a little over £7m, and it currently employs 60 direct operators and 10 staff.

The directors of Mouldal Ltd are concerned that in their existing traditional costing system there may be under- or over-costing of their products, and are considering refinements to the system through the implementation of activity based costing (ABC).

Mouldal Ltd's current costing system

Mouldal Ltd produces castings for the exterior bodywork of cars. The castings are made using aluminium casting in the company's foundry. The casting operation consists of first melting aluminium ingots, and the molten aluminum is then injected into pre-heated dies that provide moulds of the required shapes. Each separate die contains moulds for each part design. The dies are cooled to allow the molten aluminium to solidify. The parts, when cooled, are removed from the moulds and checked. Any excess bits of aluminium are snipped off by hand, and these together with any rejects are re-used by melting with new ingots. The moulded aluminium parts are then processed through sandblasting machines to give them a very high gloss finish, as required. After a final inspection, the castings are then carefully wrapped and packed into batches by hand for despatch to the customer. Any rejects are re-used and melted down with new ingots.

Under its supply contract, Mouldal makes two types of casting: a large complex casting, the LMB2, and a smaller simple casting, the SMB10. The complex casting is larger and has a more detailed shape (squiggles, curves and fins). Manufacturing the larger casting is more complex because of the more detailed features. The simple casting is smaller and has few special features.

The design, production and distribution processes at Mouldal Ltd

The following processes are used to design, produce and distribute castings, whether they are complex or simple:

1. *Design of products and processes.* Each year Resmedec plc specifies some modifications to both the complex and simple castings. Mouldal's design department specifies the design of the tools and dies, from which initial prototypes and then the final castings will be made. It also defines the required manufacturing operations.
2. *Tools and dies manufacture.* The tools and dies used in the casting process are manufactured by a number of small local toolmakers. The cost of tools and dies, and sales of product protoypes are recovered from Resmedec plc on the basis of cost plus 15%, which includes internal costs of sampling and approval and tooling design costs. This is usually recovered as a single invoiced sum (or may sometimes be amortised as an element of the piece part selling price). Prototype samples are charged to Resmedec plc plus handling charges plus a 15% uplift.
3. *Manufacturing operations.* The parts are cast in moulds, as described earlier, finished, cleaned and inspected.
4. *Shipping and distribution.* Finished castings are packed, batched and despatched to the customer.

Mouldal is operating at capacity and incurs very low marketing costs. Because of its high-quality products, Mouldal has minimal customer-service costs. But, Mouldal's business environment is very competitive with respect to the simple castings. At a recent meeting, Resmedec's purchasing director indicated that a new competitor, who makes only simple castings, was offering to supply the SMB10 casting at a price of around £215, which was below Mouldal's price of £235. Unless Mouldal lowers its selling price, it will be in danger of losing the Resmedec business for the simple casting, similar to SMB10, for the next model year. Mouldal's directors are very concerned about this development. The same competitive pressures do not exist for the complex casting, the LMB2, which Mouldal currently sells at a price of £420 per casting.

Mouldal has years of experience in manufacturing and distributing simple castings, and the directors have investigated and found that their technology and processes are very efficient in manufacturing and distributing the simple SMB10 casting. Because Mouldal often makes process improvements, the directors are confident that their technology and processes for making simple castings are similar to or better than their competitors.

However, the directors were less certain about Mouldal's capabilities in manufacturing and distributing complex castings like the LMB2. Mouldal had only recently started making this particular casting. Although the directors were pleasantly surprised to learn that Resmedec plc considered the price of the LMB2 casting to be very competitive, they were puzzled that, even at that price, it earned such large margins. Mouldal's directors were surprised that the margins were so high on this newer, less-established product, and yet low on the SMB10 product where the company had strong capabilities. Since Mouldal was not deliberately charging a low price for SMB10, the directors wondered whether the costing system overcosts the simple SMB10 casting (assigning excessive costs to it) and undercosts the complex LMB2 casting (assigning too little costs to it).

Mouldal's directors have various options that they may consider:

- give up the Resmedec business in simple castings if it really is unprofitable
- reduce the price on the simple casting and accept a lower margin
- reduce the price on the simple casting and drastically cut costs.

First, the directors needed to understand what it actually costs to make and sell the SMB10 and LMB2 castings. For sales pricing decisions, Mouldal assigns all costs, both manufacturing and non-manufacturing, to the SMB10 and LMB2 castings. (Had the focus been on costing for inventory valuation, they would only assign manufacturing costs to the castings.)

In a year, Mouldal plc works to full capacity and makes 20,000 simple SMB10 castings and 6,000 complex LMB2 castings. The costs of direct materials and direct manufacturing labour are as follows:

	SMB10	LMB2
Direct materials	£1,270,000	£750,000
Direct production labour	£880,000	£300,000

Most of the indirect costs of £2,915,000 consist of salaries paid to supervisors, engineers, manufacturing support and maintenance staff that support direct manufacturing labour. Mouldal currently uses direct manufacturing labour-hours as the only allocation base to allocate all indirect costs to the SMB10 and LMB2. In a year, Mouldal uses 87,800 total direct manufacturing labour-hours to make the small simple SMB10 castings and 28,800 direct manufacturing labour-hours to make the larger complex LMB2 castings.

Mouldal's directors were quite confident about the accuracy of the direct materials and direct manufacturing labour costs of the castings. This was because those costs could be traced directly to each of the castings. They were less certain about the accuracy of the costing system in measuring the overhead resources used by each type of casting. The directors considered that a refined costing system would provide a better measurement of the non-uniformity in the use of the overhead resources of the business.

Second, therefore, the directors decided to investigate the refining of its costing system and considering the implementation of an ABC system at Mouldal, and to identify the activities that may help explain why Mouldal incurs the costs that it currently classifies as indirect. To investigate these activities, Mouldal organised a cross-functional ABC team from design, manufacturing, distribution, and accounting and administration.

Refinement of the costing system by the Mouldal Ltd ABC team

The ABC team used the following three guidelines to refine its costing system:

I   *Use of direct cost tracing,* to classify as many of the total costs as direct costs as possible, and reduce the amount of costs classified as indirect.
II *Identification of indirect cost pools,* to expand the indirect cost pool into a number of homogeneous pools. In a homogeneous cost pool all the costs would have the same or a similar cause-and-effect relationship with the cost-allocation base.
III *Determination of cost-allocation bases,* to identify an appropriate cost-allocation base for each indirect cost pool.

The ABC team looked at the key activities by mapping all the processes needed to design, manufacture and distribute castings, and identified seven major activities:

(i)   *Design products and processes*
(ii)   *Set up the machinery to melt the aluminium ingots, align the dies and cast the moulds, and sandblast the parts*
(iii) *Operate the machines to manufacture castings*
(iv)   *Clean and maintain the moulds after the parts have been cast*
(v)   *Prepare batches of finished castings for shipment*
(vi)   *Despatch the castings to Resmedec plc*
(vii) *Administer and manage all the processes at Mouldal.*

(It should be noted that for the sake of simplicity the processes relating to the melting of aluminium ingots, casting of the moulds, and sandblasting, have been combined into one activity. In practice, of course, these are three distinctly separate processes, which would have individual cost attributes and cost-allocation bases.)

The ABC team then separated its original single overhead cost pool into seven activity-related cost pools. For each activity-cost pool, a measure of the activity performed was used as the cost-allocation base. The costs in each cost pool have a cause-and-effect relationship with the cost-allocation base. For example, Mouldal defined set-up hours as a measure of machine set-up activity and cubic metres of packages moved as a measure of distribution activity. Because each activity-cost pool related to a narrow and focused set of costs (e.g. set-up or distribution), the cost pools are homogeneous. At Mouldal, over the long run, set-up hours is a cost driver of machine set-up costs, and cubic metres of packages moved is a cost driver of distribution costs.

The Mouldal plc ABC team used a four-part cost hierarchy (defined by Cooper, who, together with Kaplan developed ABC in the 1980s). This is commonly used in ABC systems to facilitate the allocating of costs to products. It categorises costs into different cost pools on the basis of the different types of cost driver (or cost-allocation base) or different degrees of difficulty in determining cause-and-effect (or benefits-received) relationships:

(a) *Unit-level activity costs*, which are resources sacrificed on activities performed on each individual unit of a product Manufacturing operations costs (such as electricity, depreciation of machinery and equipment, and repairs) that are related to the activity of running the machines are unit-level costs, because the cost of this activity increases with each additional unit of output produced (or machine-hour).

(b) *Batch-level activity costs*, which are resources sacrificed on activities that are related to a group of units of product rather than to each individual unit of product. Purchasing costs, which include the costs of placing purchase orders, receiving materials and paying suppliers, are batch-level costs because they are related to the number of purchase orders placed rather than to the quantity or value of materials purchased.

(c) *Product-sustaining activity costs*, which are resources sacrificed on activities undertaken to support individual products. Examples may be design costs for each type of product, which depend largely on the time spent by designers on designing and modifying the particular product, and processes, and engineering costs incurred to change product designs.

(d) *Facility-sustaining activity costs*, which are resources sacrificed on activities that cannot be traced to individual products but which support the organisation as a whole. General administration costs (for example rent and security costs) are facility-sustaining costs, where it is usually difficult to find cause-and-effect relationships between the costs and a cost-allocation base. Because of the lack of a cause-and-effect relationship, these costs may be deducted from operating profit rather than allocated to products. Alternatively, if the business believes that all costs should be allocated to products, facility-sustaining costs may be allocated to products on a basis of, for example, direct manufacturing labour hours. Allocating all costs to products becomes particularly important when the businesses wants to set selling prices on a cost basis that embraces all costs.

The ABC team then set out to explain the cause-and-effect relationships and decide on the different types of cost driver relationships for each activity, and their cost-allocation base. In some cases, costs in an indirect cost pool may be traced directly to products, rather than being considered as indirect costs and dealt with on an allocation basis.

In its current system, Mouldal classifies mould-cleaning and maintenance costs as indirect costs and allocates them to products using direct manufacturing labour hours. However, the ABC team found that these costs could be traced directly to a casting because each type of casting can only be produced from a specific mould. Because mould-cleaning and maintenance costs consist of operators' wages for cleaning moulds after each batch of castings is produced, these costs are direct batch-level costs. Complex castings incur more cleaning and maintenance costs than simple castings because the moulds of complex castings are more difficult to clean, and because Mouldal produces more batches of complex castings than simple castings (see Table 1 below).

Table 1

	LMB2	SMB10	Total
Number of castings	6,000	20,000	
Castings per production batch	10	40	
Number of production batches	600	500	
Set-up time per production batch	2.3 hours	0.9 hours	
Total set-up hours	1,375 hours	450 hours	1,825 hours

Therefore, the £330,000 of the total indirect costs that were for mould-cleaning and maintenance were identified as relating directly to products. £147,000 related to the production of 20,000 SMB10 castings and £183,000 related to production of 6,000 LMB2 castings. For each of the remaining 6 activities the ABC team identified the indirect costs associated with each activity for the balance of the total indirect costs (£2,915,000 less £330,000 now treated as direct costs). The cost identified for each activity, together with the cost allocation base and overhead allocation rate is shown in Table 2 below. The table also includes an explanation of cause-and-effect relationships that supported the decisions on the choice of allocation base.

Table 2

Activity	Cost category	Total costs	Cost allocation base	Overhead allocation rate	Cause-and-effect basis of allocation base
Design	Product-sustaining	£550,000	110 parts-square-metres	£5,000 per parts-square-metres	Complex moulds require more design resources
Machine set-up	Batch level	£365,000	1,825 set-up hours	£200 per set-up hour	Set-up overheads increase as set-up hours increase
Manufacturing operations	Unit level	£780,000	7,800 machine hours	£100 per machine hour	Production overhead to support the machines increases with machine usage
Shipments	Batch level	£99,000	200 shipments	£495 per shipment	Costs of preparing shipment batches increase
Distribution	Unit level	£478,000	30,000 cubic metres	£15.95 per cubic metre	Distribution overheads increase with the cubic metres of packages shipped
Administration	Product-sustaining	£312,500	116,600 direct labour hours	£2.68 per direct labour hour	Administrative resources support direct labour hours because they increase with direct labour hours

The ABC team carried out extensive observation and measurement of each process and identified the amount of each activity required by each of the products LMB2 and SMB10, which is shown in Table 3 below:

Table 3

Activity	LMB2	SMB10	Total
Design	77 parts-square-metres	33 parts-square-metres	110 parts-square-metres
Machine set-up	1,375 set-up hours	450 set-up hours	1,825 set-up hours
Manufacturing operations	2,300 machine hours	5,500 machine hours	7,800 machine hours
Shipments	100 shipments	100 shipments	200 shipments
Distribution	10,000 cubic metres	20,000 cubic metres	30,000 cubic metres
Administration	28,800 direct labour hours	87,800 direct labour hours	116,600 direct labour hours

Required

(i) Use Mouldal Ltd's current traditional costing system to calculate the costs and profit margins in total for the company and each of its products, the SMB10 and the LMB2.

(ii) Use the data provided from the study by the Mouldal Ltd ABC team to calculate the costs and profit margins in total for the company and each of its products, the SMB10 and the LMB2, using activity based costing (ABC).

(iii) Compare the detailed total and unit cost information from i) and ii) above to identify the differences, if any, and discuss what action Mouldal Ltd may consider with regard to its pricing of the SMB10 and the LMB2.

11

Relevant costs, marginal costs and decision-making

Contents

Learning objectives

Completion of this chapter will enable you to:

- explain the scope and importance of decision-making to an organisation
- outline the decision-making process
- explain the significance of the concept of relevant costs
- apply marginal costing techniques to decision-making
- evaluate shut-down or continuation decisions
- critically compare make or buy alternatives
- consider the problem of product mix, scarce resources and limiting factors
- consider the wide range of sales pricing options
- use a decision tree to determine expected values of alternative outcomes.

Introduction

In Chapter 10 we looked at the relationship between costs, activity levels, contribution and profit. This chapter will further develop these ideas and introduce some additional ways of looking at costs. One of the most important uses of accounting and financial information is as an aid to decision-making. There are many categories of business decisions. The costs and benefits that result from each type of decision may be very different and so it is useful to identify the different categories of decisions. Broadly, decisions are to do with:

- problem-solving
- planning
- control
- investment.

This chapter outlines what decision-making means and considers the different types of decision that may be assisted by various accounting techniques. Chapter 15 has been devoted to the whole area of capital investment decision-making.

In this chapter we will outline the various types and levels of decision and the process of decision-making. The concept of relevant costs is explored in some detail and we will consider its significance in assessing the information that should be used in calculations to support decision-making. We will look at the following specific types of decision:

- whether or not to shut down a factory or a department, in a manufacturing or service environment
- whether to buy a component or part used in manufacturing from an outside supplier or to make it internally
- decisions on product or service mix and the constraints of limiting factors
- pricing policy and the alternative sales pricing options available to an entity
- decisions in which risk is a key factor, and the use of decision trees.

The scope of decision-making

The management accountant is involved with providing financial and non-financial information and analysis to enable managers to evaluate alternative proposals and to determine which courses of action they should take. However, decisions are made by managers, not by the management accountant, and the levels of authority within the management hierarchy are determined by company policy. Companies normally establish limits at each management level for each type of decision, and the level of expenditure allowed. The approval of one or more directors is normally required for all capital expenditure. Strategic decision-making is carried out at board level. Operational decisions are normally made at the middle manager level, and tactical decisions made at the junior manager level.

There are obviously different levels of decision-making and different levels and types of decisions. The decision by the chairman of Corus (formerly British Steel, now owned by Tata) about whether he should wear a blue tie or a red tie is of less significance (although perhaps not to tie-makers) than his decision on whether or not to shut down a steel-producing plant. Decisions on factory closures by Corus and many other companies have unfortunately been all too common in the UK over the past 20 or 30 years (see the Cadbury press extract below) as the manufacturing sector of the economy has shrunk to a fraction of its former size. Frequently, takeovers lead to plant closures particularly if operations can be switched to countries which have substantially lower labour costs.

Closing down a factory

The US food giant Kraft has said it is 'truly sorry' for reneging on an earlier promise to keep open Cadbury's Somerdale factory just days after it acquired the Dairy Milk maker for £11.7bn in January.

The grovelling apology came from Marc Firestone, an executive vice-president at Kraft, at a grilling by MPs yesterday over the closure, although he promised that the maker of Oreo biscuits would not close any more UK factories for the next two years.

Irene Rosenfeld, the chief executive of Kraft, had snubbed the Commons Business Select Committee meeting, sending along three executives instead, including Mr Firestone, its VP of corporate and legal affairs.

During the takeover process Kraft vowed to keep the factory open, despite the fact that Cadbury had already set in motion the process to close the Somerdale facility, at Keynsham near Bristol, and shift production to Poland with the loss of about 400 jobs.

Jack Dromey, Unite's deputy general secretary, said that Kraft had been 'utterly cynical to pretend it could reprieve the plant'. He added: 'Hopes were raised, hopes were dashed.'

On behalf of Kraft, Mr Firestone said yesterday: 'We are truly sorry about that, and I am personally sorry. I personally give you my apology for creating that uncertainty.'

In a heated session with MPs, he claimed that after the takeover had been sealed in January, Kraft had days later found out that the equipment required for manufacturing at Somerdale had already been installed in Poland. 'Tens of millions of dollars of new equipment were going into the factory during our takeover bid. We had no way of knowing', said Mr Firestone. But at least one MP laughed at his version of events and cried 'nonsense'.

Lindsay Hoyle, the Labour MP, said that Kraft's U-turn was 'remote, smug and worst of all duplicitous'.

This month, it emerged that official complaints had been made to the Takeover Panel about the comments made by Kraft concerning Somerdale.

Holding a Terry's Chocolate Orange in the air, Mr Hoyle said that Kraft had broken its promises over the Terry's factory in York. After acquiring Terry's in 1993, Kraft closed the factory.

Mr Hoyle said: 'The Vikings came to York to pillage. Kraft went to York and did exactly the same thing. You pillaged and asset-stripped the company.'

But Mr Firestone promised that Kraft would not close any more factories in the UK in the next two years, although he was unable to make any commitment beyond that. He added: 'And not withstanding any plans that are already under way, there will be no further compulsory redundancies of manufacturing employees in the UK.'

He added that it 'intends' to keep Cadbury's Dairy Milk factory in Bournville, Birmingham, open.

Source: **Kraft is 'truly sorry' for U-turn over closure of Somerdale plant,** by James Thompson © *The Independent*, 17 March 2010

Despite being the world's second largest food company Kraft acquired Cadbury during a three-year cost-cutting and restructuring exercise which involved shedding less-profitable brands, discontinuing product lines, closing plants and cutting jobs. It was perhaps inevitable that, despite assurances to the contrary, the Cadbury Somerdale plant would close in line with Kraft's corporate strategy. The impact of such plant closures is not just on the companies themselves, having much wider economic and social consequences for both the immediate areas in which they are located and for UK manufacturing in general.

The scope of decision-making includes the areas of problem-solving, planning, control and investment (see Fig. 11.1).

Problem-solving decisions

Decision-making relating to problem-solving considers relevant costs (and revenues) which are the costs (and revenues) appropriate to a specific management decision. These include incremental or **differential costs** and benefits, and opportunity costs. They are represented by future cash flows whose magnitude will vary depending upon the outcome of the management decision made. If products are sold to a retailer, the relevant costs used in the determination of the profitability of the transaction would be the cost of replacing the products, not their original purchase price, which is a sunk cost. Sunk costs, or irrecoverable costs, are costs that have been irreversibly incurred or committed to prior to a decision point and which cannot therefore be considered relevant to subsequent decisions.

An opportunity cost is the value of the benefit sacrificed when one course of action is chosen in preference to an alternative. The opportunity cost is represented by the forgone potential benefit from the best of the alternative courses of action that have been rejected.

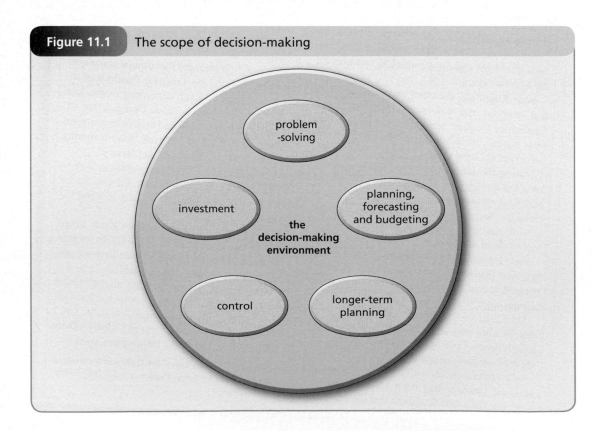

Figure 11.1   The scope of decision-making

Planning, forecasting and budgeting decisions

Planning, forecasting and budgeting decisions require best estimates of costs and the use of cost/volume/profit (CVP) analysis.

Long-term planning decisions

Longer-term planning decisions assume that in the long run all costs are variable and that scarce resources, and over- or under-capacity, are problems that can be overcome.

Control decisions

Control decisions use historical information and comparisons such as variance analysis and actual to budget comparisons.

Investment decisions

Investment decisions tend to be longer term, and cash flow and the time value of money are important appraisal factors.

Decision-making is a crucially important process within any organisation. It is used to select, hopefully, the correct future course of action in, for example:

- whether to make or buy equipment or components
- levels of order quantities
- levels of inventories held
- whether or not to replace an asset
- determination of selling prices
- contract negotiation.

Decisions also have to be made as to whether or not to invest in capital projects and on choices between investments in alternative projects, which are competing for resources. Such decisions will be considered in Chapter 15, which deals with capital investment decisions.

Routine planning decisions, including budgeting, usually require analysis of fixed and variable costs, together with revenues, over a year. These costs are often estimated and may support the use of cost/volume/profit (CVP) analysis. The usefulness of the analysis will almost certainly be enhanced by the speed and sophistication of IT spreadsheets. An example may be seen from special offers and weekend breaks seen within the UK hotel sector. Spreadsheet 'what-ifs' linked to current bookings suggest the capacity available to be offered at a special rate for specific periods (note the English Country Inns – 'Stay Sunday and Monday night for reduced rates' offer in 2010).

Decisions on short-run problems are of a non-recurring nature, where costs are incurred and benefits are received all within a relatively short period. An example is whether or not a contract should be accepted or rejected. These types of decision need identification of incremental or differential costs and revenues and a distinction between sunk costs and opportunity costs.

Investment and disinvestment decisions, such as whether to buy a new machine, or shut down a department, often have long-term consequences, and so ideally the time value of money should be allowed for, using **discounted cash flow (DCF)** techniques. The long-term consequences may span several accounting periods and the economies of more than just one country may be involved, for example international motor manufacturers with plants established throughout the world.

Longer-range decisions are made once and reviewed infrequently. They are intended to provide a continuous solution to a continuing or recurring problem. They include decisions about selling and distribution policies, for example whether to sell direct to customers or through an agent. In the long run all costs are variable. In the short term, fixed costs, or resource and capacity problems that may be encountered, can be changed or overcome over time.

Such changes may be determined by the board of directors at the strategic level, where the priorities of the business may be changed, or at the operational and tactical levels where change may be achieved through, for example, bottom-up continuous improvement initiatives. The process may therefore take several months and even years (especially, for example, when trying to sell a site or a building). The time span may be shorter; for example, UK retailers are able to announce the impact of their Christmas trading results very early in January, which suggests that analyses of variances are undertaken on a daily, or even perhaps an hourly, basis.

Control decisions involve deciding whether or not to investigate disappointing performance, and expected benefits should exceed the costs of investigation and control. Historical information such as comparison of costs, revenues or profits to budget, is used to carry out variance analysis to indicate what control decisions need to be taken. Variance analysis can be used to look at just one factory, or several factories. Manufacturers will often locate new plant and equipment in subsidiaries where there are few 'disappointing performances'.

Worked example 11.1

The UK motor manufacturer Vauxhall began producing police cars and rally cars based on its 'family saloons'.

Let's consider the short-run problems that may have been encountered by Vauxhall during the decision-making process relating to these products.

The specification of the police car was customer driven and the changes to the standard saloons could be costed in order that a price could be proposed to the customer. The operators on the production line could easily modify the existing model to the new specification.

The rally car was almost certainly going to create problems because the specification may need to change throughout the season. Production-line disruptions would inevitably ensue. The rally car would probably require specialists amongst the workforce to design and produce it.

Progress check 11.1

Why is decision-making so important to any organisation and what types of decision do they face?

The decision-making process

We have seen that it is possible to analyse decisions into five main categories:

- short-run problem decisions
- routine planning decisions
- long-range decisions
- control decisions
- investment and disinvestment decisions.

This is useful because the relevant costs and benefits are likely to differ between each type of decision. The decision-making process comprises the seven steps outlined in Figure 11.2.

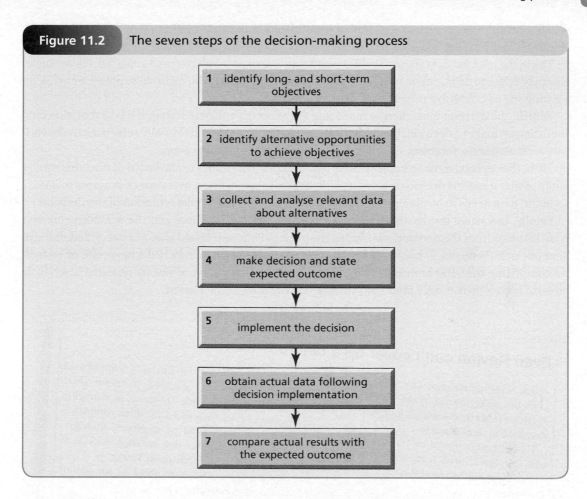

Figure 11.2   The seven steps of the decision-making process

1 identify long- and short-term objectives

2 identify alternative opportunities to achieve objectives

3 collect and analyse relevant data about alternatives

4 make decision and state expected outcome

5 implement the decision

6 obtain actual data following decision implementation

7 compare actual results with the expected outcome

First, the objectives, either long-term or short-term, need to be identified. Short-term objectives may be financial, such as:

- profit maximisation
- loss avoidance
- profit growth
- sales growth

or non-financial, such as:

- improved product quality
- customer service
- employee welfare
- environmental friendliness.

Long-term objectives may be more to do with:

- the financial risk of the company
- long-term growth
- debt or equity financing
- dividend growth
- the relationships between these factors.

Second, alternative opportunities must be identified which might contribute to achieving the company's objectives. The ability to identify opportunities, or things to do which might help the company reach its objectives, is a major test of how good management is. Failure to recognise opportunities that exist may result in decisions not taken or opportunities missed.

Third, the relevant data about each of the alternatives must be collected and analysed. For example, this may relate to decisions on whether to manufacture or buy from an external supplier, or to use an existing site or establish a new site.

Fourth, the decision must then be made and the expected outcome stated. If a board of directors, for example, makes a decision, then the minute of that decision should formally refer back to the various documentation, forecasts, etc. that are an integral part of that decision.

Fifth, the decision must be implemented. The minutes of meetings of the board of directors should confirm that a specific decision has been implemented, along with an overview of progress to date.

Sixth, data needs to be obtained about actual results following implementation of the decision.

Finally, the actual results are compared with the expected outcome, and the achievements that have resulted from the decision are evaluated. It should be appreciated that not every decision will generate achievements, as cosmetic giant Revlon found out when it launched a new suite of cosmetics comprising over 100 brands in 2005. The subsequent evaluation of results revealed a seriously adverse impact on company profits as illustrated in the press extract below.

Even Revlon can't cover up a failure

Jack Stahl has resigned from Revlon, the cosmetics maker owned by the financier Ronald Perelman, after the company's long-running woes deepened in recent months.

He has been replaced by David Kennedy, the man Mr Stahl hired from Coca-Cola, his old company, in 2002 to head Revlon's international business.

Mr Stahl, who oversaw four consecutive annual losses during his time at the helm, is leaving just a few weeks after Revlon announced a particularly disappointing second-quarter loss that was more than double the amount of the year-earlier period.

The loss was worsened by bad sales of Vital Radiance, a suite of more than 100 new cosmetic products that was meant to form a key part of Revlon's turnaround strategy.

The brand, which Mr Stahl had promised would be 'a very significant line' and a key way to entice more women over 50 to the company, was revealed to be a big disappointment when Revlon said that costs relating to Vital could knock $60 million (£32 million) from this year's profits.

The re-launch of its Almay brand also missed expectations.

Revlon said yesterday that Mr Stahl was leaving 'to pursue other interests' and that Mr Kennedy would assume his position immediately. Mr Stahl will stay on as an adviser for 30 days before leaving the company altogether.

Mr Kennedy, who was Revlon's third chief executive since 2000, joined Revlon as executive and president of Revlon's international operations and was promoted to group chief financial officer this year. He served as managing director of Coca-Cola Matil, the drink company's Australian bottler, and as a general manager. His 33-year career has also included working at Columbia Pictures and Ernst & Young.

Mr Perelman, who owns about 57 per cent of Revlon through his MacAndrews & Forbes investment firm, praised Mr Kennedy, who he said had 'restored meaningful profitability' to Revlon's international business.

Mr Kennedy, 59, has his work cut out if he is to reverse eight consecutive annual losses at Revlon – which has total liabilities of more than $2 billion – as it gets beaten by rivals such as L'Oreal and Procter & Gamble.

Kimberly Nolan, an analyst at Gimme Credit Publications, a New York-based bond research firm, said: 'Vital Radiance and Almay didn't work out as planned and didn't make the money that was hoped. Ronald Perelman is probably going to have to put more money into the company.'

Shares in Revlon fell by 2 cents, or 1.4 per cent, to close at $1.41.

Revlon reported in July that it lost $87.1 million in the three months to June 30, compared with $35.8 million in the same period last year. Revenues rose slightly from $318.3 million to $321.1 million.

Source: **Revlon chief goes as new product line fails to shine,** by Tom Bawden © *The Times*, 19 September 2006

Outline the decision-making process.

Relevant costs

The Millennium Dome project in 2000 illustrated the importance of (the lack of) appropriate planning and control of cash to be sunk into major projects. The amount that was expected to have been spent on the attraction by December 2000 (some £800m) would be a past cost already committed and spent and would therefore not be considered in any decision about to whom the attraction may ultimately be sold or for how much. However, if future cash outlays were proposed, on which a sale was dependent, then these costs would be relevant costs with regard to the sale decision.

Worked example 11.2

During the year 2009 a car manufacturer evaluated two proposals regarding the production of a new car. The car could be built in France or England.

In 2010 the company chose England.

Both relevant costs and opportunity costs would have been considered by the company in making its decision.

The relevant costs are those of setting up the production line of the new car in England and these costs could be linked back to the decision made by the board of directors. The opportunity cost was the projected profit of the alternative French production facility.

Accounting information used in absorption costing, for example, may be different from relevant information used in decision-making. Relevant information may relate to costs or revenues; compared with accounting information, it may be qualitative as well as quantitative.

Relevant costs are costs that arise as a direct consequence of a decision. These may differ between the alternative options. They are sometimes referred to as incremental or differential costs.

Relevant costs are future costs, not past costs. A decision is about the future and it cannot alter what has been done already. A cost incurred, or committed to, in the past is irrelevant to any decision that is made now.

Relevant costs are cash flows, not accounting costs. All decisions are assumed to maximise the benefit to the shareholders. The time value of money impacts on longer-term decisions but all short-term decisions are assumed to improve shareholder wealth if they increase net cash flows.

Only cash flow information is required for a decision and so costs or charges that do not reflect additional cash spend are ignored for the purpose of decision-making. It should be appreciated that depreciation is not a cash-based expense, but an entry in the accounts of the business that reflects the systematic allocation of an asset's value over the useful life of that asset.

Worked example 11.3

If a hotel group with a central booking system is required to make a decision on whether to market empty rooms at a special offer through the press, or other media such as television or the Internet, cash outflow information might have an important influence on the final decision.

Almost certainly the major cash outflow will be the cost of the advertising itself. There is an element of a 'gamble' for the company, even if it has used this strategy in the past. However, if the company follows this strategy each year then it may gain experience and an understanding of the relationship between advertising and extra bookings. It will also be able to determine the relationship between the discounts and volume of bookings and type of advertising options.

Relevant costs may also include opportunity costs. An opportunity cost is the benefit forgone by choosing one option instead of the next best alternative.

Worked example 11.4

An opportunity cost is the benefit forgone by choosing one option instead of the next best alternative.

We see many hotel websites offering rooms at discounted rates and opportunity costs would have been considered by hotel managers in making a decision to offer discounted rooms. A hotel manager would know how much cash would be lost on certain days if rooms were offered at a discounted price. The hotel manager would also know how much cash would be lost if no discounted rooms were booked. On the basis of the pattern of current rooms booked the hotel manager would know what the likely take-up would be in different periods in the future.

Unless there is some evidence to the contrary, it is always assumed that variable costs are relevant costs and that fixed costs are not relevant to a decision. However, some variable costs may include some non-relevant costs. For example, direct labour costs are normally accounted for as variable costs, but if the workforce is paid a fixed rate per person per week, in some circumstances this may be a committed cost and therefore not relevant to decision-making.

Depreciation cost per hour may be accounted for as a variable cost. But, depreciation is never a relevant cost because it is a past cost and does not represent cash flow that will be incurred in the future.

There are several costs: sunk costs; committed costs; notional costs, that are termed irrelevant to decision-making because they are either not future cash flows or they are costs which will be incurred anyway, regardless of the decision that is taken.

A sunk cost is a cost which has already been incurred and which cannot now be recovered. It is a past cost which is not relevant to decision-making. Such costs may be, for example, the costs of dedicated non-current assets and development costs already incurred. Most consumer goods currently being sold are the final version of earlier versions, which will have cost considerable sums of money to develop.

A committed cost is a future cash outflow that will be incurred whatever decision is taken about alternative opportunities. Committed costs may exist because of contracts already entered into by the company. During the year 2010, BT's Global Services division found that it had massively over-estimated the profitability of many of its long-term contracts with big corporate customers, leading to losses of £2bn for the company and three changes of chief executive in 18 months.

A **notional cost**, or imputed cost, is a hypothetical accounting cost to reflect the use of a resource for which no actual cash expense is incurred. Examples are notional rents charged by a company to its subsidiary companies, or to cost centres, for the use of accommodation that the company owns, and notional interest charged on capital employed within a cost centre or profit centre of the company.

There are many examples of the use of relevant costs in decision-making: profit planning – for example, the contribution implications of pricing and advertising decisions, and the sales mix and contribution implications of constraints on resources; profit and product mix planning – for example with regard to the contribution per limiting factor.

The following sub-sections illustrate the general rules for identifying relevant costs.

Materials

The relevant cost of raw materials is generally their current replacement cost, unless the materials are already owned and would not be replaced if used. If the materials are already owned, the relevant cost is the higher of the current resale value and the value obtained if the materials were put to alternative use. The higher of these costs is the opportunity cost. If there is no resale value and there is no other use for the materials then the opportunity cost is zero.

Depreciation

Depreciation on equipment that has already been purchased is not a relevant cost for decision-making.

Capital expenditure

The historical cost of equipment that has already been purchased is not a relevant cost for decision-making. If the capital equipment has not already been purchased, and the decision would involve such a purchase, the situation is different. The relevant cost of equipment, of which the purchase would be a consequence of the decision, can be measured in two alternative ways, using the discounted cash flow (DCF) method:

- the cost of the equipment treated as an initial cash outlay in year zero, with the relevant costs and benefits of the decision assessed over the life of the project
- the cost of the equipment converted into an annual charge to include both the capital cost and a notional interest charge over the expected life of the equipment.

Future cash costs

Future cash costs are relevant if they have a direct consequence on the decision. These are costs not yet incurred or committed to. For example, you may have an old car which you would like to sell. The price you paid for it is irrelevant to your sale decision. However, if you needed to pay out large sums of money to a garage to work on the car to make it saleable, then those future cash costs would be very relevant to your decision to sell, or not, and at what price.

Differential costs

The relevant differential cash costs are the differences between two or more optional courses of action. If we return to the example of the sale of your old car, we may find that the cost of the work required to make it saleable is prohibitive and that you may be forced to keep the car rather than sell it. However, the difference between the price quoted by the garage may be undercut sufficiently by another garage to prompt you to reverse your decision.

Worked example 11.5

A machine requires repair and the relevant costs of two different repair options are as follows:

	£
Repair machine on site	
Cost of spares	1,250
Labour cost	750
Reduction to contribution resulting from lost production	4,200
Take machine away to workshop for repair	
Cost of spares	1,250
Labour cost	400
Reduction to contribution resulting from lost production	5,800

We can prepare a statement of differential costs.

	£
Statement of differential costs	
Reduced labour cost of repair on site [750 − 400]	(350)
Lower reduction to contribution from repair on site [5,800 − 4,200]	1,600
Differential benefit of repair on site	1,250

Opportunity costs

The benefit forgone in choosing one option over the next best alternative is relevant. Many successful businesses find themselves in an expanding market, where most of their products are selling well, and each new product is becoming profitable. Inevitably, competing products from within the same company may have to be weeded out. Therefore, the company will have to forgo current benefits as a result of culling a profitable product.

The UK motor industry has several examples of product options that were dropped in favour of others. The German motor industry has seen two products dropped, only for them to reappear: the Beetle (VW) car and Boxer (BMW) motor cycle. In these cases, management decided to forgo the benefit of producing the products in favour of new models. Eventually they had to change their minds as the benefits forgone needed to be reassessed and updated versions were eventually brought back.

Sunk costs, committed costs and notional costs

None of these costs are relevant. They include, for example, costs of dedicated non-current assets and development costs already incurred.

Worked example 11.6

A company bought a computer system two years ago for £57,000. After allowing for depreciation its book value is now £19,000. Because computer technology moves on so quickly, resulting in obsolescence and price reductions, this equipment has no resale value. Although the company may continue to use the computer system for another year, with the limited facilities it provides, it would prefer to scrap it now and replace it with a much enhanced system providing many more functions.

Let's consider the implications of the company's decision to replace its computer system. The original computer system initial cost of £57,000, which now has a net book value of £19,000, is a sunk cost, and is therefore ignored in terms of a decision made to replace the computer system. The money has been spent and the asset has no alternative use.

Fixed costs

Fixed costs are not relevant costs, unless they are a direct consequence of the decision. For example, the cost of employing an extra salesman would normally be categorised as a fixed cost. Conceptually, fixed costs stay at the same level irrespective of the changes in level of activity. In practice, management needs to make decisions regarding future fixed costs. Longer-term forecasts and budgets may indicate that changes in activity levels require changes to levels of fixed costs. For example, if higher education in the UK saw the falling-off of student numbers on certain courses then that might result in the universities cutting back on their fixed overheads, such as premises and staff numbers.

Worked example 11.7

The UK saw two attractions open in London in 2000: the Millennium Dome and the London Eye. What should we consider to be the fixed costs of the two attractions?

One basic difference between the two attractions is that the Dome was to remain open for one year and the London Eye would remain open for a number of years. Obviously the majority of the Dome's fixed costs would cease with its closure, but charges like insurance would need to continue to be paid. The London Eye became popular and fully booked very quickly. Unlike the Dome, its capacity is limited to the number of passengers each gondola can hold. In the Eye's case an analysis of the fixed costs should reveal that the costs are indeed genuinely fixed and there will be little 'movement' from year to year, whereas the headlines during 2000 strongly suggested that most of the Dome's expenses were varying throughout the year!

Variable costs

Variable costs are generally relevant costs but care must be taken with regard to the provisos already outlined. Variable costs may be non-relevant costs in some circumstances, for example where a variable cost is also a committed cost.

Worked example 11.8

A company is planning a small new project that requires 1,000 hours of direct labour, costing £9 per hour. However, the company pays its direct labour workforce a fixed wage of £342 per person for a 38-hour week.

The company has a 'no redundancy' agreement, and has enough spare capacity to meet the additional hours required for the project.

What should we consider are the relevant costs relating to the new project?

The direct labour cost for accounting purposes is regarded as a variable cost of £9 per hour. But it is really a committed cost, and therefore a fixed cost of £342 per week. The relevant cost of the new project for direct labour is therefore zero.

It should be noted that the company may similarly treat depreciation of say £2.40 per hour as an accounting variable cost. However, for decision-making, depreciation is never considered as a relevant cost. It is a past cost, and therefore not a cash flow to be incurred in the future.

Attributable costs

We may consider fixed costs as comprising divisible fixed costs and indivisible fixed costs. A fixed cost is divisible if significant changes in activity volumes require increases or decreases in that cost.

An **attributable cost** is the cost per unit that could be avoided, on the average, if a product or function were discontinued entirely without changing the supporting organisational structure. An attributable cost consists of:

- short-run variable costs
- divisible fixed costs
- only those indivisible fixed costs that are traceable.

Worked example 11.9

A company employs 55 people, who are paid fixed monthly wages, within four departments in its factory. Each department is headed by a departmental manager who is paid a salary.

How should each of the staff costs be regarded in a decision relating to the possible shutdown of one of the departments?

The direct labour costs of the 55 operators are divisible fixed costs (if there were only one operator, then the direct labour cost would be an indivisible fixed cost).

Each departmental manager's salary is an indivisible fixed cost that is traceable to their department. This is because if a department were to be shut down, the manager would no longer be required and therefore no cost would be incurred.

Scarce resources

The relevant cost of a scarce resource to be included in a decision-making calculation is the benefit forgone (the opportunity cost) in using the resource in another way, in addition to the direct cost of purchasing the resource. Let's look at an example.

Worked example 11.10

Mr and Mrs Green are willing to pay £22,000 to Steamy Windows Ltd to build a conservatory. The general manager of Steamy Windows Ltd estimates that the job requires the following materials:

Material	Total units required	Units in inventory	Book value of inventory £/unit	Realisable value £/unit	Replacement cost £/unit
A	1,000	0	0.0	0.0	6.0
B	1,000	600	2.0	2.5	5.0
C	1,000	700	3.0	2.5	4.0
D	200	200	4.0	6.0	9.0

B is regularly used by Steamy Windows Ltd and if it is required for this job it needs to be replaced to meet other production demands.

C and D are in inventory because of previous overbuying, and have restricted use. No other use can be found for C, but D could be used as a substitute for 300 units of E, which currently costs £5 per unit and Steamy Windows Ltd currently has none in inventory.

Steamy Windows Ltd needs to determine the relevant costs of the project to assist the company in its their decision on whether or not it should take the job.

Relevant costs:	£	
A 1,000 × £6 per unit	6,000	replacement cost because these materials have not yet been purchased
B 1,000 × £5 per unit	5,000	replacement cost because these materials are used regularly and so the inventory items would have to be replaced
C (300 × £4 per unit) + (700 × £2.50 per unit)	2,950	300 must be bought at the replacement cost of £4 per unit, and 700 will not be replaced but could have been sold for £2.50 per unit
D (300 E × £5 per unit)	1,500	200 could be sold for £6 per unit, but this is less than the opportunity cost of substitution of 300 units of E
	15,450	

The relevant costs of the job are £15,450. If the difference of £6,550 is an acceptable level of profit to Steamy Windows Ltd, before allowing for labour and overhead costs, then the job should be accepted.

Figure 11.3   Examples of practical areas of decision-making

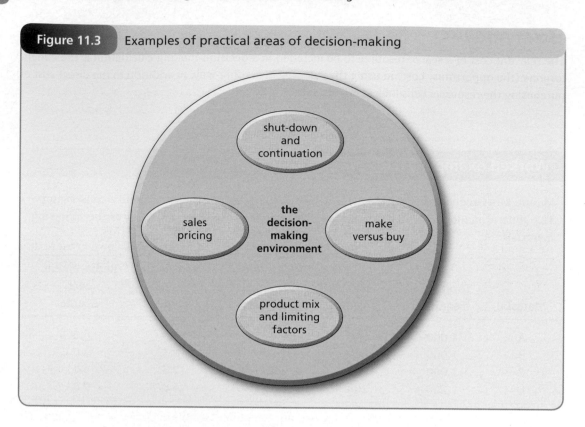

Progress check 11.3

Outline three examples of costs that are usually relevant, and three costs that are not usually relevant in decision-making.

We will now look at examples of four specific areas of decision-making, outlined in Figure 11.3.

Marginal costing and shut-down or continuation decisions

We have already discussed the importance of the marginal costing technique as an aid to costing and break-even decision-making. In the UK, during February 2010 a major steel manufacturer decided that production would cease at its plant in Redcar on Teesside with the loss of 1,600 jobs. The company explained that over-capacity forced it to cut back on production as there was no point in producing steel that would not sell. It was quite obvious from the public announcements that the company had carried out many 'what-ifs' on the corporate spreadsheets. However, it was apparently unable to justify continuation of production at the Redcar site, thus ending 160 years of steel production in the town. The following example looks at the use of marginal costing in a decision regarding the possible closure of an apparent loss-making activity.

Worked example 11.11

Ron G Choice Ltd has three departments: C chairs; D desks; T tables, manufacturing three separate ranges of office furniture. Choice Ltd's sales manager, Jim Brown, has just started a course on cost accounting and has reviewed the company's accounts for last year with renewed interest.

	C £	D £	T £
Revenue	60,000	80,000	40,000
Variable costs	40,000	60,000	34,000
Fixed costs allocated	6,000	10,000	8,000

It appeared to Jim that all was not well with the table department T. He was considering recommending to the managing director that department T should be closed down because it appeared to be making a loss. However, Jim felt he should first run his ideas past the company's accountant, Tony White, to check his figures and gain some support.

Jim provided the following analysis, using an absorption costing basis:

	C £	D £	T £	Total £
Revenue	60,000	80,000	40,000	180,000
Total costs	46,000	70,000	42,000	158,000
Profit/(loss)	14,000	10,000	(2,000)	22,000

On this basis, Jim said, department T was making a loss and should be closed.

Tony asked Jim if he had considered the position using a marginal costing basis. Jim said he had not and so Tony provided the following analysis:

	C £	D £	T £	Total £
Revenue	60,000	80,000	40,000	180,000
Variable costs	40,000	60,000	34,000	134,000
Contribution	20,000	20,000	6,000	46,000
less: Fixed costs				24,000
Profit				22,000

Tony explained to Jim that the profit for the company was the same using both techniques because there is no closing inventories adjustment involved.

However, Tony said that the way in which the fixed costs had been allocated to each department was fairly arbitrary and so perhaps they could consider what the position of Choice Ltd might be following the possible closure of department T on a marginal costing basis.

The result was as follows:

	C £	D £	T £	Total £
Revenue	60,000	80,000	–	140,000
Variable costs	40,000	60,000	–	100,000
Contribution	20,000	20,000	–	40,000
less: Fixed costs				24,000
Profit				16,000

Jim could see that closure of the tables department T would result in a reduction in total company profit of £6,000 to £16,000, compared with the original £22,000. Tony explained that this was caused by the loss of revenue of £40,000 and contribution of £6,000 derived from department T.

Jim thanked Tony for helping him avoid an embarrassing visit to the managing director's office. He would now also be better prepared for the next part of his costing course – on marginal costing!

This simple example shows that despite what the absorption costing approach indicated, department T should be kept open because it yields a positive contribution towards covering the total fixed costs.

The marginal costing approach focuses on the variable costs which are affected by the decision and separates them from the fixed costs which are unaffected by the decision and are therefore irrelevant to it. The closure of department T would not save any of the allocated fixed costs – they would then have to be shared amongst departments C and D. If the fixed costs had been directly attributable to each department rather than allocated then there would have been an £8,000 saving by closing department T. Since that is higher than the department's contribution of £6,000, then Jim's advice would have been correct to close department T.

Progress check 11.4

In what way is marginal costing useful in shut-down decisions?

Make versus buy

Make versus buy decisions are often made when a component used in one of the manufacturing processes to produce a product may either be bought in from an outside supplier or manufactured within the factory. It would seem that the choice is simply a straightforward comparison between the extra cost to make the component, the marginal cost, and the price charged by suppliers. In fact, the decision involves consideration of a number of other factors, for example:

- cost price sensitivity to changes in volumes
- accuracy of data
- reliability of bought-in and self-manufactured components
- supplier switching costs
- reliability of suppliers in terms of delivery and financial stability
- length of time the cost price will be held
- opportunity cost.

If the component were not made in-house what activities would be carried out using the relevant facilities? If other manufacturing activities have to be forgone so as to make the component in-house then there is a loss of the contribution that this work would otherwise have earned. The contribution sacrificed is the opportunity cost of not carrying out the alternative activities. The opportunity cost must be added to the marginal cost of making the component to compare with suppliers' prices in making a make versus buy decision. The technique usually used to determine loss of contribution is contribution per unit of a **key factor** (limiting factor) of production.

Worked example 11.12

Procrastinate Ltd makes a product A, which takes 30 hours using the Dragon machine. Its marginal cost and selling price are £1,400 and £2,000 respectively. Component X, which is used in the manufacture of product A, could be made on the Dragon machine in five hours with a marginal cost of £400. The best outside supplier price for one component X is £450.

Procrastinate has to decide on whether to make or buy component X.

Contribution of product A   = £2,000 − £1,400 = £600
Contribution per hour of use of the Dragon machine = £600/30   = £20

If component X is made in five hours then 5 × £20, or £100 contribution would be lost. Opportunity cost plus marginal cost = £100 + £400 = £500, which is greater than the best outside supplier price of £450, so component X should be bought rather than made in-house.

In this example, we have assumed that the Dragon machine is working at full capacity in order to calculate the opportunity cost of lost production. If this were not so and the Dragon machine were idle for a significant amount of time then there would be no loss of contribution. The only cost of making component X would then be its marginal cost of £400 which, being less than the best supplier price of £450, would indicate a decision to make in-house rather than buy.

Progress check 11.5

Illustrate the process used to make a make versus buy decision.

Product mix decisions and limiting factors

An organisation may not have access to an unlimited supply of resources to allow it to exploit every opportunity to continue indefinitely to increase contribution. Such scarce resources may include, for example:

- labour hours
- levels of labour skills
- machine capacity
- time
- market demand
- components
- raw materials
- cash
- credit facilities.

A limiting factor, or key factor, is anything that limits the activity of the organisation. The organisation must decide what mix of products or services to provide, given the restricted resources available to it, if its volume of output is constrained by limited resources. It can do this by seeking to maximise profit by optimising the benefit it obtains from the limiting factor. Machine time would be an example of a limiting factor for a company if all the machines in the company were operating at full capacity without being able to provide the output required to meet all the sales demand available to the company.

The technique used for decisions involving just one scarce resource assumes that the organisation is aiming to maximise profit. This further assumes that fixed costs are unchanged by the decision to produce more or less of each product. The technique therefore is to rank the products in order of their contribution-maximising ability per unit of the scarce resource. The following two worked examples illustrate this technique. The first example assumes that sales demand is unlimited, whilst the second example assumes given levels of sales demand.

Worked example 11.13

Need The Dough, a small village bakery, makes only two types of loaves of bread, small and large. There is unlimited demand for this bread and both products use the same skilled labour of bakers, which is in short supply. The product data are as follows:

	Small	Large
Sales price per loaf	£0.71	£0.85
Variable cost per loaf	£0.51	£0.61
Contribution per loaf	£0.20	£0.24
Minutes of skilled labour per loaf	20	30

We can determine the contribution-maximising strategy for Need The Dough.

If we consider the contribution per unit of scarce resource, one hour of skilled labour, we can see that the contribution for each loaf per hour is:

Small loaves earn	£0.60 per labour hour	[60/20 × 20p]
Large loaves earn	£0.48 per labour hour	[60/30 × 24p]

So, even though large loaves generate a larger unit contribution of 24p compared to 20p earned by small loaves, the contribution-maximising strategy for Need The Dough is to bake and sell as many small loaves as possible which generates a contribution of 60p, compared with 48p for large loaves, for each hour of scarce labour.

Worked example 11.14

Felinpot Ltd are potters who make only two products, two ornamental pots called the Bill and the Ben. The product data are as follows:

	Bill	Ben
Contribution per pot	£5	£7.20
Volume of special blue clay per pot	1 kg	2 kg
Monthly demand	470	625

In one month the maximum amount of specialist blue clay available is 1,450 kg.
We can determine the contribution-maximising strategy for Felinpot Ltd.

For each pot the contribution per unit of blue clay is:

Bill	£5/1 kg	=	£5 per kg
Ben	£7.20/2 kg	=	£3.60 per kg

The contribution-maximising strategy for Felinpot Ltd should therefore be to make Bill pots in preference to Ben pots, even though the unit contribution of a Ben is greater than a Bill.

Output of Bill pots should be maximised to meet the monthly demand of:

470 pots, using 1 kg × 470 = 470 kg	contribution	= 470 × £5 = £2,350

The balance of 980 kg of clay (1,450 kg less 470 kg) should be used to make Ben pots

980 kg/2 kg = 490 pots	contribution	= 490 × £7.20 = £3,528
	total contribution	= £5,878

Because special blue clay was in short supply every endeavour should be made to maximise the contribution to Felinpot Ltd for every kilogram of clay used. Regardless of the higher level of demand for the other product, Ben, the product with the higher contribution per kilogram of special clay used, Bill, is the one which should be produced to its maximum demand level. All the clay left over from that should then be used to produce the 'less profitable' product, Ben, in terms of its return per kilogram of special clay.

More complex actual scenarios may be encountered. For example, there may be limited sales demand and also one scarce resource. The same technique applies whereby the factors are ranked in order of their contribution per unit of scarce resource. Optimum profit is earned from the decision to produce the top-ranked products up to the limit of demand.

Many situations occur where there are two or more scarce resources. The technique of ranking items in order of contribution per unit of limiting factor cannot be used in these situations. In these cases linear programming techniques need to be used – the graphical method or the simplex (algebraic) method – which are beyond the scope of this book.

Progress check 11.6

What are limiting factors and how do they impact on decisions related to product mix?

Sales pricing

Pricing policy is just one of the four Ps, the categories of decision-making included in the 'marketing mix'. The others are the product, place (where it is sold and how it is distributed), and promotion (selling, advertising and sales promotion). Pricing decisions must have some regard for cost, in order to ensure that the selling price exceeds the average unit cost in order to make a profit. Pricing decisions must also recognise the importance of the range of factors that relate to the general heading of 'demand'.

Examples 11.15 to 11.19 look at various sales pricing methods that are concerned solely with cost, and assuming unlimited demand, that may be used to achieve a break-even position or a targeted profit. These methods illustrate both the marginal and full absorption costing approach.

Worked example 11.15

Chip Pendale's company Pendale Ltd has a maximum production output of 500 chairs. It has been asked to tender for a contract to supply 300 chairs.

The costing information for Pendale Ltd for 300 chairs (or units) is as follows:

	£
Assembly cost centre costs:	
Wages for 300 units	1,500
Materials – timber and glue	300
Direct costs	1,800
Production overheads absorbed:	
Machine maintenance	150
Machine depreciation	250
Supervision	100
	2,300
General overheads absorbed:	
Factory rent and property taxes	100
Administrative expenses	100
Heating and lighting	130
Total costs	2,630

Initially, we may assume a selling price of £11 per chair.

We will calculate the unit cost of a chair at output levels of 300 and 500 chairs, using:

(i)   absorption costing

(ii)   marginal costing

and

(iii)   compare the profits of both methods at output levels of 200, 300 and 500 chairs.

Calculation of the unit cost of a chair at output levels of 300 and 500 chairs:

		300 chairs unit costs £		500 chairs unit costs £
Wages	(£1,500/300 units)	5.00	(£2,500/500 units)	5.00
Materials	(£300/300 units)	1.00	(£500/500 units)	1.00
Variable cost per chair, unchanged for changes in output		6.00		6.00
Production overhead	(£500/300 units)	1.67	(£500/500 units)	1.00
General overhead	(£330/300 units)	1.10	(£330/500 units)	0.66
Full cost per chair		8.77		7.66

Although total fixed costs remain unchanged, the unit costs of £8.77 and £7.66 are different due to costs being based on output of either 300 or 500 units.

(i) On an absorption costing basis:

Assuming a full cost of £8.77 per chair for output of 300 units, we can consider sales volumes of 200, 300, and 500 chairs:

Chairs	200 £	300 £	500 £
Revenue at £11 per unit	2,200	3,300	5,500
Total costs at £8.77 per unit (volume × full cost per unit)	1,754	2,630	4,385
Profit	446	670	1,115

(ii) On a marginal costing basis:

Chairs	200 £	300 £	500 £
Revenue at £11 per unit	2,200	3,300	5,500
Variable costs at £6.00 per unit	1,200	1,800	3,000
Contribution	1,000	1,500	2,500
Fixed costs (the same regardless of output):			
Production overheads	500	500	500
General overheads	330	330	330
Profit	170	670	1,670

(iii)

The differences in profit between the two approaches	(276)	–	555

are due to the under- or over-charge of the fixed cost element being £8.77 − £6.00 = £2.77 × (− 100 or + 200), the volume difference against 300 chairs.

It should be noted that there may be small rounding differences in the above calculations.

Worked example 11.16

Using the data from Worked example 11.15 Pendale Ltd may consider the pricing approach of minimum pricing at specified volumes of 300 and 500 chairs.

Minimum pricing at specified volumes:

If we assume 300 units

Total revenue	= total costs which = £2,630[(300 × £6.00) + £500 + £330]
The break-even price	= £2,630/300 units = £8.77 per unit
At 500 units the break-even price	= [(500 × £6.00) + £500 + £330]/500 units
	= £3,830/500 units = £7.66 per unit

We can see that the break-even prices are equal to the fully absorbed costs per chair.

Worked example 11.17

Using the data from Worked example 11.15 Pendale Ltd may consider the effect their pricing would have on break-even volume at specified prices of £11 and £13 per chair.

Break-even volume at specified prices:

If we assume that the selling price is £11 per unit

Contribution $= \text{revenue} - \text{variable costs} = £11 - £6 = £5$ per unit

The break-even volume $= \dfrac{\text{total fixed costs}}{\text{contribution per unit}} = \dfrac{£830}{£5} = 166$ units

If we assume that the selling price is £13 per unit

Contribution $= \text{revenue} - \text{variable costs} = £13 - £6 = £7$ per unit

The break-even volume $= \dfrac{\text{total fixed costs}}{\text{contribution per unit}} = \dfrac{£830}{£7} = 119$ units

Cost-plus pricing

The technique of full cost-plus pricing requires the assessment of the total cost of a product or service, which is then marked up with a percentage, or an absolute sum, to achieve the required level of profit.

Price-taking companies have little control over the prices of their services or products, for example commodities. They may also be small companies, of which there are many in their market sector, and where there may be little to tell the difference between one product and another. Cost information is therefore very important for price takers in deciding on levels of output and product mix because they cannot do anything to influence price and so their profits are totally dependent on costs.

Price-setting companies are companies that are able to influence selling prices and may exercise discretion over the setting of prices for their products or services. These are companies that may have highly differentiated or customised products, and are market leaders. Cost information is also very important for price setters in making their pricing decisions. This is because the prices they set will be influenced by their costs, together with the actions of their competitors and their customers' perceived value of their products.

Companies may sometimes be price setters and sometimes be price takers, or they may be price setters for some products or services and price takers for others. Regardless of which they are, we can see that cost is of paramount importance.

Inaccurate cost information can result in over- or under-costing and therefore impact directly on profit, selling prices and demand. Under-costing may result in the acceptance of unprofitable business, and over-costing may result in the loss of profitable business. As we have seen in Chapter 10, inaccurate costing of products and services is most likely to result from the way in which overheads are allocated to products and services.

For inventory valuation purposes (IAS 2), products are required to be valued on an absorption costing basis. However, cost assignment for pricing should be based on direct cost tracing or cause-and-effect cost assignment, that is to say activity based costing (ABC). Some arbitrary cost allocations based on direct labour or machine hours are inevitable, for items such as general administrative costs and property costs, but an ABC approach will provide more accurate product costs. ABC also provides a better understanding of cost behaviour, which provides a sounder basis for negotiation with customers regarding selling price and order size.

Cost-plus pricing is widely used by companies for a number of reasons:

- it is simple to use and on the face of it looks factual and precise
- it may encourage price stability if all companies in the industry use it
- the impact on demand can be taken into account to some extent by adjusting mark-ups
- if a company manufactures or markets hundreds of products or services there may be difficulties in adopting more sophisticated pricing approaches that use expensive market research and complicated pricing calculations
- cost-plus pricing may be applied only to selected and relatively minor revenue items, for example on a **Pareto analysis** 80/20 basis
- cost-plus pricing may be used for guidance in price setting whilst also taking other factors into account such as levels of demand and competition.

But why use cost-plus pricing if it is likely to be changed? Well, cost-plus pricing does provide an initial approximation although it should be by no means the only information that is used for the final pricing decision. However, there are also many criticisms of cost-plus pricing because:

- it is not demand based, ignoring competition and the relationships between demand and price; cost and demand are not related
- it does not necessarily ensure that total revenue will be greater than total costs

Sheffield Hallam University
Adsetts Learning Centre (4)

Issue receipt

Title: Business accounting and finance / Tony
Davies and Ian Crawford.
ID: 1019856319
Due: 18-11-13

Total items: 1
09/11/2013 11:55 PM

To renew items or pay library fines online
go to My Library Account

Learning Centre enquiries
0114 225 3333 option 3

- it does not necessarily maximise profit
- it can lead to wrong decisions if for example costs are based on budgeted levels of activity
- selecting a suitable basis for overhead absorption, and the apportionment of shared costs, where a business produces more than one product, can be difficult
- it may ignore the distinction between variable, fixed and opportunity costs
- some estimate of demand is needed to determine the fixed costs per unit of a product or service; but how can the price be set until the volume of demand is known so as to calculate the fixed cost absorption rates – this is a vicious circle because a full cost-plus price cannot be calculated without a knowledge of demand and demand cannot be estimated without a knowledge of price

and perhaps most importantly:

- it encourages waste and a failure to control costs, because it assumes that any cost increases or overspends will be paid for by the customer – the higher the cost, the higher the selling price (but not necessarily higher profits).

The following two worked examples illustrate the use of cost-plus pricing. You should also take a look at Case Study VI which follows Chapter 16, which considers an approach to cost-plus pricing that is based on achievement of a required ROI.

Worked example 11.18

Using the data from Worked example 11.15 Pendale Ltd may consider the pricing approach of cost-plus pricing at outputs of 300 and 500 chairs.

Cost-plus pricing:
This method uses the full cost per unit plus a mark-up:

If we assume 300 units

Full cost per unit	=	£8.77
plus 25% mark-up		
New selling price	=	£11.00 (rounded up)

If we assume 500 units

Full cost per unit	=	£7.66
plus 25% mark-up		
New selling price	=	£9.60 (rounded up)

Worked example 11.19

Using the data from Worked example 11.15 Pendale Ltd may consider the pricing approach of volume required to achieve a target profit of £1,000 at a selling price of £11 per chair, and of £1,200 at a selling price of £13 per chair.

Volume required to achieve a target profit:
If we assume that the target profit is £1,000
And assume that the selling price is £11 per unit

Contribution £11 − £6 = £5 per unit

$$\text{Therefore required volume} = \frac{\text{total fixed costs} + \text{required profit}}{\text{contribution per unit}} = \frac{(£830 + £1{,}000)}{£5}$$

$$= 366 \text{ units}$$

If we assume that the target profit is £1,200
And assume that the selling price is £13 per unit

Contribution £13 − £6 = £7 per unit

$$\text{Therefore required volume} = \frac{\text{total fixed costs} + \text{required profit}}{\text{contribution per unit}} = \frac{(£830 + £1{,}200)}{£7}$$

$$= 290 \text{ units}$$

In considering each of the pricing methods we have looked at far we need to ask ourselves:

■ which selling price is most appropriate

and

■ which cost base is most appropriate?

The prices we have calculated in the worked examples have had no relationship with market demand. Neither has there been an identification of profit potential at different output or market demand levels, and there has been no attempt to maximise profit. The cost-based approach is not market-based.

Progress check 11.7

Outline four methods of sales pricing that do not make use of market data.

Maximum contribution using market data

The final sales pricing option we shall consider looks at a range of selling prices per unit and uses a graphical representation of profits and losses at various volume levels to determine the maximum contribution, and therefore maximum profit level (see Worked example 11.20).

There is difficulty in estimating a demand curve but certain practical steps can be taken to reach a pricing decision based on demand analysis as follows:

■ establish the variable cost per unit and the fixed costs for the period, and using a number of different prices construct a profit line for each price on a profit/volume (PV) chart

■ make a rough estimate of demand at each price and calculate the profit at this level of demand, and plot this profit on the profit lines on the PV chart, a different profit value for each selling price

■ join up the profit value points for each selling price and so construct a contribution curve to determine the highest point on the contribution curve which is the highest contribution and highest profit and so the approximate price that the company should consider.

Worked example 11.20

Turning again to Pendale Ltd, let's assume the following price and market information for its one product, its chair:

	p1 = £11	p2 = £12	p3 = £13	p4 = £14
Selling price per unit				
Sales volume units demand	500	420	300	250
Variable cost per unit	£6	£6	£6	£6
Contribution per unit	£5	£6	£7	£8
Total contribution	£2,500	£2,520	£2,100	£2,000

Directly attributable fixed costs are assumed to be £1,830

We will use a profit/volume (PV) chart contribution curve to determine a selling price at which profit may be maximised.

The PV chart shown in Figure 11.4 shows profit lines for each selling price plotted as p1, p2, p3, p4.
   The expected profit at each price is plotted at points A, B, C and D.

	Selling price per unit		Profit	(Contribution – Fixed costs)
p1	£11	A	£670	£2,500 – £1,830
p2	£12	B	£690	£2,520 – £1,830
p3	£13	C	£270	£2,100 – £1,830
p4	£14	D	£170	£2,000 – £1,830

The line drawn through A, B, C and D is the contribution curve which shows how contribution is maximised at or around point B and at a price of £12.

Figure 11.4   Profit/volume (PV) chart and contribution curve

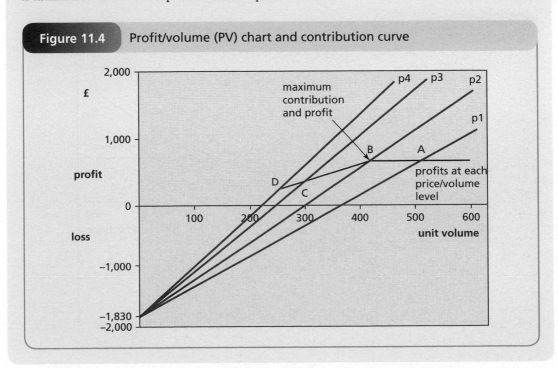

Since demand estimates at any price are likely to be approximate it may be useful to show bands of profit rather than single numbers, illustrated in Worked example 11.21.

Worked example 11.21

We may take the concept introduced in Worked example 11.20 a step further. Assume a band of demands around each of the estimated demands, for example:

a range of 480 to 520 around the estimate of 500 units
a range of 400 to 440 around the estimate of 420 units, and so on.

	Selling price per unit	Contribution per unit	Demand units	Contribution £	Profit £
p1	£11	£5	480–520	2,400–2,600	570–770
p2	£12	£6	400–440	2,400–2,640	570–810
p3	£13	£7	280–320	1,960–2,240	130–410
p4	£14	£8	230–270	1,840–2,160	10–330

We will prepare the contribution curve as a band to illustrate the selling price at which profit may be maximised.

The PV chart will then show the contribution curve as a band, as shown in Figure 11.5.

	Selling price		Profit
p1	£11	A	£570–£770
p2	£12	B	£570–£810
p3	£13	C	£130–£410
p4	£14	D	£10–£330

This indicates an optimal price of around £12.

Figure 11.5   Profit/volume (PV) chart and contribution curve band

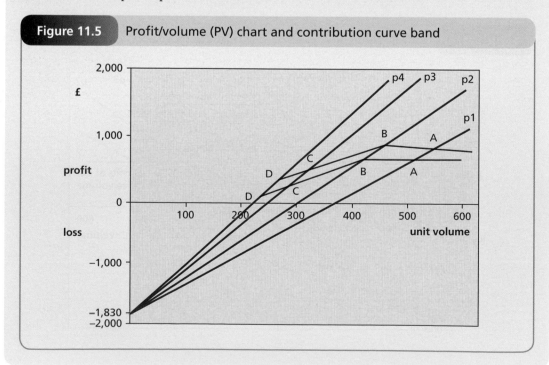

We have assumed a strong relationship in the above two worked examples between demand and price. However, it should also be remembered that demand is influenced by other factors besides price.

Risk analysis and sales pricing

The model we have used to consider market data may be further refined by providing a simple **risk analysis** by looking at the likely probabilities of demand at each selling price level. The end result of risk analysis in practice can be seen in the pricing of various computer peripherals, for example scanners and printers, where the prices are continually changing. In the PC software UK market during 2009 and 2010 major supermarkets and other retailers were stocking formerly 'sold out' software at much reduced prices.

Probabilities of occurrences may be used to weight the various estimated levels of demand at each price (and hence contribution) level to calculate **expected values**. The total expected values at each price level may then be compared. The optimum selling price is the one having the highest total expected value. This technique is illustrated in Worked example 11.22.

Worked example 11.22

We will consider the sensitivity over the selling price range £11 to £12 per unit in Worked example 11.21. The probability of actual demand volumes for chairs may in practice be determined from market research. For this example, we may assume the following probability distribution to provide an illustration of the principle. Note that the total of each of the probabilities of volumes of demand at each price totals one. This means that demand is assumed to be certainly at one of the volume levels, but we don't know with certainty which one.

Price £11		Price £11.50		Price £12	
Demand estimate units	Probability	Demand estimate units	Probability	Demand estimate units	Probability
480	0.1	410	0.3	400	0.4
490	0.2	420	0.5	420	0.4
500	0.3	430	0.2	440	0.2
510	0.3				
520	0.1				
	1.0		1.0		1.0

The profit-maximising price may then be estimated on the basis of this risk analysis, the optimum price being the price that gives the highest total expected value.

Price £11 Cont./unit £5				Price £11.50 Cont./unit £5.50				Price £12 Cont./unit £6			
Est. demand units	Cont. £	Prob.	Exp. value £	Est. demand units	Cont. £	Prob.	Exp. value £	Est. demand units	Cont. £	Prob.	Exp. value £
480	2,400	0.1	240	410	2,255	0.3	677	400	2,400	0.4	960
490	2,450	0.2	490	420	2,310	0.5	1,155	420	2,520	0.4	1,008
500	2,500	0.3	750	430	2,365	0.2	473	440	2,640	0.2	528
510	2,550	0.3	765								
520	2,600	0.1	260								
		1.0	2,505			1.0	2,305			1.0	2,496

This risk analysis would point to an optimum selling price of around £11 per unit, having the highest total expected value contribution at £2,505.

Pricing policy

We have seen that the traditional approach to sales pricing policy is full cost-plus pricing. There are some compelling reasons for its use but it also has many disadvantages. We have looked at other cost-based models like minimum pricing, and have further considered sales pricing using market data and taking account of risk and uncertainty. To complete our discussion of pricing policy three other important factors should also be considered:

- **price elasticity**: the percentage change in the quantity demanded arising from a percentage change in price
  - elastic demand is where a fall or rise in price will increase or reduce demand such that total revenue will be higher or lower than at the current price
  - inelastic demand (for example the demand for cigarettes) is the converse
- price discrimination occurs when an organisation sells the same products at different prices in two or more different markets (note the extensive use of this practice by the oil companies which sell petrol at a range of prices throughout their garages' distribution outlets in different locations)
- pricing decisions should always take account of **competitive pricing**.

In real-life business situations many further factors may impact on the company's pricing policy, for example scarcity of production resources and limiting factors of production. Profit-maximising budgets may be established through the ranking of products in order of contribution earned per unit of the scarce resource or limiting factor. However, as we have previously discussed, very often there are two or more limiting factors, in which case a linear programming model would need to be used to determine optimum solutions. Such approaches are beyond the scope of this book.

Progress check 11.9

Describe how sensitivity analysis may be used to evaluate alternative sales pricing policies.

Decision trees

A **decision tree** is a pictorial method of showing a sequence of interrelated decisions and their expected outcomes. Decision trees can incorporate both the probabilities of, and values of, expected outcomes.

Worked example 11.23

The sales department of Billy Ardtable Ltd has the opportunity to promote a new children's toy, which will provide a unit contribution of £20. Market research has indicated that if the promotion is undertaken at a cost of £50,000, there is a 60% chance of selling 50,000 units, and a 40% likelihood of selling 30,000 units. Market research has also shown that if the product is not promoted then there is a 50/50 chance of selling either quantity.

The sales manager is unsure about what he should do and has asked for advice about whether it is worthwhile promoting the product.

We first need to draw a decision tree, which shows the start point and the two alternatives of promoting or not promoting the product (see the decision tree diagram in Fig. 11.6).

The branch of the tree indicating that Ardtable should promote is labelled with the cost of that activity, £50,000.

The branch of the tree indicating that Ardtable should not promote is labelled with the cost of that activity, £0.

The next step is to label the probabilities of occurrences (sales volumes in this example) on the branches following the decision to promote, being 0.6 (60%) for sales of 50,000 toys and 0.4 (40%) for sales of 30,000 toys.

The same thing is done on the branches following the decision not to promote, being 0.5 (50%) for sales of 50,000 toys and 0.5 (50%) for sales of 30,000 toys.

The expectations of contributions are then calculated by multiplying sales volumes by unit contribution and probability.

The contribution expectation following no promotion is:

$$£500,000 + £300,000 = £800,000$$

The contribution expectation following the promotion is:

$$£600,000 + £240,000 = £840,000$$

but, the promotion option also involves a cost of £50,000 and so the net expectation is £790,000.

The £790,000 net expectation following the promotion may be compared with the net expectation from not promoting of £800,000.

On the above basis we should advise the sales manager of Billy Ardtable Ltd not to promote the sales of toys.

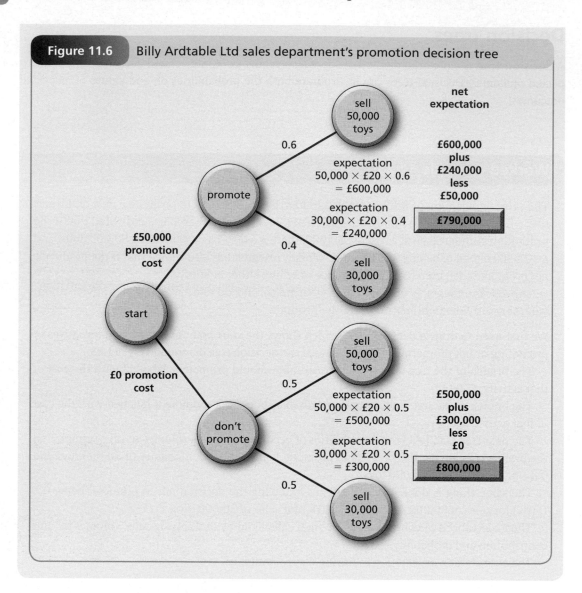

Figure 11.6   Billy Ardtable Ltd sales department's promotion decision tree

Worked example 11.23 is a very simple illustration of the use of a decision tree in decision-making. In practice, a more complex situation would require trees bearing many alternative branches and probability branches to solve the problem.

Progress check 11.10

Outline the principles involved in the use of decision trees in decision-making.

Summary of key points

■ Decision-making is of fundamental importance to organisations, for example in the areas of problem-solving, planning, control and investment.

■ The decision-making process includes identification of relevant costs, and starts with the identification of objectives. Following the implementation of decisions, the process ends with the comparison of actual results with expected outcomes.

■ Relevant costs, or incremental or differential costs, arise as a direct consequence of a decision, and may differ between alternative options.

■ Marginal costing may be used to assist in shut-down or continuation decisions.

■ Make versus buy decisions involve consideration of a wider range of factors than simply the differences in the basic cost.

■ Organisations do not have access to unlimited supplies of resources, for example, labour hours, levels of labour skills, machine capacity, time, market demand, components, raw materials and cash – a limiting factor is the lack of any resource which limits the activity of the organisation.

■ Product mix decisions are influenced by the scarcity of resources and the availability of limiting factors.

■ There are a number of reasons why cost-plus sales pricing is one of the methods most widely used to determine selling price, but there are also many disadvantages in its use and it does encourage waste and may result in a failure to control costs.

■ Sales pricing policy is just one of the four categories of decision included in the marketing mix of price, product, place and promotion, and is based on cost and market factors that influence demand for the product.

■ Decision trees enable a sequence of interrelated decisions, and their expected outcomes, to be reported pictorially.

Assessment material

Questions

Q11.1 Why is decision-making so important to organisations?

Q11.2 What are short- and long-range decisions, and control decisions?

Q11.3 What are the seven steps used in the decision-making process?

Q11.4 Use some examples to illustrate and explain what are meant by relevant costs, sunk costs and opportunity costs.

Q11.5 In what ways may marginal costing provide a better approach to decision-making than absorption costing?

Q11.6 What are the key factors that should be considered in make versus buy decisions?

Q11.7 How should limiting factors be considered if a business is seeking to maximise its profits?

Q11.8 **(i)** What are scarce resources?

   (ii) What factors does an entity need to consider to make optimising decisions related to product mix?

Q11.9 Outline the five main approaches to sales pricing decisions.

Q11.10 How may risk analysis be applied to sales pricing decisions?

Q11.11 What is a decision tree and what is its relevance as an aid to decision-making?

Discussion points

D11.1 'What is all the fuss about decision-making? Surely it's simply a question of adding up a few accounting numbers and the decision makes itself.' Discuss.

D11.2 'The selling price of a product is the amount that the average customer will pay.' Discuss.

Exercises

Solutions are provided in Appendix 3 to all exercise numbers highlighted in colour.

Level I

E11.1 *Time allowed – 45 minutes*

Eifion plc manufactures two products, A and B. The company's fixed overheads are absorbed into products on a machine hour basis, and there was full absorption of these costs in 2010. The company made a profit of £1,344,000 in 2010 and has proposed an identical plan for 2011, assuming the same market conditions as 2010. This means that Eifion plc will be working to its capacity in 2011 at the existing production level with machine hours being fully utilised. Last year's actual data are summarised below:

2010	A	B
Actual production and sales (units)	12,000	24,000
Total costs per unit	£93.50	£126.00
Selling price per unit	£107.50	£175.00
Machine hours per unit	7	3.5
Forecast demand at above selling prices (units)	18,000	30,000
Fixed costs	£1,680,000	

Required:

(i) Explain the relevance of limiting factors in the context of product mix decisions.

(ii) Prepare a profit maximisation plan for 2011 based on the data and selling prices shown for 2010.

(iii) Discuss the limitations of cost-plus pricing and how companies may overcome these in practice.

E11.2 *Time allowed – 45 minutes*

Phil Atterley Ltd is considering the promotion of a new product, which will provide a unit contribution of £2. The sales manager, Stan Palbum, has undertaken market research, which has indicated that if the promotion is undertaken at a cost of £65,000, there is a 70% chance of selling 500,000 units over the following three years, and a 30% chance of selling 300,000 units. Market research has also shown that if the product is not promoted then there is a 40% chance of selling 500,000 units, and a 60% chance of selling 300,000 units over the same time period. Stan is unsure as to whether or not it is worthwhile promoting the product.

You are required to:

(i)   Prepare a decision tree to represent the expected outcomes from promoting or not promoting the new product.

(ii) Recommend to Stan whether or not he should advise the company to promote the new product.

(iii) Outline some further financial and non-financial factors that Phil Atterley Ltd may consider in making this decision.

(iv) Briefly explain what improvements you would suggest to the information about sales over the next three years, and how this may be used to refine the decision-making process.

Level II

E11.3 *Time allowed – 60 minutes*

Hurdle Ltd makes and sells wooden fencing in a standard length. The material cost is £10 per length which requires one half-hour of skilled labour at £10 per hour (which is in quite short supply).

Hurdle Ltd has no variable overheads but has fixed overheads of £60,000 per month. Each length of fencing sells for £28, and there is a heavy demand for the product throughout the year.

A one-off contract has been offered to Hurdle Ltd to supply a variation to their standard product.

(a) The labour time for the contract would be 100 hours.

(b) The material cost would be £600 plus the cost of additional special components.

(c) The special components could be purchased from an outside supplier for £220 or could be made by Hurdle Ltd for a material cost of £100 and labour time of four hours.

You are required to advise the company:

(i)   whether the special component should be manufactured by Hurdle Ltd or purchased from the outside supplier

(ii) whether the contract should be accepted

and

(iii) how much should be charged to the customer to enable Hurdle Ltd to make a 20% mark-up on the cost of the contract.

(Hint: Do not forget to include opportunity costs in the total costs of the contract.)

E11.4   *Time allowed – 60 minutes*

Muckraker Ltd prepares four types of peat mix for supply to garden centres. Muckraker's output has increased in successive months and demand continues to increase. For example, total peat production increased from 2,580 kg April to June to 3,460 kg in the third quarter. Muckraker has now reached a crisis because output cannot be increased by more than another 5% by the current workforce, who are working flat out, and which cannot be increased. In the third quarter of its year Muckraker's financial data are as follows:

	Peat A	Peat B	Peat C	Peat D
Peat production kg	912	1,392	696	460
Selling price per kg	£8.10	£5.82	£4.96	£6.84
Cost data per kg				
Direct labour (£10 per hour)	£0.98	£0.65	£0.50	£0.85
Direct materials	£3.26	£2.45	£2.05	£2.71
Direct packaging	£0.40	£0.35	£0.30	£0.35
Fixed overheads	£1.96	£1.30	£0.99	£1.70
Total costs	£6.60	£4.75	£3.84	£5.61

Fixed overheads are absorbed on a direct labour cost basis. Another company, Bogside Products, has offered to supply 2,000 kg of peat B at a delivered price of 80% of Muckraker's selling price. Muckraker will then be able to produce extra peat A in its place up to the plant's capacity.

Should Muckraker Ltd accept Bogside Products' offer?

E11.5   *Time allowed – 60 minutes*

Ceiling Zero plc has manufactured six CZ311 aircraft for a customer who has now cancelled the order. An alternative buyer, Coconut Airways, would be prepared to accept the aircraft if certain agreed modifications were completed within one month. The Ceiling Zero contracts manager has prepared a costs schedule as a basis for establishing the minimum price that should be charged to Coconut Airways:

	£000	£000
Original cost of manufacture of six CZ311 aircraft		
Based on direct costs 100% overheads charge		6,400
less: Deposit retained when order cancelled		1,000
		5,400
Costs of modification		
Direct materials	520	
Direct labour	200	
		720
Fixed overheads at 75% of direct costs of modification [0.75 × 720]		540
Administrative expenses at 25% of direct costs [0.25 × 720]		180
Total costs		6,840
The contracts manager has suggested an additional mark-up of 25%		1,710
Suggested minimum price to Coconut Airways		8,550

Two types of material were used in the original aircraft manufacture:

- Melunium could be sold as scrap for £400,000, but it would take 60 hours of labour at £100 per hour to prepare the melunium for sale. The department required to carry out this work is particularly slack at the moment.
- Polylindeme could be sold for £300,000 and would also require 60 hours of preparation by the same department at the same rate per hour. Alternatively, polylindeme could be kept for a year and used on another contract instead of metalindeme which would cost £400,000. To do this, a further 120 hours of labour at £150 per hour would be required in addition to the 60 hours above.

The materials used in the modifications for Coconut Airways were ordered last year at a cost of £840,000. The delivery was late and the realisable value fell to £200,000. Because of this the suppliers of the materials have given Ceiling Zero a discount of £320,000. Ceiling Zero cannot use this material on any other contracts.

The direct labour for the modifications is a temporary transfer from another department for four weeks. That department usually contributes £1,000,000 per week to overhead and profits. 75% of that level could be maintained if a special piece of equipment were hired at a one-off cost of £300,000 to compensate for the reduction in the labour force.

If the aircraft were not sold, the specifications, plans and patents could be sold for £350,000.

Additional interim managers would need to be hired at £180,000 for the modifications, included in overhead costs. The fixed overhead rate included straight line depreciation (included in overheads at £140,000), staff expenses, and lighting. Hand tools will be used for the modifications. No other overheads are affected by the modifications.

Ceiling Zero's normal profit mark-up is 50%. The contracts manager has reduced this to 25% because it is felt that this is probably what Coconut Airways would be willing to pay.

> You are required to redraft the contract manager's schedule to give a more meaningful price and to explain all assumptions and alterations.

E11.6   *Time allowed – 60 minutes*

> Use the data for Muckraker Ltd from Exercise E11.4 to calculate the most profitable combination of output of peats A, B, C and D from subcontracting 2,000 kg of one of the products at a price of 80% of its selling price and producing extra quantities of another product up to Muckraker's total capacity.
>
> You should assume that demand for Muckraker's products will be sufficient to meet the extra output, and that Muckraker's levels of quality and delivery performance will be maintained.

E11.7 *Time allowed – 90 minutes*

Mr Threefingers Ltd manufactures three DIY tools, the Rimbo, the Cutzer and the Brazer. The numbers for the financial year just ended are as follows:

	Rimbo £	Cutzer £	Brazer £	Total £
Revenue	100,000	80,000	120,000	300,000
(Units sold)	(10,000)	(4,000)	(10,000)	
Variable costs	60,000	50,000	70,000	180,000
Contribution	40,000	30,000	50,000	120,000
Fixed costs	34,000	36,000	40,000	110,000
Profit/(loss)	6,000	(6,000)	10,000	10,000

£10,000 of the fixed costs of producing Cutzers are costs which would be saved if their production ceased.

Mr Threefingers Ltd is considering a number of options:

(a) Cease production of Cutzers.
(b) Increase the selling price of Cutzers by 15%.
(c) Reduce the selling price of Cutzers by 10%.
(d) Resurrect a tool which was popular 10 years ago, the Thrad, on the following basis:
 – use the resources released by ceasing production of Cutzers
 – incur variable costs of £48,000 and extra fixed costs of £12,000, for sales of 20,000 units
 – sales of 20,000 Thrads, according to market research, could be made at a price of £5 each.

(i) Evaluate the options (a) to (d), stating any assumptions that are made to support your calculations.
(ii) What other factors should be considered by Mr Threefingers Ltd in its decision on which option(s) to adopt?
(iii) Which option(s) would you recommend and why?

12

Short-term planning – the operating budget

Contents

Learning objectives

Completion of this chapter will enable you to:

- identify budgeting as one part of the strategic management process
- define a budget, its purpose and uses
- recognise the importance of forecasting within the budget process
- outline how a business may apply the budgeting process in practice
- explain the preparation of budgets for planning purposes
- prepare the elements of an operating budget and a financial budget to derive the master budget
- describe the system of responsibility accounting and identify the four different types of responsibility centre
- outline the advantages and disadvantages of ways in which divisional performance may be measured
- appreciate the motivational and behavioural aspects of budgeting
- explain the preparation of budgets for control purposes and how performance against budget may be evaluated
- identify the potential problems that may be encountered during budget preparation.

Introduction

Chapter 11 looked at decision-making as one application of the management accounting roles of problem-solving and attention-directing. This chapter looks at a further application of those roles and is concerned with how businesses attempt to plan their activities for the year ahead, or for a shorter period, to enable them to plan and maintain control of the business. Budgeting is the part of the strategic management of the business to do with planning and control. In this chapter we will consider the budget for planning and control purposes.

This chapter considers the role of forecasting in the budget process, and looks at the budget-setting process in detail. The budgeting process will be used to construct a simple budget for a company based on its organisational objectives and its best estimates of future activities.

We return to the use of budgets for control purposes in discussing the motivational aspects of budgeting and how performance against budget may be evaluated, and consider the use of return on investment (ROI) and residual income (RI) in the measurement of divisional performance. The chapter closes by identifying some of the important conflicts and problems encountered in the budgeting process.

Budgeting, planning and control

Many companies believe that the traditional annual budgeting system is unsuitable and irrelevant in rapidly changing markets. Further, they believe that budgets fail to deal with the most important drivers of shareholder value such as intangible assets like brands and knowledge. Some of these companies, like Volvo, Ikea and Ericsson, have already revised their need for annual budgets as being an inefficient tool in an increasingly changing business environment. Volvo abandoned the annual budget 10 years ago. Instead, they provide three-month forecasts and monthly board reports, which include financial and non-financial indicators. These forecasts and reports are supplemented with a two-year rolling forecast, updated quarterly, and four- and ten-year strategic plans updated yearly. It should also be noted that many of the dot.com companies that failed during the 1990s and early 2000s also felt that traditional budget methods were a little old-fashioned and irrelevant.

The budgeting process is questioned in the following article reproduced from *the Sunday Express*, with particular emphasis on the time spans over which budgets may be realistic and therefore useful. This article illustrates how impossible it is to achieve budgets set well in advance, given the changes in circumstances that will undoubtedly occur during the lifetime of a large-scale project.

There are clearly different views as to whether or not the budget is an effective and essential business tool. However, the majority of the world's most successful companies have attributed a large part of their success to their reliance on traditional formal budgeting systems. The long-term (strategic) and short-term (budget) planning processes are core management tasks that are critically important to the future survival and success of the business. The budget prepared for planning purposes, as part of the strategic planning process, is the quantitative plan of management's belief of what the business's costs and revenues will be over a specific future period. The budget prepared for control purposes, even though it may have been based on standards that may not be reached, is used for motivational purposes to influence improved departmental performance. Monitoring of actual

The accuracy of budgets

The estimated cost of the F-35 Joint Strike Fighter, the warplane due to be deployed on the UK's new aircraft carriers, has risen dramatically to $382 billion (£262 billion), according to the US Department of Defense.

The escalating cost, which is 64 per cent higher than when US firm Lockheed Martin won the F-35 contract nine years ago, increases the likelihood that the UK's coalition government will scale back its order for the stealthy aircraft in its strategic defence review.

The Ministry of Defence had been expected to order up to 150 of the jets for the RAF and Royal Navy. Major military programmes are being re-examined, however, as the MoD grapples with a budget crunch.

The US is planning to buy 2,457 of the state-of-the-art fighters, which come in three variants. The first flight of the programme's F-35C carrier variant aircraft is expected in the next few days.

British defence giant BAE Systems is building part of the fuselage of the aircraft, which could bring $30 billion into the UK.

Costs on the military programme, the world's largest, have risen for several reasons, including weight issues and underestimates of the tooling and military construction requirements.

In a separate move, cash-strapped Britain, Germany and Spain are wrangling over how many orders for A400M military transporters each nation can scrap under a new contract for the £20 billion, multinational programme.

The contract for the A400M, whose wings will be built in the UK by Airbus, is being renegotiated after the ambitious programme hit delays and ran billions over budget.

Airbus owner EADS hopes to secure a re-negotiated A400M agreement with the European launch customers by the end of July.

As part of the agreement, the partner nations (UK, Belgium, France, Germany, Luxembourg, Spain, and Turkey) are allowed to scrap a total of 10 orders for the aircraft out of the 180 on the books.

On a visit to London last week, EADS chief executive Louis Gallois said the UK, Germany and Spain were all looking at scaling back orders as budgets come under pressure.

The UK originally agreed to buy 25 A400Ms at an estimated cost of £2.5 billion. Britain wants to drop three of its planned acquisitions in the face of a massive defence budget deficit.

Meanwhile, Germany would like to ditch seven of its orders for the supersized aircraft.

Source: **Fighter jet costs rise to £260bn**, by Tracey Boles
© *Sunday Express*, 6 June 2010

performance against the budget is used to provide feedback in order to take the appropriate action necessary to reach planned performance, and to revise plans in the light of changes.

The following Worked examples 12.1 and 12.2 illustrate the importance of the preparation of business plans and what can result if there is a lack of preparation for unexpected future events.

Worked example 12.1

A business, which was involved in providing marquees and hospitality facilities for business entertaining and private parties, began to face a gradual economic downturn. The effect of this was that demand from companies started to decrease as they cut back their entertaining and hospitality budgets. The business had previously been doing very well and the proprietor felt confident of being able to continue to meet overhead payments even with a reduced sales level, because a reasonable bank balance had been built up. The proprietor did not quantify the change in position in a revised financial plan. After a few months the business needed overdraft facilities and began to delay its payments to suppliers. The bank manager was not sympathetic since he had received no prior warning of the potential problem. Goodwill with suppliers began to diminish.

The business failed, but may not have if the proprietor had:

- attempted to quantify the effect of the economic downturn on profit and cash flow
- warned the bank of the problem
- tried to negotiate the overdraft facility
- negotiated favourable terms with suppliers.

The careful preparation, and regular revision, of financial plans is vital to be prepared against the risk of unexpected events and changes in circumstances.

Worked example 12.2

The managing director of a company that manufactured and sold solid wood kitchen and dining room furniture wanted to increase the sales revenue of the business by 30% in the coming year. She had identified the requirements necessary to fulfil this increase:

- spare capacity in existing retail outlets
- additional new equipment
- one extra employee.

However, the managing director had failed to recognise the cost of financing the increased sales revenue:

- cash outflow for additional raw materials before cash flowed in from increased revenue
- financing costs of additional equipment
- additional wages.

The managing director had focused only on the positive aspects of the expansion:

- increased revenue (although sales prices remained constant)
- increased cash flowing into the business.

The business ran into cash flow problems because it did not inform its bankers of its expansion plans and therefore did not submit a business plan (projected income statement, balance sheet and cash flow) or negotiate a new overdraft facility. For any business it is crucial that any major change, whether expansion or diversification, must be quantified financially in revised business plans. Smaller businesses are particularly vulnerable and should prepare projections more frequently than on an annual basis incorporating realistic expectations for existing activities and plans for any changes in the business in order to:

- alert the business owner to risks and difficulties which may arise
- allow time for remedial action to be taken.

The broad picture of **planning** and **control** includes budgeting, **strategic planning**, **management control** and operations control. The process involves:

- identification of objectives, involving factors such as profit, market share, value, etc.
- identification of potential strategies using facts as well as opinion
- evaluation of options, including a selection of courses of action and preparation of **forecasts**
- implementation of long-term plans, and finalising the planning before going on to provide control
- monitoring of actual outcomes, which will highlight whether the **budget** was too easy or unachievable
- provision of responses regarding actual outcomes against plans through feedback.

Strategic planning

Strategic planning is the process of deciding on:

- the long-term objectives of the organisation
- changes in these objectives
- the resources used to attain these objectives
- the policies that are to govern the acquisition, use and disposition of these resources.

It is not correct to assume that strategic planning is just an extension of budgeting, but there is a close relationship between these processes. A budget is a quantified statement, for a defined period of time, which may include planned revenues, expenses, assets, liabilities and cash flows. A budget provides a focus for the organisation, aids the co-ordination of activities, and facilitates control.

The way in which a typical strategic planning process may be carried out in an organisation may be illustrated in the flow charts in Figures 12.1 and 12.2. The chart in Figure 12.1 shows how analysis is used to develop strategies and actions. The chart in Figure 12.2 shows the sequences of each step in the process and the relationship between strategic planning and budgeting.

Budgeting

The broad purposes of budgeting include:

- planning and control, through
  - exception reporting of financial and non-financial indicators, which
  - economises on managerial time, and
  - maximises efficiency

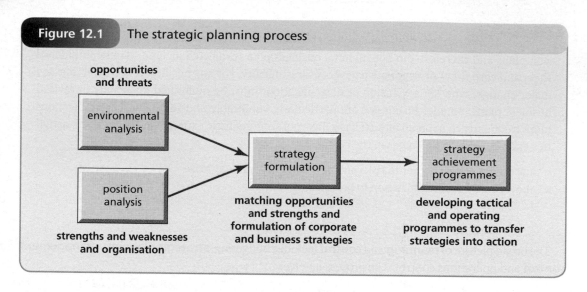

Figure 12.1   The strategic planning process

- co-ordination, which
  - assists goal congruence
- communication, through
  - the feedback process, which should
  - reduce or prevent sub-optimal performance
- motivation and alignment of individual and corporate goals, through
  - participation of many people in the budget-setting process
- evaluation of performance, to
  - facilitate control.

Budgetary control establishes a basis for internal audit by regularly evaluating departmental results. The budget process should ensure that scarce resources are allocated in an optimal way, and so enable expenditure to be controlled. Management is forced to plan ahead so that long-term goals are achieved.

The budget provides a yardstick for performance rather than relying on comparisons with past periods, since when conditions and expectations will have changed. Areas of efficiency and inefficiency are identified through reporting of **variances**, and **variance analysis** will prompt remedial action where necessary. Part of the budget process should identify the people responsible for items of cost and revenue so that areas of responsibility are clearly defined.

Planning

Planning and control are two of the most visible ways that financial and non-financial information may be used in the management control process. This is done by:

- setting standards of performance and providing feedback, and therefore
- identifying areas for improvement, by means of
- variance reports (a subject to which we shall return in more detail in Chapter 13).

Planning is the establishment of objectives and the formulation, evaluation and selection of the policies, strategies, tactics and action required to achieve them. Planning comprises long-term

---

Figure 12.2   The strategic planning relationship with budgeting

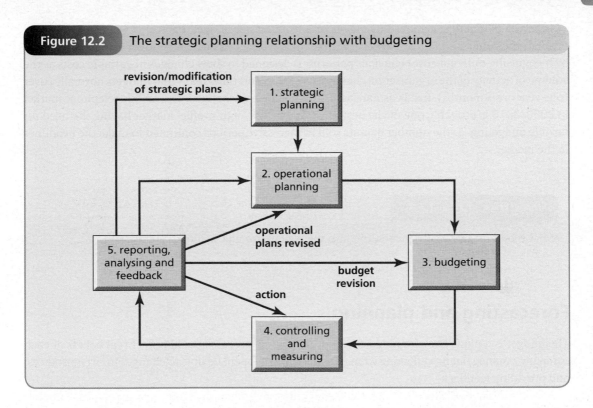

strategic planning and short-term operational planning. The latter usually refers to a period of one year. With regard to a new retail product, the strategic (long-term) plan of the business, for example, may include the aim to become profitable, and to become a market leader within three years. The short-term operational plan may be to get the product stocked by at least one leading supermarket group within 12 months.

Control

Control and monitoring are the continuous comparison of actual results with those planned, both in total and for the separate divisions within the organisation, and taking appropriate management action to correct adverse variances and to exploit favourable variances. The UK has seen the growth of 'call centres', and the media have exposed the constant monitoring by management as unpleasantly intrusive. There appears to be a high turnover of staff in these new hi-tech businesses, where they are regarded as cheap labour but do not necessarily meet management targets.

Management control is the process by which managers assure that resources are obtained and used effectively and efficiently in the accomplishment of the organisation's objectives. The UK company BP plc found itself forced into diverting extra resources into offshore oil rig inspections during 2010, following the explosion on the Deepwater Horizon rig in the Gulf of Mexico.

Operational control is concerned with day-to-day activities of organisations, and is the process of assuring that specific tasks are carried out effectively and efficiently. For example, the UK Government advanced a plan in July 2010 to allocate 80 per cent of National Health Service funding to GPs to cut £1bn of bureaucracy and transfer it to front line services.

Whereas planning is achieved by means of a fixed master budget, control is generally exercised through the comparison of actual costs with a flexible budget. A flexible budget is a budget, which by recognising different cost behaviour patterns, is designed to show changes in variable costs as the volume of activity of the organisation changes. Over the short time-spans that budgets normally cover (one year or six months), fixed costs are assumed to remain unchanged. The mobile telephone market in 2009/2010 is probably one of the best illustrations of a 'high-profile' market having the need for flexible budgeting, as the number of units sold in successive periods continued to make the headlines in the media.

> ### Progress check 12.1
>
> What is budgeting, and how does it fit into the overall strategic planning process?

Forecasting and planning

The budget is a plan. The planning activity of the budget process should reflect real beliefs of each company's management, reflecting what they think will happen, flexible to changes in circumstances, and providing feedback.

A forecast is not a budget but a prediction of future environments, events and outcomes. Forecasting is required in order to prepare budgets. This should start with projected sales volumes and market share of current and new products. Examples of forecasts by product, or sector, can be found regularly in the press, for example car sales and mobile telephone sales.

Large companies need to be very sensitive to trends and developments within their forecasting process as mistakes can prove very expensive. For example, a major UK chocolate manufacturer made too many eggs for Easter 2000, which did not sell; its forecasts and therefore its budgets were proved to be very wide of the mark, and the impact on the business was extremely costly.

In order to highlight more clearly some of the issues around forecasting it may be useful to consider it in the context of budgeting in terms of large group plcs, comprising many companies that may be either diversified or within the same industrial sector.

Sales volume projections are required to evaluate sales revenues and product margins. Marketing policy may or may not be centralised. Centralised marketing information may not always be congruent with individual company expectations and may allow little scope for negotiation.

Sales prices are usually negotiated by individual companies with their customers, to ensure that group margin targets are met. However, in the case of large group companies, relationships with major customers may mean that this is not always an autonomous process, resulting in inevitable acceptance of group agreements in many cases. Whilst this may achieve corporate goals, it may conflict with individual company objectives in trying to meet targeted gross margins. Conversely, commercial managers may try to set sales revenue budgets that may be too easily achievable through understatement of price increase expectations.

Increased market share through new innovation is commonly a primary objective of individual companies. However, new product development, financed out of internally generated funds, involves very large investments and long lead times. This creates competition for resources and at the same time also creates difficulties in trying to achieve group targets for return on investment (ROI). Resources may come off second best, but without any relaxation in product development objectives.

The production manager forecasts production resource requirements, materials and labour, based on sales revenue forecasts, inventory policies and performance improvement targets. The production manager may have an easier job in an expanding rather than a declining market.

Many companies within large groups may be suppliers and customers within the group. The prices to be charged between companies within large groups, transfer prices, are usually set by the parent company and based on predetermined formulae. Some companies within the group may lose and some companies may gain, the objective being that the group is the overall winner. As a consequence, transfer pricing may provide prices that are disagreed with and cause disputes that rarely result in acceptable outcomes for individual companies. Optimal pricing for the group must take precedence over individual company requirements to meet group profitability objectives (despite the impact on individual company profit performance bonuses!).

There are groups of companies where materials or components may be supplied from group-nominated suppliers, or certainly from suppliers where unit price is the dominant procurement criterion. Purchase indices are an important performance measure of the purchasing function, but may not relate to total procurement cost. Group purchasing performance objectives may therefore subvert those of the individual companies, which seek to minimise total costs, on which delivery costs, for example, and the impact of foreign currency exchange rate fluctuations may have a significant impact.

The above examples illustrate some important conflicts at the forecasting stage, arising from policy decisions where group goals inevitably dominate individual company goals, which in turn may also lack congruence with individual goals. Quite frequently a subsidiary company must comply with a group instruction, which may result in an apparently successful local product being dropped in favour of a group-wide product. An example of this was seen in the year 2010 where the group goals of General Motors (USA) were not appreciated by a wide cross-section of the UK community, because so many lost their jobs (and businesses) as a result of Vauxhall cutbacks and closures initiated by the group board of directors.

Forecasting usually relies on the analysis of past data to provide the patterns and trends that may be used to describe the most appropriate forecasting technique. Patterns may then be extrapolated into the future to prepare a forecast. There are many forecasting methods, qualitative and quantitative, with no one best model. It is usually a question of fitting the pattern of historical data to the model that best fits. It could be argued that it is easier to forecast the sales of ice cream than the sales of CDs by a new band. Apparently, the major music-based groups have also found this a mystery over the years.

Progress check 12.2

What is the role of forecasting in budgeting?

Qualitative forecasting

Qualitative forecasting uses expert opinion to predict future events and includes:

- the Delphi method – use of a panel of recognised experts
- technological comparisons – independent forecasters predicting changes in one area by monitoring changes in another area
- subjective curve fitting – for example, similar product life cycles for similar products like CD players and DVD players.

Quantitative forecasting

Quantitative forecasting uses historical data to try to predict the future, and includes univariate models and causal models. Univariate models predict future values of time series when conditions are expected to remain the same, for example exponential smoothing and the use of moving averages.

Causal models involve the use of the identification of other variables related to the variable being predicted. For example, linear regression may be used to forecast sales, using the independent variables of:

- sales price
- advertising expenditure
- competitors' prices.

The major UK retailers have been seen to be highly proactive in revising their sales prices and their advertising activities (and expenditure) as a result of changes in the marketplace.

Whichever method is used it is important that the basis and the methodology of the forecasting is understood. All assumptions made and the parameters of time, availability of past data, costs, accuracy required, and ease of use must be clearly stated to maintain any sort of confidence in the forecasts.

Progress check 12.3

Give examples of some of the techniques used to forecast the demand for a product.

The budget process

The budgeting process normally aims to:

- identify areas of efficiency and inefficiency
- allow people participation
- allocate responsibility to enable performance evaluation through exception reporting of actual versus budget.

Whilst participation may be encouraged, insufficient attention may be given to managers' differing motivational tendencies either to achieve success or to avoid failure. The budget process therefore may not always achieve desired results, nor provide the appropriate rewards for success.

We will use Supportex Ltd in Worked Examples 12.3 to 12.9 to illustrate a step-by-step approach to the budget preparation process.

Sales revenue and gross margin budget

The complete budget preparation process is outlined in Figure 12.3. Once the sales revenue forecast has been prepared the budgeted gross margin may be calculated. The budgeted gross margin is derived from estimated:

- sales volumes, and standard prices
- materials usage, and standard prices
- direct labour hours, and standard rates
- overhead costs.

Figure 12.3   Budget preparation flow diagram

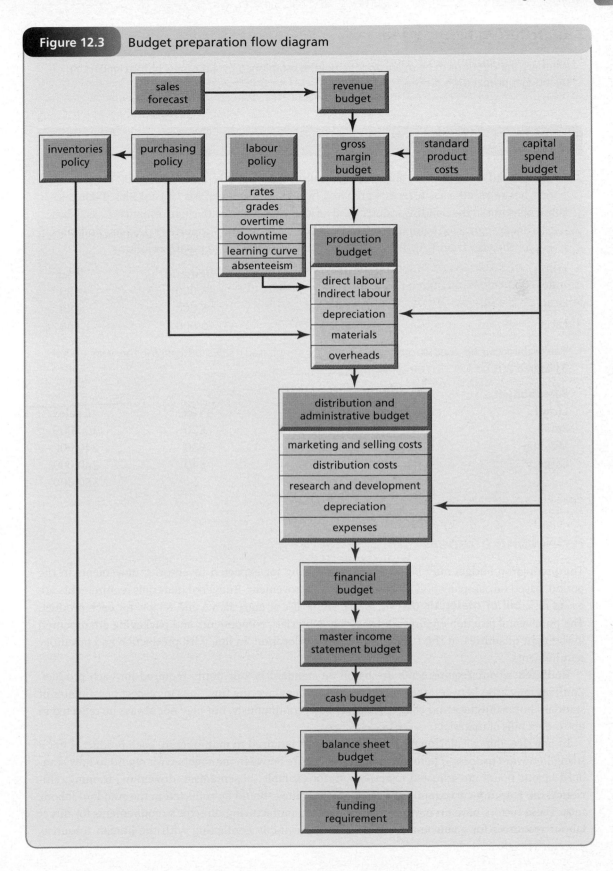

Progress check 12.4

What are the decisions to be made and the policies established by a business before embarking on the budget preparation process?

Worked example 12.3

Supportex Ltd manufactures only three specialist types of lintels: Small; Medium; Large. Supportex has received sales forecasts prepared by its sales manager, Ms Crystal Ball. Taking account of trends in the building industry and an analysis of competitive performance, Crystal has used a linear regression computer model to forecast demand for Supportex's products and sales prices for the year from 1 April 2010. Crystal Ball's sales forecast data are as follows:

Lintel	Demand	Price
Small	5,000	£20
Medium	8,000	£30
Large	6,000	£40

These data can be used to prepare a total (or un-phased) sales budget for the year ended 31 March 2011.

Sales budget

Lintel	Demand	Price	£ sales
Small	5,000	£20	100,000
Medium	8,000	£30	240,000
Large	6,000	£40	240,000
			580,000

Production budget

The production budget may be prepared by allowing for expected inventories movements in the period, based on company policy and targets for improvement. Budgeted materials requirements are based on a **bill of materials (BOM)**, which is the 'list of ingredients and recipe' for each product. The purchasing function ensures that the right materials, components and packaging are procured in the right quantities, at the right time to the right location, in line with production and inventory requirements.

Budgeted labour requirements are based on standard labour hours required for each product. Conflicts may arise between the manufacturing and engineering functions in respect of estimates of standard hours. Engineering changes may be made continuously, but may not always be reflected in up-to-date bills of materials.

In practice, the calculation of the standard hours required to manufacture each product is not a straightforward process. There is always much debate between managers with regard to how standard labour hours are adjusted in respect of, for example, absenteeism, downtime, training, efficiency, the learning curve, and the extent to which they should be reflected in the standard labour rate. These factors have an obvious impact on the manufacturing director's requirements for direct labour resources for given levels of production, inevitably conflicting with the human resources director's headcount objectives.

Many companies have structures comprising business units, each with responsibility for production areas relating to specific products and customers. Responsibility for estimating budget production overheads and indirect labour requirements is devolved to business unit managers, the remaining above-the-line overheads and indirect labour requirements being provided by quality, purchasing, logistics and maintenance managers. Each manager may also submit his or her capital expenditure requirements, which are then used for subsequent calculation of depreciation, and the assessment of cash flow implications.

Depreciation charged to production overhead is calculated based on existing plant and equipment and the plans for new plant and equipment that have been submitted by managers responsible for production and production support activities. It must be emphasised that the method of determining the depreciation charge is highly subjective, and the marketplace has seen many products last much longer than the most extreme original estimates made by managers. An example has been the Rover Mini car, which was not expected to be in production for over 50 years!

Worked example 12.4

The purchasing manager of Supportex Ltd, Arthur Daley, has obtained what he believes are the most competitive prices for materials used to make and package Supportex's products. Supportex's cost prices and the standard quantities used in each product for the budget year are as follows:

Materials	Labels	Packaging	Rubbers	Steels
Cost prices	£1	£2	£3	£6
Standard quantities				
Small	2	1	1	0.5
Medium	1	1	2	1
Large	2	2	1	1

Material handlers and operators are employed to make the Supportex products. The company's production manager, Ben Drools, has provided the following hourly rates and the standard times used in production:

	Material handlers	Operators
Hourly rates	£6	£7.50
Standard minutes		
Small	5	12
Medium	5	20
Large	10	40

Production overheads are forecast at £38,000, which are absorbed into product costs on the basis of direct labour hours.

At 31 March 2010 inventory levels have been estimated by Mr Daley at:

Finished product	Quantity	Materials	Quantity
Small	1,000	Labels	15,000
Medium	1,500	Packaging	10,000
Large	1,000	Rubbers	15,000
		Steels	10,000

The Managing Director has set Ben a target of a 20% reduction in component inventories by 31 March 2011 and the company expects finished goods inventories to be up by 10% by the same time.

Un-phased budgets for the year ended 31 March 2011 may be prepared for the following:

(i) Production
(ii) Direct labour
(iii) Unit gross profit (gross margin)
(iv) Materials usage and purchases.

(i) Production budget

	Sales units	Inventories increases	Production units
Small	5,000	100	5,100
Medium	8,000	150	8,150
Large	6,000	100	6,100

(ii) Direct labour budget

	Production units	Material handlers hours	Operators hours	
Small	5,100	425	1,020	
Medium	8,150	679	2,717	
Large	6,100	1,017	4,067	
Direct labour hours		2,121	7,804	Total 9,925 hours
Direct labour rates		£6/hour	£7.50/hour	
Direct labour cost		£12,726	£58,530	Total £71,256

(iii) Unit gross margin budget
Unit product costs

		Small £	Medium £	Large £
Materials:				
Labels		2	1	2
Packaging		2	2	4
Rubbers		3	6	3
Steels		3	6	6
	(a)	£10	£15	£15

Direct labour:		Small	Medium	Large
Material handlers		0.5 [5 × £6/60]	0.5 [5 × £6/60]	1 [10 × £6/60]
Operators		1.5 [12 × £7.50/60]	2.5 [20 × £7.50/60]	5 [40 × £7.50/60]
	(b)	£2	£3	£6

Total production overheads
£38,000 ÷ 9,925

		Small	Medium	Large
= £3.8287 per hour	(c)	£1.0848	£1.5953	£3.1906
Total unit production costs (a + b + c)	(d)	£13.0848	£19.5953	£24.1906

Sales prices	(e) £20	£30	£40
Unit gross			
margins (e − d)	£6.9152	£10.4047	£15.8094
rounded to	£6.92	£10.40	£15.81

(iv)   Materials usage budget

Units	Labels	Packaging	Rubbers	Steels
Small	10,200	5,100	5,100	2,550
Medium	8,150	8,150	16,300	8,150
Large	12,200	12,200	6,100	6,100
Total usage	30,550	25,450	27,500	16,800
Inventories 31 March 2010	15,000	10,0 00	15,000	10,000
Inventories reduction by 31 March 2011 targeted at 20% of 31 March 2010 levels	3,000	2,000	3,000	2,000

Materials purchases budget

Units	Labels	Packaging	Rubbers	Steels	
Total usage	30,550	25,450	27,500	16,800	
Inventories decrease	3,000	2,000	3,000	2,000	
Purchase requirements	27,550	23,450	24,500	14,800	
Unit costs	£1	£2	£3	£6	Total
Purchase requirements	£27,550	£46,900	£73,500	£88,800	£236,750

Distribution and administrative budget

The non-production costs of:

- marketing and selling
- distribution
- administration
- research and development

and also planned capital expenditure, are provided by managers responsible for departments such as:

- commercial and marketing
- information technology
- administration
- human resources
- engineering
- product development.

Financial budget

Finance costs and finance income from the investment of surplus funds may be estimated for the first draft budget. As the phased income statement, capital expenditure and cash budget become finalised the financial budget can be refined with a little more accuracy.

Master income statement budget

The master budget is prepared by pulling together each of the elements outlined above to provide a budgeted:

- trading account
- manufacturing account
- income statement

for the year.

These may then be phased to show expected month-by-month results. The ways in which the various items within the budget are phased are determined by the type of revenue or cost. Some items may be related to the volume of sales, or production levels, whilst others may be spread evenly on a monthly, weekly or daily basis.

The budget preparation procedure described above is usually a negotiation process between budget holders and the budget committee. Conflicts may arise as budgets are very often seen as 'finance' budgets, perceived as a pressure device, with a corresponding demotivating effect on personnel.

Problems ensue due to ignorance, or a lack of information, and very often a misunderstanding of the budget process (probably through a lack of training), which may result in generally inflated budgets. Judgement is required to identify whether apparently inflated budgets reflect real needs or some degree of 'padding' due to a fear of cutbacks. Padding relates to the overestimation of budgeted costs (or underestimation of budgeted revenues) by managers with the expectation that their budgets may be cut, so that their final agreed budgets may be at levels that they feel are achievable.

Further conflicts arise between departments within a company, through competition for resources, and also poor communication, resulting in duplication in cost budgets or padding. Examples of costs omitted, or duplicated, are health and safety costs (human resources or manufacturing?), training costs (human resources or decentralised into the operational departments?), and the question of centralised and decentralised costs generally. This often results in each department blaming the other if services are not provided, or if cost targets are not achieved.

Padding may occur where budget holders are allowed to be excessively prudent regarding costs and expenses or achievement of sales. If the company or a sector of its business is expanding, the padding may be tolerated. When competition is fierce or the industry is in decline, then the padding could prove quite harmful and lead to decisions being based on an incorrect cost base. It is inevitable that managers may be prudent when constructing their budgets, and this can take the form of putting a little extra into expense categories that may be difficult to verify, or a little less into certain categories of sales.

The budget preparation process is a continuous process of:

- setting objectives
- forecasting
- draft budget preparation
- evaluation
- feedback
- forecast and budget revisions.

Within most organisations this process continues, limited by budget preparation timetable constraints, until an acceptable final budget has been achieved.

During the budget process, cost reductions are inevitably requested from all areas within the organisation. This poses obvious dilemmas for all managers. Whilst wanting to co-operate in meeting profitability objectives, they must still maintain the same levels of service for both internal and external customers.

Worked example 12.5

Supportex Ltd has budgeted selling and administrative costs of £80,000 for the following year. The overheads and selling and administrative costs include total depreciation budgeted for the year of £23,569. There are not expected to be any financing costs over the coming year.

We will prepare a total (or un-phased) income statement budget, using absorption costing, for the year ended 31 March 2011.

Income statement master budget

	Small Total	Unit	Medium Total	Unit	Large Total	Unit	Total
Sales units	5,000		8,000		6,000		
	£		£		£		£
Sales revenue	100,000	£20	240,000	£30	240,000	£40	580,000
Cost of sales (derived from sales revenue less gross profit)	65,400		156,800		145,140		367,340
Gross profit	34,600	£6.92	83,200	£10.40	94,860	£15.81	212,660
Using unit gross margins from Worked example 12.4 (iii) Selling and administrative costs							80,000
Profit before tax							132,660

Cash budget

Cash flow is an extremely important element in the budget preparation process. The master income statement budget, together with the planned capital expenditure, the outflow of cash on non-current asset acquisitions and investments, may then be used to prepare an initial cash budget. This will also include the impact of the operating cycle:

■ materials purchases become inventory items held for a period before use, and payables to be paid out of cash at a later date
■ production uses up inventories to generate sales which become receivables to be received into cash at a later date
■ the more immediate payment of staff costs and other operational overheads.

The final cash budget, phased to show monthly cash surpluses or cash requirements, will also include the effect of non-operational items such as cash raised through the issue of shares and loans, and cash paid in respect of taxation and dividends to shareholders.

Worked example 12.6

Supportex Ltd has prepared an estimated balance sheet for 31 March 2010 as follows:

	£	£
Non-current assets	362,792	
Inventories	206,669	
Trade receivables	46,750	
Cash and cash equivalents	2,432	618,643
Trade payables	35,275	
Share capital	200,000	
Retained earnings	383,368	618,643

Customers all pay in the month following the month of sale and Arthur Daley has negotiated supplier payments to be made in the second month following the month of purchase. Direct labour, production overheads, and selling and administrative costs are all paid in the month they are incurred. There is no planned capital expenditure for the budget year and trading is expected to be evenly spread over the 12 months, except for month twelve when the changes in inventories levels are expected to occur.

We can use this to prepare a total (or un-phased) cash budget for the year ended 31 March 2011.

	£			£
Cash inflows from customers:		Cash outflows to suppliers:		
Trade receivables at 31/3/10	46,750	Trade payables at 31/3/10		35,275
Sales 2010/11	580,000	Purchases 2010/11		236,750
less: Trade receivables at		less: Trade payables at		
31/3/11 (1 month sales)	(48,333)	31/3/11 (2 months purchases)		(39,458)
	578,417			232,567
Cash outflows for overheads:		Cash outflow for capital:		zero
Production overheads	38,000	Cash outflow for tax:		zero
Selling and administrative costs	80,000	Cash outflow for dividends:		zero
less: Depreciation	(23,569)	Cash outflow for direct labour:		71,256
	94,431	Cash inflow for shares/loans:		zero

Statement of cash flows budget

	£	
Inflows from customers	578,417	
Outflows to suppliers	(232,567)	
Outflows for overheads	(94,431)	
Outflow for direct labour	(71,256)	
Budgeted cash flow 2010/11	180,163	[see Worked example 12.7]
Forecast cash balance 31/3/10	2,432	
Budgeted cash balance 31/3/11	182,595	

The calculation of the budgeted statement of cash flows, shown in Worked example 12.6, was carried out by preparing a direct statement of cash flows (see Chapter 5). This may be checked by the preparation of a more conventional indirect statement of cash flows, which is shown later in Worked example 12.9.

Balance sheet budget

The budget balance sheet may be prepared with reference to:

- information relating to sales revenue, costs, etc., from the master income statement budget
- the capital expenditure budget
- operating cycle assumptions on inventory days, collection days and payables days
- the cash budget.

As with the income statement budget and cash budget, the balance sheet budget may be phased to show the expected month-by-month financial position of the organisation.

Worked example 12.7

Using the information from the last three Worked examples 12.4 to 12.6 we can now prepare an un-phased balance sheet budget for Supportex Ltd as at 31 March 2011.

Inventories valuations at 31 March 2011	Quantity	£ unit cost (see Worked example 12.4)	£
Finished product			
Small	1,100	13.0848	14,393
Medium	1,650	19.5953	32,332
Large	1,100	24.1906	26,610
Total			73,335
Materials			
Labels	12,000	1.00	12,000
Packaging	8,000	2.00	16,000
Rubbers	12,000	3.00	36,000
Steels	8,000	6.00	48,000
Total			112,000
Budgeted inventories at 31 March 2011			185,335
Non-current assets			
Non-current assets at 31 March 2010			362,792
Budgeted depreciation 2010/11			(23,569)
Budgeted non-current assets at 31 March 2011			339,223
Retained earnings			
Retained earnings at 31 March 2010			383,368
Budgeted profit 2010/11 (see Worked example 12.5)			132,660
Budgeted retained earnings at 31 March 2011			516,028

Using the budgeted inventories, non-current assets, and retained earnings calculations above, and the budgeted cash balance, trade receivables and trade payables calculated in Worked example 12.6, we now have the complete information to construct the budgeted balance sheet as at 31 March 2011:

Balance sheet budget	£	£
Non-current assets	339,223	
Inventories	185,335	
Trade receivables	48,333	
Cash and cash equivalents	182,595	755,486
Trade payables	39,458	
Share capital	200,000	
Retained earnings	516,028	755,486

The budget balance sheet as at 31 March 2011 shown in Worked example 12.7 has been prepared by calculating the:

- effect on non-current assets of depreciation for the year 2010/11
- closing valuation of inventories at 31 March 2011
- closing valuation of trade receivables at 31 March 2011
- cash and cash equivalents balance at 31 March 2011
- closing valuation of trade payables at 31 March 2011
- addition to retained earnings, the budgeted profit for the year 2010/11.

In Worked example 12.8 we illustrate an alternative way of deriving the balance sheet that may be used in practice, which also clarifies the links between inventories movements and the income statement and its links with the balance sheet. This method requires a calculation of the materials cost of products actually sold (compared with the materials used in production in Worked example 12.4). It also requires a calculation of the direct labour and production overheads cost of products actually sold (compared with the cash paid out in Worked example 12.6). The cash paid out for direct labour and overheads in the budget year will be absorbed into the valuation of inventories of finished product. Not all that finished product will be sold in the period. Some will have remained in inventories at 31 March 2011. The same situation applied at 31 March 2010.

Therefore finished product inventories at 31 March 2011 will need to be adjusted by the amount of direct labour and overheads in their valuation that relates to the difference in the finished goods inventories level between 31 March 2010 and 31 March 2011. The balance of what is paid out for direct labour and overheads in the budget year is charged as a cost in the income statement.

Worked example 12.8

The budget balance sheet for Supportex Ltd at 31 March 2011 can be derived by plotting the expected movements for the budget year 2010/11 relating to each type of activity, and totalling across each line from the starting balance sheet 31 March 2010. This is an alternative approach to Worked example 12.7, and it shows the relationship between sales revenue, costs, cash and the balance sheet.

Materials cost of goods sold

Units	Labels		Packaging		Rubbers		Steels	
Small	[5,000 × 2]	10,000	[5,000 × 1]	5,000	[5,000 × 1]	5,000	[5,000 × 0.5]	2,500
Medium	[8,000 × 1]	8,000	[8,000 × 1]	8,000	[8,000 × 2]	16,000	[8,000 × 1]	8,000
Large	[6,000 × 2]	12,000	[6,000 × 2]	12,000	[6,000 × 1]	6,000	[6,000 × 1]	6,000
Total		30,000		25,000		27,000		16,500
Unit costs		£1		£2		£3		£6
Materials cost of sales		£30,000		£50,000		£81,000		£99,000

Total = £260,000

Direct labour in finished product inventory increase 31 March 2011

	Inventory increases	Direct labour/unit £	Inventory adjustment £
Small	100	2	200
Medium	150	3	450
Large	100	6	600
			1,250

Production overhead in finished product inventory increase 31 March 2011

	Inventory increases	Production overhead/unit (see Worked example 12.4) £	Inventory adjustment £
Small	100	1.0848	108
Medium	150	1.5953	239
Large	100	3.1906	319
			666

Sales revenue, materials purchases, depreciation, cash receipts and cash payments have previously been calculated (see Worked examples 12.3 to 12.6)

Balance sheet budget

Figures in £	Forecast 31/03/10	Revenue	Cash recs.	Purchases	Cash pays.	Depn.	Materials cost of sales	Direct labour	Production overheads	Budget 31/03/11
Non-current assets	362,792					(23,569)				339,223
Inventories	206,669			236,750			(260,000)	1,250	666	185,335
Trade receivables	46,750	580,000	(578,417)							48,333
Cash	2,432		578,417		(232,567)			(71,256)	(94,431)	182,595
	618,643									755,486
Trade payables	35,275			236,750	(232,567)					39,458
Share capital	200,000									200,000
Retained earnings	383,368	580,000				(23,569)	(260,000)	(70,006)	(93,765)	516,028
	618,643									755,486

Worked example 12.9

An unphased budgeted indirect statement of cash flows may be prepared for Supportex Ltd for the year ended 31 March 2011.

Statement of cash flows budget

	£	
Budgeted operating profit 2010/11	132,660	
plus: Depreciation	23,569	
plus: Decrease in inventories	21,334	[206,669 − 185,335] See Worked example 12.7
less: Increase in trade receivables	(1,583)	[48,333 − 46,750] See Worked example 12.6
plus: Increase in trade payables	4,183	[39,458 − 35,275]
Budgeted cash flow 2010/11	180,163	See Worked example 12.6
Forecast cash balance 31/3/10	2,432	
Budgeted cash balance 31/3/11	182,595	

The budgeted cash flow number of £180,163 can be seen to agree with the budgeted cash flow calculated in Worked example 12.6.

Progress check 12.5

Describe a typical budget preparation process.

Funding requirements

The final budget should not be accepted until the projected financial position of the business has been reviewed in terms of the adequacy, or otherwise, of funding. The budget for the forthcoming period may have been based on higher or lower activity than the previous period, or it may include new product development, or other major new projects. Risk analysis and risk assessment are essential to be carried out on each of the uncertain areas of the budget, to determine any requirement for additional funding and to safeguard the future of the business.

Additional funding may be by way of extended bank overdraft facilities, loans or additional share capital. The appropriate funding decision may be made and matched with the type of activity for which funding is required. For example, major capital expenditure projects would not normally be funded by a bank overdraft; the type of longer-term funding generally depends on the nature of the project.

Worked example 12.10

Magic Moments have planned to sell fluffy puppies between October and December to meet the Christmas demand. They have forecast the following sales at £20 each to be received in cash in the month of sale.

	Oct	Nov	Dec	Total
Units	500	750	1,500	2,750

Magic Moments have contracted to buy fluffy puppies at £12 each. They will have to buy 300 in September. Month-end inventories are planned to be:

October 30% of November sales units
November 20% of December sales units
December zero

Magic Moments must pay for fluffy puppies in the month following purchase. We will prepare:

■ a schedule of opening inventory, purchases and closing inventory in units for September to December
■ a direct cash flow forecast phased for October to January

and then consider how Magic Moments have funded their activities.

Inventories and purchases:

Units	Sep	Oct	Nov	Dec
Opening inventories	–	300	225	300
Purchases (derived)	300	425	825	1,200
Sales	–	500	750	1,500
Closing inventories	300	225	300	–

Cash flow:
Figures in £

		Oct		Nov		Dec		Jan
Opening balance		–		6,400		16,300		36,400
Cash inflow	(500 × £20)	10,000	(750 × £20)	15,000	(1,500 × £20)	30,000		–
Cash outflow	(300 × £12)	3,600	(425 × £12)	5,100	(825 × £12)	9,900	(1,200 × £12)	14,400
Closing balance		6,400		16,300		36,400		22,000

Magic Moments have funded their business through managing their operating cycle. Effectively, their payables have financed the business.

Regardless of whether higher or lower activity is expected and budgeted for future periods, it is absolutely essential that the company's bankers are kept fully informed of expectations. Bankers do not like surprises. The corporate graveyard is littered with small businesses in particular who have ignored this basic requirement.

Performance evaluation and control

The many uses of budgeting may be summarised as follows:

■ a system for optimal allocation of scarce resources, for example a factory capable of a specific process like plate glass manufacture
■ a yardstick for performance, better than past performance, since conditions may have changed
■ people participation to provide motivation for improved performance and alignment of individual and corporate goals
■ improved communication to enable co-ordination of various parts of the business and so avoid sub-optimisation

- thinking ahead to achieve long-term goals and identify short-term problems
- a system of authorisation and for clear identification of responsibility
- internal audit by evaluating efficiency and effectiveness of departmental performance for prompt remedial action as necessary
- a system of control and management by exception reporting.

Prior to budget preparation, targets may be issued, for example, for:

- sales revenue
- gross profit
- return on investment
- inventory days
- collection days
- payables days.

Whilst the responsibility for the budget usually rests with a budget committee, for the budget to achieve its aims, it is important for relevant managers to have full participation in the process and receive communication of the guidelines. Uncertainties, limiting factors and constraints, along with all assumptions, must be made available to all managers with budget responsibility.

It is by ensuring that full communication and participation take place that the most effective use may be made of budgeting as a tool of control. Actual departmental results may then be regularly reported against control budgets that have had full acceptance by the relevant managers and are based on up-to-date and realistic standards of performance. The budget is used as a tool for control of the business by monitoring actual performance and comparing how closely it is in line with the plan. For this purpose the overall budget plan is broken down into the individual elements, representing the areas of responsibility of each of the budget holders, which are called **responsibility centres**.

Responsibility centres

As part of the budgetary process, in order to co-ordinate an organisation's activities, responsibility is assigned to managers who are accountable for their actions. Each manager therefore is in charge of a responsibility centre. A responsibility centre is a department or organisational function whose performance is the direct responsibility of a specific manager. **Responsibility accounting** is the system used to measure and compare actual results against budget for each centre. Costs are traced to the activities causing them, or to the individuals knowledgeable about why they arose and who authorised them.

There are four main types of responsibility centre, and within each type, the responsibilities of the manager of each centre are defined in a different way:

- cost centre is a production or service location, function, activity or item of equipment for which costs are accumulated – the manager is accountable for costs only
- **revenue centre** is a centre devoted to raising revenue with no responsibility for costs, for example, a sales centre – the manager is responsible for revenue only (revenue centres are often used in not-for-profit organisations)
- **profit centre** is a part of the business that is accountable for both costs and revenue – the manager is responsible for revenue and costs
- **investment centre** is a profit centre with additional responsibilities for capital investment and possibly for financing, and whose performance is measured by its return on investment – the manager is responsible for investments, revenue and costs.

Responsibility must be matched with control, otherwise a manager is more likely to be demotivated. The manager must be able to influence the costs in question over specific time spans. Problems may also arise when costs may be influenced by more than one manager. Many very large businesses have pursued the policy of devolving spending responsibility down through the organisation. Employees are frequently motivated by being given spending responsibility and fully accepting control, which may be supported by sophisticated IT techniques as hardware and software has become more economic, by, for example, file sharing or remote interrogation of files.

Budget holders can only be responsible for controllable costs or revenue within their areas of responsibility. For example, a production manager may be responsible for ensuring that he or she does not exceed the number of direct labour hours allowed within their area of responsibility for a given level of output. Uncontrollable costs, for example the level of depreciation on the machines and equipment used within the production manager's department, may appear within budget holders' areas of activity but cannot realistically be used to measure performance. Further examples of such costs may be business taxes, or rents on property that may have been the subject of long-term agreements.

In a similar way, a budget holder may be responsible for controlling costs of a department that relate to sales volumes or other variable activities. The costs of that department, the variable costs and possibly the fixed costs, will vary according to the level of activity that takes place. For this reason, the budget for control purposes is flexed in line with actual levels of activity to provide more realistic levels of expected costs against which to measure performance. Flexing the budget is a topic we will discuss in detail in Chapter 13.

Progress check 12.6

Outline the system of responsibility accounting in its various forms and describe what it aims to achieve.

For control purposes, therefore, the master budget needs to be:

- phased by reporting period – usually by week, calendar month or four-week period
- broken down to provide a separate budget for each responsibility centre
- flexed to show the costs (or revenue) expected as a result of changes in activity levels from those planned within the master budget.

We will look at the mechanics of **flexed budgets** in Chapter 13, together with the method of comparison with actual performance. We shall look at the way in which standards are used for this purpose in budget preparation to enable meaningful exception reporting to be provided for analysis of differences, or variances, to the budget plan.

Divisional performance measurement

For cost control and performance measurement purposes it is necessary to measure performance at frequent intervals. Managers may be evaluated on a short-term basis monthly, quarterly or even yearly. As we discussed in Chapter 7, the measures used to consider a company's economic performance may not be the most appropriate to evaluate divisional performance of managers. Responsibility centres may be business units, divisions of a company or even companies within a group. The performance of managers of responsibility centres may be considered using the divisional performance measures of return on investment (ROI) and residual income (RI). Such short-term performance measures focus only on the performance for the particular control period.

ROI is calculated as a percentage by dividing operating profit by the investment (or net assets, which are usually averaged – see Chapter 7). It is therefore a relative measure of profitability rather than an absolute measure of profit. RI is calculated by deducting a notional interest charge for capital invested from profit before tax, and is therefore an absolute measure.

Worked example 12.11

Consider two divisions, A and B, of a company with the following results for 2009:

	Division A	Division B
Operating profit	£1m	£2m
Average net assets (investment)	£4m	£20m

The ROI for division A is 25% and for division B is 10%. Division B earns higher profits but A is more profitable on an ROI basis.

Divisional managers may, for example, be rewarded via a remuneration package, which is linked to an ROI performance measure. Since ROI tends to be low in the early stages of an investment project, managers are likely to take a short-term view in appraising investment proposals because they will be anxious to maintain their level of earnings. Managers may therefore reject proposals for such investment projects even though they may provide a satisfactorily high ROI over the longer term. The owners of the business, the shareholders, will of course be more interested in the longer-term ROI over the entire life of an investment project.

The divergence between the two points of view occurs because divisional managers and shareholders are each using different assessment criteria. The views of divisional managers and the shareholders may be brought into line if they both used the same criteria. This would mean abandoning the practice of linking a manager's remuneration directly to short-term ROI because it is likely to encourage short-term thinking.

It is sometimes claimed that RI is more likely to encourage goal congruence, but a similar lack of goal congruence to that resulting from the use of ROI may occur if divisional managers' performance is measured using RI. If divisional manager performance is based on RI then managers may decide to replace old equipment (resulting in lower ROI and worsened cash flow) to increase profit and therefore increase RI. The reduction in ROI may therefore result in a sub-optimisation decision for the company as a whole. Alternatively, if divisional manager performance is based on ROI then managers may decide to make do with old equipment, resulting in a higher ROI and improved cash flow, but which may result in a reduced RI. There have been many case studies based on UK manufacturers which showed that the age of their plant was much greater than that used by overseas competitors, which may be as a direct result of the type of divisional performance measure being used.

Worked example 12.12

Let's consider two divisions within a company that have an opportunity to invest in projects that both have an initial cost of £10m. The overall cost of capital for the company is 15% per annum. The expected operating profits from each investment and the current returns earned by the divisions are shown below:

	Division X	Division Y
Investment projects available cost	£10m	£10m
Expected operating profit	£2m	£1.3m
ROI of divisions at present	25%	9%

The expected returns from each proposed project are 20% for division X and 13% for division Y. The manager of division X would not be motivated to invest in the new project because

20% is less than the current ROI. The manager of division Y would be motivated to invest in the project because 13% is greater than the current ROI. However, both decisions are incorrect for the company as a whole. This is because the division Y project returns 2% less, and the division X project returns 5% more, than the average cost of capital for the company of 15%.

Worked example 12.13

Let's again consider the two divisions within a company that have an opportunity to invest in projects that both have an initial cost of £10m. The overall cost of capital for the company is 15% per annum. The expected operating profits from each investment are shown below:

	Division X	Division Y
Proposed investment	£10.0m	£10.0m
Expected profit before tax	£2.0m	£1.3m
Cost of capital charge (15%)	£1.5m	£1.5m
Residual income (loss)	+£0.5m	−£0.2m

On an RI basis the manager of division X will be motivated to invest and the manager of division Y will not be motivated to invest.

If a great deal of pressure is placed on managers to meet short-term performance measurement targets, there is a danger that they will take action that will improve short-term performance but that will not maximise long-term profits. For example, by skimping on expenditure on advertising, customer services, maintenance, and training and staff development costs, it is possible to improve short-term performance. However, such actions may not maximise long-term profits.

It is probably impossible to design performance measures which will ensure that maximising short-run performance will also maximise long-term performance. Some steps, however, can be taken to improve the short-term performance measures so that they minimise the potential conflict. For example, during times of rising prices, short-term performance measures can be distorted if no attempt is made to adjust for the changing price levels.

ROI and RI represent single summary measures of performance. It is virtually impossible to capture in summary financial measures all the variables that measure the success of a manager. It is therefore important that accountants broaden their reporting systems to include additional non-financial measures of performance that give clues to future outcomes from present actions (see the sections on non-financial performance indicators and the balanced scorecard in Chapter 7). For example, obtaining feedback from customers regarding the quality of service encourages managers not to skimp on reducing the quality of service in order to save costs in the short term. Other suggestions have focused on refining the financial measures so that they will reduce the potential for conflict between actions that improve short-term performance at the expense of long-term performance.

The use of ROI as a divisional performance measure has a number of deficiencies. For example, it encourages managers to accept only those investments that are in excess of their current ROI, leading to the rejection of profitable projects. Such actions may be reduced by replacing ROI with RI as the performance measure. However, as we have seen, merely changing from ROI to RI may not eliminate the short-term versus long-term conflicts. RI does enable different cost of capital percentages to be applied to different investments that have different levels of risk. It should be noted that if RI is used as the measure of divisional performance then it should be compared with budgeted or targeted levels of RI, which reflect the size of the divisional investment. However, empirical evidence indicates that RI is not widely used.

Ideally, performance measures ought to be based on future results that can be expected from a manager's actions during a period. This would involve a comparison of the present value of future cash flows at the start and end of the period, and a manager's performance would be based on the increase in present value during the period. Such a system may not be totally feasible, given the difficulty in predicting and measuring future outcomes from current actions. A variation on RI is economic value added (EVA^{TM}), which is discussed in more detail in Chapter 14. EVA aims to provide a performance measure that is highly correlated with both shareholder wealth and divisional performance. EVA is calculated by deducting from profit after tax a financial charge for the use of the company's net assets. The net assets figure reported in the company's published balance sheet is usually adjusted (in a variety of different ways) to reflect as realistic a valuation as possible of the company's net assets. The basis for the financial charge is usually the average cost of the capital used by the company.

Motivation and the behavioural aspects of budgeting

We have discussed the importance of participation and communication in the budget process and so it can be seen that key aspects of budgeting are behavioural. One of the main objectives is to influence the behaviour of the people in the organisation so that efficiency is maximised and corporate goals are attained. It is important therefore that the evaluation of performance does not degenerate into a blame culture. It follows then that motivation is an important underlying factor in ensuring that achievable budgets are set and that the managers with the responsibility for each of the elements of the budget have a very good chance of achieving their objectives.

The question of motivation is a very large subject in its own right. It is sufficient for our purposes to outline some of the many motivational factors without going into much further detail. Key motivational factors include:

- pay
- bonuses
- feedback of information
- communication and discussion of control reports
- success, and reward for target achievement
- training in the budget process
- the identification of controllable and uncontrollable costs
- the setting of fair, achievable standards
- the avoidance of short-term wins at the expense of long-term considerations, leading to dysfunctional decision-making
- flexibility in meeting the requirements of the budgeting system
- performance appraisal using budgets flexed to actual activity levels
- inclusion of non-financial performance indicators.

Many writers, including Hopwood, Argyris, Hofstede, McGregor, Becker and Green, have identified the various motivational problems which may be encountered in budgeting. The ways they have suggested these problems can be alleviated, and how motivation can be enhanced, is beyond the scope of this book, and may be followed up with further reading.

Problems in budgeting

Within most companies budgeting is a high-profile, formal process, prepared on either a yearly or half-yearly basis. The budget is prepared within the context of a company's strategic management process, and includes current year performance projections. It should ideally emphasise the strategies and priorities of the company and focus on both financial and non-financial performance.

Information provided from the budget process generally falls into the following main categories:

- sales revenue, relating to
  - customers
  - demand volumes
  - market share
  - selling price expectations
- product margins
- purchase price index expectations
- overheads
- headcount
- new product development
- capital investment
- working capital
- cash
- non-financial performance indicators, in areas such as
  - product quality
  - staff development
  - delivery performance
  - customer satisfaction.

Many companies have developed dynamic budgeting models, using packaged IT solutions that may link financial and non-financial performance measures.

The major purposes of budgeting may be identified as:

- compelling planning and forcing management to look ahead by
  - setting targets
  - anticipating problems
  - giving the organisation purpose and direction
- formalising the communication of ideas and plans to all appropriate individuals
- co-ordinating activities of different business units and departments

- establishing a system of control, by
  - allocating responsibility
  - providing a plan against which actual performance may be measured and evaluated
- motivating improved performance of personnel.

It may be seen from many job advertisements how motivation is recognised as being extremely important in providing a vital link with individual performance, which in turn links with achievement of corporate budget targets.

The emphasis given to each budget purpose varies, and is very much dependent upon:

- company policy
- the way in which information is provided and received and by whom
- the negotiating skills of each manager with the company's budget team.

Problems of conflict arise out of actual and perceived fulfilment of each of the purposes of the budget. Each area is a minefield of potential problems of conflict. For example, it was revealed in 2005 that the chief executive of a major UK retailer only wanted to hear good news about the company's position in the marketplace. The managers were afraid to give him bad news.

There are basic problems within the process of setting targets. Organisations can be very unforgiving when targets are not achieved. The budget preparation process has become easier to manage with the introduction of powerful IT resources; but it has also resulted in more accuracy required within the estimates and also within a shorter time frame.

During the budget-setting process, it is essential that individual budget holders 'buy in' to their budgets to enable subsequent meaningful monitoring and evaluation of actual performance. Their budgets, while representing difficult-to-meet targets, must also be achievable to provide the necessary motivation to reach their goals.

Responsibility must be matched with control. Costs that should be considered uncontrollable may not necessarily be treated as such in evaluating individual performance, resulting in discontent and demotivation. Similar conflicts arise if there is insufficient clarification, or if costs are controlled by more than one person; for example, special transport costs incurred to meet production needs through supplier non-performance – a manufacturing or purchasing responsibility?

Performance against budgeted costs at the operating level should be flexed to reflect current activity. This may not always happen, resulting in unfair appraisal of individual performance and misrepresentation of company performance. It is quite obvious that managers have no influence on the basic 'health' of their company's industrial sector; note the examples of mobile telephones (expanding in the UK) and coal (declining in the UK), seen in the latter part of the twentieth century.

Budgeted levels of training, particularly operator quality training, must be evaluated considering short-term profitability performance objectives and longer-term goals of zero defects. The aim must be of course to achieve both! A well-known UK car manufacturer used the pressure of telephone calls from customers direct to the factory floor, to reduce defects in the finished motor cars, especially those going into the export markets. Another UK manufacturer of motor cars required the engines to be signed for by the appropriate engineer, so that the customer could identify who was responsible for that particular engine.

Many materials may be procured in foreign currency. Should the performance of the purchasing department (responsible for supplier selection) reflect the impact of any resultant currency rate variances? Or should performance be measured using standard exchange rates prevailing at the outset, with, say, the finance department (usually responsible for hedging activities) bearing the cost of currency movements?

Major conflicts arise out of management of the operating cycle, the objective being its minimisation, through reduced receivables collection days and inventories days and extended payables days.

The company treasurer must respect this objective, while maintaining good relationships with customers and suppliers, and ensuring no threat to operations. The purchasing and manufacturing directors must ensure low inventories days, while maintaining buffer inventories to cover disasters and ensuring that schedules are met, through perhaps the use of JIT processes.

When extremely tight time constraints are imposed for the budget-setting process (which is invariably the case in practice) this may conflict with the degree of accuracy possible in reporting. It also means that top management commitment is critical in providing timely:

- direction
- communication
- feedback

required for the budget process.

The final agreed budget is inevitably a quantitative representation of future plans and targets, and the ways in which each company will reach its short-term goals. Whilst increasing attention is now paid to non-financial measures, the focus remains on performance in financial terms. That being so, traditional cost allocation methods continue to distort the way in which product profitability is reported. This, together with the short-term emphasis of the budgeting activity, therefore provides potentially misleading results. It may also have a demotivating effect on managers involved in both commercial and manufacturing activities, which may result in poor performance.

The problems encountered in the budgeting process may be summarised to include:

- the need for good planning
- difficulties with attitudes including lack of motivation, trust and honesty
- the problems in gathering information
- timeliness of the information
- the amount of detail required
- responsibility for the budget and the key performance areas within the budget.

This outline of some of the problems that may be encountered in the budgeting process may appear to give a negative perspective to its use as an instrument of planning and control. However, the conflicts, by their very nature, ideally serve to highlight the important issues and ensure that budgeting is not just a mechanical exercise carried out once or twice a year but a dynamic part of the strategic planning process contributing to successful management of the business.

Progress check 12.8

What are the key aims of budgeting and what sort of problems are encountered that may prevent those aims being met?

Summary of key points

- A budget is a plan and budgeting is one part of the strategic planning process, which is concerned with planning and control.
- Planning budgets are management's belief of what the business's costs and revenue will be over a specified future time period, the budget period.
- Control budgets are used for management motivational purposes and are used in this way to influence improved departmental performance.

- Forecasts are not plans but predictions of the future, which are required as an important pre-requisite to the budget process.

- Prior to budget preparation, in addition to forecasting, decisions must be made and policies formulated regarding inventories days and purchasing, collection days, payables days, staff costs, capital expenditure and standard costs.

- The master income statement budget is prepared from each of the elements of the operating budget: revenue; production costs; distribution costs and administrative expenses; and the financial budget.

- The master budget comprises the income statement budget, cash budget and balance sheet budget.

- Risk assessment and risk analysis should be applied to the master budget, and it must be closely reviewed in terms of additional funding requirements.

- As part of the control function of the budget, the system of responsibility accounting is used to measure actual results against budget for each of the various types of responsibility centre.

- Control budgets are usually flexed to reflect actual activity levels, and performance against budget provided from exception reporting is evaluated so that corrective actions may be implemented as appropriate.

- The preparation of budgets for planning and control purposes needs the involvement of people to provide realistic plans and the motivation for performance targets to be achieved.

- One aim of the use of economic value added (EVA) as a measure of performance is to overcome the lack of goal congruence with the whole organisation that may result from the use of ROI and RI as divisional performance measures.

- There are usually many conflicts and problems associated with the budget preparation process in most organisations, the majority of which are concerned with the 'softer' human resources issues of managers' behaviour.

Assessment material

Questions

Q12.1 **(i)** Why do businesses need to prepare budgets?

(ii) What are they used for?

Q12.2 If there are differences between budgets prepared for planning purposes and budgets prepared for control purposes, what are these differences?

Q12.3 Describe and illustrate the differences between qualitative and quantitative forecasting techniques.

Q12.4 **(i)** Give some examples of the forecasts that are required to be able to prepare the complete master budget.

(ii) What are the most suitable techniques for each of these forecasts?

Q12.5 Draw a flow diagram to illustrate the budget preparation process.

Q12.6 Explain and illustrate the way in which a business may approach the strategic management process.

Q12.7 **(i)** What are the internal and external sources of funding for a business?

   (ii) How may a business use the budget process to assess its future funding requirements?

Q12.8 How does the assignment of individual budget responsibility contribute to improved organisational performance?

Q12.9 Discuss the ways in which a budget may be used to evaluate performance.

Q12.10 Outline some of the major problems that may be encountered in budgeting.

Q12.11 Performance is frequently measured using residual income (RI) and return on investment (ROI). However, these measures are often criticised for placing too great an emphasis on short-term results, with the possible effect of damaging longer-term performance.

   (i) Discuss the issues involved in the long-term versus short-term conflict referred to above.

   (ii) Suggest some of the ways in which these issues may be reconciled.

Discussion points

D12.1 'Once I know what the forecast sales revenue is for next year I can tell you how much profit we will make within five minutes, so there's no need for this annual time-wasting and costly budgeting ritual.' Discuss.

D12.2 'The area of budgeting is a minefield of potential problems of conflict.' How can these problems be usefully used as a learning experience to ultimately improve the performance of the business?

D12.3 You are the general manager of a newly formed subsidiary company. The group managing director has declared that he has targeted your company to make a profit of £250,000 in its first year. What assumptions, decisions and policies are concerned with preparing a budget by working backwards from a starting point of budgeted profit?

Exercises

Solutions are provided in Appendix 3 to all exercise numbers highlighted in colour.

Level I

E12.1 *Time allowed – 15 minutes*

Earextensions plc set up a new business to assemble mobile phones from kits. They planned to make and sell one model only and expected to sell 441,200 units between January and June in their first year of trading. February, March and April volumes were each expected to be 20% above the preceding month and May, June and July volumes were expected to be the same as April. The selling price was £50 each.

   Cost prices for the parts used in making a phone were as follows:

Electronic assembly	**Keypad**	**Case**
£23.30	£1	£2

Operators and assemblers were employed to make the phones with the following hourly rates and standard times used in production:

	Assemblers	Operators
Hourly rate	£10	£8
Standard minutes	3	1.5

Production overheads were forecast at £4.1m, which were incurred on an equal monthly basis and absorbed into product costs on the basis of direct labour hours.

At 31 December the numbers of units in inventory were estimated at:

Finished product	Quantity	Materials	Quantity	
	zero	Electronic		
		assembly	10,000	
		Keypad	30,000	purchased in December
		Case	20,000	

Materials inventory levels at the end of each month were planned to be 50% of the following month's usage. Finished product inventory levels at the end of each month were planned to be 20% of the following month's sales.

Earextensions plc have budgeted selling costs and administrative expenses of £4.5m for the six months. The first three months were evenly spread at 60% of the total and the second three months evenly spread at 40% of the total. Production overheads included total depreciation of £50,000 budgeted for six months. Financing costs over the six months were expected to be in line with sales at 0.2% of sales value.

Earextensions plc prepared an estimated opening balance sheet for its new subsidiary at 31 December as follows:

	£	£
Non-current assets	495,000	
Inventories	303,000	
Trade receivables	–	
Cash	355,000	1,153,000
Trade payables	303,000	
Loans	450,000	
Share capital	400,000	
Retained earnings	–	1,153,000

Trade receivables were expected to be paid in the second month following the month of sale and trade payables were planned to be paid in the third month following the month of purchase. Direct labour, production overheads, and selling and administrative costs are all paid in the month in which they are incurred. There was no further planned capital expenditure during the first six months.

> **You are required to prepare a phased sales budget in units and values for the six months January to June.**

E12.2   *Time allowed – 30 minutes*

> **Using the information from Exercise E12.1 prepare a phased finished product inventories budget and a phased production budget in units for the six months January to June.**

Level II

E12.3 *Time allowed – 30 minutes*

Using the information from Exercise E12.1 prepare a unit gross margin budget and a phased direct labour budget for the six months January to June.

E12.4 *Time allowed – 30 minutes*

Using the information from Exercise E12.1 prepare a phased materials inventories, materials usage and purchases budget in units and values for the six months January to June.

E12.5 *Time allowed –30 minutes*

Using the information from Exercise E12.1 prepare a phased selling costs and administrative expenses budget, and financial budget for the six months January to June, and a phased income statement budget, using absorption costing, for the six months January to June.

E12.6 *Time allowed – 30 minutes*

Using the information from Exercise E12.1 prepare a finished product valuation budget for the six months January to June.

E12.7 *Time allowed – 30 minutes*

An extract from the financial results for 2010 for three of the operating divisions of Marx plc is shown below:

Division	Chico	Groucho	Harpo
Average net operating assets	£7.5m	£17.5m	£12.5m
Operating profit	£1.5m	£1.4m	£2.0m
Administrative expenses	£0.8m	£0.3m	£0.65m
Divisional cost of capital per annum	7%	5%	10%

Required:

(i)   Calculate the ROI for each division for 2010.

(ii) Calculate the RI for each division for 2010.

(iii) Each division is presented with an investment opportunity that is expected to yield a return of 9%.

    (a) Which division(s) would accept and which division(s) would reject the investment opportunity if divisional performance is measured by ROI, and why?

    (b) Which division(s) would accept and which division(s) would reject the investment opportunity if divisional performance is measured by RI, and why?

E12.8 *Time allowed – 60 minutes*

> Using the information from Exercise E12.1 prepare a trade payables budget and a trade receivables budget, and a phased cash budget for the six months January to June.

E12.9 *Time allowed – 60 minutes*

> Using the information from Exercise E12.1 prepare a phased balance sheet budget for the six months January to June.

E12.10 *Time allowed – 60 minutes*

Blord Ltd manufactures bookcases recommended to customers with a lyrical and romantic nature. Each bookcase retails for £75.

Blord Ltd
Balance sheet as at 30 June 2009

Assets	£
Non-current assets	
Buildings at cost	100,000
Depreciation provision	(20,000)
Equipment at cost	60,000
Depreciation provision	(25,000)
Total non-current assets	115,000
Current assets	
Inventories of raw materials (96,000 metres of timber)	192,000
Inventories of finished goods (15,000 units)	583,575
Trade receivables	300,000
Cash and cash equivalents	58,000
Total current assets	1,133,575
Total assets	1,248,575
Liabilities	
Current liabilities	
Trade payables	760,000
Net assets	488,575
Equity	
Share capital	250,000
Retained earnings	238,575
Total equity	488,575

The buildings are depreciated at 4% of cost and equipment is depreciated at 20% on a reducing balance basis. 60% of the buildings and all the equipment is used in the manufacturing process.

Blord Ltd have estimated that next year sales volumes will be:

Quarter 1	70,000
Quarter 2	80,000
Quarter 3	85,000
Quarter 4	90,000

The company makes 80% of its sales direct to the public for cash, which is received when the sales are made. 20% of the company's sales are made to trade wholesalers on one month's credit. It is expected that sales will be made evenly throughout each quarter.

You are required to:

(i)   prepare the sales budget for Blord Ltd for the year ending 30 June 2010

(ii) calculate the phased quarterly cash inflows expected from its customers over the budget year.

E12.11 *Time allowed – 60 minutes*

In order to satisfy customer demand the directors of Blord Ltd have decided that there should be an inventory of finished goods at the end of each quarter equivalent to 20% of the budgeted sales volumes for the following quarter. It is anticipated that sales volumes in both the first and second quarters of the next year will be 95,000, and the third quarter is expected to be 100,000.

You are required to prepare a production budget for each of the four quarters for the year ending 30 June 2010.

E12.12 *Time allowed – 60 minutes*

Each of Blord Ltd's bookcases is constructed from 8 metres of timber, which the company currently purchases for £2 per metre. The company does not expect the cost of timber to rise over the next financial year.

In order to ensure a smooth flow of production the company has introduced a policy for next year to ensure there is 15% of the timber required for the next quarter's production in inventory at the end of each of the preceding quarters. The timber supplier allows Blord Ltd one month's credit.

It takes 1.5 hours of direct labour to manufacture a bookcase and the company currently pays a standard wage rate of £12 per hour. In addition, it is estimated that a variable production overhead will be incurred at the rate of £2.50 per direct labour hour.

Blord Ltd anticipates that the total manufacturing fixed overheads will be £380,000 for the year, which include depreciation of equipment. Blord Ltd absorbs manufacturing fixed overheads into each product on the basis of direct labour hours.

It is anticipated that each quarter's selling and administration costs will be £1,950,000.

You are required to prepare:

(i)   the unit gross profit budget

(ii)   materials purchases and the materials usage budget

(iii) the phased quarterly cash payments expected to be made to the timber supplier, for the year ending 30 June 2010.

E12.13 *Time allowed – 60 minutes*

Use the information from E12.10 and E12.12 to prepare the direct labour budget for the year ending 30 June 2010 and the phased quarterly cash outflows.

E12.14 *Time allowed – 60 minutes*

> Use the information from E12.10 and E12.12 to prepare the manufacturing overhead budget for the year ending 30 June 2010 and the phased quarterly cash outflows.

E12.15 *Time allowed – 60 minutes*

> Use your solutions to E12.10 to E12.14 to prepare a phased quarterly cash flow budget for the year ending 30 June 2010 using the direct method.

E12.16 *Time allowed – 60 minutes*

> Use your solutions to E12.10 to E12.15 to prepare a phased quarterly income statement budget for the year ending 30 June 2010 and a balance sheet as at 30 June 2010.

13

The control budget and variance analysis

Contents

Learning objectives

Completion of this chapter will enable you to:

- use standard costing in the budget process
- use standard costing in performance evaluation and control
- identify the use of flexible budgeting in performance evaluation and control
- prepare flexed budgets in line with changes in activity levels
- explain what is meant by a variance between actual and standard performance
- appreciate the importance of variance analysis in exception reporting
- calculate the individual variances used to explain differences between actual and standard performance
- summarise variances in the form of standard cost operating statements
- explain the reasons for variances between actual and standard performance
- appreciate the differences between planning and operational variances.

Introduction

In Chapter 12 we illustrated the budget preparation process with the construction of budgets using:

- forecast volumes
- forecast selling prices
- policy decisions relating to capital expenditure and working capital
- unit product costs.

This chapter will explore in greater detail how the costs of units of a product or a process are determined. We will look at how standards may be used in the budgeting process to cost each unit or process. The budgeted unit or process cost is called its standard cost.

This chapter will explain the technique of standard costing and the ways in which actual performance may be measured and compared with the budget through the use of variance analysis. We will look at how, using standard costs, the budget may be flexed to reflect actual levels of activity, and then used to calculate individual variances. Individual variances may then be investigated to explain the reasons for the differences between actual and expected performance.

The process of explaining significant variances from standard continues to be considered as a powerful management tool. This chapter closes with an outline of the differences between planning and operational variances.

A few years ago a study by two US universities and the National Bureau of Economic Research demonstrated quite conclusively that senior executives trade off long-term economic value so as to meet short-term earnings targets to satisfy investors. This finding came two years after PricewaterhouseCoopers had castigated companies, saying that many businesses 'confuse short-term shareholder appeasement with effective cost control'. Many businesses know that this is going on – surplus cash gets committed before the year end on a use-it-or-lose-it approach to budgeting, and good projects get deferred until a period that has some slack in it – but no one does anything about it. Perhaps Homer Simpson put it best when he exclaimed: 'Marge, if you're going to get mad at me every time I do something stupid then I'm going to have to stop doing stupid things.' Maybe everyone, from line managers to finance directors to institutional investors, should be encouraged to regularly ask the question 'what stupid things have been done in order to make the company look really clever?'

Standard costing

Variance analysis is almost exclusively concerned with the comparison of performance against short-term budget targets. Short-term performance is very important. However, achieving or exceeding short-term targets should not be considered in isolation, which may ignore or be to the detriment of longer-term objectives (see the extract on the next page from *The Sunday Herald*).

Although forecasting and budgeting systems should reflect realistic expectations, it is inevitable that differences will arise between actual and expected performance. It is extremely important that the planning and budgeting process include control systems that enable accurate feedback of actual performance at the right time to the appropriate people within the organisation. Budgetary control systems should ensure that information is regularly communicated and evaluated by the key decision makers in an organisation, so that appropriate action may taken as necessary. Budgetary control systems must provide:

- fast reporting of performance
- quick response in the implementation of remedial actions
- timely revision of forecasts.

As part of the budgeting process, or at any other time when actual costs need to be compared with planned costs, a basis for comparison must be established. Standard costing provides such a basis through the setting of predetermined cost estimates.

A **standard cost** is defined as the planned unit cost of the products, components or services produced in a period, and it may be determined using many alternative bases. The main uses of standard costs are:

- measurement of business performance
- control of processes
- valuation of inventories
- establishment of selling prices.

Standards may be defined as benchmark measurements of resource usage, set in defined conditions, and can be set on a number of bases:

- on an *ex ante* (before the event) estimate of expected performance
- on an *ex post* (after the event) estimate of attainable performance
- on a prior level of performance by the same organisation
- on the level of performance achieved by comparable organisations
- on the level of performance required to meet organisational objectives.

Standards may also be set at attainable levels which assume efficient levels of operation, but which include allowances for normal loss, waste and machine downtime, or at ideal levels, which make no allowance for the above losses, and are only attainable under the most favourable conditions.

Budgeted costs and standard costs are sometimes used to mean the same thing but this is not always so. All amounts in a budget are budgeted amounts, but not all budgeted amounts are standard amounts. Budgeted costs are usually used to describe the total planned costs for a number of products. Standard amounts relate to a series of specific processes. For example, one of the processes included in producing a bottle of beer, the sticking of the label on to the bottle, is a process that includes the time and the cost of the label.

A standard product specification is a statement containing a full breakdown of the cost elements, which are included in the standard cost of a product or service. For each cost element (direct labour, direct material, overhead) a standard input quantity and a standard unit input cost are shown as well as a standard cost per unit of output produced.

A bill of materials is a detailed specification, for each product produced, of the sub-assemblies, components and materials required, distinguishing between those items that are purchased externally

When short-term targets become an obsession

They amount to nothing more than 'accounting games' or 'operating acrobatics' in the view of Warren Buffett, the 'sage of Omaha', who knows more about building company value than most people on the planet.

Most business leaders who are quizzed about them want rid of them and yet nobody actually ever seems to do anything to end the practice. Yet all that may now be about to change.

I am talking about the quarterly earnings guidance that major companies issue. These are effectively selfimposed targets which, critics argue, lead to short-termism, rather than executives and boards focusing on building the longer-term value of the business.

A significant report issued last week may just be the start of a move away from the guidance 'obsession'.

It came from the Business Roundtable Institute for Corporate Ethics (Brice) – an organisation made up of 160 American chief executives – and the CFA Institute.

As Dean Krehmeyer, executive director of Brice and one of the authors of the report published last week said: 'The obsession with short-term performance does not create value for shareholders and in many cases destroys value.'

In other words, business leaders are so busy concentrating on making the short-term targets that they lose sight of building the business for the longer term for all concerned.

But even more basic than that is the question of how much value there actually is in quarterly earnings figures. Are they really worth the paper they are written on or even the chips they are coded on?

As Bob Garratt, a corporate governance expert wrote in his excellent book The Fish Rots From The Head:

'Among its worst excesses is the notion that the CEO and CFO must sign off their quarterly results as true and accurate – does anyone know of an accounting system that can deliver true and accurate quarterly accounts? If so you will make a fortune.'

So – whisper it softly – what happens is that there is a lot of casting around within the business on the right number to give and sometimes what is arrived at is really nothing more than a guesstimate.

But once the number is out there and public then it is set in stone.

As Steve Odland, chief executive of the retailer Office Depot and head of the Business Roundtable corporate governance taskforce put it: 'Once a company puts a number out there, everybody within the business is focused on hitting the guidance rather than doing what is best for the company.'

Companies should forget the short-term and make the decisions and take the actions that will see the long-term growth of the business: real growth rather than a bit of a fudge and a gentle fiddle to make the quarterly numbers.

More companies are beginning to see the sense of this. Part of this is down to Warren Buffett's influence.

Companies in which his Berkshire Hathaway company invests, which includes Coca-Cola, Gillette and The Washington Post, dropped their quarterly figures. More recently, Intel, McDonald's, Motorola and Pfizer announced their intention to do the same.

Hopefully it will not stop there and others will begin to see the wisdom of this and follow the recommendations of the Business Roundtable report.

It calls for the earnings guidance to be replaced by more qualitative communication outlining the business's operations and what it is seeking to do and in what direction it is attempting to move.

A move away from short-termism should not stop there. As the report points out: 'Recently the directors of Coca-Cola addressed share-owner concerns about short-termism in a unique manner.

'The board adopted an "all-or-nothing" compensation in which all directors' pay consists entirely of equity-based share units payable only when longer-term company performance targets are met. The initial performance period is three years.'

As Coca-Cola chairman and chief executive officer Neville Isdell said when the move was announced in April: 'This all-or-nothing approach to board compensation aligns the interest of our directors with those of share owners more closely than any other compensation formula I have seen.'

It will be interesting to see how many businesses will conclude that things will go better if they follow the example of Coca-Cola in this respect.

That kind of scheme would really make a difference in aligning board directors' rewards with the long-term growth of the business.

Business history is littered with the corporate corpses of those who took the totally opposite approach and became hooked on the need to 'hit the guidance' quarter by quarter by any means necessary.

Most prominent of these was Enron. The recent court case heard a lot of testimony about how much pressure was on key company employees to 'make the quarter'.

As the 'growth' continued at Enron quarter after quarter, so did the pressure to continue this amazing 'winning' record. The temptations proved too great and soon profits were being booked on new business streams that were hardly launched.

Clearly, it is best for businesses not to step on to that particular carousel.

The danger is the momentum forms a 'whirlpool effect' that drags businesses under.

So, build for the long-term and communicate with your investors in a way that they can increasingly understand the business and where it's going, on its general forward momentum, and not on spectral quarterly figures that may lack substance.

Source: **How short-term thinking causes whirlpool effect**, © Ken Symon, for *The Sunday Herald*, 30 July 2006

and those which are manufactured in-house. Having established the quality and other specifications of materials required, the purchasing department estimates costs based on suppliers' prices, inflation, and the availability of bulk discounts, in order to establish direct material unit costs.

The standard direct labour cost is the planned average cost of direct labour, based on the standard time for the job and standard performance. A standard hour is the amount of work achievable, at standard efficiency levels, in one hour. Work study and analysis of the learning curve are techniques that may be used to assist in determining standard hours. The standard time for a job is the time in which a task should be completed at standard performance.

Standard performance is the level of efficiency, which appropriately trained, motivated and re-sourced employees can achieve in the long run. Initially, the time taken to produce a specific level of output is longer than the time taken after 'normal' employees have been adequately trained and have gained experience of the process. Time taken to achieve specific levels of output will reduce over time, but the amount of the reductions in time will also reduce over time until almost negligible. This is called the learning curve effect, and when time reductions have virtually ceased the curve becomes horizontal. It is that level, where the long-term time for the particular activity has been established, that may be considered standard performance for the activity. The standard direct labour cost is then calculated by multiplying a standard direct labour hour by a standard hourly rate. Direct labour rates per hour are determined with reference to the type of skills to be used, union agreements, inflation and market rates.

Progress check 13.1

What is meant by the standard cost of a product and what type of specifications and analyses are required prior to being able to calculate a standard cost?

A typical standard cost for a unit of a product may be illustrated in the following worked example.

Worked example 13.1

Applejack Ltd manufactures drums of high grade apple pie filling that uses two types of material, apples and sugar, and requires one grade of direct labour. The company additionally incurs some variable and fixed production overheads, which are absorbed into the unit costs of the product. The standard cost for a drum (one unit) of the product may be represented as follows, where overheads have been absorbed on the basis of direct labour hours.

Direct materials		£
Sugar	1 kilo at £2 per kilo =	2
Apples	2 kilos at £3 per kilo =	6
		8
Direct labour		
1 hour at £8 per hour		8
Variable production overhead		
1 hour at £2 per hour		2
Fixed production overhead		
1 hour at £3 per hour		3
Standard full production cost per drum		21

Advantages of standard costs

There are several advantages in using a standard costing system:

- it is a basis for budget preparation
- it may be used in planning and control
- it can be used to highlight areas of strength and weakness
- it can be used in evaluation of performance by comparing actual costs with standard costs and so assisting in implementation of responsibility accounting
- it should result in the use of the best resources and best methods and so increase efficiency
- it may be used as a basis for inventory valuation
- it can be used as a basis for pay incentive schemes
- it can be used for decision-making in its estimation of future costs
- it fits in with management by exception, whereby only significant variances (differences between actual and expected results) are investigated, and so making effective use of management time
  - control action is immediate because, for example, as soon as materials are issued from stores into production they can be compared with the standard materials which should be required for actual production
  - transfer prices (the prices at which goods or services are transferred from one process or department to another or from one company in the group to another) may be based on standard rather than actual costs to avoid inefficiencies in the form of excess costs.

Disadvantages of standard costs

There are also a number of disadvantages in using a standard costing system, not least of which is the difficulty in the establishment of the standard overhead rate if standard absorption costing is used as opposed to standard marginal costing.

Standard costing requires a great deal of input data, which can prove time-consuming and expensive, as can the maintenance of the cost database. The amount of detail required, together with a lack of historical detail, and lack of experience and further training requirements all add to this administrative burden.

Standard costing is usually used in organisations where the processes or jobs are repetitive. It is important to set accurate standards or else evaluation of performance will be meaningless. If the standard is weak then the comparison is of little value. However, it is difficult to strike a balance in setting accurate standards so that they both motivate the workforce and achieve the organisation's goals. There may be difficulties in determining which variances against standard are significant, and too narrow a focus on certain variances may exclude other useful information.

 If performance evaluation is linked to **management by exception**, which assumes actual equals standard unless variances contradict that, there may be attempts by managers to cover up negative results. Morale may suffer if reprimands follow poor results and managers are not praised for positive results.

Further adverse impacts on behaviour may occur if managers and supervisors feel that they do not have an overall view and are involved only in limited areas, seeing only a small part of the big picture. Responsibility accounting must also ensure that controllable and non-controllable variances are separately identified.

Operating difficulties and frustration may be encountered through, for example:

- technological and environmental factors
- assessment of standards of performance
- departmental interdependence
- variances reported at the wrong levels

- the timing of revisions to standards
- over-reaction to results
- the constant need to estimate.

It is important to remember that there is a great deal of uncertainty in setting standard costs. This can arise due to inflation, economic and political factors. Standards therefore need to be continually updated and revised – once a year is usually not often enough.

Progress check 13.2

To what extent do the advantages of the use of standard costing outweigh its disadvantages?

Types of standard

In addition to current costs there are three types of standard that may be used as the basis for a standard costing system. The use of current standards by definition relates to current circumstances with regard to performance levels, wastage and inefficiencies. It may be observed from the following explanations that 'standard costing' can be seen to be flexible and dynamic. It should not be seen as a straitjacket.

Basic standards are those that remain unchanged since the previous period and probably many previous periods. They may be used for comparison but are likely to be out of date and irrelevant. As business circumstances may change dramatically in the marketplace, so the original basic standard will not reflect the current situation.

Ideal standards are the results expected from perfect performance under perfect conditions. They assume no wastage, nor inefficiencies. However, although they may be aimed for they will be impossible to achieve and therefore provide a poor motivational tool.

Attainable standards are the results expected under normal operating conditions, having some allowances for wastage and a degree of inefficiency. Attainable standards should be set to be difficult but not impossible to achieve; they may therefore provide the most challenging targets and give the greatest motivation for achievement.

Progress check 13.3

What are the different types of standard that may be used as the basis for standard costing and which one may be the most appropriate?

Flexed budgets

We discussed flexible budgeting in Chapter 12. Control budgets need to be revised in line with actual levels of activity to provide more realistic levels of expected costs against which to measure performance. Such a revised budget is called a flexed budget, which shows the costs (and revenues) expected as a result of changes in activity levels from those planned within the master budget.

The standards chosen for use in the budget preparation are also used in the revised flexed budget to provide a method of comparison with actual performance. This method allows comparison of costs (and revenues) on a like-for-like basis and so enables meaningful exception reporting of the analysis of variances.

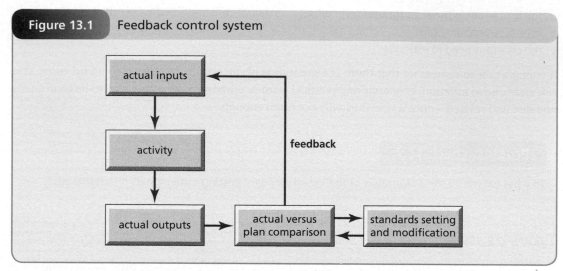

Source: Based on *CIMA Official Terminology*, 2005 ed., CIMA Publishing, Elsevier p.9.

This system of management control uses a **closed-loop system**, which allows corrective action using a feedforward or a feedback basis of control. A feedback control system is shown in Figure 13.1 and provides the measurement of differences between planned outputs and actual outputs and the modification of subsequent actions or plans to achieve future required results. Figure 13.2 illustrates a feedforward control system which forecasts differences between actual and planned outcomes and implements action before the event to avoid such differences.

Normally, fixed overheads by definition are fixed over the short term regardless of changes in the level of activity, for example units sold, units produced, number of invoices. Equally, direct labour and direct materials costs may be assumed to vary directly with sales. In practice, there is usually a wide band of activity over which direct labour costs may not vary.

Care should be taken in using the above assumptions but we may consider that they hold true for the purpose of illustration of flexed budgets and variance analysis. The variance analysis can be routine but decisions resulting from the interpretation can be far-reaching. Consider how, following the

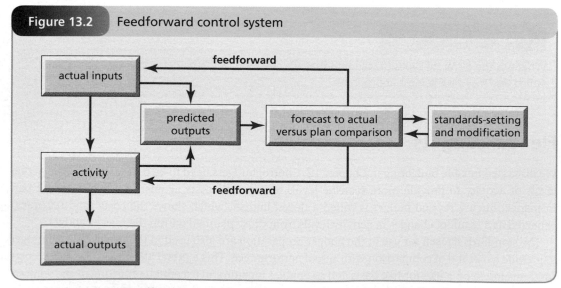

Source: Based on *CIMA Official Terminology*, 2005 ed., CIMA Publishing, Elsevier p.9.

public's reaction to buying products originating from genetically modified foodstuffs (soya or maize), many UK supermarkets publicly announced they would cease stocking them.

Progress check 13.4

Describe the way in which flexed budgets are used in a management control system.

The worked example that follows shows how a straight comparison of actual with budgeted performance may be refined through the preparation of a revised budget flexed in line with the actual activity level.

Worked example 13.2

Applejack Ltd planned to produce 600 drums of apple pie filling during September. The budget for September was prepared using the standard costs shown in Worked example 13.1. Fixed overheads are budgeted at £1,800 for September and are absorbed on the basis of direct labour hours. Variable overheads are budgeted at £1,200 for September and are absorbed on the basis of direct labour hours.

Budget costs for September

		600 units £
Production		
Direct materials		
Sugar	600 kilos at £2 per kilo =	1,200
Apples	1,200 kilos at £3 per kilo =	3,600
		4,800
Direct labour		
600 hours at £8 per hour		4,800
Variable production overhead		
600 hours at £2 per hour		1,200
Fixed production overhead		
600 hours at £3 per hour		1,800
Total production cost		12,600

600 drums of filling were planned to be produced in the month at a manufacturing cost of £12,600.

At the end of September the actual output turned out to be 650 drums as follows:

Actual costs for September

		650 units £
Production		
Direct materials		
Sugar	610 kilos at £2.10 per kilo =	1,281
Apples	1,210 kilos at £3.20 per kilo =	3,872
		5,153

Direct labour
500 hours at £9 per hour	4,500
Variable production overhead	
500 hours at £1.50 per hour	750
Fixed production overhead	
500 hours at £3.60 per hour	1,800
Total production cost	12,203

650 drums of filling were actually produced in the month at a manufacturing cost of £12,203.

The above data can be used to prepare a flexed budget for September as the basis for subsequent variance analysis.

A flexed budget for Applejack Ltd must be prepared for 650 drums output. The flexed budget will use the standard costs shown in Worked example 13.1 to show what the costs would have been if the budget had been based on 650 drums instead of 600 drums.

Flexed budget costs for September

Production		650 units £
Direct materials		
Sugar	650 kilos at £2 per kilo =	1,300
Apples	1,300 kilos at £3 per kilo =	3,900
		5,200
Direct labour		
650 hours at £8 per hour		5,200
Variable production overhead		
650 hours at £2 per hour		1,300
Fixed production overhead		
650 hours at £3 per hour		1,950
Total production cost		13,650

If 650 drums of apple pie filling had been planned to be produced in the month the standard manufacturing cost would have been £13,650.

If we compare the total manufacturing cost from the flexed budget shown in Worked example 13.2 with the total actual cost for the month, the performance looks even better than the comparison with the total budgeted cost; the total cost is £1,447 [£13,650 − £12,203] less than expected at that level of output. However, whilst the comparison of total cost is favourable, this does not tell us anything about individual performance within each element of the budget, the impacts of the differences between the actual and the flexed budget with regard to:

■ amounts of materials used
■ materials prices

- direct labour hours
- direct labour rates
- overheads.

An analysis of the detailed variances in respect of each cost can identify each element making up the cost, the unit costs and the unit quantities, and tell us something about whether the individual cost performances were good or bad. Between 2008 and 2010 the UK saw an amazing upward demand for smartphones and an overall decline in the demand for further education. Both of these sectors of the UK economy would have carried out an 'analysis of the detailed variances' during that year to assist in the determination of conclusions regarding cost performance.

Progress check 13.5

In what ways does a flexed budget provide a more realistic measure of actual performance than comparison with the original budget?

Variance analysis

A variance is the difference between a planned, budgeted or standard cost and the actual cost incurred. The same comparisons may be made for sales revenues. Variance analysis is the evaluation of performance by means of variances, whose timely reporting should maximise the opportunity for managerial action. These variances will be either favourable variances (F) or adverse variances (A). Neither should occur if the standard is correct and actual performance is as expected. A favourable variance is not necessarily good – it may be due to a weak standard. Management by exception assumes that actual performance will be the same as the standard unless variances contradict this.

Detailed variances can identify each difference within the elements making up cost or revenue by looking at unit prices and unit quantities. Variances may be due to:

- measurement errors
- use of standards that are out of date
- operations that are out of control
- random factors.

When variances occur it must then be considered whether these variances should be investigated or not. The variances may not be material (significant), or it may not be cost effective to carry out such an investigation.

Calculation of variances

Let's look at the individual variances that occurred for the month of September in Applejack's manufacture of apple pie filling in Worked example 13.3. We will analyse each of the variances and provide a detailed, line-by-line comparison of actual versus budget performance of each of the items that comprise the total actual to budget favourable variance of £397. The simplest way to start to examine the differences is to present the original budget, flexed budget and actual results in three columns for further analysis.

Worked example 13.3

We saw from Worked example 13.2 that on the face of it Applejack's performance for September was very good – higher than budget output (650 versus 600 units) at lower than budget costs (£12,203 versus £12,600).

Is it a good performance? If it is, how much of a good performance is it?

To determine how good Applejack's performance was for September we need to provide an analysis of variances to explain the favourable total cost variance of £397 against budget (£12,600 − £12,203).

Applejack Ltd's budget, actual and flexed budget (from Worked example 13.2) for the production of apple pie filling for the month of September may be summarised as follows:

		Budget		Flexed		Actual	Difference Actual – Flexed
Units		600		650		650	–
		£		£		£	£
Direct materials							
Sugar	(600 × £2)	1,200	(650 × £2)	1,300	(610 × £2.10)	1,281	19
Apples	(1,200 × £3)	3,600	(1,300 × £3)	3,900	(1,210 × £3.20)	3,872	28
		4,800		5,200		5,153	47
Direct labour							
	(600 × £8)	4,800	(650 × £8)	5,200	(500 × £9)	4,500	700
Variable production overhead							
	(600 × £2)	1,200	(650 × £2)	1,300	(500 × £1.50)	750	550
Fixed production overhead							
	(600 × £3)	1,800	(650 × £3)	1,950	(500 × £3.60)	1,800	150
Total cost		12,600		13,650		12,203	1,447

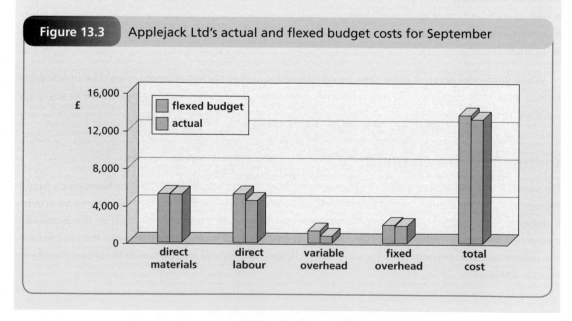

Figure 13.3 Applejack Ltd's actual and flexed budget costs for September

The graphical representation, shown in Figure 13.3, of each of the cost elements and the total of actual costs compared with the flexed budget for output of 650 units gives a broad picture of Applejack Ltd's good performance.

Let's look at the detailed variances.

We have prepared a flexed budget, which in effect gives us a new starting point against which to compare actual performance more realistically. We have therefore already built in a variance, arising out of the change in volume from 600 drums to 650 drums. At a unit cost of £21 the total of this difference, or variance, is an adverse volume variance of £1,050 (50 × £21), or £13,650 − £12,600.

Volume:

Variance 650 drums less 600 drums at a total unit cost of £21 per drum	£1,050A

We also need to consider the individual cost element variances, between actual costs £12,203 and the flexed budget costs £13,650.

Materials:

Sugar usage was 40 kilos less than it should have been at a standard cost of £2 per kilo	£80F
The sugar price was 10p more per kilo than standard for the 610 kilos used	£61A
Apples usage was 90 kilos less than it should have been at a standard cost of £3 per kilo	£270F
The apple price was 20p more per kilo than standard for the 1,210 kilos used	£242A
Total materials variance actual versus flexed budget	£47F

Direct labour:

Hours worked were 150 hours less than they should have been at a standard rate of £8 per hour	£1,200F
The labour rate was £1 more per hour than standard for the 500 hours worked	£500A
Total direct labour variance actual versus flexed budget	£700F

Variable production overhead:

Hours worked were 150 hours less than they should have been at a standard rate of £2 per hour	£300F
The overhead rate was 50p less per hour than standard for the 500 hours worked	£250F
Total variable production overhead variance actual versus flexed budget	£550F

Fixed production overhead:

Hours worked were 150 hours less than they should have been at a standard rate of £3 per hour	£450F
Hours worked were 100 less (at £3 per hour) than required to absorb total fixed costs	£300A
Total fixed production overhead variance actual versus flexed budget	£150F
Total variances [£1,050A + £47F + £700F + £550F + £150F] =	£397F
Budget total costs	£12,600
Actual total costs	£12,203
Total variance (favourable)	£397

Several variances are calculated to quantify the difference in activity or volume. Most of the other variances show the impact of:

- differences in prices
    - price variances
    - rate variances
    - expenditure variances

and

- differences in quantities
    - usage variances
    - efficiency variances

between those prices and quantities actually incurred and those which should have been expected at the actual level, or volume, of output. The exception to this is the fixed production overhead variance, which comprises a fixed production overhead expenditure variance (budget minus actual cost) and a fixed production overhead volume variance.

The total fixed production variance is the difference between:

- the actual cost

and

- the cost shown in the flexed budget.

The two components of the total fixed production volume variance are:

- the fixed production overhead efficiency variance
    - a 'normal' variance that calculates the difference between actual and flexed hours at the standard overhead absorption rate

- the fixed production overhead capacity variance
    - calculates the difference between actual and budgeted hours at the standard overhead absorption rate
    - measures the amount by which overheads have been under- or over-absorbed (under-absorbed in the Applejack example), caused by the actual hours worked differing from the hours originally budgeted to be worked.

In the Applejack worked example we have used the absorption costing approach to calculate unit standard costs for the product and therefore in the calculation of variances. Marginal costing may also be used to calculate unit standard costs for a product and calculation of variances. Some of the differences between the variances that are calculated are as one would expect, using contribution instead of profit. Another difference is in respect of production fixed costs, which of course are not absorbed into unit marginal product costs. The fixed production overhead variance using marginal costing is simply the difference between the actual and the budgeted cost.

> ### Progress check 13.6
>
> What does variance analysis tell us about actual performance that a direct analysis of differences to budget cannot tell us?

The hierarchy of variances in Figures 13.4 and 13.5 show variances using marginal costing principles and variances using absorption costing principles respectively.

Figure 13.4   Chart of variances using marginal costing principles

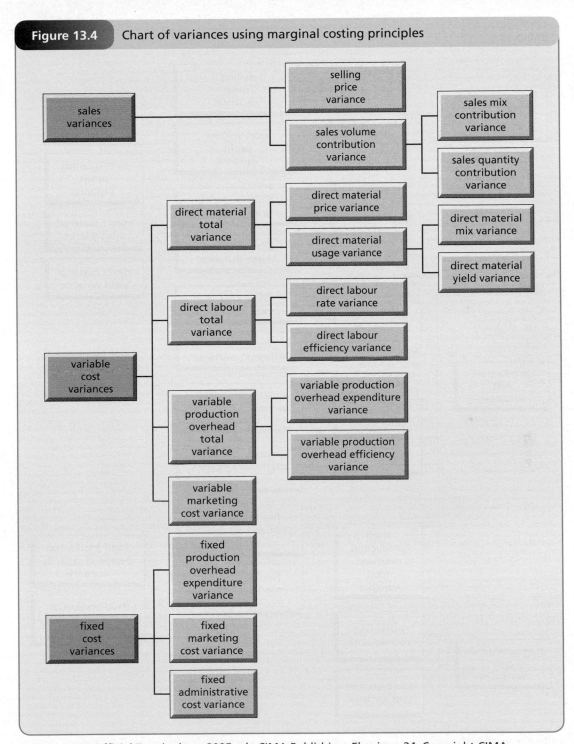

Source: *CIMA Official Terminology*, 2005 ed., CIMA Publishing, Elsevier p.34, Copyright CIMA.

A non-accountant will not usually be called upon to calculate variances. However, as a manager, it is important to appreciate clearly the way in which variances are calculated, to be better able to:

■ consider their materiality (or significance)
■ investigate the reasons for their occurrence if necessary
■ take the appropriate corrective actions.

Figure 13.5   Chart of variances using absorption costing principles

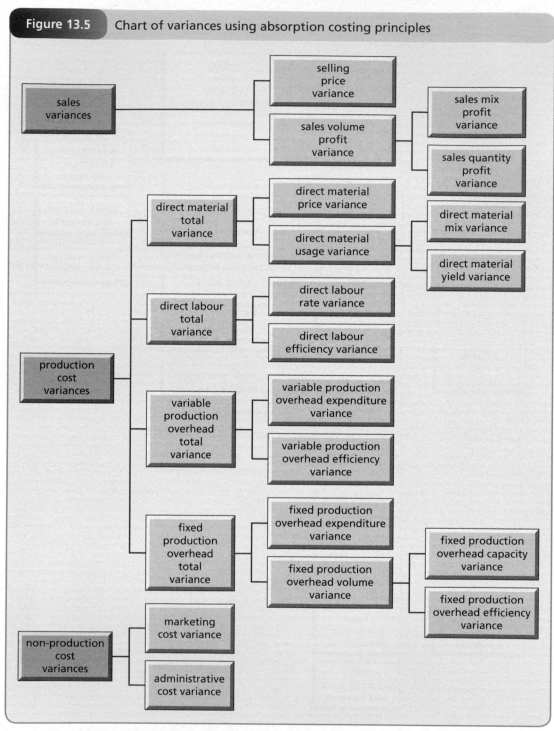

Source: *CIMA Official Terminology*, 2005 ed., CIMA Publishing, Elsevier p.35, Copyright CIMA.

An explanation of variances is usually part of the day-to-day responsibilities of most budget holding managers. Unless there is knowledge of exactly what a variance represents it is virtually impossible to begin to determine the reason why such a variance occurred. Figures 13.6 and 13.9 include the detailed formulae for the calculation of variances, on a marginal costing basis. Figures 13.7 and 13.8 include variances that apply to both absorption and marginal costing. Figures 13.10 and 13.11 include the additional variances in respect of absorption costing.

Operating statements

The comparison of actual costs and revenues with budget is normally regularly reported to management (daily, weekly or monthly) and presented in what is called an operating statement. The operating statement is usually supported by a report explaining the reasons why specific variances have occurred.

Worked examples 13.4 to 13.10 provide a comprehensive illustration of the preparation of a flexed budget and show how variances are calculated and presented in an operating statement. They also include explanations of possible reasons why the variances occurred. While not including all possible variances that may be considered according to those shown in Figures 13.4 to 13.11, these worked examples show the key variances relating to:

- sales revenue
  note how the marketing department of a company can use the results, for example UK supermarkets' consumer products special offers
- labour
  note for example how the human resources department of a company may be involved in further investigation if the variances are material
- materials
  note for example how company buyers may need to look for new sources
- overheads
  many companies move closer to their customers or to low-cost premises, for example in order to reduce overheads.

Figure 13.6   Sales variances on a marginal costing basis

> **Sales contribution variances**
>
> **Sales volume contribution**
> (budgeted sales quantity × standard contribution per unit) − (actual sales quantity × standard contribution per unit)
>
> Which can be split into:
>
> **Sales quantity contribution**
> (budgeted sales quantity × budgeted weighted average standard contribution per unit) − (total actual sales quantity × budgeted weighted average standard contribution per unit)
>
> **Sales mix contribution**
> (actual sales quantity × budgeted weighted average standard contribution per unit) − (actual sales quantity × individual standard contribution per unit)
>
> **Sales price**
> (actual sales quantity × standard selling price per unit) − actual sales revenue

Figure 13.7   Direct materials variances

Materials variances

Direct material price
(actual quantity of material purchased × standard price) − actual cost of material purchased

Direct material usage
(standard quantity for actual production × standard material cost per unit) − (actual material quantity used × standard cost per unit)

Which can be split into:

Direct material mix
(actual input quantity − standard material input quantity for the output produced) × (standard weighted average cost per input unit − standard cost per input unit)

Direct material yield
(actual material input quantity − standard material input quantity for the output produced) × standard weighted average cost per unit of material input
Or
(actual material input quantity × standard cost per unit) − (total actual material input in standard proportions × standard cost per unit)

Figure 13.8   Direct labour variances

Labour variances

Direct labour rate
(actual hours paid × standard direct labour rate per hour) − (actual hours paid × actual direct labour rate per hour)

Direct labour efficiency
(actual production in standard hours × standard direct labour rate per hour) − (actual direct labour hours worked × standard direct labour rate per hour)

Figure 13.9   Overheads variances on a marginal costing basis

Overhead variances

Variable production overhead expenditure
actual cost incurred − (actual hours worked × standard variable production overhead absorption rate per hour)

Variable production overhead efficiency
(actual hours worked × standard variable production overhead absorption rate per hour) − (actual production in standard hours × standard variable production overhead absorption rate per hour)

Fixed production overhead expenditure
budgeted fixed production overhead − actual fixed production overhead

Figure 13.10	Sales variances on an absorption costing basis

Sales profit variances

Sales volume profit
(budgeted sales quantity × standard profit per unit) − (actual sales quantity × standard profit per unit)

Which can be split into:

Sales quantity profit
(budgeted sales quantity × budgeted weighted average standard profit per unit) − (total actual sales quantity × budgeted weighted average standard profit per unit)

Sales mix profit
(actual sales quantity × budgeted weighted average standard profit per unit) − (actual sales quantity × individual standard profit per unit)

Figure 13.11	Overheads variances on an absorption costing basis

Overheads variances

Fixed production overhead volume
(actual production in standard hours × standard fixed production overhead absorption rate per hour) − budgeted fixed production overhead

Which can be split into:

Fixed production overhead efficiency
(actual hours worked × standard fixed production overhead absorption rate per hour) − (actual production in standard hours × standard fixed production overhead absorption rate per hour)

Fixed production overhead capacity
(actual hours worked × standard fixed production overhead absorption rate per hour) − (budgeted hours to be worked × standard fixed production overhead absorption rate per hour)

Worked example 13.4

Dymocks Ltd manufactures large ornamental garden pots. One is called the El Greco, the standards for which are as follows:

Direct labour	1 hour at £4 per hour
Direct materials	2 kgs at £7.50 per kg
Variable overheads	£3 per direct labour hour
Selling price	£50 per unit

Fixed overheads are budgeted at £4,000 and absorbed on a direct labour hours basis. Dymocks have budgeted to produce and sell 800 El Grecos in the month of July.

Using standard costs, the budget for El Grecos for July was:

		£
Revenue	800 × £50 per unit	40,000
Direct labour	800 × 1 hour × £4 per hour per unit	(3,200)
Direct materials	800 × 2 kg × £7.50 per kg per unit	(12,000)
Variable overheads	800 × 1 hour × £3 per direct labour hour	(2,400)
Fixed overheads	800 × 1 hour × £5 per direct labour hour	(4,000)
Budgeted profit for July		18,400

The standard profit per unit used in the budget $= \dfrac{£18,400}{800 \text{ units}} = £23$ per unit

Actual results for July were:

		£
Revenue	900 × £48	43,200
Direct labour	850 hours × £3.50 per hour	(2,975)
Direct materials	1,400 kgs × £8 per kg	(11,200)
Variable overheads		(2,750)
Fixed overheads		(5,000)
Actual profit for July		21,275

The flexed budget for July, prepared from this data, can be used to give a summary that compares the actual results for July with the budget and the flexed budget.

The flexed budget for July for sales of 900 units is:

		£
Revenue	900 × £50 per unit	45,000
Direct labour	900 × 1 hour × £4 per hour per unit	(3,600)
Direct materials	900 × 2 kg × £7.50 per kg per unit	(13,500)
Variable overheads	900 × 1 hour × £3 per direct labour hour	(2,700)
Fixed overheads	900 × 1 hour × £5 per direct labour hour	(4,500)
Flexed budgeted profit for July		20,700

The July results for Dymocks Ltd may be summarised as follows:

	Budget	Actual	Flexed	Difference Actual − Flexed
	£	£	£	£
Revenue	40,000	43,200	45,000	(1,800)
Direct labour	(3,200)	(2,975)	(3,600)	625
Direct materials	(12,000)	(11,200)	(13,500)	2,300
Variable overheads	(2,400)	(2,750)	(2,700)	(50)
Fixed overheads	(4,000)	(5,000)	(4,500)	(500)
Profit	18,400	21,275	20,700	575

The variance or the difference between the budget and the flexed budget of £2,300 (F) (£20,700 − £18,400) is only due to volume. The profit variance for sales volume is the only other variance that will need to be considered between the flexed budget and the budget. All other variances are between actual results and the flexed budget.

Worked example 13.5

Using the summary of results for Dymocks Ltd for July from Worked example 13.4 we can prepare an analysis of sales variances, and provide an explanation of why these variances might have occurred.

Sales variances

Sales volume profit

(budgeted sales quantity × standard profit per unit) − (actual sales quantity × standard profit per unit)

measuring the effect of changing sales volumes on profit

$(800 \times £23) - (900 \times £23) = £2,300$ (F)   (the profit variance of £2,300 noted in Worked example 13.4)

Sales price

(actual sales quantity × standard selling price per unit) − actual sales revenue

measuring the effect of selling prices different to those budgeted

$(900 \times £50) - £43,200 \quad = £1,800$ (A)   (see Worked example 13.4 summary)

Possible reasons for the above variances:

- selling prices are likely to affect sales volumes
- external factors such as economic recession, changes in demand, or increased competition
- prices not achievable perhaps due to lack of market research or bad planning.

Worked example 13.6

Using the summary of results for Dymocks Ltd for July from Worked example 13.4 we can prepare an analysis of materials variances, and provide an explanation of why these variances might have occurred.

Materials variances

Direct material price

(actual quantity of material purchased × standard price) − actual cost of material purchased

$(1,400 \times £7.50) - £11,200 \qquad = \quad £700$ (A)

Direct material usage

(standard quantity for actual production × standard material cost per unit) − (actual material quantity used × standard cost per unit)

$(1,800 \times £7.50) - (1,400 \times £7.50) \quad = £3,000$ (F)

Total materials variances   £2,300 (F)   (see Worked example 13.4 summary)

Possible reasons for the above variances:

- market conditions have changed
- foreign currency exchange rates may have changed (if applicable)
- supplier discounts have been reduced

- changes in the quality levels of materials used
- there may be a supplier invoicing error
- inventory control has improved
- the skills of the labour force have changed
- production methods have changed.

Note that materials price variances occur at two points: standard price compared to receipt of goods price; receipt of goods price compared to invoiced price.

Worked example 13.7

Using the summary of results for Dymocks Ltd for July from Worked example 13.4 we can prepare an analysis of direct labour variances, and provide an explanation of why these variances might have occurred.

Direct labour variances

Direct labour rate

(actual hours paid × standard direct labour rate per hour) − (actual hours paid × actual direct labour rate per hour)

(850 × £4) − (850 × £3.50)   = £425 (F)

Direct labour efficiency

(actual production in standard hours × standard direct labour rate per hour) − (actual direct labour hours worked × standard direct labour rate per hour)

(900 × £4) − (850 × £4)   = £200 (F)

Total direct labour variances   £625 (F)   (see Worked example 13.4 summary)

Possible reasons for the above variances:

- wage rate negotiations
- changes in the skills of the labour force
- better-than-expected impact of the effect of the learning curve
- impact of machinery efficiency, levels of maintenance, or use of different materials, with changed levels of quality.

Worked example 13.8

Using the summary of results for Dymocks Ltd for July from Worked example 13.4 we can prepare an analysis of variable overhead variances, and provide an explanation of why these variances might have occurred.

Variable overhead variances

Variable production overhead expenditure

actual cost incurred − (actual hours worked × standard variable production overhead absorption rate per hour)

£2,750 − (850 × £3.50)   = £225 (A)

Variable production overhead efficiency

(actual hours worked × standard variable production overhead absorption rate per hour) − (actual production in standard hours × standard variable production overhead absorption rate per hour)

$(850 \times £3.50) - (900 \times £3.50)$ = £175 (F)

Total variable overhead variances   £50 (A)   (see Worked example 13.4 summary)

Possible reasons for the above variances may be:

- related to the direct labour variances
- due to a number of individual variances within total variable overheads
- changes in the overhead rate with different levels of activity.

Worked example 13.9

Using the summary of results for Dymocks Ltd for July from Worked example 13.4 we can prepare an analysis of fixed overhead variances, and provide an explanation of why these variances might have occurred.

Fixed overhead variances

Fixed production overhead expenditure

budgeted fixed production overhead − actual fixed production overhead

£4,000 − £5,000   = £1,000 (A)

Fixed production overhead volume

(actual production in standard hours × standard fixed production overhead absorption rate per hour) − budgeted fixed production overhead

$(900 \times £5) - £4,000$ =   £500 (F)

Total fixed overhead variances   £500 (A)   (see Worked example 13.4 summary)

Possible reasons for the above variances:

- due to a number of individual variances within total fixed overheads.

Worked example 13.10

Using the variances calculated for Dymocks Ltd for July we can prepare an operating statement that reconciles the actual profit for July to the budgeted profit for July.

The actual profit for July may be reconciled with the budgeted profit by summarising the variances.

Operating statement

	£	£	£
Budget profit (Worked example 13.4)			18,400
Sales variances			
Sales volume (Worked example 13.5)	2,300 (F)		
Sales price (Worked example 13.5)	1,800 (A)	500 (F)	

Operating statement

	£	£	£
Direct materials variances			
Materials price (Worked example 13.6)	700 (A)		
Materials usage (Worked example 13.6)	3,000 (F)	2,300 (F)	
Direct labour variances			
Labour rate (Worked example 13.7)	425 (F)		
Labour efficiency (Worked example 13.7)	200 (F)	625 (F)	
Variable overheads variances			
Expenditure (Worked example 13.8)	225 (A)		
Efficiency (Worked example 13.8)	175 (F)	50 (A)	
Fixed overheads variances			
Expenditure (Worked example 13.9)	1,000 (A)		
Volume (Worked example 13.9)	500 (F)	500 (A)	
			2,875 (F)
Actual profit (Worked example 13.4)			21,275

Progress check 13.8

What are the main differences between variance analysis using marginal costing and variance analysis using absorption costing?

The reasons for variances

Although not an exhaustive list of possible causes, the following provides the reasons for most of the common variances encountered in most manufacturing and service businesses:

- direct material price: skills of purchasing department, quality of materials, price inflation, supplier discounts, foreign currency exchange rate fluctuations, invoicing errors
- direct material usage: quality of materials, labour efficiency, pilfering, inventory control, quality control
- direct labour rate: use of higher or lower skilled labour than planned, wage inflation, or union agreement
- direct labour efficiency: use of higher or lower skilled labour than planned, quality of materials, efficiency of plant and machinery, better or worse than expected learning curve performance, inaccurate time allocation – employees have to learn a new process and then repeat that process in reality many times, within times established during the learning curve evaluation
- overhead expenditure: inflation, wastage, resource usage savings, changes in services – many companies are outsourcing basic in-house services, for example accounting
- overhead efficiency: labour efficiency, efficiency of plant and machinery, technological changes
- overhead capacity: under- or over-utilisation of plant capacity, idle time.

Worked example 13.11

In Worked example 13.3 we calculated a list of variances that reconciled actual profit with budgeted profit.

In addition to the reasons for each variance, to be able to control its operations Applejack Ltd would also like to know which manager was responsible for each variance. The managers responsible may then explain the reasons and whether remedial actions may be necessary and what those actions may be.

Volume:
650 drums were produced compared to the planned 600 drums   £1,050A
**The responsibility of either the sales manager or the production
    planning manager**

Materials:
Sugar usage was 40 kilos less than standard   £80F
The responsibility of the production manager
The sugar price was 10p more per kilo than standard   £61A
The responsibility of the purchasing manager
Apples usage was 90 kilos less than the standard   £270F
The responsibility of the production manager
The apple price was 20p more per kilo than standard   £242A
The responsibility of the purchasing manager

Direct labour:
Hours worked were 150 hours less than standard   £1,200F
The responsibility of the production manager
The labour rate was £1 more per hour than standard   £500A
The responsibility of the human resources manager

Variable production overhead:
Hours worked were 150 hours less than they should have been at a standard   £300F
The responsibility of each of the managers of overhead departments
The overhead rate was 50p less per hour than standard   £250F
The responsibility of each of the managers of overhead departments

Fixed production overhead:
Hours worked were 150 hours less than they should have been at a standard   £450F
The responsibility of each of the managers of overhead departments
Hours worked were 100 less than required to absorb total fixed costs   £300A
The responsibility of each of the managers of overhead departments

Progress check 13.9

Most of the reasons for materials variances may be identified so that the appropriate corrective actions can be taken. What are the types of action that may be taken?

We have discussed the main variances (detailed in Figures 13.6 to 13.11), which are: sales variances – volume and price; labour variances – efficiency and pay rate; materials variances – usage and price; overheads variances – efficiency and expenditure; and we have already mentioned additional variances called mix variances and yield variances. Mix variances and yield variances show the effects on profit of changing the mix of products sold, and the impact of changes in the mix of input of materials and labour yielding either more or less output than expected. The key mix and yield variances are:

- sales mix variance – change in profit caused by a change in the sales mix
- materials mix variance – cost of the variation in the standard materials mix
- materials yield variance – cost of the difference between actual labour usage and that justified by actual output
- labour mix variance – cost of the variation in the standard labour grades mix
- labour yield variance – cost of the difference between actual materials usage and that justified by actual output.

Planning and operational variances

The above discussion has necessarily focused on the description, calculation and understanding of the most common variances that one may come across on a day-to-day basis in a manufacturing or service environment. Regarding each resource, such variances are normally based on the questions:

- what did it cost?

and

- what should it have cost?

or

- how long did it take?

and

- how long should it have taken?

Further light may be thrown on the reasons for differences between actual and planned performance through taking variance analysis to a greater level of sophistication than those outlined in the charts and worked examples above.

There are inevitably problems with traditional variance analyses, which are invariably due to:

- failure to distinguish variances due to an incorrect standard from those that are real operational variances
- failure to indicate which variances are controllable and which are uncontrollable
- failure to identify responsibility for variances
- lack of updating standards to current efficiency levels.

It is sufficient for our purposes to be aware of *ex post* variance analysis, which distinguishes between planning and operational variances. **Planning variances** are due to inaccuracies in the original (*ex ante*) budget. The variances between the new flexed budget that is drawn up to reflect actual conditions during the budget period (the *ex post* budget) can then be compared with actual performance to show **operational variances**. It is operational variances that may be used to evaluate individual areas of company and managerial performance and to decide on the costs and benefits of further investigation and implementation of remedial actions.

There are a number of variance investigation decision models:

- the percentage rule, which prompts investigation if variances are greater than a certain percentage of the standard
- statistical significance rule, which investigates variances that are 'unusual' occurrences using a normal distribution
- statistical control charts, which provide warning limits and action limits.

It is useful for non-financial managers to be aware of the range of ways in which variances are used, even though the detail of some of these is outside the scope of this book.

Summary of key points

- Standard costing can be used to calculate costs of units or processes that may be used in budgeted costs.

- Not all budgeted amounts are standard amounts, as the latter will be precise by nature, unlike budgeted amounts.

- Standard costing provides the basis for performance evaluation and control from comparison of actual performance against budget through the setting of predetermined cost estimates.

- A flexed budget reflects the costs or revenues expected as a result of changes in activity levels from those planned in the master budget.

- A flexed budget provides a more realistic basis for comparison of actual performance against planned performance.

- Flexed budgets enable comparison of actual costs and revenues on a like-for-like basis through the calculation of differences, or variances.

- Variances are the differences between planned, budgeted or standard costs (or revenues) and actual costs incurred and may be summarised in an operating statement to reconcile budget with actual performance.

- Variances between actual and standard performance may be investigated to explain the reasons for the differences through preparation of a complete analysis of all variances, or alternatively through the use of exception reporting that highlights only significant variances.

- Inaccuracies in original budgets may be identified through planning variances, and actual performance may then be compared with a subsequently revised budget to show operational variances.

Assessment material

Questions

Q13.1 How is standard costing used in the preparation of budgets?

Q13.2 (i)   What are the benefits of using standard costing?
   (ii) What type of standard may best ensure that those benefits are achieved?
   (iii) How are standards used to achieve those benefits?

Q13.3 Describe and illustrate the technique of flexible budgeting.

Q13.4 (i)   What is management by exception?
   (ii) How is variance analysis used to support this technique?

Q13.5 (i)   Outline the main variances that may be reported using the bases of absorption costing and marginal costing.
   (ii) What do these variances tell us about direct labour, direct materials and overhead costs?

Q13.6 Describe the main reasons why usage and efficiency variances may occur and illustrate these with some examples.

Q13.7 What are mix and yield variances?

Q13.8 (i)   Explain some of the problems associated with traditional variance reporting.
   (ii) What are planning and operational variances?

Discussion points

D13.1 'We set the budget once a year and then compare the actual profit after the end of the financial year. If actual profit is below budget, then everyone needs to make more effort to ensure this doesn't happen the following year.' Discuss.

D13.2 'The standard-setting process is sometimes seen as management's way of establishing targets that demand better and better manufacturing performance.' To what extent do you think that is true, and if it is true how effectively do you think the standard-setting process achieves that objective?

D13.3 To what extent do you think that the techniques of flexed budgets and variance analysis complicate the otherwise simple process of comparing the various areas of actual performance against budget?

D13.4 'Traditional variance analysis tends to focus on cutting costs and increasing output in a way that is detrimental to product and service quality and the longer-term viability of the business.' Discuss.

Exercises

Solutions are provided in Appendix 3 to all exercise numbers highlighted in colour.

Level I

F13.1   *Time allowed – 60 minutes*

Nilbog Ltd makes garden gnomes. It uses standard costs and has budgeted to produce and sell 130,000 Fishermen (their top-of-the-range gnome) in 2010. Nilbog's budget for the year is phased over 13 four-week periods, and production and sales revenues are spread evenly in the budget.

Budgeted standard costs and selling prices for the Fisherman are:

		£
Direct materials	3 cubic metres at £3.60 per cubic metre	10.80
Direct labour	2 hours at £6.60 per hour	13.20
Variable overheads	2 hours at £2.40 per hour	4.80
Fixed overheads	2 hours at £4.80 per hour	9.60
Standard cost of one Fisherman		38.40
Standard profit		9.60
Standard selling price		48.00

The actual results for period five, a four-week period, were:

Revenue	9,000 Fishermen at £48 each
Production	9,600 Fishermen
Purchase of direct materials	30,000 cubic metres at a cost of £115,200
Direct materials usage	28,000 cubic metres
Direct labour cost	£142,560 for 22,000 hours
Variable overhead	£44,000
Fixed overhead	£100,000

There was no work-in-progress at the start or at the end of period five. Finished goods and materials inventories are valued at standard cost.

You are required to prepare a flexed budget and an operating statement for Nilbog Ltd for period five, showing the profit for the period and all standard variances with their detailed calculations, together with an explanation of their likely causes.

F13.2   *Time allowed – 90 minutes*

Cyclops plc is an electronics business that manufactures television sets, and uses a standard costing system. The TV cabinets division of Cyclops manufactures, for sale within the company, the plastic cases for one of their most popular models, the F24. The results for the F24 for October 2010 were as follows:

	Actual	Budget
Sales units	61,200	40,800
	£	£
Revenue	348,840	244,800
Direct labour	133,280	81,600
Direct materials	114,240	81,600
Variable overheads	27,200	16,320
Contribution	74,120	65,280
Fixed overheads	25,000	20,400
Profit	49,120	44,880

The budget had been prepared for 2010 using standard costs for that year.

Sales volumes were increasing and just prior to October the TV cabinets division expected around 50% increase in sales volumes for the month. The division had unused capacity to take up this expected increase in volume. Vimla Patel had recently been appointed as commercial manager and she proposed a 30p selling price reduction per unit, which was effective from 1 October.

Melanie Bellamy, Cyclops's purchasing manager had negotiated a 4% discount on the standard prices of raw materials purchased and used from October. The production manager, Graham Brown, had been having problems with quality due to the learning curve and some operators who were still receiving training. Training had been completed by the end of September. This meant some increase in operator pay rates but the planned productivity rate was maintained and there was less materials wastage in October. The variable costs of utilities increased in October, primarily due to electricity and gas price increases.

Graham Brown was able to keep inventory levels of materials and finished product at the same level at the end of October as at the beginning of October.

You are required to:

(i)   prepare an operating statement that provides an analysis of the variances between actual and budget for October on a marginal costing basis, highlighting the performance of each of the managers

(ii)   give full explanations of why the variances may have occurred

(iii)   and (iv) prepare the same analysis and explanations as (i) and (ii) above using absorption costing

(v)   explain whether absorption costing provides the best basis for assessment of manager performance.

Level II

E13.3 *Time allowed – 90 minutes*

White Heaven Ltd manufactures a bathroom basin, the Shell and uses standard costing based on a monthly output of 50,000 units. White Heaven uses two grades of direct labour and two items of raw material.

Variable overheads include:

- indirect labour costs of material handlers and stores persons
- maintenance labour costs
- general production overheads.

Fixed overheads include:

- supervisory salaries
- other overheads such as
  - factory rent
  - electricity standing charges
  - gas standing charges.

The *ideal* standard cost of a Shell is as follows:

Direct labour	1 hour at £7.20 per hour	grade A
	0.75 hours at £6.00 per hour	grade B
Direct materials	5 kg at £2 per kg	clay
	3 kg at £4 per kg	glaze
Indirect labour	0.25 hours at £5.00 per hour	
Maintenance	0.05 hours at £10.00 per hour	
Variable overheads	15% of direct materials cost, plus	
	10% of direct labour cost	
Supervisory salaries	£95,000 per month	
Other fixed overheads	£109,000 per month	

In June 2010 adjustments were agreed as the basis for the following month's *attainable* standard costs:

- Grade A labour rates increased by 40p, grade B by 30p and indirect and maintenance labour by 20p per hour.
- Grade B labour hours increased by 0.05 hours because of process delays due to a tool change problem.
- Turnover of operators has meant recruiting some inexperienced, untrained operators:

    10% of grade A operators with 50% efficiency
    25% of grade B operators with 60% efficiency

- The clay is to be upgraded in quality with the supplier imposing a 10% surcharge.
- The glaze will be purchased in larger batches with a 12.5% discount but resulting in an increase in variable overheads to 20% of materials cost for this type of material.

> **For the July output of 49,000 Shells you are required to calculate:**
>
> **(i)**   the ideal standard cost for one Shell
> **(ii)** the attainable standard cost for a Shell for July 2010
> **(iii)** the total variance between the ideal and attainable standards.

E13.4   *Time allowed – 90 minutes*

White Heaven Ltd (see Exercise E13.3) actually produced 49,000 Shells during July 2010 and the actual costs for the month were as follows:

Direct labour	52,000 hours at £7.60 per hour	grade A
	43,500 hours at £6.30 per hour	grade B
Direct materials	247,000 kg at £2.16 per kg	clay
	149,000 kg at £3.60 per kg	glaze
Indirect labour	12,000 hours at £5.20 per hour	
Maintenance	2,250 hours at £10.20 per hour	
Variable overheads	£251,000	
Supervisory salaries	£97,000	
Other fixed overheads	£110,000	

You are required to:

(i)   calculate the variances between actual costs for July 2010 and the attainable standard
(ii)   prepare an operating statement that summarises the variances
(iii) reconcile the total actual cost for July with the expected total attainable cost
(iv)   comment on the likely reasons for each of the variances.

E13.5   *Time allowed – 90 minutes*

Millennium Models Ltd manufactured an ornamental gift for the tourist trade. The standard variable cost per unit is:

Materials	£0.85 per kg
Unit material usage	2 kg
Direct labour rate	£4.20 per hour
Standard labour per unit	42 minutes
Selling price per unit	£5.84

Fixed overhead is recovered on the basis of units produced at the rate of £0.82 per unit and Millennium Models planned to sell 4,300 units in November 2010.

In November 2010 Millennium Model's actual performance was:

Units manufactured and sold	4,100
Sales revenue	£24,805
Materials used	6,600 kg at £0.83 per kg
	1,900 kg at £0.89 per kg
Direct labour paid	2,975 at £4.50 per hour
Overheads incurred	£3,800

You are required to:

(i)   prepare an actual to budget profit reconciliation for November 2010 including an analysis of sales, materials and labour variances
(ii)   calculate the fixed overhead expenditure and fixed overhead volume variances for November 2010.

E13.6 *Time allowed – 90 minutes*

Using the information about Millennium Models Ltd from Exercise E13.5:

(i)   explain what you think are the advantages and disadvantages of the implementation of a standard costing system by Millennium Ltd

(ii)   explain how the analyses of variances may have helped Millennium Models Ltd control the business

(iii) prepare a report that explains the variance analysis you have carried out in Exercise E13.5 above and provides explanations of Millennium's performance.

E13.7 *Time allowed – 90 minutes*

The Stables is a small holiday let business in Wales.

The standard variable cost for each holiday let unit (HLU) for one holiday is:

Direct materials (food, cleaning materials, and repairs)	£120
Direct labour 15 hours at £10 per hour	£150
Variable overhead 5 hours at £1 per hour	£5

Budgeted costs and sales for the 2010 season are:

Number of holidays	50
Price per holiday	£400
Fixed overhead	£2,080

The actual outcome for one HLU for 2010 was:

Number of holidays	52
Total revenue	£19,760
Direct materials	£5,928
Direct labour (780 hours at £9 per hour)	£7,020
Variable overhead	£260
Fixed overhead	£1,950

You are required to:

(i)   Prepare a budgeted income statement for one HLU for 2010.

(ii)   Prepare an actual income statement for one HLU for 2010.

(iii) Prepare a flexed budget for one HLU that reflects the amount of actual business for 2010.

(iv)   Prepare a detailed variance analysis for one HLU and identify possible reasons for each of the variances.

(v)   Summarise the variances in an operating statement that reconciles the difference between the budgeted profit and the actual profit achieved by one HLU in 2010.

(vi)   Outline some of the problems with traditional variance analysis and explain how the identification of planning variances may assist in more accurate reporting of operational variances.

Case Study IV
ARTHURSTONE

During the 2000s, Sir William Kiloshake began work on a project that had been a dream he had wished to realise for many years.

Bill was a keen botanist and environmentalist and had been brought up close to a large country house called Arthurstone, which stood in a 500-acre estate in which there had once been extensive gardens. The house had long since gone into disrepair and the gardens had been untended for around 50 years.

Bill had brought together a consortium of experts to investigate how Arthurstone could be developed into a national educational and tourist facility.

After many years of feasibility studies, market research, soil analyses and Government grant applications, the project became a reality by 2007. The project would cost £35m to restore the building and re-establish the gardens. This was supported by a UK National Lottery grant of £17m. It was expected that around 350,000 people would visit Arthurstone every year, mostly during the summer months.

The net project cost investment of £18m (£35m total cost less £17m grant) had been obtained from sponsorship from the private sector. However, the project needed to be self-financing from its first day of opening to the public, which was 1 May 2010. The costs associated with running the house and gardens are broadly:

  Variable operational costs
  Fixed operational costs
  Variable marketing and administrative costs
  Fixed marketing and administrative costs.

The initial price for admission to Arthurstone was £6 per person.

Although market research had been carried out, there was still some uncertainty about the reliability of visitor estimates. Equally, the management of Arthurstone did not have much information about the elasticity of demand for garden attractions and were not convinced that the admission price of £6 was the optimum price. For its first year of operation there were to be no discounts for children, senior citizens, or job seekers and unemployed persons; neither were there to be volume discounts for large parties of visitors.

The following budget information relates to the first four months that Arthurstone would be open to the public:

	Month 1		Month 2		Month 3		Month 4	
	Visitors	£	Visitors	£	Visitors	£	Visitors	£
Sales revenue	85,000	510,000	90,000	540,000	95,000	570,000	85,000	510,000
Variable operational costs		153,000		162,000		171,000		153,000
Fixed operational costs		45,000		45,000		45,000		45,000
Variable marketing and administrative costs		51,000		54,000		57,000		51,000
Fixed marketing and administrative costs		52,500		52,500		52,500		52,500

The budget for 2010/2011 was prepared on the assumption that during its first year of operation there would be no visitors during the months September to April. During that period of course no variable costs would be incurred.

Required

(i)   Prepare the budgeted income statement for each of the first six months, and the total for the year to 30 April 2011, on a marginal costing basis.

(ii) Explain the reasons for the differences in profit levels between the first four months of operation (with supporting calculations).

(iii) Draw a break-even chart that shows the admission price to be charged at the break-even point for Arthurstone.

(iv) What admission price to Arthurstone should be charged to achieve a profit of 10% mark-up on full absorption costs?

(v)   What admission price to Arthurstone should be charged to achieve a target profit of £500,000 for the year May 2010 to April 2011?

(vi) What may be the possible impact of charging the prices calculated in (iv) and (v) above, and to what factors may that impact be sensitive?

(vii) At the prices calculated in (iv) and (v), by what percentage levels may the visitor numbers drop from that budgeted before Arthurstone would start to make a loss?

(viii) Prepare a short report, which includes any calculations that you consider relevant, outlining the factors that may be discussed with regard to a proposal that has been made to introduce a revised pricing structure for 2011/2012 which includes discounting for children, senior citizens, job seekers and unemployed persons, and large parties of visitors.

14

Financing the business and the cost of capital

Contents

Learning objectives

Completion of this chapter will enable you to:

- identify the different sources of finance available to an organisation
- explain the concept of gearing, and the debt/equity ratio.
- explain what is meant by the weighted average cost of capital (WACC)
- calculate the cost of equity and the cost of debt
- appreciate the concept of risk with regard to capital investment
- outline the capital asset pricing model (CAPM) and the β factor
- analyse return on equity as a function of financial structure
- explain the use of economic value added (EVA™) and market value added (MVA) as performance measures and value creation incentives.

Introduction

This chapter begins with an outline of the types of finance available to organisations to fund their long-term capital investment and short-term requirement for working capital. Financing may be internal or external to the organisation, and either short-term (shorter than one year) or medium- to long-term (longer than one year). Short-term financing is also discussed in Chapter 16, which covers working capital management.

In Chapter 15 we will deal with decisions related to capital investment. This chapter will consider a number of financing options such as leasing and Government grants, but will focus on the main sources of long-term external finance available to an entity to finance such investments: loans (or debt) and ordinary shares (or equity). We shall also discuss gearing or financial structure, which relates to the relationship between the debt and equity of the entity.

The appraisal of investment projects by a company inevitably involves calculations that use some sort of discount rate. The discount rate that is normally used is based on the company's cost of capital. A company's cost of capital is dependent on the financial structure of the entity, its relative proportions and cost of debt (loans) and cost of equity capital (shares). In Chapter 7 we introduced WACC and in this chapter we will consider its calculation and application.

We will look at how the costs of equity and debt may be determined. One of the fundamental differences between equity and debt is the risk associated with each type of financing and its impact on their cost. The capital asset pricing model (CAPM) is introduced to show how risk impacts on the cost of equity.

This chapter looks briefly at the relationship between the return on equity and the financial structure of the company. The chapter closes with an introduction to economic value added (EVA) and market value added (MVA). These measures are increasingly replacing traditional performance measures in many large companies. An outline of these recently developed techniques is considered in terms of their use as both performance measures and motivational tools.

Sources of finance

In Chapter 3 we considered some of the various types of business finance when we looked at the balance sheet. Organisations require finance for both short- and medium- to long-term requirements and the financing is usually matched with the funding requirement. Longer-term finance (longer than one year) is usually used to fund capital investment in non-current assets and other longer-term projects. Short-term finance (shorter than one year) is usually used to fund the organisation's requirement for working capital.

Both short- and long-term finance may be either internal or external to the organisation.

Internal finance may be provided from:

- retained earnings
- trade credit
- cash improvements gained from the more effective management of working capital.

Retained earnings

Retained earnings are the funds generated that are surplus to:

- the costs of adding to or replacing non-current assets
- the operational costs of running the business
- net interest charges
- tax charges
- dividend payments.

There is statistical evidence which shows that through the 2000s the majority of capital funding of UK companies continued to be derived from internal sources of finance. However, this is not free. The profit or net earnings generated from the operations of the company belongs to the shareholders of the company. There is a cost, an opportunity cost, which is the best alternative return that shareholders could obtain on these funds elsewhere in the financial markets.

It is the directors who recommend and the shareholders who vote at the annual general meeting (AGM) how much of those earnings is distributed to shareholders as dividends, the balance being held and reinvested in the business. The retained earnings of the company are increased by net profit less any dividends payable; they are part of the shareholders' funds and therefore appear within the equity of the company. Similarly any losses will reduce the retained earnings of the company. The cost of shareholders' equity is reflected in the level of dividends paid to shareholders, which is usually dependent on how well the company has performed during the year.

Trade credit, together with the more effective management of working capital, will be discussed in Chapter 16.

The main source of external short-term funding is short-term debt.

Short-term debt

Short-term financial debts are the elements of overdrafts, loans and leases that are repayable within one year of the balance sheet date. Short-term finance tends to be more expensive but more flexible than long-term debt. Short-term debt is therefore normally matched to finance the fluctuations in levels of the company's net current assets, its working capital.

Such short-term finance represents a higher risk for the borrower. Interest rates can be volatile, and an overdraft, for example, is technically repayable on demand. The company may finance its operations by taking on further short-term debt, as levels of working capital increase. Because of the higher risk associated with short-term debt, many companies adopting a conservative funding policy may accept a reduction in profitability and use long-term debt to finance not only non-current assets, but also a proportion of the company's working capital. Less risk-averse companies may use short-term debt to finance both working capital and non-current assets; such debt provides increased profitability because of its lower cost.

We will discuss each of the other sources of external finance, which are primarily long-term, and include:

- **ordinary shares** (or equity shares)
- **preference shares**
- **loan capital** (financial debt that includes bank loans, debentures and other loans)
- **hybrid finance** (for example, convertible loans)
- leasing
- UK Government funding
- European Union funding.

The two main primary sources of long-term finance available to a company, which are both external, are broadly:

- equity share capital (ordinary shares)
- debt (long-term loans, bonds and debentures).

Both types of financing have a unique set of characteristics and rights. The main ones are shown in the table in Figure 14.1.

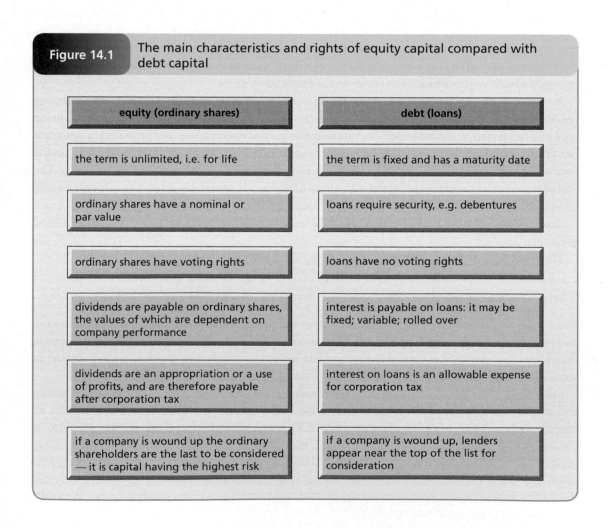

Figure 14.1 The main characteristics and rights of equity capital compared with debt capital

equity (ordinary shares)	debt (loans)
the term is unlimited, i.e. for life	the term is fixed and has a maturity date
ordinary shares have a nominal or par value	loans require security, e.g. debentures
ordinary shares have voting rights	loans have no voting rights
dividends are payable on ordinary shares, the values of which are dependent on company performance	interest is payable on loans: it may be fixed; variable; rolled over
dividends are an appropriation or a use of profits, and are therefore payable after corporation tax	interest on loans is an allowable expense for corporation tax
if a company is wound up the ordinary shareholders are the last to be considered — it is capital having the highest risk	if a company is wound up, lenders appear near the top of the list for consideration

Share capital

The share capital of a company may comprise ordinary shares and preference shares (although there are other classes of shares, which are not covered in this book). The company determines the maximum share capital that it is ever likely to need to raise and this level is called its authorised share capital. The amount of shares actually in issue at any point in time is normally at a level for the company to meet its foreseeable requirements. These shares are called the company's issued share capital which, when all the shareholders have paid for them, are referred to as fully paid-up issued share capital. Ordinary shares represent the long-term capital provided by the owners of a company, both new and existing.

In start-up businesses the ordinary shares are usually owned by the founder(s) of the business, and possibly by family and friends, or by investors seeking a gain in their value as the business grows. As a company grows it may decide:

- to raise further equity share capital, in order to finance its growth, at levels much higher than the founders of the business and/or their friends and family are willing or able to afford, or
- to sell its shares by making them publicly available and freely traded, to realise gains in their value for the founders or other investors.

The way that such businesses action these decisions is by making what are termed **initial public offerings (IPOs)** of shares in their companies. This means that shares are offered for sale to the general public and to financial institutions and are then traded (in the UK) on the London Stock Exchange or the Alternative Investment Market (AIM).

The online dating company EasyDate (see the press extract on page 554) grew rapidly from its foundation in 2005. The company listed on the AIM on 30 June 2010, raising £45m by issuing 75 million shares at 60p each. After having made a number of successful acquisitions to improve its market share, the company decided that its key strategy should be to continue to make more substantial acquisitions. For that it needed more capital, and because of the relative ease with which companies were able to raise funds on the AIM, the EasyDate founders decided that such a listing was the best strategic option for their company.

Ordinary shareholders receive a dividend at a level determined usually by company performance and not as a specific entitlement. The level of dividends is usually based on the underlying profitability of the company (Tesco plc actually advised its shareholders of this relationship in the late 1990s). Preference shareholders receive a dividend at a level that is fixed, subject to the conditions of issue of the shares, and have priority over the ordinary shareholders if the company is wound up. In addition, ordinary shareholders normally have voting rights, whereas preference shareholders do not.

If a company goes into liquidation the ordinary shareholders are always last to be repaid. Ordinary shareholders are paid out of the balance of funds that remain after all other creditors have been repaid.

Additional equity capital may be raised through increasing the number of shares issued by the company through **rights issues**. A **scrip issue** (or bonus issue) increases the number of shares with the additional shares going to existing shareholders, in proportion to their holdings, through capitalisation of the reserves of the company. No cash is called for from the shareholders.

Rights issues

In a rights issue, the right to subscribe for new shares (or debentures) issued by the company is given to existing shareholders. The 'rights' to buy the new shares are usually fixed at a price discounted to below the current market price (see Worked examples 14.1 and 14.2). A shareholder not wishing to take up a rights issue may sell the rights.

Floating on the AIM

Online dating agency EasyDate is planning for a big year. The Edinburgh-based business, which last year made £11.5m of sales and cash before charges of just under £3m, is looking to expand internationally, raise funds – possibly from a flotation – and launch a revolutionary new website that will allow those seeking a new partner to browse all the available online dating tools.

'It'll be a bit like a comparison site', says the internet, telecoms and technology entrepreneur Bill Dobbie, the 51-year-old chairman and founder of EasyDate.

The business was formed in 2005 when Dobbie teamed up with software writer Max Polyakov and has been growing steadily ever since. Last year it realised a 7pc average monthly revenue growth. But the size, scope and opportunities from the rapidly expanding global markets mean Dobbie has his sights set on still further rapid expansion. And he thinks EasyDate is well placed to capitalise on the potential due to its niche approach to online dating.

'Unlike our competition such as Match and Dating Direct, we operate a portfolio of sites and we are a niche operator', says Dobbie.

The idea is that with its basic model, systems and structure – built over five years by a team of 20 working on it full time, says Dobbie – EasyDate can launch both new niche sites itself or, as a white-label site provider, with a partner. Each will target a specific sector of society. The thinking, explains Dobbie, is that singles in their 20s, for example, need a different dating site to other demographic groups.

'There is consolidation going on in the marketplace and niches are emerging. Even companies like Match realise they can't be all things to all men. It's analogous to the drinks industry – not every pub is a Wetherspoons', he says.

The market is growing by about 20pc a year, says Dobbie, and is estimated to be worth $1bn – just over half coming from Europe. There is, he believes, still huge growth potential.

'At $20 per head per month, which is what everybody charges, that's not that many people.

'Online dating is becoming increasingly socially acceptable. People are more readily willing to say they met someone through an online dating site. There is no longer a social stigma attached to it at all. I guess it's fuelled by people being more comfortable being online and the whole social network thing.'

Alongside the niche and comparison site approach comes global growth. EasyDate's international expansion began last year.

'We are now in all the English-speaking countries and beginning to look at Spanish-speaking and others such as Sweden, Netherlands and Thailand.'

He plans to launch in Brazil this year. 'We have done some testing on the internet and if there is uptake then we'll push a little harder.

'We are test-marketing Spain now and are about to buy a Spanish database that will accelerate that expansion.'

Language is not so much an issue. 'We have an international staff and we like to keep everything in-house', he said.

The approach works. EasyDate sees £150,000 a month income from its Australian site, for example, without any of EasyDate's team of 80 having set foot in the country, says Dobbie.

'You need a critical mass', he says. 'The database is really the only barrier to entry and once you get a bit of momentum, and your database grows, it's an exponential effect.'

Buying that information by acquiring other dating companies is the fastest way to get a foothold in a new territory. And for that, EasyDate needs funds.

'We are looking at raising institutional finance – an Alternative Investment Market flotation,' says Dobbie. 'We are weighing up the options. That will give us the capital to make acquisitions, which will allow us to accelerate our foreign growth.'

Source: **Online dating site seeks to woo investors**, by Philip Smith © *Daily Telegraph*, 18 May 2010

Worked example 14.1

A company that achieves a profit after tax of 20% on capital employed has the following capital structure:

400,000 ordinary shares of £1	£400,000
Retained earnings	£200,000

In order to invest in some new profitable projects the company wishes to raise £252,000 from a rights issue. The company's current ordinary share price is £1.80.

The company would like to know the number of shares that must be issued if the rights price is: £1.60; £1.50; £1.40; £1.20.

Capital employed is £600,000 [£400,000 + £200,000]

Current earnings are 20% of £600,000 = £120,000

$$\text{Therefore, earnings per share (eps)} = \frac{£120,000}{400,000} = 30p$$

After the rights issue earnings will be 20% of £852,000 [£400,000 + £200,000 + £252,000], which equals £170,400.

Rights price £	Number of new shares £252,000/ rights price £	Total shares after rights issue £	Eps £170,400/ total shares pence
1.60	157,500	557,500	30.6
1.50	168,000	568,000	30.0
1.40	180,000	580,000	29.4
1.20	210,000	610,000	27.9

We can see that at a high rights issue share price the earnings per share are increased. At lower issue prices eps are diluted. The 'break-even point', with no dilution, is where the rights price equals the pre-rights issue capital employed per share £600,000/400,000 = £1.50.

Worked example 14.2

A company has 1,000,000 £1 ordinary shares in issue with a market price of £2.10 on 1 June. The company wished to raise new equity capital by a 1 for 4 share rights issue at a price of £1.50. Immediately the company announced the rights issue the price fell to £1.92 on 2 June. Just before the rights issue was due to be made, the share price had recovered to £2 per share, the cum rights price (the share price that includes the associated rights).

The company may calculate the theoretical ex rights price (the new market price that excludes the associated rights) as

1,000,000 shares × the cum rights price of £2	£2,000,000
250,000 shares × the issue price of £1.50	375,000
Theoretical value of 1,250,000 shares	£2,375,000

Therefore, the theoretical ex rights price is $\dfrac{£2,375,000}{1,250,000} = £1.90$ per share

Or to put it another way

Four shares at the cum rights value of £2	£8.00
One new share issued at £1.50	£1.50
	£9.50

Therefore, the theoretical ex rights price is $\dfrac{£9.50}{5} = £1.90$ per share

Long-term debt

Generally, companies try and match their financing with what it is required for, and the type of assets requiring to be financed:

- non-current assets
- long-term projects.

Long-term debt is usually less expensive and less flexible, but has less risk, than short-term debt. Long-term debt is therefore normally matched to finance the acquisition of non-current assets, which are long-term assets from which the company expects to derive benefits over several future periods.

Long-term financial debts are the elements of loans and leases that are payable after one year of the balance sheet date. Debt capital may take many forms: loans, debentures, Eurobonds, mortgages, etc. We will look at debentures, but we will not delve into the particular attributes of every type of debt capital. Suffice to say, each involves interest payment, and capital repayment and security for the loan is usually required. Loan interest is a fixed commitment, which is usually payable once or twice a year. But although debt capital is burdened with a fixed commitment of interest payable, it is a tax-efficient method of financing.

Debentures

Debentures and long-term loans are both debt, and are often taken to mean the same thing. However, loans may be either unsecured, or secured on some or all of the assets of the company. Lenders to a company receive interest, payable yearly or half-yearly, the rate of which may vary with market conditions. A debenture is a type of bond and more specifically refers to the written acknowledgement of a debt by a company, usually given under its seal, and is secured on some or all of the assets of the company or its subsidiaries. A debenture agreement normally contains provisions as to payment of interest and the terms of repayment of the principal. Other long-term loans are usually unsecured.

Security for a debenture may be by way of a floating charge, without attachment to specific assets, on the whole of the business's assets. If the company is not able to meet its obligations the floating charge will crystallise on specific assets like accounts receivable or inventories. Security may alternatively, at the outset, take the form of a fixed charge on specific assets like land and buildings.

Debentures are a tax-efficient method of corporate financing, which means that interest payable on such loans is an allowable deduction in the computation of taxable profit. For example, if corporation tax were at 30%, a 10% debenture would actually cost the company 7%, that is {10% − (10% × 30%)}.

Debentures, and other loans, may be redeemable, in which case the principal, the original sum borrowed, will need to be repaid on a specific date.

Hybrid finance

Loans may sometimes be required by companies as they move through their growth phase, and for them to finance specific asset acquisitions or projects. Disadvantages of loans are:

- the financial risk resulting from a reduction in the amount of equity compared with debt
- the commitment to fixed interest payments over a number of years
- the requirement of a build-up of cash with which to repay the loan on maturity.

Alternatively, if an increase in equity is used for this type of funding, eps (earnings per share) may be immediately 'diluted'. However, some financing is neither totally debt nor equity, but has the characteristics of both. Such hybrid finance, as it is called, includes financial instruments like convertible loans. A **convertible loan** is a 'two-stage' financial instrument. It may be a fixed interest debt or preference shares, which can be converted into ordinary shares of the company at the option of the lender. Eps will therefore not be diluted until a later date. The right to convert may usually be exercised each year at a predetermined conversion rate up until a specified date, at which time the loan must be redeemed if it has not been converted. The conversion rate may be stated as:

- a conversion price (the amount of the loan that can be converted into one ordinary share), or
- a conversion ratio (the number of ordinary shares that can be converted from one unit of the loan).

The conversion price or ratio will be specified at the outset and may change during the term of the loan. Convertibles tend to pay a lower rate of interest than straight loans, which is effectively charging lenders for the right to convert to ordinary shares. They therefore provide an additional benefit to company cash flow and cost of financing.

Progress check 14.1

What makes convertible loans attractive to both investors and companies?

Leasing

Leases are contracts between a lessor and lessee for the hire of a specific asset. Why then is leasing seen as a source of long-term financing? There are two types of leases, **operating leases** and **finance leases**, and the answer to the question lies in the accounting treatment of the latter.

Under both types of leasing contract the lessor has ownership of the asset but gives the lessee the right to use the asset over an agreed period in return for rental payments.

An operating lease is a rental agreement for an asset, which may be leased by one lessee for a period, and then another lessee for a period, and so on. The lease period is normally less than the economic life of the asset, and the lease rentals are charged as a cost in the profit and loss account as they occur. The leased asset does not appear in the lessee's balance sheet. The lessor is responsible for maintenance and regular service for assets like photocopiers, cars and PCs. The lessor therefore retains most of the risk and reward of ownership.

A finance lease relates to an asset where the present value of the lease rentals payable amounts to at least 90% of the fair market value of the asset at the start of the lease. Under a finance lease the legal title to the asset remains with the lessor, but the difference in accounting treatment, as defined by IAS 17, Leases, is that a finance lease is capitalised in the balance sheet of the lessee. A value of the finance lease is shown under non-current assets, based on a calculation of the present value of the capital part (excluding finance charges) of the future lease rentals payable. The future lease rentals are also shown as long- and short-term payables in the balance sheet. The lessee, although not the legal owner, therefore takes on the risks and rewards of ownership.

The leasing evaluation process involves appraisal of the investment in the asset itself, its outright purchase or lease, and an evaluation of leasing as the method of financing. These two decisions may be made separately in either order or they may form a combined decision, and take account of a number of factors:

- asset purchase price and residual value
- the lease rental amounts and the timing of their payments
- service and maintenance payments
- tax
    - capital allowances for purchased non-current assets
    - tax allowable expenses of lease rentals
- VAT (relating to the asset purchase and the lease rentals)
- interest rates – the general level of rates of competing financing options.

Apart from this outline of the process, the evaluation of leasing as a source of finance is beyond the scope of this book.

UK Government and European Union funding

Businesses involved in certain industries or located in specific geographical areas of the UK may from time to time be eligible for assistance with financing. This may be by way of grants, loan guarantees, and subsidised consultancy. Funding may be on a national or a regional basis from various UK Government or European Union sources.

By their very nature, such financing initiatives are continually changing in format and their areas of focus. For example, funding assistance has been available in one form or another for SMEs, the agriculture industry, tourism, former coal and steel producing areas, and parts of Wales.

This type of funding may include support for the following:

- business start-ups
- new factories
- new plant and machinery
- research and development
- IT development.

There are many examples of funding schemes that operate currently. For example, the Government, via the Department for Business, Innovation and Skills (BIS), can provide guarantees for loans from banks and other financial institutions for small businesses that may be unable to provide the security for conventional loans. Via the various regional development agencies, they may also provide discretionary selective financial assistance, in the form of grants or loans, for businesses that are willing to invest in 'assisted areas'. The BIS and Government Business Link websites, *www.bis.gov.uk* and *www.businesslink.gov.uk*, provide up-to-date information of all current funding initiatives.

The Welsh Assembly's use of European Structural Funds (ESFs) assists businesses in regenerating Welsh communities. For example, through a scheme called match funding, depending on the type of business activity and its location, ESFs can contribute up to 50% of a project's funding. The balance of the funding is provided from the business's own resources or other public or private sector funding. Websites like the Welsh European Funding Office website, *www.wefo.wales.gov.uk*, provide information on this type of funding initiative.

> ### Progress check 14.2
>
> Describe what is meant by debt and equity and give some examples of each. What are the other sources of long-term, external finance available to a company?

Gearing

In Chapter 7 when we looked at financial ratios we introduced gearing, the relationship between debt and equity capital that represents the financial structure (or capital structure) of an organisation. We will now take a look at the application of gearing and then consider worked examples that compare the use of debt capital with ordinary share capital.

The relationship between the two sources of finance, loans and ordinary shares, or debt and equity gives a measure of the gearing of the company. A company with a high proportion of debt capital to share capital is highly geared, and a company with a low proportion of debt capital to share capital is low geared. Gearing (leverage, or debt/equity) has important implications for the long-term stability of a company because of, as we have seen, its impact on financial risk.

Companies closely monitor their gearing ratios to ensure that their capital structure aligns with their financial strategy. Various alternative actions may be taken by companies, as necessary, to adjust their capital structures by increasing or decreasing their respective levels of debt and equity. An example of one of the ways in which this may be achieved is to return cash to shareholders through share repurchases. Domino's Pizza plc has had a programme of buying back shares since 2004. In November 2009 it announced a new share-repurchasing phase and had repurchased 500,000 shares by 15 February 2010. The company's annual report and accounts for the year ended 27 December 2009 reported £18.1m of cash returned to shareholders in the year through a combination of dividends and share repurchases; the company had been very cash-generative and had created £35.6m of cash in the year. Indeed the group has returned £31.7m of cash to shareholders through repurchases over the past five years. The company noted in its annual report that it monitors its overall level of financial gearing on a monthly basis to keep gearing levels within targets.

The extent to which the debt/equity is high or low geared has an effect on the earnings per share (eps) of the company:

■ if profits are increasing, then higher gearing is preferable
■ if profits are decreasing, then lower gearing or no gearing is preferred.

Similarly, the argument applies to the riskiness attached to capital repayments. If a company goes into liquidation, lenders have priority over shareholders with regard to capital repayment. So, the more highly geared the company the less chance there is of ordinary shareholders being repaid in full.

The many types of short- and long-term capital available to companies leads to complexity, but also the expectation that overall financial risks may be reduced through improved matching of funding with operational needs. The gearing position of the company may be considered in many ways depending on whether the long-term or overall capital structure is being analysed. It may also be analysed by concentrating on the income position rather than purely on the capital structure.

Financial gearing relates to the relationship between a company's borrowings, which includes debt, and its share capital and reserves. Concerning capital structure, gearing calculations may be based on a number of different capital values. All UK plcs disclose their net debt to equity ratio in their annual reports and accounts.

The two financial ratios that follow are the two most commonly used (see also Chapter 7). Both ratios relate to financial gearing, which is the relationship between a company's borrowings, which includes both prior charge capital and long-term debt, and shareholders' funds (share capital plus reserves).

$$gearing = \frac{long\text{-}term\ debt}{equity\ +\ long\text{-}term\ debt}$$

$$debt\ equity\ ratio,\ or\ leverage = \frac{long\text{-}term\ debt}{equity}$$

Worked example 14.3 illustrates the calculation of both ratios.

Worked example 14.3

Two companies have different gearing. Company A is financed totally by 20,000 £1 ordinary shares, whilst company B is financed partly by 10,000 £1 ordinary shares and a £10,000 10% loan. In all other respects the companies are the same. They both have assets of £20,000 and both make the same profit before interest and tax (PBIT).

	A £	B £
Assets	20,000	20,000
less 10% loan	–	(10,000)
	20,000	10,000
Ordinary shares	20,000	10,000

$$gearing = \frac{long\text{-}term\ debt}{equity\ +\ long\text{-}term\ debt} = \frac{0}{20,000 + 0} = 0\% \quad \frac{10,000}{10,000 + 10,000} = 50\%$$

$$debt\ equity\ ratio = \frac{long\text{-}term\ debt}{equity} = \frac{0}{20,000} = 0\% \quad \frac{10,000}{10,000} = 100\%$$

Company B must make a profit before interest of at least £1,000 to cover the interest cost of the 10% loan. Company A does not have any minimum PBIT requirement because it has no debt.

Company A is lower geared and considered less risky in terms of profitability than company B which is a more highly geared company. This is because PBIT of a lower geared company is more likely to be sufficiently high to cover interest charges and provide a return for equity shareholders.

As we have seen, gearing calculations can be made in a number of ways, and may also be based on earnings and interest relationships in addition to capital values. For example:

$$\text{dividend cover (times)} = \frac{\text{earnings per share (eps)}}{\text{dividend per share}}$$

This ratio indicates the number of times the profits attributable to the equity shareholders covers the actual dividends paid and payable for the period. Financial analysts usually adjust their calculations for any exceptional items of which they may be aware.

$$\text{interest cover (times)} = \frac{\text{profit before interest and tax}}{\text{interest payable}}$$

This ratio calculates the number of times the interest payable is covered by profits available for such payments. It is particularly important for lenders to determine the vulnerability of interest payments to a drop in profit. The following ratio determines the same vulnerability in cash terms.

$$\text{cash interest cover} = \frac{\text{net cash inflow from operations} + \text{interest received}}{\text{interest paid}}$$

Progress check 14.3

What is gearing? Outline some of the ways in which it may be calculated.

Worked example 14.4

Swell Guys plc is a growing company that manufactures equipment for fitting out small cruiser boats. Its planned expansion involves investing in a new factory project costing £4m. Chief Executive, Guy Rope, expects the 12-year project to add £0.5m to profit before interest and tax each year. Next year's operating profit is forecast at £5m, and dividends per share are forecast at the same level as last year. Tax is not expected to be payable over the next few years due to tax losses that have been carried forward.

Swell Guys last two years' results are as follows:

	Last year £m	Previous year £m
Income statement for the year ended 31 December		
Revenue	18	15
Operating costs	16	11
Operating profit	2	4
Finance costs	1	1
Profit before tax	1	3
Income tax expense	0	0
Profit after tax	1	3
Dividends	1	1
Retained profit	0	2

	Last year £m	Previous year £m
Balance sheet as at 31 December		
Non-current assets	8	9
Current assets		
Inventories	7	4
Trade and other receivables	4	3
Cash and cash equivalents	1	2
Total current assets	12	9
Total assets	20	18
Current liabilities		
Borrowings and finance leases	4	2
Trade and other payables	5	5
Total current liabilities	9	7
Non-current liabilities		
Loan	6	6
Total liabilities	15	13
Net assets	5	5
Equity		
Share capital (25p ordinary shares)	2	2
Retained earnings	3	3
Total equity	5	5

Swell Guys is considering two options:

(a) Issue of £4m 15% loan stock repayable in five years' time.
(b) Rights issue of 4m 25p ordinary shares at £1 per share after expenses.

For each of the options the directors would like to see:

(i) how the retained earnings will look for next year
(ii) how earnings per share will look for next year
(iii) how the capital and reserves will look at the end of next year
(iv) how long-term loans will look at the end of next year
(v) how gearing will look at the end of next year.

(i) **Swell Guys plc forecast income statement for next year ended 31 December**
    Operating profit £5m + £0.5m from the new project

		New debt £m	New equity £m
Operating profit		5.5	5.5
Interest payable	[1.0 + 0.6]	1.6	1.0
Profit before tax		3.9	4.5
Income tax expense		0.0	0.0
Profit after tax		3.9	4.5
Dividends		1.0	1.5
Retained profit		2.9	3.0

(ii) Earnings per share

$$\frac{\text{Profit available for ordinary shareholders}}{\text{Number of ordinary shares}} \quad \frac{£3.9\text{m}}{8\text{m}} = 48.75\text{p} \qquad \frac{£4.5\text{m}}{12\text{m}} = 37.5\text{p}$$

(iii) Capital and reserves

		As at 31 December			
		New debt		**New equity**	
		£m		**£m**	
Share capital (25p ordinary shares)	(8m shares)	2.0	(12m shares)	3.0	
Share premium account		0.0		3.0	
Retained earnings		5.9		6.0	
		7.9		12.0	
		10.0			

(iv) Long-term loans   [6 + 4]   10.0   6.0

(v) Gearing

$$\frac{\text{long-term debt}}{\text{equity} + \text{long-term debt}} \quad \frac{£6\text{m} + £4\text{m}}{£7.9\text{m} + £6\text{m} + £4\text{m}} = 55.9\% \quad \frac{£6\text{m}}{£12\text{m} + £6\text{m}} = 33.3\%$$

Progress check 14.4

Explain how a high interest cover ratio can reassure a prospective lender

The weighted average cost of capital (WACC)

The weighted average cost of capital (WACC) may be defined as the average cost of the total financial resources of a company, i.e. the shareholders' equity and the financial debt.

If we represent the market value of shareholders' equity as E and the market value of financial debt as D then the relative proportions of equity and debt to the total are:

$$\frac{E}{E + D} \text{ and } \frac{D}{E + D}$$

The cost of equity to the company is also the expected return on equity, the return the shareholders expect from their investment. If we represent the cost of shareholders' equity as e and the cost of financial debt as d, and t is the rate of corporation tax, then we can provide a formula to calculate WACC. The return on shareholder equity comprises both cash flows from dividends and increases in the share price. We will return to how the cost of equity may be derived from these in a later section in this chapter.

Interest on debt capital is an allowable deduction for purposes of corporate taxation and so the cost of share capital and the cost of debt capital are not properly comparable costs. The tax relief on debt interest should be recognised in calculating the cost of debt capital, to arrive at an

after-tax cost of debt. Therefore the cost of debt d, must be multiplied by $(1 - t)$, which is called the
tax shield, to reflect the tax benefit. The weighted average cost of capital is therefore:

$$WACC = \left\{ \frac{E}{(E + D)} \times e \right\} + \left\{ \frac{D}{(E + D)} \times d\,(1 - t) \right\}$$

The real value of a company may be determined by its WACC. The lower the WACC then the higher the net present values of its future cash flows and therefore the higher its market value. The determination of the optimum D/E ratio is one of the most difficult tasks facing the finance director.

Worked example 14.5

Fleet Ltd has the following financial structure:

$$\frac{E}{E + D} = 60\% \text{ equity to debt plus equity ratio}$$

$$\frac{D}{E + D} = 40\% \text{ debt to debt plus equity ratio}$$

$e = 15\%$ return on equity (this may be taken as given for the purpose of this example)
$d = 10\%$ lower risk, so lower than the return on equity
$t = 30\%$ rate of corporation tax

We can calculate the WACC for Fleet Ltd, and evaluate the impact on WACC of a change in capital structure to equity 40% and debt 60%.

Calculation of WACC for Fleet Ltd with the current financial structure:

$$WACC = \left\{ \frac{E}{(E + D)} \times e \right\} + \left\{ \frac{D}{(E + D)} \times d\,(1 - t) \right\}$$

$$WACC = (60\% \times 15\%) + \{40\% \times 10\%\,(1 - 30\%)\} = 11.8\%$$

If the company decides to change its financial structure so that equity is 40% and debt is 60% of total financing, then WACC becomes:

$$(40\% \times 15\%) + \{60\% \times 10\%\,(1 - 30\%)\} = 10.2\%$$

So it appears that the company has reduced its WACC by increasing the relative weight from 40% to 60% of the cheapest financial resource, debt, in its total financing. However, this may not be true in practice because as the debt/equity ratio of the company increased from 0.67 (40/60) to 1.50 (60/40) the company's financial risk has also increased. Therefore the providers of the financial resources will require a higher return on their investment. There is a well-established correlation between risk and return. So, it may not be correct to calculate the WACC using the same returns on equity and debt, as both may have increased.

One of the consequences of this is the problem for a company of calculating an accurate WACC. WACC is based on the relative proportions and costs of debt and equity capital that are continually changing as the company takes on additional debt or repays debt or issues additional share capital.

The risks and costs associated with debt capital and equity capital are different and subject to continual change, and may vary from industry to industry and between different types of business. Measurement of the D/E ratio may therefore not be a straightforward task, particularly for diversified groups of companies. Companies in different markets and indeed diversified companies that have trading divisions operating within different markets and producing different products face different levels of risk. If division A operates with a higher risk than division B then the required rate of return on A's investments should be higher than the hurdle rate of return on B's investments. The difference is 'paying' for the difference in risk. This is an important principle but very difficult to implement in practice.

In a later section, we will look at ways in which both the cost of equity and the cost of debt to the company may be determined.

There are many arguments for and against the use of WACC for investment appraisal. Its use is argued on the basis that:

■ new investments must be financed by new sources of funds – retained earnings, new share issues, new loans, and so on
■ the cost of capital to be applied to new project evaluation must reflect the cost of new capital
■ the WACC reflects the company's long-term future capital structure, and capital costs; if this were not so, the current WACC would become irrelevant because eventually it would not relate to any actual cost of capital.

It is argued that the current WACC should be used to evaluate projects, because a company's capital structure changes only very slowly over time; therefore, the marginal cost of new capital should be roughly equal to the WACC. If this view is correct, then by undertaking investments that offer a return in excess of the WACC, a company will increase the market value of its ordinary shares in the long run. This is because the excess returns would provide surplus profits and dividends for the shareholders.

The arguments against the use of WACC are based on the criticisms of the assumptions made that justify the use of WACC:

■ new investments have different risk characteristics from the company's existing operations therefore the return required by investors may go up or down if the investments are made, because their business risk is perceived to be higher or lower
■ finance raised to fund a new investment
   – may substantially change the capital structure and perceived risk of investing in the company
   – may determine whether debt or equity used to finance the project will change the perceived risk of the entire company, which
   – must be taken into account in the investment appraisal
■ many companies raise floating rate debt capital as well as fixed rate debt capital, having a variable rate that changes every few months in line with current market rates; this is difficult to include in a WACC calculation, the best compromise being to substitute an 'equivalent' fixed debt rate in place of the floating rate.

Progress check 14.5

What is WACC and why is it so important?

Cost of debt and equity capital

We have introduced the concept of risk and its correlation with returns on investments. The relationship between risk and return is also one of the key concepts relating to determination of the cost of debt and equity capital. It is an important concept and so we will briefly explore risk a little further, with regard to investments in companies. We shall discuss the cost of debt based on future income flows, that is, interest. We shall similarly discuss the cost of equity based on future income flows, that is, dividends. This will also provide an introduction to risk and the **beta factor (β)** and the **capital asset pricing model (CAPM)**.

The interest rate paid on a loan is known almost with certainty. Even if the debt carries a floating or variable interest rate it is far easier to estimate than the expected dividend flows on ordinary shares. Debt comprises debentures, loans etc., and may be corporate or government debt. Their levels of risk are different, and some debt may be secured on specific assets or the assets of a company in general.

The cost of debt is generally based on the current market rate for debt having a specific level of risk. Two of the main differences between the cost of equity and the cost of debt are:

- the different levels of risk between debt and equity
- the tax shield is applicable to interest paid on debt, but not to equity dividends paid.

The cost of servicing debt capital is based on the yearly or half-yearly interest payment, which is an allowable expense for tax. The cost of repayment of a loan, or debt, depends on the type of loan. Loans may be irredeemable and traded on the stock market, with a market value like any other security. Or loans may be redeemable at a specific date. We will look at the calculation of the cost to a company of a redeemable loan and also the cost of an irredeemable loan.

If

d = cost of debt capital
i = annual loan interest rate
L = the current market value of the loan

then, if the loan is redeemable, and if R is the loan value at redemption after n years, then:

$$L = i/(1 + d) + i/(1 + d)^2 + i/(1 + d)^3 + \cdots + (i + R)/(1 + d)^n$$

The cost of debt in the above equation can be calculated by trial and error, by interpolation, or using the appropriate Excel function.

For an irredeemable loan the interest is payable in perpetuity (for ever), so:

$$L = i/(1 + d) + i/(1 + d)^2 + i/(1 + d)^3 + \cdots \text{ to infinity}$$

which simplifies to:

$$L = i/d$$

Because interest payable on loans is an allowable deduction for corporation tax the cost of debt d is calculated by adjusting the interest rate by $(1 - t)$, the tax shield, to provide an after-tax rate of interest.

Therefore, if t = the rate of corporation tax and we rearrange the above equation then:

$$d = \frac{i \times (1 - t)}{L}$$

The value of L, the market value of the debt, is generally stated as a percentage of the nominal value of the debt.

By rearranging the formula it can be seen that L, market value of the debt, is dependent on the level of future returns, the interest rate paid, which is determined by the level of risk associated with the investment, and the rate of corporation tax:

$$L = \frac{i \times (1 - t)}{d}$$

Worked example 14.6

Owen Cash plc pays 12% interest (i) per annum on an irredeemable debt of £1m, with a nominal value of £100. The corporation tax rate (t) is currently 50%. The market value of the debt is currently £90, and therefore L, expressed as a percentage of the nominal value, is 90%.

What is Owen Cash plc's cost of debt?

$$d = \text{cost of debt capital}$$

$$d = \frac{i \times (1 - t)}{L} = \frac{12\% \times (1 - 50\%)}{90\%}$$

$$d = \frac{12\% \times 50\%}{90\%} = 6.7\%$$

In a similar way to cost of debt, the cost of equity to a company may be determined by looking at future income flows. In the case of equity or ordinary shares this future income is dividends. A difference between this method and the method applied to debt is that there is no tax relief for dividend payments.

The value of an ordinary share may be simply expressed as the present value of its expected future dividend flows:

$$S = v_1/(1 + e) + v_2/(1 + e)^2 + v_3/(1 + e)^3 + \cdots + v_n/(1 + e)^n$$

where
e = cost of equity capital
v = expected future dividends for n years
S = the current market value of the share

If dividends are expected to remain level over a period of time the formula may be simplified to:

$$S = \frac{v}{e}$$

Therefore, the cost of equity to the company would be:

$$e = \frac{v}{S}$$

Dividends payable on a particular share rarely stay constant from year to year. They may be assumed to grow at a regular rate. This so-called dividend growth model approach to the cost of equity may then be used with the above formula revised as:

$$S = v/(e - G)$$

where G = the expected future dividend growth rate, and v = next year's dividend.
The cost of equity may then be stated as:

$$e = \frac{v}{S} + G$$

Worked example 14.7

Cher Alike plc has 3m ordinary shares in issue that currently have a market price (S) of £2.71. The board have already recommended next year's dividend (v) at 17p per share. The chairman, Sonny Daze, is forecasting that dividends will continue to grow (G) at 4.2% per annum for the foreseeable future.

What is Cher Alike plc's cost of equity?

$$e = \text{cost of equity capital}$$

$$e = \frac{v}{S} + G = \frac{0.17}{2.71} + 4.2\%$$

$$e = 0.063 + 0.042 = 10.5\%$$

The cost of equity to a company may alternatively be derived using the capital asset pricing model (CAPM). We will look at this approach to risk, and at how some risk may be diversified away by using a spread (or portfolio) of investments.

Progress check 14.6

In broad terms how are the costs of debt and equity determined?

Cost of equity and risk, CAPM and the β factor

Whenever any investment is made there will be some risk involved. The actual return on investment in ordinary shares (equity capital) may be better or worse than hoped for. Unless the investor settles for risk-free securities a certain element of risk is unavoidable.

However, investors in companies or in projects can diversify their investments in a suitably wide portfolio. Some investments may do better and some worse than expected. In this way, average returns should turn out much as expected. Risk that can be diversified away is referred to as **unsystematic risk**.

Some investments are by their very nature more risky than others. This is nothing to do with chance variations in actual compared with expected returns, it is inherent risk that cannot be diversified away. This type of risk is referred to as **systematic risk** (or **market risk**). The investor must therefore accept this risk, unless he or she invests entirely in risk-free investments. In return for accepting systematic risk an investor will expect to earn a return, which is higher than the return on a risk-free investment.

The amount of systematic risk depends, for example, on the industry or the type of project. If an investor had a completely balanced portfolio of shares he or she would incur exactly the same systematic risk as the average systematic risk of the stock market as a whole, which of course is highly unlikely in practice. The capital asset pricing model (CAPM) is mainly concerned with how systematic risk is measured and how systematic risk affects required returns and share prices. It was first formulated for investments in shares on the stock exchange, but is now also used for company investments in capital projects.

CAPM considers the market return, and also the risk-free return and volatility of a share. Share-holders expect returns that are in terms of dividends and capital growth in the share price. However, actual shareholder returns may be higher or lower than expected, because of risk. Systematic risk is measured using what are known as beta factors. A beta factor (β) is the measure of the volatility of a share in terms of systematic or market risk.

CAPM is a statement of the principles outlined above. The relationship between the expected return on a company's shares, its cost of equity, and the average market return may be measured by its beta (note that $\beta = 1$ for the stock market as a whole). An investor can use the beta factor in such a way that a high factor will automatically suggest a share is to be avoided because of considerably high risk in the past. For example, a share with a β of 0.8 means less systematic risk than the market – if the market increases by 10% the share price increases by 8%; a share with a β of 1.5 means more systematic risk than the market – if the market increases by 10% the share price increases by 15%. Consider the impact on the beta factor of a company caused by the resignation from the board of the chief financial officer, together with the issue of a profits warning by the company.

CAPM may be used to calculate the return on a company's shares while making some allowance for the systematic risk relating to that company. CAPM can be stated as follows:

the expected return from a security = the risk-free rate of return, plus a premium for market risk, adjusted by a measure of the volatility of the security

If

R_s	is the expected return from an individual security
β_e	is the equity beta factor for the individual security
R_f	is the risk-free rate of return
R_m	is the return from the market as a whole
$(R_m - R_f)$	is the market risk premium

$$R_s = R_f + \{\beta_e \times (R_m - R_f)\}$$

It should be remembered that CAPM considers systematic risk only, and is based on an assumption of market equilibrium.

The β factor of a security may be calculated using the market and an individual company's information over an extended period of time as follows:

covariance of the returns of the security and the market
standard deviation of the returns of the market squared

which equals

standard deviation of the security's returns ×
correlation coefficient between the security's returns and the market returns
standard deviation of the returns of the market

This method involves collecting data on the periodic returns of the market and the particular security and using regression analysis or plotting security returns (y axis) against market returns (x axis) over a period of time. The β_e of the security is the slope of the line of best fit.

Alternatively, β values are obtainable from a variety of sources and it is perhaps easier to leave it to the experts. There are many analysts that specialise in the charting of the volatility of shares and markets, and their findings may regularly be found in the UK financial press. The Risk Measurement Service of the London Business School publishes a quarterly report of companies' beta coefficients. They calculate the betas of all major companies by regressing their monthly returns against the monthly returns of the Financial Times actuaries' all-share index over the previous five years.

A variation of the above β relationship may be used to establish an equity cost of capital to use in project appraisal. The cost of equity e, equates to the expected return from an individual security R_s, and the beta value for the company's equity capital β_e equates to the beta factor for the individual security β. CAPM is an alternative method to the dividend growth model that we discussed above, which may be used to calculate the cost of equity:

$$e = R_f + \{\beta_e \times (R_m - R_f)\}$$

Worked example 14.8

Bittaboth plc has ordinary shares in issue with a market value four times the value of its debt capital. The debt is considered to be risk-free and pays 11% (R_f) before tax. The beta value of Bittaboth's equity capital has been estimated at 0.9 (β_e) and the average market return on equity capital is 17% (R_m). Corporation tax is at 50% (t).

We can calculate Bittaboth plc's WACC.

e = cost of equity capital

$e = R_f + \{\beta_e \times (R_m - R_f)\} = 11\% + \{0.9 \times (17\% - 11\%)\}$

$e = 0.11 + (0.9 \times 0.06) = 0.164 = 16.4\%$

d = cost of debt capital

which after tax is $i \times (1 - t)$ or 11% $\times$ 50% = 5.5%

Any capital projects that Bittaboth may wish to consider may be evaluated using its WACC, which may be calculated as:

{equity/(debt + equity) ratio $\times$ return on equity} + {debt/(debt + equity) ratio $\times$ after tax cost of debt}

$$(4/5 \times 16.4\%) + (1/5 \times 5.5\%) = 14.2\%$$

14.2% is Bittaboth's weighted average cost of capital (WACC).

Progress check 14.7

Describe what is meant by systematic risk and unsystematic risk.

Return on equity and financial structure

The important formula that follows shows the return on equity (ROE) as a function of return on investment (ROI) and the financial structure, leverage or gearing of the company, where:

D = debt capital
E = equity capital
t = corporation tax rate
i = interest rate on debt
ROI = return on investment
ROE = return on equity

$$ROE = \{ROI \times (1 - t)\} + \{(ROI - i) \times (1 - t) \times D/E\}$$

Worked example 15.5 illustrates the use of this relationship and also gives a general rule derived from it.

Worked example 14.9

A hospital equipment manufacturing company, Nilby Mouth plc, makes an operating profit (PBIT) of £10m on sales of £100m and with a total investment of £60m. The investment is financed by equity (E) of £40m and debt (D) of £20m with an interest rate (i) of 10%. Assume the corporation tax rate (t) is 50%.

We will calculate:

(i)   the current return on equity (ROE)
(ii)   the ROE if financing were changed so that debt was £40m and equity was £20m
(iii)   the current ROE if operating profit were reduced to £4m
(iv)   the ROE if operating profit were reduced to £4m and if financing were changed so that debt was £40m and equity was £20m.

(Figures in £m)

(i) Calculation of return on equity (ROE)

Profit before interest and tax, or operating profit PBIT = 10

Profit before tax PBT = $10 - (20 \times 10\%) = 8$

Profit after tax PAT = $8 \times (1 - 50\%) = 4$

Return on sales ROS = $4/100 = 4\%$

Return on investment ROI (before interest and tax) = $10/60 = 16.7\%$

Debt/equity ratio D/E = $20/40 = 50\%$

ROE = $ROI \times (1 - t) + \{(ROI - i) \times (1 - t) \times D/E\}$

Return on equity ROE = $\{16.7\% \times (1 - 50\%)\} + \{(16.7\% - 10\%) \times (1 - 50\%) \times 50\%\}$

$$= 0.10025 \text{ or } 10\%$$

(ii) Calculation of ROE if financing is changed so that debt is £40m and equity is £20m

PBIT = 10   PBT = 10 − (40 × 10%) = 6   PAT = 6 × (1 − 50%) = 3

ROS = 3/100 = 3%

ROI (before interest and tax) = 10/60 = 16.7%

D/E = 40/20 = 200%

ROE = {16.7% × (1 − 50%)} + {(16.7% − 10%) × (1 − 50%) × 200%}

$\qquad$ = 0.15050 or 15%

Return on sales has reduced, whereas return on equity has increased.

(iii) Calculation of ROE if the operating profit were reduced to £4m

PBIT = 4 PBT = 4 − (20 × 10%) = 2   PAT = 2 × (1 − 50%) = 1

ROS = 1/100 = 1%

ROI (before interest and tax) = 4/60 = 6.7%

D/E = 20/40 = 50%

ROE = {6.7% × (1 − 50%)} + {(6.7% − 10%) × (1 − 50%) × 50%} = 0.02525 or 2.5%

(iv) Calculation of ROE if financing is changed so that debt is £40m and equity is £20m

PBIT = 4 PBT = 4 − (40 × 10%) = 0   PAT = 0 × (1 − 50%) = 0

ROS = 0/100 = 0%

ROI (before interest and tax) = 4/60 = 6.7%

D/E = 40/20 = 200%

ROE = {6.7% × (1 − 50%)} + {(6.7% − 10%) × (1 − 50%) × 200%} = 0.00050 or 0.05%

Return on sales and return on equity are both zero.

The general rule apparent from the relationships outlined in Worked example 14.9 is:

- when ROI is greater than i $\qquad$ the higher the D/E, the higher the ROE
- when ROI is less than i $\qquad$ the higher the D/E, the lower the ROE.

However, even if the ROI is greater than the debt interest the company's bankers may not automatically allow the D/E to increase indefinitely. The company's risk increases as the D/E or leverage increases, in terms of its commitment to high levels of interest payments, and bankers will not tolerate too high a level of risk; they will also be inclined to increase the debt interest rate as D/E increases. Shareholders will have the same reaction – they are happy with an increase in ROE but realise that they also have to face a higher risk.

For a high-growth company, to limit the shareholders' investment, the company will have a tendency to increase D/E and therefore ROE, but also the financial risk. The press (for example Questor in the *Daily Telegraph*) usually comments when a plc is seen to embark on a policy of increased borrowings and increasing its gearing ratio, which alerts the reader to 'increased financial risk'. Plcs are usually prepared and ready for such comments in order to respond with their 'defence' of such a policy.

Progress check 14.8

Discuss why bankers may refuse additional lending to a company as its debt/equity ratio increases.

Growth of a company may be looked at using income statement horizontal analyses. Use of this technique, which was covered in Chapter 8, presents all numbers in the income statement as a percentage using a base year, which is 100, for year-on-year comparison. Financial commentators usually begin articles on the performance of plcs by comparing the current year performance with the previous year, and then attempt a forecast of future performance. This is an example of a basic horizontal analysis that focuses on sales revenues and profits. Only a few companies actually succeed in growing year on year over an extended period (for example, 10 years).

Economic value added (EVA™) and market value added (MVA)

Maximisation of shareholder wealth continues to be the prime objective with which managers of companies are charged. We have considered various ways to measure managers' financial performance (see Chapter 12). The extent to which success in particular performance measures aligns with shareholder wealth is particularly relevant. Equally important are the ways in which managers are motivated to maximise shareholder wealth. As we saw in Chapter 12, in most organisations managerial remuneration provides the link between the measures of financial performance and shareholder value.

Financial performance measures such as a company's share price are commonly used to indicate how well the company is doing. However, it may be questioned how directly the share price reflects decisions that have been taken by management. In the context of managers' performance against budget targets, and the company's overall financial performance, we have previously discussed the merits and otherwise of other performance measures such as profit after tax, earnings per share, dividends, return on capital employed, and cash flow, etc. Each has its limitations, but measures based on cash flow are now becoming accepted as perhaps better indicators than profit-related measures.

During the mid-1980s, Rappaport developed shareholder value analysis, from which the American firm Stern Stewart Management Services evolved concepts known as economic value added (EVA), which we introduced in Chapter 12, and **market value added (MVA)**. Through EVA, Stern Stewart attempted to reconcile the need for a performance measure correlated with shareholder wealth, and a performance measure which was also responsive to actions taken by managers. By the mid-1990s over 200 global companies had been in discussion with Stern Stewart with regard to adoption of EVA; Lucas Varity in the UK and Coca-Cola in the USA were already successful users of EVA.

If we assume that the organisation's objective is to maximise shareholder wealth then this will be achieved if new projects are taken on and existing projects are allowed to continue only if they create value. Investment in capital projects may be made only on the basis of choosing those with a positive net present value (NPV). However, NPV cannot be applied to remuneration schemes because it is a summary measure based on projected cash flows and not realised performance.

Companies usually turn to company earnings and cash flow (which are termed flow measures) for management remuneration schemes. EVA supports the same sort of recommendations that NPV provides at the project level, but also provides a better measure of management performance because it rewards for earnings generated, whilst also including charges for the amount of capital employed to create those earnings.

If profit after tax = PAT
weighted average cost of capital = WACC
adjusted book value of net assets = NA
then we may define EVA as:

$$\text{EVA} = \text{PAT} - (\text{WACC} \times \text{NA})$$

It should be noted that to calculate EVA the PAT should be adjusted by adding back interest paid. Profit before interest paid is therefore used to calculate EVA to avoid double counting because a charge for financing is being made by deducting WACC in the calculation.

Worked example 14.10, which uses some techniques covered in Chapter 15, will illustrate the calculation of EVA and its relationship with NPV.

Worked example 14.10

A manager has to choose between three mutually exclusive projects. The company may invest:

£50,000 in project A, or
£110,000 in project B, or
£240,000 in project C

Project A is expected to generate incremental profits after tax (PAT) of £50,000 in year one, £40,000 in year two (total £90,000), after which the project is terminated.
Project B is expected to generate incremental PATs of £45,000 in year one, £70,000 in year two, £70,000 in year three (total £185,000), after which the project is terminated.
Project C is expected to generate incremental PATs of £55,000 in year one, £75,000 in year two, £80,000 in year three (total £210,000), after which the project is terminated.
The company's WACC is 10% per annum. Capital levels may be assumed to be maintained throughout the life of each project. That is, each year's new capital investment equals depreciation in that year.
Capital items are sold at their book value in the final year of each project, so free cash flow (operating cash flow less capital expenditure) will be equal to PAT each year except the final years when the capital costs are recovered.
We will assess which project the manager will choose if:

(i) his remuneration is tied to the NPV of the project
(ii) his remuneration is based on IRR
(iii) his remuneration is based on project earnings
(iv) his remuneration is based on EVA.

Using a discount rate of WACC at 10% per annum, we first calculate the NPVs of each project.

Year	Cash outflows £000	Cash inflows £000		Net cash flow £000	Discount factor at 10%	Present values £000
Project A						
0	−50			−50	1.00	−50.0
1		50		50	0.91	45.5
2		90	[40 + 50]	90	0.83	74.7
3		0		0	0.75	0.0
Total	−50	140		90		+70.2
Project B						
0	−110			−110	1.00	−110.0
1		45		45	0.91	40.9
2		70		70	0.83	58.1
3		180	[70 + 110]	180	0.75	135.0
Total	−110	295		185		+124.0

Project C

Year				Net cash flow	Discount factor	Present values
0	−240			−240	1.00	−240.0
1		55		55	0.91	50.0
2		75		75	0.83	62.3
3		320	[80 + 240]	320	0.75	240.0
Total	−240	450		210		+112.3

The IRR is the rate of return that would give an NPV of zero.

Interpolation or extrapolation techniques which we will cover in Chapter 15 may be used to derive the internal rate of return of each project.

For project C, if we assume a discount rate of 30%, we may calculate a revised NPV as follows:

Year	Cash outflows £000	Cash inflows £000	Net cash flow £000	Discount factor at 30%	Present values £000
0	−240		−240	1.00	−240.0
1		55	55	0.77	42.4
2		75	75	0.59	44.3
3		320	320	0.46	147.2
Total	−240	450	210		−6.1

We have already calculated the positive NPV for project C of £112,300 using a cost of capital of 10%. The IRR of project C must be at some point between 30% and 10% (difference 20%).

Using a similar calculation to that used in Figure 15.5 (Chapter 15):

$$\frac{£6,100}{x} = \frac{£112,300}{(20 - x)}$$

$$(£6,100 \times 20) - £6,100x = £112,300x$$

$$£122,000 = £118,400x$$

$$x = \frac{£122,000}{£118,400}$$

$$x = 1.03$$

Therefore, interpolation gives us an IRR of 30% less 1.03%, which equals 28.97% and may be rounded to 29%.

The IRRs of projects A and B may be calculated in the same way.

The cash flows, NPVs and IRRs of the three projects may be summarised as:

Project	PAT Year 1 £000	Year 2 £000	Year 3 £000	Cash out £000	Cash in Year 1 £000	Year 2 £000	Year 3 £000	Total cash flow £000	IRR %	NPV £000
A	50	40		−50	50	90 [40 + 50]		90	93	70.2
B	45	70	70	−110	45	70	180 [70 + 110]	185	53	124.0
C	55	75	80	−240	55	75	320 [80 + 240]	210	29	112.3

(i) Based on the highest NPV, project B at £124,000 is best for the company shareholders.

(ii) But if the manager's remuneration is based on IRR then he will choose project A at 93%.

(iii) If the manager is remunerated on total project earnings then he will choose project C at £210,000.

(iv) We can calculate the EVA for each project, which equals profit after tax for each period, less capital employed at the start of each period multiplied by the weighted average cost of capital.

	Project A		Project B		Project C	
	£000	EVA £000	£000	EVA £000	£000	EVA £000
Year						
1	50 − (50 × 10%)	45	45 − (110 × 10%)	34	55 − (240 × 10%)	31
2	40 − (50 × 10%)	35	70 − (110 × 10%)	59	75 − (240 × 10%)	51
3			70 − (110 × 10%)	59	80 − (240 × 10%)	56
Total		80		152		138

We may also calculate the NPV of the EVAs of each project, the present values of the EVAs:

Year	Discount factor at 10%	Project A EVA £000	NPV £000	Project B EVA £000	NPV £000	Project C EVA £000	NPV £000
1	0.91	45	41.0	34	30.9	31	28.2
2	0.83	35	29.1	59	48.9	51	42.3
3	0.75			59	44.2	56	42.0
Total		80	+70.1	152	+124.0	138	+112.5

This illustrates that EVAs actually equate to cash flows because their present values are the same as the NPV of each project. The small differences between the totals calculated for Project A and Project C are as a result of rounding differences.

If the manager is remunerated based on EVA it will be consistent with maximising NPV, which is best for shareholders.

We have seen from Worked example 14.10 that an earnings-based remuneration scheme may result in over-investment of capital whereas a scheme based on IRR may result in under-investment of capital. Use of EVA as a basis for management remuneration takes account of the fact that the use of capital is charged for by using WACC; additionally, at the project level, the present value of the EVAs gives the same result as NPVs derived from free cash flows. Compare the results in the project NPV tables with the NPVs of the EVAs of each project in Worked example 14.10.

Although the free cash flow NPVs gives the same result as the present values of the EVAs, EVA is more appropriate for remuneration schemes because, as well as being fundamentally related to shareholder value, it is a flow measure of performance. The reason is that flow measures of performance are needed for periodic remuneration because remuneration is designed to provide a flow of rewards. The other flow measure is cash flow. EVA is a better measure than that because it takes into account the cost of capital invested in the project.

Worked example 14.11

We will compute the EVA for 2008, 2009 and 2010 for a major plc from the following information.

			£m
Group cost of capital	5%		
Adjusted net assets		2010	750
		2009	715
		2008	631
Profit after tax		2010	550
		2009	526
		2008	498
Equity		2010	100
		2009	48
		2008	115
Net debt		2010	800
		2009	802
		2008	546

Year	Profit after tax £m	Adjusted net assets £m	5% cost of capital × net assets £m	EVA £m	EVA % of net profit
2010	550	750	37.50	512.50	93%
2009	526	715	35.75	490.25	93%
2008	498	631	31.55	466.45	94%

Note how the profits are being earned using borrowed funds to finance the group. The plc can earn a very high EVA by using borrowed funds.

We have talked about EVA in respect of projects, and that the present value of future EVAs equals the NPV derived from future free cash flows. At a company level, the present value of EVAs equals the market value added (MVA) of a business. This is defined as the difference between the market value of the company and the adjusted book values of its net assets.

EVA is a good financial performance measure because it answers the question of how well the company has performed in generating profits over a period, given the amount of capital tied up to generate those profits. However, the capital base is a difficult element to estimate in calculating EVA. The total net assets value on a balance sheet is not an accurate representation of either the liquidation value or the replacement cost value of the business. Stern Stewart considered more than 250 possible accounting adjustments to profit and the balance sheet to arrive at a valuation of the company's assets. In practice, most organisations find that no more than a dozen or so adjustments are truly significant, for example adding back interest to profit, and those relating to inventory valuations, depreciation calculations, goodwill and impairment, doubtful debt provision, leasing, deferred tax, and closure costs.

Further information about EVA may be obtained from the Stern Stewart's weblink at: *www.sternstewart.com/index.php?content=main*.

Worked example 14.12

We will compute the MVA for 2009 and 2010 from the following extracts from the annual report and accounts of a major plc, using the unadjusted value of net assets.

	2010	2009
Number of shares (5p)	950.2m	948.9m
Share price	278p	268p
Net assets	£1,097m	£1,437m

	2010	2009
Net assets	£1,097m	£1,437m
Market value	£2,641m	£2,543m
MVA	£1,544m	£1,106m

Progress check 14.9

What is economic value added (EVA) and what is it used for?

EVA probably does not change or add anything to the conclusions reached on the basis of conventional valuation analysis based on cash flow. EVA is primarily a behavioural tool that corrects possible distortions. However, along with most other financial measures, it fails to measure on an *ex post* basis. EVA is undoubtedly a very useful concept for measuring and evaluating management and company performance. It is not a cure for poor management and poor investment decisions but it raises the profile and the awareness of the costs of capital involved in undertaking projects and in running the business.

Summary of key points

- Sources of finance internal to a company are its retained earnings, extended credit from suppliers, and the benefits gained from the more effective management of its working capital.

- Short-term, external sources of finance include bank overdrafts and short-term loans.

- The two main sources of long-term, external finance available to a company are equity (ordinary shares), preference shares and debt (loans and debentures).

- Other sources of long-term, external finance available to UK companies include hybrid finance, leasing, and UK Government and European funding.

- Gearing, or the debt/equity ratio, is the relationship between the two sources of finance, loans and ordinary shares – a company having more debt capital than share capital is highly geared, and a company having more share capital than debt capital is low geared.

- The weighted average cost of capital (WACC) is the average cost of the total financial resources of a company, i.e. the shareholders' equity and the net financial debt, which may be used as the discount rate to evaluate investment projects, and as a measure of company performance.

- Both the cost of debt and the cost of equity are based on future income flows and the risk associated with such returns.

- A certain element of risk is unavoidable whenever any investment is made, and unless a market investor settles for risk-free securities, the actual return on investment in equity (or debt) capital may be better or worse than hoped for.

- Systematic risk may be measured using the capital asset pricing model (CAPM) and the β factor, in terms of its effect on required returns and share prices.

- The return on equity may be considered as a function of the gearing, or financial structure, of the company.

- The recently developed techniques of economic value added (EVA) and market value added (MVA) are widely becoming used in business performance measurement and as value creation incentives.

Assessment material

Questions

Q14.1   **(i)**   What are the main sources of long-term, external finance available to an organisation?

        (ii)   What are their advantages and disadvantages?

Q14.2   What are the advantages and disadvantages of convertible loans?

Q14.3   Why may leasing be considered as a long-term source of finance?

Q14.4   What are the implications for a company of different levels of gearing?

Q14.5   What are the advantages and disadvantages for a company in using WACC as a discount factor to evaluate capital projects?

Q14.6   Describe the ways in which the costs of debt and equity capital may be ascertained.

Q14.7   How does risk impact on the cost of debt and equity?

Q14.8   What is the β factor, and how may it be related to WACC?

Q14.9   How may a company's return on equity (ROE) be related to its financial structure?

Q14.10   In what way is company growth of such interest to shareholders?

Q14.11   Business performance may be evaluated to determine ways in which it can be improved upon. If managers are capable of delivering improved performance how can EVA be used to support this?

Discussion points

D14.1   The former owner and manager of a private limited company recently acquired by a large plc, of which he is now a board member, said: 'This company has grown very quickly over the past few years so that our sales revenue is now over £20m per annum. Even though we expect our revenue to grow further and double in the next two years I cannot see why we need to change our existing financing arrangements. I know we need to make some large investments in new machinery over the next two years but in the past we've always operated successfully using our existing bank overdraft facility, which has been increased as required, particularly when we've needed new equipment. I don't really see the need for all this talk about additional share capital and long-term loans.' Discuss.

D14.2   In the long run does it really matter whether a company is financed predominantly by ordinary shares or predominantly by loans? What's the difference?

D14.3   The marketing manager of a large UK subsidiary of a multinational plc: 'Surely the interest rate that we should use to discount cash flows in our appraisal of new capital investment projects should be our bank overdraft interest rate. I don't really see the relevance of the weighted average cost of capital (WACC) to this type of exercise.' Discuss.

D14.4   'Economic value added (EVA) is nothing more than just flavour of the month.' Discuss.

Exercises

Solutions are provided in Appendix 3 to all exercise numbers highlighted in colour.

Level I

E14.1   *Time allowed – 30 minutes*

A critically important factor required by a company to make financial decisions, for example the evaluation of investment proposals and the financing of new projects, is its cost of capital. One of the elements included in the calculation of a company's cost of capital is the cost of equity.

> **(i)   Explain in simple terms what is meant by the 'cost of equity capital' for a company.**

The relevant data for Normal plc and the market in general are given below.

Normal plc

Current price per share on the London Stock Exchange	£1.20
Current annual dividend per share	£0.10
Expected average annual growth rate of dividends	7%
β beta coefficient for Normal plc's shares	0.5

The market

Expected rate of return on risk-free securities	8%
Expected return on the market portfolio	12%

> **(ii)   Calculate the cost of equity capital for Normal plc, using two alternative methods:**
> **(a) the Capital Asset Pricing Model (CAPM)**
> **(b) a dividend growth model of your choice.**

E14.2   *Time allowed – 30 minutes*

Normal plc pays £20,000 a year interest on an irredeemable debenture, which has a nominal value of £200,000 and a market value of £160,000. The rate of corporation tax is 30%.

You are required to:

(i)   calculate the cost of the debt for Normal plc

(ii) calculate the weighted average cost of capital for Normal plc using the cost of equity calculated in Exercise E14.1 (ii) if Normal plc has ordinary capital of 300,000 £1 shares

(iii) comment on the impact on a company's cost of capital of changes in the rate of corporation tax

(iv) calculate Normal plc's WACC if the rate of corporation tax were increased to 50%.

Level II

E14.3   *Time allowed – 30 minutes*

Lucky Jim plc has the opportunity to manufacture a particular type of self-tapping screw, for a client company, that would become indispensable in a particular niche market in the engineering field.

Development of the product requires an initial investment of £200,000 in the project. It has been estimated that the project will yield cash returns before interest of £35,000 per annum in perpetuity.

Lucky Jim plc is financed by equity and loans, which are always maintained as two thirds and one third of the total capital respectively. The cost of equity is 18% and the pre-tax cost of debt is 9%. The corporation tax rate is 40%.

If Lucky Jim plc's WACC is used as the cost of capital to appraise the project, should the project be undertaken?

E14.4   *Time allowed – 30 minutes*

You are required to compute the MVA for 2009, 2010 and 2011 from the estimated information for a large supermarket group.

	2011	2010	2009
Number of shares	6.823m	6.823m	6.776m
Share price	261p	169p	177p
Adjusted net assets	£5,000m	£4,769m	£4,377m

E14.5   *Time allowed – 60 minutes*

Yor plc is a fast-growing, hi-tech business. Its income statement for the year ended 30 September 2010 and its balance sheet as at 30 September 2010 are shown below. The company has the opportunity to take on a major project that will significantly improve its profitability in the forthcoming year and for the foreseeable future. The cost of the project is £10m, which will result in large increases in sales, which will increase profit before interest and tax by £4m per annum. The directors of Yor plc have two alternative options of financing the project: the issue of £10m of 4% debentures at par, or a rights issue of 4m ordinary shares at a premium of £1.50 per share (after expenses).

Regardless of how the new project is financed, the directors will recommend a 10% increase in the dividend for 2010/2011. You may assume that the effective corporation tax rate is the same for 2010/2011 as for 2009/2010.

Yor plc
Income statement for the year ended 30 September 2010

	£m
PBIT	11.6
Finance costs	(1.2)
Profit before tax	10.4
Income tax expense	(2.6)
Profit for the year	7.8
Retained earnings 1 October 2009	5.8
	13.6
Dividends	(3.0)
Retained earnings 30 September 2010	10.6

Yor plc
Balance sheet as at 30 September 2010

	£m
Non-current assets	
Tangible	28.8
Current assets	
Inventories	11.2
Trade and other receivables	13.8
Cash and cash equivalents	0.7
Total current assets	25.7
Total assets	54.5
Current liabilities	
Trade and other payables	9.7
Dividends payable	1.6
Income tax payable	2.6
Total current liabilities	13.9
Non-current liabilities	
6% loan	20.0
Total liabilities	33.9
Net assets	20.6
Equity	
Share capital (£1 ordinary shares)	10.0
Retained earnings	10.6
Total equity	20.6

The directors of Yor plc would like to see your estimated income statement for 2010/2011, and a summary of the equity and debt at 30 September 2011, assuming:

(i)   the new project is financed by an issue of the debentures
(ii)   the new project is financed by the issue of new ordinary shares

To assist in clarification of the figures, you should show your calculations of:

(iii) eps for 2009/2010
(iv)   eps for 2010/2011, reflecting both methods of financing the new project

(v)   dividend per share for 2009/2010

(vi)   dividend per share for 2010/2011, reflecting both methods of financing the new project

Use the information you have provided in (i) and (ii) above to:

(vii) calculate Yor plc's gearing, reflecting both methods of financing the new project, and compare with its gearing at 30 September 2010

(viii) summarise the results for 2010/2011, recommend which method of financing Yor plc should adopt, and explain the implications of both on its financial structure.

E14.6   *Time allowed – 90 minutes*

Sparks plc is a large electronics company that produces components for CD players and iPods. It is close to the current year end and Sparks is forecasting profit after tax at £60m. The following two years' post-tax profits are each expected to increase by another £15m, and years four and five by another £10m each.

The forecast balance sheet for Sparks plc as at 31 December is as follows:

	£m
Non-current assets	500
Current assets	
Inventories	120
Trade and other receivables	160
Total current assets	280
Total assets	780
Current liabilities	
Borrowings and finance leases	75
Trade and other payables	75
Total current liabilities	150
Non-current liabilities	150
Total liabilities	300
Net assets	480
Equity	
Share capital (£1 ordinary shares)	220
Share premium account	10
Retained earnings	250
Total equity	480

Sparks plc has a large bank overdraft of £75m on which it pays a high rate of interest at 15%. The board would like to pay off the overdraft and obtain cheaper financing. Sparks also has loan capital of £150m on which it pays interest at 9% per annum. Despite its high level of debt Sparks is a profitable organisation. However, the board of directors is currently planning a number of new projects for the next year, which will cost £75m. These projects are expected to produce profits after tax of £8m in the first year and £15m a year ongoing for future years.

The board has discussed a number of financing options and settled on two of them for further consideration:

(1)   a one for four rights issue at £3.00 a share to raise £150m from the issue of 50m £1 shares

(2)   a convertible £150m debenture issue at 12% (pre tax) that may be converted into 45m ordinary shares in two years' time.

The equity share index has risen over the past year from 4,600 to the current 5,500, having reached 6,250. Sparks plc's ordinary shares are currently at a market price of £3.37. Gearing of companies in the same industry as Sparks plc ranges between 25% and 45%. In two years' time it is expected that all Sparks debenture holders will convert to shares or none will convert.

The rate of corporation tax is 50%. Repayment of the bank overdraft will save interest of £5.625m a year after tax.

The board requires some analysis of the numbers to compare against the current position:

(i)   if they make the rights issue
(ii) if they issue debentures
(iii) if the debentures are converted.

The analysis should show:

(a)   the impact on the balance sheet
(b)   the impact on the profit after tax
(c)   earnings per share
(d)   gearing
(e)   which option should be recommended to the board and why.

15

Investment appraisal
and the capital budget

Contents

Learning objectives

Completion of this chapter will enable you to:

- explain what is meant by an investment
- outline the key principles underlying investment selection methods
- explain what is meant by discounted cash flow (DCF)
- outline the strengths and weaknesses of the five investment appraisal methods
- consider investment selection using the appraisal methods of net present value (NPV) and internal rate of return (IRR)
- explain the effects of inflation, working capital requirements, length and timing of projects, taxation, and risk and uncertainty on investment appraisal calculations
- evaluate the impact of risk and the use of sensitivity analysis in decision-making
- consider the ways in which capital projects may be controlled and reviewed
- appreciate the importance of the project post-completion audit.

Introduction

We have seen in earlier chapters how the management accountant or the financial manager is involved with providing financial and non-financial information and analysis to enable managers to evaluate alternative proposals and to make decisions.

In Chapter 11 we had an introduction into the ways in which accounting and financial information may be used as an aid to decision-making. This chapter looks at the specific area of decision-making that relates to investment. Such decisions may relate to whether or not to invest in a project, or choices between investment in alternative projects which are competing for resources.

We will begin by looking at exactly what an investment is, and outlining the techniques used to decide on whether or not to invest, and how to choose between alternative investments.

We shall evaluate the advantages and disadvantages of the five main investment appraisal methods used by companies and consider examples that demonstrate their use. The most important of these are the discounted cash flow methods of net present value (NPV), and internal rate of return (IRR). The technique of discounted cash flow (DCF) will be fully explained.

In addition to the initial costs of an investment and the returns expected from it, a number of other factors usually need to be taken into account in investment decision-making. These include, for example, inflation, the need for working capital, taxation, and the length and timing of the project. We will consider the possible impact of these factors and how the effects of risk and uncertainty on the appraisal of investments may be quantified using sensitivity analysis.

Appraisal of an investment is more than an accounting exercise. An investment decision is a crucially significant and important decision for a business. It is usually a highly politically charged area in the management of an organisation, which if mismanaged is capable of destroying shareholder value. Once an investment decision has been made, the project may then be planned and implemented. This chapter closes with an introduction to the ways in which capital investment projects may be controlled and reviewed.

What is an investment?

For the accountant an **investment** appears within the assets section of the balance sheet under non-current assets. For the finance director an investment is any decision that implies expenditure 'today' with the expectation that it will generate cash inflows 'tomorrow'.

Investment decisions are extremely important because they are invariably concerned with the future survival, prosperity and growth of the organisation. A commercial organisation's primary objective of maximisation of shareholder wealth is a basic assumption that continues to hold true. Investments must be made not only to maintain shareholder wealth but more importantly to increase it. To meet the shareholder wealth maximisation objective it is crucial that those managing the organisation make optimal decisions that are based on the best information available and use of the most appropriate appraisal techniques.

At the corporate level, investment (in shares) relates to the amount that shareholders are willing to invest in the equity of a company in the expectation of future cash flows in the form of dividends and enhancement of share price. The level of future dividends and share price enhancement are in turn dependent on the extent to which the company is able to optimise returns on 'real' investment: investment in plant, machinery, working capital, new products, new projects, new businesses, and so on. There is a great deal of pressure on chief executives to ensure that profitable 'real' investments are made to provide sustained dividend growth and increasing share prices.

Investment decisions faced by companies are therefore financially driven, and so if performance is deemed inadequate or unlikely to meet shareholder expectations, then the pressure becomes even greater to identify alternative, more profitable projects. Decisions are made by managers and not by the management accountant. Levels of authority within the management hierarchy are determined by company policy. Companies normally establish limits at each management level for each type of decision, and for the level of expenditure allowed. The approval of one or more directors is normally required for all capital expenditure and for major projects.

Investment may appear in the balance sheet within non-current assets in line with the accountants' definition, for example land, buildings, plant, machinery, etc. It may also appear within the income statement in terms of public relations, staff training, or research and development. In some cases the amount of money gained as a result of making an investment is relatively easy to measure, such as cost savings, capacity increases, etc. In other cases, it may be impossible to measure the gains – company image, education, and so on. The amount of spend may be easily forecast, for example the costs of computerisation of a process to reduce the production of non-quality products. In other projects, such as research and development, costs may be more uncertain.

Regardless, an investment decision is required before spending shareholders' and lenders' funds. The decision made needs to be one that shareholders and lenders would be happy with; it is one that is expected to provide anticipated gains in real terms that greatly exceed the funds spent today, in other words a good return on the money invested. Otherwise the investment should not be made.

Progress check 15.1

Describe what is meant by investment.

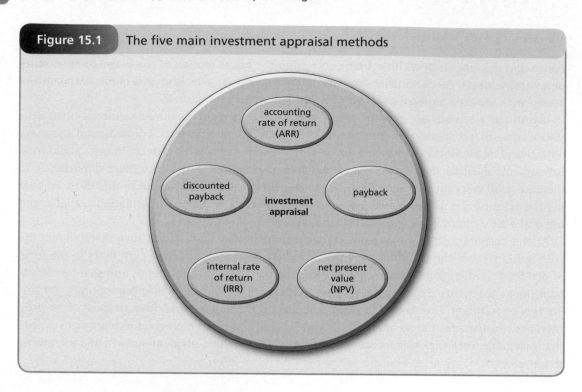

Figure 15.1   The five main investment appraisal methods

Investment appraisal methods

The five main methods used in investment appraisal are shown in Figure 15.1:

⮕ ■ the **accounting rate of return (ARR)** for appraising capital investment projects is based on profits and the costs of investment; it takes no account of cash flows or the time value of money

⮕ ■ the **payback** method for appraising capital investment projects is based on profits or cash flows, but also ignores the time value of money

⮕ ■ **net present value (NPV)** is one of the two most widely used investment decision methods, which are based on cash flow and the time value of money

⮕ ■ **internal rate of return (IRR)** is the second of the two most widely used investment decision methods, which are based on cash flow and the time value of money

⮕ ■ the **discounted payback** appraisal method is also based on cash flow and the time value of money.

We will look at examples of each of the five appraisal methods and the advantages and disadvantages of using each of them.

Accounting rate of return (ARR)

ARR is a simple measure which is sometimes used in investment appraisal. It is a form of return on capital employed. It is based on profits rather than cash flows and ignores the time value of money.

ARR may be calculated using:

$$\frac{\text{average accounting profit over the project life}}{\text{initial investment}} \times 100\%$$

There are alternative ways of calculating ARR. For example, total profit may be used instead of average profit, or average investment may be used instead of initial investment. It should be noted that in such a case if, for example, a machine originally cost £800,000 and its final scrap value was £50,000 then the average investment is £850,000/2, or £425,000. This is because the investment at the start is valued at £800,000, and the investment at the end of the project is £50,000. The average value over the period of the project is then the addition of these two values divided by two.

It should be noted that the method of calculation of ARR that is selected must be used consistently. However, ARR although simple to use is not recommended as a primary appraisal method. The method can provide an 'overview' of a new project but it lacks the sophistication of other methods (see the following explanations and methods). The impact of cash flows and time on the value of money really should be considered in investment appraisal, which we will discuss in a later section about key principles underlying investment selection criteria.

Worked example 15.1

Alpha Engineering Ltd is a company that has recently implemented an investment appraisal system. Its investment authorisation policy usually allows it to go ahead with a capital project if the accounting rate of return is greater than 25%. A project has been submitted for appraisal with the following data:

	£000	
Initial investment	100	(residual scrap value zero)
Per annum profit over the life of the project:		
Year		
1	25	
2	35	
3	35	
4	25	

The capital project can be evaluated using ARR.

$$\text{Average profit over the life of the project} = \frac{£25,000 + £35,000 + £35,000 + £25,000}{4}$$

$$= £30,000$$

$$\text{Accounting rate of return} = \frac{£30,000}{£100,000} \times 100\% = 30\%$$

which is greater than 25% and so acceptance of the project may be recommended.

Progress check 15.2

What is the accounting rate of return (ARR) and how is it calculated?

Payback

Payback is defined as the number of years it takes the future cash inflows, or profits, from a capital investment project to equal the initial investment in the project. An organisation may have a target payback period, above which projects are rejected. It is a simple but useful method and sometimes used as an initial screening process in evaluating two mutually exclusive projects. The project that pays back in the shortest time may on the face of it be the one to accept.

Worked example 15.2

Beta Engineering Ltd's investment authorisation policy requires all capital projects to pay back within three years, and views projects with shorter payback periods as even more desirable. Two mutually exclusive projects are currently being considered with the following data:

	Project 1 £000	Project 2 £000	
Initial investment	200	200	(residual scrap value zero)

Per annum cash inflows over the life of each project:

	Project 1		Project 2	
	Yearly cash flow £000	Cumulative cash flow £000	Yearly cash flow £000	Cumulative cash flow £000
Year				
1	60	60	100	100
2	80	140	150	250
3	80	220	30	280
4	90	310	10	290

The projects can be evaluated by considering their payback periods.

■ Project 1 derives total cash inflows of £310,000 over the life of the project and pays back the initial £200,000 investment three quarters of the way into year three, when the cumulative cash inflows reach £200,000 [£60,000 + £80,000 + £60,000 (75% of £80,000)].
■ Project 2 derives total cash inflows of £290,000 over the life of the project and pays back the initial £200,000 investment two thirds of the way into year two, when the cumulative cash inflows reach £200,000 [£100,000 + £100,000 (67% of £150,000)].
■ Both projects meet Beta Engineering Ltd's three-year payback criteria.
■ Project 2 pays back within two years and so is the preferred project, using Beta's investment guidelines.

Worked example 15.2 shows how payback may be used to compare projects. The total returns from a project should also be considered, in addition to the timing of the cash flows and their value in real terms. As with ARR, although its use is widespread amongst companies, payback is not recommended as a primary appraisal method. This method can also provide an 'overview' but should be the primary appraisal method used in larger companies or with regard to large projects because it ignores the time value of money.

Key principles underlying investment selection: cash flow, the time value of money and discounted cash flow (DCF)

The first two appraisal methods we have considered are simple methods that have limitations in their usefulness in making optimal capital investment decisions. The three further appraisal criteria are NPV, IRR and discounted payback. Whichever of these three methods is used, three basic principles apply: *Cash is king, Time value of money*, and *Discounted cash flow (DCF)*.

Cash is king

- Real funds can be seen in cash but not in accounting profit.
- Interest charges become payable as soon as money is made available, for example, from a lender to a borrower, not when an agreement is made or when a contract is signed.

Time value of money

Receipt of £100 today has greater value than receipt of £100 in one year's time. There are three reasons for this:

- The money could have been invested alternatively in, say, risk-free Government gilt-edged securities – in fact, the actual rate of interest that will have to be paid will be higher than the Government rate, to include a risk premium, if the investors are risk-free lenders. Generally, the higher the risk of the investment, the higher the return the investor will expect from it.
- Purchasing power will have been lost over a year due to inflation.
- The risk of non-receipt in one year's time.

Discounted cash flow (DCF)

Whichever of the three methods of appraisal is used:

- NPV
- IRR
- discounted payback,

a technique of discounting the projected cash flows of a project is used to ascertain its **present value**. Such methods are called discounted cash flow or DCF techniques. They require the use of a discount rate to carry out the appropriate calculation.

In Part I of this book (Chapters 3, 4 and 5) we discussed the differences between cash flow and profit and the advantages in using cash as a measure of financial performance.

We may assume that a specific sum of money may be held in reserve for some unforeseen future need, or used:

- to earn interest in a bank or building society account over the following year
- to buy some bottles of champagne (for example) at today's price
- to buy some bottles of champagne at the price in one year's time, which we may assume will be at a higher price because of inflation.

We may assume that the bank interest earned for one year, or the amount by which the price of champagne goes up due to inflation over one year is say 5%. Then we can see that £100 would be worth £105 if left in the bank for one year, and £100 spent on champagne today would actually buy just over £95 worth of champagne in one year's time because of its inflationary price increase.

The percentage rate by which the value of money may be eroded over one year is called the discount rate. The amount by which the value of, say, £100 is eroded over one year is calculated by dividing it by what is called the discount factor

$$\frac{£100}{(1 \ + \ \textbf{discount rate \%})}$$

So, for example, we could buy champagne in one year's time worth

$$£100/(1 \ + \ 5\%) \text{ or } £100/1.05 \ = \ £95.24$$

If the £95.24 were left for another year, and assuming that prices continued to increase at 5% per annum, we could buy champagne after a further year worth

$$£95.24/(1 \ + \ 5\%) \text{ or } £95.24/1.05 \ = \ £90.70$$

The yearly buying power continues to be reduced by application of the discount factor (or using the appropriate discount factor if the discount rate has changed). If the money is not used either to earn interest or to buy something, its value therefore normally becomes less and less. The discount factor for each year obviously depends on the discount rate. The successive year-by-year impact on £100 using an unchanging discount rate of 5% per annum may be illustrated using a simple graph showing its decreasing value from the start until the end of 10 years. The graph shown in Figure 15.2 illustrates the concept of the time value of money.

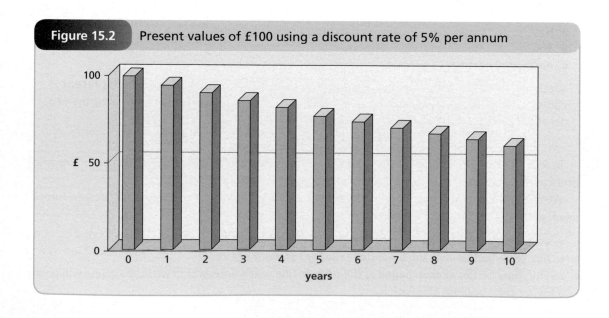

Figure 15.2 Present values of £100 using a discount rate of 5% per annum

If we consider a simple company balance sheet:

non-current assets + working capital = equity + financial debt

we can see that an investment in additional non-current assets or working capital (current assets – current liabilities) may be financed by equity or debt or by both.

Shareholders and lenders each require a return on their investment that is high enough to pay for the risk they are taking in funding the company and its assets. The expected return on equity will be higher than the cost of debt because the shareholders take a higher risk than the lenders. The average cost of these financial resources provided to the company is called the weighted average cost of capital (WACC). An important rule is that the return generated by a new investment undertaken by a company must be higher than the WACC, which reflects the discount rate – the rate of financing the investment. If, say, a company's WACC is 10%, an investment may be accepted if the expected rate of return is 15% or 16%. The importance of WACC and the significance of the debt/equity financial structure of a business was examined in detail in Chapter 14 when we looked at the cost of capital.

Other discount rates may be used, such as a borrowing interest rate or even a return on capital employed. However, the cost of capital – the WACC – is usually the hurdle rate, the opportunity cost of funds, that is used as the basis to evaluate new investments.

If r represents the cost of capital (the discount rate), and n the number of periods, e.g. years, these can be used to derive a:

present value discount factor, which is $1/(1 + r)^n$

where n may have a value from 0 to infinity.

(Note the similarity between this and the way we calculated the present values of £100 illustrated in Fig. 15.2.)

Let's consider a project where the initial investment in year 0 is I, and each subsequent year's net cash flows are CF_1, CF_2, CF_3, CF_4 and so on for n years up to CF_n. If the cost of capital (or discount rate) is r, then the present value of the cash flows is called the net present value or NPV.

Net present value of the cash flows (NPV)
$$= -I + CF_1/(1 + r)^1 + CF_2/(1 + r)^2 + \cdots + CF_n/(1 + r)^n$$

Progress check 15.4

What do we mean by discounted cash flow (DCF) and what are the principles on which it is based?

Net present value (NPV)

NPV is today's value of the difference between cash inflows and outflows projected at future dates, attributable to capital investments or long-term projects. The value now of these net cash flows is obtained by using the discounted cash flow method with a specified discount rate.

Worked example 15.3

An investment of £5,000 is made in year 0. For the purpose of NPV, year 0 is regarded as being today. The investment generates subsequent yearly cash flows of £1,000, £3,000, £3,000 and £2,000. The cost of capital is 10% per annum.

We can evaluate the investment using an NPV approach.

$$NPV = -£5,000/1.1^0 + £1,000/1.1^1 + £3,000/1.1^2 + £3,000/1.1^3 + £2,000/1.1^4$$
$$NPV = -£5,000 + (£1,000 \times 0.91) + (£3,000 \times 0.83) + (£3,000 \times 0.75) + (£2,000 \times 0.68)$$
$$NPV = -£5,000 + £910 + £2,490 + £2,250 + £1,360$$
$$NPV = +£2,010 \text{ which is greater than 0, and being positive the investment should probably be made.}$$

Such an analysis is more usefully presented in tabular form. The discount rates for each year: $1/1.1$, $1/1.1^2$, $1/1.1^3$, $1/1.1^4$, may be shown in the table as discount factor values which are calculated, or alternatively obtained from present value tables (see the extract below from the present value table in Appendix 1 at the end of this book).

Rate r % After n years	1	2	3	4	5	6	7	8	9	10	11	12
1	0.99	0.98	0.97	0.96	0.95	0.94	0.93	0.93	0.92	**0.91**	0.90	0.89
2	0.98	0.96	0.94	0.92	0.91	0.89	0.87	0.86	0.84	**0.83**	0.81	0.80
3	0.97	0.94	0.92	0.89	0.86	0.84	0.82	0.79	0.77	**0.75**	0.73	0.71
4	0.96	0.92	0.89	0.85	0.82	0.79	0.76	0.74	0.71	**0.68**	0.66	0.64
5	0.95	0.91	0.86	0.82	0.78	0.75	0.71	0.68	0.65	0.62	0.59	0.57

Tabular format of NPV analysis

Year	Cash outflows £	Cash inflows £	Net cash flow £	Discount factor	Present values £
0	−5,000		−5,000	1.00	−5,000
1		1,000	1,000	0.91	910
2		3,000	3,000	0.83	2,490
3		3,000	3,000	0.75	2,250
4		2,000	2,000	0.68	1,360
				NPV	+2,010

Progress check 15.5

What is net present value (NPV) and how is it calculated?

Internal rate of return (IRR)

The NPV of a capital investment project is calculated by:

■ discounting, using a rate of return, discount rate, or cost of capital, to obtain
■ the difference in present values between cash inflows and cash outflows.

The internal rate of return (IRR) method calculates the rate of return where the difference between the present values of cash inflows and outflows, the NPV, is zero.

$$\text{NPV} = -I + CF_1/(1 + r)^1 + CF_2/(1 + r)^2 + \cdots + CF_n/(1 + r)^n$$

Therefore if NPV = 0

$$0 = -I + CF_1/(1 + r) + CF_2/(1 + r)^2 + \cdots + CF_n/(1 + r)^n$$

By solving this equation r is the internal rate of return (IRR), the exact rate of return that the project is expected to achieve. An organisation would then undertake the project if the expected rate of return, the IRR, exceeds its target rate of return.

Solving the above equation mathematically is difficult. IRR may be determined more easily graphically and using a little trigonometry and algebra and through interpolation. This assumes a linear relationship between the NPVs of a capital investment project derived using different discount rates. If, for example, a project generates a positive NPV of £50,000 using a discount rate of 10% and a negative NPV of £5,000 using a discount rate of 20%, then the IRR (at which point NPV is zero) must be somewhere between 10% and 20%. The exact rate may be determined by interpolation as illustrated in Figure 15.3.

| Figure 15.3 | Interpolation of the internal rate of return (IRR) |

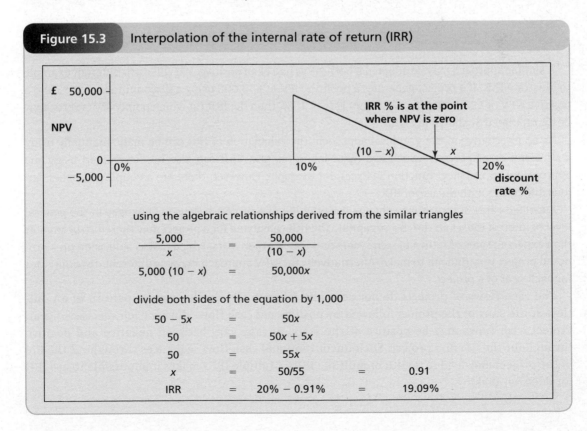

using the algebraic relationships derived from the similar triangles

$$\frac{5,000}{x} = \frac{50,000}{(10 - x)}$$

$$5,000 (10 - x) = 50,000x$$

divide both sides of the equation by 1,000

$$50 - 5x = 50x$$
$$50 = 50x + 5x$$
$$50 = 55x$$
$$x = 50/55 = 0.91$$
$$\text{IRR} = 20\% - 0.91\% = 19.09\%$$

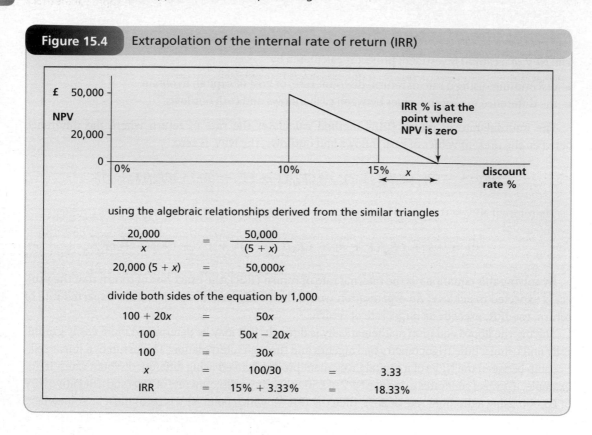

Figure 15.4   Extrapolation of the internal rate of return (IRR)

using the algebraic relationships derived from the similar triangles

$$\frac{20,000}{x} = \frac{50,000}{(5 + x)}$$

$$20,000\,(5 + x) = 50,000x$$

divide both sides of the equation by 1,000

$100 + 20x$	=	$50x$		
100	=	$50x - 20x$		
100	=	$30x$		
x	=	$100/30$	=	3.33
IRR	=	$15\% + 3.33\%$	=	18.33%

A similar approach may be adopted if both NPVs had been positive. We will use a different example to illustrate this. If a project generates a positive NPV of £50,000 using a discount rate of 10% and a positive NPV of £20,000 using a discount rate of 15%, then the IRR (at which point NPV is zero) may be extrapolated as shown in Figure 15.4.

As an alternative to the graphical approach, the calculation of IRR can be made manually using a trial and error process, which is a quite laborious task. IRR can also be determined using the appropriate spreadsheet function in Excel, for example. However, there are a couple of further serious difficulties with the use of IRR.

Expected rates of return may change over the life of a project because of changes in the general level of interest rates and the cost of capital. The IRR calculated for a project may therefore be greater than expected rates of return in some years and less in other years, which makes a decision on a proposed project very difficult to make. Alternatively, the NPV approach may use different discount rates for each year of a project.

The cash flows of projects do not normally fall into the simple, regular pattern of an outflow at the start of the project followed by positive net cash flows during each successive year. Project cash flows may be positive at the start, or may vary between negative and positive throughout the life of a project. Such unconventional cash flow sequences throughout the life of the project may lead to no IRR or multiple IRRs. Multiple IRRs makes it impossible to use IRR for decision-making.

Progress check 15.6

What is the internal rate of return (IRR) and how is it calculated?

Worked example 15.4 illustrates the use of both NPV and IRR, using conventional cash flows.

Worked example 15.4

Gamma plc is a diversified multinational group that wishes to acquire a computer system costing £600,000, which is expected to generate cash gains of £170,000 per year over five years. The computer system will have a residual value of zero after five years. The suggested cost of capital is 12% per annum. For this example we may ignore taxation. Gamma has a target IRR of 15%. Gamma plc evaluates the computer system investment by considering its IRR.

			£		
Yearly cash gains			170,000		

Year	Cash outflows £000	Cash inflows £000	Net cash flow £000	Discount factor at 12%	Present values £000
0	−600		−600	1.00	−600.0
1		170	170	0.89	151.3
2		170	170	0.80	136.0
3		170	170	0.71	120.7
4		170	170	0.64	108.8
5		170	170	0.57	96.9
				NPV	+13.7

Alternatively, using the cumulative present values in the present value tables, the present value of £1 at 12% over five years is £3.61, therefore

$$\text{NPV} = -£600{,}000 + (£170{,}000 \times 3.61) = +£13{,}700$$

The project gives a positive NPV of £13,700 over five years. If Gamma plc used NPV to appraise capital projects then acceptance of this project may be recommended because NPV is positive.

The IRR is the rate of return that would give an NPV of zero. The interpolation technique shown in Figure 15.3 may be used to derive the internal rate of return of the project.

If we assume a rate of return of 20%, the five-year cumulative discount rate is 2.99 (from the cumulative present value of £1 in the present value tables in Appendix 1).

The new NPV would be:

$$-£600{,}000 + (£170{,}000 \times 2.99) = -£91{,}700$$

(Note that if Gamma plc used NPV to appraise capital projects then acceptance of this project would not be recommended at a cost of capital of 20% because it is negative.)

We have already calculated the positive NPV of £13,700 using a cost of capital of 12%. The IRR must be at some point between 20% and 12% (difference 8%). Using a similar calculation to that used in Figure 15.3:

$$\frac{£91,700}{x} = \frac{£13,700}{(8 - x)}$$

$$£91,700(8 - x) = £13,700x$$

$$(£91,700 \times 8) - £91,700x = £13,700x$$

$$£733,600 - £91,700x = £13,700x$$

$$£733,600 = £13,700x + £91,700x$$

$$£733,600 = £105,400x$$

$$\frac{£733,600}{£105,400} = x$$

$$x = 7.0$$

Therefore, interpolation gives us an IRR of 20% less 7%, which is 13%.

If the Gamma group uses IRR to appraise capital projects then this project may be rejected as the target rate is 15%.

NPV or IRR?

We have looked at the two main capital appraisal methods, which use the DCF technique. Which method should an organisation adopt for the appraisal of capital investment projects? Which is the better method?

IRR is relatively easy to understand, particularly for non-financial managers. It can be stated in terms that do not include complicated financial jargon, for example 'a project will cost £1m and will return 20% per annum, which is better than the company's target of 15%'. NPV is not quite so clear; for example 'a project will cost £1,000,000 and have an NPV of £250,000 using the company's weighted average cost of capital of 12%'. But there are major disadvantages with the use of IRR:

■ IRR is very difficult to use for decision-making where expected rates of return may change over the life of a project
■ if project cash flows do not follow the usual 'outflow at the start of the project followed by inflows over the life of the project' the result may be no IRR, or two or more IRRs, which can lead to uncertainties and difficulties in interpretation
■ IRR should not be used to decide between mutually exclusive projects because of its inability to allow for the relative size of investments.

IRR ignores the size of investment projects, because it is a percentage measure of a return on a project rather than an absolute cash return number. Two projects, one with a large initial investment and one with a small initial investment, may have the same IRR, but one project may return many times the cash flow returned by the other project. So, if the projects were judged solely on IRR they would seem to rank equally.

If mutually exclusive projects need to be compared then the following rules for acceptance should apply:

■ is the IRR greater than the hurdle rate (usually the WACC)?

If so

■ the project with the highest NPV should be chosen assuming the NPV is greater than zero.

Progress check 15.7

What are the disadvantages in the use of internal rate of return (IRR) in the support of capital investment appraisal decisions?

Capital budgeting using NPV

A company may be considering a number of projects in which it may invest. If there is a limited amount of funds available then **capital rationing** is required. This method requires ranking the competing projects in terms of NPV per each £ of investment in each project. Investment funds may then be allocated according to NPV rankings. This capital budgeting technique is called the profitability index (PI).

Worked example 15.5

Stu VW Ltd is considering five potential new projects, which will involve a capital outlay in 2010 and will then run over the three years 2011, 2012 and 2013. The company's cost of capital is 11% per annum. The capital outlays and expected net cash inflows from each of the projects are as shown below:

Year Project	2010 £000	2011 £000	2012 £000	2013 £000
S	−40	10	30	25
T	0	5	5	5
U	−60	35	40	10
V	−80	30	50	30
W	−30	20	15	20

Each project has the capacity to be reduced to the level of available capital, which means that part investment in projects is allowed in 2010.

Capital for all projects must be paid out in 2010, but Stu VW Ltd has only £120,000 available to apply to projects in 2010 although there are no constraints on capital in subsequent years.

We will consider how Stu VW Ltd may use the limited capital available to maximise corporate value.

First we need to calculate the NPVs of each of the projects. We can then calculate the profitability index (PI) of each of the projects.

$$PI = \frac{NPV}{initial\ investment}$$

We have a constraint on the amount of capital available and so we need to rank the projects by their PIs. The rule is that the higher the PI then the higher the ranking of the project.

Project T has no capital outlay and so this project will be undertaken regardless, so long as it returns a positive NPV. The capital constraint will be divided among the other projects according to their ranking.

The NPVs of each project and their PIs have been calculated as follows:

Year	2010	2011	2012	2013		
Discount factor @ 11%	1.00	0.90	0.81	0.73		
	£000	£000	£000	£000	£000	
Project					NPV	PI
S	−40.00	9.00	24.30	18.25	11.55	0.289
T	0.00	4.50	4.05	3.65	12.20	
U	−60.00	31.50	32.40	7.30	11.20	0.187
V	−80.00	27.00	40.50	21.90	9.40	0.118
W	−30.00	18.00	12.15	14.60	14.75	0.492

Each project may be ranked according to their PIs:

Ranking	1	2	3	4	5
Project	T	W	S	U	V

Finally we can apply the capital to the projects based on the constraint of £120,000 available:

Project	£000	
T	0	full project
W	30	full project
S	40	full project
U	50	5/6 of project
V	0	no project
Total	120	

Discounted payback

The discounted payback appraisal method requires a discount rate to be chosen to calculate the present values of cash inflows and then the payback is the number of years required to repay the original investment.

Worked example 15.6

A new leisure facility project is being considered by Denton City Council. It will cost £600,000 and is expected to generate the following cash inflows over six years:

Year	£
1	40,000
2	100,000
3	200,000
4	350,000
5	400,000
6	50,000

The cost of capital is 10% per annum.
Denton City Council evaluates projects using discounted payback.

Year	Net cash flow £000	Cumulative net cash flow £000	Discount factor at 10%	Present values £000	Cumulative present values £000
0	−600	−600	1.00	−600.0	−600.0
1	40	−560	0.91	36.4	−563.6
2	100	−460	0.83	83.0	−480.6
3	200	−260	0.75	150.0	−330.6
4	350	90	0.68	238.0	−92.6
5	400	490	0.62	248.0	155.4
6	50	540	0.56	28.0	183.4
	540			NPV +183.4	

Taking a simple payback approach we can see that the project starts to pay back at nearly three quarters of the way through year four. The discounted payback approach shows that with a cost of capital of 10% the project does not really start to pay back until just over a third of the way into year five. This method also highlights the large difference between the real total value of the project of £183,400 in discounted cash flow terms, and the total value of actual cash flows of £540,000.

Progress check 15.8

What is discounted payback and how is it calculated?

Advantages and disadvantages of the five investment appraisal methods

We have discussed the five capital investment methods and seen examples of their application. The table in Figure 15.5 summarises each of the methods and the advantages and disadvantages of their practical use in investment appraisal.

It is interesting to note that even as recently as ten years ago payback still seemed to be the most popular appraisal method within UK companies, closely followed by IRR! NPV, discounted payback and ARR appeared to be equal third, sharing around the same level of popularity (see Drury, Braund, Osborne and Tayles, *A Survey of Management Accounting Practices in UK Companies* 1993, London, Chartered Association of Certified Accountants, 1993).

It should be emphasised that the whole area of capital investment appraisal is one that requires a great deal of expertise and experience. In real-life decision-making situations these types of appraisal are generally carried out by the accountant or the finance director. These sorts of longer-term decisions are concerned primarily with the maximisation of shareholder wealth, but they also impact on issues relating to the health and future development of the business. Therefore, such decisions are normally based on qualitative as well as quantitative factors.

Non-financial measures appear to be as important, if not more important, to businesses in their appraisal of new projects. These may include, for example:

- customer relationships
- employee welfare

Figure 15.5	Advantages and disadvantages of the five investment appraisal methods

	definition	advantages	disadvantages
accounting rate of return (ARR)	average accounting profit over the life of the project divided by the initial or average investment	quick and easy to calculate and simple to use	based on accounting profit rather than cash flows
		the concept of a % return is a familiar one	a relative measure and so no account is taken of the size of the project
		very similar to ROCE	ignores timing of cash flows and the cost of capital
payback	the point where the cumulative value of a project's profits or cash flows becomes positive	easily understood	ignores the timing of cash flows
		considers liquidity	ignores profits or cash flows that occur after the payback point
		looks only at relevant cash flows	ignores the cost of capital, i.e. the time value of money
net present value (NPV)	the total present values of each of a project's cash flows, using a present value discount factor	uses relevant cash flows	its use requires an estimate of the cost of capital
		allows for the time value of money	
		absolute measure and therefore useful, for example, for comparison of the change in corporate value	
		it is additive which means that if the cash flow is doubled then the NPV is doubled	
internal rate of return (IRR)	the discount factor at which the NPV of a project becomes zero	does not need an estimate of the cost of capital	it is a relative rate of return and so no account is taken of the size of the project
		because the result is stated as a % it is easily understood	its use may rank projects incorrectly
			as cash flows change signs −ve to +ve or *vice versa* throughout the project there may be more than one IRR
			it is difficult to use if changes in the cost of capital are forecast
discounted payback	the point where the cumulative value of a project's discounted cash flows becomes positive	easily understood	its use requires an estimate of the cost of capital
		considers liquidity	ignores cash flows that occur after the payback point
		looks only at relevant cash flows	
		allows for the time value of money	

- the fit with general business strategy
- competition
- availability of scarce resources such as skills and specialised knowledge.

In addition, there are a number of other important quantitative factors, which are discussed in the next section, that should also be considered in new project appraisal. The impact of taxation, for example, is sometimes forgotten with regard to the allowances against tax on the purchase of capital items and tax payable on profits, and therefore cash flows, resulting from a capital project. The uncertainty surrounding future expectations and the sensitivity of the outcome of a project to changes affecting the various elements of an appraisal calculation, are factors that also require measured assessment.

Progress check 15.9

Which technique do you think is the most appropriate to use in capital investment appraisal, and why?

Other factors affecting investment decisions

A number of further factors may have an additional impact on investment appraisal calculations:

- the effect of inflation on the cost of capital
- whether additional working capital is required for the project
- taxation
- the length of the project
- risk and uncertainty.

Inflation

If i is the real cost of capital and the inflation rate is f, then the actual (or nominal or money) cost of capital a may be calculated as follows:

$$(1 + a) = (1 + i) \times (1 + f)$$

Therefore

$$\text{actual cost of capital } a = (1 + i) \times (1 + f) - 1$$

Worked example 15.7

What is a company's real cost of capital if its actual (money) cost of capital is 11% and inflation is running at 2%?

Real cost of capital

$$i = \frac{(1 + a)}{(1 + f)} - 1$$

$$i = \frac{1.11}{1.02} - 1 = 0.088 \text{ or } 8.8\%$$

This would normally then be rounded to say 9% and forecast cash flows that have not been adjusted for inflation may then be discounted using this real cost of capital. Alternatively, if forecast cash flows have been adjusted for inflation, then these money cash flows would be discounted using the company's actual cost of capital. The result is approximately the same using either method.

Working capital

Any increases in working capital required for a project in addition to long-term asset investments need to be shown as cash outflows as necessary in one or more years, offset by cash inflows to bring the total to zero by the end of the project.

Worked example 15.8

Delta Precision plc, a manufacturing company, has the opportunity to invest in a machine costing £110,000 that will generate net cash inflows from the investment of £30,000 for five years, after which time the machine will be worth nothing. Cost of capital is 10% per annum. We may ignore inflation and taxation in our evaluation of the project using NPV.

Year	Cash outflows £000	Cash inflows £000	Net cash flow £000	Discount factor at 10%	Present values £000
0	−110		−110	1.00	−110.0
1		30	30	0.91	27.3
2		30	30	0.83	24.9
3		30	30	0.75	22.5
4		30	30	0.68	20.4
5		30	30	0.62	18.6
				NPV	+3.7

The positive NPV of £3,700 would indicate acceptance of this investment.

Suppose that in addition to the above factors, for this project Delta required:

■ £20,000 working capital in year 1
■ £40,000 working capital in year 2, but then
■ zero working capital in years 3, 4 and 5.

The revised cash flows would be:

Year	0 £000	1 £000	2 £000	3 £000	4 £000	5 £000	Total £000
Investment	−110						−110
Cash inflows		30	30	30	30	30	150
Working capital {		−20		20			0
capital {			−40	40			0
Total	−110	10	−10	90	30	30	40

The total cash flow of the project is still the same at £40,000, but the timings of the cash flows are different.

Year	Net cash flows £000	Discount factor	Present values £000
0	−110	1.00	−110.0
1	10	0.91	9.1
2	−10	0.83	−8.3
3	90	0.75	67.5
4	30	0.68	20.4
5	30	0.62	18.6
		NPV	−2.7

The need for, and the timing of, working capital gives a negative NPV of £2,700 which would now indicate rejection of this investment.

Taxation

In practice, tax must always be allowed for in any capital investment appraisal calculations. The following two examples provide an introduction to this topic, which illustrate the principles.

Worked example 15.9

Epsilon Ltd is a company that manufactures and distributes consumer products. It is currently considering the acquisition of a machine costing £2,700,000 to market a new product.

The machine will be worth nothing after 10 years but is expected to produce 10,000 units of a product per year during that period, with variable costs of £35 per unit.

The product can be sold for £120 per unit.
Fixed costs directly attributed to this product will be £300,000 per year.
The company's cost of capital is 10% per annum.
We may assume that all costs and revenues are paid and received during each year.

We may further assume that corporation tax is paid in the year that profit is made and calculated at 40% of profit, and that for tax purposes each year's depreciation is equal to capital allowances.

The acquisition of the machine can be NPV.

	£000	
Sales revenue	1,200	[10,000 × £120]
Variable costs	(350)	[10,000 × £35]
Depreciation	(270)	[2,700,000 over 10-year life]
Fixed costs	(300)	
Taxable profit	280	
Corporation tax at 40%	(112)	[based on taxable profit plus depreciation less capital allowances]
Profit after tax	168	
Add back depreciation	270	[non-cash flow]
Yearly cash flow	438	

Using the cumulative present value tables (see Appendix 1) the present value of £1 at 10% over 10 years is £6.15, therefore:

$$\text{NPV} = -£2,700,000 + (£438,000 \times 6.15) = -£6,300$$

The NPV is less than 0 and the project is therefore not acceptable.

Corporation tax is normally payable by a company in the year following the year in which profit is earned. If a project lasts for say four years then cash flow in respect of tax must be shown in the fifth year. The length of the project is then effectively five years. Tax payable in respect of operating profit must be shown separately from cash flows in respect of capital allowances. The first investment year is normally shown as year 0 and the first tax allowance year is therefore year one.

Worked example 15.10

Zeta plc has the opportunity to invest in a machine costing £100,000 that will generate cash profits of £30,000 per year for the next four years after which the machine would be sold for £10,000. The company's after tax cost of capital is 8% per annum.

We may assume:

- corporation tax at 30%
- annual writing down allowances in each year are on the investment reducing balance at 25%
- there will be a balancing charge or allowance on disposal of the machine.

We can consider whether the investment should be made, using an NPV approach.

Capital allowances:

Year	Opening balance £	Capital allowance at 25% £	Balancing allowance/ (charge) £	Closing balance £
0	100,000	25,000		75,000
1	75,000	18,750		56,250
2	56,250	14,063		42,187
3	42,187	10,547		31,640
4	31,640	7,910		23,730
	23,730			
Proceeds	10,000		13,730	
Total		76,270	13,730	

Note that the totals of the capital allowances and balancing allowance equal £90,000, the net cost of the machine £100,000 less £10,000.

Next, we can calculate the taxable profit and the tax payable.

Year	0 £	1 £	2 £	3 £	4 £
Profits		30,000	30,000	30,000	30,000
Capital allowances	25,000	18,750	14,063	10,547	21,640
Taxable profit	−25,000	11,250	15,937	19,453	8,360
Tax receivable/ (payable) at 30%	7,500	(3,375)	(4,781)	(5,836)	(2,508)

Because profits are cash profits can now calculate the net cash flows and the present values of the project:

Year	Investment £	Cash profits £	Tax £	Net cash flow £	Discount factor at 8% pa	Present values £
0	−100,000			−100,000	1.00	−100,000
1		30,000	7,500	37,500	0.93	34,875
2		30,000	−3,375	26,625	0.86	22,897
3		30,000	−4,781	25,219	0.79	19,923
4	10,000	30,000	−5,836	34,164	0.74	25,281
5			−2,508	−2,508	0.68	−1,705
					NPV	+1,271

The positive NPV of £1,271 would indicate acceptance of this investment.

Capital investment decisions take on a wider dimension for international corporations with the consideration of a further factor, the uncertainty associated with foreign currency exchange rate fluctuations. For UK-based companies this has had a particular significance over the past few years with the uncertainty surrounding the UK's non-adoption of the euro. Foreign currency exchange rate risk is not discussed in this chapter but is an important topic that was introduced in Chapter 3.

Progress check 15.10

Why and how should inflation and working capital be allowed for in making capital investment decisions?

The press extract below illustrates the factors involved in (and the implications of) making investment decisions. When Bosch opened its alternator factory in Cardiff in 1989 the decision was aided by the belief that the UK was undergoing a renaissance as an automobile manufacturer. In addition, more than £20m of grants were received by Bosch from the Welsh Development Agency in a bid to

The impact of high UK costs on investments by large foreign companies

About 900 jobs are to be lost in South Wales as Bosch prepares to shut a car parts factory next year.

The privately owned German engineering group blamed its decision to pull out of Wales on the economic slump, which has hit the car industry hard. The Unite union described the news as a 'terrible blow'.

Management confirmed the closure to workers at the plant in Miskin near Cardiff on Thursday, after a three-month consultation, during which they had to decide whether to shed 300 jobs and carry on with a smaller operation, or close the plant completely in 2011.

The division in charge of the plant will now recommend to the Bosch board that production should be phased out. The consultation is being extended until February as unions and staff try to thrash out redundancy terms.

The factory, which makes alternators for German carmakers including BMW and Daimler's Mercedes-Benz, is scheduled to shut in the summer of next year. Production will be transferred to Hungary, where labour costs are 65% of those in Cardiff.

The move is a serious blow to south Wales. The other major employer in the region is Corus, the steelmaker, which itself is cutting more than 1,000 jobs at Port Talbot, along the M4 from Miskin.

Unite's regional officer, David Lewis, said: 'There should have been some alternative at a site this size, with the number of people they employ, that the company could have looked for.' While acknowledging that there was overcapacity in

several divisions of Bosch, he added: 'Everyone is bitterly disappointed that there's not a hope of something being retained.'

Bosch, which is set to make its first operating loss for six decades, said demand for alternators had dropped dramatically, with sales down 45% last year.

The global recession has hit carmakers around the world, with General Motors and Chrysler going bankrupt last year and needing US government aid to survive. The luxury marques BMW and Daimler both saw sales slip by 13%, according to figures released yesterday, as government scrappage schemes led to a move towards smaller and more fuel-efficient vehicles.

'I deeply regret that we could not find a solution for the Cardiff plant', said Stefan Asenkerschbaumer, president of the Bosch starter motors division, who rejected the alternative plan to keep the plant open with the loss of 300 jobs.

'I have spent time in a previous role as plant manager in Cardiff and I know first-hand the dedication and commitment of the employees here. Therefore, this is for me personally one of the toughest decisions in my career.'

The worst economic downturn for many decades had 'left its mark' on the Bosch group, he said.

The Welsh assembly government offered Bosch employees its full support.

Source: 'Terrible blow' to Wales as car parts factory is shut with loss of 900 jobs: Bosch plant near Cardiff to close in summer of 2011, by Julia Kollewe © *The Guardian*, 16 January 2010

improve the economy of an area that had been adversely affected by the massive reduction in the coal industry. However, circumstances change and the factors that attracted overseas investment in the past may often be seen as no longer financially attractive now.

The same press extract highlights an additional factor influencing investment decisions – the cost of labour. The labour cost differentials between the UK and, for example, China and Eastern Europe have resulted increasingly in companies making new investments in countries like Poland, the Czech Republic, Hungary and China. While a willing and abundant workforce in the Cardiff region (along with government grants) attracted Bosch 20 years ago, a competitive advantage in the depressed car industry could more recently be achieved from cost reductions in emerging countries. Changes, such as a gradual shift in the market toward smaller more fuel-efficient and lower emission vehicles, have impacted on the company's profits to the extent that in April 2010 Bosch announced its first operating loss in sixty years.

Risk and uncertainty and decision-making – sensitivity analysis

In our earlier discussion on the decision-making process we talked about comparing actual results following implementation of the decision with the expected outcome. Our own experience tells us that actual outcomes usually differ considerably from expected outcomes. In terms of capital investment, the greater the timescale of the project the more time there is for more things to go wrong; the larger the investment, the greater may be the impact.

As a final step in evaluation of the investment in a project it is prudent to carry out some sort of **sensitivity analysis**. Sensitivity analysis may be used to assess the risk associated with a capital investment project. A project having a positive NPV may on the face of it seem viable. It is useful to calculate how much the NPV may change should there be changes to the factors used in the appraisal exercise. These factors are shown in Figure 15.6.

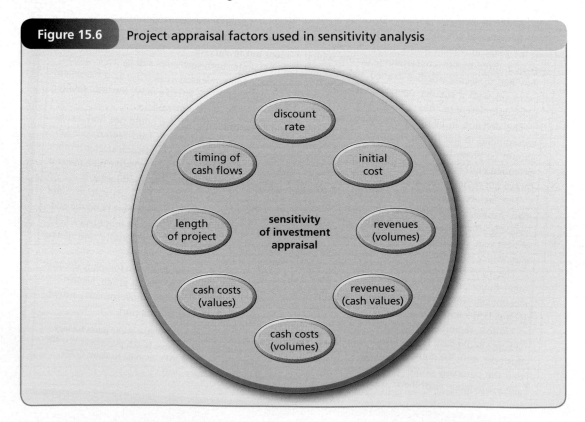

Figure 15.6 Project appraisal factors used in sensitivity analysis

Sensitivity may be evaluated through numerical analysis, which is illustrated in Worked examples 15.10 to 15.14. Sensitivity may also be shown graphically:

- NPV may be plotted on the y vertical axis
- the percentage change in the variable factors, used in the appraisal, may be plotted on the x horizontal axis.

This process may be carried out for each variable, for example:

- sales
- cost savings
- investment
- scrap value.

The most sensitive variable is the one with the steepest gradient.

Worked example 15.11

Theta Ltd has the opportunity to invest in a project to make a new product with an initial cost of £100,000 that will generate estimated net cash flows of £35,000 at the end of each year for five years. The company's cost of capital is 12% per annum. For simplicity we can ignore the effects of tax and inflation.

The cumulative present value tables show us the annuity factor over five years at 12% per annum at 3.61 (see Appendix 1).

Therefore the NPV of the project is:

$$-£100,000 + (£35,000 \times 3.61)$$
$$= -£100,000 + £126,350$$
$$NPV = +£26,350$$

The positive NPV of £26,350 would indicate going ahead with the investment in this project.

We can consider the sensitivity analysis of the project to changes in the initial investment.

Initial investment

The NPV of the project is £26,350. If the initial investment rose by £26,350 to £126,350 (£100,000 + £26,350) the NPV would become zero and it would not be worth taking on the project. This represents an increase of 26.4% on the initial investment.

Worked example 15.12

Using the data from Worked example 15.11 we can evaluate the sensitivity of the annual cash flows from the project, using an NPV approach.

Annual cash flow

If we again consider what needs to happen to bring the NPV to zero then

$$NPV = 0 = -£100,000 + (a \times 3.61)$$

where a is the annual cash flow

$$a = £100,000/3.61$$
$$a = £27,700$$

which is a reduction of 20.9% from the original per annum cash flow of £35,000.

Worked example 15.13

Using the data from Worked example 15.11 we can evaluate the sensitivity of cost of capital on the project for Theta Ltd, using an NPV approach.

Cost of capital
When the NPV is zero we can calculate the internal rate of return (IRR). If the cost of capital is greater than the IRR then the project should be rejected.

In this example we therefore first need to calculate the cumulative discount factor at which the NPV is zero.

$$\text{NPV} = 0 = -£100,000 + (£35,000 \times d)$$

Where d is the cumulative discount factor for five years

$$d = £100,000/£35,000$$
$$d = 2.857$$

The cumulative present value tables show us that the annuity factor over five years of 2.86 represents a discount rate of 22%.

The IRR is therefore approximately 22%, which is an 83.3% increase over the cost of capital of 12%.

Worked example 15.14

Using the data from Worked example 15.11 we can evaluate the sensitivity of the length of the project for Theta Ltd, using an NPV approach.

Length of project
The original project was five years for which we calculated the NPV at £26,350. We may consider what would be the effect if the project ended after say four years or three years.

If the project was four years, the cumulative discount factor (from the tables) is 3.04 so the NPV of the project is:

$$-£100,000 + (£35,000 \times 3.04)$$
$$= -£100,000 + £106,400$$
$$\text{NPV} = +£6,400$$

The positive NPV of £6,400 still indicates going ahead with the investment in this project.

If the project was three years the cumulative discount factor (from the tables) is 2.40 so the NPV of the project is:

$$-£100,000 + (£35,000 \times 2.40)$$
$$= -£100,000 + £84,000$$
$$\text{NPV} = +£16,000$$

The negative NPV of £16,000 indicates not going ahead with the investment in this project if the length of the project drops below four years, which is the year in which NPV becomes negative. This is a change of 20% (that is a drop from five years to four years).

Worked example 15.15

Each of the sensitivities that have been calculated in Worked examples 15.11 to 15.14 may be summarised and we can draw some conclusions about the sensitivity of the project that are apparent from the summary.

The sensitivity analysis that we have carried out is more usefully summarised for each of the factors we have considered, to show:

- the values used in the original appraisal
- the critical values of those factors
- the percentage change over the original values that they represent.

Factor	Original value	Critical value	% change
Initial investment	£100,000	£126,350	26.4
Annual cash flow	£35,000	£27,700	−20.9
Cost of capital	12%	22%	83.3
Length of project	5 years	4 years	−20.0

We may draw the following conclusions from our sensitivity analysis:

- none of the factors used in the appraisal was critical, their critical values all being +/− 20%
- cost of capital is the least critical factor at 83.3%, which is useful to know since the accuracy of the calculation of cost of capital may not always be totally reliable.

The same technique of sensitivity analysis may be used as an early warning system before a project begins to show a loss. It can be seen from the factors outlined in this section that a board of directors should request a sensitivity analysis on major projects. In the UK, between 2007 and 2010 we saw several projects within the construction industry become very unprofitable, as the timing of project cash flows critically impacted on their viability.

However, there are limitations to the use of sensitivity analysis. In the worked examples we have considered we have looked at the effect of changes to individual factors in isolation. In reality two or more factors may change simultaneously. The impact of such changes may be assessed using the more sophisticated technique of linear programming. A further limitation may be the absence of clear rules governing acceptance or rejection of the project and the need for the subjective judgement of management.

When we looked at risk and sales pricing in Chapter 11 we saw that we may apply probabilities to estimated demand estimates at different pricing levels to derive expected values. In the same way, cash flows from investments may be weighted by their probabilities of occurrence to calculate an expected NPV.

Worked example 15.16

Kappa plc has the opportunity of engaging in a two-year project for a specific client. It would require an initial investment in a machine costing £200,000. The machine is capable of running three separate processes. The process used will depend on the level of demand from the client's final customers. Each process will therefore generate different yearly net cash flows, each with a different likelihood of occurrence. The company's cost of capital is 15% per annum.

The forecast probabilities and net cash flows for each year are:

Process	Probability of occurrence	Per annum cash flow
Process 1	0.5	£150,000
Process 2	0.1	£15,000
Process 3	0.4	£90,000
	1.0	

The total of the probabilities is 1.0, which indicates that one of the options is certain to occur. Even though one process will definitely be used should Kappa take on the project?

We first need to use the probabilities to calculate the weighted average of the expected outcomes for each year.

Process	Cash flow £	Probability	Expected cash flow £
1	150,000	0.5	75,000
2	15,000	0.1	1,500
3	90,000	0.4	36,000
Expected per annum cash flows			112,500

To calculate the expected NPV of the project we need to discount the expected annual cash flows using the discount rate of 15% per annum.

Year	Expected cash flow £	Discount rate at 15%	Expected present value £
1	112,500	0.87	97,875
2	112,500	0.76	85,500
Total	225,000		183,375
Initial investment (year 0)			200,000
Expected NPV			−16,625

The negative expected NPV of £16,625 indicates that Kappa plc should reject investment in this project.

Although the technique of expected net present value is a clear decision rule with a single numerical outcome there are caveats:

- this technique uses an average number which in the above example is not actually capable of occurrence
- use of an average number may cloud the issue if the underlying risk of outcomes worse than the average are ignored
- if the per annum cash flow from process 1 had been £300,000, the expected NPV would have been highly positive, but consider the impact on Kappa if, for example, the client had actually required the use of process 2.

Progress check 15.11

Risk and uncertainty increasingly impact on investment decisions. What are these risk factors, and how may we evaluate their impact?

Control of capital investment projects

Once a project has been appraised and a sensitivity analysis carried out and the approval has been given at the relevant level in the organisation, project controls must be established and then post-project completion audits carried out. The controls cover the three main areas of:

- capital spend – note the number of subjective areas where things can go wrong
- project-timing – delays appear to be 'routine' in many major projects as evidenced almost daily in the financial press
- benefits – evidenced almost as frequently in the financial press, this is another area where things may not turn out as planned.

Capital spending limits are usually put in place by most organisations with levels of spend requiring authorisation at the appropriate managerial level. Capital expenditure proposals should be documented to show:

- project details, including costs, benefits and the life of the project
- appraisal calculations and comparisons with the organisation's targets
- assumptions
- names of the project manager and the project team
- name(s) and signature(s) of the manager(s) authorising the project
- the period(s) in which expenditure should take place.

Material delays in capital spend or in the progress of the project should prompt a resubmitted proposal together with the reasons for delay. A good project manager with the appropriate level of responsibility and authority should ensure that projects run to plan.

Benefits from projects are not easy to control because they are usually derived over many years. The importance of having a good project manager in place cannot be overemphasised. He or she should ensure that expected benefits actually materialise and are as large in value as anticipated. The project manager should also ensure that costs are kept in line with expectation.

Post-implementation audits should be carried out for all projects if possible. Although after the event corrective action cannot usually be taken, variances may be analysed to use the project as an information and learning tool:

- to appraise manager performance
- to identify strengths and weaknesses in forecasting and estimating techniques
- to identify areas of improvement in the capital investment process
- to advertise the fact that both project and manager performance are being monitored.

Progress check 15.12

In what ways can we ensure that capital investment projects are adequately controlled?

Summary of key points

- An investment requires expenditure on something 'today' that is expected to provide a benefit in the future.
- The decision to make an investment is extremely important because it implies the expectation that expenditure today will generate future cash gains in real terms that greatly exceed the funds spent today.
- '£100 received today is worth more than £100 received in a year's time' is an expression of what is meant by the 'time value of money'.
- The technique of discounted cash flow discounts the projected net cash flows of a capital project to ascertain its present value, using an appropriate discount rate, or cost of capital.
- The principles underlying the investment appraisal techniques that use the DCF method are cash flow (as opposed to profit) and the time value of money.
- Five main methods are used to appraise investments: accounting rate of return (ARR); payback; net present value (NPV); internal rate of return (IRR); and discounted payback – the last three being discounted cash flow (DCF) techniques.
- Additional factors impacting on investment criteria calculations are: the effect of inflation on the cost of capital; working capital requirements; length of project; taxation; risk and uncertainty.
- There may be a number of risks associated with each of the variables included in a capital investment appraisal decision: estimates of initial costs; uncertainty about the timing and values of future cash revenues and costs; the length of project; variations in the discount rate.
- Sensitivity analysis may be used to assess the risk associated with a capital investment project.
- To establish the appropriate levels of control, the appointment of a good project manager, with the appropriate level of responsibility and authority, and regular project reviews are absolute essentials to ensure that projects run to plan.
- The techniques of capital investment appraisal require a great deal of expertise and experience, and further training should be received before attempting to use them in real life decision-making situations.

Assessment material

Questions

Q15.1 **(i)** What is capital investment?

(ii) Why are capital investment decisions so important to companies?

Q15.2 Outline the five main investment appraisal methods.

Q15.3 Describe the two key principles underlying DCF investment selection methods.

Q15.4 What are the advantages in the use of NPV over IRR in investment appraisal?

Q15.5 What are the factors that impact on capital investment decisions?

Q15.6 **(i)** What is meant by risk with regard to investment?

(ii) How does sensitivity analysis help?

Q15.7 Describe how capital investment projects may be controlled and reviewed.

Discussion points

D15.1 'I know that cash and profit are not always the same thing but surely eventually they end up being equal. Therefore, surely we should look at the likely ultimate profit from a capital investment before deciding whether or not to invest?' Discuss.

D15.2 'This discounted cash flow business seems like just a bit more work for the accountants to me. Cash is cash whenever it's received or paid. I say let's keep capital investment appraisal simple.' Discuss.

D15.3 'If you don't take a risk you will not make any money.' Discuss.

Exercises

Solutions are provided in Appendix 3 to all exercise numbers highlighted in colour.

Level I

E15.1 *Time allowed – 30 minutes*

Global Sights & Sounds Ltd (GSS) sells multi-media equipment and software through its retail outlets. GSS is considering investing in some major refurbishment of one of its outlets, to enable it to provide improved customer service, until the lease expires at the end of four years. GSS is currently talking to two contractors, Smith Ltd and Jones Ltd. Whichever contractor is used, the improved customer service has been estimated to generate increased net cash inflows as follows:

Year	£
1	75,000
2	190,000
3	190,000
4	225,000

Smith:

The capital costs will be £125,000 at the start of the project, and £175,000 at the end of each of years 1 and 2.

Jones:

The capital costs will be the same in total, but payment to the contractor can be delayed. Capital payments will be £50,000 at the start of the project, £75,000 at the end of each of years one, two and three, and the balance of capital cost at the end of year four. In return for the delayed payments the contractor will receive a 20% share of the cash inflows generated from the improved services, payable at the end of each year. In the interim period, the unutilised capital will be invested in a short-term project in another department store, generating a cash inflow of £60,000 at the end of each of years one, two and three.

It may be assumed that all cash flows occur at the end of each year.

The effects of taxation and inflation may be ignored.

> You are required to advise GSS Ltd on whether to select Smith or Jones, ignoring the time value of money, using the appraisal basis of:
>
> (i) accounting rate of return (ARR), and
> (ii) comment on the appraisal method you have used.

E15.2 *Time allowed – 30 minutes*

> Using the information on Global Sights & Sounds Ltd from Exercise E15.1, you are required to advise GSS Ltd on whether to select Smith or Jones, ignoring the time value of money, using the appraisal basis of:
>
> (i) payback, and
> (ii) comment on the appraisal method you have used.

E15.3 *Time allowed – 60 minutes*

Rainbow plc's business is organised into divisions. For operating purposes, each division is regarded as an investment centre, with divisional managers enjoying substantial autonomy in their selection of investment projects. Divisional managers are rewarded via a remuneration package, which is linked to a return on investment (ROI) performance measure. The ROI calculation is based on the net book value of assets at the beginning of the year. Although there is a high degree of autonomy in investment selection, approval to go ahead has to be obtained from group management at the head office in order to release the finance.

Red Division is currently investigating three independent investment proposals. If they appear acceptable, it wishes to assign each a priority in the event that funds may not be available to cover all three. The WACC (weighted average cost of capital) for the company is the hurdle rate used for new investments and is estimated at 15% per annum.

The details of the three proposals are as follows:

	Project A £000	Project B £000	Project C £000
Initial cash outlay on non-current assets	60	60	60
Net cash inflow in year 1	21	25	10
Net cash inflow in year 2	21	20	20
Net cash inflow in year 3	21	20	30
Net cash inflow in year 4	21	15	40

Taxation and the residual values of the non-current assets may be ignored.
Depreciation is straight line over the asset life, which is four years in each case.

You are required to:

(i)   evaluate the three investment proposals with regard to divisional performance, using ROI and RI

(ii) evaluate the three investment proposals with regard to company performance, using a DCF approach

(iii) explain any divergence between the two points of view, expressed in (i) and (ii) above, and outline how the views of both the division and the company can be brought into line.

Level II

E15.4   *Time allowed – 30 minutes*

Using the information on Global Sights & Sounds Ltd from Exercise E15.1, you are required to advise GSS Ltd on whether to select Smith or Jones, using the appraisal basis of:

(i)   net present value (NPV), using a cost of capital of 12% per annum to discount the cash flows to their present value, and

(ii) comment on the appraisal method you have used.

E15.5   *Time allowed – 30 minutes*

Using the information on Global Sights & Sounds Ltd from Exercise E15.1, you are required to advise GSS Ltd on whether to select Smith or Jones, using the appraisal basis of:

(i)   discounted payback, using a cost of capital of 12% per annum to discount the cash flows to their present value, and

(ii) comment on the appraisal method you have used.

E15.6   *Time allowed – 45 minutes*

Using the information on Global Sights & Sounds Ltd from Exercise E15.1, you are required to advise GSS Ltd on whether to select Smith or Jones, using the appraisal basis of:

(i)   internal rate of return (IRR), and

(ii) comment on the appraisal method you have used.

E15.7 *Time allowed – 45 minutes*

In Exercise E15.1 we are told that a 20% share of the improved cash inflow has been agreed with Jones Ltd.

You are required to:

(i) calculate the percentage share at which GSS Ltd would be indifferent, on a financial basis, as to which of the contractors Smith or Jones should carry out the work

(ii) outline the other factors, in addition to your financial analyses in (i), that should be considered in making the choice between Smith and Jones.

E15.8 *Time allowed – 60 minutes*

Alive & Kicking Ltd (AAK) owns a disused warehouse in which a promoter runs regular small gigs. There are currently no facilities to provide drinks. The owners of AAK intend to provide such facilities and can obtain funding to cover capital costs. This would have to be repaid over five years at an annual interest rate of 10%.

The capital costs are estimated at £120,000 for equipment that will have a life of five years and no residual value. To provide drinks, the running costs of staff, etc., will be £40,000 in the first year, increasing by £4,000 in each subsequent year. AAK proposes to charge £10,000 per annum for lighting, heating and other property expenses, and wants a nominal £5,000 per annum to cover any unforeseen contingencies. Apart from this, AAK is not looking for any profit as such from the provision of these facilities, because it believes that there may be additional future benefits from increased use of the facility. It is proposed that costs will be recovered by setting drinks prices at double the direct costs.

It is not expected that the full sales level will be reached until year three. The proportions of that level estimated to be reached in years one and two are 40% and 70% respectively.

You are required to:

(i) calculate the sales that need to be achieved in each of the five years to meet the proposed targets

(ii) comment briefly on four aspects of the proposals that you consider merit further investigation.

You may ignore the possible effects of taxation and inflation.

E15.9 *Time allowed – 90 minutes*

Lew Rolls plc is an international group that manufactures and distributes bathroom fittings to major building supply retailers and DIY chains. The board of Rolls is currently considering four projects to work with four different customers to develop new bathroom ranges (toilet, bidet, bath, basin and shower).

Rolls has a limit on funds for investment for the current year of £24m. The four projects represent levels of 'luxury' bathrooms. The product ranges are aimed at different markets. The lengths of time to bring to market, lives of product and timings of cash flows are different for each product range.

The Super bathroom project will cost £3m and generate £5m net cash flows spread equally over five years.

The Superluxury bathroom project will cost £7m and generate £10m net cash flows spread equally over five years.

The Executive bathroom project will take a long time to start paying back. It will cost £12m and generate £21m net cash flows, zero for the first two years and then £7m for each of the next three years.

The Excelsior bathroom project will cost £15m and generate £10m net cash flows for two years.

For ease of calculation it may be assumed that all cash flows occur on the last day of each year.

Projects may be undertaken in part or in total in the current year, and next year there will be no restriction on investment. Lew Rolls plc's cost of capital is 10%.

You are required to:

(i) calculate the NPV for each project

(ii) calculate the approximate IRR for each project

(iii) advise on the acceptance of these projects on the basis of NPV or IRR or any other method of ranking the projects.

(iv) What are the advantages of the appraisal method you have adopted for Lew Rolls plc?

(v) What other factors should be used in the final evaluations before the recommendations are implemented?

E15.10 *Time allowed – 90 minutes*

A UK subsidiary of a large multinational group plc is considering investment in four mutually exclusive projects. The managing director, Indira Patel, is anxious to choose a combination of projects that will maximise corporate value.

At the current time the company can embark on projects up to a maximum total of £230m. The four projects require the following initial investments:

£20m in project Doh
£195m in project Ray
£35m in project Mee
£80m in project Fah

The projects are expected to generate the following net cash flows over the three years following each investment. No project will last longer than three years.

Project Year	Doh £m	Ray £m	Mee £m	Fah £m
1	15	45	15	20
2	30	75	25	25
3		180	60	100

The company's WACC is 12% per annum, which is used to evaluate investments in new projects. The impact of tax and inflation may be ignored.

Advise Indira with regard to the projects in which the company should invest on the basis of maximising corporate value, given the limiting factor of the total funds currently available for investment.

Case Study V
COMPUTACORE LTD

Computacore Ltd produces and sells a range of computer systems. After-sales service work is carried out by local subcontractors, approved by Computacore Ltd. The managing director is considering Computacore carrying out all or some of the work itself and has chosen one area in which to experiment with the new routine.

Some of the computer systems are so large that repair or service work can only be done on site at customers' premises. Others are small enough for subcontractors to take back to their local repair workshops, repair them, and re-deliver them to the customer. If the company does its own after-sales service, it proposes that customers would bring these smaller items for repair to a local company service centre which would be located and organised to deal with visitors.

There is a list price to customers for the labour content of any work done and for parts used. However, the majority of the after-sales service work is done under an annual service contract taken out by customers on purchasing a computer system; this covers the labour content of any service work to be done, but customers pay for parts used.

Any labour or parts needed in the first six months are provided to the customer free of charge under Computacore's product guarantee, and subcontractors are allowed by the company a fixed sum of 2.5% of the selling price of each appliance to cover this work. These sums allowed have proved to be closely in line with the work needed over the past few years.

The price structure is as follows:

Parts
The price to the subcontractor is the Computacore Ltd cost plus 15%
The price to customer is the subcontractor price plus 30%

Labour
The price to the subcontractor is:
80% of list price for work done under a service contract
75% of list price for work not done under a service contract

Records show that 70% by value of the work has to be carried out at customers' premises, whilst the remainder can be done anywhere appropriate.

The annual income Computacore Ltd currently receives from subcontractors for the area in which the experiment is to take place is as follows:

Parts

Under service contract	£360,000
Not under service contract	£120,000

Labour

Under service contract	£600,000
Not under service contract	£240,000
	£1,320,000

The company expects the volume of after-sales work to remain the same as last year for the period of the experiment.

Computacore Ltd is considering the following options:

(a) setting up a local service centre at which it can service small computer systems only – work at customers' premises would continue to be done under subcontract

(b) setting up a local service centre to act only as a base for its own employees who would only service appliances at customers' premises – servicing of small computer systems would continue to be done under subcontract

(c) setting up a local combined service centre plus base for all work – no work would be subcontracted.

If the company were to do service work, it has estimated that annual fixed costs would be budgeted as follows:

	Option		
	(a)	(b)	(c)
	£000	£000	£000
Staff costs			
Managers	180	100	200
Stores	90	70	100
Repair and service	310	1,270	1,530
Rent, business property taxes and lighting	350	100	900
Van and car hire, and transport costs	70	460	470

Required

(i) Prepare an appropriate financial analysis to evaluate each of the alternative options, compared with the current position.

(ii) Recommend which of the three options Computacore Ltd should adopt on the basis of your financial analysis.

(iii) Identify and comment on the non-financial factors, relevant to your recommendation, which might favourably or adversely affect the customer.

(iv) Outline the factors that may be discussed if Computacore Ltd were to propose the establishment of a 'call centre' within or outside the UK, to deal with after-sales service and organisation and scheduling of repair and service work.

16

Working capital management

Contents

Learning objectives

Completion of this chapter will enable you to:

■ explain what is meant by working capital and by the operating cycle

■ describe the management and control of the working capital requirement

■ outline some of the working capital policies that may be adopted by companies

■ implement the systems and techniques that may be used for the management and control of inventories, and optimisation of inventory levels

■ outline a system of credit management and the control of trade receivables

■ consider the management of trade payables as an additional source of finance

■ use the operating cycle to evaluate a company's working capital requirement performance

■ consider the actions and techniques to achieve short-term and long-term cash flow improvement.

Introduction

Chapters 14 and 15 have been concerned with the longer-term elements of the balance sheet: investments and the alternative sources of funds to finance them. This chapter turns to the shorter-term elements of the balance sheet, the net current assets (current assets less current liabilities) or working capital, which is normally supported with short-term financing, for example bank overdrafts. The chapter begins with an overview of the nature and purpose of working capital.

An emphasis is placed on the importance of good management of the working capital requirement (WCR) for the sustained success of companies. The techniques that may be used to improve the management of inventories, trade receivables and trade payables are explored in detail.

Regular evaluation of the operating cycle may be used to monitor a company's effectiveness in the management of its working capital requirement. Optimisation of working capital is an objective that reduces the extent to which external financing of working capital is required. However, there is a fine balance between minimising the costs of finance and ensuring that sufficient working capital is available to adequately support the company's operations.

This chapter will close by linking working capital to the effective management of cash and by considering some of the ways that both long-term and short-term cash flow may be improved.

Working capital and working capital requirement

The balance sheet is sometimes presented showing all the assets in one part of the balance sheet and all the liabilities in another part of the balance sheet. This may be said to be a little unsatisfactory since the various categories within the assets section and within the liabilities heading are very different in nature. Cash, for example, is a financial asset and has very different characteristics to non-current assets and to inventories.

If we consider the following relationship:

$$\text{assets} = \text{equity} + \text{liabilities}$$

it may be rewritten as

$$\text{non-current assets} + \text{inventories} + \text{trade receivables} + \text{prepayments} + \text{cash}$$
$$=$$
$$\text{equity} + \text{financial debt} + \text{trade payables} + \text{accruals}$$

This may be further rewritten to show homogeneous items on each side of the = sign as follows:

$$\text{equity} + \text{financial debt} - \text{cash}$$
$$=$$
$$\text{non-current assets} + \text{inventories} + \text{trade receivables} - \text{trade payables} - \text{accruals} + \text{prepayments}$$

Therefore

> **equity**
> **=**
> **non-current assets + inventories + trade receivables − trade payables −**
> **accruals + prepayments − financial debt + cash**

Financial debt comprises two parts:

- long-term debt (loans repayable after one year, in accounting terms)
- short-term debt (overdrafts and loans repayable within one year, in accounting terms)

and so from substitution and rearranging the equation we can see that:

$$\text{equity} + \text{long-term debt}$$
$$=$$
$$\text{non-current assets} + \text{inventories} + \text{trade receivables} - \text{trade payables} - \text{accruals} + \text{prepayments} - \text{short-term debt} + \text{cash}$$

or

> **equity + long-term debt = non-current assets + working capital**

Therefore, equity plus long-term financial debt is represented by non-current assets plus, as we saw in Chapter 3, working capital (WC)

> **WC = inventories + trade receivables − trade payables − accruals + prepayments −**
> **short-term financial debt + cash**

Inventories, of course, comprise raw materials, finished product and work in progress (including their share of allocated and apportioned production overheads).

Figure 16.1 The operating cycle

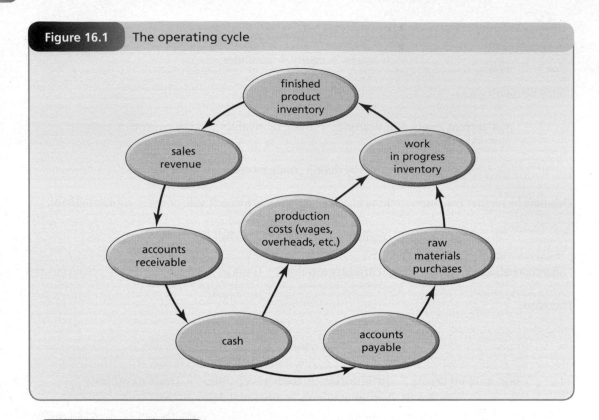

Progress check 16.1

Explain briefly the main components of working capital, using an example of a UK plc.

The need for working capital – the operating cycle

The interrelationship of each of the elements within working capital may be represented in the operating cycle (Fig. 16.1), which was introduced in Chapter 3 when we looked at the balance sheet.

The operating cycle includes:

■ acquisition of raw materials and packaging, which are at first stored in warehouses prior to use, are invoiced by suppliers and recorded by the company in accounts payable, and then normally paid for at a later date

■ use of materials and packaging in the manufacturing process to create partly completed finished goods, work in progress, stored as inventory in the company's warehouses

■ use of materials, packaging, and work in progress to complete finished goods, which are also stored as inventory in the company's warehouses

■ despatch of finished goods from the warehouses and delivery to customers, who accept the products for which they will pay

■ recording as sales by the company its deliveries to customers, which are included in its accounts receivable, and normally paid by customers at a later date

■ use of cash resources to pay overheads, wages and salaries

■ use of cash resources to pay trade payables for production overheads and other expenses

■ use of cash resources to pay trade payables for raw materials.

A company with a low number of operating cycle days is likely to have a better operating cash position than a similar company with a high number of operating cycle days.

Worked example 16.1

We can identify which of the following categories may be included within a company's operating cycle:

- plant and machinery
- trade payables
- investments in subsidiaries
- cash
- work in progress
- patents
- accounts receivable
- fixtures and fittings.

Non-current assets are not renewed within the operating cycle. The following items extracted from the above list relate to non-current assets:

plant and machinery	patents
investments in subsidiaries	fixtures and fittings

The remaining categories therefore relate to the operating cycle, as follows:

accounts payable	cash
work in progress	accounts receivable

The company therefore uses some of its funds to finance its inventories, through the manufacturing process, from raw materials to finished goods, and also the time lag between delivery of the finished goods or services and the payments by customers of accounts receivable. Short-term funds, for example bank overdrafts, are needed to finance the working capital the company requires as represented in the operating cycle. Many companies use the flexibility of the bank overdraft to finance fluctuating levels of working capital.

Progress check 16.2

How is a company's need for investment in operations explained by the operating cycle?

Working capital requirement (WCR)

We have seen that

$$\text{equity} + \text{long-term debt} + \text{short-term debt} - \text{cash}$$
$$=$$
$$\text{non-current assets} + \text{inventories} + \text{trade receivables} - \text{trade payables} - \text{accruals}$$
$$+ \text{prepayments}$$

From this equation we can see that the total financial resources of the company are equity plus long- and short-term financial debt minus cash. This represents the total money invested in the company, and is called the total investment. Therefore

$$\text{total investment}$$
$$=$$
$$\text{non-current assets} + \text{inventories} + \text{trade receivables} - \text{trade payables} - \text{accruals}$$
$$+ \text{prepayments}$$

The total investment in the company can therefore be seen to comprise broadly two elements:

- investment in non-current assets
- investment in operations

where the investment in operations is

> **inventories + trade receivables − trade payables − accruals + prepayments**

which is called the working capital requirement (WCR).

Stated in words, the WCR is telling us something very important: the company has to raise and use some of its financial resources, for which it has to pay, to invest in its operating cycle. These financial resources are specifically for the company to purchase and create inventories, while it waits for payments from its customers. The impact of this is decreased by the fact that suppliers also have to wait to be paid. Added to this is the net effect of accruals and prepayments. Prepayments may be greater than accruals (requiring the use of funds) or accruals may be greater than prepayments (which is a source of funds).

In most manufacturing companies the WCR is positive. The smaller the WCR, the smaller are the total financial resources needed, and the more liquid is the company. Some businesses, for example supermarkets, may have limited inventories and zero accounts receivable, but high accounts payable. In such cases WCR may be negative and these companies are effectively able to finance acquisition of non-current assets with funds payable to their suppliers.

Worked example 16.2

From the balance sheet of Flatco plc for 2010 and the comparatives for 2009 (see Fig. 16.2), and the additional information shown in Figure 7.5 in Chapter 7 we may calculate the working capital requirement for 2010 and the working capital requirement for 2009.

Figures in £000
Working capital requirement:

WCR = inventories + trade receivables − trade payables − accruals + prepayments

WCR for 2010 = 311 + 573 − 553 − 82 + 589 = 838

WCR for 2009 = 268 + 517 − 461 − 49 + 617 = 892

Throughout this chapter we will use the financial statements of Flatco plc, an engineering company, shown in Figures 16.2 and 16.3 and the additional information in Figure 7.5 in Chapter 7, to illustrate the calculation of the key working capital ratios. The income statement is for the year ended 31 December 2010 and the balance sheet is as at 31 December 2010. Comparative figures are shown for 2009.

Progress check 16.3

What is meant by working capital requirement (WCR)?

Figure 16.2   Flatco plc balance sheets as at 31 December 2009 and 2010

Flatco plc Balance sheet as at 31 December 2010	2010 £000	2009 £000
Assets		
Non-current assets		
Tangible	1,884	1,921
Intangible	416	425
Investments	248	248
Total non-current assets	2,548	2,594
Current assets		
Inventories	311	268
Trade and other receivables	1,162	1,134
Cash and cash equivalents	327	17
Total current assets	1,800	1,419
Total assets	4,348	4,013
Liabilities		
Current liabilities		
Borrowings and finance leases	50	679
Trade and other payables	553	461
Current tax liabilities	50	44
Dividends payable	70	67
Provisions	82	49
Total current liabilities	805	1,300
Non-current liabilities		
Borrowings and finance leases	173	–
Trade and other payables	154	167
Deferred tax liabilities	–	–
Provisions	222	222
Total non-current liabilities	549	389
Total liabilities	1,354	1,689
Net assets	2,994	2,324
Equity		
Share capital	1,200	1,000
Share premium account	200	200
Retained earnings	1,594	1,124
Total equity	2,994	2,324

Working capital (WC)

Working capital (WC) is normally defined as:

$$\text{current assets} - \text{current liabilities}$$

or

$$WC = \text{inventories} + \text{trade receivables} - \text{trade payables} - \text{accruals} + \text{prepayments} - \text{short-term debt} + \text{cash}$$

Figure 16.3 Flatco plc income statements for the years ended 31 December 2009 and 2010

Flatco plc
Income statement for the year ended 31 December 2010

	2010 £000	2009 £000
Revenue	3,500	3,250
Cost of sales	(2,500)	(2,400)
Gross profit	1,000	850
Distribution costs	(300)	(330)
Administrative expenses	(250)	(160)
Other income	100	90
Operating profit	550	450
Finance income	111	80
Finance costs	(71)	(100)
Profit before tax	590	430
Income tax expense	(50)	(44)
Profit for the year from continuing operations	540	386
Profit for the year from discontinued operations	–	–
Profit for the year	540	386

Therefore

$$\text{WC} = \text{WCR} - \text{short-term debt} + \text{cash}$$

The difference between WC and WCR can be seen to be cash less short-term financial debt.

The financial analyst considers the definitions of long- and short-term in a different way to the accountant, thinking of long-term as 'permanent' or 'stable' and so will consider WC in an alternative way by calculating the difference between the stable financial resources of the company and its long-term use of funds, its non-current assets.

Since

$$\text{equity} + \text{short-term debt} + \text{long-term debt} - \text{cash}$$
$$=$$
$$\text{non-current assets} + \text{inventories} + \text{trade receivables} - \text{trade payables} - \text{accruals} + \text{prepayments}$$

and

$$\text{WC} = \text{inventories} + \text{trade receivables} - \text{trade payables} - \text{accruals} + \text{prepayments}$$
$$- \text{short-term financial debt} + \text{cash}$$

an alternative representation of working capital is

$$\text{WC} = \text{equity} + \text{long-term debt} - \text{non-current assets}$$

As a general rule, except in certain commercial circumstances WC should always be positive in the long run because if it were negative then the company would be financing its (long-term) non-current assets with short-term debt. Renewal of such debt represents a major liquidity risk. It is the same thing as, say, financing one's house purchase with an overdraft. Since WC has to be positive and the aim should be for WCR to be as small as possible, or even negative, there is a dilemma as to the acceptability of either positive or negative cash. The answer really depends on the quality of the WCR.

If net cash is negative then short-term debt is higher than the cash balance and so WCR is financed partly with short-term debt. So the question may be asked 'will the company suffer the same liquidity risk as with a negative WC?' If inventories are of high-quality champagne, the value of which will probably rise year by year, or if the trade receivables are, say, blue chip companies with no credit risk, then a bank is likely to finance such WCR with no restrictions. If the quality of the WCR is poor the bank is unlikely to finance the WCR with short-term debt. The management and control of each of the elements of WCR: inventories; trade receivables; trade payables, must be considered in terms of both their quality and their level. We will look at each of these elements in the sections that follow.

> ### Progress check 16.4
>
> What is meant by working capital (WC)? How may it differ in a manufacturing company compared with a supermarket retailer?

Working capital policy

Companies should ideally adopt a policy of matching financing with the type of investment being made in new assets and projects. Such a policy finances the long-term investment in non-current assets with long-term funding such as loans, bonds, equity and retained earnings. The financing of its investment in operations, its short-term working capital requirement (WCR), offers a number of options to a company. Choices may be made between internal and external finance. The external financing of the WCR is usually provided by bank overdraft. This is because of its flexibility in accommodating the fluctuating nature of net current assets. However, this incurs a relatively high cost – short-term interest rates are normally higher than long-term interest rates.

The servicing costs of bank overdrafts, and other short-term funding, are not insignificant and so it is of obvious benefit for companies to maintain their overdraft facility requirements at minimum levels. Such requirements may be reduced by the adoption of appropriate policies with regard to the level of investment in working capital that a company chooses to operate.

The working capital policy adopted will be dependent on individual company objectives that may often be influenced by the type of business and the commercial or industrial sector in which it operates. The choice of policy inevitably presents a conflict between the goals of profitability and liquidity, and there is a range of working capital policies that may be chosen that lie somewhere between the following two approaches:

- aggressive
- conservative.

If the company adopts an aggressive working capital policy then for a given level of activity it will aim to operate with low levels of inventories and cash. This type of policy is adopted in order to increase profitability. However, it is a high-risk strategy that provides little flexibility for the company, and may result in:

- an inability to meet customer demand because of stock-outs
- poor customer relationships or loss of customers because of tight credit terms
- an inability to meet current commitments or pay suppliers because of cash shortages, and therefore a danger of interrupted supply of materials or services.

If the company adopts a conservative working capital policy then for a given level of activity it will aim to operate with higher levels of inventories and cash. This type of policy is adopted in order to increase liquidity. It is a policy that provides greater flexibility, but its higher levels of inventories and cash will result in reduced profitability because of:

- the high costs of holding inventories (see the later section about inventory management)
- extended credit terms meaning that cash is received from customers later and therefore has to be funded by short-term overdraft, which incurs high interest costs
- the opportunity cost of holding cash, which is the return that could otherwise have been earned from investment in profitable projects (which may be mitigated to some extent with interest earned from short-term lending of cash surplus to immediate requirements).

A conservative working capital policy presents lower levels of risk for the company because of:

- customer demand being easier to meet with less likelihood of stock-outs
- good customer relationships and customer retention because of favourable credit terms
- the ability to meet current commitments and pay suppliers and therefore avoiding interrupted supply of materials or services.

Any working capital policy adopted that lies between the two extremes of conservative and aggressive may be tailored to suit the requirements of the business and its particular market. A company cannot determine the 'right' working capital policy with absolute precision. However, it may benchmark similar companies in its particular industrial sector.

For example, companies like automotive manufacturers, house builders, and retailers of fashion items and non-perishable goods will inevitably need to hold relatively high levels of materials, work in progress and finished products, and will therefore have relatively higher levels of working capital. On the other hand, companies like supermarkets, food companies, and retailers of fast-moving and perishable goods will have a much higher turnover of inventories and therefore lower levels of working capital. Additionally, supermarkets have only cash customers and therefore zero trade receivables, and are also able to extend their credit with suppliers, and so their working capital tends to be extremely low or negative, or even highly negative as currently seen in Tesco plc.

Working capital is the 'lubricant' of the investment in a company's operations, enabling the 'engine' of the business, its investment in non-current assets, to be most effectively exploited. An under-utilisation of non-current assets can result in higher inventory levels, which increase the working capital requirement and therefore the requirement for additional short-term financing and its associated costs. Reductions in levels of the WCR reduce the requirement for financing and its associated costs. Maintenance of optimal, and therefore more manageable, levels of the WCR increase levels of **efficiency** and **effectiveness** and, as we have seen above, additionally contribute to increased profitability and a reduction in the requirement for external financing.

Regardless of the policies adopted, the improved management of working capital may have a significant impact on the level of requirement for external and internal financing. Good management of their working capital requirement by companies can therefore be seen to be crucially important to both their short- and long-term success.

Progress check 16.5

Why is the good management of the working capital requirement (WCR) crucial to company success?

Inventories management

In Chapter 10 we discussed how lean accounting can provide the relevant information and measurements to support and encourage lean thinking throughout an organisation. The lean enterprise uses less of everything to provide more, which results from the control and elimination of waste in all its forms. The Japanese quality guru Taiichi Ohno identified seven main areas of waste (called *muda* by Ohno), which relate to inventories to a large extent in terms of their handling, their movement and their storage, in addition to the levels held and the proportion of defective and obsolete inventories (see *The Toyota Production System*, Productivity Press, 1988). These areas of waste emphasise the importance for companies to identify and take the appropriate action for improvement in this aspect of the management of working capital.

Overproduction

Overproduction is the most serious area of waste, which discourages the smooth flow of goods and services and inhibits quality, and productivity, and communication, and causes increases in inventories and

- leads to excessive lead and storage times
- leads to a lack of early detection of defects
- results in product deterioration
- creates artificial work rate pressures
- causes excessive work in progress
- leads to dislocation of operations and poorer communications
- encourages the push of unwanted goods through the system, for example, through the use of bonus systems.

Pull systems and *kanban* provide opportunities to overcome overproduction.

Waiting

Waiting waste occurs when there is no moving or work taking place and

- affects materials, products and people
- should be used for training, maintenance or *kaizen* but not overproduction.

Transportation

Transportation waste is incurred from unnecessary movement and double-handling and

- may result in damage and deterioration – for example, in 1999 and 2000 the UK car manufacturers Rover and Vauxhall found themselves with unsold or excess inventories of vehicles being stored for too long in the open air, and were then forced to cut back production because of storage and damage problems
- increased distance means slower communication or feedback of poor quality, therefore slower corrective action.

Inappropriate processing

Inappropriate processing waste often results from complex solutions to simple procedures, such as

- the use of large inflexible machines instead of small flexible ones, which encourages overproduction to recoup the investment in them

■ poor layout leading to excessive transportation and poor communications – the ideal is to use the smallest machine for the required quality located next to the preceding and succeeding operations
■ the lack of sufficient safeguards, for example, *poka yoke* and *jidoka*, leading to poor quality.

Unnecessary inventories

The holding of unnecessary inventories is a waste that leads to increased lead times, the need for more space, and therefore higher storage costs and

■ prevents rapid identification of problems
■ discourages communication,

which all lead to hidden problems that can be identified only by reducing inventories.

Unnecessary motion

Unnecessary motion waste refers to the importance of **ergonomics** for quality and productivity.

Quality and productivity are ultimately affected by operators stretching unnecessarily, bending and picking up, leading to undue exertion and tiredness.

Product defects

Product defects waste is a direct money cost and provides an opportunity to improve performance. It is an area that is therefore a target for immediate *kaizen* activity.

An example of the problems of overproduction resulting in excessive inventories can be seen from the press extract below. Its immediate effect is to increase the length of the operating cycle and increase the need for further funding, the cost of which has a negative impact on profitability. The other further effects of high inventory levels have an additional downward impact on profit from the cost of increased waste in the ways we have examined above.

The Marks & Spencer press extract illustrates the serious impact on businesses of not clearing inventories. For retailers, increasing their inventory levels before Christmas ensures that customer demand will be met, but the skill is to gauge just what that demand will be. Christmas 2008 was celebrated during a time of deep recession and many stores feared that they would be left with unsold inventories after Christmas. To try and avoid that they engaged in a huge wave of offers and price reductions in an attempt to stimulate customer spending. Not all retailers survived the recession, and Woolworths (mentioned in the press extract) closed its business in late December 2008.

Inventory levels should be optimised so that neither too little is held to meet orders nor too much is held so that waste occurs. The forecasting of inventory requirements must be a part of the management process. In addition, inventory level optimisation requires the following:

■ establishment of robust inventories purchase procedures
■ appropriate location and storage of inventories
■ accurate and timely systems for the recording, control and physical checks of inventories
■ monitoring of inventory turnover performance
■ implementation of effective inventories management and reorder systems.

Progress check 16.6

Briefly explain how electronic point of sales (EPOS) provides a system of monitoring inventory turnover performance.

The problem of too much inventory

Shops are slashing prices this Christmas in the hope that millions of people will scorn the credit crunch.

They are offering discounts of up to 40 per cent to spur buyers into action.

A one-day Marks & Spencer sale last week caught other stores on the hop and inspired a rush of copycat price cuts across Britain.

The good news is that the discounting is likely to continue.

Stores fearing a bleak Christmas as families are hit by soaring bills and fuel costs have decided to slash profit margins rather then leave shelves full.

They fear shoppers will be even less prepared to spend in the New Year and are terrified that they could be left with piles of unsold stock unless they cut prices now.

House of Fraser has already entered the price war by announcing a two-day sale this week.

A spokesman said yesterday: 'In the light of numerous discount events this week, we have decided to offer our customers similar opportunities.

'On Thursday and Friday, House of Fraser will also offer up to 25 per cent off our normal trading prices, with our own brands such as Linea, Untold and Episode all having a limited edition discount of 40 per cent.'

London's New West End Company, a retail organisation representing 600 stores in Oxford Street, Regent Street, Bond Street and 12 neighbouring streets, said the sales war was unprecedented.

Spokesman Jace Tyrrell said: 'This coming week is pay week for a lot of people and you can expect to see more sales announced to try to cash in on full pay packets. It will continue right up to Christmas.

'Retailers are fighting for their lives out there and they will continue slashing prices and cutting their profit margins.

'Sixty of our members are opening at 7am this Friday to try to sell more.

'Shops will use any and every tactic and everyone knows that sales work.

'The shops may not like it but it is the best possible news for the rest of us. There will be some unbelievable bargains out there.' Asda chief executive Andy Bond said that many stores were slashing prices in panic because of the economic climate.

'People are not holding their nerve', he said. 'There is a little bit of panic out there, although conversely this is good for consumers.' A spokesman for Kent's Bluewater shopping centre, recently rated one of the top 10 retail areas in Britain, said that the number of shoppers had increased by 15 per cent this November, compared to last year.

The centre, just off the M25, is a magnet for overseas shoppers seeking British bargains.

Bhs began 20 per cent off 'mega days' on Friday, continuing today.

John Lewis has renewed its pledge never to be undersold, even if competitors slash their prices in sales.

The Arcadia Group, owners of Wallis and Dorothy Perkins, is also running a 20 per cent off sales week, starting today.

Marks & Spencer said its surprise sale last week was a huge success and it will continue to run promotions on single sections.

The British Retail Consortium said the record interest rate cut was good news as it was likely to restore consumer confidence in time for the Christmas period. H Samuel has reduced a Citizen watch from £169 to £69, The Perfume Shop is offering Emporio Armani perfume and aftershave at £14.99, down from £36.99, and Zavvi is selling a boxed set of all 10 seasons of Friends for £49.99, down from £199.99.

Argos is offering a third off bicycles and Game has cut the price of an Xbox 360 from £259.99 to £199.99.

However, a growing list of retailers are facing the threat of administration. Woolworths is fighting to stay in business and one administrator said he was busier than he had ever been.

Source: **Christmas chopping: stores hacking prices to make Britain defy the credit crunch,** by David Jarvis and Emily Fox © *Sunday Express*, 23 November 2008

Inventory purchase

For cash flow (and operational efficiency) purposes it is crucial that efficient and effective sales order, materials procurement and inventory control systems are in place and operated by highly trained staff. Authority levels for the appropriate purchasing and logistics managers must be established for both price and quantities, for initial orders and reorders.

Inventory location

A variety of options exist for the location of inventories and the ways in which they may be stored. Related items of inventories may be grouped together, or they may be located by part number, or by frequency of pick, or located based on their size or weight.

Inventory recording and physical checks

Ideally, all inventory transactions should be recorded simultaneously with their physical movement. Inventory turnover must be regularly reviewed so that damaged, obsolete and slow-moving inventory may be disposed of, possibly at discounted sales prices or for some scrap value.

In cash terms, holding on to unsaleable inventories is a 'waste' of the highest order. It uses up valuable space and time and needs people to manage it. It clogs up the system and reduces efficient order fulfilment and represents money tied up in assets of little or no value. Businesses need to move on and dispose of old, obsolete and slow-moving inventories.

Progress check 16.7

What are the ways in which improvements in a company's management of inventories may contribute to achievement of optimisation of its level of working capital requirement (WCR)?

It is inevitable that inventories will be required to be physically counted from time to time, to provide a check against inventory records. This may be by way of a complete physical count two or three times a year, with one count taking place at the company's financial year-end. Alternatively, physical **cycle counts** may take place continuously throughout the year. This system selects groups of inventories to be counted and checked with inventory records in such a way that all inventories are checked two, three, four or more times up to maybe 12 times a year, dependent on such criteria as value or frequency of usage.

Inventory ratios

You may recall from the sections in Chapter 7 about financial ratios that one of the efficiency ratios related to inventory turnover is a measure used to monitor inventories levels:

$$\text{inventories days} = \frac{\text{inventories value}}{\text{average daily cost of sales in period}}$$

Inventories days (or inventory turnover) is the number of days that inventories could last at a forecast or the most recent usage rate. This may be applied to total inventories, finished goods, raw materials, or work in progress. The weekly internal efficiency of inventory utilisation is shown in the following ratios:

$$\frac{\text{finished goods}}{\text{average weekly despatches}} \qquad \frac{\text{raw materials}}{\text{average weekly raw material usage}} \qquad \frac{\text{work in progress}}{\text{average weekly production}}$$

Inventory ratios are usually calculated using values but may also be calculated for individual inventory lines using quantities where appropriate:

$$\text{inventory weeks} = \frac{\text{total inventories units}}{\text{average weekly units cost of sales}}$$

Financial analysts usually only have access to published accounts and so they often calculate the inventory weeks ratio using the total closing inventories value in relation to the cost of sales for the year.

Worked example 16.3

From Flatco plc's balance sheet and income statement for 2010 and the comparatives for 2009, we may calculate the inventory turnover for 2010 and the inventories days (inventory turnover) for 2009.

$$\text{inventories days 2010} = \frac{\text{inventories value}}{\text{average daily cost of sales in period}} = \frac{£311}{£2,500/365}$$

$$= 45 \text{ days (6.5 weeks)}$$

$$\text{inventories days 2009} = \frac{£268}{£2,400/365} = 41 \text{ days (5.9 weeks)}$$

The performance for 2009, 2010 and future years may be more clearly presented in a trend analysis. If 2009 was the first year in the series, then 41 days may be expressed as the base of 100. The 45 days for the year 2010 is then expressed as 110 [$45 \times 100/41$], and so on for subsequent years. Comparison of 110 with 100 more clearly shows its significance than the presentation of the absolute numbers 45 and 41.

ABC and VIN analysis

The appropriate level of control of inventories may be determined through assessment of the costs of control against the accuracy required and the potential benefits. Use of a Pareto analysis (80/20 analysis) allows selective levels of control of inventories through their categorisation into A items, B items and C items. The ABC method uses Pareto to multiply the usage of each inventory item by its value, ranking from the highest to the lowest and then calculating the cumulative result at each level in the ranking.

A items, for example, may be chosen so that the top five inventory items make up 60% of the total value. Such items would then be continuously monitored for unit-by-unit replenishment. B items, for example, may be chosen from say 60% to 80% of the total value. Such items would be subject to automated systematic control using cycle counts, with levels of inventories replenished using economic order quantities (see page 638). C items, for example, may be identified as the 20% of inventories remaining – 'the trivial many' in financial terms. These inventories may be checked by sample counting; because of their low value, more than adequate levels may be held.

Other important factors impact on the choice of inventory levels. Total acquisition costs must be considered rather than simply the unit purchase price. There may be requirements to provide items of inventory using a just in time approach (see the section dealing with JIT later in this chapter). The cost of not having a particular item in inventory, even though it may itself have a low cost, may be significant if it is an integral part within a process. Consequently, in addition to ABC categories, inventories are usually allocated vital/important/nice to have (VIN) categories, indicating whether they are:

- vital (V) – out of inventory would be a disaster
- important (I) – out of inventory would give significant operational problems or costs
- nice to have (N) – out of inventory would present only an insignificant problem.

Progress check 16.8

Describe how inventory turnover may be regularly monitored.

Economic order quantity (EOQ)

A simplistic model called EOQ, or the 'economic order quantity' model, aims to reconcile the problem of the possible loss to a business through interruption of production, or failure to meet orders, with the cost of holding inventories levels large enough to give security against such loss. EOQ may be defined as the most economic inventory replenishment order size, which minimises the sum of inventory ordering costs and inventory holding costs. EOQ is used in an 'optimising' inventory control system.

If

$$P = \text{the £ cost per purchase order}$$
$$Q = \text{order quantity of each order in units}$$
$$N = \text{annual units usage}$$
$$S = \text{annual £ cost of holding one unit}$$

then

the annual cost of purchasing
= cost per purchase order × the number of orders to be placed in a year
(which is the annual usage divided by quantity ordered per purchase)

or $\qquad P \times N/Q$
or $\qquad PN/Q$

the annual cost of holding inventory
= annual cost of holding one unit in inventory × average number of units held in inventory
$$= 0.5Q \times S \text{ or } QS/2$$

The minimum total cost occurs when the annual purchasing cost equals the annual holding cost,

or $\qquad PN/Q = QS/2$

Cross-multiplication gives

$$2PN = Q^2/S$$
$$\text{or} \quad Q^2 = 2PN/S$$

Therefore when the quantity ordered is the economic order quantity:

$$\mathbf{EOQ = \sqrt{2PN/S}}$$

Let's look at a simple example.

Worked example 16.4

E.C.O. Nomic & Sons, the greengrocers, buy cases of potatoes at £20 per case.

£ cost of one purchase order	P = £5 per order
Number of cases turned over in a year	N = 1,000 cases (units)
Annual £ cost of holding one case	S = 20% of purchase price

$$S = 20\% \times £20 = £4$$

The economic order quantity

$$EOQ = \sqrt{2PN/S} = \sqrt{2 \times 5 \times 1,000/4}$$
$$EOQ = \sqrt{2,500}$$
$$EOQ = 50 \text{ cases of potatoes per order}$$

EOQ illustrates the principle of inventory ordering and inventory holding optimisation but it is extremely limited. In practice, significant divergences from the EOQ may result in only minor cost increases:

- the optimum order quantity decision may more usually be dependent on other factors like storage space, storage facilities, purchasing department resources, logistical efficiency, etc.
- costs of purchasing and holding inventories may be difficult to quantify accurately so the resultant EOQ calculation may be inaccurate
- in periods of changing prices, interest rates, foreign currency exchange rates, etc., continual recalculation is required that necessitates constant updates of all purchasing department and warehouse records of purchases and inventories – computerised systems can assist in providing the answers to some of the financial 'what-ifs' presented by changes in the business environment.

The emphasis over the past couple of decades on inventory minimisation or inventory elimination systems through the implementation of, for example, JIT, *kanban* and vendor managed inventory (VMI) has reinforced the disadvantages of holding large inventories. High inventory levels reduce the risk of disappointing customers, but it is a costly process not only in the inherent cost of the inventory itself, but in the cost resulting from the 'wastes' identified by Ohno that we discussed earlier in this chapter.

Progress check 16.9

Outline the basic conflict that might arise between the marketing department and the finance department when discussing the practical application of an economic order quantity (EOQ) system.

Just in time (JIT), materials requirement planning (MRP) and optimised production technology (OPT)

Just in time (JIT)

Just in time (JIT) is sometimes incorrectly referred to as an inventory reduction or a zero inventory system. JIT is a philosophy that is a response to two key factors: the reduction in product life cycles and the increase in levels of quality required from demanding customers.

JIT is a management philosophy that incorporates a 'pull' system of producing or purchasing components and products in response to customer demand. In a JIT system products are pulled through the system from customer demand back down through the supply chain to the level of materials and components. The consumer buys, and the processes manufacture the products to meet this demand. The consumer therefore determines the schedule.

The JIT system contrasts with a 'push' system where levels of **buffer stock** (inventories) are built up between each process within and between purchasing, manufacturing and sales. In a push system, products are produced to schedule, and the schedule may be based on:

- a 'best guess' of demand
- last year's sales
- intuition.

Some of the key principles and techniques of waste elimination, which in turn support improved inventory management, are embraced within the implementation of the JIT process:

- total quality control (TQC), which embraces a culture of waste elimination and 'right first time'
- *kanban* which is a system of signals used to control inventories levels and smooth the rate of production, for example using cards to prompt top-up of materials or components driven by demand from the next process
- set-up time reduction for reduced manufacturing batch sizes
- *heijunka*, which is the smoothing of production through levelling of day-to-day variations in schedules in line with longer-term demand
- *jidoka*, or autonomation, where operators are empowered to stop the line if a quality problem arises, avoiding poor quality production and demanding immediate resolution of the problem
- improved production layout
- *poka yoke* (mistake-proofing) fail-safe devices, supporting *jidoka* by preventing parts being fitted in the wrong way, so that poor quality is not passed to the next stage in the production process
- employee involvement including self-quality and operator first-line maintenance
- multi-skilling of employees for increased flexibility
- supplier development for higher quality and greater reliability of supply – in the UK, M&S, for example, has publicised its adoption of this practice.

Two other approaches to inventory management:

- **materials requirement planning (MRP)**, its development into **manufacturing resource planning (MRPII)**, and
- optimised production technology (OPT)

are sometimes seen as alternatives to JIT, but in fact may be used to complement JIT systems.

> **Progress check 16.10**
>
> Explain briefly what benefits might be gained by both supplier (manufacturer) and customer (national retailer) if they work jointly on optimisation of inventories levels and higher quality levels.

Materials requirement planning (MRP)

MRP is a set of techniques, which uses the bill of materials (BOM), inventory data and the **master production schedule** to calculate future requirements for materials. It essentially makes recommendations to release material to the production system. MRP is a 'push' approach that starts with forecasts of customer demand and then calculates and reconciles materials requirements using basic mathematics. MRP relies on accurate BOMs and scheduling **algorithms**, EOQ analyses and allowances for wastage and shrinkage.

Optimised production technology (OPT)

OPT is a philosophy, combined with a computerised system of shop-floor scheduling and capacity planning, that differs from a traditional approach of balancing capacity as near to 100% as possible and then maintaining flow. It aims to balance flow rather than capacity. Like JIT, it aims at improvement of the production process and is a philosophy that focuses on factors such as:

- manufacture to order
- quality
- lead times
- batch sizes
- set-up times

and has important implications for purchasing efficiency, inventory control and resource allocation.

OPT is based on the concept of throughput accounting (TA), which was outlined in Chapter 8, developed by Eli Goldratt and vividly portrayed in his book *The Goal* (Gower, 1984). The aim of OPT is to make money, defined in terms of three criteria: throughput (which it aims to increase), and inventory and operating expense, which should at the same time both be reduced. It does this by making better use of limited capacity through tightly controlled finite scheduling of bottleneck operations, and use of increased process batch sizes, which means producing more of a high-priority part once it has been set up on a bottleneck machine.

> **Progress check 16.11**
>
> In the UK there are several low-volume car manufacturers. Make an attempt to relate the optimised production technology (OPT) philosophy to their operations.
>
> (*Hint*: Research Morgan Cars of Malvern and Ascari Cars of Banbury.)

Factory scheduling is at the root of OPT and the critical factor in OPT scheduling is identification and elimination or management of bottlenecks. OPT highlights the slowest function. This is crucially important in OPT: if one machine is slowing down the whole line then the value of that machine at that time is equivalent to the value of the whole production line. Conversely, attention paid to improving the productivity of a non-bottleneck machine will merely increase inventories.

Trade receivables and credit management

All companies that sell on credit to their customers should maintain some sort of system of credit control. Improved debt collection is invariably an area that produces significant, immediate cash flow benefits from the reduction of trade receivable balances. It is therefore an area to which time and resources may be profitably devoted.

Cash flow is greatly affected by the policies established by a company with regard to:

- the choice of customers
- the way in which sales are made
- the sales invoicing system
- the speedy correction of errors and resolution of disputes
- the means of settlement
- the monitoring of customer settlement performance
- the overdue accounts collection system.

These are all areas that can delay the important objective of turning a sale into an account receivable and an account receivable into cash in the shortest possible time. Each area of policy involves a cost. Such costs must be weighed against the levels of risk being taken.

Customers and trading terms

Sales persons are enthusiastic to make sales. It is important that they are also aware of the need to assess customer risk of the likelihood of slow payment or non-payment. If risks are to be taken then this must be with prior approval of the company and with an estimate of the cost of the risk included within the selling price. Similar limits and authorisations must be in place to cover credit periods, sales discounts and the issue of credit notes.

Credit checks should always be made prior to allowing any level of credit to a potential new customer. Selling on credit with little hope of collection is a way of running out of cash very quickly and invariably resulting in business failure. The procedure for opening a new account must be a formal process that shows the potential customer that it is something that the organisation takes seriously. Many risky customers may thus be avoided.

Before a new account is agreed to be opened, at least three references should be obtained: one from the customer bank and two from high-profile suppliers with whom the customer regularly does business. It is important that references are followed up in writing with requests as to whether there are any reasons why credit should not be granted. A credit limit should be agreed that represents minimum risk, but at a level that the customer can service. It should also be at a level within which the customer's business may operate effectively.

A copy of the latest annual and interim accounts of a potential customer should be requested from the Registrar of Companies. These will indicate the legal status of the company, who the owners are, and its financial strength. These accounts are by their nature historical. If large volumes of business are envisaged then details of future operations and funding may need to be discussed in more detail with the potential customer. If such large contracts involve special purchases then advance payments should be requested to reduce any element of risk.

Having established relationships with creditworthy customers a number of steps may be taken to further minimise risk associated with ongoing trading:

- sale of goods with reservation of title (**Romalpa clause**) – the goods remain in the ownership of the selling company until they are paid for, and may be recovered should the customer go into liquidation
- credit insurance cover in respect of customers going into liquidation and export risk
- passing of invoices to a factoring company for settlement; the factoring company settles the invoices, less a fee for the service, which therefore provides a type of insurance cover against non-payment – a factoring company can be used as a source of finance, enabling short-term funds to be raised on the value of invoices issued to customers.

The measures adopted should be even more rigorous in their application to the supply of goods or services to businesses abroad. This is because of the inevitable distance, different trading conditions, regulations, currencies and legislation.

Progress check 16.13

What are the ways in which improvements in the management of trade receivables and credit management may contribute to achievement of optimal levels of working capital requirement (WCR)?

Settlement methods

Payment collection methods should be agreed with all customers at the outset. The use of cheques, though still popular, is becoming a costly and ineffective collection method. Cash, credit card receipts and automated electronic transfers are the main methods used by retailers and regular speedy banking is the cornerstone of efficient use of funds. Bankers' drafts are the next best thing to cash but should be avoided because of the risk involved through their potential for accidental or fraudulent loss. Electronic mail transfers are frequently used for settlement by overseas companies. These tend to be costly and have been known to 'get lost' in the banking systems. **Letters of credit** together with sight drafts are frequently used for payments against large contracts.

Extreme care needs to be taken with letters of credit, which are a minefield of potential problems for non-settlement. Letters of credit must be completed providing full details and with the requisite numbers of copies of all supporting documentation. The conditions stipulated must be fully complied with and particularly regarding delivery of goods at the right time at the right location and in the quantity, quality and condition specified.

Electronic collection methods continue to increase in popularity. Direct debit payments are an option where settlement may be made on presentation of agreed sales invoices to the bank. Personal banking is now a feature of the Internet. As its use and level of sophistication continues to be developed, corporate banking transactions conducted through the Internet will inevitably become a major feature. Absolute control is required over both receivables and payables transactions, and all businesses benefit from the strict adherence to administrative routines by the staff involved. Successful control of cash and cheques requires well-thought-out procedures. Examples may be seen in the formal recording that takes place in the systems adopted in high-volume businesses.

One of the most acceptable methods is payment through **BACS**, the bankers' automated clearing services. The BACS method requires customers to register as BACS users and to specify the type of payment pattern they wish to adopt for settlement of their suppliers' accounts or payroll. Every week, or two weeks or every month, companies supply details of payments to be made – names of payees and amounts. These are then settled by BACS exactly on the day specified and with only one payment transaction appearing on the bank statement. This means that the problems of cost of individual cheques and the uncertainty of not knowing when each payment will be cleared are avoided.

Cash takings must be strictly controlled in terms of a log and the issue of receipts. Regular physical counts must be carried out and cash banked twice daily or at least once daily. Cheques may be lost in the mail, or bear wrong dates, or wrong amounts, or the customer may have forgotten to sign. One person should be nominated to receive and bank cash and cheques. A separate person should manage accounts receivable in order to maintain internal control.

Sales invoices

The sales invoicing system must ensure that prompt, accurate invoices are submitted to customers for all goods and services that are provided. A control system needs to be implemented to prevent supply without a subsequent sales invoice being issued. An invoicing delay of just one day may result in one month's delay in payment. Incorrect pricing, VAT calculations, invoice totalling and customer names and addresses may all result in delay. A customer is unlikely to point out an undercharged invoice.

Sales invoices may be routinely followed up with statements of outstanding balances. The credit period offered to customers should obviously be as short as possible. Care should be taken in offering cash discounts for immediate or early payment. This is invariably a disadvantage. Many customers will take the discount but continue to take the extended credit. This is something that may not even be spotted by staff responsible for checking and processing receipts from customers, which effectively results in an unauthorised cost being incurred by the business.

Trade receivables ratios

Another of the efficiency ratios from the sections in Chapter 7 about financial ratios relates to trade receivables collection days, which is a measure used to monitor customer settlement performance.

$$\text{collection days} = \frac{\text{trade receivables} \times 365}{\text{revenue}}$$

Collection days indicate the average time taken, in calendar days, to receive payment from credit customers. Adjustment is needed if the ratio is materially distorted by VAT or other taxes. Currently, UK sales for exports to countries abroad are not applicable for VAT. Other forms of sales tax may be applicable to sales revenues in some countries.

Worked example 16.5

From the balance sheet and income statement of Flatco plc for 2010, and the comparatives for 2009, and the additional information shown in Figure 7.5 in Chapter 7 we may calculate the collection days for 2010 and the collection days for 2009.

$$\text{collection days 2010} = \frac{\text{trade receivables} \times 365}{\text{revenue}} = \frac{£573 \times 365}{£3,500} = 60 \text{ days}$$

$$\text{collection days 2009} = \frac{£517 \times 365}{£3,250} = 58 \text{ days}$$

A similar trend analysis to that described in Worked example 16.3 may be used for greater clarification of performance.

If in 2009, 58 days = 100, then the year 2010 collection days would = 103.

Progress check 16.14

Describe how customer settlement performance may be regularly monitored.

Collection policy

As a great many experienced businessmen may confirm, perhaps the key factor underlying sustained, successful collection of accounts receivable is identification of 'the person' within the customer organisation who actually makes things happen and who can usually speed up the processing of a payment through the company's systems. Payments are usually authorised by the finance director or managing director or the accountant. However, 'the person' is the one who prepares payments and pushes them under the nose of the appropriate manager for signature. Cultivation of a good relationship with 'the person' within each customer organisation is an investment that usually pays massive dividends.

The benefit of issue of regular monthly statements of account to customers may be questioned. Most companies pay on invoice and so a brief telephone call to confirm that all invoices have been received, to check on the balance being processed for payment, and the payment date, usually results in settlement. Issue of a statement is usually of greater benefit as an *ad hoc* exercise to resolve queries or when large numbers of transactions are involved.

A routine should be established for when settlement of invoices becomes overdue. This process should include having a member of staff who has the specific responsibility for chasing overdue accounts – a credit controller. Chasing overdue accounts by telephone is usually the most effective method. It allows development of good working relationships with customers to enable problems to be quickly resolved and settled.

It is absolutely essential that accurate accounts receivable information is available, up-to-date in terms of inclusion of all invoices that have been issued and allowing for all cash received, before calling a customer to chase payment. It is also imperative that immediately errors are identified, for example errors in invoicing, they are corrected without delay. These are two of the commonest areas used by customers to stall payment and yet the remedy is within the hands of the company!

An indispensable information tool to be used by the credit controller should be an up-to-date **aged accounts receivable report** giving full details of all outstanding invoices (see Fig. 16.4). This shows the totals of accounts receivable from all customers at a given date and also an analysis of the outstanding invoices in terms of the time between the date of the report and the dates on which the invoices were issued.

In addition, it is useful to have available the full details of each customer's payment record showing exactly what has been paid and when, going back perhaps one year. To provide a historical analysis and assist in resolving possible customer disputes, computerised systems may be used to hold customer data going back many years, for future retrieval. The friendly agreement of the facts on a customer account on the telephone usually goes a very long way towards obtaining settlement in accordance with agreed terms.

Perhaps one of the most effective methods of extracting payment from a customer with an overdue account is a threat to stop supply of goods or services. If a debt continues to be unpaid then the next step may be a chasing letter that shows that the organisation means business and will be prepared to follow up with legal action. Prior to sending any such letter the facts should be checked and double-checked – people and computers make mistakes! This letter should clearly explain what is expected and what the implications may be for non-compliance with agreed terms. A solicitor's letter should

| Figure 16.4 | Example of an aged accounts receivable report |

Hannagan plc
Aged Accounts Receivable as at 30 September 2010

Customer name	total balance	up to 30 days	over 30, up to 60 days	over 60, up to 90 days	over 90 days
	£	£	£	£	£
Alpha Chemicals Ltd	16,827	7,443	8,352	635	397
Brown Manufacturing plc	75,821	23,875	42,398	6,327	3,221
Caramel Ltd	350,797	324,776	23,464	2,145	412
.	.	.	.	.	.
.	.	.	.	.	.
.	.	.	.	.	.
.	.	.	.	.	.
Zeta Ltd	104,112	56,436	43,565	3,654	457
Total	4,133,714	2,354,377	1,575,477	184,387	19,473
% ageing		56.96%	38.11%	4.46%	0.47%

probably not be considered, as a rule of thumb, before an invoice is, say, 90 days overdue from its expected settlement date.

The last resort is to instruct a solicitor to take action against a customer for non-payment. Small debts may be recovered through the small claims court. The costs are low and the services of a solicitor are not necessarily required. Large debts may be recovered by suing the customer for non-payment. This is an expensive and very time-consuming business. The use of the last resort measures that have been outlined should be kept to a minimum. Their use may be avoided through a great deal of preliminary attention being paid to the recruitment of excellent staff, and the establishment of excellent systems, robust internal controls, and a formal credit control system.

Progress check 16.15

What are some of the ways in which the settlement of accounts receivable from customers may be speeded up?

Trade payables management

The balance sheet category of trade and other payables that are payable within one year comprises taxes, National Insurance, VAT, etc. and accounts payable to suppliers of materials, goods and services provided to the company. Payments to the government are normally required to be made promptly.

Trade payables are sometimes considered a 'free' source of finance because if a company has not paid a supplier then it is able to hold onto and use that cash. However, this really is not the case and unpaid trade payables are not a free method of borrowing money. A supplier is likely to charge a higher price for a product if it is paid 90 days after delivery than if it is paid 30 days after delivery. The following worked example illustrates this point.

Worked example 16.6

A supplier may offer Justin Time Ltd payment terms of 90 days from delivery date. If Justin Time Ltd alternatively proposes to the supplier payment terms of 60 days from delivery date the supplier may, for example, offer 1% (or 2%) discount for settlement 30 days earlier.

Annual cost of discount:

$$\text{At 1\% discount} \quad \frac{365 \times 1\%}{30} = 12.2\% \text{ per annum}$$

$$\text{At 2\% discount} \quad \frac{365 \times 2\%}{30} = 24.3\% \text{ per annum}$$

A discount of 1% for settlement one month early is equivalent to over 12% per annum (and a discount of 2% is over 24% per annum). Consequently, it becomes apparent that the supplier's selling price must have included some allowance for financial charges; accounts payable are therefore not a free debt.

Many companies habitually delay payments to suppliers, in order to improve cash flow, either to the point just before relationships break down or until suppliers refuse further supply. Trade payables may be paid more slowly than the agreed terms to gain a short-term cash advantage, but even as a short-term measure this should only be regarded as temporary. It is very short-term thinking and obviously not a strategy that creates an atmosphere conducive to the development of good supplier relationships. A more systematic approach to the whole purchasing and payables system is the more ethical and professional means of providing greater and sustainable benefits. This is an approach followed by the majority of UK plcs, which is now supported by changes in legislation that were introduced during 1999/2000.

With regard to suppliers, overall business effectiveness and improved control over cash flow may be better served by establishment of policies, in much the same way as was suggested should apply to customers, with regard to:

- the choice of suppliers
- the way in which purchases are made
- the purchase invoicing system
- the speedy correction of errors and resolution of disputes
- the means of settlement
- the monitoring of supplier payment performance.

Progress check 16.16

Explain whether or not trade payables are a 'free' or even a cheap source of finance for a company, and why.

Suppliers and trading terms

New suppliers should be evaluated perhaps even more rigorously than customers with particular regard to quality of product, quality and reliability of distribution, sustainability of supply, and financial stability. Appropriate controls must be established to give the necessary purchasing authority to a minimal number of procurement managers. This role requires highly skilled buyers who are able to source the right-quality product for the job at the best total acquisition price (base price, delivery, currency risk, etc.), in the delivery quantities and frequencies required and at the best possible terms. Their authority must be accompanied by rules governing:

- which suppliers may be dealt with
- acceptable ranges of product
- purchase volumes
- price negotiation
- discounts
- credit terms
- transaction currencies
- invoicing
- payment methods
- payment terms.

Terms of trading must be in writing. Most companies print their agreed terms on their purchase orders.

Payment methods

Payments to suppliers should be made in line with terms of trading, but advantages may be gained from cheaper payment methods that provide better control than through the issue of cheques. For example, the payables system may automatically prepare weekly payment schedules and trigger automated electronic payments (for example, BACS) directly through the bank. Alternatively, submission of correct supplier invoices directly to the company's bank may also be used to support automatic payment in line with agreed terms. Provided that adequate controls are put in place to check and monitor such transactions these methods provide a cost-effective method of controlling cash outflows and may be an invaluable aid to cash planning.

Purchase invoices

Integrated purchase order, inventory control and payables systems, preferably computerised, should be used to control approval of new suppliers, trading terms, prices, etc. When supplier invoices are received by the organisation they must match completely with goods or services received and be matched with an official order. An efficient recording system should allow incorrect deliveries or incorrect invoices to be quickly identified, queried and rectified. The recording system should verify the credit terms for each invoice.

Progress check 16.17

What are some of the ways in which payments to suppliers may be improved to the mutual benefit of the company and its suppliers?

Trade payables ratios

Another of the efficiency ratios, from the sections in Chapter 7 about financial ratios, relates to payables days, which is a measure used to monitor supplier payment performance.

$$\text{payables days} = \frac{\text{trade payables} \times 365}{\text{cost of sales (or purchases)}}$$

Payables days indicate the average time taken, in calendar days, to pay for supplies received on credit. Adjustment is needed if the ratio is materially distorted by VAT or unusual trading terms.

Worked example 16.7

From the balance sheet and income statement of Flatco plc for 2010, and the comparatives for 2009, and the additional information shown in Figure 7.5 in Chapter 7 we may calculate the payables days for 2010 and the payables days for 2009.

$$\text{payables days 2010} = \frac{\text{trade payables} \times 365}{\text{cost of sales}} = \frac{£553 \times 365}{£2,500} = 81 \text{ days}$$

$$\text{payables days 2009} = \frac{£461 \times 365}{£2,400} = 70 \text{ days}$$

A trend analysis may also be calculated in the same way as discussed in Worked examples 16.3 and 16.5.

Payment policy

The priority for the accounts payable manager must be to maintain the level of payables and cash outflows in line with company policy, but at all times ensuring absolutely no interruption to any manufacturing processes or any other operations of the business. Fundamental to this is the development of good working relationships with suppliers so that problems may be quickly resolved and settled, thus avoiding any threats to supply.

The accounts payable manager must have accurate accounts payable information that is up-to-date in terms of all invoices received, invoices awaited and payments made. In the same way as the credit controller deals with customer queries it is also imperative that the accounts payable manager requests corrections of invoice errors, immediately errors are identified. The accounts payable manager should have access to an up-to-date **aged accounts payable report** (see Fig. 16.5). This shows the totals of accounts payable to all suppliers at a given date and also an analysis of the balances in terms of the time between the date of the report and the dates of the invoices from suppliers.

The accounts payable manager should also have available detailed reports of all unpaid invoices on each account, and full details of each supplier's payment record showing exactly what has been paid and when, going back perhaps one year. The availability for use of correct, up-to-date information goes a long way to ensuring the avoidance of the build-up of any potential disputes.

Figure 16.5	Example of an aged accounts payable report

Hannagan plc
Aged Accounts Payable as at 31 December 2010

Supplier name	total balance	up to 30 days	over 30, up to 60 days	over 60, up to 90 days	over 90 days
	£	£	£	£	£
Ark Packaging plc	9,800	4,355	2,555	445	2,435
Beta Plastics plc	45,337	32,535	12,445	144	213
Crown Cases Ltd	233,536	231,213	2,323	.	.
.	.	.	.	.	.
.	.	.	.	.	.
.	.	.	.	.	.
.	.	.	.	.	.
Zonkers Ltd	89,319	23,213	21,332	12,321	32,453
Total	**3,520,811**	**2,132,133**	**1,142,144**	**123,213**	**123,321**
% ageing		**60.56%**	**32.44%**	**3.50%**	**3.50%**

Progress check 16.18

Describe how supplier payment performance may be regularly monitored.

Operating cycle performance

The operating cycle, or working capital cycle, which was illustrated in Figure 16.1, is the period of time which elapses between the point at which cash begins to be expended on the production of a product and the collection of cash from the customer. It determines the short-term financing requirements of the business. For a business that purchases and sells on credit the cash operating cycle may be calculated by deducting the average payment period for suppliers from the average inventory turnover period and the average customer's settlement period.

operating cycle (days) = inventories days + collection days − payables days

The operating cycle may alternatively be calculated as a percentage:

$$\text{operating cycle \%} = \frac{\text{working capital requirement}}{\text{(inventories + trade receivables − trade payables)}}$$
$$\text{revenue}$$

Worked example 16.8

From the working capital requirement information shown in Worked example 16.2 and the inventories days, collection days and payables days calculated in Worked examples 16.3, 16.5 and 16.7, we may calculate the operating cycle in days and % for Flatco plc for 2010 and 2009.

Operating cycle days:

$$\text{Operating cycle } 2010 = \text{inventories days} + \text{collection days} - \text{payables days}$$

$$= 45 + 60 - 81 = 24 \text{ days}$$

$$\text{Operating cycle } 2009 = 41 + 58 - 70 = 29 \text{ days}$$

Operating cycle %:

$$\text{Operating cycle \% } 2010 = \frac{\text{working capital requirement}}{\text{revenue}}$$

$$= \frac{(£311 + £573 - £553) \times 100\%}{£3,500} = 9.5\%$$

$$\text{Operating cycle \% } 2009 = \frac{(£268 + £517 - £461) \times 100\%}{£3,250} = 10.0\%$$

From this example we can see that Flatco plc's operating cycle has improved by five days from 2009 to 2010, an improvement of 0.5%. The deterioration in collection days and inventory turnover in this example has been more than offset by the increase in payables days. Despite the overall improvement, this must be a cause for concern for the company which should therefore set targets for improvement and action plans to reduce its average customer collection period and reduce its number of inventories days.

Overtrading

We have seen how important to a company is its good management of WCR. Personal judgement is required regarding choice of optimal levels of working capital appropriate to the individual company and its circumstances. This generally leads to the quest for ever-reducing levels of working capital. However, there is a situation called overtrading which occurs if the company tries to support too great a volume of trade from too small a working capital base.

Overtrading is a condition of a business which enters into commitments in excess of its available short-term resources. This can arise even if the company is trading profitably, and is typically caused by financing strains imposed by a lengthy operating cycle or production cycle. Overtrading is not inevitable. If it does occur then there are several strategies that may be adopted to deal with it, including for example:

- reduction in business activity to consolidate and give some breathing space
- introduction of new equity capital rather than debt, to ease the strain on short-term resources
- drastically improve the management of working capital in the ways which we have outlined.

This chapter has dealt with working capital and the working capital requirement (WCR). We have looked specifically at management of the WCR. The appreciation by managers of how working capital operates, and its effective management, is fundamental to the survival and success of the company. Cash and short-term debt are important parts of working capital, the management of which we shall consider in the section that follows.

Progress check 16.19

How may a company's investment in operations, its operating cycle, be minimised? What are the potential risks to the company in pursuing an objective of minimisation?

Cash improvement techniques

We have already discussed how profit and cash flow do not mean the same thing. Cash flow does not necessarily equal profit. However, all elements of profit may have been or will be at some time reflected in cash flow. It is a question of timing and also the quality of each of the components of profit:

- day-to-day expenses are usually immediately reflected in the cash book as an outflow of cash
- non-current assets may have been acquired with an immediate outflow of cash, but the cost of these assets is reflected in the profit and loss account through depreciation which is spread over the life of the assets
- sales of products or services are reflected as revenue in the profit and loss account even though cash receipts by way of settlement of sales invoices may not take place for another month or two or more
- some sales invoices may not be paid at all even though the sales revenue has been recognised and so will subsequently be written off as a cost to bad debts in the profit and loss account
- purchases of materials are taken into inventories and may not be reflected in the profit and loss account as a cost for some time after cash has been paid to the suppliers even though credit terms may have been agreed with suppliers and inventory may not yet have been used.

Cash flow is therefore importantly linked to business performance, or profit, which may fluctuate from period to period. There is also a significant impact from non-profit items, which may have a more permanent effect on cash resources.

The non-profit and loss account items that affect short-term and long-term cash flow may be identified within each of the areas of the balance sheet (see Fig. 16.6).

The short-term cash position of a business can be improved by:

- reducing current assets
- increasing current liabilities.

The long-term cash position of a business can be improved by:

- increasing equity
- increasing non-current liabilities
- reducing the net outflow on non-current assets.

We shall consider each of these actions for improvement in the cash position of the business.

Progress check 16.20

Profit and cash do not always mean the same thing. Why is operating profit different from operating cash flow?

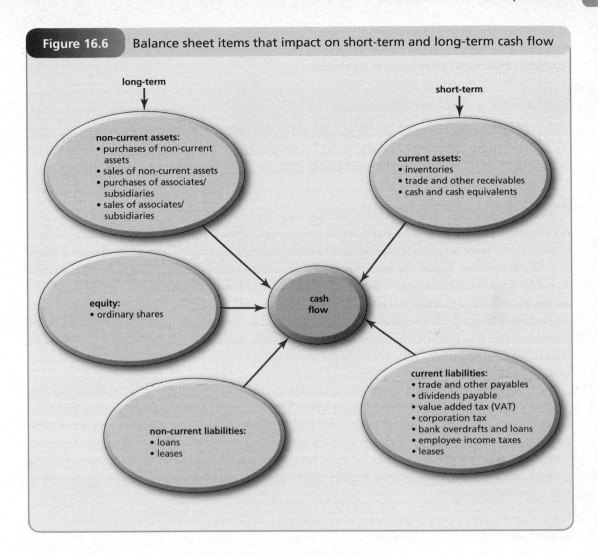

Figure 16.6   Balance sheet items that impact on short-term and long-term cash flow

Short-term cash flow improvement

Inventories levels

Inventories levels should be optimised so that neither too little is held to meet orders nor too much held so that waste occurs. It is a fine balance that requires planning, control and honesty. Many companies either hide or are prepared to turn a blind eye to inventory errors, over-ordering or over-stocking because managers do not like to admit their mistakes, and in any case the higher the inventory then the higher the reported profit!

For cash flow (and operational efficiency) purposes it is crucial to put in place:

- efficient sales order systems
- materials procurement systems
- inventory control systems

operated by highly trained staff.

Inventory turnover must be regularly reviewed so that damaged, obsolete and slow-moving inventories may be disposed of at discounted sales prices or for some scrap value if possible. In cash terms, hanging on to unsaleable inventories is a 'waste' of the highest order. It uses up valuable space and time and needs people to manage it. It clogs up the system, hinders efficient order fulfilment and represents money tied up in assets of little value.

Trade and other receivables

Accounts receivable arise from sales of products or services. The methods employed in making sales, the sales invoicing system, the payment terms, and the cash collection system, are all possible areas that can delay the important objective of turning a sale into cash in the shortest possible time.

Cash and cash equivalents

Whichever method is used for collection from customers, debts will ultimately be converted into a balance in the bank account. It is important to recognise that the balance shown on the bank statement is not the 'real' balance in the bank account. It is very important for a company to frequently prepare a bank reconciliation that details the differences between the company's cash book and its bank statement on a given date. However, it should be noted that the bank statement balance does not represent 'cleared' funds. **Cleared funds** are funds that have actually been cleared through the banking system and are available for use. It is this balance, if overdrawn, which is used to calculate overdraft interest. There are software packages which routinely monitor bank charges and many users have obtained a refund from their bank.

The difference between the bank statement balance and the cleared balance is the 'float' and this can very often be a significant amount. The cleared balance information should be received from the bank and recorded so that it can be monitored daily. Cash requirements should be forecast in some detail say six months forward and regularly updated. Cleared funds surplus to immediate requirements should be invested. This may be short-term, even overnight, into, say, an interest-bearing account, or longer-term into interest-bearing investments or the acquisition of capital equipment or even other businesses.

Trade and other payables

Accounts payable may be paid more slowly than the agreed terms to gain a short-term cash advantage, but even as a short-term measure this should only be regarded as temporary. A more systematic approach to the whole purchasing and payables system is a more ethical and professional approach that may provide greater and sustainable benefits.

Ordering anything from a third party by any individual within the organisation is a commitment to cash leaking out at some time in the future. Tight controls must be in place to give such authority to only the absolute minimum of employees. This authority must be accompanied by rules governing:

- which suppliers may be dealt with
- acceptable ranges of product
- purchase volumes
- price negotiation
- discounts
- credit terms
- transaction currencies
- invoicing
- payment methods
- payment terms.

A tightly controlled and computerised system of:

■ integrated purchase order
■ inventory control
■ payables

must also feature countersigned approval of, for example:

■ new suppliers
■ terms
■ price ranges.

When supplier invoices are received by the organisation they must match absolutely with goods or services received and be matched with an official order. The recording system should verify the credit terms for each invoice. If payments are made by cheque, then the cheques should always bear two signatures as part of the company's control system.

Cash improvements may be gained from the purchasing and accounts payables system in a number of ways. The starting point must be a highly skilled buyer or buyers who are able to source the right quality product for the job at the best total acquisition price (base price plus delivery costs plus allowance for currency risk, for example), in the delivery quantities and frequencies required and at the best possible terms.

Further gains may be achieved from efficient recording systems that allow incorrect deliveries or incorrect invoices to be quickly identified, queried and rectified. Payments should be made in line with terms but advantages may be gained from less costly payment methods and better control than the issue of cheques. For example, the payables system may automatically prepare weekly payment schedules and trigger automated electronic payments directly through the bank.

Alternatively, submission of correct supplier invoices directly to the company's bank may also be used to support automatic payment in line with agreed terms. Provided that adequate controls are put in place to check and monitor such transactions they provide a cost-effective method of controlling cash outflows and cash planning.

Bank overdrafts and loans

If a bank overdraft facility is required by a company, then the lowest possible interest rate should be negotiated. As with the purchase of any service, it pays to shop around to obtain the best deal. Bank interest charges should be checked in detail and challenged if they look incorrect – all banks make mistakes. Computer software packages are available to routinely monitor bank charges.

A bank statement should be received routinely by the company weekly, or daily, and should always be thoroughly checked. A detailed monthly schedule of bank charges should be requested from the bank and checked very carefully. These charges should be strictly in line with the tariff of charges agreed at the outset with the bank. In the same way as interest charges, bank charges should be challenged if they look incorrect.

At all times minimisation of both bank interest and bank charges must be a priority. This can be achieved by cash-flow planning and optimisation of the methods of receipts into and payments out of the bank account. If several bank accounts are held they should be seriously reviewed and closed unless they are really essential and add value to the business.

Corporation tax

Taxation on corporate profit is a complicated and constantly changing area. Tax experts may be engaged to identify the most tax-efficient ways of running a business. At the end of the day, if a business is making profits then tax will become payable. Obvious cash gains may be made from knowing when the tax payment dates are and ensuring they are adhered to. Penalties and interest charges for late and non-payment are something to avoid.

Value added tax (VAT)

Value added tax (VAT) is probably an area that is even more complicated than corporate taxation. VAT does not impact on the profit of the business. Businesses are unpaid collectors of VAT. If a business is registered for VAT (currently mandatory for businesses with sales revenue of £70,000 or more) it is required to charge VAT at the appropriate rate on all goods and services that are vatable. Accurate records must be maintained to account for all such VAT. Such VAT output tax, as it is called, must be paid over to HMRC every three months or every month, whichever has been agreed.

VAT charged by suppliers, or input tax, may be offset against output tax so that the net is paid over monthly or quarterly. If input tax exceeds output tax, the VAT is refunded by HMRC. It is important to note that VAT offices look very carefully at trends on VAT returns. A return that is materially different to the trend will usually result in a visit from a VAT inspector who will carry out an extremely rigorous audit of all accounting records.

It may benefit an organisation to choose to account either monthly or quarterly for VAT. In the same way as for corporate taxation, great care must be taken to submit correct VAT returns, and pay VAT on the correct date to avoid any penalties or interest charges.

Employee income taxes

In the UK, taxes are collected by companies and paid to the Government on behalf of employees. Such taxes include Pay As You Earn (PAYE) taxation and National Insurance (NI) contributions, which must be deducted at source by UK companies from payments to employees. Salaries net of PAYE and NI are paid to employees, and the PAYE and NI and a further contribution for employer's NI is then paid to HMRC. Employees may be paid weekly or monthly and then PAYE and NI are paid over to the HMRC by the 19th of the following month. In exceptional circumstances HMRC may allow an odd day's delay. However, as with all other taxes, payment on the due date without fail is the best advice to avoid unnecessary outflows of cash in penalties and interest for non-compliance.

Dividends payable

Dividends are payable to shareholders by companies as a share of the profits. They are not a cost or a charge against profits but are a distribution of profits. There are some factors for consideration regarding cash flow. The timing of dividend payments is within the control of the company. Dividends may therefore be paid on dates that are most convenient in terms of cash flow and it is important to remember to include them in cash planning.

Progress check 16.21

Which areas within the income statement and the balance sheet may be considered to identify improvements to the short-term cash position of a company?

Worked example 16.9

An extract from Flatco plc's balance sheet as at 31 December 2010 and 2009 is shown below. From it we can see that trade receivables at 31 December 2009 were £517,000. Sales revenue was £3,250,000 and so collection days for 2009 were 58 days. Trade receivables at 31 December 2010 were £573,000, sales revenue was £3,500,000 and collection days for 2010 had worsened to 60 days. Although new cash collection procedures and a reinforced credit control department were introduced in the latter part of 2010, it was too early to see an improvement by December 2010. A report published on the industry for 2009 indicated that the average time customers took to pay was 35 days, with the best-performing companies achieving 25 days.

We will calculate the range of savings that Flatco would expect if it were to implement the appropriate measures to achieve average performance, or if it improved enough to match the best performers. We may assume that sales revenue is more or less evenly spread throughout the year. Flatco's profit before tax for 2009 was £430,000. The average bank interest paid or earned by Flatco plc was 9% per annum.

Flatco plc
Extract of the balance sheet as at 31 December 2010

	2010 £000	2009 £000
Current assets		
Inventories	311	268
Trade receivables	573	517
Prepayments	589	617
Cash and cash equivalents	327	17
	1,800	1,419

	Flatco		Average (derived)		Best (derived)
Trade receivables	£517,000		£312,000		£223,000
Revenue	£3,250,000		£3,250,000		£3,250,000
Collection days	58		35		25
Gain per annum		[517 – 312]	£205,000	[517 – 223]	£294,000
Interest saved or earned at 9% per annum			£18,450		£26,460
Improvement to profit before tax			[£18,450 × 100/£430,000] +4.3%		[£26,460 × 100/£430,000] +6.2%

Assuming that Flatco plc's new credit control procedures become effective, at current trading levels it should result in a profit improvement of between 4.3% and 6.2% per annum.

Long-term cash flow improvement

Equity

Shareholders' capital has many advantages in providing a means of improving long-term cash flow. Provision of additional equity by the shareholders immediately strengthens the balance sheet. It also indirectly strengthens the profit position because equity (ordinary shares) does not bear a commitment to pay interest. Additional equity is an investment in future business, which will ultimately result in dividends payable from successful trading.

When owners of the organisation provide additional equity, a personal cost is imposed on them in that the funding is from their own capital. It also may dilute their own stake or percentage of the business. Private equity firms or venture capitalists may be another source of equity. This carries the same advantages but also the expectation of rewards is much higher than those from interest-bearing loans.

Loans

Long-term loans have certain advantages, particularly for the acquisition of non-current assets, even though they carry a commitment to regular interest payments which may bear a fixed or variable rate. The period of the loan may be matched with the life of the asset and the agreed repayment schedule may be included in the cash flow plan with reasonable certainty.

Borrowing is always a big decision regardless of the amount. It has a cost and always has to be repaid. The ability to service any borrowing and the ability to repay must be assessed before making the decision to borrow. The real payback on borrowing for investment in non-current assets and working capital should be calculated and cheaper alternatives such as:

- re-use of equipment
- renovation of equipment
- renegotiated terms of trading

fully explored before borrowing.

A disadvantage of long-term loans is that they are invariably secured by lenders on the company's existing non-current assets or those to be acquired, or on other long-term or short-term assets. This requirement for security may limit the company's flexibility with regard to its future short-term or long-term borrowing requirements.

If a company needs to acquire land and buildings in order to trade it has a choice of purchasing leasehold or freehold, or renting. Purchase of premises additionally takes an organisation immediately into the property business. While property prices are rising, this speculation may appear attractive. However, it does represent some risk to the organisation – property speculation has proved disastrous to many companies in the past – and it may result in a lack of flexibility. If a company needs to expand or relocate it may not be able to achieve this quickly and may be hampered by the fixed cost of owning a property.

Renting or short leases may present lower risk and greater opportunities in terms of location and flexibility and with regular payments that may be included in the cash flow plan. It also gives the organisation further financing opportunities, by not having a fixed liability of a loan secured on property.

Leasing

Leasing may be used for financing acquisitions of non-current assets. A lease may be an operating lease (short-term) or a finance lease (long-term). An operating lease requires the payment of lease rentals, which are treated as an operating cost. A finance lease incurs interest charges on the capital amount of the lease, and depreciation on the asset, which are charged against profits. The term of a finance lease is matched with the expected life of the asset acquired. Cash flow may be planned in advance whichever method is chosen.

Purchases of non-current assets

The acquisition of non-current assets may represent an immediate outflow of cash. Cash-rich organisations may see advantages in outright purchases. However, the majority of organisations generally need to seek alternative funding. The sources of such funding may be from shares, loans or leasing, either within the UK or from overseas.

The use of an overdraft facility is not usually appropriate for acquisition of non-current assets. Non-current assets by definition have a long life and may be permanent in nature. An overdraft is repayable on demand, which is suitable for working capital requirements but is a risk if used to finance, for example, some machinery which may have an expected life of say 15 years.

Sales of non-current assets

Sales of non-current assets are an obvious means of raising funds. However, the opportunity cost of disposal of an asset must be considered prior to disposal and this should be considered in real terms using discounted cash flows with some allowance for inflation and taxation. An alternative may be to consider the sale of the asset to a leasing company, which then leases it back to the company.

Cash management

Any cash improvement exercise should include the factors we have discussed, which should also be regularly reviewed. However, in order to maintain control over cash flow it is crucial that a cash flow plan or statement is prepared on a month-by-month or week-by-week basis for, say, six months ahead.

The phased cash flow plan should be updated weekly or monthly. It may be continually reviewed and revised in the light of actual performance, and for advantage to be taken of opportunities for improvement through savings and rephasing as a result of consideration of the factors we have discussed above.

The recruitment of honest and reliable staff to deal with the control of cash and working capital is extremely important. Insufficient attention to this point together with a lack of frequent, appropriate training in credit control and cash management is a common occurrence, much to the cost of many companies. Many customers may detect a weak system of credit control and take advantage, resulting in considerable delays in payment of invoices.

Effective, integrated, computerised purchasing, inventory control, order processing and sales invoicing systems are the tools necessary for trained and motivated staff to optimise the use of cash resources and safeguard the company's assets. It should be appreciated that until a customer has paid an invoice it remains an asset, which is effectively under the direct control of another business.

Progress check 16.22

Which areas within the income statement and the balance sheet may be considered to identify improvements to the long-term cash position of a company?

Cash shortage is a common reason for business failure. However, businesses that are cash-rich may also fail to take full advantage of opportunities to maximise the return on capital employed in the business. Such opportunities may include:

- acquisition of new businesses
- investment in research and development
- investment in new products
- lending to gain the most tax-efficient returns.

All investments should, as a matter of company policy, be appraised using one of the recognised discounted cash flow techniques. A realistic company cost of capital should be used to determine whether each project is likely to pay back an acceptable return.

If surplus funds are to be invested for short-term returns, the most tax-efficient investments should be sought. An understanding of the relationship between risk and reward is a prerequisite. High-risk investment strategies should only be undertaken if the downside risk is fully understood, and the consequences are what the business could bear and survive should the worst happen. In both the UK and USA there have been some high-profile failures of deposit-takers, resulting in massive losses by the depositors (note the collapse of BCCI in the UK).

Companies should endeavour to maintain good relationships with their bankers at all times (good or bad), with regular meetings and the provision of up-to-date information on company performance, plans and new initiatives. The bank should ensure that bank statements, daily cleared bank balance positions, and detailed financial information relating to loans, interest and bank charges are provided to the company as frequently as required. The company's finance department should regularly and thoroughly check their accuracy, and challenge the bank with regard to incorrect bank charges and interest. All slow-moving or inactive accounts, particularly, for example, old currency accounts opened for one-off contracts, should be closed to avoid incurring continuing account maintenance charges.

Summary of key points

- The operating cycle of working capital (WC), the net of current assets less current liabilities, is the period of time which elapses between the point at which cash begins to be expended on the production of products or services, and the collection of cash from customers.
- The difference between working capital (WC) and working capital requirement (WCR) is cash less short-term financial debt (bank overdrafts and short-term loans).
- The working capital requirement is normally financed by bank overdraft because of its flexibility in accommodating the fluctuating nature of net current assets, but note the generally higher cost of short-term financing.
- Effective management and control of inventories requires their appropriate location and storage, establishment of robust inventory purchase procedures and reorder systems, and accurate and timely systems for recording, control and physical check of inventories.
- Effective management and control of trade receivables requires establishment of appropriate policies covering choice of the way in which sales are made, the sales invoicing system, the means of settlement, and the implementation of a credit management and overdue accounts collection system.
- Although not free, trade payables provide the company with an additional source of finance.
- Effective management and control of trade payables requires the establishment of appropriate policies covering choice of suppliers, the way in which purchases are made, the purchase invoicing system, and the means of settlement.

■ Regular measurement of the operating cycle, which determines the short-term financing requirements of the business, enables the company to monitor its working capital performance against targets and identify areas for improvement.

■ The short-term cash position of an organisation may be improved by reducing current assets, or by increasing current liabilities.

■ The long-term cash position of an organisation may be improved by increasing equity, increasing long-term liabilities, and reducing the net outflow on non-current assets.

Assessment material

Questions

Q16.1 Describe how a company's financing of its investment in operations may be different from its financing of its investment in non-current assets.

Q16.2 (i) Explain the differences between working capital (WC) and working capital requirement (WCR).
(ii) What are the implications for companies having either negative or positive WCs or WCRs?

Q16.3 Outline the policy options available to a company to finance its working capital requirement (WCR).

Q16.4 Outline the processes and techniques that may be used by a company to optimise its inventories levels.

Q16.5 (i) Explain what is meant by economic order quantity (EOQ).
(ii) Describe some of the more sophisticated inventory management systems that the EOQ technique may support.

Q16.6 Describe the areas of policy relating to the management of its customers on which a company needs to focus in order to minimise the amount of time for turning sales into cash.

Q16.7 Outline the processes involved in an effective collections and credit management system.

Q16.8 Describe the policies and procedures that a company may implement for effective management of its suppliers.

Q16.9 (i) What is meant by overtrading?
(ii) What steps may be taken by a company to avoid the condition of overtrading?

Q16.10 Describe
(i) a review of the operating cycle, and
(ii) an appropriate action plan that may be implemented to improve the short-term cash position of a business.

Q16.11 (i) For what reasons may some companies require increases in long-term cash resources?
(ii) What sources are available to these companies?

Discussion points

D16.1 If working capital is the 'lubricant' of a company's investment in its operations that enables its investment in non-current assets to be most effectively exploited, how does the company choose the best method of lubrication and how often should this oil be changed?

D16.2 'Management of working capital is simply a question of forcing suppliers to hold as much inventory as we require for order and delivery at short notice, and extending payment as far as possible to the point just before they refuse to supply, and putting as much pressure as possible on customers by whatever means to make sure they pay within 30 days.' Discuss.

D16.3 'A manufacturing company that adopts a policy of minimising its operating cycle may achieve short-term gains in profitability and cash flow but may suffer longer-term losses resulting from the impact on its customer base and its ability to avoid disruption to its production processes.' Discuss.

Exercises

Solutions are provided in Appendix 3 to all exercise numbers highlighted in colour.

Level I

E16.1 *Time allowed – 30 minutes*

Oliver Ltd's sales revenue budget for 2010 is £5,300,000. Oliver Ltd manufactures components for television sets and its production costs as a percentage of sales revenue are:

	%
Raw materials	40
Direct labour	25
Overheads	10

Raw materials, which are added at the start of production, are carried in inventory for four days and finished goods are held in inventory before sale for seven days. Work in progress is held at levels where products are assumed to be 25% complete in terms of labour and overheads.

The production cycle is 14 days and production takes place evenly through the year. Oliver Ltd receives 30 days' credit from suppliers and grants 60 days' credit to its customers. Overheads are incurred evenly throughout the year.

> **What is Oliver Ltd's total working capital requirement?**

E16.2 *Time allowed – 45 minutes*

Coventon plc's income statement for the year ended 30 June 2010, and its balance sheet as at 30 June 2010 are shown below. The chief executive of Coventon has set targets for the year to 30 June 2011, which he believes will result in an increase in PBT for the year. The marketing director has forecast that targeted collection days of 60 would result in a reduction in sales of 5% from 2010 but also a £30,000 reduction in bad debts for the year. The same gross profit percentage is expected in 2011 as 2010 but inventories days will be reduced by 4 days. The CEO has set further targets for 2011: savings on administrative expenses and distribution costs of £15,000 for the year; payables days to be rigidly adhered to at 30 days in 2011. One third of the loan was due to be repaid on 1 July 2010, resulting in a proportionate saving in interest payable. (Note: Coventon plc approximates its payables days and inventories days using cost of sales at the end of the year rather than purchases for the year.)

Coventon plc
Income statement for the year ended 30 June 2010

	£000
Revenue	2,125
Cost of sales	(1,250)
Gross profit	875
Distribution and administrative costs	(300)
Operating profit	575
Finance costs	(15)
Profit before tax	560
Income tax expense	(125)
Profit for the year	435
Retained profit 1 July 2009	515
	950
Dividends	(125)
Retained profit 30 June 2010	825

Coventon plc
Balance sheet as at 30 June 2010

	£000
Non-current assets	
Intangible	100
Tangible	1,875
Total non-current assets	1,975
Current assets	
Inventories	125
Trade receivables	425
Prepayments	50
Cash and cash equivalents	50
Total current assets	650
Total assets	2,625
Current liabilities	
Borrowings and finance leases	50
Trade payables	100
Accruals	150
Dividends payable	125
Income tax payable	125
Total current liabilities	550

Coventon plc
Balance sheet as at 30 June 2010

	£000
Non-current liabilities	
Loan	250
Total liabilities	800
Net assets	1,825
Equity	
Share capital	1,000
Retained earnings	825
Total equity	1,825

You are required to calculate the following:

(i)   operating cycle days for 2009/2010
(ii) operating cycle days for 2010/2011
(iii) the expected value of inventories plus trade receivables less trade payables as at 30 June 2011
(iv) the PBT for 2010/2011.

E16.3   *Time allowed – 45 minutes*

Trumper Ltd has recently appointed a new managing director who would like to implement major improvements to the company's management of working capital. Trumper's customers should pay by the end of the second month following delivery. Despite this they take on average 75 days to settle their accounts. Trumper's sales revenue for the current year is estimated at £32m, and the company expects bad debts to be £320,000.

The managing director has suggested an early settlement discount of 2% for customers paying within 60 days. His meetings with all the company's major customers have indicated that 30% would take the discount and pay within 60 days; 70% of the customers would continue to pay within 75 days on average. However, the finance director has calculated that bad debts may reduce by £100,000 for the year, together with savings of £20,000 on administrative costs.

Trumper Ltd has a bank overdraft facility to finance its working capital on which it pays interest at 12% per annum.

The managing director would like to know how Trumper may gain from introducing early settlement discounts, if it is assumed that sales revenue levels would remain unchanged. The managing director would also like suggestions as to how the company may reduce its reliance on its bank overdraft, perhaps through better management of its trade receivables, and whether the bank overdraft is the best method of financing its working capital.

Level II

E16.4   *Time allowed – 45 minutes*

Josef Ryan Ltd has experienced difficulties in getting its customers to pay on time. It is considering the offer of a discount for payment within 14 days to its customers, who currently pay after 60 days. It is estimated that only 50% of credit customers would take the discount, although administrative cost savings of £10,000 per annum would be gained. The marketing director believes that sales would be unaffected by the discount. Sales revenue for 2006 has been budgeted at £10m. The cost of short-term finance for Ryan is 15% per annum.

> **What is the maximum discount that Josef Ryan Ltd may realistically offer?**

E16.5   *Time allowed – 45 minutes*

Worrall plc's sales revenue for 2009 was £8m. Costs of sales were 80% of sales revenue. Bad debts were 2% of sales. Cost of sales variable costs were 90% and fixed costs were 10%. Worrall's cost of finance is 10% per annum. Worrall plc allows its customers 60 days' credit, but is now considering increasing this to 90 days' credit because it believes that this will increase sales. Worrall plc's sales manager estimated that if customers were granted 90 days' credit, sales may be increased by 20%, but that bad debts would increase from 2% to 3%. The finance director calculated that such a change in policy would not increase fixed costs, and neither would it result in changes to trade payables and inventories.

> **Would you recommend that Worrall plc increase customer credit to 90 days?**

E16.6   *Time allowed – 45 minutes*

Chapman Engineering plc has an annual sales revenue of £39m, which are made evenly throughout the year. At present the company has a bank overdraft facility on which its bank charges 9% per annum.

Chapman Engineering plc currently allows its customers 45 days' credit. One third of the customers pay on time, in terms of total sales value. The other two thirds pay on average after 60 days. Chapman believes that the offer of a cash discount of 1% to its customers would induce them to pay within 45 days. Chapman also believes that two-thirds of the customers who now take 60 days to pay would pay within 45 days. The other third would still take an average of 60 days. Chapman estimates that this action would also result in bad debts being reduced by £25,000 a year.

> (i)   What is the current value of trade receivables?
> (ii)   What would the level of trade receivables be if terms were changed and 1% discount was offered to reduce collection days from 60 days to 45 days?
> (iii) What is the net annual cost to the company of granting this discount?
> (iv)   Would you recommend that the company should introduce the offer of an early settlement discount?
> (v)   What other factors should Chapman consider before implementing this change?
> (vi)   Are there other controls and procedures that Chapman could introduce to better manage its trade receivables?

E16.7   *Time allowed – 60 minutes*

Sarnico Ltd, a UK subsidiary of a food manufacturing multinational group, makes sandwiches for sale by supermarkets. The group managing director, Emanuel Recount, is particularly concerned with Sarnico's cash position. The financial statements for 2010 are as follows:

Income statement for the year ended 30 September 2010

	£m	£m
Revenue		49
less: Cost of sales		
Opening inventories	7	
add: Purchases	40	
	47	
less: Closing inventories	10	37
Gross profit		12
Expenses		(13)
Loss for the year		(1)

Balance sheet as at 30 September 2010

	£m
Non-current assets	15
Current assets	
Inventories	10
Trade receivables	6
Total current assets	16
Total assets	31
Current liabilities	
Bank overdraft	11
Trade payables	4
Total current liabilities	15
Non-current liabilities	
Loans	8
Total liabilities	23
Net assets	8
Equity	
Ordinary share capital	3
Retained earnings	5
Total equity	8

We may assume that trade receivables and trade payables were maintained at a constant level throughout the year.

(i) Why should Emanuel Recount be concerned about Sarnico's liquidity?

(ii) What is the 'operating cycle'?

(iii) Why is the operating cycle important with regard to the financial management of Sarnico?

(iv) Calculate the operating cycle for Sarnico Ltd.

(v) What actions may Sarnico Ltd take to improve its operating cycle performance?

E16.8   *Time allowed – 60 minutes*

Refer to the balance sheet for Flatco plc as at 31 December 2010, and its income statement for the year to 31 December 2010 shown at the beginning of Chapter 16.

A benchmarking exercise that looked at competing companies within the industry revealed that on average collection days for 2010 were 33 days, average payables days were 85 days, and average inventories days were 32 days. The exercise also indicated that in the best-performing companies in the industry the time that customers took to pay was 24 days, with payables days at 90 days and inventories days at 18 days.

> You are required to calculate the range of values of savings that Flatco may achieve in 2011 (assuming the same activity levels as 2010) if it were to implement the appropriate measures to achieve average performance or if it improved enough to match the best performers.
>
> You may assume that sales revenue is more or less evenly spread throughout the year. The average bank interest paid and earned by Flatco plc is 9% per annum.

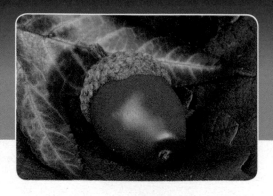

Oak Ltd is a UK manufacturing company that assembles one product called the Acorn. Oak Ltd bases its pricing policy on the pricing policy of the General Motors Corporation, outlined in an article by Albert Bradley back in the 1920s (see below).

The data that follow relate to the operations of Oak Ltd during the forthcoming year:

Investment in plant and other non-current assets	£1m
Required return on investment (ROI)	20% before tax
Annual capacity	400,000 Acorns

Factory and selling costs per Acorn:

Materials	£3.75
Assembly labour	£0.60
Overhead	£1.90
Total	£6.25

The factory and selling costs have been determined as being 60% fixed costs and 40% variable costs.

Working capital comprises inventories of raw materials, work in progress and finished product, receivables and cash, which are all assumed to be in direct proportion to factory and selling costs and in total are turned over on average five times a year.

* * *

On 1 January 1927 in the USA, Albert Bradley published an article in the *National Association of Cost Accountants (NACA) Bulletin*, which described the General Motors Corporation (GM) pricing policy. At the time of writing the article, Mr Bradley was the general assistant treasurer of GM. He later became its vice-president, then executive vice-president, and then chairman of the board of directors. The following notes are a summary of the main points from Mr Bradley's article.

General policy

Return on investment is the basis of the General Motors policy with regard to the pricing of product. The return on investment is the highest average long-term rate of return over a protracted period of time that can be expected, consistent with a healthy growth of the business.

The necessary rate of return on capital will vary between separate sectors of industry as a result of differences in their economic situations, and within each industry primarily because of the relatively greater efficiency of certain producers.

The fundamental policy with regard to pricing product and expansion of the business requires a decision as to the normal average rate of plant operation. The relationship between assumed normal average rate of operation and practical annual capacity is known as standard volume.

The basis of GM's pricing policy is standard volume and required return on investment.

Standard volume

Costs of production and distribution per unit of product vary with fluctuation in volume because of the fixed or non-variable nature of some of the expense items. Productive materials and productive labour may be considered costs which are 100 per cent variable, since within reasonable limits the aggregate varies directly with volume, and the cost per unit of product therefore remains uniform.

Among the items classified as manufacturing burden (overhead) there exist varying degrees of fluctuation with volume. Manufacturing expenses include 100 per cent fixed expenses such as depreciation, since within the limits of plant capacity the aggregate will not change, but the amount per unit of product will vary in inverse ratio to the output.

Manufacturing expenses also include 100 per cent variable expenses, such as inspection and material handling, since the amount per unit of the product is unaffected by volume. Between the classes of 100 per cent fixed and 100 per cent variable is a large group of expense items that are partially variable, such as light, heat, power and salaries.

In the General Motors Corporation, standard burden rates are developed for each burden centre, so that there will be included in costs a reasonable average allowance for manufacturing expense. In order to establish this rate, it is first necessary to obtain an expression of the estimated normal average rate of plant operation.

The rate of plant operation is affected by such factors as general business conditions, extent of seasonal fluctuation in sales, policy relating to inventory levels, and plant capacity. Each factor should be carefully considered before making additions to existing plants, in order that there may be a logical relationship between assumed normal average rate of plant operation and practical annual capacity.

A standard burden rate is then developed, which represents the proper absorption of burden in costs at standard volume. In periods of low volume, the unabsorbed manufacturing expense is charged directly against profits as unabsorbed burden, while in periods of high volume, the over-absorbed manufacturing expense is credited to profits, as over-absorbed burden.

Return on investment

Before an enterprise can be considered successful and worthy of continuation or expansion, however, still another element of cost must be reckoned with. This is the cost of capital including an allowance for profit.

Thus, the calculation of standard prices of products necessitates the establishment of standards of capital requirement as well as expense factors, representative of the normal operating condition. The standard for capital employed in fixed assets is expressed as a percentage of factory cost, and the standards for working capital are expressed in part as a percentage of sales, and in part as a percentage of factory cost.

The amount tied up in working capital items should be directly proportional to the volume of business. For example, raw materials on hand should be in direct proportion to the manufacturing requirements – so many days' supply of this material, so many days' supply of that material, and so on – depending on the condition and location of sources of supply, transportation conditions, etc. Work in process should be in direct proportion to the requirements of finished production, since it is dependent on the length of time required for the material to pass from the raw to the finished state, and the amount of labour and other charges to be absorbed in the process. Finished product should be in direct proportion to sales requirements. Accounts receivable should be in direct proportion to sales, being dependent on terms of payment and efficiency of collections.

Conclusion

The basic pricing policy stated in terms of the economic return attainable is a policy, and it does not absolutely dictate the specific price. At times, the actual price may be above, and at other times below, the standard price. The standard price calculation affords a means not only of interpreting actual or proposed prices in relation to the established policy, but at the same time affords a practical demonstration as to whether the policy itself is sound. If the prevailing price of a product is found to be at variance with the standard price other than to the extent due to temporary causes, it follows that prices should be adjusted; or else, in the event of conditions being such that prices cannot he brought into line with the standard price, the conclusion is necessarily drawn that the terms of the expressed policy must be modified.

You are required to use the same pricing technique for Oak Ltd, as that outlined by Albert Bradley for GM, to:

(i)   calculate the standard selling price of an Acorn

(ii) calculate the standard selling price of an Acorn if production was only at 75% of capacity.

You should also

(iii) outline the assumptions on which this pricing policy is made, and some of its limitations

(iv) explain the possible impacts on Oak Ltd of production at less than full capacity.

APPENDICES

Contents

Outline of Appendices

Appendix 1 provides discounted cash flow tables, which show the present value of £1 on both a yearly, and a cumulative year basis, up to 15 years for discount rates from 1% up to 50% per annum.

Appendix 2 includes schedules of all current International Accounting Standards (IASs) and International Financial Reporting Standards (IFRSs).

Appendix 3 contains solutions to around 45% of the chapter-end exercises, which include a mix of both Level I and Level II exercises. They refer to the chapter-end exercise numbers which are highlighted in colour. This allows you to attempt the exercises at the end of each chapter and then check on your understanding of the key points and how well you have been able to apply the various learning topics and techniques. Further exercises are included on the book's accompanying website.

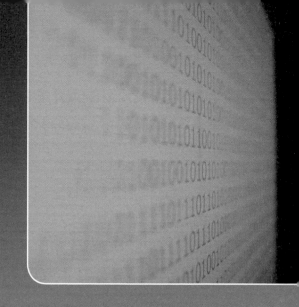

Appendix 1

Present value tables

Present value of £1

The table shows the value of £1 to be received or paid, using a range of discount rates (r) after a given number of years (n). The values are based on the formula $V_n r = (1 + r)^{-n}$

Rate r % After n years	1	2	3	4	5	6	7	8	9	10	11	12
1	0.99	0.98	0.97	0.96	0.95	0.94	0.93	0.93	0.92	0.91	0.90	0.89
2	0.98	0.96	0.94	0.92	0.91	0.89	0.87	0.86	0.84	0.83	0.81	0.80
3	0.97	0.94	0.92	0.89	0.86	0.84	0.82	0.79	0.77	0.75	0.73	0.71
4	0.96	0.92	0.89	0.85	0.82	0.79	0.76	0.74	0.71	0.68	0.66	0.64
5	0.95	0.91	0.86	0.82	0.78	0.75	0.71	0.68	0.65	0.62	0.59	0.57
6	0.94	0.89	0.84	0.79	0.75	0.70	0.67	0.63	0.60	0.56	0.53	0.51
7	0.93	0.87	0.81	0.76	0.71	0.67	0.62	0.58	0.55	0.51	0.48	0.45
8	0.92	0.85	0.79	0.73	0.68	0.63	0.58	0.54	0.50	0.47	0.43	0.40
9	0.91	0.84	0.77	0.70	0.64	0.59	0.54	0.50	0.46	0.42	0.39	0.36
10	0.91	0.82	0.74	0.68	0.61	0.56	0.51	0.46	0.42	0.39	0.35	0.32
11	0.90	0.80	0.72	0.65	0.58	0.53	0.48	0.43	0.39	0.35	0.32	0.29
12	0.89	0.79	0.70	0.62	0.56	0.50	0.44	0.40	0.36	0.32	0.29	0.26
13	0.88	0.77	0.68	0.60	0.53	0.47	0.41	0.37	0.33	0.29	0.26	0.23
14	0.87	0.76	0.66	0.58	0.51	0.44	0.39	0.34	0.30	0.26	0.23	0.20
15	0.86	0.74	0.64	0.56	0.48	0.42	0.36	0.32	0.27	0.24	0.21	0.18

Rate r % After n years	13	14	15	16	17	18	19	20	30	40	50
1	0.88	0.88	0.87	0.86	0.85	0.85	0.84	0.83	0.77	0.71	0.67
2	0.78	0.77	0.76	0.74	0.73	0.72	0.71	0.69	0.59	0.51	0.44
3	0.69	0.67	0.66	0.64	0.62	0.61	0.59	0.58	0.46	0.36	0.30
4	0.61	0.59	0.57	0.55	0.53	0.52	0.50	0.48	0.35	0.26	0.20
5	0.54	0.52	0.50	0.48	0.46	0.44	0.42	0.40	0.27	0.19	0.13
6	0.48	0.46	0.43	0.41	0.39	0.37	0.35	0.33	0.21	0.13	0.09
7	0.43	0.40	0.38	0.35	0.33	0.31	0.30	0.28	0.16	0.09	0.06
8	0.38	0.35	0.33	0.31	0.28	0.27	0.25	0.23	0.12	0.07	0.04
9	0.33	0.31	0.28	0.26	0.24	0.23	0.21	0.19	0.09	0.05	0.03
10	0.29	0.27	0.25	0.23	0.21	0.19	0.18	0.16	0.07	0.03	0.02
11	0.26	0.24	0.21	0.20	0.18	0.16	0.15	0.13	0.06	0.02	0.01
12	0.23	0.21	0.19	0.17	0.15	0.14	0.12	0.11	0.04	0.02	0.008
13	0.20	0.18	0.16	0.15	0.13	0.12	0.10	0.09	0.03	0.013	0.005
14	0.18	0.16	0.14	0.13	0.11	0.10	0.09	0.08	0.03	0.009	0.003
15	0.16	0.14	0.12	0.11	0.09	0.08	0.07	0.06	0.02	0.006	0.002

Cumulative present value of £1

The table shows the present value of £1 per annum, using a range of discount rates (r), receivable or payable at the end of each year for n years.

Rate r % After n years	1	2	3	4	5	6	7	8	9	10	11	12
1	0.99	0.98	0.97	0.96	0.95	0.94	0.94	0.93	0.92	0.91	0.90	0.89
2	1.97	1.94	1.91	1.89	1.86	1.83	1.81	1.78	1.76	1.74	1.71	1.69
3	2.94	2.88	2.83	2.78	2.72	2.67	2.62	2.58	2.53	2.49	2.44	2.40
4	3.90	3.81	3.72	3.63	3.55	3.47	3.39	3.31	3.24	3.17	3.10	3.04
5	4.85	4.71	4.58	4.45	4.33	4.21	4.10	3.99	3.89	3.79	3.70	3.61
6	5.80	5.60	5.42	5.24	5.08	4.92	4.77	4.62	4.49	4.36	4.23	4.11
7	6.73	6.47	6.23	6.00	5.79	5.58	5.39	5.21	5.03	4.87	4.71	4.56
8	7.65	7.33	7.02	6.73	6.46	6.21	5.97	5.75	5.54	5.34	5.15	4.97
9	8.57	8.16	7.79	7.44	7.11	6.80	6.52	6.25	6.00	5.76	5.54	5.33
10	9.47	8.98	8.53	8.11	7.72	7.36	7.02	6.71	6.42	6.15	5.89	5.65
11	10.37	9.79	9.25	8.76	8.31	7.89	7.50	7.14	6.81	6.50	6.21	5.94
12	11.26	10.58	9.95	9.39	8.86	8.38	7.94	7.54	7.16	6.81	6.49	6.19
13	12.13	11.35	10.64	9.99	9.39	8.85	8.36	7.90	7.49	7.10	6.80	6.42
14	13.00	12.11	11.30	10.56	9.90	9.30	8.75	8.24	7.79	7.37	6.98	6.63
15	13.87	12.85	11.94	11.12	10.38	9.71	9.11	8.56	8.06	7.61	7.19	6.81

Rate r % After n years	13	14	15	16	17	18	19	20	30	40	50
1	0.89	0.88	0.87	0.86	0.85	0.85	0.84	0.83	0.77	0.71	0.67
2	1.67	1.65	1.63	1.61	1.59	1.57	1.55	1.53	1.36	1.22	1.11
3	2.36	2.32	2.28	2.25	2.21	2.17	2.14	2.11	1.81	1.59	1.41
4	2.97	2.91	2.86	2.80	2.74	2.69	2.64	2.59	2.17	1.85	1.61
5	3.52	3.43	3.35	3.27	3.20	3.13	3.06	2.99	2.44	2.04	1.74
6	4.00	3.89	3.78	3.69	3.59	3.50	3.41	3.33	2.64	2.17	1.82
7	4.42	4.29	4.16	4.04	3.92	3.81	3.71	3.61	2.80	2.26	1.88
8	4.80	4.64	4.49	4.34	4.21	4.08	3.95	3.84	2.93	2.33	1.92
9	5.13	4.95	4.77	4.61	4.45	4.30	4.16	4.03	3.02	2.38	1.95
10	5.43	5.22	5.02	4.83	4.66	4.49	4.34	4.19	3.09	2.41	1.97
11	5.69	5.45	5.23	5.03	4.83	4.66	4.49	4.33	3.15	2.44	1.98
12	5.92	5.66	5.42	5.20	4.99	4.79	4.61	4.44	3.19	2.46	1.99
13	6.12	5.84	5.58	5.34	5.12	4.91	4.71	4.53	3.22	2.47	1.99
14	6.30	6.00	5.72	5.47	5.23	5.01	4.80	4.61	3.25	2.48	1.99
15	6.46	6.14	5.85	5.58	5.32	5.09	4.88	4.68	3.27	2.48	2.00

Appendix 2

IFRSs and IASs

International Financial Reporting Standards (IFRSs) in force in the year 2010

IFRS 1	First-time adoption of international financial reporting standards
IFRS 2	Share-based payment
IFRS 3	Business combinations
IFRS 4	Insurance contracts
IFRS 5	Non-current assets held for sale and discontinued operations
IFRS 6	Exploration for and evaluation of mineral resources
IFRS 7	Financial instruments: disclosures
IFRS 8	Operating segments (to replace IAS 14)
IFRS 9	Financial instruments (with effect from 1 January 2013 to replace IAS 39)

International Accounting Standards (IASs) in force in the year 2010

IAS 1	Presentation of financial statements
IAS 2	Inventories
IAS 7	Statement of cash flows
IAS 8	Accounting policies, changes in accounting estimates, and errors
IAS 10	Events after the reporting period
IAS 11	Construction contracts
IAS 12	Income taxes
IAS 16	Property, plant and equipment
IAS 17	Leases
IAS 18	Revenue
IAS 19	Employee benefits
IAS 20	Accounting for Government grants and disclosure of Government assistance
IAS 21	The effects of changes in foreign exchange rates
IAS 23	Borrowing costs
IAS 24	Related party disclosures
IAS 26	Accounting and reporting by retirement benefit plans
IAS 27	Consolidated and separate financial statements
IAS 28	Investments in associates
IAS 29	Financial reporting in hyperinflationary economies
IAS 31	Interests in joint ventures
IAS 32	Financial instruments: presentation
IAS 33	Earnings per share
IAS 34	Interim financial reporting
IAS 36	Impairment of assets
IAS 37	Provisions, contingent liabilities and contingent assets
IAS 38	Intangible assets
IAS 39	Financial instruments: recognition and measurement
IAS 40	Investment property
IAS 41	Agriculture

Appendix 3

Solutions to selected exercises

Solutions are provided for the chapter-end exercise numbers highlighted in colour.

Chapter 2

E2.1 Hall

Hall Ltd
Income statement for the years ended 31 December 2009 and 2010

	2010 £	2009 £
Sales revenue	12,000	11,000
Cost of sales	8,000	7,000
Gross profit	4,000	4,000
Expenses	3,000	2,500
Net profit	1,000	1,500

Working
2009
Cost of sales: opening inventories £600 + purchases £7,100 less closing inventories £700.

2010
Cost of sales: opening inventories £700 + purchases £8,300 less closing inventories £800 less the obsolete inventories of £200.

Cost of sales for 2010 must exclude obsolete inventories as it has not been sold.

Expenses £2,800 plus the obsolete inventories £200.

E2.2 Accruals

(i)
The invoices for the common utilities rarely coincide with accounting period ends. To ensure that costs up to the year end are appropriately included, an adjustment is required for the consumption between the invoice date and year end.

(ii)

	Debit £	Credit £
Profit and loss account		
Electricity to 15 December 2010	10,000	
Accruals for charges 16 to 31 December 2010	300	
Total electricity costs for the year 2010	10,300	
Gas to 20 December 2010	5,000	
Accruals for charges 21 to 31 December 2010	150	
Total gas costs for the year 2010	5,150	
Balance sheet		
Electricity accrual at 31 December 2010		300
Gas accrual at 31 December 2010		150
Total accruals at 31 December 2010		450

E2.7 Correcting Entries

31 December 2010

	Debit £	Credit £
(i)		
Profit and loss account		
Rent	2,400	
Profit and loss account		
Car hire		2,400
Correction of account error		
(ii)		
Profit and loss account		
Discount allowed		20
Balance sheet		
Accounts receivable control account	20	
Customer settlement discount		
(iii)		
Profit and loss account		
Car insurance	1,200	
Balance sheet		
Motor vehicle non-current assets account		1,200
Correction of account error		
(iv)		
Profit and loss account		
Building repairs	3,500	
Balance sheet		
Buildings non-current assets account		3,500
Correction of account error		

E2.8 Etcoakco

(i)

	Debit £	Credit £
Capital		
Transaction 1		100,000
Balance c/f	100,000	
	100,000	100,000
Balance b/f		100,000
@ 1/1/10		

	Debit £	Credit £
Cash		
Transaction 1	100,000	
Transaction 2		50,000
Transaction 3		7,000
Transaction 5		400
Transaction 10	27,600	
Balance c/f		70,200
	127,600	127,600
Balance b/f	70,200	
@ 1/1/10		

	Debit £	Credit £
Non-current assets – shop		
Transaction 2	50,000	
Balance c/f		50,000
	50,000	50,000
Balance b/f @ 1/1/10	50,000	
Printing and stationery expenses		
Transaction 5	400	
Balance c/f		400
	400	400
Balance b/f @ 1/1/10	400	
Inventories		
Transaction 6	31,250	
Transaction 9		27,500
Balance c/f		3,750
	31,250	31,250
Balance b/f @ 1/1/10	3,750	
Receivables		
Transaction 7	23,000	
Transaction 8	27,600	
Transaction 10		27,600
Balance c/f		23,000
	50,600	50,600
Balance b/f @ 1/1/10	23,000	

	Debit £	Credit £
Non-current assets – fittings and equipment		
Transaction 3	7,000	
Transaction 4	20,000	
Balance c/f		27,000
	27,000	27,000
Balance b/f @ 1/1/10	27,000	
Payables		
Transaction 4		20,000
Transaction 6		31,250
Balance c/f	51,250	
	51,250	51,250
Balance b/f @ 1/1/10		51,250
Sales revenue		
Transaction 7		23,000
Transaction 8		27,600
Balance c/f	50,600	
	50,600	50,600
Balance b/f @ 1/1/10		50,600
Cost of sales		
Transaction 9	27,500	
Balance c/f		27,500
	27,500	27,500
Balance b/f @ 1/1/10	27,500	

Solutions to parts **(ii)**, **(iii)** and **(iv)** may provide an introduction to inventories valuation, cost of sales and alternative uses of funds, covered in Chapters 3, 4 and 5 of this book.

Chapter 3

E3.3 Trainer

Trainer plc
Balance sheet as at 31 December 2010

	£000
Non-current assets	
Land and buildings	320
Plant and machinery cost	200
Plant and machinery depreciation provision	(80)
Total non-current assets	440
Current assets	
Inventories	100
Trade receivables	100
Cash and cash equivalents	73
Total current assets	273
Total assets	713
Current liabilities	
Trade payables	130
Accruals	5
Income tax payable	20
Total current liabilities	155
Net assets	558
Equity	
Ordinary shares	320
Retained earnings	238
Total equity	558

Working	£000
Revenue	1,000
Cost of sales	600
Gross profit	400
Expenses	(120)
Bad debt	(2)
Depreciation	(20)
Profit before tax	258
Income tax expense (also within *Current Liabilities*)	(20)
Net profit	238

E3.6 Gorban

Gorban Ltd
Balance sheet as at 31 December 2010

	Per TB £				£
Non-current assets					
Tangible assets	235,000		29,368		264,368
Depreciation provision	(30,165)				(30,165)
Total non-current assets	204,835				234,203
Current assets					
Inventories	51,420		48,000		99,420
Trade receivables	42,500			(10,342)	32,158
Doubtful debts provision	(1,725)			(1,870)	(3,595)
Cash and cash equivalents	67,050	(20,000)	(29,368)	50,000	67,682
Total current assets	159,245				195,665
Total assets	364,080				429,868
Current liabilities					
Trade payables	35,112				35,112
Accruals		1,173			1,173
Total current liabilities	35,112				36,285
Non-current liabilities					
Loan	20,000	(20,000)			
Total liabilities	55,112				36,285
Net assets	308,968				393,583
Equity					
Share capital	200,000			50,000	250,000
Retained earnings	108,968	(1,173)	48,000	(1,870)	(10,342)	143,583
Total equity	308,968				393,583

E3.7 Pip

Pip Ltd
Balance sheet as at 31 December 2010

	£000	Working
Non-current assets		
Land and buildings	100,000	
Plant and equipment	100,000	[150,000 − 50,000]
Total non-current assets	200,000	
Current assets		
Inventories	45,000	[50,000 − 5,000]
Trade receivables	45,000	[50,000 − 5,000]
Cash and cash equivalents	11,000	[10,000 + 1,000]
Total current assets	101,000	
Total assets	301,000	

Current liabilities

Borrowings	10,000
Trade payables	81,000
Total liabilities	91,000
Net assets	210,000

Equity

Ordinary shares (issued)	100,000
Retained earnings	110,000
Total equity	210,000

Note that the intangible assets, brands worth £10,000 in the opinion of the directors, have not been included in the balance sheet on the assumption that they are not purchased brands. Under IAS 38, Intangible Assets, only brand names that have been purchased may be capitalised and included in the balance sheet.

Chapter 4

E4.3 CDs

Overview

Inventories are dealt with in IAS 2, Inventories, which states that they should be valued at the lower of cost and net realisable value. Retailers can (and do) take the retail value of their inventories (by category) and deduct the gross profit (by category) as an estimate of cost.

(i)   This inventory should be valued at £5,000 (cost) as it is selling consistently.

(ii)   This inventory should not be in the balance sheet at any value, as it will not generate any cash in the future.

(iii)   As in (i) above this inventory can be valued at £1,000 (cost) for balance sheet purposes. As there are more risks associated with holding single artist CDs the inventory levels should be continually reviewed.

(iv)   In this situation the selling pattern has changed and the posters have stopped selling. The posters must not appear in the balance sheet as they will not generate any future cash.

E4.4 Partex

	2008 £	2009 £	2010 £
(i) Balance sheet as at 31 December – accounts receivable			
Accounts receivable including debts to be written-off	88,000	110,000	94,000
Write-off of debts to profit and loss account (1)	(4,000)	(5,000)	(4,000)
	84,000	105,000	90,000
	–	3,360	4,200
Doubtful provision at 4% of accounts receivable (2)	(3,360)	(4,200)	(3,600)
Trade receivables at end of year	80,640	104,160	90,600

(ii) Profit and loss account year ended 31 December – bad and doubtful debts

Bad debts written-off (1)	4,000	5,000	4,000
	–	(3,360)	(4,200)
Doubtful debt provision at 4% of accounts receivable (2)	3,360	4,200	3,600
Bad and doubtful debts charge for year	7,360	5,840	3,400

E4.5 Tartantrips

(i) Sum of the digits depreciation

The company needs to decide on the economic life of the asset (say 10 years in this example) and its esti-mated residual value at the end of its life (£1m in this example).

Cost	£5,000,000
Residual value	£1,000,000
Amount to be written-off over 10 years	£4,000,000

Over 10 years the digits 10 + 9 + 8 . . . 2 + 1 add up to 55

Depreciation in year 1 is 10/55 × £4,000,000	=	£727,272
Depreciation in year 2 is 9/55 × £4,000,000	=	£654,545
Depreciation in year 3 is 8/55 × £4,000,000	=	£581,818
and so on until		
Depreciation in year 9 is 2/55 × £4,000,000	=	£145,546
Depreciation in year 10 is 1/55 × £4,000,000	=	£72,727
Total depreciation for 10 years		£4,000,000

(ii) Straight line depreciation

This method is very simple to operate. The company needs to decide on the economic life of the asset and its residual value at the end of its life (as above). The annual depreciation will be:

Depreciation per year is £4,000,000 divided by 10 years = £400,000 per year

It can be seen that there is a constant charge to the annual profit and loss account for the systematic alloca-tion of the depreciable amount of the non-current asset.

(iii) Reducing balance depreciation

This method is quite different to the straight line method because the depreciation charge is much higher in the earlier years of the life of the asset. The same sort of estimates are required: economic life, residual value, which are used in a reducing balance formula to calculate each year's depreciation.

The reducing balance formula where d is the percentage depreciation to charge on the written down value of the asset at the end of each year is:

$d = 1 - \sqrt[10]{1,000,000/5,000,000} = 14.9\%$ (which may also be calculated using the Excel DB function)

Depreciation in year 1 is 14.9% of £5,000,000	=	£745,000
Depreciation in year 2 is 14.9% of £4,255,000	=	£633,995
Depreciation in year 3 is 14.9% of £3,621,005	=	£539,530
and so on until year 10		
The total depreciation for 10 years is		£4,000,000

E4.8 Retepmal

			£	£
Revenue				266,000
Cost of sales				
		Opening inventories 31 March 2009	15,000	
	plus	Purchases	150,000	
	less	Closing inventories 31 March 2010	(25,000)	140,000
Gross profit				126,000
Distribution costs [40,000 + 3,000]				43,000
Administrative expenses [50,000 − 5,000 + 3,000]				48,000
Profit before tax				35,000
Income tax expense				19,000
Profit for the year				16,000
Dividend				7,000
Retained earnings				9,000

Balance sheet as at 31 March 2010

	£
Non-current assets [95,000 + 40,000 + 30,000 − 3,000]	162,000
Current assets	
Inventories	25,000
Trade receivables	75,000
Prepayments	5,000
Cash and cash equivalents	35,000
Total current assets	140,000
Total assets	302,000
Current liabilities	
Trade payables	54,000
Accruals	3,000
Income tax payable	19,000
Dividends payable	7,000
Total current liabilities	83,000
Net assets	219,000
Equity	
Share capital	80,000
Retained earnings [130,000 + 9,000]	139,000
Total equity	219,000

Chapter 5

E5.1 Candyfloss

(i)   Candyfloss cash flow six months to 30 June 2010 using the direct method

	£000
Operating activities	
Receipts from customers	76.0
Payments	
Flowers suppliers	59.5
Employees	5.0
Other overheads:	
Rent	4.0
Operating expenses	7.0
	75.5
Cash inflow from operating activities	0.5
Investing activities	
Purchase of lease	15.0
Lease fees	1.0
Purchase of van	14.5
Cash outflow from investing activities	30.5
Financing activities	
Loan	3.0
Issue of shares	18.0
Cash inflow from financing activities	21.0
Decrease in cash and cash equivalents for the period	(9.0)

(ii)   Candyfloss income statement for the 6 months to 30 June 2010

	£000	
Revenue	84.0	[76.0 + 8.0]
Cost of flowers	54.0	[59.5 + 4.0 − 9.5]
Operating expenses	8.0	[7.0 + 1.0]
Wages	5.0	
	67.0	
Gross profit	17.0	
Overheads		
Rent	2.0	
Depreciation	1.5	[(14.5 − 2.5)/4 × 50% for the half year]
Bad debts	1.5	
	5.0	
Profit for period	12.0	

(iii) The difference between the cash flow and profit for the period is

−£9,000 − £12,000 = −£21,000

Both cash and profit give an indication of performance.

The profit of £12,000 may be compared with the cash inflow from operating activities of £500.

	Profit	Operating cash flow	Differences
	£000	£000	
Revenue/receipts	84.0	76.0	sales 8 not yet paid by customers
Bad debts	(1.5)		sales assumed will never be paid
Flowers	(54.0)	(59.5)	9.5 in inventory and 4 not yet paid for
Wages	(5.0)	(5.0)	
Operating expenses	(8.0)	(7.0)	1 not yet paid
Rent	(2.0)	(4.0)	2 rent paid in advance
Depreciation	(1.5)		1.5 not cash
	12.0	0.5	

(iv) **A number of items in the income statement are subjective and open to various different methods of valuation:**

Bad debts	1.5	different subjective views as to whether customers may pay or not
Inventories	9.5	different valuation methods
Depreciation	1.5	different bases may be used

- additionally cash flow shows how much was paid out for the lease and for the van and what financing was obtained
- cash flow gives a clear picture of the financial performance, looked at alongside the balance sheet which shows the financial position at a point in time
- looking at the income statement from period to period it is difficult to compare performance with that of similar businesses because of different approaches to asset valuation.

E5.4 Medco

Medco Ltd
Cash generated from operations for the year ended 31 December 2010
Indirect cash flow method

	£
Profit before tax	2,400
Depreciation charge	2,000
Loss on disposal of tangible asset	500
Adjust finance (income)/costs	100
Increase in inventories	(1,000)
Increase in trade and other receivables	(1,000)
Decrease in trade and other payables	(2,000)
Cash generated from operations	1,000
Interest paid	(100)
Income tax paid	(400)
Net cash inflow from operating activities	500

Statement of cash flows for the year ended 31 December 2010

	£000
Cash flows from operating activities	
Cash generated from operations	1,000
Interest paid	(100)
Income tax paid	(400)
Net cash inflow from operating activities	500
Cash flows from investing activities	
Purchases of tangible assets	(12,500)
Proceeds from sales of tangible assets	2,000
Net cash outflow from investing activities	(10,500)
Cash flows from financing activities	
Proceeds from issue of ordinary shares [20,000 − 15,000]	5,000
Proceeds from borrowings [2,000 − 1,000]	1,000
Dividends paid to equity shareholders	(750)
Net cash inflow from financing activities	5,250
Decrease in cash and cash equivalents in the year	(4,750)
Cash and cash equivalents and bank overdrafts at beginning of year	6,000
Cash and cash equivalents and bank overdrafts at end of year	1,250

E5.6 Victoria

(i)

(a)	£000
Increase in retained earnings 2010 over 2009 from balance sheet	500
Add tax payable	320
Add dividends payable	480
Therefore profit before tax is	1,300

(b)	£000
Profit before tax	1,300
Add debenture interest	100
Therefore operating profit is	1,400

(ii)

Victoria plc
Cash generated from operations for the year ended 30 June 2010
Indirect cash flow method

	£000
Profit before tax	1,300
Depreciation charge	200
Adjust finance (income)/costs	100
Increase in inventories	(1,400)

Increase in trade and other receivables	(680)
Decrease in trade and other payables	(200)
Cash used from operations	(680)
Interest paid	(100)
Income tax paid	(300)
Net cash outflow from operating activities	(1,080)

Statement of cash flows for the year ended 30 June 2010

	£000
Cash flows from operating activities	
Cash used from operations	(680)
Interest paid	(100)
Income tax paid	(300)
Net cash outlow from operating activities	(1,080)
Cash flows from investing activities	
Purchases of tangible assets	(2,100)
Net cash outflow from investing activities	(2,100)
Cash flows from financing activities	
Proceeds from issue of ordinary shares	2,740
Dividends paid to equity shareholders	(360)
Net cash inflow from financing activities	2,380
Decrease in cash and cash equivalents in the year	(800)
Cash and cash equivalents and bank overdrafts at beginning of year	200
Cash and cash equivalents and bank overdrafts at end of year	(600)

Analysis of cash and cash equivalents and bank overdrafts as at 30 June 2010

	At 30 June 2009 £000	At 30 June 2010 £000
Cash and cash equivalents	200	–
Bank overdrafts	–	(600)
Cash and cash equivalents and bank overdrafts	200	(600)

E5.7 Sparklers

Sparklers plc
Cash generated from operations for the year ended 31 October 2010
Indirect cash flow method

	£m
Profit before tax	40.80
Depreciation charge	10.10
Loss on disposal of tangible asset	1.40

Adjust finance (income)/costs	0.48
Increase in inventories	(20.00)
Increase in trade and other receivables	(36.40)
Decrease in trade and other payables	8.40
Cash generated from operations	4.78
Interest paid	(0.56)
Income tax paid	(6.40)
Net cash outflow from operating activities	(2.18)

Statement of cash flows for the year ended 31 October 2010

	£m
Cash flows from operating activities	
Cash generated from operations	4.78
Interest paid	(0.56)
Income tax paid	(6.40)
Net cash outflow from operating activities	(2.18)
Cash flows from investing activities	
Purchases of tangible assets	(23.60)
Proceeds from sales of tangible assets	2.00
Interest received	0.08
Net cash outflow from investing activities	(21.52)
Cash flows from financing activities	
Proceeds from borrowings	0.30
Dividends paid to equity shareholders	(10.20)
Net cash outflow from financing activities	(9.90)
Decrease in cash and cash equivalents in the year	(33.60)
Cash and cash equivalents and bank overdrafts at beginning of year	1.20
Cash and cash equivalents and bank overdrafts at end of year	(32.40)

Analysis of cash and cash equivalents and bank overdrafts as at 31 October 2010

	At 31 October 2009	At 31 October 2010
	£000	£000
Cash and cash equivalents	1.20	–
Bank overdrafts	–	(32.40)
Cash and cash equivalents and bank overdrafts	1.20	(32.40)

Working

	£m	£m
Depreciation		
Depreciation 31 October 2010		21.50
Depreciation 31 October 2009	19.00	
Depreciation on assets sold in 2010	(7.60)	(11.40)
Charge for the year 2010		10.10
Loss on sale of assets		
Proceeds on sale		2.00
Net book value: cost	11.00	
depreciation	(7.60)	(3.40)
Loss on sale		(1.40)
Dividends paid		
Dividends payable at 31 October 2009		6.00
Dividends declared for 2010: preference		0.20
ordinary interim		4.00
ordinary final		12.00
		22.20
Less dividends payable at 31 October 2010		12.00
Dividends paid during 2010		10.20
Purchase of non-current assets		
Non-current assets 31 October 2010		47.80
Non-current assets 31 October 2009	35.20	
Cost of non-current assets sold	(11.00)	(24.20)
Non-current assets purchased 2010		23.60

You should refer to the relevant sections in Chapter 5 to check your assessment of the reasons for the increased overdraft.

Chapter 6

E6.1 Share options

Past governments have made employee share option schemes tax efficient and therefore schemes are now very common amongst plcs.

Many plcs have found that their share prices react to specific management policies and decisions, for example takeovers and disposals of businesses. Users of financial information can assess these decisions, knowing of the options awarded to the directors.

Many plcs have found that they can only keep and attract high calibre managers by including share options in their remuneration packages.

Investing institutions demand more and more information regarding directors' remuneration. This can influence their basic hold or buy or sell decisions. The financial press frequently includes criticism of specific companies.

E6.2 Perks

Directors are not the owners of the company (although sometimes directors may own shares in the company). The shareholders own the company and appoint the directors to manage it on their behalf.

Any monies (expenses) that a director takes from the company will affect the annual profit.

Annual dividends are paid from the annual profits. The shareholders approve the accounts at the AGM, which includes remuneration of the directors.

If the directors hide information regarding their remuneration and benefits from the shareholders, then that part of the accounts may not show a true and fair view of the situation.

E6.3 Contracts

Before the UK Corporate Governance Code of Practice was introduced, shareholders found that their directors had powers that were increasing, especially regarding length of contract and compensation for loss of office.

The Cadbury and Greenbury committees recommended that directors' contracts should be no longer than (first) three years (Cadbury) and then one year (Greenbury). These committees had looked at the evidence presented to them. Hampel (1998) provided that the contracts should be one year or less.

The financial press regularly comments on the compensation paid to a director, where company performance has been acknowledged to be poor. There is always reference to the length of outstanding directors' contracts.

Shareholders can decide whether to hold or buy or sell shares if they have advance information on the type of contracts being awarded to the executive directors of their company.

UK financial institutions have also become proactive regarding the length of directors' contracts issue. They have noted that in the past too many highly paid directors were awarding themselves contracts in which compensation for loss of office was very expensive to pay. Currently it often costs companies potentially many millions of pounds to buy out a chief executive from just a one-year contract.

E6.7 Tomkins

Equity shareholders are the owners of the company, and the level of their dividends usually varies with levels of profits earned by the company.

Directors are appointed by the shareholders, and remunerated for their efforts. Major multinational companies are difficult to manage successfully over a long period of time. The remuneration of directors should reflect that difficulty.

The information that has been given about Tomkins plc shows that there was an executive director who earned a basic salary of just below £1 million a year, an amount which most shareholders would like to see disclosed in the accounts and discussed at the AGM.

The bonus of £443,000 would also have generated some interest amongst the institutions and individual shareholders. Institutions (and the UK Government) are seen to put pressure on directors if they feel pay awards are excessive.

The consultancy agreement for a non-executive director may also have been of interest to the various users of the notes to the accounts.

Chapter 7

E7.1 Priory

(i) Net debt to equity

	2009	2010	2011
Net debt	100	250	800
Equity	300	500	800
Debt/equity (%)	33%	50%	100%

(ii) Long-term loans to equity and long-term loans – gearing

	2009	2010	2011
Long-term loans	200	200	600
Equity plus long-term loans	500	700	1,400
Gearing (%)	40%	29%	43%

E7.2 Freshco

Profitability ratios for Freshco plc for 2010 and the comparative ratios for 2009
Gross profit (or gross margin, GM)

$$\frac{\text{Gross profit \%}}{2010} = \frac{\text{gross profit}}{\text{revenue}} = \frac{£204 \times 100\%}{£894} = 22.8\%$$

$$\frac{\text{Gross profit \%}}{2009} = \frac{£166 \times 100\%}{£747} = 22.2\%$$

Profit before interest and tax, PBIT (or operating profit)

$$\frac{\text{PBIT \%}}{2010} = \frac{\text{operating profit}}{\text{revenue}} = \frac{£83 \times 100\%}{£894} = 9.3\%$$

$$\frac{\text{PBIT \%}}{2009} = \frac{£82 \times 100\%}{£747} = 11.0\%$$

Profit for the year (profit after tax, PAT, or return on sales, ROS)

$$\frac{\text{PAT \%}}{2010} = \frac{\text{net profit}}{\text{revenue}} = \frac{£56 \times 100\%}{£894} = 6.3\%$$

$$\frac{\text{PAT \%}}{2009} = \frac{£54 \times 100\%}{£747} = 7.2\%$$

Return on capital employed, ROCE (return on investment, ROI)

$$\frac{\text{ROCE \%}}{2010} = \frac{\text{operating profit}}{\substack{\text{total assets} - \text{current liabilities} \\ \text{(average capital employed)}}} = \frac{£83 \times 100\%}{(£233 + £233)/2} = \frac{£83 \times 100\%}{£233} = 35.6\%$$

$$\frac{\text{ROCE \%}}{2009} = \frac{£82 \times 100\%}{(£233 + £219)/2} = \frac{£82 \times 100\%}{£226} = 36.3\%$$

Return on equity, ROE

$$\frac{\text{ROE \%}}{2010} = \frac{\text{PAT}}{\text{equity}} = \frac{£56 \times 100\%}{£213} = 26.3\%$$

$$\frac{\text{ROE \%}}{2009} = \frac{£54 \times 100}{£166} = 32.5\%$$

Capital turnover

$$\frac{\text{Capital turnover}}{2010} = \frac{\text{revenue}}{\text{average capital employed in year}} = \frac{£894}{£233} = 3.8 \text{ times}$$

$$\frac{\text{Capital turnover}}{2009} = \frac{£747}{£226} = 3.3 \text{ times}$$

Report on the profitability of Freshco plc

Sales for the year 2010 increased by 19.7% over the previous year, but it is not clear whether from increased volumes, new products, or higher selling prices.

Gross profit improved by 0.6% to 22.8% of sales revenue, possibly from increased selling prices and/or from lower costs of production.

Operating profit dropped by 1.7% to 9.3% of sales despite the improvement in gross profit, because of higher levels of distribution costs and administrative expenses.

ROCE declined from 36.3% to 35.6%, indicating a less effective use of funds by Freshco.

Return on equity dropped by 6.2% to 26.3%. This was because the profit for the year after tax remained fairly static but equity was increased through an issue of shares and increases in general reserves and retained earnings.

Capital turnover for 2010 increased to 3.8 times from 3.3 in 2009, reflecting the significant increases in sales levels in 2010 over 2009.

E7.4 Freshco

Liquidity ratios for Freshco plc for 2010 and the comparative ratios for 2009

Current ratio

$$\frac{\text{Current ratio}}{2010} = \frac{\text{current assets}}{\text{current liabilities}} = \frac{£208}{£121} = 1.7 \text{ times}$$

$$\frac{\text{Current ratio}}{2009} = \frac{£191}{£107} = 1.8 \text{ times}$$

Quick ratio

$$\frac{\text{Quick ratio}}{2010} = \frac{\text{current assets} - \text{inventories}}{\text{current liabilities}} = \frac{£208 - £124}{£121} = 0.7 \text{ times}$$

$$\frac{\text{Quick ratio}}{2009} = \frac{£191 - £100}{£107} = 0.8 \text{ times}$$

Defensive interval

$$\frac{\text{Defensive interval}}{2010} = \frac{\text{quick assets}}{\text{average daily cash from operations}} = \frac{£208 - £124}{(£80 + £894 - £70)/365} = 34 \text{ days}$$

$$\frac{\text{Defensive interval}}{2009} = \frac{£191 - £100}{(£60 + £747 - £80)/365} = 46 \text{ days}$$

Report on the liquidity of Freshco plc

The current ratio and the quick ratio have both dropped slightly to 1.7 times and 0.7 times respectively. However, the defensive interval has dropped significantly from 46 days to 34 days at which level the company could potentially survive if there were no further cash inflows.

Net cash flow from operations improved from £54m in 2009 to £62m in 2010. Investments in non-current assets were at lower levels in 2010 and matched by a reduction in long-term financing (debentures).

E7.8 Laurel

(i)

Profitability ratios for Hardy plc for 2010 and the comparative ratios for 2009 and 2008
Gross profit

$$\frac{\text{Gross profit \%}}{2010} = \frac{\text{gross profit}}{\text{revenue}} = \frac{£161 \times 100\%}{£456} = 35.3\%$$

Gross profit %
2009
$= \dfrac{£168 \times 100\%}{£491} = 34.2\%$

Gross profit %
2008
$= \dfrac{£142 \times 100\%}{£420} = 34.0\%$

Profit before interest and tax, PBIT (or operating profit)

PBIT %
2010
$= \dfrac{\text{operating profit}}{\text{revenue}} = \dfrac{£52 \times 100\%}{£456} = 11.4\%$

PBIT %
2009
$= \dfrac{£61 \times 100\%}{£491} = 12.4\%$

PBIT %
2008
$= \dfrac{£50 \times 100\%}{£420} = 11.9\%$

Profit for the year, or profit after tax, PAT

PAT %
2010
$= \dfrac{\text{net profit}}{\text{revenue}} = \dfrac{£20 \times 100\%}{£456} = 4.4\%$

PAT %
2009
$= \dfrac{£28 \times 100\%}{£491} = 5.7\%$

PAT %
2008
$= \dfrac{£25 \times 100\%}{£420} = 6.0\%$

Return on capital employed, ROCE (return on investment, ROI)

ROCE %
2010
$= \dfrac{\text{operating profit}}{\text{total assets} - \text{current liabilities}} = \dfrac{£52 \times 100\%}{(£284 + £292)/2} = \dfrac{£52 \times 100\%}{£288} = 18.1\%$

ROCE %
2009
$= \dfrac{£61 \times 100}{(£237 + £284)/2} = \dfrac{£61 \times 100\%}{£260.5} = 23.4\%$

ROCE % 2008 is not available because we do not have the capital employed number for 31 March 2007.

Return on equity, ROE

ROE %
2010
$= \dfrac{\text{PAT}}{\text{equity}} = \dfrac{£20 \times 100\%}{£223} = 9.0\%$

ROE %
2009
$= \dfrac{£28 \times 100\%}{£215} = 13.0\%$

ROE %
2008
$= \dfrac{£25 \times 100\%}{£199} = 12.6\%$

Capital turnover

Capital turnover
2010
$= \dfrac{\text{revenue}}{\text{average capital employed in year}} = \dfrac{£456}{£288} = 1.6 \text{ times}$

Capital turnover
2009
$= \dfrac{£491}{£260.5} = 1.9 \text{ times}$

Capital turnover 2008 is not available because we do not have the capital employed number for 31 March 2007.

Report on the profitability of Hardy plc

Sales for the year 2010 were 7.1% lower than sales in 2009, which were 16.9% above 2008. It is not clear whether these sales reductions were from lower volumes, fewer products, or changes in selling prices.

Gross profit improved from 34.0% in 2008 to 34.2% in 2009 to 35.3% in 2010, possibly from increased selling prices and/or from lower costs of production.

Operating profit to sales increased from 11.9% in 2008 to 12.4% in 2009 but then fell to 11.4% in 2010, despite the improvement in gross profit, because of higher levels of distribution costs and administrative expenses.

ROCE dropped from 23.4% to 18.1%, reflecting the lower level of operating profit. Return on equity increased from 12.6% in 2008 to 13.0% in 2009 but then fell sharply in 2010 to 9.0%. This was because of the large fall in profit after tax in 2010.

Capital turnover was reduced from 1.9 times in 2009 to 1.6 in 2010, reflecting the fall in sales levels in 2010 compared with 2009.

Efficiency ratios for Hardy plc for 2010 and the comparative ratios for 2009 and 2008

Collection days

$$\text{Collection days 2010} = \frac{\text{trade receivables} \times 365}{\text{revenue}} = \frac{£80 \times 365}{£465} = 63 \text{ days}$$

$$\text{Collection days 2009} = \frac{£70 \times 365}{£491} = 52 \text{ days}$$

$$\text{Collection days 2008} = \frac{£53 \times 365}{£420} = 46 \text{ days}$$

Payables days

$$\text{Payables days 2010} = \frac{\text{trade payables} \times 365}{\text{cost of sales}} = \frac{£38 \times 365}{£295} = 47 \text{ days}$$

$$\text{Payables days 2009} = \frac{£38 \times 365}{£323} = 43 \text{ days}$$

$$\text{Payables days 2008} = \frac{£26 \times 365}{£277} = 34 \text{ days}$$

Inventories days (inventory turnover)

$$\text{Inventory days 2010} = \frac{\text{inventories}}{\text{average daily cost of sales in period}} = \frac{£147}{£295/365} = 182 \text{ days (26.0 weeks)}$$

$$\text{Inventories days 2009} = \frac{£152}{£323/365} = 172 \text{ days (24.5 weeks)}$$

$$\text{Inventories days 2008} = \frac{£118}{£277/365} = 155 \text{ days (22.2 weeks)}$$

Operating cycle days

$$\text{Operating cycle 2010} = \text{inventories days} + \text{collection days} - \text{payables days} = 182 + 63 - 47$$

$$= 198 \text{ days}$$

$$\text{Operating cycle 2009} = 172 + 52 - 43 = 181 \text{ days}$$

$$\text{Operating cycle 2008} = 155 + 46 - 34 = 167 \text{ days}$$

Operating cycle %

$$\text{Operating cycle \%} \atop 2010 = \frac{\text{working capital requirement}}{\text{revenue}}$$

$$= \frac{(£147 + £80 - £38) \times 100\%}{£456} = 41.4\%$$

$$\text{Operating cycle \%} \atop 2009 = \frac{(£152 + £70 - £38) \times 100\%}{£491} = 37.5\%$$

$$\text{Operating cycle \%} \atop 2008 = \frac{(£118 + £53 - £26)}{£420} = 34.5\%$$

Asset turnover

$$\text{Asset turnover} \atop 2010 = \frac{\text{revenue}}{\text{total assets}} = \frac{£456}{£385} = 1.18 \text{ times}$$

$$\text{Asset turnover} \atop 2009 = \frac{£491}{£374} = 1.31 \text{ times}$$

$$\text{Asset turnover} \atop 2008 = \frac{£420}{£303} = 1.39 \text{ times}$$

Report on the efficiency performance of Hardy plc

Average collection days worsened successively over the years 2008, 2009 and 2010 from 46 to 52 to 63 days. This was partly mitigated by some improvement in the average payables days which increased from 34 to 43 to 47 days over the same period. The average inventories days worsened from 155 to 172 to 182 days over 2008, 2009 and 2010. Therefore, mainly because of the poor receivables collection performance and increasingly high inventories levels, the operating cycle worsened from 167 days in 2008 to 181 days in 2009 and to 198 days in 2010 (operating cycle 34.5% to 37.5% to 41.4%). Asset turnover reduced from 1.39 to 1.31 times from 2008 to 2009 and then to 1.18 in 2010, reflecting the degree to which sales revenue had dropped despite increasing levels of total assets.

Liquidity ratios for Hardy plc for 2010 and the comparative ratios for 2009 and 2008

Current ratio

$$\text{Current ratio} \atop 2010 = \frac{\text{current assets}}{\text{current liabilities}} = \frac{£253}{£93} = 2.7 \text{ times}$$

$$\text{Current ratio} \atop 2009 = \frac{£251}{£90} = 2.8 \text{ times}$$

$$\text{Current ratio} \atop 2008 = \frac{£197}{£66} = 3.0 \text{ times}$$

Quick ratio

$$\text{Quick ratio} \atop 2010 = \frac{\text{current assets} - \text{inventories}}{\text{current liabilities}} = \frac{£253 - £147}{£93} = 1.1 \text{ times}$$

$$\text{Quick ratio} \atop 2009 = \frac{£251 - £152}{£90} = 1.1 \text{ times}$$

$$\text{Quick ratio} \atop 2008 = \frac{£197 - £118}{£66} = 1.2 \text{ times}$$

Defensive interval

$$\text{Defensive interval} \atop 2010 = \frac{\text{quick assets}}{\text{average daily cash from operations}}$$

$$= \frac{£253 - £147}{(£70 + £456 - £80)/365} = 87 \text{ days}$$

$$\text{Defensive interval} \atop 2009 = \frac{£251 - £152}{(£53 + £491 - £70)/365} = 76 \text{ days}$$

The defensive interval for 2008 is not available because we do not have the trade receivables number for 31 March 2007.

Report on the liquidity of Hardy plc
The current ratio and the quick ratio have both dropped over the 3 years from 3.0 to 2.7 times, and 1.2 times to 1.1 times respectively. The defensive interval has increased from 76 days to 87 days at which level the company could potentially survive if there were no further cash inflows.

(ii) There are a number of areas that require further investigation. The following five ratios may be particularly useful to assist this investigation:

■ return on capital employed, ROCE
■ receivables collection days
■ payables days
■ inventories days
■ current ratio.

(iii) The relevant information has not been provided to enable the following investment ratios to be calculated for Hardy plc, which would have improved the analysis of Hardy plc's performance:

Earnings per share, eps
Cannot be calculated because we do not have details of the number of ordinary shares in issue.

Dividend per share
Cannot be calculated because we do not have details of the number of ordinary shares in issue.

Dividend cover
Cannot be calculated because we have not been able to calculate earnings per share, eps, and dividend per share.

Dividend yield %
Cannot be calculated because we have not been able to calculate dividend per share, and we do not have the market prices of the company's shares.

Price/earnings ratio, P/E
Cannot be calculated because we have not been able to calculate earnings per share, and we do not have the market prices of the company's shares.

Capital expenditure to sales %
Cannot be calculated because we do not have details of capital expenditure.

Capital expenditure to gross non-current assets %
Cannot be calculated because we do not have details of capital expenditure.

Chapter 8

E8.11 Alcoholic drinks group

Five-year income statement

Horizontal analysis

	Year 5	Year 4	Year 3	Year 2	Year 1
Revenue	108.4	107.3	107.5	106.9	100.0
Gross profit	93.9	92.2	93.5	91.7	100.0
Other investment income	(470.8)	(195.8)	(370.8)	200.0	100.0
Operating profit	107.5	99.1	104.6	89.1	100.0
Finance cost	48.5	55.9	63.7	92.2	100.0
Profit before tax	122.6	110.2	115.1	88.3	100.0
Income tax expense	107.0	103.7	100.4	102.1	100.0
Profit after tax	129.5	113.0	121.5	82.3	100.0
Minority interests	106.9	103.4	106.9	75.9	100.0
Profit for the year	130.7	113.5	122.3	82.6	100.0
Dividends	124.5	127.4	117.7	108.9	100.0
Retained earnings	135.9	102.1	126.1	61.0	100.0
Earnings per share	124.9	104.6	113.2	81.5	100.0
Interest cover	220.4	177.6	163.3	95.9	100.0
Dividend cover	95.7	87.0	100.0	78.3	100.0

Vertical analysis

	Year 5	Year 4	Year 3	Year 2	Year 1
Revenue	100.0	100.0	100.0	100.0	100.0
Gross profit	20.3	20.1	20.4	20.1	23.4
Other investment income	2.4	1.0	1.9	(1.0)	(0.6)
Operating profit	22.7	21.1	22.3	19.1	22.9
Finance cost	(2.1)	(2.4)	(2.8)	(4.0)	(4.7)
Profit before tax	20.6	18.7	19.5	15.1	18.2
Income tax expense	(5.5)	(5.4)	(5.2)	(5.3)	(5.5)
Profit after tax	15.1	13.4	14.3	9.8	12.7
Minority interests	(0.7)	(0.6)	(0.7)	(0.5)	(0.7)
Profit for the year	14.5	12.7	13.7	9.3	12.0
Dividends	(6.2)	(6.5)	(5.9)	(5.5)	(5.4)
Retained earnings	8.2	6.3	7.7	3.8	6.6

Revenue

The horizontal analysis shows an increase in sales of 8.4% over the five years, most of which was gained from year two over year one. Since year two, sales have not increased materially.

Gross profit

The horizontal analysis shows a drop in gross profit of 6.1% of sales over the five years. The vertical analysis shows that gross profit at 23.4% of sales in year one has dropped to 20.3% of sales in year five. The group may have been suffering from increased competition as its brands failed to continue to maintain their profitability.

Operating profit
The horizontal analysis shows an increase in operating profit of 7.5% of sales over the five years, despite the drop in gross profit levels. This is due to the extremely large gains in investment income. The vertical analysis shows that operating profit has been maintained fairly level over the five years at 22.9% of sales in year one to 22.7% of sales in year five.

Finance cost
The horizontal analysis shows a drop in interest paid by year five to less than half the level in year one. The vertical analysis bears this out, showing interest paid of 2.1% of revenue in year five compared with 4.7% of sales in year one. The group's borrowings were probably significantly reduced as little expansion has taken place, indicated by a reliance on mature markets and a lack of new ideas. The increased interest cover confirms the loan repayments.

Profit for the year
The horizontal analysis reflects a small increase in profit levels from 12.0% of revenue in year one to 14.5% of revenue in year five. The vertical analysis shows a steady increase in profit over the years except for a drop in year two, because of the negative investment income and high interest payments in that year.

Dividends
The level of dividends has been up and down over the years but year five is slightly higher at 6.2% of sales than year one which was 5.4% of sales, as shown in the vertical analysis. Dividend cover has been maintained at around two times.

Earnings per share
The horizontal analysis shows an increase of almost 25% in earnings per share in year five compared with year one, having recovered from a dip in earnings in year four.

Chapter 9

E9.1 Bluebell Woods

(i) Absorption costing

$$\text{Overhead absorption rate} = \frac{\text{budgeted fixed production cost}}{\text{budgeted units of production}} = \frac{£3,526}{4,300} = £0.82 \text{ per unit}$$

	£
Selling price per unit	5.84

Total production costs per unit

		£
Direct material	[£0.85 × 2 kg]	1.70
Direct labour	[42 × £4.20/60]	2.94
Variable production overhead		0.12
Variable production cost		4.76
Fixed production overhead		0.82 see above
Full production cost per unit		5.58

Four-week standard profit statement

		£
Sales revenue	[4,300 × £5.84]	25,112
Cost of sales		
Direct material	[4,300 × £1.70]	7,310
Direct labour	[4,300 × £2.94]	12,642
Variable production overhead	[4,300 × £0.12]	516
Fixed production overhead	[4,300 × £0.82]	3,526
		23,994
Profit for the period		1,118

(ii) Marginal costing

	£
Selling price per unit	5.84

Variable production costs per unit

		£
Direct material	[£0.85 × 2 kg]	1.70
Direct labour	[42 × £4.20 / 60]	2.94
Variable production overhead		0.12
Variable production cost		4.76

Four-week standard profit statement

		£
Sales revenue	[4,300 × £5.84]	25,112
Variable cost of sales	[4,300 × £4.76]	20,468
Contribution		4,644
Fixed production overhead		3,526
Profit for the period		1,118

E9.4 Rocky

Income statements for July and August on an absorption costing basis

	Per unit £	July Units	£	£	August Units	£	£
Sales revenue	10.00	4,400		44,000	5,000		50,000
Production costs:							
Variable	7.50	5,300	39,750		4,400	33,000	
Fixed	0.50	5,300	2,650		4,400	2,200	
		5,300	42,400		4,400	35,200	
Opening inventories	8.00	0	0		900	7,200	
Closing inventories	8.00	900	7,200		300	2,400	
Cost of sales	8.00	4,400		35,200	5,000		40,000

Gross profit	2.00	4,400		8,800	5,000		10,000
Selling and administrative costs			7,200			7,200	
(Under)/over absorption of fixed production costs	0.50		350			800	
				7,550			8,000
Net profit				1,250			2,000

E9.5 Rocky

Income statements for July and August on a marginal costing basis

	Per unit £	July			August		
		Units	£	£	Units	£	£
Sales revenue	10.00	4,400		44,000	5,000		50,000
Production costs:							
Variable	7.50	5,300	39,750		4,400	33,000	
Opening inventories	7.50	0	0		900	6,750	
Closing inventories	7.50	900	6,750		300	2,250	
Marginal cost of sales	7.50	4,400		33,000	5,000		37,500
Contribution	2.50	4,400		11,000	5,000		12,500
Fixed costs							
Production costs			3,000			3,000	
Selling and administrative costs			7,200	10,200		7,200	10,200
Net profit				800			2,300

Chapter 10

E10.1 Profit

Contribution for January = sales revenue − variable costs

$$= £320,000 - £240,000$$

$$= £80,000$$

Contribution to sales revenue ratio % $= \dfrac{£80,000 \times 100\%}{£320,000} = 25\%$

$$\text{£ revenue at break-even point} = \frac{\text{fixed costs}}{\text{contribution to revenue ratio \%}}$$

$$\text{£240,000} = \text{fixed costs}/25\%$$

$$\text{Fixed costs} = \text{£60,000}$$

$$\textbf{Profit for January} = \text{contribution} - \text{fixed costs}$$

$$= \text{£80,000} - \text{£60,000}$$

$$= \text{£20,000}$$

E10.2 Break-even

$$\text{Contribution for January} = \text{profit} + \text{fixed costs}$$

$$= \text{£10,000} + \text{£30,000}$$

$$= \text{£40,000}$$

$$\text{Contribution to revenue ratio \%} = \frac{\text{£40,000} \times 100\%}{\text{£120,000}} = 33.3\%$$

$$\textbf{£ revenue at break-even point} = \frac{\text{fixed costs}}{\text{contribution to revenue ratio \%}}$$

$$= \text{£30,000}/33.3\%$$

$$= \text{£90,000}$$

E10.3 Break-even and profit

Selling price $= $ £15

Marginal cost $= $ £9

Contribution $= $ £6

$$\text{Contribution to revenue ratio \%} = \frac{\text{£6} \times 100\%}{\text{£15}} = 40\%$$

$$\textbf{£ revenue at break-even point} = \frac{\text{fixed costs}}{\text{contribution to revenue ratio \%}}$$

$$= \text{£30,000}/40\%$$

$$= \text{£75,000}$$

$$\textbf{Profit for January} = \text{contribution} - \text{fixed costs}$$

$$= (40\% \times \text{£120,000}) - \text{£30,000}$$

$$= \text{£48,000} - \text{£30,000}$$

$$= \text{£18,000}$$

E10.4 Seivad

(i)

Unit contribution = selling price − variable costs

$$= £30 − (£10 + £7 + £8)$$

$$= £5$$

Planned contribution for 2010 = 20,000 × £5

$$= £100,000$$

(ii)

Profit = contribution − fixed costs

Planned profit for 2010 = £100,000 − £70,000

$$= £30,000$$

(iii)

Planned revenue for 2010 = 20,000 × £30

$$= £600,000$$

Planned contribution for 2010 = £100,000

Contribution to revenue ratio % $= \dfrac{£100,000}{£600,000} × 100\% = 16.67\%$

£ revenue at break-even point $= \dfrac{\text{fixed costs}}{\text{contribution to revenue ratio \%}}$

$$= £70,000/16.67\%$$

$$= £419,916$$

(iv)

Number of units at break-even point $= \dfrac{\text{£ revenue at break-even point}}{\text{selling price}}$

$$= £419,916/£30$$

$$= 13,998 \text{ units}$$

(It should be noted that the correct break-even point is £420,000 sales and 14,000 units. £419,916 and 13,998 units are the result of using a rounded-up contribution ratio of 16.67%.)

(v)

Margin of safety (sales revenue) = planned revenue − break-even sales value

$$= £600,000 − £419,916$$

$$= £180,084$$

(vi)

Margin of safety (sales units) = planned sales units − break-even sales units

$$= 20,000 − 13,998$$

$$= 6,002 \text{ units}$$

(vii)

Revised profit for 2010 = (20,000 × unit contribution) − (£70,000 + 20%)

(£30,000 + 10%) = (20,000 × unit contribution) − (£70,000 + 20%)

$$(20,000 \times \text{unit contribution}) = (£30,000 + 10\%) + (£70,000 + 20\%)$$

$$= £33,000 + £84,000$$

$$= £117,000$$

Unit contribution $= \dfrac{£117,000}{20,000}$

$$= £5.85$$

Selling price $=$ unit contribution $+$ unit variable costs

$$= £5.85 + £25$$

$$= £30.85$$

E10.8 Abem

(i) Cost per unit using conventional methods:

	Product A £	Product B £	Product C £
Direct labour ($\frac{1}{2}$, $1\frac{1}{2}$, 1 hours $\times$ £8)	4.00	12.00	8.00
Direct materials	20.00	10.00	25.00
Prime cost	24.00	22.00	33.00
Overhead ($1\frac{1}{2}$, 1, 3 hours $\times$ £25)	37.50	25.00	75.00
Cost per unit	61.50	47.00	108.00

(ii) Total overhead may be calculated from multiplying total machine hours by the overhead absorption rate per machine hour.

Total machine hours

$$(750 \times 1\tfrac{1}{2})\,[\text{Product A}] + (1,975 \times 1)\,[\text{Product B}] + (7,900 \times 3)\,[\text{Product C}] = 26,800 \text{ hours}$$

Total overhead is therefore $(26,800 \times £25) = £670,000$.

This may be apportioned to activities using the percentages given:

Activity	%	Apportionment (£)	Cost driver
Set-ups	35	234,500	Set-ups
Machining	20	134,000	Machine hours
Materials handling	15	100,500	Movements
Inspection	30	201,000	Inspections
		670,000	

The relevant cost driver for each activity is taken from the question.

$$\text{rate per set-up} = \frac{\text{Budgeted set-up cost}}{\text{Number of set-ups}} = \frac{£234,500}{670} = £350$$

$$\text{rate per machine hour} = \frac{\text{Budgeted machine cost}}{\text{Number of machine hours}} = \frac{£134,000}{26,800} = £5$$

$$\text{rate per movement} = \frac{\text{Budgeted handling cost}}{\text{Number of movements}} = \frac{£100,500}{120} = £837.50$$

$$\text{rate per inspection} = \frac{\text{Budgeted inspection cost}}{\text{Number of inspections}} = \frac{£201,000}{1,000} = £201$$

	Product A	Product B	Product C
	£	£	£
Set-up costs:			
70, 120, 480 set-ups × £350	24,500	42,000	168,000
divided by 750, 1,975, 7,900 units	32.67	21.27	21.27
Machine costs: 1½, 1, 3 hours × £5	7.50	5.00	15.00
Materials handling costs:			
10, 20, 90 movements × £837.50	8,375	16,750	75,375
divided by 750, 1,975, 7,900 units	11.17	8.48	9.54
Inspection costs:			
150, 180, 670 inspections × £201	30,150	36,180	134,670
divided by 750, 1,975, 7,900 units	40.20	18.32	17.05

Cost per unit	Product A	Product B	Product C
	£	£	£
Prime cost (from (i))	24.00	22.00	33.00
Overhead: Set-up cost	32.67	21.27	21.27
Machine cost	7.50	5.00	15.00
Handling cost	11.17	8.48	9.54
Inspection cost	40.20	18.32	17.05
Cost per unit	115.54	75.07	95.86

(iii) Comparative cost per unit	Product A	Product B	Product C
	£	£	£
Using machine hour rate	61.50	47.00	108.00
Using ABC	115.54	75.07	95.86
Difference	54.04	28.07	(12.14)

These are very significant differences. If the cost driver information is reasonably accurate, then the existing absorption rate causes the high-volume product (C) to heavily subsidise the other two, which have lower volumes. Product costs may therefore be inaccurate, with implications for inventory valuation and profit. Also, to the extent that they are based on cost, selling prices may be too low for A and B, while being too high for C. A and B may thus be selling at a loss, whereas C's sales volume may be depressed by an artificially high price.

Chapter 11

E11.1 Eifion

(i)
A limiting factor is anything which limits the activity of a business. Examples of limiting factors, or key factors, are a shortage of supply of a resource or a restriction on sales demand at a particular price. A

business should seek to optimise the benefit it obtains from the limiting factor. If a company has a short-term capacity constraint then its product mix should be based on maximising its contribution per limiting factor.

(ii)

Existing capacity $= (12,000 \times 7) + (24,000 \times 3.5)$
$\qquad\qquad\qquad = \underline{168,000 \text{ machine hours}}$

Fixed cost per unit $= £1,680,000/168,000$
$\qquad\qquad\qquad\qquad = \underline{£10 \text{ per machine hour}}$

	A	B
	£	£
Total cost per unit	93.50	126.00
Fixed cost per unit	70.00 (7 × £10)	35.00 (3.5 × £10)
Variable cost per unit	23.50	91.00
Selling price per unit	107.50	175.00
Contribution per unit	84.00	84.00
Contribution per machine hour	12.00 (£84/7)	24.00 (£84/3.5)

Machine hours are fully utilised at the existing production level. Therefore, demand (18,000 + 30,000 = 48,000 units) is in excess of current capacity. Profits will be maximised by concentrating on B, since this yields the larger contribution per machine hour. In order to meet the maximum demand for B, 105,000 (30,000 × 3.5) machine hours will be required. The remaining capacity of 63,000 hours (168,000 − 105,000) should be allocated to producing 9,000 (63,000/7) units of A. The total profit for this output level is as follows:

		£
A (9,000 × £84 contribution per unit)	=	756,000
B (30,000 × £84 contribution per unit)	=	2,520,000
Contribution		3,276,000
Less: fixed costs		1,680,000
Profit		1,596,000

(iii)

You should refer to the relevant section in Chapter 11 to check on the limitations of cost-plus pricing. In practice, one solution to the problems of cost-plus pricing is to estimate likely demand (which should be known from past experience in the case of established products) and calculate an absorption rate on this assumed volume of output. Provided that actual volume equals or exceeds the estimated volume of sales, the company will achieve (or exceed) its target profit.

Another solution is to set a price on the basis of a budgeted production volume and allow inventories to build up for a time if demand is below production volume at this price. A price review can be made when demand conditions are known better, and either of the following actions could be taken:

■ a price reduction could be made to stimulate demand if this seems appropriate
■ production volumes could be reduced and prices raised if necessary in recognition of the lack of demand for the product at the original budgeted volumes.

E11.2 Phil Atterley

(i)

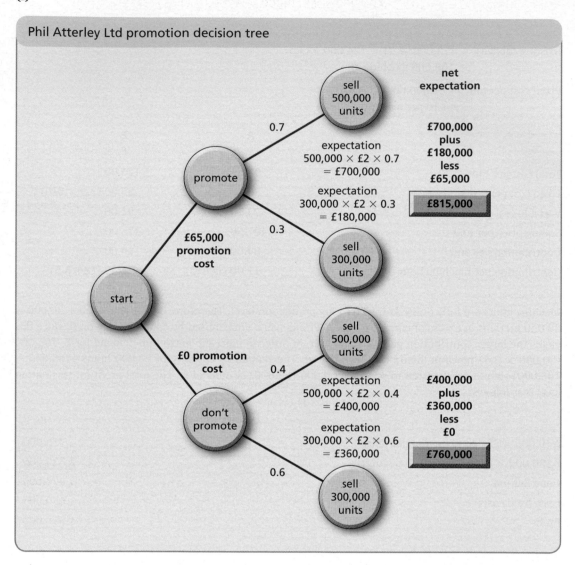

Phil Atterley Ltd promotion decision tree

net expectation

sell 500,000 units

0.7

promote

expectation
500,000 × £2 × 0.7
= £700,000

£700,000
plus
£180,000
less
£65,000

expectation
300,000 × £2 × 0.3
= £180,000

£815,000

£65,000 promotion cost

0.3

sell 300,000 units

start

sell 500,000 units

£0 promotion cost

0.4

don't promote

expectation
500,000 × £2 × 0.4
= £400,000

£400,000
plus
£360,000
less
£0

expectation
300,000 × £2 × 0.6
= £360,000

£760,000

0.6

sell 300,000 units

The branch of the tree indicating that Phil Atterley Ltd should promote is labelled with the cost of that activity £65,000.

The branch of the tree indicating that Phil Atterley Ltd should not promote is labelled with the cost of that activity £0.

The probabilities of occurrences are labelled on the branches following the decision taken to promote, being 0.7 (70%) for sales of 500,000 units and 0.3 (30%) for sales of 300,000 units.

Similarly, the same thing is done on the branches following the decision not to promote, being 0.4 (40%) for sales of 500,000 units and 0.6 (60%) for sales of 300,000 units.

(ii)

The expectations of contributions are then calculated by multiplying sales volumes by unit contribution and probability.

The contribution expectation following no promotion is:

$$£400,000 + £360,000 = £760,000$$

The contribution expectation following the promotion is:

$$£700,000 + £180,000 = £880,000$$

but, the promotion option also involves a cost of £65,000 and so the net expectation is £815,000.

The £815,000 net expectation following the promotion may be compared with the net expectation from not promoting of £760,000.

On the above basis we can recommend to Stan to advise the company to promote the sales of its new product.

(iii)

There are a number of further factors that Phil Atterley Ltd may consider when making this decision, for example:

- accuracy of market research information
- cost of obtaining market research information
- cost of getting perfect information
- risk analysis
- sensitivity analysis
- working capital requirements
- return on investment
- opportunity costs
- demand for competing products
- prices of competing products
- product life cycle.

(iv)

Information may be usefully obtained about the years in which sales may be achieved and the possible different probabilities of these occurring in each year. Use of an appropriate cost of capital would enable calculation of the net present values of the expected outcomes of each decision. This may provide a more realistic comparison, particularly if the timing of cash flows was significantly different following whether or not promotion was undertaken or if the cost of capital was significantly high.

E11.3 Hurdle

(i)

In view of the scarcity of labour, labour hours are obviously a key factor. Since any new work undertaken by the company will entail diverting labour from the standard product (for which there is heavy demand) the first thing that must be done is to find a contribution per hour of the key factor.

Standard product

	£	£
Selling price		28
Marginal cost:		
Materials	10	
Labour 0.5 hours × £10 per hour	5	15
Contribution		13
Contribution per labour hour (£13 ÷ 0.5 hours)		26

Make-versus-buy decision for the special component

Making the component

		£
Materials cost		100
Labour cost	4 hours at £10 per hour	40
Opportunity cost	4 hours at £26 per hour	104
Total cost to make special component		244

Since the component can be purchased for only £220 then it is cheaper for the company to buy it rather than make it.

(ii)

The contract costs can now be calculated assuming that the special component may be purchased.

		£
Materials cost		600
Special component		220
Labour cost	100 hours at £10 per hour	1,000
Opportunity cost	100 hours at £26 per hour	2,600
Total cost of contract		4,420

The contract may be accepted by the company if the contract price is greater than £4,420.

(iii)

If a 20% mark-up is required by the company then the contract price should be £4,420 plus 20%, which is £5,304.

Chapter 12

E12.1 Earextensions

Sales price   £50

	Jan	Feb	Mar	Apr	May	Jun	Total
Sales budget							
Units	50,000	60,000	72,000	86,400	86,400	86,400	441,200
£	2,500,000	3,000,000	3,600,000	4,320,000	4,320,000	4,320,000	22,060,000

E12.2 Earextensions

	Jan	Feb	Mar	Apr	May	Jun	Total
Production budget (units)							
Opening inventories	0	12,000	14,400	17,280	17,280	17,280	0
Production	62,000	62,400	74,880	86,400	86,400	86,400	458,480
Sales	50,000	60,000	72,000	86,400	86,400	86,400	441,200
Closing inventories	12,000	14,400	17,280	17,280	17,280	17,280	17,280

E12.3 Earextensions

Production overheads

Direct labour hours

Assemblers	3.0 × 458,480	1,375,440 minutes	=	22,924 hours
Operators	1.5 × 458,480	687,720 minutes	=	11,462 hours
Total	4.5 × 458,480	2,063,160 minutes	=	34,386 hours

Total production overheads £4,100,000

$$\text{Production overheads per direct labour hour} \quad \frac{£4,100,000}{34,386} = £119.235 \text{ per hour} = £1.987 \text{ per minute}$$

Unit gross margin budget

			£	£	£
Sales price					50.000
Unit cost					
Direct labour	Assemblers	3 minutes @ £10 per hour	0.5000		
	Operators	1.5 minutes @ £8 per hour	0.2000		
				0.7000	
Materials	Electronic assembly		23.3000		
	Keypad		1.0000		
	Case		2.0000		
				26.3000	
Overheads	4.5 minutes @ £1.987 per minute			8.9426	
					35.9426
Unit gross margin					14.0574

	Jan	Feb	Mar	Apr	May	Jun	Total
Direct labour budget (£)							
Production units							
× £0.70 per unit	43,400	43,680	52,416	60,480	60,480	60,480	320,936

E12.4 Earextensions

	Jan	Feb	Mar	Apr	May	Jun	Total
Materials purchases and usage budget (units)							
Electronic assembly							
Opening inventories	10,000	31,200	37,440	43,200	43,200	43,200	10,000
Purchases	83,200	68,640	80,640	86,400	86,400	86,400	491,680
Usage	62,000	62,400	74,880	86,400	86,400	86,400	458,480
Closing inventories	31,200	37,440	43,200	43,200	43,200	43,200	43,200
Keypad							
Opening inventories	30,000	31,200	37,440	43,200	43,200	43,200	30,000
Purchases	63,200	68,640	80,640	86,400	86,400	86,400	471,680
Usage	62,000	62,400	74,880	86,400	86,400	86,400	458,480
Closing inventories	31,200	37,440	43,200	43,200	43,200	43,200	43,200

	Jan	Feb	Mar	Apr	May	Jun	Total
Case							
Opening inventories	20,000	31,200	37,440	43,200	43,200	43,200	20,000
Purchases	73,200	68,640	80,640	86,400	86,400	86,400	481,680
Usage	62,000	62,400	74,880	86,400	86,400	86,400	458,480
Closing inventories	31,200	37,440	43,200	43,200	43,200	43,200	43,200

Materials purchases and usage budget (£)

Electronic assembly £23.30 per unit

	Jan	Feb	Mar	Apr	May	Jun	Total
Opening inventories	233,000	726,960	872,352	1,006,560	1,006,560	1,006,560	233,000
Purchases	1,938,560	1,599,312	1,878,912	2,013,120	2,013,120	2,013,120	11,456,144
Usage	1,444,600	1,453,920	1,744,704	2,013,120	2,013,120	2,013,120	10,682,584
Closing inventories	726,960	872,352	1,006,560	1,006,560	1,006,560	1,006,560	1,006,560

Keypad £1.00 per unit

	Jan	Feb	Mar	Apr	May	Jun	Total
Opening inventories	30,000	31,200	37,440	43,200	43,200	43,200	30,000
Purchases	63,200	68,640	80,640	86,400	86,400	86,400	471,680
Usage	62,000	62,400	74,880	86,400	86,400	86,400	458,480
Closing inventories	31,200	37,440	43,200	43,200	43,200	43,200	43,200

Case £2.00 per unit

	Jan	Feb	Mar	Apr	May	Jun	Total
Opening inventories	40,000	62,400	74,880	86,400	86,400	86,400	40,000
Purchases	146,400	137,280	161,280	172,800	172,800	172,800	963,360
Usage	124,000	124,800	149,760	172,800	172,800	172,800	916,960
Closing inventories	62,400	74,880	86,400	86,400	86,400	86,400	86,400

E12.5 Earextensions

Overheads, selling, administrative, financial costs budget (£)

	Jan	Feb	Mar	Apr	May	Jun	Total
Production overheads (£4,100,000 less depreciation £50,000)	675,000	675,000	675,000	675,000	675,000	675,000	4,050,000
Selling costs and administrative expenses	900,000	900,000	900,000	600,000	600,000	600,000	4,500,000
Interest (0.2% of sales)	5,000	6,000	7,200	8,640	8,640	8,640	44,120

Income statement budget

	Jan	Feb	Mar	Apr	May	Jun	Total
Sales units	50,000	60,000	72,000	86,400	86,400	86,400	441,200
Figures in £							
Sales revenue	2,500,000	3,000,000	3,600,000	4,320,000	4,320,000	4,320,000	22,060,000
Cost of sales	1,797,130	2,156,556	2,587,866	3,105,440	3,105,440	3,105,440	15,857,872
Gross profit	702,870	843,444	1,012,134	1,214,560	1,214,560	1,214,560	6,202,128
Selling, administrative and interest costs	905,000	906,000	907,200	608,640	608,640	608,640	4,544,120
(Loss)/profit	(202,130)	(62,556)	104,934	605,920	605,920	605,920	1,658,008
Cumulative (loss)/ profit	(202,130)	(264,686)	(159,752)	446,168	1,052,088	1,658,008	

E12.6 Earextensions

	Jan	Feb	Mar	Apr	May	Jun	Total
Finished product inventory valuation budget							
@ £35.9426/unit							
	£431,311	£517,573	£621,088	£621,088	£621,088	£621,088	
Over (under) absorption of production overheads units	76,413	76,413	76,413	76,413	76,413	76,413	458,480
	62,000	62,400	74,880	86,400	86,400	86,400	458,480
	14,413	14,013	1,533	(9,987)	(9,987)	(9,987)	0
@ £8.9426/unit	£128,893	£125,316	£13,712	£(89,307)	£(89,307)	£(89,307)	£0
Cumulative inventories adjustment	£128,893	£254,208	£267,920	£178,614	£89,307	£0	
Total finished goods inventories	£560,204	£771,782	£889,008	£799,702	£710,395	£621,088	

E12.7 Marx

(i)

	Chico	Groucho	Harpo
Average net operating assets	£7.5m	£17.5m	£12.5m
Operating profit	£1.5m	£1.4m	£2.0m
ROI%	20%	8%	16%
Ranking of ROI%	1	3	2

(ii)

	Chico	Groucho	Harpo
Average net operating assets	£7.5m	£17.5m	£12.5m
Divisional WACC	7%	5%	10%
Operating profit	£1.5m	£1.4m	£2.0m
Administrative expenses	£0.80m	£0.30m	£0.65m
	£0.70m	£1.10m	£1.35m
Notional financial charge			
(WACC × average net operating assets)	£0.525m	£0.875m	£1.250m
RI	£0.175m	£0.225m	£0.100m
Ranking of RI	2	1	3

(iii)

(a) The ROI % of each division is currently above its WACC with Chico being by far the best performer, followed by Harpo and then Groucho.

Chico and Harpo would be reluctant to pursue an investment opportunity that is expected to yield a return of 9% because they both currently earn 20% and 16% respectively.

In the case of Chico this represents a lost opportunity for Marx plc because taking on the investment would add value since Chico's WACC is 2% lower than the project's 9%.

Harpo's decision not to take on the investment is in the best interest of Marx plc since Harpo's WACC is 7% above the project's 9%.

Groucho would be keen to pursue an investment opportunity that is expected to yield a return of 9% because it currently earns only 8%.

Groucho's decision to take on the investment is also in the best interest of Marx plc since Groucho's WACC is 4% below the project's 9%.

(b) The current RI of Groucho is the highest, followed by Chico and then Harpo.

If performance is measured using RI, then Chico and Groucho would take on an investment opportunity that yields 9% because even after capital charges on net operating assets at 7% and 5% respectively it would add to their residual incomes.

If performance is measured using RI, Harpo would not take on an investment opportunity that yields 9% because after the capital charge on net operating assets at 10% there would be a reduction to residual income.

E12.8 Earextensions

Trade receivables budget (£)

Sales revenue		Jan	Feb	Mar	Apr	May	Jun
	2,500,000	2,500,000	2,500,000				
	3,000,000		3,000,000	3,000,000			
	4,320,000			3,600,000	3,600,000		
	4,320,000				4,320,000	4,320,000	
	4,320,000					4,320,000	4,320,000
	4,320,000						4,320,000
Total trade receivables		2,500,000	5,500,000	6,600,000	7,920,000	8,640,000	8,640,000

Trade payables budget (£)

Materials purchases		Jan	Feb	Mar	Apr	May	Jun
	303,000	303,000	303,000				
	2,148,160	2,148,160	2,148,160	2,148,160			
	1,805,232		1,805,232	1,805,232	1,805,232		
	2,120,832			2,120,832	2,120,832	2,120,832	
	2,272,320				2,272,320	2,272,320	2,272,320
	2,272,320					2,272,320	2,272,320
	2,272,320						2,272,320
Total trade payables		2,451,160	4,256,392	6,074,224	6,198,384	6,665,472	6,816,960

Cash flow budget (£)

	Jan	Feb	Mar	Apr	May	Jun	Total
Customer receipts	0	0	2,500,000	3,000,000	3,600,000	4,320,000	13,420,000
Supplier payments	0	0	303,000	2,148,160	1,805,232	2,120,832	6,377,224
Direct labour	43,400	43,680	52,416	60,480	60,480	60,480	320,936
Overheads	675,000	675,000	675,000	675,000	675,000	675,000	4,050,000

	Jan	Feb	Mar	Apr	May	Jun	Total
Selling costs and administrative expenses	900,000	900,000	900,000	600,000	600,000	600,000	4,500,000
Interest	5,000	6,000	7,200	8,640	8,640	8,640	44,120
Total payments	1,623,400	1,624,680	1,937,616	3,492,280	3,149,352	3,464,952	15,292,280
Cash flow	(1,623,400)	(1,624,680)	562,384	(492,280)	450,648	855,048	(1,872,280)
Opening balance	355,000	(1,268,400)	(2,893,080)	(2,330,696)	(2,822,976)	(2,372,328)	355,000
Closing balance	(1,268,400)	(2,893,080)	(2,330,696)	(2,822,976)	(2,372,328)	(1,517,280)	(1,517,280)

E12.9 Earextensions

Balance sheet budget (£)

	Dec	Jan	Feb	Mar	Apr	May	Jun	Depreciation per month
Non-current assets	495,000	486,666	478,332	470,000	461,666	453,333	445,000	8,333
Inventories	303,000	1,380,764	1,756,454	2,025,168	1,935,862	1,846,555	1,757,248	
Trade receivables	0	2,500,000	5,500,000	6,600,000	7,920,000	8,640,000	8,640,000	
Cash	355,000	(1,268,400)	(2,893,080)	(2,330,696)	(2,822,976)	(2,372,328)	(1,517,280)	
	1,153,000	3,099,030	4,841,706	6,764,472	7,494,552	8,567,560	9,324,968	
Trade payables	303,000	2,451,160	4,256,392	6,074,224	6,198,384	6,665,472	6,816,960	
Loans	450,000	450,000	450,000	450,000	450,000	450,000	450,000	
Share capital	400,000	400,000	400,000	400,000	400,000	400,000	400,000	
Retained earnings	0	(202,130)	(264,686)	(159,752)	446,168	1,052,088	1,658,008	
	1,153,000	3,099,030	4,841,706	6,764,472	7,494,552	8,567,560	9,324,968	

E12.10 Blord

(i)

	Quarter 1 £	Quarter 2 £	Quarter 3 £	Quarter 4 £	Total £
Sales revenue	5,250,000	6,000,000	6,375,000	6,750,000	24,375,000
	(£75 × 70k)	(£75 × 80k)	(£75 × 85k)	(£75 × 90k)	

(ii)

	Quarter 1 £	Quarter 2 £	Quarter 3 £	Quarter 4 £	Total £
Opening receivables	300,000	350,000	400,000	425,000	1,475,000
Per bal. sheet 30/6/09		(£5.25m × 20%/3)	(£6.00m × 20%/3)	(£6.375m × 20%/3)	

	Quarter 1 £	Quarter 2 £	Quarter 3 £	Quarter 4 £	Total £
Cash inflow from customers					
Cash sales					
(80% of quarterly sales)	4,200,000	4,800,000	5,100,000	5,400,000	19,500,000
Credit sales					
Opening receivables + 20% sales revenue − closing receivables	1,000,000	1,150,000	1,250,000	1,325,000	4,725,000
Total cash inflows	5,200,000	5,950,000	6,350,000	6,725,000	24,225,000
Trade receivables at 30 June 2010				450,000	
				($£6.75m \times 20\%/3$)	

E12.11 Blord

Units	Quarter 1	Quarter 2	Quarter 3	Quarter 4	Total
Opening finished goods inventories (per balance sheet)	15,000	16,000	17,000	18,000	15,000
plus Production (by deduction)	71,000	81,000	86,000	91,000	329,000
less Sales (given)	70,000	80,000	85,000	90,000	325,000
Closing finished goods inventories	16,000	17,000	18,000	19,000	19,000
	($20\% \times 80k$)	($20\% \times 85k$)	($20\% \times 90k$)	($20\% \times 95k$)	

E12.12 Blord

(i)

329,000 bookcases have been budgeted to be produced during the budget year ending 30 June 2010.

Direct labour hours $= 329,000 \times 1.5 = 493,500$ DLH

Fixed overhead rate $= £380,000/493,500 = £0.77$ per DLH

Unit gross profit budget

	£	£	
Unit selling price		75.000	
Unit costs			
Direct materials	16.000		($8 \times £2$)
Direct labour	18.000		($1.5 \times £12$)
Variable overhead	3.750		($1.5 \times £2.50$)
Fixed overhead	1.155		($1.5 \times £0.77$)
Unit cost		38.905	
Unit gross profit		36.095	

(ii)

Estimated production budget for the first and second quarters of the year ending 30 June 2011 (the year following the budget year)

Units	Quarter 1	Quarter 2	Quarter 3
Opening inventories (see E12.11)	19,000	19,000	20,000
plus Production (by deduction)	95,000	96,000	
less Sales (given) (see E12.11)	95,000	95,000	100,000
Closing inventories	19,000	20,000	
	(20% × 95k)	(20% × 100k)	

Budgeted production for first quarter of the year ending 30 June 2011 (the year following the budget year) is therefore 95,000 units.

Unit materials purchases and materials usage budget for the year ending 30 June 2010

Units	Quarter 1	Quarter 2	Quarter 3	Quarter 4	Total
Opening inventories (per balance sheet)	96,000	97,200	103,200	109,200	96,000
plus Purchases (by deduction)	569,200	654,000	694,000	732,800	2,650,000
less Usage (see E12.11)	568,000 (8m × 71k)	648,000 (8m × 81k)	688,000 (8m × 86k)	728,000 (8m × 91k)	2,632,000
Closing inventories (see E12.11 and above)	97,200	103,200	109,200	114,000	114,000
	(15% × 8m × 81k)	(15% × 8m × 86k)	(15% × 8m × 91k)	(15% × 8m × 95k)	

£ materials purchases and material usage budget for the year ending 30 June 2010

(budgeted units × £2 cost per metre)

	Quarter 1 £	Quarter 2 £	Quarter 3 £	Quarter 4 £	Total £
Opening inventories	192,000	194,400	206,400	218,400	192,000
Purchases	1,138,400	1,308,000	1,388,000	1,465,600	5,300,000
Usage	1,136,000	1,296,000	1,376,000	1,456,000	5,264,000
Closing inventories	194,400	206,400	218,400	228,000	228,000

(iii)
Phased cash payments to timber supplier

	Quarter 1 £	Quarter 2 £	Quarter 3 £	Quarter 4 £	Total £
Opening payables (per balance sheet)	760,000	379,467	436,000	463,667	760,000
plus Purchases (see above)	1,138,400	1,308,000	1,388,000	1,465,600	5,300,000
less Payments (by deduction)	1,518,933	1,251,467	1,360,333	1,440,734	5,571,467
Closing payables (Purchases/3)	379,467	436,000	463,667	488,533	488,533

E12.13 Blord

	Quarter 1	Quarter 2	Quarter 3	Quarter 4	Total
Production (units)	71,000	81,000	86,000	91,000	329,000
Labour hours per unit	1.5	1.5	1.5	1.5	1.5
Total direct labour hours	106,500	121,500	129,000	136,500	493,500
Labour rate per hour (£)	12	12	12	12	12
Total direct labour cost (£) and quarterly cash flows	1,278,000	1,458,000	1,548,000	1,638,000	5,922,000

E12.14 Blord

Depreciation calculation (see E12.10)
Buildings cost £100k × 4% = £4,000 for the year 2010
Equipment reducing balance £60k − £25k = £35k × 20% = £7,000 for the year 2010
Total budget depreciation for the year ending 30 June 2010 = £11,000

60% of building depreciation relates to manufacturing = 60% × £4,000 = £2,400 for the year
or £2,400/4 = £600 per quarter
100% of equipment depreciation relates to manufacturing = £7,000 for the year
or £7,000/4 = £1,750 per quarter
Total quarterly depreciation relating to manufacturing = £600 + £1,750 = £2,350

	Quarter 1	Quarter 2	Quarter 3	Quarter 4	Total
Budgeted direct labour hours	106,500	121,500	129,000	136,500	493,500
Variable overhead rate per DLH	£2.50	£2.50	£2.50	£2.50	
Total variable overhead (£)	266,250	303,750	322,500	341,250	1,233,750
Fixed manufacturing overhead (£)	95,000	95,000	95,000	95,000	380,000
Total manufacturing overheads (£)	361,250	398,750	417,500	436,250	1,613,750
less Depreciation re manufacturing (£)	2,350	2,350	2,350	2,350	9,400
Total manufacturing overheads cash outflow(£)	358,900	396,400	415,150	433,900	1,604,350

E12.15 Blord

	Quarter 1 £	Quarter 2 £	Quarter 3 £	Quarter 4 £	Total £
Total selling and administrative costs	1,950,000	1,950,000	1,950,000	1,950,000	7,800,000
less Depreciation (£11,000/4 − £2,350)	400	400	400	400	1,600
Selling and admin cash outflow	1,949,600	1,949,600	1,949,600	1,949,600	7,798,400

Phased statement of cash flows budget for the year ending 30 June 2010
Direct method

	Quarter 1 £	Quarter 2 £	Quarter 3 £	Quarter 4 £	Total £
Receipts (see E12.10(i))	5,200,000	5,950,000	6,350,000	6,725,000	24,225,000
Payments					
Timber supplier (E12.12)	1,518,933	1,251,467	1,360,333	1,440,734	5,571,467
Direct labour (E12.13)	1,278,000	1,458,000	1,548,000	1,638,000	5,922,000

Manufacturing overheads (E12.14)	358,900	396,400	415,150	433,900	1,604,350
Selling and administrative costs	1,949,600	1,949,600	1,949,600	1,949,600	7,798,400
Total payments	5,105,433	5,055,467	5,273,083	5,462,234	20,896,217
Quarterly cash flow	94,567	894,533	1,076,917	1,262,766	3,328,783
Opening cash balance	58,000	152,567	1,047,100	2,124,017	58,000
Closing cash balance	152,567	1,047,100	2,124,017	3,386,783	3,386,783

E12.16 Blord

Phased income statement budget for the year ending 30 June 2010

	Quarter 1 £	Quarter 2 £	Quarter 3 £	Quarter 4 £	Total £
Sales revenue	5,250,000	6,000,000	6,375,000	6,750,000	24,375,000
Cost of sales (by deduction)	2,723,351	3,112,401	3,306,926	3,501,452	12,644,130
Gross profit	2,526,649	2,887,599	3,068,074	3,248,548	11,730,870
	($£36.095 \times 70k$)	($£36.095 \times 80k$)	($£36.095 \times 85k$)	($£36.095 \times 90k$)	
Selling and administrative costs	1,950,000	1,950,000	1,950,000	1,950,000	7,800,000
Profit	576,650	937,600	1,118,075	1,298,550	3,930,870

Balance sheet budget as at 30 June 2010

£

Assets

Non-current assets

Buildings at cost	100,000	
Depreciation provision	(24,000)	see E12.14 £20k + £4k
Equipment at cost	60,000	
Depreciation provision	(32,000)	see E12.14 £25k + £7k
Total non-current assets	104,000	

Current assets

Inventories of raw materials (114,000 metres of timber × £2)	228,000	see E12.12
Inventories of finished goods (19,000 units × £38.905)	739,195	see E12.11 and E12.12
Trade receivables	450,000	see E12.10
Cash	3,386,783	see E12.15
Total current assets	4,803,978	
Total assets	4,907,978	

	£	
Liabilities		
Current liabilities		
Trade payables	488,533	see E12.12
Net assets	4,419,445	
Equity		
Share capital	250,000	
Retained earnings	4,169,445	£238,575 + £3,930,870
Total equity	4,419,445	

Chapter 13

E13.1 Nilbog

Flexed budget

	Budget	Flexed	Actual
Units (Fishermen)			
Opening inventory finished goods	0	0	0
Unit production	10,000	9,600	9,600
Unit sales	10,000	9,000	9,000
Closing inventory finished goods	0	600	600
Cubic yards (materials)			
Opening inventory materials	0	0	0
Materials purchases	30,000	30,800	30,000
Materials usage	30,00	28,800	28,000
Closing inventory materials	0	2,000	2,000

		Budget £		Flexed £		Actual £	Actual to flexed budget variances		
							Variance	£	Working
Sales revenue	(10,000 × 48)	480,000	(9,000 × 48)	432,000	(9,000 × 48)	432,000	sales price	0	
Opening inventories:									
Finished goods		0		0		0			
Materials		0		0		0			
Materials purchased	(10,000 × 3 × 3.6)	(108,000)	((9,600 × 3 + 2,000) × 3.6)	(110,880)	(30,000 × 3.84)	(115,200)	materials price	(7,200)	30,000 × (3.6 − 3.84)
							materials usage	2,880	(30,800 − 30,000) × 3.6
Direct labour	(10,000 × 2 × 6.6)	(132,000)	(9,600 × 2 × 6.6)	(126,720)	(22,000 × 6.48)	(142,560)	labour rate	2,640	22,000 × (6.6 − 6.48)
							labour efficiency	(18,480)	(19,200 − 22,000) × 6.6
Variable overhead	(10,000 × 2 × 2.4)	(48,000)	(9,600 × 2 × 2.4)	(46,080)	(22,000 × 2.0)	(44,000)	overhead spend	8,800	22,000 × (2.4 − 2.0)
							overhead efficiency	(6,720)	(19,200 − 22,000) × 2.4
Fixed overhead	(10,000 × 2 × 4.8)	(96,000)		(96,000)		(100,000)	overhead spend	(4,000)	96,000 − 100,000
Closing inventories:									
Finished goods		0	(600 × 38.4)	23,040	(600 × 38.4)	23,040			
Materials		0	(2,000 × 3.6)	7,200	(2,000 × 3.6)	7,200			
Net profit		96,000		82,560		60,480		(22,080)	
Net profit £ per unit		9.60		9.17		6.72			
									Flexed budget to budget variances
							sales volume	(9,600)	(10,000 − 9,000) × 9.6
							fixed overhead volume	(3,840)	(10,000 × 2) × 4.8 − (9,600 × 2) × 4.8
							total variances	(35,520)	actual minus budget profit

Operating statement for period 5 in 2010 (4 weeks)

			£
Budget sales revenue	10,000 × £48		480,000
Standard cost of sales	10,000 × £38.4		384,000
Budgeted profit			96,000

Variances	Favourable	Unfavourable	
	£	£	
Sales volume		9,600	
Materials			
Price		7,200	
Usage	2,880		
Direct labour			
Rate	2,640		
Efficiency		18,480	
Variable overhead			
Expenditure	8,800		
Efficiency		6,720	
Fixed overhead			
Expenditure		4,000	
Volume		3,840	
	14,320	49,840	(35,520)
Actual profit			60,480

Inventories are valued at standard cost at each month end so that a true month activity is reported, not previous inadequacies.

Variances	Favourable	Unfavourable	Likely causes of variances
	£	£	
Sales volume		9,600	An extra 1,000 units had been planned for period 5 at £9.60 per unit standard profit.
Materials			
Price		7,200	Factors may be economic, currency fluctuations or poor standards.
Usage	2,880		Low defects, better quality, better inventory control, different production methods, improved labour training.
Direct labour			
Rate	2,640		Lower grade, union negotiation, less overtime.
Efficiency		18,480	Machine breakdowns, rework (but not apparent from materials usage).

Variable overhead

Expenditure	8,800		Poor standard, tighter cost control.
Efficiency		6,720	Machine breakdowns, rework (but not apparent from materials usage).

Fixed overhead

Expenditure		4,000	Poor standard, tighter cost control.
Volume		3,840	Under-recoveries of fixed overhead because of low volumes.
	14,320	49,840	

E13.2 Cyclops

Note: minor differences are the result of roundings

(i)

	Budget	Flexed	Actual			Variances
Units	40,800	61,200	61,200			
	£	£	£			£
Sales	244,800	367,200	348,840	sales price		
	40,800 × £6.00		61,200 × £5.70	61,200 × £0.30		18,360A
Materials	81,600	122,400	114,240	materials		
	40,800 × £2.00		61,200 × £1.87	61,200 × £0.13		8,160F
Labour	81,600	122,400	133,280	labour		
	40,800 × £2.00		61,200 × £2.18	61,200 × £0.18		10,880A
Overhead	16,320	24,480	27,200	overhead		
	40,800 × £0.40		61,200 × £0.44	£24,480 − £27,200		2,720A
Contribution	65,280	97,920	74,120			23,800A
Contribution/unit	£1.60					
	£65,280/40,800					
Volume variance	65,280	97,920		sales		
	budget profit − flexed budget =		£1.60 × (40,800 − 61,200)			32,640F
				Total variances		8,840F
					£	£
Budget contribution						65,280
Sales variances						
Price	30p price reduction				18,360A	
Volume	50% increase				32,640F	14,280F
Materials						
Price	4% discount				4,896F	
Usage	savings on wastage				3,264F	8,160F
Labour	use of more highly paid and skilled staff					10,880A
Overhead	higher electricity and gas supplies					2,720A
Actual contribution						74,120

(ii)

You should refer to the relevant section in Chapter 13 to check your solution.

(iii)

	Budget	Flexed	Actual		Variances
Units	40,800	61,200	61,200		
	£	£	£		£
Contribution	65,280	97,920	74,120	as (i) above	23,800A
Fixed overhead	20,400	20,400	25,000	spend	4,600A
Profit	44,880	77,520	49,120		
Profit per unit	£1.10				
	£44,880/40,800				

Volume variance				sales	
	44,880	77,520		£1.10 × (61,200 − 40,800)	22,440F
	budget profit −	flexed budget	=	fixed overhead	
				£0.50 × (61,200 − 40,800)	10,200F
				Total variances	4,420F

				£	£
Budget profit					44,880
Sales variances					
Price	30p price reduction			18,360A	
Volume	as above			22,440F	4,080F
Materials					
Price	4% discount			4,896F	
Usage	savings on wastage			3,264F	8,160F
Labour	use of more highly paid and skilled staff				10,880A
Variable overhead	higher electricity and gas supplies				2,720A
Fixed overhead					
Spend	(£20,400 − £25,000)			4,600A	
Volume	as above			10,200F	5,600F
Actual profit					49,120

(iv)

You should refer to the relevant section in Chapter 13 to check your solution.

(v)

Using absorption costing the sales volume variance now becomes £22,440 favourable, based on profit rather than contribution. The difference of £10,200 is shown as a favourable volume variance due to increased recovery of fixed overheads due to the higher volume of sales.

The spend variance for fixed overheads is £4,600 and may be due to a number of reasons: poor budgeting; operations out of control; unforeseen cost price increases, etc.

It may be argued that fixed overheads should not be included in performance reports because they are fixed and therefore uncontrollable by nature. However, as we can see in the example of Cyclops in actuality some responsibility and accountability should be assigned to them.

If absorption costing is used it goes some way to ensuring that all costs are covered in pricing decisions. However, in situations of spare capacity it may mean that products are overpriced in tendering for new business which may then be lost. If a marginal basis were used a contribution may be provided towards meeting those fixed overheads.

E13.3 White Heaven

(i) Ideal standard cost per Shell

		£	£
Direct materials			
Clay	5 kg × £2.00	10.00	
Glaze	3 kg × £4.00	12.00	
			22.00
Direct labour			
Grade A	1 hour × £7.20	7.20	
Grade B	0.75 hours × £6.00	4.50	
			11.70
Indirect labour	0.25 hours × £5.00	1.25	
Maintenance	0.05 hours × £10.00	0.50	
Variable overhead			
Direct materials	15% × £22.00	3.30	
Direct labour	10% × £11.70	1.17	
			6.22
Total variable costs			39.92
Fixed overhead cost			
Supervisors' salaries	£95,000/50,000	1.90	
Other	£109,000/50,000	2.18	
			4.08
Ideal standard cost per Shell			44.00

(ii)
Grade A direct labour

Originally 1 operator working for 1 hour made 1 Shell
Or, 10 operators each working for 1 hour made 10 Shells
Now 1 operator working for 1 hour makes 0.5 Shells
And 9 operators each working for 1 hour make 9 Shells
So 10 operators each working for 1 hour make 9.5 Shells
So 1 Shell takes $\frac{10}{9.5}$ hours = 1.053 hours

The rate is now £7.20 + £0.40 or £7.60 per hour
Therefore 1 Shell costs 1.053 hours × £7.60 = £8.00 direct labour

Grade B direct labour

Originally 1 operator working for 0.75 hours made 1 Shell
Or, 10 operators each working for 0.75 hours made 10 Shells
Now 1 operator working for 0.80 hours would ideally make 1 Shell

Or, 10 operators each working for 0.80 hours would ideally make 10 Shells
But 2.5 operators working for 0.80 hours only make 0.6 Shells each or 1.5 Shells
And 7.5 operators each working for 0.80 hours make 1 Shell each or 7.5 Shells
So 10 operators each working for 0.80 hours make 9 Shells
So 1 Shell takes $\frac{8}{9}$ hours = 0.889 hours

The rate is now £6.00 + £0.30 or £6.30 per hour
Therefore 1 Shell costs 0.889 hours × £6.30 = £5.60 direct labour

Attainable standard cost per Shell

		£	£
Direct materials			
Clay	£10.00 + 10%	11.00	
Glaze	£12.00 − 12.5%	10.50	
			21.50
Direct labour			
Grade A	see workings	8.00	
Grade B	see workings	5.60	
			13.60
Indirect labour	0.25 hours × £5.20	1.30	
Maintenance	0.05 hours × £10.20	0.51	
Variable overhead			
Direct material			
Clay	15% × £11.00	1.65	
Glaze	20% × £10.50	2.10	
Direct labour	10% × £13.60	1.36	
			6.92
Total variable costs			42.02
Fixed overhead cost			
Supervisors' salaries	£95,000/50,000	1.90	
Other	£109,000/50,000	2.18	
			4.08
Attainable standard cost per Shell			46.10

(iii)
Ideal standard cost per Shell = £44.00 × 49,000 units = £2,156,000
Attainable standard cost per Shell = £46.10 × 49,000 units = £2,258,900
Variance = £2.10 × 49,000 units = £102,900

E13.5 Millennium

	Budget	Flexed	Actual		Variances
Units	4,300	4,100	4,100		
	£	£	£		£
Sales	25,112	23,944	24,805	price	
	4,300 × £5.84	4,100 × £5.84	4,100 × £6.05	4,100 × (£5.84 − £6.05)	861F
Materials	7,310	6,970	7,169	price	
	4,300 × 2 × £0.85	4,100 × 2 × £0.85	(6,600 × £0.83) +(1,900 × £0.89)	8,500 × (£0.8434 − £0.85)	56F
				usage	
				£0.85 × (8,500 − 8,200)	255A
Labour	12,642	12,054	13,387.50	rate	
	4,300 × 0.7 × £4.20	4,100 × 0.7 × £4.20	2,975 × £4.50	2,975 × (£4.50 − £4.20)	892.50A
				efficiency	
				£4.20 × (2,870 − 2,975)	441A
Contribution	5,160	4,920	4,248.50		
Fixed	3,526	3,526	3,800	spend	
overhead	4,300 × £0.82			£3,526 − £3,800	274A
Profit	1,634	1,394	448.50		
Profit per unit	£0.38				
	£1,634/4,300				

Volume

variance

					sales	
	1,634	1,394		=	£0.38 × (4,100 − 4,300)	76A
	budget profit − flexed budget				fixed overhead	
					£0.82 × (4,100 − 4,300)	164A
Total variances						1,185.50A

	£	£
Budget profit		1,634
Sales variances		
Price	861F	
Volume	76A	785F
Materials variances		
Price	56F	
Usage	255A	199A
Labour variances		
Rate	892.50A	
Efficiency	441A	1,333.50A
Fixed overhead variances		
Spend	274A	
Volume	164A	438A
Actual profit		448.50

Chapter 14

E14.3 Lucky Jim

If shareholders' equity is E and the financial debt is D then the relative proportions of equity and debt in the total financing are:

$$\frac{E}{E + D} \text{ and } \frac{D}{E + D}$$

$$\frac{E}{E + D} = 2/3$$

$$\frac{D}{E + D} = 1/3$$

Cost of equity $e = 18\%$
Return on financial debt $d = 12\%$
WACC $= (2/3 \times 18\%) + ((1/3 \times 9\% \, (1 - 40\%))$
$\qquad = 12\% + 1.8\% = 13.8\%$

The present value of future cash flows in perpetuity $= \dfrac{\text{annual cash flows}}{\text{annual discount rate \%}}$

$$\frac{£35,700}{0.138} = £253,623$$

Net present value, NPV $= £253,623 - £200,000 = £53,623$
Using WACC to discount the cash flows of the project, the result is a positive NPV of £53,623 and therefore the project should be undertaken.

E14.4 Supermarket

	2011	2010	2009
Adjusted net assets	£5,000m	£4,769m	£4,377m
Market value	£17,808m	£11,531m	£11,995m
MVA	£12,808m	£6,762m	£7,618m

E14.5 Yor

(i)

Yor plc
Income statement for the year ended 30 September 2011

	using debentures £m	using shares £m
PBIT	15.6	15.6
Finance costs	(1.6)	(1.2)
Profit before tax	14.0	14.4
Income tax expense	(3.5)	(3.6)
Profit for the year	10.5	10.8
Retained earnings 1 October 2010	10.6	10.6
	21.1	21.4
Dividends	(3.3)	(4.6)
Retained earnings 30 September 2011	17.8	16.8

(ii)

Yor plc
Equity and debt as at 30 September 2011

	using debentures £m	using shares £m
Share capital (£1 ordinary shares)	10.0	14.0
Share premium account (4m × £1.50)		6.0
Retained earnings	17.8	16.8
	27.8	36.8
Loans	30.0	20.0

(iii)

$$\text{earnings per share } 2010 = \frac{\text{profit available for ordinary shareholders}}{\text{number of ordinary shares in issue}} = \frac{£7.8m}{10m}$$

$$= 78p$$

(iv)
using debentures

$$\text{earnings per share } 2011 = \frac{£10.5m}{10m} = £1.05$$

using shares

$$\text{earnings per share } 2011 = \frac{£10.8m}{14m} = 77p$$

(v)

$$\text{dividend per share } 2010 = \frac{\text{total dividends paid to ordinary shareholders}}{\text{number of ordinary shares in issue}} = \frac{£3.0m}{10m}$$

$$= 30p$$

(vi)

using debentures

$$\text{dividend per share } 2011 = \frac{£3.3m}{10m} = 33p$$

using shares

$$\text{dividend per share } 2011 = \frac{£4.6m}{14m} = 33p$$

(vii)

$$\text{gearing} = \frac{\text{long-term debt}}{\text{equity} + \text{long-term debt}}$$

	using debentures	**using shares**
2010	**2011**	**2011**
$\dfrac{£20.0m}{£20.6m + £20.0m} = 49.3\%$	$\dfrac{£30.0m}{£27.8m + £30.0m} = 51.9\%$	$\dfrac{£20.0m}{£36.8m + £20.0m} = 35.2\%$

(viii)

Summary of results

Figures in £m

	2010	using debentures 2011	using shares 2011
Profit for the year	7.8	10.5	10.8
Dividends	(3.0)	(3.3)	(4.6)
Retained earnings for year	4.8	7.2	6.2

The use of debentures to finance the new project will increase the 2010/2011 profit for the year after tax, available for dividends, by £2.7m or 34.6%, whereas if shares were used the increase would be £3.0m or 38.5%. Earnings per share will be increased to £1.05 (+27p) and decreased to 77p (−1p) respectively. However, retained earnings would be increased by £2.4m (50%) and £1.4m (29.2%) respectively. The difference is because the gain from the lower interest cost in using shares is more than offset by the increase in dividends.

Dividend per share will be increased from 30p to 33p per share regardless of which method of financing is used.

Gearing at 30 September 2010 was 49.3%. If debentures are used to finance the new project then gearing will increase to 51.9%, but if shares are used to finance the new project then gearing will decrease to 35.2%. This represents a higher financial risk for the company with regard to its commitments to making a high level of interest payments. The company is therefore vulnerable to a downturn in business and also the possibility of its loans being called in and possible liquidation of the company.

Chapter 15

E15.3 Rainbow

(i)

From a divisional point of view

Divisional managers are rewarded via a remuneration package which is linked to an ROI performance measure. Therefore they are likely to take a short-term view in appraising the investment proposals because they will be anxious to maintain their earnings. They would be interested in the short-term effect on ROI and perhaps on residual income.

Project A

	Year			
	1 £000	2 £000	3 £000	4 £000
NBV of asset at beginning of year	60	45	30	15
Net cash inflow	21	21	21	21
Depreciation	15	15	15	15
Operating profit	6	6	6	6
Imputed interest at 15%	9	7	5	2
Residual income	(3)	(1)	1	4
ROI %	(6/60) 10.0	(6/45) 13.3	(6/30) 20.0	(6/15) 40.0

Project B

	Year			
	1 £000	2 £000	3 £000	4 £000
NBV of asset at beginning of year	60	45	30	15
Net cash inflow	25	20	20	15
Depreciation	15	15	15	15
Operating profit	10	5	5	–
Imputed interest at 15%	9	7	5	2
Residual income	1	(2)	–	(2)
ROI %	16.7	11.1	16.7	–

Project C

	Year			
	1 £000	2 £000	3 £000	4 £000
NBV of asset at beginning of year	60	45	30	15
Net cash inflow	10	20	30	40
Depreciation	15	15	15	15
Operating profit	(5)	5	15	25
Imputed interest at 15%	9	7	5	2
Residual income	(14)	(2)	10	23
ROI %	(8.3)	11.1	50.0	166.7

Red Division is likely to reject project A because of the potential adverse effect on the manager's remuneration in year one.

Similarly, project C is also likely to be rejected due to adverse results in the early years, despite the long-term profitability of the project.

Project B is the most likely to be accepted if the manager takes a short-term view to protect his or her remuneration in the coming year, although the decision will be affected by the division's current level of ROI.

(ii)
From a company point of view
The company is likely to appraise the projects using discounted cash flow.

Year	15% discount factor	Project A Cash flow £000	Project A Present value £000	Project B Cash flow £000	Project B Present value £000	Project C Cash flow £000	Project C Present value £000
1	0.87	21	18.27	25	21.75	10	8.70
2	0.76	21	15.96	20	15.20	20	15.20
3	0.66	21	13.86	20	13.20	30	19.80
4	0.57	21	11.97	15	8.55	40	22.80
	2.86		60.06		58.70		66.50
Initial investment			60.00		60.00		60.00
Net present value			0.06		(1.30)		6.50

From the company point of view project A may be acceptable although the NPV is very small and there is no room for possible error in the estimates and the risk of a negative return would be very great. The final decision will depend, among other things, on the risk premium built into the cost of capital.

Project B would be unacceptable whereas project C would be acceptable from a company point of view.

(iii)
Probable decision

Project	Division	Company
A	Reject	Accept
B	Accept	Reject
C	Reject	Accept

The table shows that there is unlikely to be goal congruence between the company and the manager of Red Division.

The divergence between the two points of view has occurred because they are each using different assessment criteria. The views of the division and the company can be brought into line if they both use the same criteria in future. This would mean abandoning the practice of linking a manager's remuneration directly to short-term ROI because this is likely to encourage short-term thinking since ROI tends to be low in the early stages of an investment.

On the other hand it would be difficult to link remuneration to the net present value of individual projects because of the problems of disentanglement and the length of time before all the costs and benefits arise.

The specific problem with project A could be overcome through the use of annuity depreciation instead of the straight line method. The constant cash flows will then result in a smoother ROI profile over the life of the project. The manager would then be more likely to make the same decision as the company, although it depends to an extent on the division's current level of ROI.

The company may consider introducing the use of economic value added (EVA) as a measure of performance, which may be suitable for both divisional and economic performance.

E15.8 AAK

(i)

Year	Equipment £000	Running costs £000	Lighting, heating, etc. £000	Total outflow £000	10% discount rate	Present value £
0	120			120	1.00	120,000
1		40	15	55	0.91	50,050
2		44	15	59	0.83	48,970
3		48	15	63	0.75	47,250
4		52	15	67	0.68	45,560
5		56	15	71	0.62	44,020
Present value						355,850

We can assume that the annual sales revenue at the full level is S. We first need to calculate the present value of each year's expected sales.

Year	Sales revenue	10% discount rate	Present value
1	$0.4S$	0.91	$0.364S$
2	$0.7S$	0.83	$0.581S$
3	$1.0S$	0.75	$0.750S$
4	$1.0S$	0.68	$0.680S$
5	$1.0S$	0.62	$0.620S$
Present value			$2.995S$

$$\text{Contribution} = \text{sales} - \text{variable costs}$$

Because the prices of drinks are to be set at double their direct (variable) costs then half of the total present value of sales $2.995S$ must represent direct costs and the other half must represent contribution.

$$\text{Therefore contribution} = \frac{2.995S}{2}$$

$$= 1.4975S \text{ which is the present value of the contribution from the drinks}$$

To break even at an annual interest rate of 10% the present value of the contribution from drinks must equal the present value of the total outgoings, which is £355,850.

$$1.4975S = £355,850$$
$$S = £237,629$$

Therefore the required sales revenue of drinks in each year are:

Year		£
1	£237,629 × 40%	95,052
2	£237,629 × 70%	166,341
3		237,629
4		237,629
5		237,629

(ii)

Aspects of the proposals that require further investigation:

■ Can the facilities be used outside normal opening hours for alternative uses in order to increase the contribution?
■ Has market research been carried out to support the belief that there will be additional future benefits?
■ Will the proposed cost plus drinks pricing methods result in competitive prices?
■ Perhaps there is a better way for this project to utilise the space and the capital, and perhaps food may be an option.

E15.9 Lew Rolls

(i)

Year	10% DF	20% DF	Super CF £m	Super 10% DCF £m	Super 20% DCF £m	Superlux CF £m	Superlux 10% DCF £m	Superlux 20% DCF £m	Exec CF £m	Exec 10% DCF £m	Exec 20% DCF £m	Excel CF £m	Excel 10% DCF £m	Excel 20% DCF £m
0	1.00	1.00	−3	−3	−3	−7	−7	−7	−12	−12	−12	−15	−15	−15
1	0.91	0.83	1	0.91	0.83	2	1.82	1.66	0	0	0	10	9.10	8.30
2	0.83	0.69	1	0.83	0.69	2	1.66	1.38	0	0	0	10	8.30	6.90
3	0.75	0.58	1	0.75	0.58	2	1.50	1.16	7	5.25	4.06	0	0	0
4	0.68	0.48	1	0.68	0.48	2	1.36	0.96	7	4.76	3.36	0	0	0
5	0.62	0.40	1	0.62	0.40	2	1.24	0.80	7	4.34	2.80	0	0	0
Total			2	0.79	−0.02	3	0.58	−1.04	9	2.35	−1.78	5	2.40	0.20

(ii)

Calculation of IRR

From the table above calculate the IRR for each of the projects using interpolation or extrapolation as shown in Figures 15.3 and 15.4 in Chapter 15 to obtain:

	Super	Superlux	Exec	Excel
IRR	19.8%	13.6%	15.7%	20.9%
Ranking of projects (highest IRR ranked 1st)	2	4	3	1

(iii)

Net present value

NPV of each project	£790,000	£580,000	£2,350,000	£2,400,000
NPV per £ invested	£0.263	£0.083	£0.196	£0.160
Ranking	1	4	2	3

NPV per £ invested is the more reliable evaluation method for appraisal of this project therefore, given the £24m total investment constraint, the decision should be to invest:

	£m	NPV per £ invested	NPV £
Super	3	£0.263	790,000
Exec	12	£0.196	2,350,000
Excel	9	£0.160	1,440,000
Superlux	0	£0.083	0
Optimum total NPV			£4,580,000

If IRR rankings were used to make the investment decision:

	£m	NPV per £ invested	NPV £
Excel	15	£0.160	2,400,000
Super	3	£0.263	790,000
Exec	6	£0.196	1,175,000
Superlux	0	£0.083	0
Total NPV			£4,365,000
			which is not optimal

(iv) and **(v)**
You should refer to the relevant sections in Chapter 15 to check your solutions.

Chapter 16

E16.1 Oliver

Production costs

		£	
Raw materials	[40% × £5,300,000]	2,120,000	held in inventory on average four days
Direct labour	[25% × £5,300,000]	1,325,000	finished goods held in inventory on average seven days
Overheads	[10% × £5,300,000]	530,000	
		3,975,000	

The production cycle is 14 days

Working capital requirement

			£		£
Raw materials	[£2,120,000 × 4/365]			=	23,233
Work in progress					
Raw materials	[£2,120,000 × 14/365]	=	81,315		
Direct labour	[£1,325,000 × 14/365 × 25%]	=	12,705		
Overheads	[£530,000 × 14/365 × 25%]	=	5,082		
					99,102
Finished goods	[£3,975,000 × 7/365]			=	76,233
Trade receivables	[£5,300,000 × 60/365]			=	871,223
Trade payables	[£2,120,000 × 30/365]			=	(174,247)
Total working capital requirement					895,544

E16.5 Worrall

Cost of sales is 80% of sales

Variable cost of sales	80% × 90%	=	72% of sales
Therefore			
Contribution		=	28% of sales

Proposed trade receivables

Sales revenue, increased by 20% is	120% × £8m = £9.6m		
Credit allowed increased to 90 days	£9.6m × 90/365	=	£2,367,123
Current trade receivables	£8m × 60/365	=	£1,315,068
Increase in trade receivables		=	£1,052,055

Gains

Increase in contribution	(£9.6m − £8.0m) × 28%	=	£448,000

Losses

Increase in bad debts	(3% × £2,367,123) − (2% × £1,315,068)	=	£44,713
Increase in financing costs	£1,052,055 × 10%	=	£105,206
Total losses			£149,919
Net gain per annum			£298,081

The net gain to Worrall Ltd is £298,081 per annum and so an increase to 90 days' credit may be recommended.

Glossary of key terms

absorption costing A method of costing that, in addition to direct costs, assigns all, or a proportion of, production overhead costs to cost units by means of one or a number of overhead absorption rates.

accountability concept Management accounting presents information measuring the achievement of the objectives of an organisation and appraising the conduct of its internal activities in that process. In order that further action can be taken, based on this information, it is necessary at all times to identify the responsibilities and performance of individuals within the organisation.

accountancy The practice or profession of accounting.

accounting The classification and recording of monetary transactions, the presentation and interpretation of the results of those transactions in order to assess performance over a period and the financial position at a given date, and the monetary projection of future activities arising from alternative planned courses of action.

accounting adjustments Accounting entries that do not arise from the basic transactions of cash and invoices. Adjusting entries are made for depreciation, bad and doubtful debts, closing inventories, prepayments, and accruals.

accounting concepts The principles underpinning the preparation of accounting information. Fundamental accounting concepts are the broad basic assumptions which underlie the periodic financial statements of business enterprises.

accounting period The time period covered by the accounting statements of an entity.

accounting policies The specific accounting bases selected and consistently followed by an entity as being, in the opinion of the management, appropriate to its circumstances and best suited to present fairly its results and financial position (FRS 18 and Companies Act).

accounting rate of return (ARR) Annual profit divided by investment. It is a form of return on capital employed. Unlike NPV and IRR, it is based on profits, not cash flows.

accounting standard Authoritative statement of how particular types of transaction and other events should be reflected in financial statements. Compliance with accounting standards will normally be necessary for financial statements to give a true and fair view (ASB).

Accounting Standards Board (ASB) A UK standard-setting body set up in 1990 to develop, issue and withdraw accounting standards. Its aims are to 'establish and improve standards of financial accounting and reporting, for the benefit of users, preparers and auditors of financial information'.

accounts payable (or **purchase ledger**) A subsidiary ledger that contains all the personal accounts of each individual supplier or vendor, and records every transaction for goods and services with each supplier since the start of their relationship with the company. The total of the balances on each individual supplier account at any time is reflected in an accounts payable control account within the general ledger, and is reported in the balance sheet as trade payables.

accounts receivable (or **sales ledger**) A subsidiary ledger that contains all the personal accounts of each individual customer, and records every transaction for goods and services with each customer since the start of their relationship with the company. The total of the balances on each individual customer account at any time is reflected in an accounts receivable control account within the general ledger, and is reported in the balance sheet as trade receivables.

accruals Allowances made for costs and expenses payable within one year of the balance sheet date but for which no invoices have yet been recorded.

accruals concept The principle that revenues and costs are recognised as they are earned or incurred, and so matched with each other, and dealt with in the profit and loss account of the period to which they relate, irrespective of the period of receipt or payment. Where a conflict arises, this concept is subservient to the prudence concept.

acid test ratio See quick ratio.

activity based costing (ABC) An approach to costing and monitoring of activities which involves tracing resource consumption and costing final outputs. Resources are assigned to activities and activities to cost objects based on consumption estimates. Activities utilise cost drivers to attach activity costs to outputs.

activity based management (ABM) A system of management which uses activity based cost information for a variety of purposes including cost reduction, cost modelling and customer profitability analysis.

aged accounts payable report The amount owed to each individual supplier, classified by age of debt.

aged accounts receivable report The amount owed by each individual customer, classified by age of debt.

algorithm A process or set of rules used for a mathematical calculation.

allocation The charging to a cost centre of those overheads which result solely from the existence of that cost centre.

amortisation In the same way that depreciation applies to the charging of the cost of tangible non-current assets over their useful economic lives, amortisation is the systematic write-off of the cost of an intangible asset, relating particularly to the passage of time, for example leasehold premises (IAS 38 and IFRS 3).

annual report and accounts A set of statements which may comprise a management report (in the case of companies, a directors' report), an operating and financial review (OFR), and the financial statements of the entity.

apportionment The charging to a cost centre of a fair share of an overhead on the basis of the benefit received by the cost centre in respect of the facilities provided by the overhead.

asset A right or other access to future economic benefits which can be measured reliably and are controlled by an entity as a result of past transactions or events (IAS 16).

attainable standard A standard that assumes efficient levels of operation, but which includes allowances for normal loss, waste and machine downtime.

attributable cost The cost per unit that could be avoided, on average, if a product or function were discontinued entirely without changing the supporting organisational structure.

audit A systematic examination of the activities and status of an entity, based primarily on investigation and analysis of its systems, controls and records. A statutory annual audit of a company is defined by the APB as an independent examination of, and expression of an opinion on, the financial statements of the enterprise.

Auditing Practices Board (APB) A body formed in 1991 by an agreement between the six members of the Consultative Committee of Accountancy Bodies, to be responsible for developing and issuing professional standards for auditors in the United Kingdom and the Republic of Ireland.

auditor A professionally qualified accountant who is appointed by, and reports independently to, the shareholders, providing an objective verification to shareholders and other users that the financial statements have been prepared properly and in accordance with legislative and regulatory requirements; that they present the information truthfully and fairly; and that they conform to the best accounting practice in their treatment of the various measurements and valuations.

audit report An objective verification to shareholders and other users that the financial statements have been prepared properly and in accordance with legislative and regulatory requirements; that they present the information truthfully and fairly; and that they conform to the best accounting practice in their treatment of the various measurements and valuations.

BACS (bankers' automated clearing services) An electronic bulk clearing system generally used by banks and building societies for low-value and/or repetitive items such as standing orders, direct debits and automated credits such as salary payments.

bad debt A debt which is considered to be uncollectable and is, therefore, written off either as a charge to the profit and loss account or against an existing doubtful debt provision.

balance sheet The balance sheet is a section of the general ledger that records all asset, liability and shareholders' equity account transactions. The balance sheet report is a statement of the financial position of an entity at a given date disclosing the assets, liabilities and accumulated funds such as shareholders' contributions and reserves, prepared to give a true and fair view of the financial state of the entity at that date. The balance sheet is one of the three key financial statements.

balanced scorecard An approach to the provision of information to management to assist strategic policy formulation and achievement. It emphasises the need to provide the user with a set of information which addresses all relevant areas of performance in an objective and unbiased fashion. The information provided may include both financial and non-financial elements, and cover areas such as profitability, customer satisfaction, internal efficiency and innovation.

bank reconciliation A detailed statement reconciling, at a given date, the cash balance in an entity's cash book with that reported in a bank statement.

basic standard A standard that remains unchanged since the previous period and probably many previous periods, that may be used for comparison but is likely to be out of date and irrelevant.

benchmarking The establishment, through data gathering, of targets and comparators, whereby relative levels of performance (and particularly areas of underperformance) can be identified. By the adoption of identified best practices it is hoped that performance will improve.

beta factor (β) The measure of the volatility of the return on a share relative to the market. If a share price were to rise or fall at double the market rate, it would have a beta factor of 2. Conversely, if the share price moved at half the market rate, the beta factor would be 0.5.

bill of materials (BOM) A detailed specification, for each product produced, of the sub-assemblies, components and materials required, distinguishing between those items which are purchased externally and those which are manufactured in-house.

bonus issue See scrip issue.

bookkeeping Recording of monetary transactions, appropriately classified, in the financial records of an entity, either by manual means or otherwise.

bottleneck An activity within an organisation which has a lower capacity than preceding or subsequent activities, thereby limiting throughput. Bottlenecks are often the cause of a build-up of work-in-progress and idle time.

break-even point The level of activity at which there is neither profit nor loss, ascertained by using a break-even chart or by calculation.

budget A quantified statement, for a defined period of time, which may include planned revenues, expenses, assets, liabilities and cash flows.

buffer stock A level of extra inventory that is maintained to form a buffer against running out of inventories due to supply bottlenecks.

business entity concept The concept that financial accounting information relates only to the activities of the business entity and not to the activities of its owners.

Cadbury Committee Report of the Cadbury Committee (December 1992) on the Financial Aspects of Corporate Governance, set up to consider issues in relation to financial reporting and accountability, and to make recommendations on good practice, relating to:

- responsibilities of executive and non-executive directors
- establishment of company audit committees
- responsibility of auditors

- links between shareholders, directors and auditors
- any other relevant matters.

The report established a Code of Best Practice, now succeeded by the UK Corporate Governance Code.

capital asset pricing model (CAPM) A theory which predicts that the expected risk premium for an individual share will be proportional to its beta, such that the expected risk premium on a share is equal to beta multiplied by the expected risk premium in the market. Risk premium is defined as the expected incremental return for making a risky investment rather than a safe one.

capital expenditure The cost of acquiring, producing or enhancing non-current assets.

capital rationing This is a restriction on an organisation's ability to invest capital funds, caused by an internal budget ceiling being imposed on such expenditure by management (soft capital rationing), or by external limitations being applied to the organisation, for example when additional borrowed funds cannot be obtained (hard capital rationing).

cash (and cash equivalents) Cash and cash equivalents comprise cash on hand and demand deposits, together with short-term, highly liquid investments that are readily convertible to a known amount of cash (IAS 7).

cash book A book of original entry that includes details of all receipts and payments made by an entity. The details normally include transaction date, method of payment or receipt, amount paid or received, bank statement value (if different), name of payee or payer, general ledger allocation and coding.

cash flow statement See statement of cash flows.

cash interest cover Net cash inflow from operations plus interest received, divided by interest paid, calculates the number of times the interest payable is covered by cash flow available for such payments.

cash payment A cash payment is the transfer of funds from a business to a recipient (for example, trade creditor or employee).

cash receipt A cash receipt is the transfer of funds to a business from a payer (for example, a customer).

cleared funds Cleared funds are funds that have actually been cleared through the banking system and are available for use. It is the cleared funds balance, if overdrawn, which is used to calculate overdraft interest.

closed-loop system A control system that includes a provision for corrective action, taken on either a feedback or a feedforward basis.

closing inventories All trading companies buy inventories with the intention of reselling, at a profit, to a customer. At the end of each accounting period, the company will have unsold inventories that will be sold during a subsequent accounting period. Unsold inventories are termed 'closing inventory' which is deducted from opening inventory plus purchases (to derive cost of sales), and will appear in the balance sheet as inventories (within current assets).

collection days Average trade receivables divided by average daily sales on credit terms indicates the average time taken, in calendar days, to receive payment from credit customers.

Combined Code of Practice The successor to the Cadbury Code, established by the Hampel Committee. The code consists of a set of principles of corporate governance and detailed code provisions embracing the work of the Cadbury, Greenbury and Hampel Committees. It was, itself, succeeded by the UK Corporate Governance Code in 2010.

common size analysis See horizontal analysis.

competitive pricing Setting a price by reference to the prices of competing products.

computerised accounting system This is a system that maintains business transactions on a computer on a long-term basis.

conceptual frameworks of accounting The statements of principles, which provide generally accepted guidance for the development of new financial information reporting practices and the review of current reporting practices.

concurrent engineering A means of reducing product development time and cost by managing development processes so they can be implemented simultaneously rather than sequentially.

consistency concept The principle that there is uniformity of accounting treatment of like items within each accounting period and from one period to the next.

consolidated accounts The consolidated financial statements which present financial information for the group as a single economic entity, prepared using a process of adjusting and combining financial information from the individual financial statements of a parent undertaking and its subsidiary undertakings (IAS 27).

contingent liability A possible obligation that arises from past events and whose existence will be confirmed only by the occurrence of one or more uncertain future events not wholly within the entity's control; or a present obligation that arises from past events but is not recognised because:

  - it is not probable that a transfer of benefits will be required to settle the obligation or
  - the amount of the obligation cannot be measured with sufficient reliability (IAS 37).

continuing operations Operations not satisfying all the conditions relating to discontinued operations (see below).

contribution Sales value less variable cost of sales, which may be expressed as total contribution, contribution per unit, or as a percentage of sales.

control The power to govern the financial and operating policies of an entity so as to obtain benefits from its activities (IAS 24).

controllability concept Management accounting identifies the elements or activities which management can or cannot influence, and seeks to assess risk and sensitivity factors. This facilitates the proper monitoring, analysis, comparison and interpretation of information which can be used constructively in the control, evaluation and corrective functions of management.

convertible loan A loan which gives the holder the right to convert to other securities, normally ordinary shares, at a predetermined date and at a predetermined price or ratio.

corporate governance The system by which companies are directed and controlled. Boards of directors are responsible for the governance of their companies. The shareholders' role in governance is to appoint the directors and the auditors and to satisfy themselves that an appropriate governance structure is in place.

corporate social responsibility (CSR) Corporate social responsibility is the decision-making and implementation process that guides all company activities in the protection and promotion of international human rights, labour and environmental standards and compliance with legal requirements within its operations and in its relations to the societies and communities where it operates. CSR involves a commitment to contribute to the economic, environmental and social sustainability of communities through the ongoing engagement of stakeholders, the active participation of communities impacted by company activities and the public reporting of company policies and performance in the economic, environmental and social arenas (*www.bench-marks.org*).

corporation tax Tax chargeable on companies resident in the UK, or trading in the UK through a branch or agency, as well as on certain unincorporated associations (FRS 16 and IAS 12).

cost The amount of expenditure (actual or notional) incurred on, or attributable to, a specified thing or activity. To cost something is to ascertain the cost of a specified thing or activity. Cost also relates to a resource sacrificed or forgone, expressed in a monetary value.

cost centre A production or service location, function, activity or item of equipment for which costs are accumulated and to which they are charged.

cost driver Any factor which causes a change in the cost of an activity. For example, the quality of parts received by an activity is a determining factor in the work required by that activity and therefore affects the resources required. An activity may have multiple cost drivers associated with it.

cost object The thing that we wish to determine the cost of.

cost of quality (COQ) The cost of quality may be defined as the additional cost incurred in non-added-value activities and events in a business in fully satisfying customers' agreed requirements for products and services delivered. It is the cost both of not doing the right things and not doing things right first time.

cost of sales The sum of direct cost of sales, adjusted for closing inventories, plus manufacturing overhead attributable to the sales. Direct costs include the wages and salaries costs of time worked on products, and the costs of materials used in production. Manufacturing overheads include the wages and salaries costs of employees not directly working on production, and materials and expenses incurred on activities not directly used in production but necessary to carry out production. Examples are cleaning materials and electricity costs.

cost unit A unit of product or service in relation to which costs are ascertained.

creative accounting A form of accounting which, while complying with all regulations, nevertheless gives a biased (generally favourable) impression of a company's performance.

cross-function management Horizontal cross-departmental organisation as opposed to the traditional vertical, functional, 'chimney' organisation.

cross-sectional analysis Cross-sectional analysis provides a means of providing a standard against which performance can be measured and uses ratios to compare different businesses at the same points in time (see inter-company comparison).

current assets Cash or other assets, for example inventories, receivables and short-term investments, held for conversion into cash in the normal course of trading.

current liabilities Liabilities which fall due for payment within one year. They include that part of long-term loans due for repayment within one year.

current ratio Current assets divided by current liabilities is an overall measure of liquidity.

cycle count The process of counting and valuing selected inventory items at different times, on a rotating basis, so that all inventories are counted two, three, four or more times each year.

debenture The written acknowledgement of a debt by a company, usually given under its seal, and normally containing provisions as to payment of interest and the terms of repayment of principal. A debenture may be secured on some or all of the assets of the company or its subsidiaries.

debt One of the alternative sources of capital for a company, also called long-term debt or loans.

debt/equity ratio A gearing ratio that relates to financial gearing, which is the relationship between a company's borrowings, which includes both prior charge capital and long-term debt, and its ordinary shareholders' funds (share capital plus reserves).

decision tree A pictorial method of showing a sequence of interrelated decisions and their expected outcomes. Decision trees can incorporate both the probabilities of, and values of, expected outcomes, and are used in decision-making.

defensive interval Quick assets (current assets excluding inventories) divided by average daily cash from operations, shows how many days a business could survive at its present level of operating activity if no inflow of cash was received from sales or other sources.

depreciation The systematic allocation of the depreciable amount of an asset over its useful life (IAS 16). Depreciation should be allocated so as to charge a fair proportion of the total cost (or valuation) of the asset to each accounting period expected to benefit from its use.

depreciation provision The amount of depreciation that has cumulatively been charged to the profit and loss account, relating to a non-current asset, from the date of its acquisition. Non-current assets are stated in the balance sheet at their net book value (or written-down value), which is usually their historical cost less the cumulative amount of depreciation at the balance sheet date.

differential cost The difference in total cost between alternatives, calculated to assist decision-making.

direct cost A traceable cost, or expenditure, which can be economically identified with and specifically measured in respect of a relevant cost object.

direct labour Labour costs which can be economically identified with and specifically measured in respect of a relevant cost object.

direct materials Materials costs which can be economically identified with and specifically measured in respect of a relevant cost object.

direct method A method of calculating cash flow from operating activities as the net of operating cash receipts and payments that is summarised for inclusion in the statement of cash flows. It is a time-consuming process that is not as straightforward as the indirect method.

director A person elected under the company's articles of association to be responsible for the overall direction of the company's affairs. Directors usually act collectively as a board and carry out such functions as are specified in the articles of association or the Companies Acts, but they may also act individually in an executive capacity.

discontinued operations A discontinued operation is a component of an entity that either has been disposed of or is classified as held for sale and: represents either a separate major line of business or a geographical area of operations, and:

- is part of a single coordinated plan to dispose of a separate major line of business or geographical area of operations

or

- is a subsidiary acquired exclusively with a view to resale and the disposal involves loss of control (IFRS 5).

discounted cash flow (DCF) The discounting of the projected net cash flows of a capital project to ascertain its present value, using a yield or internal rate of return (IRR), net present value (NPV) or discounted payback.

discounted payback The number of years required to repay an original investment using a specified discount rate.

dividend An amount payable to shareholders from profits or distributable reserves. Dividends are normally paid in cash, but scrip dividends, paid by the issue of additional shares, are permissible. Listed companies usually declare two dividends each year, an interim dividend based on the mid-year profits and a final dividend based on annual profit.

dividend cover Earnings per share divided by dividend per share indicates the number of times the profits attributable to the equity shareholders cover the actual dividends payable for the period.

double-entry bookkeeping The system of bookkeeping based on the principle that every financial transaction involves the simultaneous receiving and giving of value, and is therefore recorded twice.

doubtful debt A debt for which there is some uncertainty as to whether or not it will be settled, and for which there is a possibility that it may eventually prove to be bad. A doubtful debt provision may be created for such a debt by charging it as an expense to the profit and loss account.

doubtful debt provision An amount charged against profit and deducted from trade receivables to allow for the estimated non-recovery of a proportion of the debts.

dual aspect concept The rule that provides the basis for double-entry bookkeeping, reflecting the practical reality that every transaction always includes both the giving and receiving of something.

earnings per share (eps) Profit after tax less preference share dividends divided by the number of ordinary shares in issue measures the return per share of earnings available to shareholders.

EBITDA Earnings before interest, tax, depreciation and amortisation.

economic value added (EVA™) EVA is a measure developed by the US consultancy firm Stern Stewart. EVA equals profit after tax (plus interest payable) adjusted for distortions in operating performance (such as goodwill, extraordinary losses and operating leases) minus a charge for the use of the capital employed to create that profit (calculated by multiplying the adjusted book value of net assets of the company by its weighted average cost of capital).

effectiveness The utilisation of resources such that the output of the activity achieves the desired result. In other words, efficiency alone is not enough – efficiency in areas from which optimised output is what is required to be effective (to avoid being a 'busy fool').

efficiency The achievement of either maximum useful output from the resources devoted to an activity, or the required output from the minimum resource input.

electronic point of sale (EPOS) EPOS systems process sales transactions electronically and scan and capture real-time product information at the point of sale. The systems range from networked cash registers in retail and wholesale outlets with links to business computer systems, to larger systems that link point-of-sale information with warehousing, suppliers ordering systems, customer databases and online web stores.

environmental reporting A statement included within the annual report and accounts that sets out the environmental policies of the company and an explanation of its environmental management systems and responsibilities. The environmental report may include reporting on the performance of the business on environmental matters in qualitative terms regarding the extent to which it meets national and international standards. It may also include a quantitative report on the performance of the business on environmental matters against targets, together with an assessment of the financial impact.

equity The total investment of the shareholders in the company, the total value of book wealth. Equity comprises capital, share premiums and retained earnings.

ergonomics The study of the efficiency of persons in their working environment.

euro The common currency that is used in most of the member countries of the European Union, which came into being on 1 January 1999. Financial transactions and/or financial reporting of member states may now be undertaken in either the functional domestic currencies, or in euros.

ex ante Means before the event. An *ex ante* budget, or standard, is set before a period of activity commences, and is based on the best information available at that time on expected levels of cost, performance, etc.

expected value The financial forecast of the outcome of a course of action multiplied by the probability of achieving that outcome. The probability is expressed as a value ranging from zero to 1.

ex post Means after the event. An *ex post* budget, or standard, is set after the end of a period of activity, when it can represent the optimum achievable level of performance in the conditions which were experienced. Thus the budget can be flexed, and the standards can reflect factors such as unanticipated changes in technology and in price levels.

finance director The finance director of an organisation is actively involved in broad strategic and policy-making activities involving financial considerations. The finance director provides the board of directors with advice on financing, capital expenditure, acquisitions, dividends, the implications of changes in the economic environment, and the financial aspects of legislation. The finance director is responsible for the planning and control functions, the financial systems, financial reporting, and the management of funds.

finance lease A lease is a contract between a lessor and a lessee for the hire of a specific asset. The lessor retains ownership of the asset but gives the right to the use of the asset to the lessee for an agreed period in return for the payment of specified rentals (IAS 17). A finance lease transfers substantially all the risks and rewards of ownership of the asset to the lessee.

financial accounting Financial accounting is the function responsible for the periodic external reporting, statutorily required, for shareholders. It also provides such similar information as required for Government and other interested third parties, such as potential investors, employees, lenders, suppliers, customers and financial analysts.

financial instrument Any contract that gives rise to both a financial asset of one entity and a financial liability or equity instrument of another entity. Financial instruments include both primary financial instruments – such as bonds, debtors, creditors and shares – and derivative financial instruments whose value derives from the underlying assets.

financial management The management of all the processes associated with the efficient acquisition and deployment of both short- and long-term financial resources. Within an organisation, financial management assists operations management to reach their financial objectives.

Financial Reporting Standards (FRSs) The accounting standards of practice published by the Accounting Standards Board since 1 August 1990, and which gradually replaced the Standard Statements of Accounting Practice (SSAPs), which were published by the Accounting Standards Committee up to 1 August 1990.

financial statements Summaries of accounts, whether to internal or external parties, to provide information for interested parties. The three key financial statements are: income statement; balance sheet; statement of cash flows. Other financial statements are: report of the auditors; statement of recognised gains and losses; statement of changes in equity.

financing The section of the statement of cash flows that shows the long-term funds raised by or repaid by the company during an accounting period.

finished product Finished product or finished goods are manufactured goods ready for sale or despatch.

first in first out (FIFO) Assumes that the oldest items of inventory or costs are the first to be used. It is commonly applied to the pricing of issues of materials, based on using first the costs of the oldest materials in inventory, irrespective of the sequence in which actual material usage takes place. Closing inventories are therefore valued at relatively current costs.

fixed cost A cost which is incurred for an accounting period, and which, within certain output or turnover limits, tends to be unaffected by fluctuations in the levels of activity (output or sales revenue).

flexed budget The budgeted cost ascribed to the level of activity achieved in a budget centre in a control period. It comprises variable costs in direct proportion to volume achieved and fixed costs as a proportion of the annual budget.

flotation (or a new issue of shares) A flotation is the obtaining of a listing by a company on a stock exchange, through the offering of its shares to the general public, financial institutions or private-sector businesses.

forecast A forecast is a prediction of future events and their quantification for planning purposes.

fraudulent trading An offence committed by persons who are knowingly party to the continuance of a company trading in circumstances where creditors are defrauded or for other fraudulent purposes. Generally, this means that the company incurs more debts at a time when it is known that those debts will not be met. Persons responsible for so acting are personally liable without limitation for the debts of the company. The offence also carries criminal penalties.

gearing Financial gearing calculations can be made in a number of ways. Gearing is generally seen as the relationship between a company's borrowings, which include both prior charge capital (capital having a right of interest or preference shares having fixed dividends) and long-term debt, and its ordinary shareholders' funds (share capital plus reserves).

general ledger Also called the nominal ledger, contains all accounts and transactions relating to assets, expenses, revenue and liabilities.

going concern concept The assumption that the entity will continue in operational existence for the foreseeable future.

goodwill The difference between the consideration transferred and the net of the acquisition-date amounts of the identifiable assets acquired and the liabilities assumed (IFRS 3). If the difference above is negative, the resulting gain is recognised as a bargain purchase in the income statement.

gross profit (or gross margin) Gross profit is the difference between sales revenue and the total cost of sales.

Hampel Committee The 1998 report of the Hampel Committee on Corporate Governance was set up to conduct a review of the Cadbury Code and its implications:

- – review of the role of directors
- – matters arising from the Greenbury Study Group on directors' remuneration
- – role of shareholders and auditors
- – other relevant matters.

The Hampel Committee was responsible for the corporate governance Combined Code of Practice.

heijunka The smoothing of production through the levelling of schedules. This is done by sequencing orders in a repetitive pattern and smoothing the day-to-day variations in total orders to correspond to longer-term demand.

historical cost concept The normal basis of accounting prescribed by IAS 16 for published accounts that uses a system of accounting in which all values are based on the historical costs incurred.

horizontal analysis (or **common size analysis**) An analysis of the income statement (or balance sheet) that allows a line-by-line analysis of the accounts with those of the previous year. It may provide over a number of years a trend of changes showing either growth or decline in these elements of the accounts through calculation of annual percentage growth rates in profits, sales revenue, inventories or any other item.

hybrid finance A financial instrument that has the characteristics of both debt and equity.

ideal standard A standard that is only attainable under the most favourable conditions and makes no allowance for normal loss, waste and machine downtime.

impairment In accordance with IAS 36, an asset is impaired when its book value exceeds its recoverable amount. The recoverable amount is the greater of the net selling price of the asset and the discounted cash flow expected to arise from the use of the asset over its remaining life. If the recoverable amount is less than the book value then the asset's value should be impaired with the loss of value being charged to the income statement. The asset must then be depreciated for future periods on its revised carrying amount, which is the amount at which the asset is recognised in the balance sheet after deducting accumulated depreciation and accumulated impairment losses.

income statement The income statement shows the profit or loss generated by an entity during an accounting period by deducting all expenses from all revenues, its financial performance. It measures whether or not the company has made a profit or loss on its operations during the period, through producing and selling its goods or services. The income statement is one of the three key financial statements.

indirect cost An indirect cost is a cost that is untraceable to particular units. It is expenditure on labour, materials or services that cannot be economically identified with a specific saleable cost unit. Such costs have to be allocated, that is, assigned to a single cost unit, cost centre, cost account or time period. The term 'burden' used by American companies is synonymous with indirect costs or overheads.

indirect method A method of calculating cash flow from operating activities which uses the starting point of profit before tax. Profit before tax for the period must then be adjusted for depreciation, as well as movements in inventories, receivables and payables over the same period to derive the net cash flow from operating activities.

inflation A general increase in the price level over time. In a period of hyperinflation the rate at which the price level rises has become extremely high, and possibly out of control.

initial public offering (IPO) An IPO is a company's first public sale of its shares. Shares offered in an IPO are often, but not always, those of young, small companies seeking outside equity capital and a public market for their shares. Investors purchasing shares in IPOs generally must be prepared to accept considerable risks for the possibility of large gains.

insolvency The inability of a company, partnership or individual to pay creditors' debts in full after realisation of all the assets of the business.

intangible non-current assets Intangible non-current assets are identifiable non-monetary assets without physical substance that are controlled by the entity as a result of past events (for example, purchase or self-creation), and from which future economic benefits are expected to flow. These assets include computer software, patents and copyrights (IAS 38).

interdependency concept Management accounting, in recognition of the increasing complexity of business, must access both internal and external information sources from interactive functions such as marketing, production, personnel, procurement and finance. This assists in ensuring that the information is adequately balanced.

interest cover Profit before interest and tax divided by interest payable, calculates the number of times the interest payable is covered by profits available for such payments. It is particularly important for lenders to determine the vulnerability of interest payments to a drop in profit.

inter-company comparison Systematic and detailed comparison of the performance of different companies generally operating in a common industry. Normally the information distributed by the scheme administrator (to participating companies only) is in the form of ratios, or in a format that prevents the identity of individual scheme members from being identified.

internal audit The UK Institute of Internal auditors defines internal audit as an independent appraisal function established within an organisation to examine and evaluate its activities as a service to the organisation. The objective of internal auditing is to assist members of the organisation in the effective discharge of their responsibilities. To this end, internal auditing furnishes them with analyses, appraisals, recommendations, counsel and information concerning the activities reviewed.

internal control As defined in the Cadbury Report, it is the whole system of controls, financial or otherwise, established in order to provide reasonable assurance of:

- effective and efficient operation
- internal financial control
- compliance with laws and regulations.

internal rate of return (IRR) The annual percentage return achieved by a project, at which the sum of the discounted cash inflows over the life of the project is equal to the sum of the discounted cash outflows.

International Accounting Standards (IASs) The international financial reporting standards issued by the IASC, which are very similar to the UK's SSAPs and FRSs.

International Accounting Standards Board (IASB) The IASB is the body that is responsible for setting and publishing International Financial Reporting Standards (IFRSs). It was formed on 1 April 2001 and succeeded the International Accounting Standards Committee (IASC) which had been formed in 1973. The parent body of the IASB is the International Accounting Standards Committee Foundation, which was incorporated in the USA in March 2001, and was also responsible for issuing International Accounting Standards (IASs).

International Financial Reporting Standards (IFRSs) The international financial reporting standards issued by the IASB, which incorporate the IASs, issued by the IASC. IASs are very similar to the UK's SSAPs and FRSs.

inventories Inventories, according to IAS 2, comprise:

- assets held for sale in the ordinary course of business (finished goods)
- assets in the production process for sale in the ordinary course of business (work in progress) and
- materials and supplies that are consumed in production (raw materials).

inventory days Inventories value divided by average daily cost of sales, which measures the number of days' inventories at the current usage rate.

investment Any application of funds which is intended to provide a return by way of interest, dividend or capital appreciation.

investment centre A profit centre with additional responsibilities for capital investment and possibly for financing, and whose performance is usually measured by its return on investment. Its manager is responsible for investments, revenues and costs.

jidoka Autonomation, which increases productivity through eliminating the non-value-adding need for operators to watch machines, thus freeing them for more productive work, for example quality assurance.

just in time (JIT) The management philosophy that incorporates a 'pull' system of producing or purchasing components and products in response to customer demand, which contrasts with a 'push' system where inventories act as buffers between each process within and between purchasing, manufacturing and sales.

kaizen Continuous improvement in all aspects of performance, at every level within the organisation.

kanban A signal, for example a card used in JIT production to prompt top-up of materials or components driven by demand from the next process.

key factor (or **limiting factor**) Anything which limits the activity of an entity. An entity seeks to optimise the benefit it obtains from the limiting factor. Examples are a shortage of supply of a resource or a restriction on sales demand at a particular price.

last in first out (LIFO) Assumes that the last item of inventory received is the first to be used.

lean accounting Lean accounting is concerned with the financial performance of a company that has implemented lean processes. Lean means using less of everything to provide more, and in greater variety, through the control and elimination of waste in all its forms. It may include the organisation of costs by value stream, changes in the way that inventories may be valued, and a modification of the financial statements and the reporting of non-financial information.

leave of the court This is where the court will make a decision after hearing all the relevant information.

letter of credit A document issued by a bank on behalf of a customer authorising a third party to draw funds to a specified amount from its branches or correspondents, usually in another country, when the conditions set out in the document have been met.

liabilities An entity's obligations to transfer economic benefits as a result of past transactions or events (IAS 37).

life cycle costing The maintenance of physical asset records over the entire asset life, so that decisions concerning the acquisition, use or disposal of the asset can be made in a way that achieves the optimum assets usage at the lowest possible cost to the business. The term may be applied to the profiling of cost over a product's life, including the pre-production stage, and to company and industry life cycles.

limited company (Ltd) A Ltd company is one in which the liability of members for the company's debts is limited to the amount paid and, if any, unpaid on the shares taken up by them.

limiting factor (or **key factor**) Anything which limits the activity of an entity. An entity seeks to optimise the benefit it obtains from the limiting factor. Examples are a shortage of supply of a resource or a restriction on sales demand at a particular price.

linear programming The use of a series of linear equations to construct a mathematical model. The objective is to obtain an optimal solution to a complex operational problem, which may involve the production of a number of products in an environment in which there are many constraints.

loan capital Also called debt, relates to debentures and other long-term loans to a business.

management accounting The application of the principles of accounting and financial management to create, protect, preserve and increase value so as to deliver that value to the stakeholders of profit and not-for-profit enterprises, both public and private. Management accounting is an integral part of management, requiring the identification, generation, presentation, interpretation and use of information relevant to:

- formulating business strategy
- planning and controlling activities
- decision-making
- efficient resource usage
- performance improvement and value enhancement
- safeguarding tangible and intangible assets
- corporate governance and internal control.

management by exception The practice of focusing on activities which require attention and ignoring those which appear to be conforming to expectations.

management control The process by which managers assure that resources are obtained and used effectively and efficiently in the accomplishment of the organisation's objectives.

manufacturing resource planning (MRPII) An expansion of material requirements planning (MRPI) to give a broader approach than MRPI to the planning and scheduling of resources, embracing areas such as finance, logistics, engineering and marketing.

marginal costing A costing technique whereby each unit of output is charged with variable production costs. Fixed production costs are not considered to be real costs of production, but costs which provide the facilities for an accounting period that enable production to take place.

margin of safety The difference between the break-even point and an anticipated or existing level of activity above that point.

market value added (MVA) The difference between the market value of the company and the adjusted book values of its assets.

master production schedule A time-phased statement (usually computerised) of how many items are to be produced in a given period (like a giant timetable), based on customer orders and demand forecasts.

materiality Information is material if its omission or misstatement could influence the economic decisions of users taken on the basis of financial information. Materiality depends on the size of the item or error judged in the particular circumstances of its omission or misstatement.

materiality concept Information is material if its omission or misstatement could influence the economic decisions of users taken on the basis of the financial statements. Materiality depends on the size of the item or error judged in the particular circumstances of its omission or misstatement. Thus, materiality provides a threshold or cut-off point rather than being a primary qualitative characteristic that information must have if it is to be useful.

materials requirement planning (MRPI or MRP) A system that converts a production schedule into a listing of the materials and components required to meet that schedule, so that adequate inventory levels are maintained and items are available when needed.

mission The mission of an organisation, not necessarily written, is its general sense of purpose and underlying inherent beliefs that creates and reflects a 'common thread', common values and culture, throughout the organisation. An organisation's written mission statement usually includes a summary of goals and policies together with its purpose and what business it is in, what it provides and for whom it exists, its values and commitment to its employees and suppliers, its policies and behaviour standards and principles of business, quality and professionalism, and its strategy and long-term vision.

money measurement concept Most quantifiable data are capable of being converted, using a common denominator of money, into monetary terms. The money measurement concept holds that accounting deals only with those items capable of being translated into monetary terms, which imposes a limit on the scope of accounting reporting to such items.

net assets The excess of the book value of assets over liabilities, including loan capital. This is equivalent to net worth, which is used to describe the paid-up share capital and reserves.

net debt The total borrowings of the company net of liquid resources. Net debt excludes non-equity shares because, although similar to borrowings, they are not actually liabilities of the entity. Net debt excludes receivables and payables because, whilst they are short-term claims on and sources of finance to the entity, their main role is as part of the entity's trading activities.

net present value (NPV) The difference between the sums of the projected discounted cash inflows and outflows attributable to a capital investment or other long-term project.

net realisable value The amount for which an asset could be disposed, less any direct selling costs (IAS2).

non-current assets Or fixed assets, are any assets, tangible or intangible, acquired for retention by an entity for the purpose of providing a service to the business, and not held for resale in the normal course of trading. These include, for example, equipment, machinery, furniture, fittings, computers, software and motor vehicles that the company has purchased to enable it to meet its strategic objectives; such items are not renewed within the operating cycle.

non-current liabilities Liabilities which fall due for payment after one year. They include that part of long-term loans due for repayment after one year.

non-executive director A director who does not have a specific functional role within the company's management. The usual involvement of non-executive directors is to attend board meetings and chair corporate governance committees.

non-financial performance indicators Measures of performance based on non-financial information which may originate in and be used by operating departments to monitor and control their activities without any accounting input. Non-financial performance measures may give a more timely indication of the levels of performance achieved than do financial ratios, and may be less susceptible to distortion by factors such as uncontrollable variations in the effect of market forces on operations.

non-related company A company in which a business has a long-term investment, but over which it has no control or influence. If control exists then the company is deemed to be a subsidiary.

notional cost A cost used in product evaluation, decision-making and performance measurement to represent the cost of using resources which have no conventional 'actual cost'. Notional interest, for example, may be charged for the use of internally generated funds.

off balance sheet financing The funding of operations in such a way that the relevant assets and liabilities are not disclosed in the balance sheet of the company concerned.

operating cycle The operating cycle, or working capital cycle, is calculated by deducting payables days from inventory days plus receivables collection days. It represents the period of time which elapses between the point at which cash begins to be expended on the production of a product or service and the collection of cash from the customer.

operating gearing The relationship of fixed costs to total costs. The greater the proportion of fixed costs, the higher the operating gearing, and the greater the advantage to the business of increasing sales volume. If sales drop, a business with high operating gearing may face a problem from its high level of fixed costs.

operating lease A lease is a contract between a lessor and a lessee for the hire of a specific asset. The lessor retains ownership of the asset but gives the right to the use of the asset to the lessee for an agreed period in return for the payment of specified rentals (IAS 17). An operating lease is a lease other than a finance lease, where the lessor retains most of the risks and rewards of ownership.

operating profit Operating profit is calculated from gross profit plus or minus all operating revenues and costs, excluding interest and taxation. It is the profit of an entity regardless of its financial structure.

operational variance A classification of variances in which non-standard performance is defined as being that which differs from an *ex post* standard. Operational variances can relate to any element of the standard product specification.

opportunity cost The value of the benefit sacrificed when one course of action is chosen, in preference to an alternative. The opportunity cost is represented by the forgone potential benefit from the best rejected course of action.

optimised production technology (OPT) OPT is a manufacturing philosophy combined with a computerised system of shop-floor scheduling and capacity planning. It is a philosophy that focuses on factors such as manufacture to order, quality, lead times, batch sizes and set-up times, and differs from a traditional approach of balancing capacity as near 100 per cent as possible and then maintaining flow. The aim of OPT is to balance flow rather than capacity. The goal of OPT is to make money by increasing throughput and reducing inventories and operating expenses, by making better use of limited capacity by tightly controlled finite scheduling of bottleneck operations.

ordinary shares Shares which entitle the holders to the remaining divisible profits (and, in a liquidation, the assets) after prior interests, for example payables and prior charge capital, have been satisfied.

overhead absorption rate A means of attributing overhead to a product or service, based, for example, on direct labour hours, direct labour cost or machine hours.

overhead over- and under-absorption (or overhead over- and under-recovery) The difference between overhead incurred and overhead absorbed, using an estimated rate, in a given period.

Pareto analysis An analysis of a frequency distribution with a small proportion (say 20%) of the items accounting for a large proportion (say 80%) of the total. Examples may be seen in around 80% of sales of a company being derived from about 20% of its customers, and 80% of the value of its inventories being held in 20% of its items.

payables days Average trade payables divided by average daily purchases on credit. It indicates the average time taken, in calendar days, to pay for supplies received on credit.

payback The number of years it takes the cash inflows from a capital investment project to equal the cash outflows. An organisation may have a target payback period, above which projects are rejected.

period cost A cost which relates to a time period rather than to the output of products or services.

periodicity concept The requirement to produce financial statements at set time intervals. With regard to companies, this requirement is embodied in the Companies Act 2006.

planning The establishment of objectives, and the formulation, evaluation and selection of the policies, strategies, tactics and action required to achieve them. Planning comprises long-term strategic planning and short-term operational planning, the latter being usually for a period of up to one year.

planning variance A planning or revision variance is a classification of variances caused by *ex ante* budget allowances being changed to an *ex post* basis.

poka yoke Failsafe devices, support *jidoka* by preventing parts being mounted or fitted in the wrong way and alerting operators by flashing lights or sounding buzzers – it is a method of spotting defects, identifying, repairing and avoiding further defects.

policy deployment The process of internalising improvement policies throughout the company from translation of customer requirements, through each process of specification, design, etc. to final manufacturing and delivery.

post balance sheet events Favourable and unfavourable events that occur between the balance sheet date and the date on which the financial statements are approved by the board of directors.

preference shares Shares carrying a fixed rate of dividend, the holders of which, subject to the conditions of issue, have a prior claim to any company profits available for distribution. Preference shares may also have a prior claim to the repayment of capital in the event of a winding-up.

prepayments Prepayments include prepaid expenses for services not yet used, for example rent in advance or electricity charges in advance, and also accrued income. Accrued income relates to sales of goods or services that have occurred and have been included in the profit and loss account for the trading period but have not yet been invoiced to the customer.

present value The cash equivalent now of a sum receivable or payable at a future date.

price earnings ratio (P/E) The market price per ordinary share divided by earnings per share shows the number of years it would take to recoup an equity investment from its share of the attributable equity profit.

price elasticity A measure of the responsiveness of the demand for a product or service to a change in the price of that product or service. Products with an inelastic demand show relatively little changes in demand to relatively large changes in price (for example, the necessities of life) – demand is therefore not significantly price sensitive. Products with an elastic demand show relatively large changes in demand to relatively small changes in price.

profit and loss account The profit and loss account is the section of the general ledger that records all revenue and expense transactions. See also income statement, which is a report that summarises the profit and loss account transactions.

profit before tax (PBT) Operating profit plus or minus net interest.

profit centre A department or division of a business, or a company within a group, which is accountable for both costs and revenues. Its manager is responsible for revenues and costs.

profit for the year Or profit after tax (PAT), is profit before tax (PBT) minus corporation tax.

provision An amount charged against profit to provide for an expected liability or loss even though the amount or date of the liability or loss is uncertain (IAS 37).

prudence concept The principle that revenue and profits are not anticipated, but are included in the income statement only when realised in the form of either cash or other assets, or the ultimate cash realisation can be assessed with reasonable certainty; provision is made for all known liabilities (expenses and losses) whether the amount of these is known with certainty or is a best estimate in the light of information available.

public limited company (plc) A plc is a company limited by shares or by guarantee, with a share capital, whose memorandum states that it is public and that it has complied with the registration procedures for such a company. A public company is distinguished from a private company in the following ways: a minimum issued share capital of £50,000; public limited company, or plc, at the end of the name; public company clause in the memorandum; freedom to offer securities to the public.

pull system A system whose objective is to produce or procure products or components as they are required for use by internal and external customers, rather than for inventory. This contrasts with a 'push' system, in which inventories act as buffers between processes within production, and between production, purchasing and sales.

purchase invoice A document received from a supplier by an entity showing the description, quantity, prices and values of goods or services received.

purchase invoice daybook A list of supplier invoices recording their dates, gross values, values net of VAT, the dates of receipt of the invoices, the names of suppliers, and the general ledger allocation and coding.

purchase ledger See accounts payable.

qualified accountant A member of the accountancy profession, and in the UK a member of one of the six professional accountancy bodies: CIMA; ICAEW; ICAS; ICAI; ACCA; CIPFA.

quick ratio (or **acid test ratio**) Quick assets (current assets excluding inventories) divided by current liabilities, measures the ability of the business to pay accounts payable in the short term.

raw materials Goods purchased for incorporation into products for sale.

realisation concept The principle that increases in value should only be recognised on realisation of assets by arm's-length sale to an independent purchaser.

receiver A person appointed by secured creditors or by the court to take control of company property, usually following the failure of the company to pay principal sums or interest due to debenture holders whose debt is secured by fixed or floating charges over the assets of the company. The receiver takes control of the charged assets and may operate the company's business with a view to selling it as a going concern. In practice receivership is closely followed by liquidation.

Registrar of Companies (in some countries the Chamber of Commerce) Government official agency that is responsible for initial registration of new companies and for collecting and arranging public access to the annual reports of all limited companies.

relevancy concept Management accounting must ensure that flexibility is maintained in assembling and interpreting information. This facilitates the exploration and presentation, in a clear, understandable and timely manner, of as many alternatives as are necessary for impartial and confident decisions to be taken. This process is essentially forward-looking and dynamic. Therefore, the information must satisfy the criteria of being applicable and appropriate.

relevant cost Cost appropriate to a specific management decision.

reliability concept Management accounting information must be of such quality that confidence can be placed in it. Its reliability to the user is dependent on its source, integrity and comprehensiveness.

repayable on demand This refers to the definition of cash where there is a loss of interest if cash is withdrawn within 24 hours.

reporting entity A public or private limited company required to file its annual report and accounts with the Registrar of Companies.

reserves Retained profits or surpluses. In a not-for-profit entity these are described as accumulated funds. Reserves may be distributable or non-distributable.

residual income (RI) Profit before tax less an imputed interest charge for invested capital, which may be used to assess the performance of a division or a branch of a business.

responsibility accounting A system in which a budget holder is given responsibility for all revenues and costs that can be traced to clearly defined areas of their responsibility.

responsibility centre A department or organisational function whose performance is the direct responsibility of a specific manager.

retained earnings (or retained profit) Profits that have not been paid out as dividends to shareholders, but retained for future investment by the company, and reported on a cumulative basis within the equity section of the balance sheet.

return on capital employed (ROCE) ROCE, or return on investment (ROI), is the profit before interest and tax divided by average capital employed. It indicates the profit-generating capacity of capital employed.

return on investment (ROI) See return on capital employed (ROCE).

revenue (or sales, or sales revenue) is the gross inflow of economic benefits (cash, receivables, other assets) arising from the ordinary operating activities of an entity, such as sales of goods, sales of services, interest, royalties and dividends (IAS 18).

revenue centre A centre devoted to raising revenue with no responsibility for costs, for example, a sales centre. Its manager is responsible for revenues only. Revenue centres are often used in not-for-profit organisations.

revenue expenditure Expenditure on the manufacture of goods, or the provision of services, or on the general conduct of the entity, which is charged to the profit and loss account in the accounting period of sale. This includes repairs and depreciation of non-current assets as distinct from the provision of these assets.

reverse engineering The decomposition and analysis of competitors' products in order to determine how they are made, their costs of production and the way in which future development may proceed.

rights issue The raising of new capital by giving existing shareholders the right to subscribe to new shares or debentures in proportion to their current holdings. These shares are usually issued at a discount to the market price. A shareholder not wishing to take up a rights issue may sell the rights.

risk A condition in which there exists a quantifiable dispersion in the possible outcomes from any activity. For example: credit risk – the risk that a borrower may default on his or her obligations; currency risk – the possibility of loss or gain due to future changes in exchange rates.

risk analysis The evaluation and quantification of all currently known uncertainty, in order to predict likely outcomes and identify strategies for reducing risk to an acceptable level and controlling residual risk.

risk management The process of understanding and managing the risks that the organisation is inevitably subject to in attempting to achieve its corporate objectives. For management purposes, risks are usually divided into categories such as: operational; financial; legal compliance; information; personnel.

Romalpa clause A contractual clause, named after a case in which its effect was litigated in 1976, by which the ownership of goods is to remain with the seller until they have been paid for. This can provide a useful protection for the seller in the event of the buyer's insolvency. Its value may be questionable if the goods are mixed with other goods in a manufacturing process or if they are resold to a third party.

sales invoice A document prepared by an entity showing the description, quantity, prices and values of goods delivered or services rendered to a customer.

sales invoice daybook A list of customer invoices recording their dates, gross values, values net of VAT, the names of customers, and the general ledger allocation and coding.

sales ledger See accounts receivable.

scrip issue (or **bonus issue**) The capitalisation of the reserves of a company by the issue of additional shares to existing shareholders, in proportion to their holdings. Such shares are normally fully paid-up with no cash called for from the shareholders.

segmental reporting The inclusion in a company's report and accounts of analysis of turnover, profits and net assets by class of business and by geographical segments (IFRS 8).

semi-variable cost A cost containing both fixed and variable components and which is thus partly affected by a change in the level of activity.

sensitivity analysis A modelling and risk assessment technique in which changes are made to significant variables in order to determine the effect of these changes on the planned outcome. Particular attention is thereafter paid to variables identified as being of special significance.

separate valuation concept In determining the aggregate amount of any asset or liability, the amount of each individual asset or liability making up the aggregate must be determined separately (IAS 16).

share A fixed identifiable unit of capital which has a fixed nominal or face value, which may be quite different from the market value of the share.

share capital The book value of share capital, reported in the equity section of the balance sheet, is the number of shares issued by the company multiplied by the nominal value of the shares.

share premium account The difference in price between the original nominal value of shares and the price new investors will have to pay for shares issued by the company.

small to medium-sized enterprises (SMEs) SMEs are currently defined, by the European Union, as enterprises which have fewer than 250 employees and which have either an annual turnover not exceeding 50 million euro, or an annual balance sheet total not exceeding 43 million euro. In the UK, the thresholds are less than 250 employees, annual turnover not exceeding £25.9m and a balance sheet total not exceeding £12.9m (Companies Act 2006).

spreadsheet A spreadsheet is a type of computer software package developed in the late 1970s and used in a variety of business operations. The spreadsheet is named after the accountant's manual spreadsheet in which text or numbers or formulae are displayed in rows and columns. Spreadsheet programs enable information to be introduced that automatically and speedily affects entries across the entire spreadsheet. Complex spreadsheet programs exist that enable the transfer of spreadsheet information through word processing techniques, and there are also three-dimensional spreadsheets for multi-department, multi-division and multi-company budgeting, planning and modelling.

standard A benchmark measurement of resource usage, set in defined conditions.

standard cost The planned unit cost of the products, components or services produced in a period. The standard cost may be determined on a number of bases. The main uses of standard costs are in performance measurement, control and inventory valuation and in the establishment of selling prices.

statement of affairs Details submitted to the Official Receiver during the winding-up of a company identifying the assets and liabilities of the company. The details are prepared by the company directors, or other persons specified by the Official Receiver, and must be submitted within 14 days of the winding-up order or the appointment of a provisional liquidator.

statement of cash flows (or cash flow statement) A statement that summarises the inflows and outflows of cash for a period, classified under the following standard headings (IAS 7):

 – operating activities
 – investing activities
 – financing activities.

 The statement of cash flows is one of the three key financial statements.

Statement of Principles (SOP) for Financial Reporting The UK conceptual framework of accounting issued by the Accounting Standards Board in 1999.

Statements of Standard Accounting Practice (SSAPs) The accounting standards of practice published by the Accounting Standards Committee up to 1 August 1990.

strategic planning A process of deciding on the objectives of an organisation, the resources used to attain these objectives, and on the policies that are to govern the acquisition, use and disposition of these resources. The results of this process may be expressed in a strategic plan, which is a statement of long-term goals along with a definition of the strategies and policies that will ensure achievement of those goals.

subsidiary companies A subsidiary company, defined by IAS 27, is a company for which another company (the parent company) owns more than half the voting shares or has power:

 – over more than one half of the voting rights by virtue of an agreement with other investors
 or
 – to govern the financial and operating policies of the entity under a statute or an agreement
 or
 – to appoint or remove the majority of the members of the board of directors
 or
 – to cast the majority of votes at a meeting of the board of directors.

substance over form concept Where a conflict exists, the structuring of reports should give precedence to the representation of financial reality over strict adherence to the requirements of the legal reporting structure.

sunk cost A cost which has already been incurred and which cannot now be recovered.

SWOT analysis Performing a SWOT analysis is a means of gaining a clear picture of the Strengths, Weaknesses, Opportunities and Threats, which make the organisation what it is. SWOT analysis can apply across diverse management functions and activities, but is particularly appropriate to the early stages of formulating strategy.

systematic risk (or market risk) Some investments are by their very nature more risky than others. This is nothing to do with chance variations in actual compared with expected returns; it is inherent risk that cannot be diversified away.

target cost A product cost estimate derived by subtracting a desired profit margin from a competitive market price. This may be less than the planned initial product cost, but will be expected to be achieved by the time the product reaches the mature production stage.

tax shield A reduction in corporation tax payable due to the use of tax-allowable deductions against taxable income, for example the corporation tax relief on debt interest that should be recognised in calculating the cost of debt capital to calculate an after-tax cost of debt.

theory of constraints (TOC) An approach to production management which aims to maximise sales revenue less materials (throughput), whilst simultaneously reducing 'inventory' and operational expense. It focuses primarily on factors which act as constraints to this maximisation.

throughput The rate of production of a defined process over a stated period of time. Rates may be expressed in terms of units of products, batches produced, turnover, or other meaningful measurements.

throughput accounting (TA) A method of performance measurement which relates production and other costs to throughput. Throughput accounting product costs relate to usage of key resources by various products.

top-down process A top-down approach usually relates to a particular type of budgeting process where a budget allowance is set or imposed without permitting the ultimate budget holder to have the opportunity to participate in the budgeting process.

total productive maintenance (TPM) Where first-line maintenance, cleaning, checking for irregularities, leaks etc., and simple maintenance, become the responsibility of operators rather than of the maintenance department.

total quality control (TQC) A concept of the quality operation of a business that includes policy deployment, quality control teams, cross-function quality groups, 5S techniques of good housekeeping, the seven tools of quality, and the Deming cycle of plan-do-check-act, to involve everyone in all areas of the business to meet customer needs.

total quality management (TQM) An integrated and comprehensive system of planning and controlling all business functions so that products or services are produced which meet or exceed customer expectations. TQM is a philosophy of business behaviour, embracing principles such as employee involvement, continuous improvement at all levels and customer focus, as well as being a collection of related techniques aimed at improving quality. In addition to the features included in TQC, TQM additionally includes JIT, *heijunka* and *jidoka*.

trade payables An amount reported in the balance sheet in respect of money owed by suppliers, persons or entities, as a consequence of the receipt of goods or services in advance of payment.

trade receivables An amount reported in the balance sheet in respect of money owed to customers, persons or entities, as a consequence of goods or services provided on credit.

treasury management The corporate handling of all financial matters, the generation of external and internal funds for business, the management of currencies and cash flows, and the complex strategies, policies and procedures of corporate finance.

trial balance The list of account balances in a double-entry accounting system. If the records have been correctly maintained, the sum of the debit balances will equal the sum of the credit balances, although certain errors such as the omission of a transaction or erroneous entries will not be disclosed by a trial balance.

true and fair view The requirement for financial statements prepared in compliance with the Companies Act to 'give a true and fair view' overrides any other requirements. Although not precisely defined in the

Companies Act this is generally accepted to mean that accounts show a true and fair view if they are unlikely to mislead a user of financial information in giving a false impression of the company.

UK Corporate Governance Code The corporate governance code applicable to listed companies, issued by the Financial Reporting Council (FRC) in June 2010, and described as a 'guide only in general terms to principles, structure and processes'.

unit cost The average cost of a product or service unit based on total costs and the number of units produced.

unsystematic risk Risk that can be diversified away.

value added statement An alternative presentation of the traditional profit and loss account that measures the wealth created by a company through its activities, through value added by the business rather than the profit earned by the business. It shows how value added is distributed among the relevant parties: employees; lenders; shareholders; Government; and the amount to provide maintenance and expansion of the business.

value added tax (VAT) A tax charged on most goods and services that VAT-registered businesses provide in the UK and other countries. VAT is charged when a VAT-registered business sells to either another business or to a non-business customer. In the UK, there are three rates of VAT, depending on the goods or services the business provides. The current rates are: standard (20%); reduced (5%); zero (0%).

value analysis A technique for examination, by multi-disciplined teams, of design attributes and any other factors affecting the cost of the product, to identify and implement the means of achieving the specified purpose most economically at the required standard of quality and reliability. Value analysis is the broad term usually used to include both value analysis and value engineering. Value engineering applies to products under development, whilst value analysis applies to products currently in production.

value engineering The method of value analysis that applies to products under development.

variable cost A cost that varies in direct proportion to the volume of activity.

variance The difference between a planned, budgeted or standard cost and the actual cost incurred. The same comparisons may be made for revenues.

variance analysis The evaluation of performance by means of variances, whose timely reporting should maximise the opportunity for managerial action. These variances will be either favourable variances (F) or adverse variances (A).

vendor managed inventory (VMI) The management of inventories on behalf of a customer by the supplier, the supplier taking responsibility for the management of inventories within a framework that is mutually agreed by both parties. Examples are seen in separate supermarket racks maintained and stocked by merchandising groups for such items as spices, and car parts distributors topping up the shelves of dealers/garages, where the management of inventories, racking and shelves is carried out by the merchandising group or distributor.

vertical analysis An analysis of the income statement (or balance sheet) in which each item is expressed as a percentage of the total. The vertical analysis provides evidence of structural changes in the business such as increased profitability through more efficient production.

voluntary winding-up A voluntary winding-up of a company occurs where the company passes a resolution that it shall liquidate and the court is not involved in the process. A voluntary winding-up may be made by the members (the shareholders) of the company or by its creditors, if the company has failed to declare its solvency.

weighted average cost of capital (WACC) The average cost of the company's finance (equity, debentures, bank loans) weighted according to the proportion each element bears to the total pool of capital. Weighting is usually based on market valuations, current yields and costs after tax.

window dressing A creative accounting practice in which changes in short-term funding have the effect of disguising or improving the reported liquidity position of the reporting organisation.

working capital Also called net current assets, is the capital available for conducting day-to-day operations of an organisation; normally the excess of current assets over current liabilities.

working capital requirement Inventories plus receivables plus prepayments less payables less accruals. This investment in the operating cycle represents the financial resources specifically required for the company to purchase and create inventories while it waits for payments from its customers.

work in progress (WIP) Products or services in intermediate stages of completion.

wrongful trading Wrongful trading occurs where a director knows or ought to have known before the commencement of winding-up that there was no reasonable prospect of the company avoiding insolvency and he/she does not take every step to minimise loss to creditors. If the court is satisfied of this it may (i) order the director to contribute to the assets of the business, and (ii) disqualify him/her from further involvement in corporate management for a specified period (Insolvency Act 1986).

Index

The names of companies mentioned in the book are in **bold** type. Definitions of key terms may be found on the pages that are highlighted in **colour**.